Volume I

$HANDBOOK OF $$$$$$HEALTH $$$$$$$$CARE $$ACCOUNTING $$AND FINANCE SECOND EDITION

Edited by

William O. Cleverley, Ph.D., CPA

Professor of Health Services Management
and Accounting
Graduate Program in Hospital
and Health Services Management
The Ohio State University
Columbus, Ohio

AN ASPEN PUBLICATION®
Aspen Publishers, Inc.
Rockville, Maryland
1989

Library of Congress Cataloging-in-Publication Data

Handbook of health care accounting and finance/edited by
William O. Cleverley.--2nd. ed.
p. cm.
"An Aspen publication."
Includes bibliographies and indexes.
ISBN: 0-8342-0056-2
1. Health facilities--Finance. 2. Health facilities--Accounting.
3. Health facilities--Business management. I. Cleverley, William O.
[DNLM: 1. Economics, Hospital--United States.
2. Financial Management. WX 157 H236]
RA971.3.H24   1989   362.1'1'0681--dc19
DNLM/DLC
for Library of Congress
88-37545
CIP

Aspen Publishers, Inc., grants permission for photocopying for limited personal or internal use.
This consent does not extend to other kinds of copying, such as copying for general
distribution, for advertising or promotional purposes, for creating new collective works,
or for resale. For more information, address Aspen Publishers, Inc.,
Permissions Department, 1600 Research Boulevard, Rockville, Maryland 20850.

Editorial Services: Marsha Davies

Library of Congress Catalog Card Number: 88-37545
ISBN: 0-8342-0056-2

Printed in the United States of America

1 2 3 4 5

To my wife
Linda S. Cleverley

8

Table of Contents

Volume I

PART 1—CONTROLLERSHIP

Volume II

Contributors

Seth Allcorn
Administrator
Department of Medicine
Strong Memorial Hospital
Rochester, New York

Jane M. Bachmann
Manager
Laventhol and Horwath
Chicago, Illinois

Allwyn J. Baptist
Partner
Laventhol and Horwath
Chicago, Illinois

James E. Bennett
McKinsey and Company
Toronto, Ontario, Canada

Michael L. Caine
Partner
Arthur Andersen & Co.
Charlotte, North Carolina

Robert J. Caswell
Associate Professor
Graduate Program in Hospital and Health
    Services Administration
The Ohio State University
Columbus, Ohio

Marcus V. Cavanagh
Senior Vice President
McDonald & Company Securities, Inc.
Columbus, Ohio

Stephen A. Claiborn, Ph.D.
Managing Director
Shearson Lehman Hutton, Inc.
Houston, Texas

John F. Clarkin
Director
Coopers & Lybrand
Philadelphia, Pennsylvania

Richard V. Clausing, CPA
Manager
Arthur Andersen & Co.
Chicago, Illinois

William O. Cleverley, Ph.D. , CPA
Professor of Health Services Management and
    Accounting
Graduate Program in Hospital and Health
    Services Management
The Ohio State University
Columbus, Ohio

Diane Cornwell
Partner
Arthur Andersen & Co.
Chicago, Illinois

xxi

Marguerite A. Daniels
Manager, Marketing Clinical Systems
SMS
Malvern, Pennsylvania

Donna Daugherty
Consultant
Arthur Andersen & Co.
Dallas, Texas

Dale G. Deatsch
Senior Manager
Ernst & Whinney
Chicago, Illinois

J. Keith Deisenroth
Partner
Ernst & Whinney
Los Angeles, California

David K. Dennis, Ph.D., CPA
Associate Professor
School of Business and Administration
Duquesne University
Pittsburgh, Pennsylvania

Jesse F. Dillard, Ph.D.
Associate Professor of Accounting
The Ohio State University
Columbus, Ohio

Maria E. DiMauro
Product Manager, IBHS
SMS
Malvern, Pennsylvania

Timothy D. Dixon
Vice President and Manager
Healthcare Division
Society National Bank
Cleveland, Ohio

Jerome R. Gardner
Vice President, Audit Services
Oklahoma Health Care Corporation
Oklahoma City, Oklahoma

Martha Garner
Senior Manager
Price Waterhouse
St. Louis, Missouri

Edward A. Grant
Partner
Arthur Andersen & Co.
Chicago, Illinois

Myra J. Green
Partner
Choate, Hall & Stewart
Boston, Massachusetts

Jeffrey T. Grover
Manager
The Raleigh Group
Cleveland, Ohio

David A. Hampshire
Senior Manager
Ernst & Whinney
Cleveland, Ohio

Robert E. Haskell
Advisory Systems Designer
SMS
Malvern, Pennsylvania

John F. Hill
Director of Finance
Benedictine Health System
Duluth, Minnesota

William H. Hranchak
Manager
Arthur Andersen & Co.
Los Angeles, California

Norman Jaspan
President
Norman Jaspan Associates, Inc.
New York, New York

Kenneth F. Johnson
President
Strategic Healthcare Systems, Inc.
Winthrop, Maine

Kenneth Kaufman
Managing Director
Kaufman, Hall & Associates
Northfield, Illinois

83388

888

Alan G. Seidner
President
The Alan G. Seidner Company
Investment Management and Consulting
Pasadena, California

Geoffrey B. Shields
Partner
Gardner, Carton & Douglas
Chicago, Illinois

Adam P. Sielicki, Jr., CPCU, ARM
Executive Vice President
Insurance Buyers' Council, Inc.
Baltimore, Maryland

Patricia A. Simone
Senior Product Analyst
SMS
Malvern, Pennsylvania

Robert A. Snyder
Executive Director, Payment and
  Benefit Management Department
Blue Cross and Blue Shield Association
Chicago, Illinois

James D. Suver, DBA, CMA, FHFMA
Director, Programs in Health Administration
University of Colorado
Denver, Colorado

Dawson Taylor
Partner
Arthur Andersen & Co.
Seattle, Washington

Jay E. Toole
Partner
Arthur Andersen & Co.
Atlanta, Georgia

Glenn T. Troyer, Esq.
Partner
Locke, Reynolds, Boyd & Wetsell
Indianapolis, Indiana

Susan J. Velleman
Managing Director
William M. Mercer Meidinger Hansen, Inc.
Boston, Massachusetts

Matthew B. Weekley
Chief Financial Officer
Memorial Hospital of Union County
Marysville, Ohio

Robert G. Waldeck
Senior Manager
Ernst & Whinney
Columbus, Ohio

R. Steven Wilder
Partner
Arthur Young & Company
Columbus, Ohio

Frank G. Williams, Ph.D.
Associate Professor
School of Health Administration and Policy
Arizona State University
Tempe, Arizona

Robert Yagi
Vice President
Moody's Investors Service
New York, New York

David Zimmerman
President
Zimmerman & Associates
Hales Corners, Wisconsin

Gary Zmrhal
Partner
Arthur Andersen & Co.
Indianapolis, Indiana

Andrew E. Zuckerman, Esq.
Sanders, Schnabel and Brandenburg
Washington, D.C.

Preface

In the second edition of *Handbook of Health Care Accounting and Finance*, as in the first edition, the objective is to provide a readily available source of reference materials on financial management topics for health care executives. The major reasons for rewriting include the dramatic changes in the nature of payment for health care services, most notably the Medicare shift from cost payment to prospective rates. Major changes in other areas affecting health care financial management were also evident. These changes include capital formation regulations, tax reform provisions, information technology developments, and many others. Most of the chapters in this second edition represent major revisions and in some cases completely new topics.

The first edition of the *Handbook of Health Care Accounting and Finance* was very well received. The book won the Association of American Publishers' award for the best book in business, management, and economics in 1982. The same categorization scheme used in the first edition is repeated in the second edition. The topics were categorized using the Financial Executives Institute (FEI) framework. In that scheme, financial management activity is split into controller or treasurer functions:

Controller
1. Planning for control
2. Reporting and interpreting
3. Evaluating and consulting
4. Tax administration
5. Government reporting
6. Protection of assets
7. Economic appraisal

Treasurer
1. Provision of capital
2. Investor relations
3. Short-term financing
4. Banking and custody
5. Credits and collection
6. Investments
7. Insurance

It is customary in the financial management field to refer to the controllership activities as accounting and the treasurership activities as finance—hence the title of this book is *Handbook of Health Care Accounting and Finance*. However, it is important to bear in mind that underlying the more popular division into accounting and finance is the more functional division of financial management into controllership and treasurership activities.

The FEI categorization scheme is reflected in the following major categories of this book:

Controllership
1. Financial accounting
2. Cost accounting and analysis
3. Management planning and control
4. Tax administration

5. Payment
6. Information systems
7. Quantitative methods
8. Regulation and legal issues

Treasurership
1. Provision of funds
2. Working capital management
3. Insurance

While the above categorization scheme seems to show a greater emphasis on the controllership area, this may be illusory. For example, some of the categories listed in the controllership area (e.g., payment or regulation and legal issues) might arguably fall in the treasurership area. In sum, since the categorization scheme and the placement of individual topics or chapters can be debated, the important point is whether the coverage is comprehensive. I believe that the reader will find that this second edition of the *Handbook of Health Care Accounting and Finance* provides a wealth of information that is timely, relevant, and authoritative.

Acknowledgments

I am indebted to a great number of individuals for ideas, assistance, and support in the development of this book. I am especially grateful for the love and support of my wife, Linda, to whom this book is dedicated. For 21 years she has supported me in every aspect of my career and has helped to provide a beacon of direction in all my efforts.

I am also especially grateful to the many authors who have contributed to this book. Obviously a book of this scope would not have been possible without them. The time which many of them devoted to this project cut deeply into their own well-deserved personal time and came at a great cost. I have thoroughly enjoyed the opportunity that I have had to work with them in the development of this book and to get to know many of them as individuals. Simply acknowledging them does not seem sufficient recognition. However, I know of no other way to recognize them except to say thank you for a job well done.

I am also grateful to a large number of people at Aspen Publishers for countless hours in the development and production of this book. They have always maintained the highest degree of professionalism and have made the very complex task of coordination and management bearable.

I must also recognize the efforts of Lee Bolzenius. She provided administrative and typing support that in many cases was above and beyond the call of duty.

Finally, I wish to recognize the support of my three children, Michelle, Meredith, and Jamie. While they did not contribute directly to this book, they are my greatest source of pride and satisfaction.

Part I
Controllership

Financial Accounting

Chapter 1

General Principles of Accounting

William O. Cleverley
Professor, Graduate Program in Hospital and Health Services Management
The Ohio State University

Information does not happen by itself; it must be generated by an individual or a formally designed system. Financial information is no exception. The accounting system generates most financial information to provide quantitative data, primarily financial in nature, that are useful in making economic decisions about economic entities.

FINANCIAL VERSUS MANAGERIAL ACCOUNTING

Financial accounting is the branch of accounting that provides general-purpose financial statements or reports to aid a large number of decision-making groups, internal and external to the organization, in a variety of decisions. The primary outputs of financial accounting are four financial statements that will be discussed in Chapter 2 (see Exhibits 2-1, 2-2, 2-3, 2-4, and 2-5).

1. balance sheet
2. statement of revenues and expenses
3. statement of changes in financial position
4. statement of changes in fund balance

This chapter is reprinted from *Essentials of Health Care Finance*, 2nd ed., by W.O. Cleverley, pp. 49–65, Aspen Publishers, Inc., © 1986.

The field of financial accounting is restricted in many ways regarding how certain events or business transactions may be accounted for. The term *generally accepted accounting principles* is often used to describe the body of rules and requirements that shape the preparation of the four primary financial statements. For example, an organization's financial statements that have been audited by an independent certified public accountant (CPA) would bear the following language:

> In our opinion, the aforementioned financial statement presents fairly the financial position of the XYZ Company at December 31, 1986, and the results of its operations and changes in its financial position for the year ended, in conformity with generally accepted accounting principles applied on a basis consistent with that of the preceding year.

Financial accounting is not limited to preparation of the four statements. An increasing number of additional financial reports are being required, especially for external users for specific decision-making purposes. This is particularly important in the health care industry. For example, hospitals submit cost reports to a number of third-party payers, such as Blue Cross, Medicare, and Medicaid. They also submit financial reports to a large number of regulatory agencies, such as planning agencies, rate review agencies, service associations, and many others. In addition, CPAs often prepare financial projections that are used by investors in capital financing. These statements, although not usually audited by independent CPAs, are, for the most part, prepared in accordance with the same generally accepted accounting principles that govern the preparation of the four basic financial statements.

Managerial accounting is primarily concerned with the preparation of financial information for specific purposes, usually for internal users. Since this information is used within the organization, there is less need for a body of principles restricting its preparation. Presumably, the user and the preparer can meet to discuss questions of interpretation. Uniformity and comparability of information, which are desired goals for financial accountants, are clearly less important to management accountants.

PRINCIPLES OF ACCOUNTING

Here we are concerned with both sets of accounting information—financial and managerial. Although managerial accounting has no formally adopted set of principles, it relies strongly on financial accounting principles. Understanding the principles and basics of financial accounting is therefore critical to understanding both financial and managerial accounting information.

The case example in our discussion of the principles of financial accounting is a newly formed, nonprofit community hospital, which we shall refer to as "Alpha Hospital."

Accounting Entity

Obviously, in any accounting there must be an entity for which the financial statements are being prepared. Specifying the entity upon which the accounting will focus defines the information that is pertinent. Drawing these boundaries is the underlying concept behind the accounting entity principle.

Alpha Hospital is the entity for which we will account and prepare financial statements. We are not interested in the individuals who may have incorporated Alpha or other hospitals in the community but solely in Alpha Hospital's financial transactions.

Defining the entity is not as clear-cut as one might expect. Significant problems arise, especially when the legal entity is different from the accounting entity. For example, if one doctor owns a clinic through a sole proprietorship arrangement, the accounting entity may be the clinic operation, whereas the legal entity includes the doctor and the doctor's personal resources as well. A hospital may be part of a university or government agency, or it might be owned by a large corporation organized on a profit or nonprofit basis. Indeed, many hospitals have now become subsidiaries of holding companies as a result of corporate restructuring. Careful attention must be paid to the definition of the accounting entity in these situations. If the entity is not properly defined, evaluation of its financial information may be useless at best and misleading at worst.

The common practice of municipalities directly paying the fringe benefits of municipal employees employed in the hospital illustrates this situation. Such expenses may never show up in the hospital's accounts, resulting in an understatement of the expenses associated with running the hospital. In many cases, this may produce a bias in the rate-setting process.

Money Measurement

Accounting in general, but financial accounting in particular, is concerned with measuring economic resources and obligations and their changing levels for the accounting entity under consideration. The accountant's yardstick for measuring is not metered to size, color, weight, or other attributes; it is limited exclusively to money. However, there are significant problems in money measurement, which will be discussed shortly.

Economic resources are defined as scarce means, limited in supply, but essential to economic activity. They include supplies, buildings, equipment, money, claims to receive money, and ownership interests in other enterprises. The terms *economic resources* and *assets* may be interchanged for most practical purposes. Economic obligations are responsibilities to transfer economic resources or provide services to other entities in the future, usually in return for economic resources received from other entities in the past through the purchase of assets, the receipt of services, or the acceptance of loans. For most practical purposes, the terms *economic obligations* and *liabilities* may be used interchangeably.

In most normal situations, assets exceed liabilities in money-measured value. Liabilities represent the claim of one entity on another's assets; any excess, or remaining residual interest, may be claimed by the owner. In fact, for entities with ownership interest, this residual interest is called "owner's equity."

In most nonprofit entities, including health care organizations, there is no residual ownership claim. Any assets remaining in a liquidated not-for-profit entity, after all liabilities have been dissolved, legally become the property of the state. Residual interest is referred to as "fund balance" for most health care organizations.

In the Alpha Hospital example, assume that the community donated $1 million in cash to the hospital at its formation, hypothetically assumed to be December 31, 1986. At that time, a listing of its assets, liabilities, and fund balance would be prepared in a balance sheet and read as below:

Alpha Hospital Balance Sheet
December 31, 1986

Assets
Cash $1,000,000

Liabilities and Fund Balance
Fund balance $1,000,000

Duality

One of the fundamental premises of accounting is a very simple arithmetic requirement: the value of assets must always equal the combined value of liabilities and residual interest, which we have called fund balance. This basic accounting equation, the *duality principle*, may be stated as follows:

Assets = Liabilities + Fund Balance

This requirement means that a balance sheet will always balance—the value of the assets will always equal the value of claims, whether liabilities or fund balance, on those assets.

Changes are always occurring in organizations that affect the value of assets, liabilities, and fund balance. These changes are called transactions and represent the items that interest accountants. Examples of transactions are borrowing money, purchasing supplies, and constructing buildings. The important thing to remember is that each transaction must be carefully analyzed under the duality principle to keep the basic accounting equation in balance.

To better understand how important this principle is, let us analyze several transactions in our Alpha Hospital example.

- *Transaction No. 1*. On January 2, 1987, Alpha Hospital buys a piece of equipment for $100,000. The purchase is financed with a $100,000 note from the bank.
- *Transaction No. 2*. On January 3, 1987, Alpha Hospital buys a building for $2,000,000, using $500,000 cash and issuing $1,500,000 worth of 20-year bonds.
- *Transaction No. 3*. On January 4, 1987, Alpha Hospital purchases $200,000 worth of supplies from a supply firm on a credit basis.

If balance sheets were prepared after each of these three transactions, they would appear as follows:

- *Transaction No. 1*

Alpha Hospital Balance Sheet
January 2, 1987

Assets

Cash	$1,000,000
Equipment	100,000
Total	$1,100,000

Liabilities and Fund Balance

Notes payable	$ 100,000
Fund balance	1,000,000
Total	$1,100,000

Assets: Increase $100,000 (equipment increases by $100,000)
Liabilities: Increase $100,000 (notes payable increase by $100,000)

• *Transaction No. 2*

Alpha Hospital Balance Sheet
January 3, 1987

Assets

Cash	$ 500,000
Equipment	100,000
Building	2,000,000
Total	$2,600,000

Liabilities and Fund Balance

Notes payable	$ 100,000
Bonds payable	1,500,000
Fund balance	1,000,000
Total	$2,600,000

Assets: Increase $1,500,000 (cash decreases by $500,000 and building increases by $2,000,000)
Liabilities: Increase $1,500,000 (bonds payable increase by $1,500,000)

• *Transaction No. 3*

Alpha Hospital Balance Sheet
January 4, 1987

Assets

Cash	$ 500,000
Supplies	200,000
Equipment	100,000
Building	2,000,000
Total	$2,800,000

Liabilities and Fund Balance

Accounts payable	$ 200,000
Notes payable	100,000
Bonds payable	1,500,000
Fund balance	1,000,000
Total	$2,800,000

Assets: Increase $200,000 (supplies increase by $200,000)
Liabilities: Increase $200,000 (accounts payable increase by $200,000)

In each of these three transactions, the change in asset value is matched by an identical change in liability value. Thus, the basic accounting equation remains in balance.

It should be noted that, as the number of transactions increases, the number of individual asset and liability items also increases. In most organizations, there is a very large number of these individual items, which are referred to as accounts. The listing of these accounts is often called a chart of accounts; it is a useful device for categorizing transactions related to a given health care organization. There is already significant uniformity among hospitals and other health care facilities in the chart of accounts used; however, there is also pressure, especially from external users of financial information, to move toward even more uniformity.

Cost Valuation

Many readers of financial statements make the mistake of assuming that reported balance sheet values represent the real worth of individual assets or liabilities. Asset and liability values reported in a balance sheet are based on their historical or acquisition cost. In most situations, asset values do not equal the amount of money that could be realized if the assets were sold. However, in many cases the reported value of a liability in a balance sheet is a good approximation of the amount of money that would be required to extinguish the indebtedness.

Examining the alternatives to historical cost valuation helps clarify why the cost basis of valuation is used. The two primary alternatives to historical cost valuation of assets and liabilities are market value and replacement cost valuation.

Valuation of individual assets at their market value sounds simple enough and appeals to many users of financial statements. Creditors are often especially interested in what values assets would bring if liquidated. Current market values give decision makers an approximation of liquidation values.

The market value method's lack of objectivity is, however, a serious problem. In most normal situations, established markets dealing in secondhand merchandise do not exist. Decision makers must rely on individual appraisals. Given the current state of the art of appraisal, two appraisers are likely to produce different estimates of market value for an identical asset. Accountants' insistence on objectivity in measurement thus eliminates market valuation of assets as a viable alternative.

Replacement cost valuation of assets measures assets by the money value required to replace them.

This concept of valuation is extremely useful for many decision-making purposes. For example, management decisions to continue delivery of certain services should be affected by the replacement cost of resources, not their historical or acquisition cost—which is considered to be a sunk cost, irrelevant to future decisions. Planning agencies or other regulatory agencies should also consider incorporating estimates of replacement cost into their decisions to avoid bias. Considering only historical cost may improperly make old facilities appear more efficient than new or proposed facilities and projects.

While replacement cost may be a useful concept of valuation, it too suffers from lack of objectivity in measurement. Replacement cost valuation depends upon *how* an item is replaced. For example, given the rate of technological change in the general economy, especially in the health care industry, few assets today would be replaced with like assets. Instead, more refined or capable assets would probably be substituted. What is the replacement cost in this situation? Is it the cost of the new, improved asset or the present cost of an identical asset that would most likely *not* be purchased? Compound this question by the large numbers of manufacturers selling roughly equivalent items and you have some idea of the inherent difficulty and subjectivity in replacement cost valuation.

Historical cost valuation, with all its faults, is thus the basis that the accounting profession has chosen to value assets and liabilities in most circumstances. Accountants use it rather than replacement cost largely because it is more objective. There is currently some fairly strong pressure from inside and outside the accounting profession to switch to replacement cost valuation, but it is still uncertain whether this pressure will be successful.

One final, important point should be noted. At the time of initial asset valuation, the values assigned by historical cost valuation and replacement cost valuation are identical. The historical cost value is most often criticized for assets that have long useful lives, such as building and equipment. Over a period of many years, the historical cost and replacement cost values tend to diverge dramatically, partly because general inflation in our economy erodes the dollar's purchasing power. A dollar of today is simply not as valuable as a dollar of ten years ago. This problem could be remedied, without sacrificing the objectivity of historical cost measurement, by selecting a unit of purchasing power as the unit of measure. Transactions would then not be accounted in dollars but in dollars of purchasing power at a given point in time, usually the year for which the financial statements are being prepared. We will discuss this issue later when we talk about the stable monetary unit principle.

Accrual Accounting

Accrual accounting is a fundamental premise of accounting. It means that transactions of a business enterprise are recognized in the time period to which they relate, not necessarily in the time periods in which cash is received or paid.

It is quite common to hear people talk about an accrual versus a cash basis of accounting. Most of us think in cash basis terms. We measure our personal, financial success during the year by how much cash we took in. Seldom do we consider such things as wear and tear on our cars and other personal items or the differences between earned and uncollected income. Perhaps if we accrued expenses for items like depreciation on heating systems, air conditioning systems, automobiles, and furniture, we might see a different picture of our financial well-being.

The accrual basis of accounting significantly affects the preparation of financial statements in general; however, its major impact is on the preparation of the statement of revenues and expenses. The following additional transactions for Alpha Hospital illustrate the importance of the accrual principle:

- *Transaction No. 4*. Alpha Hospital bills patients $100,000 on January 16, 1987, for services provided to them.
- *Transaction No. 5*. Alpha Hospital pays employees $60,000 for their wages and salaries on January 18, 1987.
- *Transaction No. 6*. Alpha Hospital receives $80,000 in cash from patients who were billed earlier in Transaction No. 4 on January 23, 1987.

• *Transaction No. 7*. Alpha Hospital pays the $200,000 of accounts payable on January 27, 1987, for the purchase of supplies that took place on January 4, 1987.

Balance sheets prepared after each of these transactions would appear as follows:

• *Transaction No. 4*

Alpha Hospital Balance Sheet
January 16, 1987

Assets

Cash	$ 500,000
Accounts receivable	100,000
Supplies	200,000
Equipment	100,000
Building	2,000,000
Total	$2,900,000

Liabilities and Fund Balance

Accounts payable	$ 200,000
Notes payable	100,000
Bonds payable	1,500,000
Fund balance	1,100,000
Total	$2,900,000

Assets: Increase $100,000 (accounts receivable increase by $100,000)
Fund balance: Increases $100,000

• *Transaction No. 5*

Alpha Hospital Balance Sheet
January 18, 1987

Assets

Cash	$ 440,000
Accounts receivable	100,000
Supplies	200,000
Equipment	100,000
Building	2,000,000
Total	$2,840,000

Liabilities and Fund Balance

Accounts payable	$ 200,000
Notes payable	100,000
Bonds payable	1,500,000
Fund balance	1,040,000
Total	$2,840,000

Assets: Decrease by $60,000 (cash decreases by $60,000)
Fund balance: Decreases $60,000

• *Transaction No. 6*

Alpha Hospital Balance Sheet
January 23, 1987

Assets

Cash	$ 520,000
Accounts receivable	20,000
Supplies	200,000
Equipment	100,000
Building	2,000,000
Total	$2,840,000

Liabilities and Fund Balance

Accounts payable	$ 200,000
Notes payable	100,000
Bonds payable	1,500,000
Fund balance	1,040,000
Total	$2,840,000

Assets: No change (cash increases by $80,000; accounts receivable decrease by $80,000)

• *Transaction No. 7*

Alpha Hospital Balance Sheet
January 27, 1987

Assets

Cash	$ 320,000
Accounts receivable	20,000
Supplies	200,000
Equipment	100,000
Building	2,000,000
Total	$2,640,000

Liabilities and Fund Balance

Accounts payable	$ 0
Notes payable	100,000
Bonds payable	1,500,000
Fund balance	1,040,000
Total	$2,640,000

Assets: Decrease by $200,000 (cash decreases by $200,000)
Liabilities: Decrease by $200,000 (accounts payable decrease by $200,000)

In Transactions Nos. 4 and 5, there is an effect upon Alpha Hospital's residual interest or its fund balance. In Transaction No. 4, an increase in fund balance occurred due to the billing of patients for services previously rendered. Increases in fund balance or owner's equity resulting from the sale of goods or delivery of services are called revenues. It should be noted that this increase occurred even though no cash was actually collected until January 23, 1987, illustrating the accrual principle of accounting. Recognition of revenue occurs when the revenue is earned, not necessarily when it is collected.

In Transaction No. 5, a reduction in fund balance occurs. Costs incurred by a business enterprise to provide goods or services that reduce fund balance or owner's equity are called expenses. Under the accrual principle, expenses are recognized when assets are used up or liabilities incurred in the production and delivery of goods or services, not necessarily when cash is paid.

The difference between revenue and expense is often referred to as *net income*. In the hospital and health care industry, this term may be used interchangeably with the term *excess of revenues over expenses*.

The income statement or statement of revenues and expenses summarizes the revenues and expenses of a business enterprise over a defined period of time. If an income statement is prepared for the total life of an entity, that is, from inception to dissolution, it happens that the value for net income would be the same under both an accrual and a cash basis of accounting.

In most situations, frequent measurements of revenue and expense are demanded, creating some important measurement problems. Ideally, under the accrual accounting principle, expenses should be matched to the revenue that they helped create. For example, wage, salary, and supply costs can usually be easily associated with revenues of a given period. However, in certain circumstances, the association between revenue and expense is impossible to discover, necessitating the accountant's use of a systematic, rational method of allocating costs to a benefiting time period. In the best example of this procedure, costs such as those associated with building and equipment are spread over the estimated useful life of the assets through the recording of depreciation.

To complete the Alpha Hospital example, we will assume that the financial statements must be prepared at the end of January. Before they are prepared, certain adjustments must be made to the accounts to adhere fully to the accrual principle of accounting. The following adjustments might be recorded:

- *Adjustment No. 1.* There are currently $100,000 of patient charges that have been incurred but not yet billed.

- *Adjustment No. 2.* There is currently $50,000 worth of unpaid wages and salaries for which employees have performed services.

- *Adjustment No. 3.* A physical inventory count indicates that $50,000 worth of initial supplies have been used.

- *Adjustment No. 4.* The equipment of Alpha Hospital has an estimated useful life of ten years, and the cost is being allocated over this time period. On a monthly basis, this amounts to an allocation of $833 per month.

- *Adjustment No. 5.* The building has an estimated useful life of 40 years, and the cost of the building is being allocated equally over its estimated life. On a monthly basis, this amounts to $4,167.

- *Adjustment No. 6.* While no payment has occurred on either notes payable or bonds payable, it must be recognized that there is an interest expense associated with using money for this one-month time period. This interest expense will be paid at a later date. Assume that the note payable carries an interest rate of eight percent and the bond payable carries an interest rate of six percent. The actual amount of interest expense incurred for the month of January would be $8,167 ($667 on the note and $7,500 on the bond payable).

The effects of these adjustments on the balance sheet of Alpha Hospital, and on the ending balance sheet that would be prepared after all the adjustments were made, are presented on the following page.

Adjustment	Amount of Change	Account(s) Increased	Account(s) Decreased
No. 1	$100,000	Fund balance	None
		Accounts receivable	None
No. 2	50,000	Wages and salaries payable	Fund balance
No. 3	50,000	None	Fund balance, supplies
No. 4	833	None	Fund balance, equipment
No. 5	4,167	None	Fund balance, building
No. 6	8,167	Interest payable	Fund balance

Alpha Hospital Balance Sheet
January 31, 1987

Assets		Liabilities and Fund Balance	
Cash	$ 320,000	Wages and salaries payable	$ 50,000
Accounts receivable	120,000	Interest payable	8,167
Supplies	150,000	Notes payable	100,000
Equipment	99,167	Bonds payable	1,500,000
Building	1,995,833	Fund balance	1,026,833
Total	$2,685,000	Total	$2,685,000

It is also possible to prepare the following statement of revenues and expenses:

Alpha Hospital
Statement of Revenues and Expenses
for Month Ended January 31, 1987

Revenues	$200,000
Less expenses	
Wages and salaries	$110,000
Supplies	50,000
Depreciation	5,000
Interest	8,167
Total	$173,167
Excess of revenues over expenses	$ 26,833

Note that the difference between revenue and expense during the month of January was $26,833, the exact amount by which the fund balance of Alpha Hospital changed during the month. Alpha Hospital began the month with $1,000,000 in its fund balance account and ended with $1,026,833. This illustrates an important point to remember in the reading of financial statements: *the individual financial statements are fundamentally related to one another*.

Stable Monetary Unit

The money measurement principle of accounting discussed earlier restricted accounting measures to money. In accounting in the

U.S., the unit of measure is the U.S. dollar. At the present time, no adjustment to changes in the general purchasing power of that unit is required in financial reports; a 1972 dollar is assumed to be equal in value to a 1987 dollar. This permits arithmetic operations, such as addition and subtraction. If this assumption were not made, addition of the unadjusted historical cost values of assets acquired in different time periods would be inappropriate, like adding apples and oranges. Current, generally accepted accounting principles incorporate the *stable monetary unit principle*.

This principle may not seem to pose any great problems. In fact, when the inflation rate was less than two percent annually, it did not. However, given the recent high rates of inflation, the effects of assuming a stable monetary unit can be quite dramatic. Imagine that the inflation rate in the economy is currently 100 percent, compounded monthly. The hypothetical entity under consideration is a neighborhood health center that has all its expenses, except payroll, covered by grants from governmental agencies. Its employees have a contract that automatically adjusts their wages to changes in the general price level. (With a monthly inflation rate of 100 percent, it is no wonder.) Assume that revenues from patients are collected on the first day of the month following the one in which they were billed, but that the employees are paid at the beginning of each month. Rates to patients are set so that the excess of revenues over expenses will be zero. With the first month's wages set equal to $100,000, the income and cash flow positions that result for the first six months of the year are shown in the chart.

Note the tremendous difference between income and cash flow. While the income statement would indicate a break-even operation, the cash balance at the end of June would be a negative $3,150,000. Obviously, the health center's operations cannot continue indefinitely in light of the extreme cash hardship position imposed.

Fortunately, the rate of inflation in our economy is not 100 percent. However, smaller rates of inflation compounded over long periods of time could create similar problems. For example, setting rates equal to historical cost depreciation of fixed assets leaves the entity with a significant cash deficit when it is time to replace the asset. Yet, currently many third-party payers do in fact limit reimbursement to unadjusted historical cost depreciation, and few health care organizations actually set rates at levels necessary to recover replacement cost.

Fund Accounting

Fund accounting is a system in which an entity's assets and liabilities are segregated in the accounting records. Each fund may be thought of as an independent entity with its own self-balancing set of accounts. The basic accounting equation discussed under the duality principle must be satisfied for each fund—assets must equal liabilities plus fund balance for the particular fund in question. This is, in fact, how the term *fund balance* developed; a fund balance originally represented the residual interest for a *particular fund*.

Fund accounting is widely employed by nonprofit, voluntary health care facilities, especially

	Income Flows			Cash Flows		
	Expense	Revenue	Net Income	Inflow	Outflow	Difference
January	$ 100,000	$ 100,000	0	$ 50,000*	$ 100,000	(50,000)
February	200,000	200,000	0	100,000	200,000	(100,000)
March	400,000	400,000	0	200,000	400,000	(200,000)
April	800,000	800,000	0	400,000	800,000	(400,000)
May	1,600,000	1,600,000	0	800,000	1,600,000	(800,000)
June	3,200,000	3,200,000	0	1,600,000	3,200,000	(1,600,000)
	$6,300,000	$6,300,000	0	$3,150,000	$6,300,000	(3,150,000)

*Equal to the revenue billed in December.

hospitals. It is not a basic concept or principle of accounting like those previously discussed, but it is a feature peculiar to accounting for many health care organizations. It evolved primarily for use in stewarding funds donated by external parties who imposed stipulations on the usage of those monies.

Two major categories of funds are presently used in the hospital industry and in other health care facilities: They are restricted and unrestricted. A restricted fund is one in which a third party, outside the entity, has imposed certain restrictions on the use of donated monies or resources. There are three common types of restricted funds:

1. specific-purpose funds
2. plant replacement and expansion funds
3. endowment funds

Specific-purpose funds are donated by individuals or organizations and restricted for purposes other than plant replacement and expansion or endowment. Monies received from governmental agencies to perform specific research or other work are examples of specific-purpose funds.

Plant replacement and expansion funds are restricted for use in plant replacement and expansion. Assets purchased with these monies are not recorded in the fund. When the monies are used for plant purposes, the amounts are transferred to the unrestricted fund. For example, if $200,000 in cash from the plant replacement fund were used to acquire a piece of equipment, the equipment and fund balance of the unrestricted fund would be increased.

Endowment funds are contributed to be held intact for generating income. The income may or may not be restricted for specific purposes. Some endowments are classified as *term* endowments. That is, after the expiration of some time period, the restriction on use of the principal is lifted. The balance is then transferred to the unrestricted fund.

Unrestricted funds have no third-party donor restrictions imposed upon them. In some cases, the governing board of the organization may restrict use, but, since this is not an external or third-party restriction, the funds are still classified as unrestricted. Sometimes, the unrestricted fund is referred to as the general or operating fund.

CONVENTIONS OF ACCOUNTING

The accounting principles discussed up to this point are important in the preparation of financial statements. However, several widely accepted conventions modify the application of these principles in certain circumstances. We shall discuss three of the more important conventions:

1. conservatism
2. materiality
3. consistency

Conservatism affects the valuation of some assets. Specifically, accountants use a "lower of cost or market rule" for valuing inventories and marketable securities. The "lower of cost or market" rule means that the value of a stock of inventory or marketable securities would be its actual cost or market value, whichever is less. For these resources, there is a deviation from cost valuation to market valuation whenever market value is lower.

Materiality permits certain transactions to be treated out of accordance with generally accepted accounting principles. This might be permitted because the transaction does not materially affect the presentation of financial position. For example, theoretically, paper clips have an estimated useful life greater than one year. However, the cost of capitalizing this item and systematically and rationally allocating it over its useful life is not justifiable; the difference in financial position that would be created by not using generally accepted accounting principles would be immaterial.

Consistency limits the accounting alternatives that can be used. In any given transaction, there is usually a variety of available, generally acceptable accounting treatments. For example, generally accepted accounting principles permit the use of double-declining balance, sum-of-the-year digits, or straight-line methods for allocating the costs of depreciable assets over their estimated useful life; but the consistency convention limits an entity's ability to change from one acceptable method to another. Recall that the opinion paragraph in a CPA's audit report assures that generally accepted accounting principles have been applied on a basis *consistent* with that of the previous year.

SUMMARY

In this chapter we have discussed the importance of generally accepted accounting principles in deriving financial information. Although these principles are formally required only in the preparation of audited financial statements, they influence the derivation of most financial information. An understanding of some of the basic principles is critical to an understanding of financial information in general.

Six specific principles of accounting were discussed in some detail:

1. accounting entity
2. money measurement
3. duality
4. cost valuation
5. accrual accounting
6. stable monetary unit

In addition to these, the general importance of fund accounting, as it relates to the hospital and health care industry, was discussed. The chapter concluded with a discussion of three conventions that may modify the application of generally accepted accounting principles in specific situations.

Chapter 2

Financial Statements

William O. Cleverley
Professor, Graduate Program in Hospital and Health Services Management
The Ohio State University

Understanding the principles of accounting is a critical first step in understanding financial statements. However, the format and language of financial statements may be unintelligible to the occasional reader. In this chapter we discuss in some detail the four major general-purpose financial statements:

1. balance sheet
2. statement of revenues and expenses
3. statement of changes in financial position
4. statement of changes in fund balances

In addition, we examine the footnotes to the financial statements.

The balance sheet and statement of revenues and expenses are more widely published and used than the other two statements. Understanding them enables a reader to use the other two financial statements and financial information in general. Therefore, in the following discussion, we pay major attention to the balance sheet and statement of revenues and expenses.

The balance sheets examined in the following two sections illustrate the separation of funds into unrestricted and restricted categories. Restricted funds are not available for general

operating purposes. The duality principle can also be seen operating in these balance sheets. Assets equal liabilities plus fund balance in both restricted and unrestricted balance sheets. In both cases, the entity being accounted for is Omega Hospital.

BALANCE SHEET: UNRESTRICTED FUNDS

Current Assets

Assets that are expected to be exchanged for cash or consumed during the operating cycle of the entity (or one year, whichever is longer) are classified as current assets on the balance sheet. The operating cycle is the length of time between acquisition of materials and services and collection of revenue generated by them. Since the operating cycle for most health care organizations is significantly less than one year (perhaps three months or less), current assets are predominantly those that may be expected to be converted into cash or used to reduce expenditures of cash within one year.

Cash

Cash represents the funds on hand in bill or coin form or in savings or checking accounts. It does not include funds restricted in some way,

This chapter is reprinted from *Essentials of Health Care Finance*, 2nd ed., by W.O. Cleverley, pp. 67–93, Aspen Publishers, Inc., © 1986.

for example, cash funds restricted for investment in retirement plans or self-insurance plans.

Marketable Securities

Marketable securities, or short-term investments, comprise another major category of cur-

rent assets that often shows up on balance sheets, although it is not shown in Exhibit 2-1. In some cases, cash and marketable securities are combined. This is not considered bad reporting because the liquidity of marketable securities allows them to be treated as cash for most purposes. Marketable securities are short-term in-

Exhibit 2-1 Balance Sheet for Omega Hospital, Unrestricted Funds

Omega Hospital Balance Sheet
Unrestricted Funds June 30, 1987
(with comparative figures for 1986)

	June 30	
	1987	1986
Assets		
Current assets		
Cash	$ 376,766	$ 46,073
Accounts receivable		
Patients (less contractual allowances from third–party payers of $278,000 in 1987 and $248,000 in 1986, and allowance for doubtful accounts of $330,000 in 1987 and $295,000 in 1986)	3,675,531	2,846,266
Other	272,144	260,070
Inventories	325,720	255,176
Prepaid expenses	343,640	289,806
Total current assets	4,993,801	3,697,391
Property and equipment		
Land and improvements	413,809	408,557
Buildings and equipment	11,191,834	10,776,959
Building additions in progress	25,741,801	18,199,040
Other construction in progress	377,317	36,502
	37,724,761	29,421,058
Allowances for depreciation	6,745,307	6,106,815
Total property and equipment	30,979,454	23,314,243
Other assets		
Board-designated investments	98,328	102,470
Total	$36,071,583	$27,114,104
Liabilities reserve and fund balance		
Current liabilities		
Accounts payable—trade	$ 797,966	$ 760,920
construction contractor	1,665,797	1,724,878
Advances from third–party payers	142,051	—
Loan payable—restricted fund	—	554,689
Accrued expenses	1,341,393	868,091
Payroll deductions	127,478	143,017
Current maturities or mortgages payable	222,386	—
Total current liabilities	4,297,071	4,051,595
Mortgages payable	21,515,300	14,440,202
Loan payable—restricted fund	1,390,905	—
Total liabilities	27,203,276	18,491,797
Deferred revenue	56,000	76,000
Fund balance	8,812,307	8,546,307
Total	$36,071,583	$27,114,104

vestments that meet two criteria. First, management must intend to sell or convert them to cash within a year's time. This is guaranteed if the maturity of the investment is less than one year. Second, they must have a readily available and active market. Marketable securities are valued at their cost or market value, whichever is lower. This is one of the few exceptions to the cost valuation principle.

Accounts Receivable

Accounts receivable represent legally enforceable claims on customers for prior services or goods. In Omega Hospital, there are two categories of accounts receivable: patient and other. Other accounts receivable in a health care organization imply revenue derived from sources other than patient services. For example, Omega Hospital has a physician's office building, a parking ramp, and a number of educational programs. Accounts receivable may exist in one or all of those areas.

Patient accounts receivable are usually the largest accounts receivable item and, for that matter, the largest single current asset item in the balance sheet. Omega Hospital is no exception—it has an estimated $3,675,531 in accounts receivable that will eventually result in cash. The actual dollar amount of accounts receivable is higher but is reduced by estimated allowances.

A characteristic of hospitals and other health care organizations that makes their accounts receivable different from those of most other organizations is that the charges actually billed to patients are quite often settled for substantially less than the amounts charged. The differences are also known as allowances. Four major categories of allowances are used to restate accounts receivable to expected, realizable value:

1. charity allowances
2. courtesy allowances
3. doubtful account allowances
4. contractual allowances

A charity allowance is the difference between established service rates and amounts actually charged to indigent patients. Many health care facilities, especially clinics and other ambulatory care settings, have a policy of scaling the normal charge by some factor based on income. A courtesy allowance is the difference between established rates for services and rates billed special patients, such as employees, doctors, and clergy. A doubtful account allowance is the difference between rates billed and amounts expected to be recovered. For example, a medically indigent patient might actually receive services that have an established rate of $100, but be billed only $50. If it is anticipated that the patient will not pay even the $50, then that $50 will show up as a doubtful account allowance.

In most situations, contractual allowances represent the largest deduction from accounts receivable. A contractual allowance is the difference between rates billed to a third-party payer, such as Medicare, and the amount that will actually be paid by that third-party payer. For example, a Medicare patient may receive hospital services priced at $4,000 but actually pay the hospital only $3,000 for those services, based upon the patient's diagnosis-related group (DRG) classification. If this account is unpaid at the fiscal year end, the financial statements would include the net amount to be paid, $3,000, as an account receivable. Accounts receivable represent the amount of cash expected to be received, not the gross prices charged. Since most major payers—such as Medicare, Medicaid, and Blue Cross—have a contractual relationship that permits payment on a basis other than charges, contractual allowances can be, and usually are, very large.

It is important to note that the allowances are estimates and will, in all probability, differ from the actual value of accounts receivable that will eventually be written off. For example, Omega Hospital shows an expected value of accounts receivable to be collected as $3,675,531 in 1987, but it actually has $4,283,531 of outstanding accounts receivable.

Net accounts receivable	$3,675,531
Contractual allowances	278,000
Doubtful account allowance	330,000
Accounts receivable gross	$4,283,531

Since estimation of allowances is so critical to the reported value of accounts receivable, the methodology should be scrutinized. Just how was the estimate developed? Has the estimating method been used in the past with any degree of reliability? An external audit performed by an independent certified public accountant (CPA) can usually provide the required degree of reliability and assurance.

Inventories

Inventories in a health care facility represent items that are to be used in the delivery of health care services. They may range from normal business office supplies to highly specialized chemicals used in a laboratory.

Prepaid Expenses

Prepaid expenses represent expenditures already made for future service. In Omega Hospital, they may represent prepayment of insurance premiums for the year, rents on leased equipment, or other similar items. For example, an insurance premium for a professional liability insurance policy may be $600,000 per year, due one year in advance. If this amount were paid on January 1, then on June 30, $300,000, or one-half the total, would be shown as a prepaid expense.

Property and Equipment

This category is sometimes called fixed assets or shown more descriptively as plant property and equipment. Items in this category represent investment in tangible, permanent assets; they are sometimes referred to as the capital assets of the organization. These items are shown at the historical cost or acquisition cost, reduced by allowances for depreciation.

Land and Improvements

Land and improvements represent the historical cost of the earth's surface owned by the health care facility and the historical cost of any improvements erected on it. Such improvements might include water and sewer systems, roadways, fences, sidewalks, shrubbery, and parking lots. While land may not be depreciated, land

improvements may. Land held for investment purposes is not shown in this category but will appear as an investment in the other assets section.

Buildings and Equipment

Buildings and equipment represent all buildings and equipment owned by the entity and used in the normal course of its operations. These items are also stated at historical cost. Buildings and equipment not used in the normal course of operations should be reported separately. For example, real estate investments would not be shown in the fixed asset or plant property and equipment section but in the other assets section. Equipment in many situations is classified into three categories: (1) *fixed equipment*—affixed to the building in which it is located, including items such as elevators, boilers, and generators; (2) *major movable equipment*—usually stationary but capable of being moved, including reasonably expensive items such as automobiles, laboratory equipment, and x-ray apparatus; and (3) *minor equipment*—usually low in cost with short estimated useful lives, including such items as wastebaskets, glassware, and sheets.

Construction in Progress

Construction in progress represents the amount of money that has been expended on projects that are still not complete at the date the financial statement is published. In Omega Hospital, there are currently $25,741,801 of building additions in progress and $377,317 of other construction in progress. When these projects are completed, the values will be charged to buildings and equipment.

Allowance for Depreciation

Allowance for depreciation represents the accumulated depreciation taken on the asset to the date of the financial statement. The concept of depreciation is important and useful in a wide variety of decisions. The following example illustrates the depreciation concept: A $500 desk is purchased and depreciated over a five-year life. The balance sheet values are presented on the following page.

	Year				
	1	2	3	4	5
Historical equipment cost	$500	$500	$500	$500	$500
Allowance for depreciation	100	200	300	400	500
Net	$400	$300	$200	$100	$ 0

In the case of Omega Hospital, there is $6,745,307 of accumulated depreciation at June 30, 1987. The historical cost base for this amount is probably fairly close to $11,191,834, the historical cost value of buildings and equipment. In reality, the figure is slightly higher because land improvements are also depreciated and would be included in the accumulated depreciation total. This means that 60.26 percent of the historical cost of present facilities has been depreciated in prior years. As the ratio of allowance for depreciation to building and equipment increases, it usually signifies that a physical plant will need replacement in the near future. Omega Hospital appears to be in such a situation, which may partially explain the current construction.

Other Assets

Other assets are assets that are neither current nor involve plant and equipment. Typically, they are either investments or intangible assets. In the case of Omega Hospital, all other assets consist of investments that have been board-restricted; they must be shown in the unrestricted balance sheet because the board restriction does not qualify as a third-party restriction. However, they are shown separately in the unrestricted balance sheet to identify the restriction.

Two major intangible asset items that show up in some health care facility balance sheets are goodwill and organization costs. Goodwill represents the difference between the price paid to acquire another entity and the fair market value of the acquired entity's assets, less any related obligations or liabilities. Goodwill shows up mainly in proprietary facilities, although it is also being increasingly seen in voluntary not-for-profit organizations as they acquire other health care entities. Organization costs are expended for legal and accounting fees and other items incurred at the formation of the entity. The cost of these items is usually amortized over some allowable life.

Current Liabilities

Current liabilities are obligations that are expected to require payment in cash during the coming year or operating cycle, whichever is longer. Like current assets, they are generally expected to be paid in one year's time.

Accounts Payable

Accounts payable may be thought of as the counterpart of accounts receivable. They represent the entity's promise to pay money for goods or services it has received. In the Omega Hospital example, two types of accounts payable appear, one resulting from normal activity, called accounts payable—trade, the other due to the construction contractor for work in process, referred to as accounts payable—construction contractor.

Advances from Third Parties

Advances from third parties constitute an account that is somewhat peculiar to the health care industry. In some situations, a third-party payer, Blue Cross particularly, will pay a health care entity a sum in advance of the provision of services. Since the entity must generally invest its resources prior to payment, this advance partially offsets the entity's requirement for a cash outflow and helps meet the financial requirements of the health care facility. An additional advantage is that the advance may reduce the amount of money a health care provider must borrow; this in turn reduces interest expense and thereby keeps costs down in the long run.

Accrued Expenses

Accrued expenses are obligations that result from prior operations. They are thus a present right or enforceable demand. The accruing of interest expense with the passage of time, discussed in Chapter 1, is an example. Other examples of accrued expenses are payroll, vacation pay, tax deductions, rent, and insurance. In some cases, especially payroll, accrued expenses are disaggregated to show material categories. Omega Hospital does not do this, but it does show a separate listing of payroll deductions.

Payroll Deductions

Payroll deductions represent amounts withheld from employees' wages to meet a variety of federal, state, and local obligations, for example, social security contributions and income taxes.

Current Maturities of Long-Term Debt

Current maturities of long-term debt represent the amount of principal that will be repaid on the indebtedness within the coming year. It does not equal the total amount of the payments that will be made during that year. Total payments include both interest and principal; current maturities of long-term debt include just the principal portion. For example, if at the June 30 fiscal year close, a total of $360,000 ($30,000 per month) will be paid on long-term indebtedness during the coming year and, of this amount, only $120,000 is principal payment, then $120,000 would be shown as a current maturity of long-term debt.

Noncurrent Liabilities

Noncurrent liabilities include obligations that will not require payment in cash for at least one year or more. Omega Hospital shows two types of noncurrent liabilities, mortgages payable and loan payable from restricted fund.

Mortgage Payable

Mortgage payable is one source of long-term indebtedness. The adjective mortgage implies that the indebtedness is collateralized by a lien on some set of the entity's assets. Other examples of long-term debt are bonds payable and notes payable.

Loan Payable—Restricted Fund

Omega Hospital also has a noncurrent liability described as a loan payable from restricted funds. This brings up an important issue. Just how valid is this liability? The debt is, after all, owed to the entity itself. Note that at June 30, 1986, the indebtedness of $554,689 is classified as a current liability, but on June 30, 1987, the indebtedness of $1,390,905 is classified as noncurrent. This transfer from current liabilities to noncurrent liabilities causes some speculation about the validity of the indebtedness. However, it must be remembered that a restricted fund is one in which a third party has imposed some restrictions on use. The validity of the loan, as well as the separation of funds, depends upon the legitimacy of those restrictions.

Deferred Revenue

Deferred revenue is not classified as liability or fund balance. Deferred revenue means cash or other assets received prior to the actual recognition of the amount as revenue. Typically, in the health care industry, the deferred revenue account is used to recognize timing differences between the receipt of cash and the recognition of it as revenue. For example, Omega Hospital may have used some form of accelerated depreciation for cost-reimbursement purposes but used straight-line depreciation for financial reporting. Specifically, in the desk illustration discussed earlier, straight-line depreciation in the first year would be $100. If the sum-of-the-year digits depreciation method were used for reimbursement purposes, first year depreciation would be $167. The difference ($67) would be recorded as deferred revenue. At the conclusion of the useful life of this asset, the deferred revenue account would be zero.

Fund Balance

Fund balance, as discussed earlier, represents the difference between assets and the claim to those assets by third parties or liabilities. Increases in this account balance usually arise from one of two sources: (1) contributions or (2) earnings.

In the nonprofit health care industry, there is usually no separation in the fund balance account to recognize these two sources. Thus, there is no indication of how much of Omega Hospital's fund balance of $8,812,307 was earned and how much was contributed. Financial statements prepared for proprietary entities do show this breakdown. Earnings of prior years, reduced by dividend payments to stockholders, are shown in an account labeled retained earnings.

In any given year, however, it is possible to determine the sources of change in fund balance by examining the statement of changes in fund balance (see Exhibit 2-5). For example, in fiscal year 1987, transfers from the plant replacement and renovation fund, a restricted fund, accounted for all the increase in fund balance. These transfers more than offset the operating loss of $226,247 for the period.

The value of the fund balance account at any point in time is often confused with the cash position of the entity. However, cash and fund balance will hardly ever be equal. In most situations, the cash balance will be far less than fund balance. For example, Omega Hospital has $8,812,307 in fund balance at June 30, 1987, but only $376,766 in cash at the same date. Thus, the assumption that the $8,812,307 reported as fund balance can be converted into cash is a false assumption.

BALANCE SHEET: RESTRICTED FUNDS

The balance sheet of Omega Hospital has a separate accounting for four funds that third parties have restricted (see Exhibit 2-2):

1. specific-purpose fund
2. research fund
3. endowment fund
4. plant replacement and renovation fund

It is possible to think of these four funds as separate balance sheets, each satisfying the basic accounting equation of

$$Assets = Liabilities + Fund\ Balance$$

For example, Omega Hospital's plant replacement and renovation fund has a balance of $3,378,408, which must equal its assets because no liabilities exist. The assets of the plant replacement and renovation fund consist of $1,681,258 in cash and money market investments, $306,245 in pledges receivable, and $1,390,905 in loans receivable from unrestricted funds.

Omega Hospital Balance Sheet
Plant Replacement and Renovation Fund

Assets

Cash and money market investments	$1,681,258
Pledges receivable	306,245
Loan receivable—unrestricted fund	1,390,905
Total	$3,378,408

Fund Balance

Fund balance	$3,378,408

This arithmetic is also representative of the other three funds.

The use of the cost valuation principle can be seen clearly in the investments of the endowment fund. In 1986 and 1987, the market value of the investments was less than their historical cost, but cost valuation continued to be used. In reality, Omega Hospital does not have $685,815 in endowment fund investments; it has only a realizable value of $575,431. This difference could be caused by poor investment management or external limitations on investment imposed by the stipulations of the initial gift. Regardless of the reason, the hospital has seen a decline in its initial donated value of $110,384 (see Exhibit 2-2).

Pledges receivable is an account that may be unfamiliar to many individuals. It represents a

Exhibit 2-2 Balance Sheet for Omega Hospital, Restricted Funds

Omega Hospital
Balance Sheet
Restricted Funds
June 30, 1987
(with comparative figures for 1986)

	June 30	
	1987	1986
Assets		
Cash and money market investments		
Specific-purpose funds	$ 117,889	$ 92,156
Research funds	57,848	46,347
Endowment funds	62,161	52,096
Plant replacement and renovation fund	1,681,258	2,248,863
Investments—endowment funds, at cost (approximate market value $575,431 in 1987 and $538,000 in 1986)	685,815	685,815
Plant replacement and renovation fund		
Pledges receivable	306,245	678,662
Loan receivable from unrestricted fund	1,390,905	554,689
	$4,302,121	$4,358,628
Fund balance		
Specific-purpose funds	$ 117,889	$ 92,156
Research funds	57,848	46,347
Endowment funds		
Free care	598,426	598,426
Scholarships	111,529	112,212
Other	38,021	27,273
Plant replacement and renovation fund	3,378,408	3,482,214
	$4,302,121	$4,358,628

legally enforceable commitment from a third party. In the case of Omega Hospital, $306,245 of pledges are currently outstanding as of June 30, 1987. These pledges are restricted and must be used for plant replacement and renovation. Restricted in this way, they will never have to be reported as income by Omega Hospital. Depending upon management's objectives, it may or it may not be advantageous to restrict the majority of gifts. For example, a hospital faced with regulatory controls on income may wish to restrict all pledges so that it will not have to report them as income. Nonetheless, it is important to recognize such sources of unreported income in the assessment of a health care entity's financial strength.

STATEMENT OF REVENUES AND EXPENSES

The statement of revenues and expenses (Exhibit 2-3) has become a financial statement of increasing importance, both in the proprietary and nonproprietary sectors. It gives a better picture of operations in a given time period than a balance sheet does. A balance sheet summarizes the wealth position of an entity at a given point in time by delineating its assets, liabilities, and fund balance. An income statement provides information concerning *how* that wealth position was changed through operations.

An entity's ability to earn an excess of revenue over expenses is an important variable in many external and internal decisions. A series of income statements indicates this ability well. Creditors use income statements to determine the entity's ability to pay future and present debts; management and rate-regulating agencies use them to assess whether current and proposed rate structures are adequate.

The *entity principle* is an important factor in analyzing and interpreting the statement of revenue and expense. Income, the excess of revenue over expenses, comes from a large number of individual operations within a health care entity

Exhibit 2-3 Statement of Revenues and Expenses for Omega Hospital

Omega Hospital
Statement of Revenue and Expense
Year Ended June 30, 1987
(with comparative figures for 1986)

	Year Ended June 30	
	1987	1986
Hospital services		
Patient service revenue	$23,448,220	$19,814,924
Allowances and uncollectible accounts	1,208,376	751,475
Patient service revenue, before contractual allowances	22,239,844	19,063,449
Other operating revenue	665,160	614,834
Total operating revenue	22,905,004	19,678,283
Operating expenses		
Nursing services	7,331,032	6,329,254
Other professional services	7,273,611	6,303,910
General services	3,769,307	3,086,584
Fiscal services	1,002,768	869,857
Administrative services	2,871,246	1,902,813
Provision for depreciation	549,799	470,609
Interest expense	156,695	85,266
Total operating expenses	22,954,458	19,048,293
Excess (deficiency) of operating revenues over operating expenses	(49,454)	629,990
Nonoperating revenues	11,126	67,989
Excess (deficiency) of revenues over expenses	(38,328)	697,979
Professional office building services		
Excess of expenses over revenues	(80,420)	—
Parking ramp service		
Excess of expenses over revenues	(107,499)	—
Excess (deficiency) of revenues over expenses	$(226,247)	$ 697,979

and is aggregated in the statement of revenue and expense. For example, reports on minor breakdowns may be required on a departmental basis for some decisions; little can be said about specific rates and their adequacy within a health care facility if departmental statements of revenue and expense are not available. Such statements are in fact frequently available and should be used. Here, however, our focus is on the general-purpose statement of revenue and expense, which is an aggregate of individual departments' income.

Revenue

Generally speaking, revenue in a health care facility comes from three sources:

1. operations related to patient services
2. operations not related to patient services
3. nonoperating sources

Patient Service Revenue

Patient service revenue in most facilities is by far the largest source of revenue. Omega Hospital reported $23,448,220 of patient service revenue in 1987. This amount is stated at its gross or billed value and does not reflect what amounts were actually collected or expected to be collected. To determine what was or will be collected, the gross figure must be reduced by estimates of the four categories of allowances discussed earlier in the chapter. Omega Hospital had $1,208,376 of allowances and uncollectible accounts in 1987, which yielded a net patient service revenue of $22,239,844. Net patient service revenue reflects the amount of revenue that will be realized in cash payments; it measures what is or will be collected, not what was charged.

Earlier discussion of accounts receivable briefly mentioned the four categories of allowances (charity, courtesy, contractual, and uncollectible) that must be estimated to state accounts receivable properly in terms of realizable cash value. Note that the value of the esti

mated allowances for accounts receivable in 1987 (see Exhibit 2-1) is

$$\$278{,}000 + \$330{,}000 = \$608{,}000$$

This figure is significantly less than the amount shown in the statement of revenue and expenses for allowances, $1,208,376. This kind of difference is quite common. Remember that the balance sheet value reflects the estimated allowances for accounts still outstanding, whereas the statement of revenue and expenses reflects the allowance for all patient service revenue billed during the year.

Certain categories of patient service revenue are important in decision making. Payment source is especially important. Some common categories of payment sources are

- Medicare
- Medicaid
- Blue Cross
- commercial insurance
- self-pay
- other

Identification of these categories is critical to setting rates and making many other financial decisions, such as in the projection of short-term cash flow and collection efforts. Ordinarily, this information is available within the entity, although it is not usually published in general-purpose financial statements. Departmental breakdowns of data are also useful in many decisions and are available internally, but they are not usually published in general-purpose financial statements.

Other Operating Revenue

Other operating revenue is generated from normal, day-to-day operations not directly related to patient care. It is usually classified by source into three categories: (1) educational programs, (2) grants, and (3) miscellaneous. Revenue from such educational programs as nursing, medicine, laboratory, and x-ray technology may generate tuition and other fees that show up in this category. Omega Hospital had a relatively large dollar amount of other operating revenue— $665,160 in 1987—much of it representing tuition from educational programs.

Grants from research projects or projects run by federal or other agencies are also reported as other operating revenue. Omega Hospital has some monies in this category, as shown in the statement of changes in fund balances (see Exhibit 2-5). A transfer of $75,775 as other operating revenue was made from the restricted research fund to the unrestricted fund in 1987.

Miscellaneous sources of other operating revenue include such items as revenue from office rentals, cafeteria and gift shop sales, and parking lot fees. It is important to note that this revenue is not always offset against its related expenses. As a result, it is sometimes impossible to determine whether the operations were profitable or not. If they are minor or immaterial, their value determination is not an important problem. However, Omega Hospital believes that its parking lot and professional office building operations are significant enough to warrant separate reporting. Therefore, in Omega's statement of revenue and expenses, this revenue is netted against related expenses, rather than appearing just as other operating revenue.

Nonoperating Revenue

Nonoperating revenue is revenue not related to patient care or to normal day-to-day operations. Major categories of nonoperating revenue are (1) unrestricted gifts, (2) unrestricted income from endowments, and (3) miscellaneous.

Unrestricted gifts—gifts with no restrictions on use—are treated as nonoperating revenue. Omega Hospital had relatively few of these gifts in the two years for which we have information. However, it did receive a large dollar amount of gifts restricted for plant replacement and renovation in the past, as evidenced by the values for pledges receivable shown in the restricted balance sheet.

If income from an endowment is not restricted, it may be used for general operating purposes and treated as nonoperating revenue. The statement of changes in fund balances (see Exhibit 2-5) shows that only $2,018 of income was designated as nonoperating revenue in 1987. Revenue from miscellaneous sources includes income from unrestricted funds; rentals of facilities not used in operations, such as farm land or apartments; and, in some cases, the fair market value of services donated by volunteers.

Operating Expenses

In these days of increasing concern over health care costs, decision makers are paying more attention to health care facilities' operating expenses. Generally speaking, there are two ways that expenses may be categorized: (1) by cost or responsibility center or (2) by object or type of expenditure.

In most general-purpose financial statements, costs are reported by cost center or department. Omega Hospital breaks down expenses into five major categories of departments:

1. nursing service areas
2. other professional service areas
3. general service areas
4. fiscal service areas
5. administrative service areas

Nursing service and other professional services could also be classified as revenue departments. They provide services directly to patients, for which there is a charge. General, fiscal, and administrative services are indirect or support-area services; they are not direct patient services, but rather support the nursing and other professional service areas.

Two expenses, depreciation and interest, are listed by object or type of expense category. As explained in the next chapter, these two expense categories are critical to many decisions and require separate reporting.

It should be noted that expense and expenditure (or payment and cash) may not be equivalent in any given period. For example, a health care facility may incur an expenditure of $1 million to buy a piece of equipment but may charge only $200,000 as depreciation expense in a given

year. In general, expenditure reflects the payment of cash, while expense recognizes prior expenditure that has produced revenue. In general,
there are three major categories of expenditures
that are not treated as expenses:

1. retirement or repayment of debt
2. investment in new fixed assets
3. increases in working capital or current
   assets

One major category of expense—depreciation
on fixed assets—does not involve a cash expenditure. In addition, other normal accruals, such
as vacation and sick leave benefits, may be recognized as expense but involve no immediate
cash outlay.

STATEMENT OF CHANGES IN FINANCIAL POSITION

The statement of changes in financial position
is designed to give additional information on the
flow of funds within an entity. As we have noted,
the concept of expense does not necessarily give
decision makers information on funds flow. The
statement of changes in financial position is
designed to give information on the flow of funds
within an entity and to summarize the sources
that make funds available and the uses for those
funds during a given period.

Funds are usually defined as working capital.
This is true for Omega Hospital, as shown in its
statement of changes in financial position (see
Exhibit 2-4). Major categories of fund sources
include

Exhibit 2-4 Statement of Changes in Financial Position for Omega Hospital, Unrestricted Funds

Omega Hospital
Statement of Changes in Financial Position
Unrestricted Funds
Year Ended June 30, 1987

	12 Months to June 30, 1987
Source of funds	
Net operating income before depreciation	$ 500,345
Nonoperating income	11,126
Professional office building income before depreciation	(2,883)
Parking ramp income before depreciation	31,253
Loan from restricted funds	1,390,905
Increase in mortgage payable	7,075,098
County construction grant	128,000
Decrease in other assets	4,142
Transferred from restricted fund for plant renovation and equipment	364,247
Total sources of funds	$9,502,233
Uses of funds	
Purchase of fixed assets	888,538
Construction of new facilities	7,542,761
Decrease in deferred revenue	20,000
Increase in working capital	1,050,934
Total uses of fund	$9,502,233
Changes in working capital	
Increase in current assets	$1,296,410
Less increase in current liabilities	245,476
Increase in working capital	$1,050,934

- income-related sources
- debt financing
- sale of assets

Major uses of funds include

- purchase of fixed assets
- repayment of debt
- increases in working capital

Income-related sources represent the difference between revenue and expenses, plus the related depreciation expense. Depreciation is added back to income because depreciation does not involve an actual expenditure of cash or funds. Many financial analysts refer to the sum of depreciation and net income as cash flow. In Omega Hospital, net operating income before depreciation was $500,345, which equals $549,799 of depreciation less the $49,454 operating loss.

STATEMENT OF CHANGES IN FUND BALANCE

The statement of changes in fund balance for both unrestricted and restricted funds merely accounts for the changes in fund balance during the year. Information on flows between restricted and unrestricted funds and flows into the entity that are restricted can be obtained from this statement.

In fiscal years 1986 and 1987, Omega Hospital had a lot of activity in the plant replacement and renovation fund (see Exhibit 2-5). The fund received $363,000 in county construction grants, earned $412,530 in interest on its investment, and received $174,383 in pledges. Such transactions are never reported as income in a statement of revenues and expenses, but they did have a very positive effect on Omega Hospital's financial position. Close scrutiny of the statement of changes in fund balance can detect many of these flows.

Exhibit 2-5 Statement of Changes in Fund Balance for Omega Hospital

Omega Hospital
Statement of Changes in Fund Balances
Year Ended June 30, 1987,
with Comparative Figures for 1986

	Year Ended June 30	
	1987	1986
Unrestricted funds		
Balance at beginning of year	$8,546,307	$7,129,625
Excess (deficiency) of revenues over expenses	(226,247)	697,979
Transfers from plant replacement and renovation fund to purchase property and equipment		
County construction grant	128,000	235,000
Renovation construction	302,032	450,110
Other donations and bequests	62,215	33,593
Balance at end of year	$8,812,307	$8,546,307

Exhibit 2-5 continued

	Year Ended June 30	
	1987	1986
Restricted funds		
Specific-purpose funds		
Balance at beginning of year	$ 92,156	$ 83,586
Increases		
Contributions	40,019	30,472
Grants	28,397	10,478
Nursing school tuition and fees	57,851	47,312
Nursing student loan repayments	4,585	5,404
Transfer from endowment funds	3,781	3,912
Total increases	134,633	97,578
Decreases		
Specific-purpose disbursements	24,512	19,482
Transfers to unrestricted fund		
Operating revenue or expense	51,037	42,085
Nursing student scholarships	13,148	12,116
Property and equipment	14,134	—
Transfer to plant replacement and renovation fund	—	8,079
Student loan cancellation and repayment of government student loan advances and contra-adjustments	6,069	7,246
	108,900	89,008
Balance at end of year	$ 117,889	$ 92,156
Research funds		
Balance at beginning of year	$ 46,347	$ 44,942
Increases		
Contributions and bequests	3,688	1,584
Grants	83,588	151,208
Total increases	87,276	152,792
Decreases		
Transfers to unrestricted funds (operating revenues)	75,775	151,387
Balance at end of year	$ 57,848	$ 46,347

Exhibit 2-5 continued

	Year Ended June 30	
	1987	1986
Endowment funds		
Balance at beginning of year	$ 737,911	$ 741,133
Increases		
Income from investments	43,898	49,430
Decreases		
Transfers to unrestricted funds		
Operating revenue	22,311	36,497
Nonoperating revenue	2,018	2,022
Endowment fund disbursements	5,723	10,221
Transfers to specific-purpose funds	3,781	3,912
Total decreases	33,833	52,652
Balance at end of year	$ 747,976	$ 737,911
Plant replacement and renovation fund		
Balance at beginning of year	$3,482,214	$3,539,497
Increases		
Contributions	2,125	2,015
County construction grant	128,000	235,000
Interest earned	187,667	224,863
Donated equipment	62,215	25,514
Transfer from specific-purpose funds	—	8,079
Pledges receivable from building fund campaign	8,434	165,949
Total increases	388,441	661,420
Decreases		
Transfers to unrestricted fund		
County construction grant	128,000	235,000
Renovation construction	302,032	450,110
Donated property and equipment	62,215	33,593
Total decreases	492,247	718,703
Balance at end of year	$3,378,408	$3,482,214

Exhibit 2-6 Notes to Financial Statements

Notes to Financial Statements
ABC Medical Center
June 30, 1987

- Note A—Significant accounting policies

Inventories: Inventories are stated at the lower of first-in, first-out cost or market value.

Property and equipment: Property and equipment are stated on the basis of cost or approximate fair value at date of donation. Depreciation, which includes amortization of assets under capital leases, is computed principally by the straight-line method, using rates designed to amortize the cost of such assets over their estimated useful lives. Expenditures for maintenance, repairs, and renewals are charged to operations as they are incurred and betterments are capitalized. The ABC Medical Center eliminates from the accounts the cost and related allowances for property and equipment sold or retired, and any resulting gains or losses are included in operations concurrently.

Investments: Investments in marketable securities are generally stated at cost or fair market value at date of donation.

Cost reimbursement activities with third-party payers: A significant portion of the medical center's revenues is received under contractual arrangements with the Medicare, Medicaid, and Blue Cross programs, whereby the medical center is paid based on allowable costs, as defined. Amounts received under these programs are generally less than at the established billing rates, and the difference is accounted for as a contractual adjustment. Preliminary settlements are subject to redetermination by the responsible agency. The medical center's management believes that adequate provision for anticipated adjustments has been made in the financial statements.

The provision for contractual adjustments is based on revenues and expenses reported for financial statement purposes. The medical center's deferred revenue results from timing differences between expenses reported in the financial statements and currently allowable cost, as defined by third-party payers. The timing differences result primarily from recognizing sick pay on the accrual basis and computing depreciation by the straight-line method for financial reporting, whereas the cash basis and accelerated depreciation accounting methods, respectively, are used for certain reimbursement programs.

Income taxes: The medical center is a nonprofit corporation and has been granted an exemption from the payment of income taxes.

Specific-purpose and endowment funds: The medical center recognizes these resources as revenue during the period in which the expenditures are made for the purpose intended by the donor.

Reclassifications: Certain amounts reported for 1986 have been reclassified to conform with the current year's presentation, with no impact on financial condition.

- Note B—Restatement of 1986 financial statements

The 1986 financial statements for the ABC Medical Center have been restated to reflect proper application of a cost-reimbursement principle that was clarified in connection with an intermediary audit of the medical center's 1986 third-party cost reports. The provision for contractual adjustments has been increased by $600,000 for 1986, resulting in a reduction of revenues in excess of expenses in the same amount.

During 1987, the medical center elected to change the reporting treatment of the plant replacement and renovation fund and the loan repayment sinking fund, which had been established to comply with related loan agreements. Previously, these funds had been reported as restricted funds in the medical center's financial statements. Current industry financial reporting practice indicates that funds such as these, established by requirements of nondonor third parties, should be reported in the unrestricted fund. Balances in these funds are now reported in the unrestricted fund as noncurrent assets. Balances for 1986 have been restated to conform with the 1987 presentation, including nonoperating income, which has been increased by $270,000, representing investment earnings on these funds during 1986.

- Note C—Construction in progress

Construction in progress includes expenditures relating to the renovation of existing facilities. The remaining estimated costs to complete, $7,006,980, will be financed through the proceeds from revenue bonds issued in July 1986 (see Note D).

Exhibit 2-6 continued

• Note D—Long-term debt

On July 15, 1986, the XYZ Hospital Finance Authority issued Series A Revenue Bonds on behalf of the ABC Medical Center in the principal amount of $11,565,000 to finance the renovation of the center's facilities. The proceeds from the bonds were placed with a trustee. The medical center received from the trustee $10,859,500 in exchange for an FHA-insured mortgage note. The mortgage, together with revenues from the project, secures the bonds. The trustee placed the remaining proceeds into a debt service fund, which will be used along with payments on the mortgage by the medical center to make principal and interest payments to the bondholders. The loan agreement requires the medical center to maintain a mortgage reserve fund for use in the event of default. This fund had a balance of $227,148 at June 30, 1987. It is the obligation of the medical center to make loan repayments and any other payments required to pay the interest, principal, and redemption premium, if any, on the bonds.

Long-term debt at June 30, 1987, and 1986, consisted of the following:

	1987	1986
FHA-insured mortgage note, payable in monthly installments of $131,403, including interest at 8.1% plus .5% insurance fee secured by first mortgage on all property, due on December 31, 2004	$14,695,319	$15,065,393
HHS-guaranteed loan, payable in monthly installments of $79,980, including interest at 7.9% with an interest subsidy of 3% (effective interest rate at 4.9%), secured by second mortgage on all property, due on October 1, 2002	8,193,082	8,492,616
FHA-insured mortgage note, payable in equal monthly installments commencing May 1, 1990, including interest at 11%, secured by third mortgage on all property, due April 1, 2010	10,859,500	
Notes payable to the State Hospital Finance Authority, payable in varying monthly installments including interest ranging from 8.75% to 10.95%, secured by equipment with a carrying value of $2,416,937 at June 30, 1987	2,286,732	1,254,913
Note payable with monthly installments of $12,849, including interest at 15%, secured by certain equipment with a carrying value of $352,114 at June 30, 1987	337,164	
Capitalized lease obligations		24,280
	$36,371,797	$24,837,202
Less current maturities	1,331,951	926,361
Totals	$35,039,846	$23,910,841

The FHA loan due 2005 and HHS loan agreements require that, among other things, the medical center maintain a loan repayment fund to be accumulated from that part of its revenue attributable to depreciation expense. The fund is to be sufficient to pay the principal amounts due on the loans and the cost of certain equipment replacement. Such amount must be deposited not less than annually in a separate fund to ensure the accumulation of interest. Withdrawals from the fund may be made only as prescribed in the agreements.

Principal maturities of long-term debt for the four years subsequent to June 30, 1988, are as follows: 1989—$1,488,583; 1990—$1,705,082; 1991—$1,568,827; 1992—$1,375,734.

Interest cost of $124,000 was capitalized in 1987 in connection with the medical center's construction and renovation program.

• Note E—Leases

Future minimum payments, by year and in the aggregate, under noncancelable operating leases with initial or remaining terms of one year or more, consisted of the following at June 30, 1987:

1988	$412,926
1989	107,190
1990	83,488
1991	65,659
1992	7,500
Total minimum lease payments	$676,763

Exhibit 2-6 continued

Rental expense under the operating leases, all of which constituted minimum rentals, aggregated $415,000 in 1987 and $407,000 in 1986.

• Note F—Pension plan

The ABC Medical Center has a pension plan covering substantially all of its employees. Pension expense was $1,013,982 in 1987 and $1,188,746 in 1986. The medical center's policy is to fund pension cost accrued, including amortization of past service cost over 30 years.

Accumulated plan benefit information, as estimated by consulting actuaries, and plan net assets for the medical center's plan are as follows:

| | January 1 | |
	1987	1986
Actuarial present value of accumulated plan benefits:		
Vested	$3,930,249	$6,735,207
Nonvested	441,289	833,814
	$4,371,538	$7,569,021
Net assets available for benefits	$8,261,777	$8,354,398

The reduction in the actuarial present value of accumulated plan benefits is due primarily to the actuary's use of different mortality tables in the 1987 computation. In addition, on July 1, 1986, annuities were purchased for all retirees of record on that date by the plan's previous trustee. Therefore, there is no liability remaining for that group of participants.

The actuarial present value of accumulated plan benefits for the plan is estimated by the consulting actuaries using an assumed rate of return of 7½%.

• Note G—Liability risk insurance

The ABC Medical Center maintains a program of self-insurance for all professional liability and patient general liability risks for claims up to $100,000 per claim and $800,000 in the aggregate. The program is supplemented with a comprehensive excess insurance policy up to $11,000,000 per claim and $13,000,000 in the aggregate. Provision for self-insurance charged to operations was $268,452 in 1987 and $102,897 in 1986. Comprehensive excess insurance premiums were $562,740 and $548,538 in 1987 and 1986, respectively.

The medical center is aware of certain incidents that may result in the assertion of additional claims, and other claims may be asserted arising from services provided to patients in the past. An estimate of the ultimate cost of such potential claims has been provided in the financial statements. The medical center's management believes that the provision for potential claims is adequate.

• Note H—Commitments

The medical center utilized funds from the Hill-Burton program in 1973 and, consequently, must provide a certain volume of uncompensated services each year through 1993. The medical center has provided uncompensated services (1987—$719,069; 1986—$882,211) that exceed the requirements for each of the years ended June 30, 1987, and 1986.

SUMMARY

In this chapter we have discussed the contents of four general-purpose financial statements:

1. balance sheet
2. statement of revenues and expenses
3. statement of changes in financial position
4. statement of changes in fund balances

Primary attention was directed at the first two, balance sheet and statement of revenues and expenses, which provide a basis for most financial information.

Our attention in this chapter was directed at understanding the basic information available in these four financial statements. The next two chapters will discuss how that information can be interpreted and used in actual decision making.

FOOTNOTES TO FINANCIAL STATEMENTS

The footnotes to financial statements are an integral part of the total financial report. There is usually a wealth of information contained in them, and they should never be ignored. Some of the major categories of information in such footnotes are

- summary of significant accounting policies
- description of long-term debt
- description of leases
- discussion of pension plans
- discussion of contingent liabilities and professional liability arrangements

A set of footnotes to an actual financial report is shown in Exhibit 2-6 (they do not relate to the financial statements of Omega Hospital). These notes provide detail in all of the areas listed above, plus several others.

Chapter 3

Accounting for Inflation

William O. Cleverley
Professor, Graduate Program in Hospital and Health Services Management
The Ohio State University

To adjust for the effects of changing price levels, the Financial Accounting Standards Board (FASB), in September 1979, issued the "Statement of Financial Accounting Standards No. 33." The major provisions of this statement require supplementary information in the following five areas for fiscal years ended on or after December 25, 1979:

1. income from continuing operations adjusted for the effects of general inflation
2. purchasing power gain or loss
3. income from continuing operations on a current cost basis
4. current cost amounts of inventory and property, plant, and equipment at the end of the fiscal year
5. increases or decreases in current cost amounts of inventory and property, plant, and equipment, net of inflation

The FASB statement applies to public enterprises that either have total assets in excess of $1 billion or have inventory and property, plant, and equipment (before deducting accumulated depreciation) of more than $125 million. It is likely that the reporting requirements of the

FASB Statement No. 33, perhaps in a modified form, will be extended to a much larger set of business organizations in the future.

The rationale for these changes in financial reporting stems from the inaccuracy and inability of present unadjusted historical cost reports to measure financial position accurately in an inflation-riddled economy. Unless inflationary pressures in the economy are removed, it seems logical to assume that alternative financial reporting systems that can account for the effects of changing price levels will be adopted. It also seems logical to expect that the accounting profession will eventually extend alternative reporting requirements to all business organizations. Hospitals and other health care organizations will, in all probability, be included.

At present, the effect of these financial reporting changes has not been clearly demonstrated. Thus, many individuals have formed beliefs and expectations about financial reporting changes that may not be accurate.

The major purpose of this chapter is to discuss and describe the major alternatives for reflecting the effects of inflation in financial statements. Specific methods are described, and the adjustments that need to be made to convert historical cost statements are illustrated. This discussion should provide a basis for understanding and using financial statements that have been adjusted for inflation.

This chapter is reprinted from *Essentials of Health Care Finance*, 2nd ed., by W.O. Cleverley, pp. 97–113, Aspen Publishers, Inc., © 1986.

REPORTING ALTERNATIVES

Methods of financial reporting can be categorized along two dimensions: (1) the method of asset valuation and (2) the unit of measurement. Two major methods of asset valuation are (1) acquisition (or historical) cost and (2) current (or replacement) value.

Asset valuation at acquisition cost means that the value of the asset is not changed over time to reflect changing market values. Amortization of the value may take place, but the basis is the acquisition cost. Depreciation is recorded, using the acquisition, or historical, cost of the asset. Utilizing an acquisition cost valuation method postpones the recognition of gains or losses from holding assets until the point of sale or retirement. Current valuation of assets revalues the assets in each reporting period. The assets are stated at their current value rather than their acquisition cost. Likewise, depreciation expense is based on the current value, not the historical cost. Current valuation recognizes gains or losses from holding assets prior to sale or retirement.

There are also two major alternative units of measurement in financial reporting: (1) nominal, or unadjusted, dollars and (2) constant dollars measured in units of general purchasing power. Use of a nominal dollar unit of measurement simply means that the attribute being measured is the number of dollars. From an accounting perspective, a dollar of one year is no different from a dollar of another year. No recognition is given to changes in the purchasing power of the dollar, because the attribute is not measured. The major outcome associated with the use of this measurement unit is that gains or losses, regardless of when they are recognized, are not adjusted for changes in purchasing power. For example, if a piece of land that was acquired for $1 million in 1967 were sold for $5 million in 1987, it would have generated a $4 million gain, regardless of changes in the purchasing power of the dollar during the 20-year period.

A constant dollar measuring unit reports the effects of all financial transactions in terms of constant purchasing power. The units that are usually used are the purchasing power of the dollar at the end of the reporting period or the average during the fiscal year. The measurement is made by multiplying the unadjusted, or nominal, dollars by a price index to convert to a measure of constant purchasing power. In periods of inflation, when using a constant dollar measuring unit, gains from holding assets are reduced, while losses are increased. Thus, in the above land sale example, the initial acquisition cost would be restated to 1987 dollars to reduce the gain:

Sale price of land (1987 dollars)	$5,000,000
Less acquisition cost restated (1987 dollars)	2,038,504
Gain on sale	$2,961,496

Constant dollar measurement has a further significant effect upon financial reporting: The gains or losses created by holding monetary liabilities or assets during periods of purchasing power changes are recognized in the financial reporting. For example, an entity that owed $25 million during a year when the purchasing power of the dollar decreased by ten percent would report a $2.5 million (0.10 × $25 million) purchasing power gain. All gains or losses would be recognized, regardless of the valuation basis used.

Monetary assets and liabilities are defined as those items that reflect cash or claims to cash that are fixed in terms of the number of dollars, regardless of changes in prices. Almost all liabilities are monetary items, whereas monetary assets consist primarily of cash, marketable securities, and receivables. Purchasing power gains or losses are recognized on monetary items because there is an assumption that the gains or losses are already realized, since repayments or receipts are fixed.

The interfacing of the valuation basis and the unit of measurement basis produces four alternative financial reporting methods (see Table 3-1). Each of the four methods is a possible basis for financial reporting. The unadjusted historical cost (HC) method represents the present method used by accountants; the other three methods are alternatives that would provide some degree of inflationary adjustment not present in the HC method. Both of the constant

Table 3-1 Alternative Financial Reporting Bases

Unit of Measurement	Asset Valuation Method	
	Acquisition Cost	Current Value
Nominal dollars	Unadjusted historical cost (HC)	Current value (CV)
Constant dollars	Historical cost-general price level adjusted (HC-GPL) (FASB #33 constant dollar accounting)	Current value-general price level adjusted (CV-GPL) (FASB #33 current cost accounting)

dollar methods, historical cost-general price level adjusted (HC-GPL) and current value-general price level adjusted (CV-GPL), are required by FASB Statement No. 33. The HC-GPL method is referred to as historical cost/constant dollar accounting, while the CV-GPL method is referred to as current cost accounting.

Table 3-2 summarizes the effects the four reporting methods would have upon three major income statement items: (1) depreciation expense, (2) purchasing power gains or losses, and (3) unrealized increases in replacement values. However, the net effect of the changes in these items upon net income for an individual institution cannot be predicted; the composition and age of the assets, as well as the prior patterns

of financing, will determine whether the net effect will be positive or negative, and to what degree.

USES OF FINANCIAL REPORT INFORMATION

The measurement of financial position is an important function, and its results are useful to a great variety of decision makers, both internal and external to the organization. Changes in financial reporting methods will unquestionably alter the resulting measures of financial position reported in financial statements. These changes are quite likely to produce changes in the decisions that are based on the financial reports (see Figure 3-1).

Lenders represent an important category of financial statement users who may change their decisions on the basis of a new financial reporting method. The lender's major concern is the relative financial position of both the individual firm and the industry. A decrease in the relative financial position of the industry could seriously affect both the availability and the cost of credit. If, for a variety of reasons, new measurements of financial position make the health care industry appear weaker than other industries, financing terms could change. Particularly for the health care industry, which is increasingly dependent

Table 3-2 Major Effects of Alternative Reporting Methods upon Net Income Measurement

Reporting Method	Impact Variables		
	Depreciation Expense	Purchasing Power Gains/Losses	Unrealized Gains in Replacement Value
Unadjusted historical cost (HC)	No change	No change/not recognized	No change/not recognized
Historical cost-general price level adjusted (HC-GPL)	Increase/GPL depreciation is recognized	Gain or loss/depends upon the *net* monetary asset position	No change/not recognized
Current value (CV)	Increase will recognize current replacement cost	No change/not recognized	Gain/will recognize increase in replacement cost
Current value-general price level adjusted (CV-GPL)	Increase will recognize current replacement cost	Gain or loss/depends upon the *net* monetary asset position	Gain/will recognize increase in replacement cost but will reduce the amount by changes in the GPL

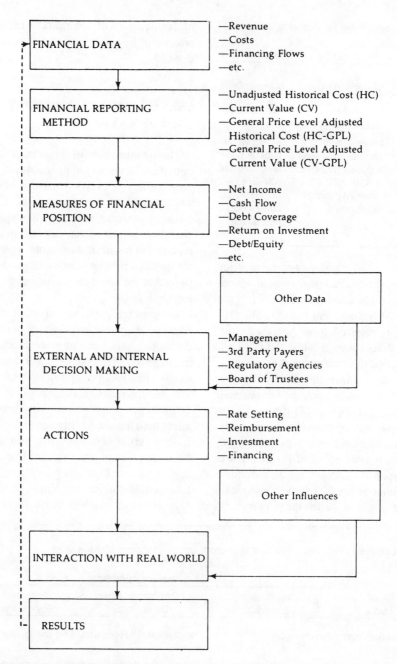

Figure 3-1 Financial Data in Decision Making

upon debt financing, the importance of financial reporting method changes cannot be overstated. Research on the results of changing to an HC-GPL method has shown that the relative financial positions of individual firms and industries are also likely to change.

Changes in financial reporting methods could also have an effect upon decisions reached by regulatory and rate-setting organizations. As a result of such changes, comparisons of costs across institutions may be more meaningful than they were before. For example, the capital costs of institutions that operate in relatively new physical plants may not be compared with the unadjusted historical capital costs of older facilities. Without these adjustments, new facilities may appear to have higher costs and thus be less efficient, whereas in fact the opposite may be true.

The actions of interested community leaders who have access to, and make decisions based on, financial statements might also be affected by reporting method changes. For example, suppose that individual, corporate, and public agency giving is in part affected by reported income. Many in fact regard reported income as a basic index of need, and the relationship between income and giving seems logical. Thus, since each of the alternative financial reporting methods we have discussed will produce a different measure of income, total giving in each case could be affected.

Internal management decisions might also change with a new financial reporting method. Perhaps the most obvious example of such a change would be in rate setting. Studies have shown that, in the nonprofit hospital industry, rates are closely aligned with reported costs. Thus, changes in costs produced by a financial reporting change are likely to affect rates.

CASE EXAMPLE: WILLIAMS CONVALESCENT CENTER

In the remainder of this chapter, we show how adjustments are made in the income statement and balance sheet of Williams Convalescent Center, a 120-bed skilled and intermediate care facility, to take into account the effects of inflation. The center's two financial statements are shown in Exhibits 3-1 and 3-2. You will note that values are reported for each of three reporting methods:

1. unadjusted historical cost (HC)
2. historical cost-general price level adjusted (HC-GPL)
3. current value-general price level adjusted (CV-GPL)

In this discussion, we do not describe or apply the current value (CV) method. This method is not being seriously considered by the accounting profession at this time, and it is not likely to be considered in the future. The CV method suffers from a serious flaw: it does not recognize the effects of changing price levels upon equity. In short, the CV method would treat increases in the replacement cost of assets as a gain and not restate them for changes in purchasing power.

Table 3-3 presents values for the Consumer Price Index (CPI). CPI is the price index that is used by the accounting profession at the present time to adjust financial statements for the effects of inflation.

Price Index Conversion

The two methods (HC and HC-GPL) we have selected to adjust the financial statements of the Williams Convalescent Center both utilize a constant dollar as the unit of measurement. This means that purchasing power, not the dollar, is the unit of measurement. That is, all reported values in the financial statements are expressed in dollars of a specified purchasing power. Usually the purchasing power used is the period end value. In our case example, Williams Convalescent Center uses the purchasing power as of December 31, 1984.

Restatement of nominal or unadjusted dollars to constant dollars is a relatively simple process, at least conceptually. All that is required are three pieces of information:

1. unadjusted value of the account in historical or nominal dollars
2. a price index that reflects the purchasing power in which the unadjusted value is currently expressed
3. a price index that reflects the purchasing power at the date the account is to be restated

For example, Williams Convalescent Center's long-term debt at December 31, 1983, is $1,203 (see Exhibit 3-2) (000s omitted). To express that amount in constant dollars as of

Exhibit 3-1 Statement of Income for the Williams Convalescent Center

	Historical Cost 1984	Constant Dollar (Historical Cost–General Price Level Adjusted) 1984	Current Cost (Current Value–General Price Level Adjusted) 1984
Williams Convalescent Center Statement of Income (000s Omitted)			
Operating revenues	$3,556	$3,625	$3,625
Operating expenses	3,253	3,316	3,316
Depreciation	74	177	185
Interest	102	104	104
Net income	$ 127	$ 28	$ 20
Purchasing power gain from holding net monetary liabilities during the year	—	$ 43	$ 43
Increase in specific prices of property, plant, and equipment during the year	—	—	$ 136
Less effect of increase in general price level	—	—	$ 144
Increase in specific prices over (under) increase in the general price level	—	—	$ (8)
Change in equity due to income transactions	$ 127	$ 71	$ 55

December 31, 1984, the following adjustment would be made:

$$\text{Unadjusted amount} \times \frac{\text{Price index converting to}}{\text{Price index converting from}}$$

$$= \text{Constant dollar value}$$

$$\$1,203 \times \frac{315.5}{303.5} = \$1,251$$

The value of the beginning long-term debt for the center would be $1,251 expressed in purchasing power as of December 31, 1984. The adjustment method described above is the same for all other accounts. The price index to which the conversion is made is usually the price index at the ending balance sheet date (December 31,

1984, in our example). The price index from which the conversion is made represents the purchasing power in which the account is currently expressed. This value will vary depending upon the classification of the account as either monetary or nonmonetary.

Monetary versus Nonmonetary Accounts

When restating financial statements from one based on a historical cost method to one based on a constant dollar method, it is critical to distinguish between monetary accounts and nonmonetary accounts. Monetary accounts are automatically stated in current dollars and therefore require no price-level adjustments. Monetary items, discussed earlier in this chapter,

Exhibit 3-2 Balance Sheet for the Williams Convalescent Center

Williams Convalescent Center
Balance Sheets
(000s omitted)

	Historical Cost 1983	Historical Cost 1984	Constant Dollar (Historical Cost–General Price Level Adjusted) 1984	Current Cost (Current Value–General Price Level Adjusted) 1984
Current assets				
Cash	$ 98	$ 21	$ 21	$ 21
Accounts receivable	217	249	249	249
Supplies	22	27	27	27
Prepaid expenses	36	36	36	36
Total current assets	$ 373	$ 333	$ 333	$ 333
Property and equipment				
Land	200	200	530	525
Building and equipment	2,102	2,228	5,333	5,570
	2,302	2,428	5,863	6,095
Less accumulated depreciation	783	844	2,020	2,186
Total	1,519	1,584	3,843	3,909
Investments	161	596	596	596
Total assets	$2,053	$2,513	$4,772	$4,838
Current liabilities	412	493	493	493
Long-term debt	1,203	1,478	1,478	1,478
Partners' equity	438	542	2,801	2,867
	$2,053	$2,513	$4,772	$4,838

Table 3-3 Consumer Price Index, Year-End Values

Year	CPI
1970	119.1
1971	123.1
1972	127.3
1973	138.5
1974	155.4
1975	166.3
1976	174.3
1977	186.1
1978	202.9
1979	229.9
1980	258.4
1981	283.4
1982	292.4
1983	303.5
1984	315.5

Source: United States Department of Labor, Bureau of Labor Statistics

Williams Convalescent Center

	Unadjusted	Conversion Factor	Constant Dollars
Beginning long-term debt (12/31/83)	$1,203	315.5/303.5	$1,251
− Repayment (6/30/84)	152	315.5/309.5	155
+ New debt (6/30/84)	427	315.5/309.5	435
Ending long-term debt (12/31/84)	$1,478		$1,531
− Actual ending long-term debt (12/31/84)			$1,478
Purchasing power gain			$ 53

consist of cash or claims to cash or promises to pay cash that are fixed in terms of dollars, regardless of price-level changes. Nonmonetary accounts require price-level adjustments in order to be stated in current dollars.

Because of the fixed nature of monetary items, holding them during a period of changing price levels creates a gain or loss. This can be seen in the data from the Williams Convalescent Center (000s omitted).

The above data assume that a repayment and new issue occurred at the midpoint of the year, June 30, 1984. The price index at that point would have been approximately 309.5. This resulted from taking the average of the beginning and ending values, (303.5 + 315.5)/2. In constant dollars, the Williams Convalescent Center would have reported $1,531 of long-term debt at December 31, 1984. However, the actual value of the long-term debt at that date was $1,478. The difference of $53 represents a purchasing power gain to the center during the year. Because the price level increased during 1984, the value of the long-term debt actually owed by the center declined when measured in constant purchasing power.

Nonmonetary asset accounts must always be restated to purchasing power at the current date. The price index at the time of acquisition represents the price index from which the conversion is made. The price index at the current date represents the index to which the conversion is made. To illustrate the adjustment, assume that the building and equipment account of Williams Convalescent Center has the following age distribution:

Year Acquired	Cost	Conversion Factor	Constant Dollar Cost (12/31/84)
1970	$1,500	315.5/119.1	$3,974
1978	401	315.5/202.9	624
1981	201	315.5/283.4	224
1984	126	315.5/315.5	126
	$2,228		$4,948

The above data show that assets with a historical cost of $2,228 represent $4,948 of cost when stated in dollars as of December 31, 1984. The latter value is much more meaningful than the former as a measure of actual asset cost in 1984. It provides the center with a measure of cost that is expressed in dollars as of the current date and thus better represents its actual investment. Depreciation expense should also be restated in 1984 dollars in order to portray accurately the center's actual cost of using its building and equipment in the generation of current revenues.

Adjusting the Income Statement

Operating Revenues

If one assumes that revenues are realized equally throughout the year, it simplifies the restatement significantly. If the assumption is valid, and in most cases it is, it means that the revenues can be considered realized at the midpoint of the year, in our case, June 30, 1984. As already noted, the price index at June 30, 1984, can be assumed to be the average of the beginning and ending price index, or 309.5. The restated operating revenue would be calculated as follows:

$$\$3,556 \times 315.5/309.5 = \$3,625$$

Operating Expenses

Based on the same assumption that was used with operating revenues, the adjustment for operating expenses would be

$$\$3,253 \times 315.5/309.5 = \$3,316$$

It should be noted that operating expenses do not include depreciation or interest. Separate adjustments for these two items may be required.

Depreciation

The depreciation expense adjustment is different from the earlier adjustments in two ways. First, depreciation expense represents an amortization of assets purchased over a long period of time, usually many years. This means that the midpoint conversion method used for operating revenues and operating expenses is clearly not appropriate. Second, the adjustment methods for the constant dollar and current cost methods diverge. Depreciation expense may vary considerably because the current cost of the assets may differ dramatically from the constant dollar cost. Remember, a price index represents price changes for a large number of goods and services; specific price changes of individual assets may vary significantly from that index.

Constant Dollar Adjustment. There are two methods that can be used to adjust depreciation expense to a constant dollar amount. The most accurate method is to perform an adjustment for each individual asset. This can be a time-consuming process, however, and may not be worth the effort.

Alternatively, an average acquisition date can be estimated by first determining the average age of the assets, as follows:

$$\text{Average age} = \frac{\text{Accumulated depreciation}}{\text{Depreciation expense}}$$

$$= \frac{\$844}{\$74} = 11.4 \text{ years}$$

If one uses straight-line depreciation, this way of estimating average age is reasonably reliable. For the Williams Convalescent Center, an average of 11.4 years would imply that the assets

were purchased sometime in 1973. Interpolation would yield a price index of 131.8. Depreciation expense in 1984 expressed in constant dollars thus would be

$$\$74 \times 315.5/131.8 = \$177$$

Current Cost Adjustment. The identification of the current cost of existing physical assets is a subjective and complex process. To many individuals, the current cost method provides little additional value, compared with the constant dollar method. Whether it will be eventually eliminated and replaced by the constant dollar method is not clear at this time.

The first issue to address in the adjustment is the definition of current cost. By and large, current cost can be equated to the replacement cost of the assets. In short, we must determine what the cost of replacing assets in today's dollars would be. This could be estimated through a variety of techniques, using, for example, insurance appraisals or specific price indexes. In the case of the Williams Convalescent Center, we will assume that a recent insurance appraisal indicated a replacement cost of $5,570 for buildings and equipment. With this estimate, depreciation expense could be adjusted as follows:

$$\frac{\text{Appraisal cost}}{\text{Historical cost}} \times \text{Depreciation expense}$$

$$= \text{Restated depreciation expense}$$

$$\frac{\$5,570}{\$2,228} \times \$74 = \$185$$

Interest Expense

We will again assume that interest expense is paid equally throughout the year. This assumption would produce the following interest expense adjustment:

$$\$102 \times 315.5/309.5 = \$104$$

Purchasing Power Gains or Losses

A purchasing power gain results if one is a net debtor during a period of rising prices, while a purchasing power loss results if one is a net creditor during such a period. In most health care firms, purchasing power gains result because liabilities exceed monetary assets. A firm is thus paying its debts with dollars that are cheaper than the ones it received.

To calculate purchasing power gains or losses, net monetary asset positions must first be calculated. The net monetary position for the Williams Convalescent Center is presented below.

Monetary assets	Beginning (12/31/83)	Ending (12/31/84)
Cash	$ 98	$ 21
Accounts receivable	217	249
Prepaid expenses	36	36
Investments	161	596
Monetary assets	$ 512	$ 902
Monetary liabilities		
Current liabilities	$ 412	$ 493
Long-term debt	1,203	1,478
Monetary liabilities	$ 1,615	$ 1,971
Net monetary assets	$(1,103)	$(1,069)

The actual calculation of the purchasing power gain for the Williams Convalescent Center is given in the next chart.

	Actual Dollars	Conversion Factor	Constant Dollars
Beginning net monetary liabilities	$1,103	315.5/303.5	$1,147
− Decrease	34	315.5/309.5	35
Ending net monetary liabilities	$1,069		$1,112
− Actual			$1,069
Purchasing power gain			$ 43

Because the center was in a net monetary liability position during the year, it experienced a purchasing power gain of $43. This value is not an element of net income; it is rather shown below the net income line in Exhibit 3-1. It thus affects the change in equity.

Increase in Specific Prices over General Prices

The adjustment to take into account an increase in specific prices over general prices is made only in the current cost method. The constant dollar method does not recognize any increases (or reductions) in prices that are different from the general price level. In short, no gains or losses from holding assets are permitted in the constant dollar method.

The calculations involved in this adjustment can be terribly complex. In our Williams Convalescent Center example, we will make some assumptions to simplify the arithmetic without impairing the reader's conceptual understanding of the adjustment. We will assume the following data:

Insurance appraisal of buildings and equipment, 12/31/83	$5,015
Insurance appraisal of buildings and equipment, 12/31/84	$5,570
Appraised value of land, 12/31/83	$ 500
Appraised value of land, 12/31/84	$ 525
New equipment bought on 12/31/84	$ 126

The following data show the increase in specific prices over general prices.

	Buildings & Equipment	Land	Total
Ending appraised value less acquisitions	$5,444	$525	$5,969
− Accumulated depreciation on appraised value	2,186	—	2,186
Ending net appraised value	$3,258	$525	$3,783
Beginning appraised value	$5,015	$500	$5,515
− Accumulated depreciation on appraised value	1,868	—	1,868
Net appraised value	$3,147	$500	$3,647
Increase in specific prices during the year			$ 136
Effect of increase in general price level	$3,647 × [(315.5/303.5) − 1.0]		$ 144
Increase in specific prices over general price level			$ (8)

These data show that, during 1984, the value of physical assets held by the Williams Convalescent Center did not increase more than the general price level. This may be a positive sign for the center if it is not contemplating a sale. The replacement cost for its assets is increasing less than the general price level. Therefore, revenues could increase less than the general price level and replacement could still be ensured.

Adjusting the Balance Sheet

Monetary Items

None of the monetary items—cash, accounts receivable, supplies, prepaid expenses, investments, current liabilities, and long-term debt—requires adjustment. The values of these items already reflect current dollars.

Land

In our discussion of the increase in specific prices over the general price level in the Williams Convalescent Center's income statement, we assumed an appraisal value for land of $525. That value will be used here with the current cost method. With the constant dollar method, we will assume that the land was acquired in 1970 for $200. To restate that amount to purchasing power as of December 31, 1984, the following calculation would be made:

$$\$200 \times 315.5/119.1 = \$530$$

Buildings and Equipment

Values for the center's buildings and equipment and the related accumulated depreciation have already been cited for the current cost method. We will assume those same values here. This produces a value for buildings and equipment of $5,570 (000s omitted) based upon an appraisal. The value for accumulated depreciation was derived as follows:

Adjusted accumulated depreciation =

Unadjusted accumulated depreciation $\times$

$$\frac{\text{Appraised value } - \text{ Current year acquisitions}}{\text{Historical cost } - \text{ Current year acquisitions}}$$

$$\$2,186 = \$844 \times \frac{(\$5,570 - \$126)}{(\$2,228 - \$126)}$$

The constant dollar method values can be derived by using the estimated average age of plant. In earlier discussions relating to depreciation expense, we computed the average age to be 11.4 years and the related price index at acquisition to be 131.8. With this information the following values result:

Buildings and equipment
$$= \$2,228 \times 315.5/131.8 = \$5,333$$

Accumulated depreciation
$$= \$844 \times 315.5/131.8 = \$2,020$$

Equity

We will not discuss the equity calculations in any detail here. It is enough for our purposes to recognize that equity is a derived figure. Equity must equal total assets less liabilities. In our Williams Convalescent Center example, this generates values of $2,801 for the constant dollar method and $2,867 for the current cost method.

SUMMARY

Financial reporting suffers from its current reliance on the unadjusted HC valuation concept. Inflation has made many of the reported values in current financial reports meaningless to decision makers. The example used in this chapter illustrates this point. The total asset investment of Williams Convalescent Center is approximately 100 percent larger when adjusted for inflation under the current cost or constant dollar method. Net income, on the other hand, decreased. The result is a dramatic deterioration in return on investment—the single most important test of business success.

The following table summarizes return on assets and return on equity for the Williams Convalescent Center.

	Historical Cost	Constant Dollar	Current Cost
Net income/Total assets	5.1%	0.6%	0.4%
Change in equity due to income transactions/Total assets	5.1	1.5	1.1
Net income/Equity	23.4	1.0	0.7
Change in equity due to income transactions/Equity	23.4	2.5	1.9

These reductions are so drastic, they would prompt an investor seriously to question the continuation of the present investment, let alone replacement. More profitable avenues of investment may very likely be available.

To the extent that our Williams Convalescent Center example is representative of many health care firms—and it probably is—decisions regarding health care business continuation must be seriously evaluated. It is imperative that health care companies, like all other businesses, adjust their financial reports to reflect inflation. Whether the method used is current cost or constant dollar is not the issue. The important point is that ignoring the effects of inflation is unwise at best.

Chapter 4

External Audits

Lloyd B. Morgan
Partner, Arthur Andersen & Co.
Richard V. Clausing
Manager, Arthur Andersen & Co.

With increasing government regulation and public pressure for accountability, management and board members of most health care institutions feel as if they are buried under an avalanche of auditors—government auditors from the Department of Health and Human Services (HHS) and the Internal Revenue Service (IRS); intermediary auditors for the Health Care Financing Administration (HCFA); insurance company auditors; internal auditors; state auditors; and, last but not least, auditors from the institution's certified public accounting (CPA) firm.

Given this audit-filled climate, management and directors may have the following questions:

- How does an external audit differ from internal and governmental audits?
- Why is an external audit necessary?
- Is such an audit required?
- How can value be provided to the institution from the audit process?
- What do external auditors do?
- How much will it cost and how should an auditing firm be selected?

The answers to these questions are somewhat different for each institution. However, this chapter addresses each of these considerations to help readers come to their own conclusions about the cost-benefit relationship of involving an external, independent auditor for their institutions.

WHAT IS AN EXTERNAL AUDIT?

While there have been and will continue to be many changes in the health care industry, the basics of an audit remain virtually unchanged. An external audit is an examination of an entity's financial statements that are derived from its accounting processes. This audit examination is performed by a CPA whose objective is to express an independent opinion on the financial statements. To put the concept of an external audit into perspective, it is useful to understand the difference between auditing and authoring the financial statements.

The trustees and management of an entity are responsible for adopting sound accounting policies, for maintaining an adequate and effective system of accounts, for safeguarding assets, and for devising a system of internal control that will help to ensure the production of accurate financial statements. These responsibilities collectively may be referred to as authoring financial statements and other data derived from the accounting processes. Although auditors may influence the form and content of financial statements or other data by proposing various adjustments and modifications, the entity's management and trustees have the final decision-making authority over the form and content of the financial statements and other data furnished to creditors, regulatory agencies, and others. The auditor has sole responsibility for the report or opinion issued on these statements. Since most institutions are interested in receiving an unqualified auditors' report (a clean opinion) on their financial statements, management and trustees will ultimately accept the auditors' professional recommendations. Clearly, the responsibilities of management and trustees and those of the independent auditors are different and separate.

EXAMINATIONS BY THIRD-PARTY PAYERS

The scope and quality of an external audit are different from an examination made by the intermediary for a third-party payer, which focuses primarily on matters directly affecting the level of reimbursement, rather than the overall financial condition of the entity. Because qualifications and training of the payers' examiners vary from payer to payer or from state to state, the examination is not necessarily performed by persons having the qualifications of CPAs. Their audit procedures often vary, depending on the examiners' abilities, state, or payer procedures and time restraints.

EXAMINATIONS BY INTERNAL AUDITORS

An internal auditor generally performs certain selected tests and procedures of financial data and operating procedures and controls, rather than a full audit of the financial statements taken as a whole. Their primary objective is to determine whether the institution's policies and procedures are being followed by staff and management and to recommend procedural changes to improve the effectiveness of internal operations and controls.

Internal auditors generally report to the chief financial officer and in some cases to the chief executive officer, even though they should, and often do, have some involvement with the board. While internal auditors should be encouraged by management to maintain a stance independent from the regular-line organization, they can never have the same degree of independence as the external, independent CPA since they are salaried by the institution. Nevertheless, a strong internal audit department can strengthen internal control and thus help to minimize the cost of an external audit, as the independent auditors may be able to reduce the scope of their testing if a well-directed internal audit program has been followed.

WHY IS AN EXTERNAL AUDIT NEEDED?

For many health care institutions, an external audit is required by a third party. Most public and private debt arrangements require annual audited financial statements. In some states, an audit is required by Blue Cross or as a result of state rate regulations.

Even if an external audit is not required, management and the board of trustees should consider carefully whether such an audit is desirable to help them fulfill their basic responsibilities and to provide them with positive support and recommendations concerning operations and financial matters.

The trustees have a responsibility to those who elect or appoint them to monitor all major activities of the health care entity. The trustees and management are required to understand the financial condition of the entity and to ensure that the results of its operations are fairly presented and disclosed. An independent audit is invaluable in fulfilling this responsibility. In addition to examining the entity's financial statements and issuing an opinion thereon, the external auditor should provide an independent business perspective on the total operation. This perspective, combined with the auditor's business, financial, accounting, and industry knowledge, often results in recommendations for management improvement, payment or revenue maximization, and tax-planning opportunities.

Not-for-profit health care institutions receive funds in the form of payments, grants, and gifts from many sources—private individuals, commercial insurers, public agencies, and businesses. Each of these parties has a vested interest in the institution and has the right to receive regular information about its financial condition and the results of operations. Reliable and consistent financial information is important to maintaining consumer and philanthropic support, and confidence in financial statements is significantly enhanced when the statements have been audited by an external public accountant.

WHICH STATEMENTS DO THE AUDITORS EXAMINE?

Auditors may be engaged to examine and report on basic annual financial statements, interim financial statements, or any number of special-purpose financial data or statements.

Most commonly, an audit is conducted at year-end and consists of an examination of an entity's balance sheet as of the year-end and the related statements of revenues and expenses and cash flows for that year. The usual purpose of such an audit is to enable the independent CPA to render an opinion on whether the financial statements present fairly the financial position of the entity as of the balance sheet date, and the results of its operations and changes in its cash flows for that period, in conformity with generally accepted accounting principles.

An audit also may consist of an examination of other financial statements or other data. Under certain circumstances, for example, the independent CPA may examine and report on

- financial statements presented on a basis of accounting other than generally accepted accounting principles (e.g., cash-basis financial statements)
- specified elements, accounts, or items of a financial statement, such as amounts paid or payable to third parties, contributions to an employee benefit plan, or amounts receivable from third parties
- compliance with certain provisions of contractual agreements, such as loan agreements

- financial information presented in a prescribed form or schedule that requires a prescribed form of auditors' report; and
- financial projections

Under certain circumstances, independent auditors may examine and report on interim financial statements or perform a limited review of annual financial statements. Such reviews consist primarily of inquiries of company personnel and an analytical review of the financial data. These reviews are substantially narrower in scope than the examination made in accordance with generally accepted auditing standards and do not result in the expression of a full opinion by the auditor. The report on such limited work indicates only that the auditor is not aware of any material modifications that should be made to the financial statements.

GENERALLY ACCEPTED AUDITING STANDARDS

Most reports issued by independent CPAs state, ''We conducted our audits in accordance with generally accepted auditing standards. Those standards require that we plan and perform the audit to obtain reasonable assurance about whether the financial statements are free of material misstatement.'' Generally accepted auditing standards provide a common reference that defines for the auditors, the client, and third-party users of these statements the professional characteristics and competence of the auditing firm, the nature of the examination and what it is intended to accomplish, and the meaning of the auditors' report.

Generally accepted auditing standards guide every public accounting firm's practice. Auditing standards are different from auditing procedures. Procedures relate to specific tasks, whereas standards measure the quality of the performance of the tasks and guide the selection of the tasks by providing overall objectives. Auditing standards are general in nature, while auditing procedures are specific. Auditing standards guide the recruitment and training of personnel, the conduct of the audit, the auditors' report, the scope of the firm's practice, and the ethical conduct of the firm and its personnel.

The membership of the American Institute of Certified Public Accountants (AICPA) has adopted a series of generally accepted auditing standards to which all members must adhere. The standards require, among other things, that audits be performed only by adequately trained persons who are to maintain an independent mental attitude and exercise due professional care; that audits must be adequately planned and supervised; that sufficient evidence must be examined and internal control must be studied; and that the reports issued by the independent CPA must be in conformance with certain defined standards.

SUFFICIENT COMPETENT EVIDENTIAL MATTER

To minimize the risk that the CPA may reach a wrong conclusion, one of the generally accepted auditing standards requires that "sufficient competent evidential matter" be obtained. Evidential matter supporting financial statements consists of the underlying accounting data and all available corroborating information, such as checks, invoices, contracts, work sheets, or general ledgers. Competent evidence is considered to be that which is valid and relevant. For example, evidential matter can be obtained from independent sources outside an entity by direct confirmation. Accounting data developed from systems where internal control techniques are strong are generally more reliable than data developed under less satisfactory conditions of internal control. Direct knowledge, which may be obtained through physical examination, observation, computation, or inspection, is usually more persuasive than information obtained indirectly. Nevertheless, in most cases, the auditor must rely on evidence that is persuasive rather than absolutely convincing.

The word *sufficient* relates to the amount of data studied. It is impracticable and too costly for the auditor to obtain all pertinent evidential matter or to review all transactions in a year in any one area of the audit. Choices must be made.

When selecting the evidential matter to be obtained, the audit team exercises professional judgment in establishing the audit scope or the tests of the accounting records and other auditing procedures considered necessary. The factors the auditor considers include internal controls, matters likely to require particular attention, the possibility of errors and irregularities, internal auditing, and transactions with related parties. Of these, internal controls are the most significant factor.

STUDY OF INTERNAL ACCOUNTING CONTROL SYSTEMS

Institutions establish systems of internal control to provide reasonable assurance that assets are safeguarded and that the financial records are reliable. Auditing standards require a proper study and evaluation of these internal control systems. It is very important that such study include the internal controls surrounding the computer systems, since they are an integral part of the overall system of internal control.

There are two basic and interrelated reasons why an entity's financial statements may be materially wrong in some important respect. First, material errors or irregularities may occur in the accounting systems by which the financial statements are developed. Second, these errors or irregularities may not be detected by the normal internal review or even auditing procedures of internal or external auditors.

A strong system of internal accounting control sharply reduces the first of these risks. When such a system exists and has a long-term track record of accuracy, the auditor relies, to some extent, on an entity's accounting system to produce financial statements that are not affected by material errors or irregularities. This means that fewer tests need to be made to meet the auditing standard requiring sufficient competent evidential matter.

However, the auditor cannot rely completely on internal accounting controls, since these have limitations. They normally are established and maintained by management to provide reasonable, but not absolute, assurance that the objectives are achieved considering the relationship of probable costs and likely benefits. Even where well-designed internal control techniques are in effect, undetected errors or irregularities could arise from a variety of causes, including misunderstandings, mistakes in judgment, carelessness, or even management fraud or employee collusion. Thus, the auditor relies on both internal controls and examination of evidence as bases for an opinion.

The extent to which the auditor relies on internal controls in a particular audit engagement is an informed judgmental determination that is based on a study and evaluation of the internal accounting controls as they existed during the period covered by the audit. In performing a study of internal control, the auditor must first gain an understanding of the system and then perform tests in order to gain a reasonable degree of assurance that the procedures were operating effectively.

In order to understand the accounting procedures and controls, the auditor spends a considerable amount of time in discussion with accounting personnel and operating personnel who are involved in initiating and processing transactions. The auditor can also gain a great deal of initial information through review of flow charts, procedures manuals, job descriptions, and critical forms.

Gaining an understanding of the processing of transactions and identifying the controls being used can be an informative experience for management if approached on a positive basis. The better the auditor understands the entity being audited, the better the audit and the more helpful the suggestions the auditor is able to make in the management letter.

To help the institution that is facing an external audit, let us discuss briefly how an auditor might approach such a study.

Regardless of how simple or complex the entity, the auditor spends considerable time referring to existing documentation and discussing the accounting system. The auditor is not required to gain detailed knowledge of all processing procedures affecting all types of transactions but rather to concentrate on those types of transactions and the related systems of control that materially affect the financial statements.

Business Cycles and Functions

As a first step, the auditor generally segregates a client's business and the related accounting systems into four or five cycles of business activity, such as revenue, treasury, expenditure, financial reporting, and payroll. A cycle is a grouping of similar economic events that must be reflected in the financial statements. Once the cycles are identified, the auditor identifies the significant categories of transactions that flow through each cycle and the functions that are performed within each cycle to recognize, authorize, process, classify, and report the transaction. The auditor should then have a thorough understanding of the flow of transactions and how they are processed through the system.

Control Objectives and Techniques

The auditor identifies certain desirable internal control objectives for each cycle and the internal control techniques used to achieve these objectives. These control techniques are identified primarily by discussion with the entity's personnel. The auditor asks questions to help identify the critical techniques being used, such as

- How can erroneous transactions go undetected?
- How would lost or duplicate transactions be caught?
- How could unauthorized changes to programs or procedures be made and would they be caught?
- How could authorization requirements be circumvented?
- Could anything go wrong as transactions pass from one system or function to another?
- What assurance is there that the reported data from the edit or validation process will be corrected and re-entered?

The auditor will evaluate the techniques to identify only those necessary to attain a reasonable degree of assurance that the transactions are being processed correctly.

Compliance Tests

Once the auditor has identified the necessary control techniques, tests are performed to determine whether the techniques were operating effectively during the entire period being audited. These tests are referred to as compliance tests.

Substantive Tests

Auditing standards require the auditor to obtain sufficient evidential matter, which is gathered through tests of details of transactions and balances and analytical reviews of ratios and trends. These tests are referred to as substantive tests. The extent of the required substantive tests is inversely proportional to the amount of reliance the auditor has decided to place on internal control.

Report on Internal Control

Auditors are required by auditing standards to communicate to senior management or the board any material weaknesses in internal control that come to their attention during an audit. However, unless the auditors are specifically requested to issue a separate internal control report, they will not typically do so. Most auditors communicate suggestions for improvement in internal control through their management letter. This letter will also include other administrative or financial matters that the auditor wishes to bring to the attention of the board or management.

THE AUDITORS' REPORT

A key concept underlying the independent audit is that the financial statements constitute the representations of an entity's management of its financial position and the results of operation for a particular period. The purpose of the auditors' report is to express an opinion on the entity's financial statements. Prior to 1934, the last paragraph in the standard short-form auditors' report usually started with the words, "We certify that in our opinion. . . ." It was natural that the report came to be called an auditors' certificate. Since the auditors' report does not certify but rather expresses an opinion, the use of the word *certificate* has diminished because it implies a degree of exactitude that is not present in the financial statements. The more appropriate term in use today is *report*.

Auditors generally issue a short-form or a long-form report, depending upon the nature of the engagement. The short-form report is most common. The report is generally addressed to the entity or board, the shareholders or members. The report typically contains three paragraphs, the first setting forth the responsibilities of management and that of the auditors, the second setting forth the scope of the audit, and the third expressing the auditors' opinion. The standard wording used in a short-form report is shown in Exhibit 4-1.

The report is dated on the date the auditor completes fieldwork. The auditor is responsible for reviewing events and transactions occurring between the balance sheet date and the report date. If the auditor learns of any significant events or transactions that require either adjustment to or disclosure in the financial statements covered by the auditors' report, these events or transactions must be reflected in the financial statements or related footnotes.

In some circumstances, the auditor may issue a long-form report. In addition to the basic financial statements, this report generally includes supplemental information such as detailed financial schedules, statistical data, or explanatory comments. In certain circumstances, long-form reports can be very lengthy and detailed and can discuss specific audit procedures performed and the results of those specified procedures.

An example of another paragraph added to the standard short-form three-paragraph report is shown in Exhibit 4-2.

Generally, the auditor issues the standard short-form report, which includes the auditors' opinion to the effect that the financial statements are fairly presented in accordance with generally accepted accounting principles. This is referred to as an *unqualified opinion*.

Exhibit 4-1 Typical Short-Form Report

Independent Auditors' Report

To A Hospital:

We have audited the accompanying balance sheets of A Hospital as of December 31, 19X2 and 19X1, and the related statements of income, funds, and cash flows for the years then ended. These financial statements are the responsibility of the Hospital's management. Our responsibility is to express an opinion on these financial statements based on our audits.

We conducted our audits in accordance with generally accepted auditing standards. Those standards require that we plan and perform the audit to obtain reasonable assurance about whether the financial statements are free of material misstatement. An audit includes examining, on a test basis, evidence supporting the amounts and disclosures in the financial statements. An audit also includes assessing the accounting principles used and significant estimates made by management, as well as evaluating the overall financial statement presentation. We believe that our audits provide a reasonable basis for our opinion.

In our opinion, the financial statements referred to above present fairly, in all material respects, the financial position of A Hospital as of December 31, 19X2 and 19X1, and the results of its operations and its cash flows for the years then ended in conformity with generally accepted accounting principles.

March 15, 19X3   XYZ & Co., CPA

However, the auditor may issue a qualified opinion, a disclaimer of opinion, or an adverse opinion under certain circumstances or conditions, including the following:

- The scope of the auditors' examination may be affected by conditions or restrictions that prevent the auditor from carrying out all the auditing procedures considered necessary. As examples, management might instruct the auditor not to send confirmations of accounts receivable to patients or customers, or the condition of the accounting records might not allow the auditor to examine sufficient evidential matter.
- The financial statements may be prepared using an accounting principle that is not generally accepted, which produces a result materially different from that obtained using a principle that is generally accepted.
- Information such as footnote disclosures, which are required to present the financial statements fairly, is omitted. Examples of matters that need to be disclosed are liens on assets, contingent liabilities, affiliated or controlling interests and the nature and magnitude of transactions with such interests or with management, and certain subsequent events.

Not all of the matters that should be disclosed can be enumerated here, but this listing is generally indicative of the matters or conditions that are required to be disclosed.

Occasionally, auditors of a hospital or other health care institution may be required to amend their opinion because a disputed amount due from a third-party payer or the impact of a malpractice claim cannot be estimated with any degree of certainty, especially in cases where disputed issues involve material amounts.

Exhibit 4-2 Additional Paragraph of a Typical Long-Form Report

Our examination has been made primarily for the purpose of forming the opinion stated in the preceding paragraph. The data contained in pages (or exhibits) . . . to . . . , inclusive, of this report, although not considered necessary for a fair presentation of financial position, are presented as supplementary information and have been subjected to the audit procedures applied in the examination of the basic financial statements. In our opinion, these data are fairly stated in all material respects in relation to the basic financial statements taken as a whole.

Depending on prior experience with such disputes, the auditor may not be able to determine the outcome of the dispute and would be required to communicate this major uncertainty through an additional paragraph in the auditor's report.

SELECTING AN AUDITOR

Selecting an independent CPA is an important decision. Because the relationship probably will last for many years, management and the board must give the selection careful attention.

Public accounting firms vary in size, from small local firms to large international firms. Each possesses differing degrees of expertise in various industries. Firms also differ in the nature and extent of the supplementary consulting services they are able to provide to their clients. While a firm's reputation and its ability to perform an audit are major considerations, the firm selected should also be able to provide advice to the entity in other areas, such as payment and contracting issues, systems reviews and installations, feasibility studies, merger and acquisition assistance, purchase investigations, and income tax consultation.

The external auditor provides an independent business perspective and should be able to offer advice on all aspects of the entity's operations. Usually, persons with a broad base of health care industry experience can perform such services most effectively.

No firm should be excluded from consideration on the basis of size alone. While small firms may not have the range of personnel or industry expertise to serve large health care institutions, there are occasions when such a relationship may be appropriate. On the other hand, large firms often devote a considerable amount of their practice to serving small clients. The larger firms offering a wide diversity of services generally charge a higher per diem rate than the small local or regional firm that has less overhead.

Both management and directors should evaluate what a firm can offer in relation to the services the institution requires now and in the foreseeable future. Each firm under consideration should be requested to submit a written proposal setting forth its general qualifications; a listing of similar engagements it has performed; the estimated cost of an audit (in terms of total dollars and hours required); the proposed timing of the examination; and, particularly, the names and qualifications of individuals who will be assigned to the engagement. Preferably, the individuals assigned should have proven experience in the industry. The proposals should be reviewed initially by the administrator or chief executive officer, who will present opinions to the board or its committee. The board should decide which firms to pursue.

After the choice of firms has been narrowed, management and the directors should meet with representatives of the firm, including individuals who will be assigned to the engagement. The firms should be questioned about their experience in various areas, methods and scope of internal control reviews, management letters, and other subjects that will enable the board to assess the firm's competence and methods before making its final selection.

Once a firm has been chosen and notified of its appointment, the work of developing a solid client-auditor relationship begins. Careful selection of a firm, with due consideration of the institution's needs and requirements measured against the qualifications of the firm and the individuals who will be assigned to the engagement, should result in a mutually beneficial relationship.

AUDIT FEES

Audit fees generally are directly related to the number of hours worked by the auditors. The established hourly or per diem rates of public accounting firms are, therefore, one factor in calculating the audit fee. The per diem rates vary in relation to the size of, and services offered by, the public accounting firm. Assuming a firm has been chosen wisely, the per diem rate should not be an overwhelming consideration in evaluating the cost of an audit.

The number of hours the auditors must spend to complete an audit are variable depending on factors such as

- size and complexity of the entity
- quality of internal control
- reputation of the entity, its board members and officers, and the auditors' experience with them
- management's accessibility, attitude, cooperation, and communication
- prior and present existence of related-party transactions, litigation, errors, and irregularities
- existence and effectiveness of an audit committee

THE CLIENT-AUDITOR RELATIONSHIP

Cooperation and communication between management and the independent auditors begin when the auditors are appointed by the board. The final decision as to the appointment of auditors should be that of the board and not management, as management's work will be reviewed.

Before an audit begins, the auditors usually meet with management and the board to review the overall audit plan and discuss the estimated fees. After the planning is complete, the auditors send a letter to management setting forth the arrangements for the upcoming audit. This letter should convey a clear understanding of the basic arrangements: what the auditors will examine; the general scope of the examination (including a reference to their review of internal control); and an estimate of the fees. Any supplemental services, such as tax return preparation or preparation of loan compliance reports, should also be included.

AUDIT COMMITTEES

In recent years, the boards of many institutions, both public and private, have formed audit committees. Board members have a responsibility for monitoring the entity's financial reporting. Trustees have been held liable for failure to discharge their responsibilities for financial reporting. Financial reporting has become increasingly complex and, at the same time, the

public has a growing awareness of its occasional deficiencies. The independent auditors and board members can best discharge their responsibilities for financial reporting by discussing all aspects of the business as it relates to such reporting. Formation of an audit committee is often a more efficient method of operation than full board participation. Board members serving on the committee should be those persons who possess the greatest degree of financial expertise.

An audit committee should

- recommend to the board the independent auditors to be selected
- discuss with the independent auditors the scope of their audit
- discuss with the independent auditors and management the entity's accounting principles and policies and the reporting practices followed, including the impact of alternative accounting principles
- discuss with the internal auditors the adequacy of the entity's accounting and financial systems and internal controls
- be aware of all work (audit, tax, reimbursement, and systems) that the public accounting firm performs for the entity
- discuss with the independent auditors the results of their audit, along with matters of controversy (resolved or unresolved) with management
- review and determine what action is required as a result of significant weaknesses in internal control noted during the annual audit, and management's evaluation of such weaknesses (the audit committee should determine appropriate action on the basis of its cost-benefit evaluation)
- review any memorandums prepared by the independent auditors setting forth any questionable activities or payments noted during their audit work

Management also should make presentations to the audit committee in connection with its responsibility for the financial statements.

The committee should determine the number and timing of its meetings with the auditors. The frequency of the meetings depends on the committee's overall responsibilities and the number and significance of the matters it must oversee. Most audit committees meet with the independent auditors and financial management at least twice a year.

The purpose of the first meeting is usually to discuss the general scope of the audit, major anticipated audit problems, the entity's general accounting policies and reporting practices, and any recent changes in such policies and practices. The initial meeting also may include a review of the entity's financial affairs and related matters with the chief financial officer and a discussion of activities and plans for the coming year with the entity's internal auditor. Such a meeting also may be an appropriate time to discuss possible changes in the company's system of internal accounting controls.

The purpose of the audit committee's final meeting of the year is to review the results of the audit, the financial statements, the auditors' report and any suggestions for improvements in accounting procedures, and internal accounting controls developed during the audit examination. The committee also should question the independent auditors about any major services provided during the past year and the results of such work.

Other questions the committee may wish to address to the independent auditors are as follows:

- Was management's cooperation satisfactory?
- How did management respond to suggestions for improvement in the entity's system of internal accounting control? Are there any serious weaknesses still not corrected?
- What adjustments were proposed during the course of the audit? Are these adjustments indicative of deficiencies in the entity's annual or interim reporting system?
- How may this entity's accounting policies be characterized in relation to others in the industry?
- Are there any accounting policies that management should consider changing? Why?

- Have the entity's policies and procedures been reviewed with respect to possible conflicts of interest, political contributions, bribes, or kickbacks? How? What were the results of this review?
- Did the scope of the audit include a review of officers' expense reports? Are the entity's procedures for approval of such expense reports adequate?
- Is the entity making effective use of its computers?
- Does the entity's internal audit function appear to be properly organized and staffed? Is it operating effectively? In what areas did the internal auditors assist in this year's audit? Could their role be expanded?

Additional meetings should be held as circumstances warrant. Meetings often are scheduled prior to board meetings so that the committee can give the board a timely report on its activities. It also is common to excuse management participants from a portion of the meeting so that committee members can, if they wish, question the auditors without management present.

Audit committee members should concentrate more on what the audit ultimately contributes to their company. They can be more effective if they deal less with the actual process of auditing and more with its benefits.

UNIQUE ASPECTS OF HEALTH CARE AUDITING

Every industry presents special problems for auditors. In most commercial companies, inventory is a significant asset and requires unique auditing techniques. Many of the assets of a financial institution are negotiable instruments, requiring the auditors to apply special auditing procedures.

In health care institutions, inventory is generally insignificant and negotiable assets are typically held in safekeeping. Nevertheless, numerous aspects of health care entities present the auditors special problems and challenges. Management and the board should understand these problems to participate effectively in planning discussions with the auditors. The following paragraphs highlight certain of the more challenging aspects of auditing health care institutions.

Accounts receivable from patients and third-party payers and the related contractual allowances are very significant and require special consideration by the auditors. Because bills are generally paid by a third party, it is usually difficult for the auditor to confirm directly with the patient the dollar amount owed. The auditor must carefully evaluate the various alternative procedures that can be adopted to obtain reasonable assurance that the accounts receivable are bona fide and properly stated.

The amount of contractual allowances is probably the most difficult aspect of a health care institution's financial statements to audit. For this reason, the auditors typically review the completed year-end cost report and Medicare reports of cases paid before they can be satisfied that the contractual allowance is appropriately computed.

Many hospitals have a significant amount of investments that may be restricted, unrestricted, or board-designated. Often, these investments relate to a special-purpose gift, grant funds, or building projects. Accounting for and auditing the income earned and the principal transactions of the related funds can be complex, especially where numerous special-purpose funds are present.

Institutions that retain a portion of their malpractice liability risks also present unique problems for the auditor, who must determine whether the amount provided and accrued is adequate. This is especially true in the early years of a retained risk program, when historical data have not yet been accumulated. Because of the subjective considerations involved in establishing the reserve, the auditors engage in discussions with the risk manager, other key executives, and the actuary.

These difficult auditing problems can be minimized if the board, management, and other accounting personnel prepare for the audit by carefully analyzing these areas and preparing, as practicable, written analyses and other documentation to explain and support the recorded amounts. The most significant factor in minimizing auditing problems is a strong and effective system of internal control.

SUMMARY

An external audit can be valuable. Audited financial statements are generally afforded a higher degree of credibility by readers and users. An external audit can help the board most effectively fulfill its responsibility to monitor the entity's financial condition and reporting. The audit should be performed in accordance with generally accepted auditing standards by independent public accountants who have been carefully selected. The auditors should issue an opinion on the financial statements and should prepare a management letter that makes recommendations for improvements in internal controls, accounting procedures, and other administrative matters. The auditors should provide positive support to management and the board from an independent business perspective and offer advice in matters such as financial performance, capital expansion, and financing and taxes. For management and the board to reap the greatest benefit from the client-auditor relationship, the channels of communication should be open and used freely and frequently.

BIBLIOGRAPHY

American Institute of Certified Public Accountants. *Hospital Audit Guide*. 5th ed. New York: American Institute of Certified Public Accountants, Inc., 1985.

Arthur Andersen & Co. *Challenges of Today's Audit Committee*. Arthur Andersen & Co., Fall 1988.

Guide to Studying and Evaluating Internal Accounting Controls. Arthur Andersen & Co., 1987.

Rossi, Joseph J., Jr., and Thomas R, Prince. "Selecting a CPA Firm." *Hospital Progress* 60, no. 4 (April 1978): pp. 62–66.

Chapter 5

Financial Reporting Issues

Martha Garner
Senior Manager, Price Waterhouse

Richard G. Kleiner
Partner, Price Waterhouse

OVERVIEW

This chapter deals with reporting issues that are unique or have special importance in health care organizations.

According to a recent survey conducted jointly by Price Waterhouse and the Healthcare Financial Management Association (HFMA),[1] the main development affecting hospital financial reporting trends in the 1980s did not come as the result of a pronouncement from the Financial Accounting Standards Board (FASB), the American Institute of Certified Public Accountants (AICPA), or any other standard-setting body. Rather, it came from the federal government, which issued regulations on September 1, 1983, implementing the prospective payment system (PPS) for Medicare inpatient hospital services. This change in the payment methodology for the Medicare program, one of the nation's largest purchasers of health care services, caused an upheaval in the traditional methods of delivery and financing of health care services. A myriad restructurings and alliances followed, with health care organizations em-

Portions of this chapter are adapted from *Hospital Financial Reports: A Survey*, with permission of Healthcare Financial Management Association, © 1987. Copies of this book are available from HFMA, Two Westbrook Corporate Center, Suite 700, Westchester, Illinois, 60153.

barking on long-range strategic plans to ensure their survival. New types of providers appeared on the scene. An era of all-out competition for limited dollars had begun—an era that is expected to see the closure of a significant number of the nation's hospitals by the year 2000, and equally significant changes in the way in which those that survive will conduct their businesses.

The increased level of competition in health care delivery and the amount of attention being directed toward rising health care costs are factors causing the accounting and financial reporting practices of health care organizations to be subjected to increased scrutiny. This increase in activity will continue as we move into the decade of the 1990s. Both FASB and the AICPA now have projects under way that have significant implications for the industry's financial statements.

During the course of a major project to develop a framework of concepts that underlie all financial accounting and reporting, FASB devoted a great deal of attention to studying issues pertaining to organizations characterized as "nonprofit," a classification that includes not-for-profit health care providers. In doing so, FASB identified five important not-for-profit issues it felt should be addressed in standards projects. These are recognition of depreciation; accounting for contributions; definition of the reporting entity; display of financial position and results of operations; and accounting for investments, particularly income of restricted investments. The depreciation project was completed with the issuance of an FASB statement on that topic in August 1987;[2] the standards it contained had no real impact on the health care community because most providers have been recording and disclosing depreciation all along. Work is currently underway on the projects concerning contributions, the reporting entity, display issues, and investments.

The AICPA is also currently active in the area of health care accounting and reporting matters. The changes that have come about in the 15 years since the AICPA's *Hospital Audit Guide* was first issued have diminished that guide's usefulness. Recognizing this, the AICPA's Health Care Committee and Hospital Audit Guide Task Force have been working on a draft of a revised accounting and audit guide for the health care industry. The proposed guide would expand the scope of the present *Guide* to cover "entities whose principal operations involve providing health services to individuals." Its provisions would therefore provide long-awaited accounting guidance to nursing homes, continuing care retirement communities (CCRCs), home health agencies, and clinics and other ambulatory care organizations, in addition to hospitals. Intertwined with this project are separate but related projects concerning accounting for HMOs and CCRCs, deferred reimbursement costs, single-fund reporting, and consolidations.

Sources of Health Care Generally Accepted Accounting Principles

The financial statements of health care entities should be prepared in conformity with generally accepted accounting principles (GAAP). The *Hospital Audit Guide* states that the Statements and Interpretations issued by FASB, and the Opinions and Accounting Research Bulletins (ARBs) issued by its predecessors, the Accounting Principles Board (APB) and the Committee on Accounting Procedure, should be followed in reporting on the financial statements prepared by

health care entities unless they are "inapplicable." Governmental providers must also comply with pronouncements issued by the Governmental Accounting Standards Board (GASB). (Questions about "applicability," however, have long been raised by a paragraph in Accounting Research Bulletin No. 43 that indicates that authoritative pronouncements are primarily directed to for-profit organizations, unless the issuing body specifically states otherwise. To assist in resolving this issue, the AICPA's Not-for-Profit Committee is working on a project dealing with the applicability of the main body of GAAP to not-for-profit organizations.)

Under the hierarchy of GAAP established by Statement on Auditing Standards No. 43, *Omnibus Statement on Auditing Standards* (see Exhibit 5-1), only FASB (or GASB, in the case of governmental providers) can officially establish accounting principles that must be complied with in financial statements prepared under the accounting profession's code of ethics. Until recently, FASB and its forerunners directed their standards efforts primarily to accounting issues that affected a broad range of companies across industry lines, as opposed to industry-specific matters. Industry issues were left to others to resolve, primarily by the industry committees of the AICPA.

Health care was one of the industries with unique accounting considerations; therefore, in 1972 the AICPA's Committee on Health Care Institutions issued the first edition of the *Hospital Audit Guide*. Since that time the committee has issued six statements of position (SOPs) that have amended or supplemented conclusions originally set forth in the *Guide*. The AICPA, therefore, has been and continues to be the primary source of guidance relating to specific accounting principles for health care organizations.

This arrangement is not without problems, however.

- Because pronouncements of the AICPA's committees are considered to be a secondary source of accounting principles, their use in the preparation of financial statements is not mandatory under the AICPA's code of ethics. Therefore, the AICPA's guides and SOPs have less authority (and somewhat less consistent application in practice) than do statements issued by FASB or GASB.*

- Because each of the AICPA committees focused on its own industry's unique needs, different accounting treatments were sometimes prescribed for similar issues. This created diversity in practice across industry lines, especially among not-for-profit organizations.
- Some of the conclusions published by the committees now conflict with conclusions that have been reached by FASB in its standards projects.
- Because the guides and SOPs are not part of FASB's official accounting literature, FASB cannot amend them or even provide interpretations when questions arise.

In 1979, FASB announced its plan to remedy these problems by "extracting" the specialized industry principles from a number of guides and SOPs and issuing them as FASB statements. Thereafter, each industry would have technically sanctioned GAAP, and FASB would have the authority to make changes and provide interpretations when needed. FASB Statement No. 32 and its companion, FASB Statement No. 56, identify the guides and SOPs containing the principles to be extracted. They also designate these industries' accounting and reporting principles as being "preferable" until such time as FASB completes its work and issues standards for that industry. In practice, this means that hospitals using accounting principles other than those recommended by the AICPA's Health Care Committee would not be required to adopt the provisions of the *Hospital Audit Guide* and its related SOPs; however, if they should ever elect to make a change in an accounting principle, the change should be to a "preferable" principle.

The "extraction" project for health care principles is still incomplete. As FASB considered the guides that had been issued for different types of not-for-profit organizations (one being the *Hospital Audit Guide*),* discrepancies were noted with regard to certain fundamental principles. Therefore, FASB decided first to develop broad concepts of reporting for nonprofit organizations (i.e., a conceptual framework) to use as a basis for developing consistent standards. To date, FASB has issued six Statements of Financial Accounting Concepts that represent a Category *d* source of GAAP (as other accounting literature). These statements do not in and of themselves constitute standards; rather, they provide a common foundation and basic reasoning process on which to consider merits of alternatives when questions arise.

After the *Hospital Audit Guide* was issued, new accounting and disclosure issues continued to arise in the health care community. Because of its due-process requirements, the AICPA could not act swiftly to issue position statements on these topics; the preparation of an issues paper, its consideration by FASB, and the subsequent preparation and exposure of an SOP normally take several years. The health care industry was in dire need of interim guidance. Action was taken in 1975 when the leadership of HFMA founded its Principles and Practices Board. This committee, which is still active today, consists of distinguished individuals in the field of health care finance who set forth advisory recommendations on health care accounting and reporting issues. Although statements by the HFMA's Principles and Practices Board fall into Category *d* (least authoritative) of the hierarchy of GAAP shown in Exhibit 5-1, they are of great value in that they can be issued relatively quickly to disseminate well-thought-out opinions, along with views on the issues and relevant background information, to the health care community.

Governmental providers must deal with an additional set of unique reporting considerations. In 1978, the AICPA issued SOP 78-7, *Financial Accounting and Reporting by Hospi-*

*They are, however, designated as another source of established accounting principles that must be considered by an individual who seeks to express an opinion on financial statements. Justification may be required for financial statements that contain departures from the recommendations of these pronouncements.

*The other guides were those for colleges and universities, voluntary health and welfare organizations, and certain (other) nonprofit organizations.

Exhibit 5-1 Hierarchy of Health Care Related GAAP

No single reference source exists for all GAAP. The sources of established accounting principles are generally as follows:

Level of Authority	Include These Sources		Which Contain These Health Care-Specific References
Officially established accounting principles (most authoritative) *(Category a)*	FASB Statements	SFAS 32	Specialized Accounting and Reporting Principles and Practices in AICPA Statements of Position and Guides on Accounting and Auditing Matters
	GASB Statements*		
	FASB Interpretations	SFAS 56	Designation of AICPA . . . SOP 81-2 Concerning Hospital-Related Organizations As Preferable for Purposes of Applying APB Opinion 20
	APB Opinions		
		SFAS 93	Recognition of Depreciation by Not-for-Profit Organizations
Other sources of established accounting principles *(Category b)*	AICPA Industry Audit and Accounting Guides	—	*Hospital Audit Guide*
		SOP (no number)	Clarification of Accounting, Auditing, and Reporting Practices Relating to Hospital Malpractice Loss Contingencies
	AICPA Statements of Position	SOP 78-1	Accounting by Hospitals for Certain Marketable Equity Securities
		SOP 78-7	Financial Accounting and Reporting by Hospitals Operated by a Governmental Unit
	FASB Technical Bulletins	SOP 81-2	Reporting Practices Concerning Hospital-Related Organizations
		SOP 85-1	Financial Reporting by Not-for-Profit Health Care Entities for Tax-Exempt Debt and Certain Funds Whose Use Is Limited
		SOP 87-1	Accounting for Asserted and Unasserted Medical Malpractice Claims of Health Care Providers and Related Issues
			FASB Technical Bulletin No. 79-5: Meaning of the Term "Customer" As It Applies to Health Care Facilities under FASB Statement No. 14

Category		References
c	AICPA Accounting Interpretations Prevalent Industry Practices	No References
Other accounting literature (least authoritative) **d**	APB Statements AICPA Issues Papers FASB Concepts Statement Pronouncements of professional associations or regulatory agencies Minutes of FASB meetings Minutes of FASB's "Emerging Issues Task Force" meetings Textbooks and articles	Statements 1–9 of HFMA's Principles and Practices Board EITF Issue No. 86-2: Accounting for retroactive wage adjustments affecting Medicare payments EITF Issue No. 86-12: Accounting by insureds for claims-made insurance policies

Note: Category references are taken from Statement on Auditing Standards No. 43, *Omnibus Statement on Auditing Standards*. Generally, the accountant should look first to Category *a* for guidance. If no guidance on a particular topic is found at this level, he or she should consider whether the treatment is specified by a source from Categories *b* or *c*. In the absence of a pronouncement in (*a*), (*b*), or (*c*), other accounting literature may be considered, depending on its relevance in the circumstances.

*Only apply to facilities operated by a state or local government unit. For these entities, GASB pronouncements stand higher in the hierarchy than do FASB pronouncements.

Source: Price Waterhouse, 1987.

tals Operated by a Governmental Unit. Questions had arisen concerning the financial accounting and reporting practices that should be followed by hospitals operated by governmental units, due to an overlap between the jurisdiction of the *Hospital Audit Guide* (all hospitals) and the audit guide for state and local government units. In the interest of promoting comparability of financial statements within the hospital industry, the AICPA concluded that hospitals operated by governmental units should follow the requirements of the *Hospital Audit Guide*.

Nearly a decade later, the jurisdictional problem reappeared. In 1984, after nearly five years of discussion, the Financial Accounting Foundation (FAF) established a structural agreement under which responsibility for standards setting was divided between GASB (for governmental units) and FASB (for all other entities). Unfortunately, instead of focusing on issues unique to governmental accounting and reporting, GASB has interpreted its powers under the structural agreement very broadly and has exercised its right to rule on *all* transactions of *all* governmental entities. This includes governmental health care providers, which therefore may one day end up with accounting standards and financial statements that are very different from those of corresponding providers in other sectors.

HFMA and many others involved in the health care industry hold that a characteristic of ownership should not be a basis for differences in accounting for nonownership issues. Consequently, the FAF is being urged to re-evaluate the situation and take action to relieve any confusion that the creation of GASB has caused.

UNIQUE ASPECTS OF HOSPITAL FINANCIAL REPORTING

Investor-Owned versus Not-for Profit Status

One significant characteristic of the health care industry is that distinctions are made for financial reporting purposes between facilities that are investor-owned and those that are operated as nonprofit organizations. According to Robert Anthony,[3] the basic difference between investor-owned companies and others fundamentally lies along the same lines as the distinction made for income tax purposes between for-profit (i.e., taxable) and not-for-profit (i.e., tax-exempt) organizations.

Nonprofit health care organizations are generally governed in their financial reporting by the AICPA's *Hospital Audit Guide*. Although in practice many proprietary (investor-owned) facilities use formats similar to those contained in the *Hospital Audit Guide*, their statements are subject to the same reporting requirements as are other traditionally commercial enterprises.

Attempts to establish different accounting and reporting principles for facilities classified as nonprofit have drawn fire from the health care community. The majority of nonprofit health care providers do not differ from their proprietary counterparts with regard to the nature of the business they conduct. For many, their nonprofit status arose simply from receiving tax exemption or having been established by a governmental entity. Yet for accounting and reporting purposes, FASB has grouped tax-exempt health care providers with other "nonbusiness" organizations (FASB's terminology), such as churches, museums, and voluntary health and welfare organizations.

FASB has acknowledged, however, that the word *nonbusiness* is not a synonym for *not-for-profit*. Investor-owned and nonprofit health care facilities alike must seek to generate a profit on their operations. An excess of revenues over expenses is required to enable an entity to meet its financial obligations, to improve its patient care, to keep pace with new technology, and to expand its facilities when necessary.

For accounting purposes, the fundamental distinction between the two statuses lies in the composition of the entity's equity or "net assets." The equity of a proprietary enterprise may be increased through investments of assets by owners who may, from time to time, receive distributions of assets from the entity. (Therefore, investor-owned facilities must generate sufficient after-tax net income to provide their owners with a reasonable return on their ownership interests.) Not-for-profit organizations, on the other hand, do not issue defined ownership interests in exchange for contributions of capital. Rather, their net assets (assets minus liabilities) often are increased by receipts of assets from contributors, donors, or grantors who give such funds unilaterally; they do not expect to receive repayment of the funds, nor do they expect to receive any return on the funds. Their only interest may be in how the organization makes use of their contributions.

Since the nature of their "businesses" are comparable, most health care financial professionals believe that the financial statements of for-profit and not-for-profit providers should be prepared in a comparable manner, based on comparable standards, with their fundamental differences highlighted so that they are apparent to the financial statements' users. To date, FASB has not issued any standards that require different accounting by nonprofit providers for transactions found commonly in the for-profit environment.

Single-Fund versus Multi-Fund Reporting

Since many institutional health care providers were developed as community organizations or as instrumentalities of a government organization, fund accounting similar to that used in government was generally adopted for record keeping and financial reporting purposes. In fund accounting, an organization is expressed as a self-balancing group of accounts composed of assets, liabilities, and fund balances. A *general fund* is used to account for resources available for general operating purposes and a separate *restricted fund* (or funds) is used to account for donor-restricted resources. This segregation of restricted resources is necessary because the provider has a fiduciary responsibility to use these funds only for the purposes specified by the donor; they are not available for general operating purposes.

Many users of financial statements who are accustomed to statements prepared in the traditional "business" format are often confused by the fund accounting concept. They find fragmented data presented in columns on a single statement or in a succession of separate statements, each of which deals with a piece of the organization; there appears to be no "bottom line."

For this reason, interest is growing in the preparation of single-fund statements. This approach displays all asset, liability, and net asset amounts in a single aggregated balance sheet, with fund differentiation indicated by notation in the net asset section and disclosure in the notes to the financial statements. Single-fund reporting gives appropriate recognition to the fact that the health care organization is a single entity and not a series of separate entities (funds), and therefore more closely parallels financial reporting in other business organizations.

The first guidance on single-fund reporting appeared in March 1986, when HFMA's Principles and Practices Board issued its Statement No. 8, *The Use of Fund Accounting and the Need for Single Fund Reporting by Institutional Healthcare Providers*. HFMA recommended that single-fund reporting be used by all institutional health care providers for all general-purpose financial statements. According to Statement No. 8, gifts, bequests, and grants that are restricted by donors for specific operating purposes . . . "for additions to property, plant and equipment, or for endowment purposes . . ." should be reported in the general fund with noncurrent assets and labeled as "assets whose use is limited." A contra-amount, depending on the nature of the limitations on the use of resources, should be reflected as deferred revenue, a liability, or in net assets, with appropriate footnote disclosure.

In December of that same year, FASB published its Statement of Financial Accounting Concepts No. 6, *Elements of Financial Statements*. This statement sets forth the concept that, although some not-for-profit organizations may choose to classify assets and liabilities into fund groups, information about those fund groupings is not a necessary part of general-purpose external financial reporting. It suggests that recognizing limitations on net assets, even in cases of stringent legal limitations, is sufficient.

Use of a single-fund presentation for external financial reporting has no effect on the opinion rendered in the accountants' report. In addition, its use does not imply that the organization would not continue to keep detailed records on a fund-type basis. Internally, the organization would continue to carry out its stewardship responsibility and ensure that donor-restricted resources are used only for specified purposes.

No authoritative literature currently exists that favors one presentation over another; however, the AICPA has two projects under way that are expected to provide guidance in this area. The AICPA's Not-for-Profit Committee has established a task force to work on issues relating to financial statement display. The task force will prepare an issues paper for FASB's consideration that may serve as a springboard for future FASB activity in this area. In addition, the AICPA's Health Care Committee has added a project to its agenda aimed at issuing an SOP on single-fund reporting by not-for-profit providers.

BASIC FINANCIAL STATEMENTS

The information contained in this section is directed primarily toward the preparation of financial statements by not-for-profit hospitals, since GAAP is currently provided only for hospitals. The AICPA's proposed revised audit guide, tentatively entitled *Audits of Providers of Health Care Services*, will contain recommendations and illustrative financial statements for other types of providers as well; these are expected to be generally consistent with the format used for nonprofit hospital statements.*

Investor-owned health care entities generally follow the financial reporting requirements of other investor-owned businesses.

Balance Sheet

Most nonprofit hospitals use the term *balance sheet* for the statement of financial position. Assets and liabilities reflected on the balance sheet of the general fund (defined below) are usually classified as current or long-term, with prior year balances presented for comparative purposes.

---

*The final version of the proposed guide is tentatively expected to be released sometime in 1989.

It is essential that a clear separation be made on the balance sheet between *general funds* (resources available for general operating purposes) and *donor-restricted funds* (contributed resources that must be used as directed by the donor). This segregation of restricted resources is necessary because the health care entity has a fiduciary responsibility to use these funds only for the purposes specified by the donor; they may not be used for general operating purposes. Donor-restricted funds generally fall into one of five categories: funds for specific operating purposes, funds for additions to property and equipment, endowment funds, and the less commonly seen loan funds and annuity and living trust funds. These classifications are discussed further under "Gifts, Grants, and Pledges."

The sample balance sheet appearing in the *Hospital Audit Guide* presents general and restricted balance sheets in a layered format. While the layered presentation traditionally has been most commonly used, other formats such as columnar and single-fund are also found in practice. In Exhibits 5-2 and 5-3 a single-fund presentation is compared with a layered presentation.

The general fund section of the balance sheet often will include a special category of funds under a caption such as "assets whose use is limited." This classification is used to report any funds that are set aside for specific uses under terms of debt indentures, trust agreements, and third-party payment or other similar arrangements.[4] It also includes any assets that have been earmarked by a facility's governing board for identified purposes; these are commonly referred to as "board-designated funds." If the balance sheet is prepared in a single-fund format, the entity's donor-restricted funds may also be reflected under this caption.

Aside from the separate presentation of any donor-restricted funds, the primary difference between a balance sheet prepared for a proprietary provider and one prepared for a not-for-profit provider is in the presentation of the "net assets" section. In proprietary financial statements, net assets are referred to as *owners' equity*; in not-for-profit statements, they are known as *fund balance*.

Exhibit 5-2 Example of Layered Format of Balance Sheet*

Assets	December 31, 19X2	19X1	Liabilities and Fund Balance	December 31, 19X2	19X1
		General Funds			
Current assets	$12	$ 9	Current liabilities	$ 6	$ 5
Property, plant, and equipment	39	37	Long-term debt	12	9
Assets whose use is limited	9	5	Fund balance	42	37
Total general fund assets	$60	$51	Total general fund liabilities and fund balance	$60	$51
		Donor-Restricted Funds			
Specific-purpose funds:			Specific-purpose funds:		
Assets	$ 5	$ 4	Fund balance	$ 5	$ 4
Endowment funds:			Endowment funds:		
Assets	$11	$10	Fund balance	$11	$10

*Details of classification are omitted to simplify presentation.

Exhibit 5-3 Example of Single-Fund Format of Balance Sheet*

Assets	December 31, 19X2	19X1	Liabilities and Fund Balance	December 31, 19X2	19X1
Current assets	$12	$ 9	Current liabilities	$ 6	$ 5
Property, plant, and equipment	39	37	Long-term debt	12	9
Assets whose use is limited:			Fund balance:		
By board for capital improvements	9	5	Temporarily restricted by donors	5	4
By donors for specific uses	16	14	Permanently restricted by donors	11	10
			General	42	37
Total assets	$76	$65	Total liabilities and fund balance	$76	$65

*Details of classification are omitted to simplify presentation.

Statement of Revenues and Expenses

The statement of revenues and expenses is the equivalent of the conventional income statement in the nonprofit hospital environment. It reports the revenues generated from the provision of services and the expenses incurred in providing those services, and it is widely used to judge the performance of hospital management.[5]

Income statements of industrial corporations often appear in a single-step format. All revenues are grouped together at the top of the state-ment, and expenses are grouped in the lower portion of the statement. Net income (before provision for income taxes) is then determined in a single step by subtracting total expenses from total revenues.[6] Hospitals, on the other hand, customarily present their income statements in a multiple-step format that depicts the results of operations through a series of intermediate sub-totals. The multiple-step format is considered by many to provide a more useful indication of the nature and sources of hospital income because it emphasizes the facility's income (or loss) from operations before consideration of nonoperating revenues.[7]

The "steps" of a hospital income statement traditionally have been

- patient service revenue
- deductions from revenue
- net patient service revenue
- other operating revenue
- total operating revenue
- operating expenses
- income (loss) from operations
- nonoperating revenue
- excess (deficit) of revenue over expenses

Patient service revenues historically have been reported at their gross billing values, with revenue deductions (i.e., third-party payer contractual allowances, charity allowances, and other allowances and discounts) subtracted in a separate step to arrive at net patient service revenue. However, as fewer and fewer third-party purchasers pay for hospital services at established rates, presentation of the gross revenue amount becomes less meaningful. Therefore, the industry is moving toward a net revenue presentation, with disclosure of deductions from revenue in a footnote. (This is discussed in more detail under "Third-Party Payment Issues.")

Operating expenses normally are classified along functional lines, except that depreciation and interest expense are usually set forth separately. The most commonly used classifications are as follows:

- functional descriptions
  - nursing services
  - other professional services
  - general services
  - administrative services
  - fiscal services
  - professional care of patients
  - leasehold and property
  - dietary
  - depreciation
  - interest
- natural descriptions
  - salaries and wages
  - professional fees

- payroll taxes and employee benefits
- supplies (and other expenses)
- purchased services
- insurance
- depreciation
- interest expense

The operating results for nonprofit hospitals are reflected in a subtotal designated as "income (loss) from operations." Controversy abounds as to where the dividing line should lie in determining whether certain elements of revenue should be classified as "operating" or "nonoperating." In commercial business enterprises, "operating income" or "income from operations" generally includes revenues from the sale of products or services whose costs are included in "operating expenses." When interest, dividends, rents, and royalties are peripheral to the companies' major operating objective, they are usually reported under captions such as "other revenue" or "other income."[8]

Nonprofit hospitals must make tougher distinctions. The appropriate classification of some types of nonpatient revenue, such as unrestricted gifts or unrestricted income from investments, presents no problem because of specific guidance contained in the 1972 Hospital Audit Guide. Other types of revenue, such as restricted contributions utilized and certain types of investment income and gains or losses, are not adequately addressed by the Guide; this gives preparers of financial statements a great deal of latitude for interpretation within the boundaries of GAAP. Consequently, a great deal of inconsistency exists among hospitals in whether they classify nonpatient revenues above or below the operations line.

Both the AICPA and HFMA's Principles and Practices Board are addressing this diversity in practice. Both the AICPA's draft proposed audit guide and an exposure draft of a statement by the HFMA's Principles and Practices Board entitled The Presentation of Nonpatient Service Revenue and Related Issues state that revenues that are not directly related to an entity's ongoing or principal operations should not be included in operating income. Donor-restricted contributions should be included in operations to the extent that related expenses are included in operations, and investment income directly related to certain operating costs is properly classified as operating revenue.

Donor-restricted contributions that have not yet been used for their intended purposes should *not* be reflected in the statement of revenue and expenses. These should instead flow through a statement of changes in fund balances prepared for the restricted fund (or group of funds).

After nonoperating revenue is added to the income or loss from operations, the bottom line of the income statement reflects either an "excess of revenues over expenses" or an "excess of expenses over revenues." This is the amount by which net assets (fund balance or equity) in the statement of changes in fund balance will be increased or decreased as a result of the facility's operations.

Presentation of extraordinary items is basically the same in hospital financial statements as it is in other businesses. The criteria for classification as an extraordinary item are set forth in APB Opinion No. 30, *Reporting the Results of Operations: Reporting the Effects of Disposal of a Segment of a Business, and Extraordinary, Unusual and Infrequently Occurring Events and Transactions.*

It is debatable as to whether the write-off (reversal) of previously recorded Medicare timing differences related to capital costs meets the criteria of an extraordinary item as defined by APB Opinion No. 30. When this situation is encountered, the criteria should be evaluated based on the specific facts and circumstances in each situation. This is further discussed under "Third-Party Payment Issues."

Gains or losses on early retirement of tax-exempt debt, if material, must always be classified as extraordinary, according to FASB Statement No. 4, *Reporting Gains and Losses from Extinguishment of Debt.*

Another relatively rare item that requires special treatment in the statement of revenues and expenses is the prior-period adjustment. The criteria for reporting prior-period adjustments are set forth in paragraphs 10 and 11 of FASB Statement No. 16, *Prior Period Adjustments* (as amended).

With all of these considerations, the statement of revenues and expenses has the potential to become an extremely detailed document. Some facilities present a great deal of detail; others present income statements that are highly condensed, providing only summary totals of major classifications of revenue and expense. Details, if desired, may also be presented in the accompanying notes or in supplemental schedules or statements. Each hospital must determine the level of detail that it feels is most meaningful for full disclosure.

Statement of Changes in Fund Balance(s)

The statement of changes in fund balance is the nonprofit hospital's equivalent of the statement of changes in stockholders' equity prepared by the investor-owned business. The use of fund accounting usually results in the fragmentation of a nonprofit hospital's net assets into one or more separate fund balance accounts. As discussed earlier, a fund balance is the excess of assets over liabilities existing within a particular fund. A statement of changes in fund balances, then, should report all changes that have occurred during the reporting period in all fund balance accounts maintained by the hospital.

A hospital's excess of revenues over expenses (or excess of expenses over revenues) will constitute at least part of the change in its net assets during a period. Net assets may also be affected by reclassifications between restricted and general funds (such as when a temporary endowment expires and the funds become available for general operating purposes), or by reclassifications between restricted funds. Therefore, it is important that a statement of changes in fund balance be presented for all funds. FASB Concepts Statement No. 6 states:

> Since donor-imposed restrictions affect the types and levels of service a not-for-profit organization can provide, whether an organization has maintained certain classes of net assets may be more significant than whether it has maintained net assets in the aggregate. For example, if net assets were maintained in a period only because permanently restricted endowment contributions made up for a decline in unrestricted net assets, information focusing on the

aggregated change might obscure the fact that the organization had not maintained the part of its net assets that is fully available to support services in the next period.*

Statement of Changes in Financial Position

In November 1987, FASB issued its Statement No. 95, *Statement of Cash Flows*. This statement superseded APB Opinion No. 19, *Reporting Changes in Financial Position*; it requires that the statement of changes in financial position be replaced by a statement of cash flows in financial statements prepared for fiscal years ending after July 15, 1988. Nonprofit organizations, however, are specifically excluded from the scope of FASB Statement No. 95 because of current AICPA activities in the area of financial statement display.

In this regard, the AICPA's Not-for-Profit Committee has established a task force to determine how the financial position and results of operations of not-for-profit organizations should be displayed in financial statements. The task force will prepare an issues paper for FASB's consideration that should serve as a springboard for future FASB activity in this area. In the meantime, voluntary nonprofit organizations will technically continue to be governed by the provisions of APB Opinion No. 19; however, since most providers believe that the provisions of FASB Statement No. 95 should be applied to not-for-profit health care entities, it is likely that the revised audit guide will recommend this guidance as well when it is issued in final form.

GASB has issued an exposure draft of a statement requiring governmental entities that use "proprietary fund" accounting (such as governmental health care providers) to adopt cash flow reporting. The exposure draft's provisions parallel those of FASB Statement No. 95 except that more categories are used for classifying cash transactions; the "operating" category is more narrowly focused; and "net cash provided by operations" is reconciled to net *operating* income rather than net income for the year.

---

*Paragraph 106.

Authoritative guidance is not clear as to whether nonoperating revenue should be included or excluded in the determination of cash provided by operating activities. The results of a 1985 survey of hospital reporting practices conducted jointly by Price Waterhouse and HFMA indicated a distinct preference to exclude such revenue.[9]

General Footnote Disclosures

APB Opinion No. 22, *Disclosure of Accounting Policies*, requires inclusion of a description of all significant accounting policies as an integral part of a set of financial statements. While recognizing the need for flexibility, the opinion expresses a preference for a separate summary to precede the notes to the financial statements or to be placed as the initial note, and suggests the title "Summary of Significant Accounting Policies." In practice this is usually accomplished in an initial note. The accounting principles and practices most frequently described in the summary are

- principles of financial statement preparation (specifying organizations included in the financial statements)
- revenue recognition
- contractual agreements with third-party payers
- definition of cash equivalents
- inventory valuation
- investment valuation
- property, plant, and equipment: capitalization policies and depreciation and amortization policies
- gifts, grants, and bequests (including the treatment of pledges)
- existence of restricted funds/assets limited as to use
- financing and deferred costs
- interest capitalization
- deferred revenue
- pensions: accounting and funding

The appendix to SOP 85-1, *Financial Reporting by Not-for-Profit Health Care Entities for*

Tax-Exempt Debt and Certain Funds Whose Use Is Limited, states that the accounting policies footnote should describe the differences between general funds, including those limited as to use, and restricted funds.

Health care organizations are subject to the same reporting requirements as those of other organizations and should disclose appropriate information (if applicable) in the notes to the financial statements with regard to such matters as

- leases
- income taxes
- earnings per share
- stock-option plan commitments
- contingent liabilities

Investor-owned health care companies registered with the Securities and Exchange Commission (SEC) must comply with that body's reporting requirements as well, in such ways as including management's discussion and analysis of financial condition and results of operations for the most recent three years, along with liquidity and capital requirements. SEC registrants are also required to include selected financial data for five years in their annual reports to shareholders. These companies customarily include other supplementary information and analyses common to any large publicly-held company, such as summaries of financial highlights.

RELATED ORGANIZATIONS

In its exposure draft *Institutional Healthcare Providers Are Businesses*, HFMA's Principles and Practices Board noted that there has been a widespread movement to diversify the activities of institutional health care providers. This diversification has been reflected in the recent proliferation of multiple corporations, as well as in increased activity in the area of mergers and acquisitions. Such changes in organizational structure are often undertaken to recognize diverse activities more appropriately, enhance access to capital, respond to regulatory pressures, help the hospital to compete more effectively, or protect assets.

A major catalyst in this movement has been the implementation of Medicare's PPS, which has radically changed the ways in which health care services are financed (and delivered). In addition, the increased use of alternative-delivery health care providers such as nursing homes and home health agencies has decreased utilization of inpatient hospital services. Such changes, coupled with an increasing awareness of the costs of providing services, have forced all providers to become more efficient; they have also fostered a competitive environment in which many institutions must search for ways to survive.

One effect of PPS has been a trend to restructure nonprofit hospital organizations to enhance their ability to provide "other sources of revenue." Such plans were designed to provide a means of increasing revenue that would not be affected by control programs or other constraints. In a typical reorganization, nonmedical support functions (such as management services, electronic data processing, and laundry) are sold or otherwise transferred to separate organizations that, in turn, sell their services to the hospital as well as to others. Other subsidiary organizations may also be formed to carry on taxable commercial activities (such as real estate operations) that a nonprofit provider could not conduct without jeopardizing its tax-exempt status.

Besides encouraging corporate reorganizations, another effect of PPS has been to fuel significant increases in merger and consolidation activity, especially among investor-owned providers. Historically, the most common way in which a single health care organization became a multi-institutional system was through constructing other facilities.[10] A faster alternative is the business combination,[11] in which organizations can rapidly expand "horizontally" (i.e., a hospital purchasing another hospital) or "vertically" (i.e., a hospital purchasing a home health agency) by merging with each other or by the acquisition of one by another.

However, expansion has not been limited solely to the for-profit sector. The traditionally non-expansionist not-for-profit sector has also become active by developing numerous alternatives to acquisition by large investor-owned chains. Many hospitals located in the same service area have merged together to achieve economies of scale and to fight problems such as cost containment and decreased utilization. Large not-for-profit hospitals have acquired smaller hospitals; others have formed affiliations to position themselves for survival in the industry.[12] Although nonprofit hospitals have long encouraged the creation of foundations, auxiliaries, guilds, and similar organizations to enhance their financial well-being, these types of related organizations are more important today than ever before, since increasing percentages of hospital revenues are derived from Medicare, Medicaid, and other third-party payer programs that often do not provide adequate funds to pay for new services and equipment.

The upsurge in merger and acquisition activity shows no sign of stopping. It is predicted that 15 to 20 percent of all hospitals will close during the decade of the 1990s. Those that survive are likely to be owned by or affiliated with a multihospital system or third-party insurer or payer.[13]

Limited guidance is available to address the problems arising in the preparation of the financial statements of multientity health care systems; this has resulted in a proliferation of recent activity by FASB, the AICPA, and HFMA's Principles and Practices Board. The guidance available at the time of this writing is discussed below.

Corporate Reorganizations

In a typical corporate reorganization, a standalone hospital moves to a multientity structure; therefore, new legal entities are created. After the restructuring has taken place, the restructured provider retains most of the activities that are essentially inherent in its direct health care mission, while other activities (e.g., ambulance service, real estate holding, or fund raising) are parceled out to separate but related entities.

The most common types of reorganizations are

- *Push up.* The provider "pushes up" nonprovider operations (such as fund raising, investing, and other non-health care

activities, as well as activities of other types of providers, such as an attached nursing home) to a newly-created parent corporation. This parent corporation, which becomes the controlling entity, has tax-exempt status as a publicly supported foundation or a "supporting" organization; the provider becomes a subsidiary. In the course of the reorganization, all but the provider's operating assets are transferred to the parent.

- *Drop down.* A tax-exempt entity creates one or more new controlled entities, thereby making itself a parent company. The provider operations are then "dropped down" to the status of a controlled entity. Some assets may be transferred in this type of reorganization, such as the transfer of investment property to a new real estate operation or the transfer of endowment funds to a foundation.

- *Unrelated entities.* A reorganization may create other entities that are not under common control. The most common example of this relationship is the creation of a separate fund-raising organization (also called a development foundation), which solicits funds for the benefit of the provider but is not legally under the control of the provider. Both the provider and foundation would normally be tax-exempt. The foundation may also serve as the parent company for other types of operations, such as real estate and taxable activities.[14]

As seen here, transfers of assets between entities are common in many reorganizations, yet no authoritative guidance specifically addresses how transfers between entities under common control in a reorganization should be accounted for. HFMA's Principles and Practices Board put forth some tentative advisory recommendations in an exposure draft entitled *Accounting and Reporting Issues Related to Corporate Reorganizations Involving Tax-Exempt Institutional Healthcare Providers*, which was issued in May 1987.

The exposure draft states that, in a reorganization, transfers of assets between the controlling and controlled entities should flow through their respective fund balance accounts; such transactions should not be reflected in revenue or expense. This is based on the generally accepted accounting principle that transactions of a capital nature should not be included in net income.[15]

Transfers of assets may also occur after a reorganization has taken place. Typical situations involving assets transferred subsequent to a reorganization, and the exposure draft's recommendations related to each, are as follows:

- *Contributions*. An entity that receives contributions (such as a development foundation) may transfer these funds to a related entity (such as a hospital). The transferring organization may not remove any restrictions originally imposed on the use of the funds by the donors; however, they may impose additional restrictions, which must be complied with by the organization that receives the funds.
- *Return of capital*. If a provider transfers assets to an entity it creates in the course of a reorganization, and the related entity subsequently returns all or a portion of this capital contribution, the funds returned to the provider should be recorded directly in the provider's fund balance. This conclusion is also based on the provision of APB Opinion No. 9 that states that capital transactions shall be excluded from the determination of net income.
- *Transfer of profits*. The exposure draft also addresses transactions in which a provider transfers an amount equivalent to its profits from operations to another member of its controlled group. The HFMA's Principles and Practices Board likens this to payment of dividends, because dividends also represent distribution of all or a portion of an organization's profits. The board recommends that this type of transfer flow through the provider's fund balance, consistent with its recommended treatment of a transfer of assets at the time of a reorganization.

Another issue addressed in the exposure draft involves the appropriate valuation of nonmonetary assets transferred in a reorganization. APB Opinion No. 29, *Accounting for Nonmonetary Transactions*, specifically excludes from its scope transfers of nonmonetary assets between companies or persons under common control. However, the logic it contains is used by some preparers of financial statements to justify the valuation at historical cost of assets transferred within a controlled group. APB Opinion No. 29 indicates that in certain specific situations where an exchange is not essentially the culmination of an earnings process, the value of the assets transferred should be based on their "recorded amount" (i.e., historical cost).* Since transfers between entities under common control are also not a result of the earnings process, those who take this position argue that it would be inappropriate to record an increased value in the transferee's records by recording the transfer at any basis other than historical cost. The exposure draft also cites support for recording transfers of nonmonetary assets at historical cost in certain circumstances from APB Opinion No. 16, *Business Combinations*, and its related interpretations.

Mergers and Acquisitions

A business combination occurs when two or more organizations are brought together into one accounting entity. In contrast to a reorganization, which creates new legal entities, a combination results in fewer legal entities. APB Opinion No. 16, *Business Combinations*, outlines two acceptable methods for accounting for business combinations: the purchase method and the pooling-of-interests method. The pooling-of-interests method may be used only if the combination meets certain specified criteria; combinations that do not meet all of these criteria should be accounted for by using the purchase method.

The pooling-of-interests method accounts for a business combination as the combining of the ownership interests of two or more companies brought together by the exchange of equity interests. No acquisition of one by the other is recognized because their respective ownership inter-

---

*The APB recognized only two types of exchanges to which this applies; both are highly specific.

ests are "pooled." No purchase or sale is involved; therefore, the assets and liabilities of each entity are carried forward in the combined corporation at their recorded amounts. Aggregate income is not changed, since the total resources are not changed; the reported income of the entities for prior periods are combined and reported as income of the combined corporation.

The purchase method accounts for a business combination as the acquisition of one enterprise by another. Unlike the pooling-of-interests method, which brings assets and liabilities forward into the new corporation at their former *book* values, the purchase method requires the acquired assets to be recorded on the books of the acquiring corporation at their *fair* values. Any difference between the purchase price and the sum of the fair values of assets acquired, less liabilities assumed, is recorded as goodwill. In the year of acquisition, the results of operations of the purchaser include the results of operations of the acquired organization from the date of acquisition, based on its cost to the acquiring enterprise.

Financial Reporting Considerations

FASB Statement No. 94, *Consolidation of All Majority-Owned Subsidiaries*; Accounting Research Bulletin No. 51, *Consolidated Financial Statements*; and APB Opinion No. 18, *The Equity Method of Accounting for Investments in Common Stock*; establish GAAP for presenting ownership of one organization by another in general-purpose financial statements.

Until recently, the decision of which subsidiaries to consolidate and which to reflect by using the equity method often has not been clear-cut. Authoritative pronouncements left room for differences of opinion and exercise of judgment. Some organizations prepared consolidated or combined statements, some used the equity method, and others made footnote disclosure only. To eliminate this growing diversity in practice, FASB undertook a major project entitled "The Reporting Entity, Including Consolidations and the Equity Method," to consider issues related to the concept of reporting entity, consolidation, application of the equity meth-

od, and accounting for various types of joint ventures.

By December 1986, the board's deliberations on the concept of reporting entity had proceeded far enough to make clear that consolidation of all majority-owned subsidiaries whose control was not in question was consistent with all of the other reporting entity concepts under consideration. Therefore, the board separated that issue from the remainder of the project and published its conclusions in FASB Statement No. 94, *Consolidation of All Majority-Owned Subsidiaries*. This statement amended Accounting Research Bulletin No. 51 by requiring consolidation of all majority-owned subsidiaries, except in circumstances where control is either temporary or does not rest with the majority owner.

The provisions of FASB Statement No. 94 must be applied in financial statements prepared for fiscal years after December 15, 1988, although earlier application is encouraged. Comparative financial statements for earlier periods, including those of the year of adoption, shall be restated.

Conditions for Consolidation

FASB Statement No. 94 amends ARB No. 51 to require that consolidated financial statements be prepared whenever one entity in a reporting group has a direct or indirect "controlling financial interest" in other members of the group, unless control is temporary or does not rest with the majority owners. ARB No. 51 had previously allowed presentation of separate statements for subsidiaries with "nonhomogeneous" operations, large minority interests, or foreign locations if doing so would make the parent companies' financial statements "more meaningful" to their users than consolidated statements would be.

FASB Statement No. 94 continues to allow exceptions in circumstances in which control is temporary or does not rest with the majority owners (in legal reorganizations or bankruptcies, for instance); however, the appropriateness of these exceptions is being examined as FASB's reporting entity project continues. The cost method has usually been employed to account for majority-owned subsidiaries that meet either of these criteria.[16] Statement No. 94 does not specify which accounting method should be used; preparers of financial statements must therefore be governed by existing literature. APB Opinion No. 18, however, effectively (although not explicitly) requires such organizations to be accounted for by the cost method.*

Prior to issuance of Statement No. 94, companies with material investments in majority-owned subsidiaries that were not consolidated were required to present summarized information regarding the assets, liabilities, and results of operations (or separate statements) for such subsidiaries in their financial statements. Statement No. 94 requires those companies that will be forced to change their policy of nonconsolidation (i.e., those that were previously unconsolidated for reasons of nonhomogeneity or other restrictive consolidation policies) to continue to disclose this information after consolidation is accomplished.

Conditions Requiring Use of the Equity Method

Consolidated statements generally must be prepared for controlled subsidiaries. Control is usually determined by majority ownership (more than 50 percent).

If the investor owns less than 50 percent but exercises "significant influence" over the investee, APB Opinion No. 18 states that the equity method should be used to account for the investment. Significant influence is presumed if the ownership interest is 20 percent or greater.

Opinion No. 18 states that an investment accounted for under the equity method should be shown in the investor's balance sheet as a single line item. Similarly, an investor's share of the investment's earnings or losses should ordinarily be shown in its income statement as a single

amount (except when extraordinary items or prior-period adjustments exist).

Specific Guidance for Health Care

The whole area of multi-organization health care systems requires judgment in determining the most meaningful financial statement presentation, since the health care-specific literature currently available did not contemplate the complex systems that are now being developed (such as multiple not-for-profit organizations and taxable entities under common parents) when it was issued.

In August 1981 the AICPA's Health Care Committee issued SOP 81-2, *Reporting Practices Concerning Hospital-Related Organizations*, in an attempt to homogenize a growing diversity of reporting practices. SOP 81-2 amended the 1972 *Hospital Audit Guide*, providing guidance in determining the circumstances in which nonprofit organizations should be considered to be "related" to a hospital for financial statement purposes, and setting forth the disclosure requirements for those organizations in hospital financial statements.

Nowhere is specific guidance currently provided for providers other than hospitals. Working drafts of the proposed audit guide *Audits of Providers of Health Care Services* incorporate the conclusions of SOP 81-2 with one major change: the word *hospital* has been replaced with the phrase *health care entity* throughout to make the conclusions of the original SOP applicable to all providers covered by the proposed guide.

HFMA's Principles and Practices Board takes a similar view in its exposure draft of an advisory statement entitled *Accounting and Reporting Issues Related to Corporate Reorganizations Involving Tax-Exempt Institutional Healthcare Providers*. The exposure draft advises that the guidance on related parties contained in SOP 78-10, *Accounting Principles and Reporting Practices for Certain Non-Profit Organizations*, could be construed to apply to tax-exempt hospital-related organizations, since they are not covered by any existing audit guide. The provisions of SOP 78-10 are very similar to those of SOP 81-2; consolidated or combined financial

---

*Footnote No. 4 of APB Opinion No. 18 (as amended) states that the limitations to consolidation specified in ARB No. 51 (that is, where control is temporary or does not rest with the majority owner) should also be applied as limitations to the use of the equity method.

statements should be presented when "control" exists and any one of three circumstances related to sole beneficiary status exists.

What Is a Hospital-Related Organization?

According to SOP 81-2, a separate organization is considered to be related to a hospital if either of the following two conditions exist:

1. The hospital controls the separate organization through contracts or other legal documents that provide the hospital with the authority to direct the separate organization's activities, management, and policies.
2. The hospital is the sole beneficiary of the organization.

Ownership of a majority voting interest in another company or organization ordinarily constitutes control in a for-profit company. However, nonprofit organizations are not "owned"; as a result, control is more difficult to determine. FASB Statement No. 57, *Related Party Disclosures*, defines control as "the possession, direct or indirect, of the power to direct or cause the direction of the management and policies of an enterprise through ownership, by contract, or otherwise."*

SOP 81-2 is more explicit with regard to determining sole beneficiary status, which is evidenced by the existence of any of the following three circumstances:

1. The organization has solicited funds to be used by the hospital.
2. The hospital has transferred resources to the organization, and substantially all of the organization's resources are held for the benefit of the hospital.
3. The organization operates primarily for the benefit of the hospital, and has been assigned certain of the hospital's functions.

---

*Paragraph 24(b).

If either the "control" or "sole beneficiary" condition is met, then the hospital and the separate organization are related, and the hospital must determine whether combination, consolidation, or financial statement disclosure is required.

SOP 81-2 directs hospitals to look to ARB No. 51 for guidance on whether or not consolidation or combination is appropriate. If the hospital has a controlling financial interest in the related organization (as defined in ARB No. 51), then combined or consolidated financial statements should be presented (see "Applicability of FASB Statement No. 94 to Not-for-Profit Providers"). As discussed under "Conditions for Consolidation," controlling financial interest is usually evidenced by ownership of more than 50 percent of an organization's voting stock. Since tax-exempt organizations usually do not issue stock, the definition of whether a controlling financial interest exists depends upon a careful evaluation of the facts and circumstances in each situation.

Preliminary research by the FASB in the not-for-profit phase of its "reporting entity" project indicates that both consolidation based on control and consolidation based on legal entity boundaries are found in present practice.[17]

If the hospital does not have a controlling financial interest in the related organization, consolidation is not appropriate; but if that same hospital controls and is the sole beneficiary of the related organization's activities, then it should disclose summarized financial data pertaining to the related organization in the notes to its financial statements. This would include information such as total assets, total liabilities, changes in fund balance, total revenue, total expenses, and amount of distributions to the hospital. In addition, the hospital should disclose the nature of its relationship with the related organization.

Additional disclosures are required if the related organization holds significant amounts of funds designated for the hospital or if material transactions have taken place between the hospital and the related organization. In either of these cases, SOP 81-2 states that the hospital should disclose the existence and nature of the relationship(s). If material transactions have taken place, the hospital must describe and quantify the transactions in accordance with FASB Statement No. 57. These would include

- a description of the transactions, including transactions to which no amounts or nominal amounts were ascribed, for each of the periods for which income statements are presented, and such other information deemed necessary to an understanding of the effects of the transactions on the financial statements
- the dollar amounts of transactions for each of the periods for which income statements are presented and the effects of any change in the method of establishing the terms from that used in the preceding period
- amounts due from or to related parties as of the date of each balance sheet presented and, if not otherwise apparent, the terms and manner of settlement

In addition to the above, Statement No. 57 requires disclosure of the nature of control relationships that could result in operating results or financial positions significantly different from those that would have been obtained if the enterprises were autonomous, regardless of whether there are transactions between the related parties.

If the hospital does not have a controlling financial interest, does not control the activities of the related organization, or is not the sole beneficiary of the related organization's activities, then no disclosure of the relationship is required unless the related organization holds significant amounts of funds designated for the hospital, or unless there have been material transactions between the hospital and the organization. Those specific situations should be disclosed as described above.

One additional aspect should be considered. Nonprofit organizations are required to operate in accordance with their charters. Their unique legal form gives substance to the argument that they are separate organizations that cannot be controlled in the same manner as those in which a majority voting interest is owned. Therefore, in circumstances where it is deemed appropriate

to combine the financial statements of certain related nonprofit organizations, the notes to such financial statements should disclose clearly any resulting limitations on the mutual availability of resources among the entities, the basis for the combination, and other pertinent information. Legal ramifications also influence the question of consolidating or combining the financial statements of not-for-profit organizations. These ramifications vary from state to state and therefore can result in different practices by a state.

Applicability of FASB Statement No. 94 to Not-for-Profit Providers

The issuance of FASB Statement No. 94 has raised questions about its applicability to not-for-profit providers, because of the confusion regarding the general applicability of authoritative (i.e., FASB, APB, or ARB) pronouncements to not-for-profit organizations. Page 3 of the *Hospital Audit Guide* states that authoritative pronouncements should be followed in reporting on hospital financial statements unless they are "inapplicable." However, ARB No. 43 indicates that authoritative pronouncements are primarily directed to for-profit organizations, unless the issuing body specifically states otherwise.

SOP 81-2 directs a hospital that is related to another organization to look to ARB No. 51 for guidance on whether the financial statements should be consolidated or combined; however, under the hierarchy of GAAP, SOPs are considered "preferable" principles, not authoritative principles. If a hospital elected to adopt this "preferable principle" (i.e., to follow ARB No. 51), but decided that combination or consolidation was inappropriate only because the operations of the majority-owned subsidiary were not homogeneous with those of the parent, then the hospital must prepare consolidated financial statements, since FASB Statement No. 94 removed the exception for non-homogeneity. This would be the only circumstance under which a hospital would be *required* to consolidate a previously unconsolidated majority-owned subsidiary under FASB Statement No. 94, although hospitals are certainly free to voluntarily *elect* consolidation or combination.

Future Developments

As discussed under "Financial Reporting Considerations," the reporting entity issue for not-for-profit organizations is currently being considered by FASB as part of an overall project on the reporting entity, including consolidations and the equity method. This project consists of three phases, the last of which will address not-for-profit organizations. The first phase, which will develop an entity concept for investor-owned enterprises, is expected to provide the basis for a reporting entity concept for not-for-profit organizations as well.

The AICPA's Health Care Committee also has underway a project aimed at providing interim guidance to not-for-profit health care enterprises that elect to prepare consolidated/combined financial statements; the project will not, however, address the issue of *when* to consolidate or combine the financial statements of health care enterprises, as this issue is being covered by the FASB project.

Joint Ventures

Joint ventures are agreements or organizations in which participating parties share the rewards—and risks—of business. They can provide an opportunity for hospitals to expand beyond their traditional markets in a way that allows them to share project costs and enjoy reduced financial risks. Because there are other investors, usually less capital is required than if the hospital were attempting to start the venture on its own.

Three basic structural models, with many variations, exist for hospital joint ventures:

1. separate corporations
2. partnerships (general and limited)
3. contractual arrangements (undivided interests)

FASB is addressing the accounting for investments in joint venture entities in its project entitled "The Reporting Entity, Including Consolidations and the Equity Method." So far, FASB has designated joint ventures organized as separate entities, such as corporations or partnerships, as "investments in jointly-controlled entities," while joint ventures arranged via contracts (undivided interests) are referred to as "participation in joint operations."

Until this project is completed, we must look to existing literature for guidance. APB Opinion No. 18 (as amended by FASB Statement No. 94) states that the equity method should be used for investments in common stock of corporate joint ventures, which are enterprises owned and operated by a small group of businesses for the mutual benefit of the group's members. Although Opinion No. 18 does not contain any specific references to the applicability of the equity method for accounting for investments in partnerships or undivided interests, an AICPA interpretation of Opinion No. 18 states that many of its provisions would be appropriate in accounting for investments in unincorporated entities as well.[18] The interpretation states that most investor-partners reflect partnership profits and losses in their financial statements in the same manner as do investors in corporate joint ventures (i.e., by the equity method). It concludes that many of the provisions of Opinion No. 18 would therefore be appropriate for partnership arrangements,* if the facts and circumstances indicate that the rights of an unincorporated investor are similar to those of an investor in a corporate joint venture. Therefore, investments in partnerships generally should be reflected in the financial statements of the investor in accordance with the provisions of Opinion No. 18; that is, the investment should be shown in the balance sheet of the investor as a single amount, and the investor's share of partnership earnings or losses should ordinarily be shown in

---

*The interpretation applies the same guidance to unincorporated joint venture arrangements; however, this guidance will likely be changed, based on FASB's preliminary conclusions regarding treatment of undivided interests (see next paragraph in text).

the income statement of the investor as a single amount except for extraordinary items and prior-period adjustments.

FASB has reached tentative conclusions with regard to accounting by those ventures referred to as "participation in joint operations" (i.e., undivided interests). In these, the investor owns an undivided interest in each asset and is proportionately liable for its share of each liability; in other words, no legal entity exists between the investor and the assets and liabilities of the venture. In FASB's research on the reporting entity project, the most common practice noted was for each joint venturer's financial statements to reflect its pro rata share of each of the venture's assets, liabilities, revenues, and expenses, rather than to account for it as an equity investment in which each investor has a proportionate interest.[19] FASB has tentatively agreed that this method of accounting, known as the pro rata share method, is the most appropriate for this type of joint venture.

If the above methods are not considered to be appropriate for investments in partnerships or unincorporated joint ventures, the cost method of accounting should be used.

MALPRACTICE LOSS CONTINGENCIES AND INSURANCE COVERAGE

The trend toward increased litigation during the 1970s and 1980s, primarily involving malpractice claims, has had a dramatic impact on the cost and availability of liability insurance. Despite efforts to reduce malpractice claims through means of risk-management programs and attempts to resolve such claims through arbitration agreements, the number of claims against providers of health care services has continued to grow. As a result, insurance carriers have substantially increased malpractice premium rates or limited the amount of risk they are willing to take, or both.

In response to the increases in malpractice claims exposure, complexities, and claim amounts, the AICPA's Health Care Committee issued an SOP in 1978 entitled *Clarification of*

Accounting, Auditing and Reporting Practices Relating to Hospital Malpractice Loss Contingencies. This SOP, which amended relevant sections of the *Hospital Audit Guide*, provided limited guidance in accounting for, auditing, and disclosing potential losses from uninsured malpractice claims in accordance with the provisions of Statement of Financial Accounting Standards No. 5, *Accounting for Contingencies*, and FASB Interpretation No. 14, *Reasonable Estimation of the Amount of Loss*. Basically, the SOP requires that loss contingencies be accrued only when (1) it is probable that an asset has been impaired or a liability incurred at the date of the financial statements and (2) the amount of loss can be reasonably estimated.

Unfortunately, this simple guidance has not been sufficient. Additional questions have arisen for which neither the *Guide* nor the SOP provides adequate guidance; therefore, diversity has arisen in practice. In addition, the litigious environment has created changes in the traditional methods used to insure hospitals against medical malpractice losses. Instead of traditional occurrence-based insurance policies, many hospitals have turned to alternatives such as retrospectively rated policies, claims-made policies, or single- or multiprovider captive insurance companies. Some hospitals dropped all such commercial coverage and established self-insurance trusts to fund the costs of uninsured claims and related expenses. Others have no protection whatsoever and must attempt to pay such costs, when they arise, out of general funds. This has compounded the diversity of accounting practices because no specific guidance has been available with regard to these transactions.

As a basis for reducing the existing diversity of practice and providing guidance on accounting for these issues, the Accounting Standards Division of the AICPA issued SOP 87-1, *Accounting for Asserted and Unasserted Medical Malpractice Claims of Health Care Providers and Related Issues*, in March 1987. SOP 87-1 answers many of the questions regarding circumstances in which an accrual should be made. It defines, for accounting purposes, the two major categories of malpractice loss contingencies as *asserted* and *unasserted* claims. It states that the ultimate costs of asserted and unasserted claims (including costs of litigation and settlement) should be accrued when the incidents occur that give rise to the claims, if it is probable that losses have been sustained from the incidents and if the amount can be estimated reasonably. Estimated losses should be reviewed and changed, if necessary, in each successive set of financial statements, with the amounts of the changes recognized currently as additional expense or reductions of expense. Accrued unpaid claims and expenses that are expected to be paid during the normal operating cycle should be classified as current liabilities; all other accrued unpaid claims and expenses should be classified as noncurrent liabilities.

SOP 87-1 also provides guidelines on estimating the amount of losses for asserted and unasserted claims, and states that industry experience may be used in estimating the expected amount of such claims in certain cases. If a provider cannot estimate losses arising from a particular category of claims, no accrual for these claims should be made; however, the contingency should be disclosed in the notes to the financial statements as required by FASB Statement No. 5.

SOP 87-1 does not address the issue of the appropriateness of discounting accrued medical malpractice claims (i.e., measuring the cost of malpractice claims at the present value of the estimated future payments). SOP 87-1 states that, until the discounting issue is resolved, health care providers that discount accrued malpractice claims should disclose the carrying amount of accrued malpractice claims that are presented in the financial statements at their net present value, along with the range of interest rates used to discount those claims.

Multiprovider and Wholly Owned Captive Insurance Companies

An insurance company owned by two or more health care providers that underwrites malpractice insurance for its owners is referred to as a *multiprovider captive* insurance company.

When such a company is a subsidiary of a provider and provides malpractice insurance primarily to its parent, it is referred to as a *wholly owned captive* insurance company.

As with other types of coverage, financial statements of a provider insured through a wholly owned captive should include a provision for estimated losses from uninsured asserted and unasserted claims as stipulated above. This provision may be accounted for directly in the financial statements of the health care provider or included through consolidation of the financial statements of the captive.

The premiums on many policies issued by multiprovider captives are retrospectively rated. A provider insured by a multiprovider captive under a retrospectively rated policy should account for the premiums in the same manner as discussed in "Retrospectively Rated Premium Policies," depending on whether the experience portion is based on individual or group loss history. If the policy is based on the experience of the group, the provider must assess whether the economic substance of the captive is sufficient to relieve the provider from further liability.

In practice, financial statements generally have not disclosed the method of accounting for captive insurance companies. SOP 87-1 specifies that financial statements should disclose the fact that a provider is insured by a multiprovider captive, along with its ownership percentage in the captive.

Claims-Made Policies

A claims-made policy covers only those claims that are reported to the insurance carrier during the policy term (or continuation thereof). If such a policy is not continually renewed or if "tail coverage" is not obtained when the policy is discontinued, a provider is uninsured for claims reported after the termination of the policy, even if the incidents occurred during the period in which the policy was in force. Guidance in accounting for claims-made policies can be found in SOP 87-1 and in minutes from 1986 meetings of FASB's Emerging Issues Task Force.

To the extent estimable, providers insured under claims-made policies should recognize a liability in the financial statements for estimated costs of claims that arose during the policy term but were not reported to the insurance carrier until after the expiration date.* This should be done unless the provider has purchased tail coverage and included the cost of the premium as expense in the financial statements for that period.

Tail coverage is insurance designed to cover malpractice claims incurred before, but reported after, cancellation or expiration of a claims-made policy. If tail coverage is not purchased and included in expense of the period, the estimated cost of purchasing tail coverage would not be a relevant factor in determining the amount of incurred but not reported (IBNR) loss to be accrued. However, if a policy offers an option to purchase tail coverage at a premium not to exceed a specified fixed maximum amount, this can effectively impose a ceiling on the estimated IBNR liability if the liability does not exceed the limits in the tail coverage policy and the insured intends to purchase the coverage. Purchase of tail coverage does not, however, eliminate the hospital's need to determine whether an additional liability should be accrued because of policy limits or other factors.

The amount of expense to be reported in the financial statements is equal to the annual premium plus the difference between the IBNR accrual at the beginning of the year and the anticipated accrual at the end of the year. The minutes of FASB's Emerging Issues Task Force meetings on this issue provide specific guidance regarding the amount of expense to be recognized each period in interim financial statements.[20]

*This directly conflicts with a provision of the 1978 SOP that would not require a hospital in these circumstances to accrue a liability if it provided written representation to its auditor that it intended to obtain tail coverage. Although it was not specifically stated, the Accounting Standards Division of the AICPA intended that if any provisions of SOP 87-1 and the *Hospital Audit Guide* (as amended by the 1978 SOP) were in conflict, then the conclusions in SOP 87-1 should be applied. Therefore, the guidance for accounting for claims-made policies in SOP 87-1 supersedes the guidance contained in the 1978 SOP.

Retrospectively Rated Premium Policies

An insurance policy with a premium that is adjustable based on actual experience during the policy term is known as a retrospectively rated policy. Under this type of policy, a deposit premium is generally paid to the insurer at the beginning of the coverage period. This usually consists of a minimum premium (representing the insurance company's expenses and profits) and an additional amount for estimated claims experience. The portion based on experience is adjusted during the term of the policy, subject to any minimum and maximum premium limitations defined in the contract. The experience portion can be based on the loss history of a single insured or on a group of insureds.

The amount to be recognized as expense should be based on an estimate of the total premium ultimately to be paid. For a provider whose ultimate premium under this type of policy is based primarily on its own loss experience, the minimum premium should be charged to expense, and estimated losses from asserted and unasserted claims in excess of the minimum premium should be accrued. However, estimated losses should not be accrued in excess of any stipulated maximum premium.

For providers whose premiums primarily are based on the experience of a group, the initial premium should be amortized to expense pro rata over the policy term. Additional premiums or refunds should be accrued based on the group's experience to date, which includes provision for the ultimate cost of asserted and unasserted claims before the financial statement date, whether reported or unreported. These hospitals should disclose that they are insured under a retrospectively rated policy and that premiums are accrued based on the ultimate cost of the experience to date of a group of providers.

Self-Insurance Programs

SOP 87-1 also addresses certain issues with respect to the accounting and reporting for malpractice loss contingencies under partial or full self-insurance programs. Included among these issues are questions of whether trusteed self-insurance funds should be excluded from the financial statements of the hospital, and whether the computation of the amount required to be funded into a self-insurance trust can be equated with the amount of malpractice loss that can or should be accrued for financial reporting purposes in accordance with FASB Statement No. 5.

Estimated losses from asserted and unasserted claims should be accrued and reported as they are for the other types of coverage; expense for the period should not be based on the amounts funded. The amount required to be funded into a self-insurance trust is determined actuarially on a prospective basis. That is, the actuarial valuation is made at the beginning of a fiscal year in order to determine the contribution to be made during that year. Such valuation usually includes a provision for adverse deviation or "cushion" and uses broad averages of expected losses for comparable institutions, rather than the hospital's actual prior experience. The intent of the funding program is to produce, through a smooth pattern of contributions over a future period of time, a fund that will protect adequately the hospital's financial stability.

In contrast, the amount accruable for financial reporting purposes is determined retrospectively, at the end of a reporting period (or the balance sheet date). The amount accrued must give consideration to the hospital's actual prior experience and recognize only asserted and unasserted claims relating to incidents that have already occurred. Accrual of a liability relates to incidents of the past, not the future. The purpose here is the proper timing of recognition of the loss for financial reporting purposes, and not the funding or payment thereof.

According to the proposed SOP, trust funds established to pay malpractice claims should be included in the provider's financial statements and classified as general funds in accordance with SOP 85-1, *Financial Reporting by Not-for-Profit Health Care Entities for Tax-Exempt Debt and Certain Funds Whose Use Is Limited* (see "Balance Sheet"). If the hospital has classified any asserted or unasserted claims as current liabilities, a portion of the fund equal to the amount of assets expected to be required to satisfy these liabilities should correspondingly be classified in current assets. Otherwise, such funds should be classified as noncurrent.

Revenues of the trust fund should be included with other operating revenues, and the administrative expense of the trust fund should be included with other administrative expenses. The financial statements should disclose the existence of the trust fund; if the trust is irrevocable, that fact should also be disclosed.

LONG-TERM DEBT

The capital requirements for replacement, expansion, and modernization of health care facilities have expanded significantly in the past few years. Increased capital expenditures have been required to implement new medical technology, meet increasing service demands, and comply with more stringent health and safety codes. As charitable giving has declined in relative importance, hospitals, nursing homes, and other providers have turned with increasing frequency to the issuance of bonds and other debt obligations to finance these expenditures.

Tax-Exempt Financing

Tax-exempt revenue bonds are limited obligations of a governmental agency authorized to issue tax-exempt bonds, such as a city, county, or financing authority established by a state. The arrangements take many forms. In some cases, a mortgage lien is granted to the governmental agency issuing the bonds; in others, the governmental agency may take title to the property and lease it to the provider for an amount sufficient to cover the debt service on the issue. Regardless of the arrangements, principal and interest on these types of bonds are payable solely from revenues of the health care provider operating the facilities. In most cases this means that the health care provider is, in substance, both the debtor and owner of the related assets. Accordingly, the bonds are usually shown as debt obligations of the provider, and the related proceeds of the debt issue (or the asset purchased or constructed with the proceeds) are shown as assets of the provider.

Funds Held under Bond Indentures

Among the many provisions normally included in the bond indentures of publicly issued debt are requirements to set aside funds annually from operations to ensure that bond principal and interest payments and other requirements are met. Usually these debt reserve funds are placed under the control of a trustee.

In nonprofit health care organizations there have historically been two major issues relative to accounting for these indentured funds. One concerns the proper balance sheet classification of both the assets required to be set aside under the bond indenture and the related indebtedness. The second issue is whether investment income on indentured assets should be accounted for as a direct credit to fund balance, as other operating revenue, as nonoperating revenue, or as an offset against interest expense. Both of these issues are addressed in an SOP issued by the AICPA in 1985 entitled *Financial Reporting by Not-for-Profit Health Care Entities for Tax-Exempt Debt and Certain Funds Whose Use Is Limited* (SOP 85-1). SOP 85-1 amended the *Hospital Audit Guide* and created a new balance sheet caption, "Assets (Funds) Whose Use Is Limited." By definition, these assets include proceeds of debt issues and funds of a health care entity deposited with a trustee and limited to use in accordance with the requirements of an indenture or similar document, along with other types of assets. (See under "Balance Sheet" for more information on other types of assets whose use is limited.)

According to SOP 85-1, assets whose use is limited under terms of a bond indenture should be reported in the noncurrent section of the balance sheet, with an accompanying contra-account reflecting the portion that is required to satisfy current debt service requirements. The offset to this contra-account should appear in current assets. Debt issued by a financing authority for the benefit of a health care entity should be reported as a liability in the general funds section of the entity's balance sheet.

Investment income related to borrowed funds (i.e., proceeds of debt issues) held by a trustee (other than interest that is capitalized as part of a construction project) should be included in the facility's results of operations. Two approaches are offered for displaying this information in financial statements:

1. The gross amount of interest income can be reported separately as other operating revenue.
2. A net presentation of the income and related interest expense may be shown in either operating expenses or other operating revenue, whichever is appropriate, with the offsetting amount disclosed parenthetically.

Investment income related to funds held by a trustee that are not "borrowed funds" should be reported as nonoperating revenue.

Bond Issuance Costs

Bond discount and other financing costs are deferred and written off over the life of the bond issue. According to APB Opinion No. 21, *Interest on Receivables and Payables*, any debt discount or premium should be amortized over the life of the debt using the interest method. However, no specific guidance exists that indicates a preferable method (or methods) of amortization, or the term of the amortization, for other financing costs. HFMA's Principles and Practices Board addressed this issue in its advisory Statement No. 4, *Reporting of Certain Transactions Arising in Connection with the Issuance of Debt*. The board recommended that financing costs be amortized over the life of the debt issue using a constant-rate method (such as the interest method or the bonds-outstanding method).

Advance Refunding

An advance refunding of an outstanding bond issue can be used to reduce long-term interest costs, consolidate debt, or eliminate restrictive loan covenants. Proceeds from an advance refunding can be used actually to retire the existing debt through call provisions, or they may be used to satisfy the existing debt through defeasance provisions.

In an "in-substance" defeasance transaction, an amount that will be sufficient to pay the interest, call premiums and principal of the old debt (when invested at a given rate of return) is placed in trust and irrevocably restricted to satisfy specific debt. Because the effect of an in-substance defeasance is essentially the same as extinguishment (i.e., retirement) of debt, the debt is considered to be extinguished for financial reporting purposes and should be removed from the financial statements, even though the debtor may not be legally released from being the primary obligor under the old debt obligation.

The accounting and reporting requirements for advance refundings are dealt with in APB Opinion No. 26, *Early Extinguishment of Debt*. This opinion requires that the difference between the net carrying amount of the extinguished debt (amount due at maturity adjusted for unamortized premium, discount, and cost of issuance) and the reacquisition price (amount paid on extinguishment, including call premium and miscellaneous costs of reacquisition) be recognized in the determination of net income of the period of extinguishment as a gain or loss. Opinion No. 26 specifically prohibits the amortization of any gain or loss to future periods.

In response to requests for clarification of the circumstances that constitute extinguishment, FASB issued Statement No. 76, *Extinguishment of Debt*, in November 1983. Statement No. 76 amends Opinion No. 26 by making it applicable to all extinguishments of debt, whether early or not, and provides guidance regarding the circumstances that constitute an extinguishment of debt.

FASB Statement No. 4, *Reporting Gains and Losses from Extinguishment of Debt*, provides guidance regarding the financial statement classification of the gain or loss resulting from extinguishments of debt. It requires any such gain or loss, if material, to be classified as an extraordinary item, net of any related income tax or third-party payment effect. (This does not apply, however, to gains or losses from extinguishments of debt made to satisfy sinking-fund requirements, which a facility must meet within one year of the date of the extinguishment.)

A gain or loss on extinguishment of debt in an advance refunding or refinancing may be treated differently for third-party payment purposes. The differences in treatment between GAAP and third-party payment rules may give rise to a timing difference. The treatment of these timing differences is discussed more fully under "Third-Party Payment Issues."

Governmental Entities

Unless otherwise specified, pronouncements issued by GASB apply to financial reporting by all state and local governmental entities. In March 1987, GASB issued its Statement No. 7, *Advance Refundings Resulting in Defeasance of Debt*. The disclosure guidance it provides is applicable to all governmental entities (including governmental hospitals) and is effective for fiscal periods beginning after December 15, 1986. According to the statement, all governmental entities that defease debt through an advance refunding should provide a general description of the transaction in the notes to the financial statements in the year of the refunding. At a minimum, these should include (1) the difference between the cash flows required to service the old debt and the cash flows required to service the new debt and complete the refunding, and (2) the economic gain or loss resulting from the transaction. In subsequent years, entities having an in-substance defeasance (as opposed to a defeasance in fact) should disclose the amount of the defeased debt, if any, that remains outstanding at year-end.

Interest during Construction

In 1979, FASB issued its Statement No. 34, *Capitalization of Interest Costs*, which specified appropriate practices for accounting for interest during construction. According to Statement No. 34, interest income derived from investment of borrowed funds should not be offset against capitalized interest costs. This guidance was changed in 1982 when FASB issued its Statement No. 62, *Capitalization of Interest Cost in Situations Involving Certain Tax-Exempt Borrowings and Certain Gifts and Grants*. This statement amended Statement No. 34 to provide that capitalized interest cost should be reduced by interest earned on the "borrowed funds" if the proceeds of the tax-exempt borrowings are externally restricted to finance the acquisition of specified qualifying assets or to service the related debt.

THIRD-PARTY PAYMENT ISSUES

One of the more unique aspects of the health care industry is the existence and interaction of third-party payers. In most enterprises that provide services to the public, the recipient of the services is also the one who pays for them. In health care, however, a majority of the services provided are paid for, in whole or in part, by the government or private insurance companies on behalf of the recipient. Payments by such third-party payers as Medicare, Medicaid, and Blue Cross/Blue Shield are based on a contractual agreement between the health care provider and the contracting program or agency. A provider agrees to service program beneficiaries in return for a payment amount that will be determined by a formula or established at a predetermined rate. Therefore, payment is generally made with little or no regard to a provider's established rates. As a result, most providers record a "contractual allowance" or "contractual adjustment" in their financial statements to recognize the difference between the established rates for covered services and the amounts paid by third parties. The unique financial reporting issues with respect to such third-party payer arrangements include (1) the appropriate reporting of revenues from services rendered (to patients, residents, and the like); (2) settlement of prior-period cost reports; and (3) matters related to timing differences.

Revenue Recognition and Contractual Allowances

The *Hospital Audit Guide* states that "patient service revenue should be accounted for at established rates, regardless of whether the hospital expects to collect the full amount." The established rate has customarily been defined as a single rate, or price, for each service that will apply to the entire patient population. Yet, as discussed above, third-party payers have for years paid amounts other than the hospital's charges for the services they purchased. In addition, more and more hospitals are contracting with HMOs, preferred provider organizations, and comprehensive medical plans for payments at rates that are less than established charges. These payment amounts (along with any deductible and coinsurance amounts) represent payment in full; the hospital has no legal authority to seek additional payment from the patient or anyone else for the difference between the charges and the amount actually paid. Therefore, the amount traditionally shown in financial statements as "gross revenue" is becoming less and less meaningful to users of those financial statements.

The exposure draft of the revised health care audit guide called for "service" revenue (a generic term encompassing the gross revenue of many types of providers) to be reported *net* of contractual allowances, allowances for uncompensated services, and other allowances in the statement of revenues and expenses. This approach is also supported by HFMA's Principles and Practices Board Statement No. 7, which calls for recording "the amount that a payer has an obligation to pay."[21] If deemed necessary, contractual allowances may be disclosed in the notes to the financial statements; the provisions for uncollectible accounts and charity care should be disclosed if they are material.

Under a cost-based payment system, the calculation of the contractual allowance is relatively simple, and a clear revenue cutoff can be established for patients remaining in the hospital as of the balance sheet date. When payment is made on a prospective basis, however, the amount to be received is determined independently of the patients' actual length of stay or the charges actually incurred; therefore, an absolute cutoff point for revenue recognition purposes does not exist.

The exposure draft of the revised audit guide recommended that a methodology be employed by the hospital to estimate properly the net revenue earned on such patients. It stated that such a calculation could be estimated on the basis of the actual or national mean length of stay, or by using any other methodology that properly matches revenue with expenses.

Final Settlement of Prior-Period Cost Reports

Some third-party payers retrospectively determine final amounts reimbursable for services rendered to their beneficiaries based on allowable costs. After the close of the fiscal period, a determination is made of the "cost" of the services provided to the program's beneficiaries. This is compared with payments made during the year, and the difference is recorded as receivable from or payable to the program. Although final settlement is actually made in a subsequent period, the amount is usually subject to reasonable estimation and should be recorded in the provider's financial statements for the period during which the services were rendered.

No matter how precisely a provider may strive to estimate such final settlements, differences are likely to occur between the actual settlement and the amount accrued at the end of a reporting period. The *Hospital Audit Guide* specifically addresses the manner of accounting for differences between the amount accrued at the end of a reporting period and the eventual final settlement amount determined by the third-party payer. Since such accruals are generally susceptible of reasonable estimation, the *Guide* states that any differences from over- or underaccruals should be included in the statement of revenues and expenses as an adjustment to the appropriate allowance accounts in the period in which the final settlement is determined. Differences should not be reported as prior-period adjustments (i.e., as an adjustment of the beginning retained earnings or unrestricted fund balance) unless they meet the criteria set forth in paragraphs 10 and 11 of FASB Statement No. 16, *Prior Period Adjustments* (as amended).

Timing Differences

Prior to the implementation of PPS, Medicare paid hospitals based upon the estimated costs of providing services to program beneficiaries. As with income tax regulations, Medicare reporting regulations have not always followed GAAP. Under cost-based payment, therefore, certain expenses may be reimbursed in a different

accounting period than that in which they were recognized for financial reporting purposes. This results in a timing difference, as described in the *Hospital Audit Guide*. The third-party payment effect of a timing difference should be deferred so that revenues and expenses of the period will be properly matched. In later years, the deferred revenue (or cost) will be eliminated when the effect of the timing difference is reversed.

Under cost-based Medicare payment, timing differences commonly resulted from

- recognizing contributions to a self-insurance trust as an expense for cost reporting purposes, while accruing estimated liabilities to determine expense for financial reporting purposes
- determining the gain or loss on extinguishment of debt differently for cost reporting and financial reporting
- establishing different useful lives on property and equipment for cost reporting purposes and financial reporting purposes
- recording capitalized interest net of interest income for Medicare, and in accordance with GAAP for financial reporting purposes
- making a contribution to a pension fund after the Medicare payment deadline and accruing the total expense for financial statement purposes

With the initiation of PPS, the AICPA Health Care Committee's Task Force on Federal Health Care Legislation prepared an article on the impact of PPS on timing differences that was published jointly by *Healthcare Financial Management* magazine and the *Journal of Accountancy* in their November 1984 issues.[22] To date, this article remains the most authoritative source of GAAP (as "other accounting literature") on this topic. The conclusions it contains with regard to three areas of costs are discussed below.

1. *Costs related to inpatient care (other than capital costs).* Under PPS, payments to be received by a hospital generally are not affected by the inpatient operating costs they report; therefore, the timing of when

these expenses are included in the Medicare cost report and when they are recognized for financial reporting purposes no longer has any effect on Medicare payments received by the hospital. No timing differences related to inpatient services for Medicare patients should be recorded after a facility enters the PPS program.

This also means that timing differences related to such costs that were carried over from prior years would never reverse. Therefore, their status changes from temporary to permanent. The task force stated that deferred debits or credits resulting from these timing differences should be written off in the year when it is determined that they would not be realized (generally the fiscal year prior to the first year under the PPS program). They further stated that such transactions should flow through the statement of revenues and expenses and not through fund balance.

Whenever timing differences are eliminated, the accounting treatment of the deferred Medicare benefits or revenues that are eliminated, if significant, should be disclosed in the financial statements. The task force acknowledged that the point is debatable as to whether this type of write-off meets the criteria of an extraordinary item as defined by APB Opinion No. 30, *Reporting the Results of Operations: Reporting the Effects of Disposal of a Segment of a Business, and Extraordinary, Unusual and Infrequently Occurring Events and Transactions.* Opinion No. 30 defines the criteria for extraordinary items as an event or transaction that is both unusual in nature and infrequently occurring; these criteria should be evaluated based on the specific facts and circumstances in each situation. If an extraordinary presentation is not considered to be appropriate, the task force stated that it may be appropriate to emphasize the transaction by reflecting it as a separate line item in the statement of revenues and expenses.

2. *Costs associated with outpatient care (other than capital costs).* These costs are excluded from PPS because no official patient classification system presently exists for outpatient cases. The portion of hospital operating costs that are allocated to outpatient care therefore may continue to create timing differences after a hospital enters the PPS program. The task force stated that hospitals should continue to record timing differences related to these costs, if material, until legislation is passed to incorporate them into the PPS rates. Generally, these timing differences are not material in relation to the financial statements taken as a whole.

3. *Capital costs.* Since Medicare presently pays hospitals for capital costs on a cost basis (subject to certain limitations), timing differences arising from the reporting of these costs are not currently affected by PPS. Until enacted legislation (and implementing regulations) provide sufficient guidelines for determining financial measurement of the effects of changes in reimbursement policy, hospitals should continue to account for any capital-related timing differences.

Hospitals that are not covered under PPS are subject to payment limitations on cost increases. Therefore, if a hospital is increasing costs beyond the limit, temporary timing differences (or portions of them) could eventually become permanent. The task force stated that such timing differences should be analyzed and written off, if appropriate, in the year it is determined that they are unlikely to reverse.

Disclosure

A hospital's financial statements should include appropriate disclosure describing major third-party payment programs and activity and the accounting policies related thereto. Disclosure should include such information as the names and description of major programs, their basis of payment, and the status of audits and settlements of prior cost reporting periods, if applicable. Total deductions from gross service revenue or specific components of deductions from gross service revenue may be disclosed if deemed necessary. Uncertainties of future recovery of deferred reimbursement assets due to effects of expected future changes in definitive legislation should be disclosed if the effects are expected to be material to the financial statements.

PENSION AND OTHER EMPLOYEE BENEFIT PLANS

The latest steps in the evolution of pension obligation measurement and recognition were accomplished with FASB's issuance of Statements No. 87, *Employers' Accounting for Pensions*, and No. 88, *Employers' Accounting for Settlements and Curtailments of Defined Benefit Pension Plans and for Termination Benefits*, in late 1985.

Statement No. 87 supersedes APB Opinion No. 8, *Accounting for the Cost of Pension Plans*, FASB Statement No. 36, *Disclosure of Pension Information*, and FASB Interpretation No. 3, *Accounting for the Cost of Pension Plans Subject to the Employee Retirement Income Security Act of 1974*, for all but governmental providers (see below). It does not change any of the requirements set forth in FASB Statement No. 35, *Accounting and Reporting by Defined Benefit Pension Plans*, relating to reporting by defined-benefit pension plans.* Statement No. 87 requires employers to use a standardized method for measuring net periodic pension cost over the employee's service life, to disclose more information about their plans in the notes to financial statements, and to recognize a liability when the accumulated benefit obligation exceeds the fair value of plan assets.

Table 5-1 summarizes the major changes between APB Opinion No. 8 and FASB Statement No. 87.

FASB Statement No. 88 supersedes FASB Statement No. 74, *Accounting for Special Ter-*

---

*FASB Statement No. 75, *Deferral of the Effective Date of Certain Accounting Requirements for Pension Plans of State and Local Government Units*, indefinitely deferred the effective date of FASB Statement No. 35 for pension plans sponsored by state and local governmental units.

mination Benefits Paid to Employees. Under the provisions of this statement, previously deferred gains or losses associated with the termination or curtailment of the plan are to be recognized in earnings when a pension obligation is settled.

Simultaneous adoption of FASB Statements No. 87 and No. 88 is required. Providers having at least one plan with more than 100 participants must adopt all provisions except those pertaining to recording a minimum liability for the fiscal year beginning after December 15, 1986. Nonpublic providers having defined-benefit plans with 100 or fewer participants are required to adopt all provisions in their fiscal year beginning after December 15, 1988; for all other providers, the provisions of the statement are effective for fiscal years beginning after December 15, 1986, except for the minimum liability provisions, which are applicable for fiscal years beginning after December 15, 1988.

Governmental Providers

In September 1986, GASB issued its Statement No. 4, *Applicability of FASB Statement No. 87, "Employers' Accounting for Pensions," to State and Local Government Employers*. The GASB statement provided that state and local government employers should not change their accounting and reporting of pension activities to conform with FASB Statement No. 87 because GASB had a similar project in process. The GASB believed that needless confusion would result from implementing the FASB statement and shortly thereafter having to implement a GASB statement.

In November 1986, GASB issued its Statement No. 5, *Disclosure of Pension Information by Public Employee Retirement Systems and State and Local Governmental Employers*. In this statement, GASB sets forth standards for disclosure of pension information in notes to financial statements and in required supplementary information. (Until pension *accounting* guidance is provided in a future GASB statement or statements, governmental entities should continue to account for pensions in accordance with the pronouncements specified in GASB State-

Table 5-1 Major Changes between APB Opinion No. 8 and FASB Statement No. 87

Major Provision	APB Opinion No. 8	FASB Statement No. 87
Recognition of additional liability	Legal obligation in excess of amounts accrued	Excess of accumulated benefit obligation over the fair value of plan assets
Recognition of other elements when additional liability is required	Deferred charge	Intangible asset to the extent of unrecognized prior-service cost; reduction of equity for any excess
Method used to calculate normal cost	Any "acceptable actuarial cost method"	Based on terms of the plan
Method and period of amortization of prior-service cost arising from plan amendments	Systematic and rational; specifies minimum and maximum; maximum = 10% of original cost	Assignment of equal amounts to each future period of service of each employee active at amendment date expected to receive benefits
Method of amortizing unrecognized actuarial gains and losses	Various	Any method consistently applied, subject to a minimum based on the "corridor" method
Period or rate for amortizing unrecognized actuarial gains and losses	10 to 20 years	Minimum rate to spread amount outside the corridor over average remaining service period
Selection of actuarial assumptions	Not addressed; both explicit and implicit found in practice	Explicit; rate at which obligation could be effectively settled used for discounting and for service and interest cost; expected long-term rates used for return on assets

Source: Reprinted from *Employers' Accounting for Pensions and for Settlements and Curtailments of Defined Benefit Pension Plans and for Termination Benefits: Understanding and Applying FASB 87 and 88*, Price Waterhouse, © 1986.

ment No. 1, *Authoritative Status of NCGA [National Council on Governmental Accounting] Pronouncements and AICPA Industry Audit Guide*. For hospitals, this would most likely involve continued compliance with the requirements of APB Opinion No. 8 and FASB Statement No. 74. Because Statement No. 74 is specifically referred to in GASB Statement No. 4, it is assumed that the provisions of FASB Statement No. 88 are also not applicable to governmental entities.)

The disclosure requirements of this statement differ in some respects from those required by FASB Statement No. 87. In particular, the FASB statement requires disclosure of two pen-

sion obligation amounts (one calculated *with* salary progression, the other calculated *without*), while the GASB statement requires disclosure of only one amount, calculated *with* salary progression. Regarding interest rate assumptions, the GASB and FASB statements differ in that the GASB statement requires use of a long-term rate as a basis for determining the discount rate. Finally, the disclosure requirements of the GASB statement exceed those of the FASB statement by requiring presentation of ten-year trend data.

Small employers (as defined in the statement) may disclose the actuarial accrued liability developed from specified actuarial funding methods, instead of the standardized measure of the pension obligation required of larger entities. These smaller entities are also exempted from the requirement for actuarial updates.

GIFTS, GRANTS, AND PLEDGES

Gifts, grants, and pledges are important sources of revenue for many nonprofit providers. Such revenues may be received from a variety of sources, with a wide range of restrictions or stipulations attached. While such revenues are usually realized in cash, they may also be received in the form of donated supplies, investments, property, equipment, or services.

Many nonprofit providers have a mixture of funds with no limitations or restrictions on their use (i.e., available for any purpose at the discretion of the governing board); "funds limited as to use" (set aside for specific uses by the provider's board of trustees or set aside under terms of bond indentures or trust agreements); and "donor-restricted funds" (funds given by donors or grantors for specific uses). From a financial reporting standpoint, it is important that gifts, grants, and pledges be recorded in the proper fund and disclosed in such a way that the reader is fully aware of their amount and any restrictions on their use. This reporting is predicated upon the proper delineation of those resources that are donor-restricted and those that are not (see "Single-Fund versus Multi-Fund Reporting").

Unrestricted Contributions

According to the *Hospital Audit Guide*, gifts, grants, and bequests that are not restricted by donors (unrestricted contributions) should be reported as nonoperating revenue in the statement of revenues and expenses. The proposed revised guide *Audits of Providers of Health Care Services* may recommend that unrestricted contributions be recorded as operating or nonoperating revenue depending on whether they are central and ongoing or peripheral to the provider's operations.

Restricted Contributions

Gifts, grants, and pledges that are restricted by donors generally fall into five categories:

1. funds for specific operating purposes
2. funds for additions to property, plant, and equipment
3. endowment funds
4. loan funds
5. annuity and living trust funds

If a contribution is designated to be used for a specific operating purpose, it should initially be accounted for as a direct addition to a restricted fund balance. In the period in which it is utilized (expensed) for the purpose specified by the donor, the resources should be transferred to the general fund and reported as revenue* in the statement of revenues and expenses.

Funds restricted by donors for additions to property, plant, and equipment are initially added to the restricted fund balance. In the period when such resources are expended for the purpose intended by the donor, they should be reported as a transfer from the restricted fund balance to the general fund balance. They do not flow through income because they are considered to be additions to the permanent capital of the hospital. Contributions restricted for retirement of debt principal would also be reported in this manner.

Endowment funds may be classified as either *pure* (principal may not be expended) or *term* (principal may be expended at some specified point in time). Upon receipt, both types should be reported as restricted funds in the balance sheet. With respect to term endowments, disclosure should be made in the notes to the financial statements as to the term of the endowment and the purpose for which the principal may be ultimately used. Upon satisfaction of the term, the resources should be reported in the statement of revenues and expenses if they will be available for general operating purposes; if their use is restricted for a specific purpose, they should be

---

*If the resources are used to support free care, the applicable amounts are reported as an offset to the allowance for free care.

reflected as a transfer to a specific-purpose or other restricted-type fund.

Valuation of Noncash Donations

Hospitals often receive gifts in the form of donated supplies, investments, property or equipment, or services of individuals. Historically, donations of property and equipment have been recorded in the general fund balance at their fair market value on the date of contribution, unless designated for endowment or other restricted purposes. However, it appears that the revised guide *Audits of Providers of Health Care Services* may recommend that such contributions be recorded initially in a restricted fund, and transferred to the general fund when the asset is placed in service. This is consistent with the prescribed treatment of cash contributions that are restricted for the acquisition of property and equipment.

The *Hospital Audit Guide* states that donated supplies and materials should be reported as other operating revenue in the statement of revenues and expenses, while donated securities are reported as nonoperating revenue. Working drafts of the proposed revised guide indicate that the AICPA may recommend that preparers of financial statements be guided by Concepts Statement No. 6 in determining the appropriate classification of donated noncapital assets. According to Concepts Statement No. 6, revenues and gains should be classified as ''operating'' if they are associated with a provider's ongoing or central operations and as ''nonoperating'' if they are peripheral or incidental to the provision of health care services, or if they stem from events that are beyond management's control.

According to the *Hospital Audit Guide*, the fair value of donated services should be recorded when the equivalent of an employer-employee relationship exists and there is an objective basis for valuing the services. Lay-equivalent amounts should be recorded as expense with the credit to nonoperating revenue. The working draft of the revised audit guide proposes that donated services not be recorded at all unless certain specific criteria are met. FASB also has a project currently under way entitled ''Account-

ing for Contributions.'' This project is of major significance to tax-exempt health care providers, because FASB standards take precedence over AICPA SOPs and audit guides if their conclusions differ. As this publication goes to press, FASB has tentatively agreed that *if* donated goods and services are reported in financial statements, then fair market value is the appropriate basis to be used; however, no conclusion has been reached as to whether such transactions should be reported. FASB has also tentatively agreed that donated goods should be recorded and donated services disclosed unless they create or enhance a continuing asset; this is essentially the same treatment recommended in the draft of the revised audit guide.

Pledges

Pledges should be included in the provider's balance sheet at their estimated net realizable value. Their balance sheet classification as general or restricted depends on the existence of any donor restrictions placed on the use of the amounts received, as does their inclusion either in nonoperating revenue or in fund balance upon receipt. Unrestricted pledges are reported as revenue in the period in which the pledge is made; restricted pledges are initially recorded in the appropriate donor-restricted fund balance. Unrestricted pledges that apply to a period beyond the balance sheet date should be accounted for as deferred revenue.

FASB is also considering pledges as part of its ''contributions'' project discussed previously. Issues under consideration regarding accounting for pledges include the following:

- Should conditional pledges—those that depend on specified events yet to occur—be recognized in financial statements or merely disclosed?
- What is the distinction between conditional promises and pledges with donor-imposed restrictions?
- What if a promised asset is received before donor-imposed conditions or restrictions have been fulfilled?

- Should a liability be recognized by the donor of a pledge?

Both an exposure draft and a final statement setting forth standards for contribution accounting are expected to be released in 1989.

SUBSEQUENT EVENTS

The AICPA's Statement on Auditing Standards (SAS) No. 1, *Codification of Auditing Standards and Procedures*, defines "subsequent events" as material events that occur after the balance sheet date but before issuance of the financial statements and independent accountant's report, which require adjustment of, or disclosure in, the financial statements. When issuing an opinion, the independent accountant is concerned with the financial position at a given date and the results of operations and the cash flows for a period up to that particular date. However, because of their potential impact, the accountant must evaluate the effect of subsequent events in order to determine the need for adjustment to the financial statements on which he or she is reporting, or for additional disclosures necessary for a fair presentation of such statements.

Section 560 of SAS No. 1 is the authoritative reference on subsequent events. SAS No. 1 embraces a "clean cutoff" concept that generally requires that the accounting effect of subsequent events be recognized in the period in which they occur. However, two general types of subsequent events are identified in SAS No. 1, each of which requires different accounting and reporting treatment in the financial statements.

Type I Events

Type I events are those that provide additional evidence with respect to conditions that existed at the balance sheet date and affect the estimates inherent in the process of preparing the financial statements for the period ending on that date. The financial statements should be adjusted for any changes in estimates resulting from the use of evidence provided by this type of event. Examples of such events are

- collection of receivables or settlement or determination of liabilities on a basis substantially different from that previously recorded, if the event giving rise to change in assessment is associated with conditions that existed at the balance sheet date or represent the culmination of conditions that existed over a relatively long period of time
- realization of loss on sale of investments, inventories, or properties held for sale when the subsequent act of sale merely confirms a previously existing unrecognized loss

Some subsequent events of this type may require only a reclassification of amounts previously recorded. As an example, if all or a portion of a long-term loan is prepaid after the balance sheet date, a corresponding amount of the loan should be reclassified as a current liability in that balance sheet.

Type II Events

Type II events are those that provide evidence with respect to conditions that did not exist at the balance sheet date but arose subsequent to that date. The financial statements covering the period ending on that date are not to be adjusted for subsequent events of this type, but disclosure of the event may be necessary to keep the financial statements from being misleading. These events are comprised of extraordinary or unusual transactions that can be measured and that have a determinable, significantly beneficial or detrimental effect on financial position at the time of occurrence or in the future.

Some examples of Type II events applicable to health care organizations are as follows:

- business combinations
- issuing new notes, bonds or other indebtedness
- damage from fire, flood, or other casualty
- settlement of litigation when the event giving rise to the claim took place subsequent to the balance sheet date
- sale of land
- adoption of welfare, pension, or compensation plans

• declaration of certain unusual cash or stock dividends, or adoption of stock option plans (for-profit providers only)

Events of this nature may be of such significance that the historical financial statements require disclosure beyond the usual narrative disclosure in the notes to the financial statements. In such circumstances, it may be necessary to supplement the historical financial statements with pro forma financial statements giving retroactive effect to such events. It is not possible to state which of the above events would require such pro forma presentation and which would require only note disclosure. Only after all of the facts and circumstances, including materiality, have been considered, can the disclosure that results in the most meaningful presentation be selected.

Disclosure—General

In practice, the classification of events as Type I or Type II can be extremely difficult and requires careful consideration and judgment.

When there is no clear answer, it is usually prudent to treat a subsequent event loss as a Type I event and a subsequent event gain as a Type II event.

Type I subsequent events, which require adjustment of the financial statements, generally do not need to be specifically disclosed in the financial statements unless disclosure is otherwise required by GAAP.

Type II events may be reported in any of the following ways:

• explanatory description in notes to the financial statements
• parenthetical explanations in the statements or notes
• references in the financial statements to information included elsewhere in the same document
• pro forma financial data giving retroactive effect
• explanatory paragraph included in the independent accountant's report on the financial statements

---

NOTES

1. Price Waterhouse and Healthcare Financial Management Association (HFMA), *Hospital Financial Reports: A Survey* (Westchester, Ill.: HFMA, 1987), p. 2.

2. Financial Accounting Standards Board (FASB), Statement of Financial Accounting Standards No. 93, *Recognition of Depreciation by Not-for-Profit Organizations* (Stamford, Conn.: FASB, August 1987).

3. Robert N. Anthony, *Financial Accounting in Nonbusiness Organizations: An Exploratory Study of Conceptual Issues* (Stamford, Conn.: FASB, 1978), p. 164.

4. American Institute of Certified Public Accountants (AICPA), Statement of Position (SOP) 85-1, *Financial Reporting by Not-for-Profit Health Care Entities for Tax-Exempt Debt and Certain Funds Whose Use Is Limited* (New York: AICPA, 1985), paragraph 23(c).

5. L. Vann Seawell, *External and Internal Reporting by Hospitals* (Westchester, Ill.: HFMA, 1984), p. 48.

6. Ibid., p. 56.

7. Ibid.

8. HFMA Principles and Practices (P&P) Board, "The Presentation of Nonpatient Service Revenue and Related Issues," exposure draft of a proposed P&P Board Statement (Westchester, Ill.: HFMA, May 29, 1987), p. 7.

9. Price Waterhouse and Healthcare Financial Management Association, *Hospital Financial Reports*, p. 61.

10. Steven A. Finkler and Sandra L. Horowitz, "Merger and Consolidation: An Overview of Activity in Healthcare Organizations," *Healthcare Financial Management* (January 1985): 22.

11. Ibid.

12. Ibid., 28.

13. Barrett L. Boehm and John A. Witt, "The Patient Lived but the Hospital Died," *Today's Executive* 9, no. 2 (Spring 1986): 17.

14. HFMA P&P Board, "Accounting and Reporting Issues Related to Corporate Reorganizations Involving Tax-Exempt Institutional Healthcare Providers," exposure draft of a proposed P&P Board Statement, issued May 29, 1987.

15. AICPA Accounting Principles Board (APB), Opinion No. 9, *Reporting the Results of Operations* (New York: AICPA), paragraph 28.

16. FASB, "Consolidation of All Majority-Owned Subsidiaries," exposure draft of FASB Statement No. 94, issued December 16, 1986, paragraph 12.

17. FASB, *Status Report*, October 13, 1987, p. 5.

18. AICPA, "Investments in Partnerships and Ventures," *The Equity Method of Accounting for Investments in Common Stock: Accounting Interpretations of APB Opinion No. 18* (New York: AICPA, 1971).

19. FASB, *Action Alert*, November 25, 1987, p. 2.

20. FASB Emerging Issues Task Force, Issues Summary 86-12, "Accounting by Insureds for Claims-Made Insurance Policies," suppl. no. 2, May 22, 1986.

21. HFMA P&P Board Statement No. 7, "The Presentation of Patient Service Revenue and Related Issues," *Healthcare Financial Management* (April 1986): 79.

22. "Medicare Changes Create Accounting, Reporting, and Auditing Problems," *Healthcare Financial Management* (November 1984): 28–38; and "Medicare's New Prospective Payment System: Accounting and Auditing Implications," *Journal of Accountancy* (November 1984): 162–171.

BIBLIOGRAPHY

American Institute of Certified Public Accountants (AICPA) Accounting Principles Board (APB). Opinion No. 8, *Accounting for the Cost of Pension Plans*. New York: AICPA, 1966.

_____. Opinion No. 9, *Reporting the Results of Operations*, 1966.

_____. Opinion No. 16, *Business Combinations*, 1970.

_____. Opinion No. 18, *The Equity Method of Accounting for Investments in Common Stock*, 1971.

_____. Opinion No. 21, *Interest on Receivables and Payables*, 1971.

_____. Opinion No. 22, *Disclosure of Accounting Policies*, 1972.

_____. Opinion No. 26, *Early Extinguishment of Debt*, 1972.

_____. Opinion No. 29, *Accounting for Nonmonetary Transactions*, 1973.

_____. Opinion No. 30, *Reporting the Results of Operations: Reporting the Effects of Disposal of a Segment of a Business, and Extraordinary, Unusual and Infrequently Occurring Events and Transactions*, 1973.

_____. "Investments in Partnerships and Ventures," *The Equity Method of Accounting for Investments in Common Stock: Accounting Interpretations of APB Opinion No. 18*, 1971.

AICPA Accounting Standards Division (AcSEC). Statement of Position (SOP) 78-7, *Financial Accounting and Reporting by Hospitals Operated by a Governmental Unit*, 1978.

_____. SOP 78-10, *Accounting Principles and Reporting Practices for Certain Non-Profit Organizations*, 1978.

_____. SOP 81-2, *Reporting Practices Concerning Hospital-Related Organizations*, 1981.

_____. SOP 85-1, *Financial Reporting by Not-for-Profit Health Care Entities for Tax-Exempt Debt and Certain Funds Whose Use Is Limited*, 1985.

_____. SOP 87-1, *Accounting for Asserted and Unasserted Medical Malpractice Claims of Health Care Providers and Related Issues*, 1987.

_____. "Audits of Providers of Health Care Services," exposure draft of a proposed industry audit and accounting guide, issued March 15, 1988.

AICPA Auditing Standards Division. SOP, *Classification of Accounting, Auditing, and Reporting Practices Relating to Malpractice Loss Contingencies*, 1978.

_____. Statement on Auditing Standards (SAS) No. 1, *Codification of Auditing Standards and Procedures*, 1972.

_____. SAS No. 43, *Omnibus Statement on Auditing Standards*, 1982.

_____. ARB No. 43, *Restatement and Revision of Accounting Research Bulletins*, 1953.

AICPA Committee on Accounting Procedure. Accounting Research Bulletin (ARB) No. 51, *Consolidated Financial Statements*, 1959.

AICPA, *Hospital Audit Guide*. 5th ed. New York: AICPA, 1985.

AICPA Task Force on Federal Health Care Legislation. "Medicare Changes Create Accounting, Reporting, and Auditing Problems." *Healthcare Financial Management* (November 1984): 28–38.

_____. "Medicare's New Prospective Payment System: Accounting and Auditing Implications." *Journal of Accountancy* (November 1984): 162–71.

Anthony, Robert N. *Financial Accounting in Nonbusiness Organizations: An Exploratory Study of Conceptual Issues*. Stamford, Conn.: Financial Accounting Standards Board (FASB), 1978.

Boehm, Barrett L., and John A. Witt. "The Patient Lived but the Hospital Died." *Today's Executive* 9, no. 2 (Spring 1986): 17–20.

Employers' Accounting for Pensions and for Settlements and Curtailments of Defined Benefit Pension Plans and for Termination Benefits: Understanding and Applying FAS 87 and 88. New York: Price Waterhouse, 1986.

FASB. *Action Alert*, No. 87-47, November 25, 1987.

_____. *Status Report*, No. 189, October 13, 1987.

_____. Statement of Financial Accounting Standards (SFAS) No. 4, *Reporting Gains and Losses from Extinguishment of Debt*, 1975.

_____. SFAS No. 5, *Accounting for Contingencies*, 1975.

_____. SFAS No. 16, *Prior Period Adjustments*, 1977.

_____. SFAS No. 34, *Capitalization of Interest Costs*, 1979.

_____. SFAS No. 35, *Accounting and Reporting by Defined Benefit Pension Plans*, 1980.

_____. SFAS No. 36, *Disclosure of Pension Information*, 1980.

_____. SFAS No. 57, *Related Party Disclosures*, 1982.

_____. SFAS No. 62, *Capitalization of Interest Cost in Situations Involving Certain Tax-Exempt Borrowings and Certain Gifts and Grants*, 1982.

_____. SFAS No. 74, *Accounting for Special Termination Benefits Paid to Employees*, 1983.

_____. SFAS No. 75, *Deferral of the Effective Date of Certain Accounting Requirements for Pension Plans of State and Local Government Units*, 1983.

_____. SFAS No. 76, *Extinguishment of Debt*, 1983.

_____. SFAS No. 87, *Employers' Accounting for Pensions*, 1985.

_____. SFAS No. 88, *Employers' Accounting for Settlements and Curtailments of Defined Benefit Pension Plans and for Termination Benefits*, 1985.

_____. SFAS No. 93, *Recognition of Depreciation by Not-for-Profit Organizations*, 1987.

_____. "Consolidation of All Majority-Owned Subsidiaries," exposure draft of FASB Statement No. 94, issued December 16, 1986.

_____. SFAS No. 94, *Consolidation of all Majority-Owned Subsidiaries*, 1987.

_____. SFAS No. 95, *Statement of Cash Flows*, 1987.

_____. Interpretation No. 3, *Accounting for the Cost of Pension Plans Subject to the Employee Retirement Income Security Act of 1974*, 1974.

_____. Interpretation No. 14, *Reasonable Estimation of the Amount of Loss*, 1976.

_____. Statement of Financial Accounting Concepts (SFAC) No. 6, *Elements of Financial Statements*, 1985.

_____. Emerging Issues Task Force (EITF). Issues Summary 86-12, "Accounting by Insureds for Claims-Made Insurance Policies," Supplement No. 2, May 22, 1986.

Finkler, Steven A., and Sandra L. Horowitz. "Merger and Consolidation: An Overview of Activity in Healthcare Organizations." *Healthcare Financial Management* (January 1985): 19–28.

Governmental Accounting Standards Board (GASB). Statement No. 1, *Authoritative Status of NCGA Pronouncements and AICPA Industry Audit Guide*. Norwalk, Ct.: GASB, 1984.

_____. Statement No. 4, *Applicability of FASB Statement No. 87, "Employers' Accounting for Pensions," to State and Local Government Employers*, 1986.

_____. Statement No. 5, *Disclosure of Pension Information by Public Employee Retirement Systems and State and Local Governmental Employers*, 1986.

_____. Statement No. 7, *Advance Refundings Resulting in Defeasance of Debt*, 1987.

Healthcare Financial Management Association (HFMA), Principles and Practices (P&P) Board. Statement No. 4, *Reporting of Certain Transactions Arising in Connection With the Issuance of Debt*. Westchester, Ill.: HFMA, 1982.

_____. Statement No. 8, *The Use of Fund Accounting and the Need for Single Fund Reporting by Institutional Healthcare Providers*, 1986.

_____. "The Presentation of Nonpatient Service Revenue and Related Issues." exposure draft of a proposed P&P Board Statement, issued May 29, 1987.

_____. "Accounting and Reporting Issues Related to Corporate Reorganizations Involving Tax-Exempt Institutional Healthcare Providers." exposure draft of a proposed P&P Board Statement, issued May 29, 1987.

Price Waterhouse and Healthcare Financial Management Association. *Hospital Financial Reports: A Survey*. Westchester, Ill.: HFMA, 1987.

Seawell, L. Vann. *External and Internal Reporting by Hospitals*. Westchester, Ill.: HFMA, 1984.

_____. *Hospital Financial Accounting: Theory and Practice*. Westchester, Ill.: HFMA, 1975.

Cost Accounting and Analysis

Chapter 6

Cost Concepts and Decision Making

William O. Cleverley
Professor, Graduate Program in Hospital and Health Services Management
The Ohio State University

In previous chapters, we have focused on understanding and interpreting the financial information prepared by the financial accounting system and presented in general-purpose financial statements. This chapter is directed more narrowly at the utilization of cost information in decision making. Cost information is produced by the cost accounting system of an entity. In most situations, it is shaped by the financial accounting system and the generally accepted principles of financial accounting. However, it is flexible, since it usually provides information for identifiable and specific decision-making groups, such as budgetary cost variance reports to department managers, cost reports to third-party payers, and forecasted project cost reports to planning agencies.

Cost is a noun that never really stands alone. In most situations, two additional pieces of information are added that enhance the meaning and relevance of the cost statistic.

First, the object being costed is defined. For example, we might say that the cost of routine nursing care in Willkram Hospital is $200. Objects of costing are usually of two types:

1. products (outputs or services)
2. responsibility centers (departments or larger units)

Quite often, we oversimplify this classification system and refer to cost information about products as *planning information* and cost information about responsibility centers as *control information*.

Second, usually an adjective is added to modify cost. For example, we might say that the *direct* cost of routine nursing care in Willkram Hospital is $100. A number of major categories of adjective modifiers refine the concept of cost; they are all used to improve the decision-making process by precisely defining cost to make it more relevant to decisions.

This chapter discusses some of the basic concepts of cost used in cost analysis. It is important to explain this jargon if decision makers are to use cost information correctly. Different concepts of cost are required for different decision purposes. In most situations, these concepts require specific, unique methodologies for cost measurement.

CONCEPTS OF COST

Cost may be categorized in a variety of ways to meet decision makers' specific needs. How-

This chapter is reprinted from *Essentials of Health Care Finance*, 2nd ed., by W.O. Cleverley, pp. 191–216, Aspen Publishers, Inc., © 1986.

ever, in most situations, the total value of cost is the same. Using one cost concept in place of another simply slices the total cost pie differently. For example, in Exhibit 6-1 the total cost of a laboratory for June 1986, was $21,360. Of that amount, $20,000 could be classified as direct cost and $1,360 as indirect cost. However, classifying costs by controllability might determine that $15,000 of the laboratory cost was controllable and $6,360 was not controllable. The total cost, however, is the same in both cases.

This brings us to another important point. Since, in most cases, different concepts of cost simply slice total cost in different ways, there may be underlying relationships between the various concepts of costs. For example, direct costs and controllable costs may be related. In many situations, there are standard rules of thumb that may be used to relate cost measures.

The difference between cost and expense is another crucial definitional point. Accountants have traditionally defined cost in a way that leads one to think of cost as an expenditure. However, in most reported cost statistics, the definition is usually one of expense, not necessarily expenditure. For example, in Exhibit 6-1 depreciation is listed as a cost. However, depreciation is not an actual expenditure of cash but an amortization of

prior cost. In the present context, unless otherwise indicated, when we are discussing cost statistics, the terms *cost* and *expenses* may be used interchangeably.

For purposes of discussion, we examine below the four major categories within which costs can be classified:

1. traceability to the object being costed
2. behavior of cost to output or activity
3. management responsibility for control
4. future versus historical

Traceability

Of all cost classifications, traceability is the most basic. Two major categories of costs classified by traceability are (1) direct costs and (2) indirect costs. A direct cost is specifically traceable to a given cost objective. For example, the salaries, supplies, and other costs of Exhibit 6-1 are classified as direct costs of the laboratory. Indirect costs cannot be traced to a given cost objective without resorting to some arbitrary method of assignment. In Exhibit 6-1, depreciation, employee benefits, and costs of other departments would be classified as indirect costs.

Not all costs classified as indirect may actually be indirect, however. In some situations, they could be redefined as direct costs. For example, it might be possible to calculate employee benefits for specific employees; these costs could then be charged to the departments where the employees worked and thus become direct costs. However, the actual costs of performing these calculations might be prohibitive.

The classification of a cost as either direct or indirect depends on the given cost objective. This is a simple observation, but one that is forgotten by many users of cost information. For example, the $20,000 of direct cost identified in Exhibit 6-1 is a direct cost only with respect to the laboratory department. If another cost objective is specified, the cost may no longer be direct. For example, dividing the $20,000 of direct costs by the number of relative value units (RVUs) yields a direct cost per RVU of $2.00. But this is not really true. The direct cost of any

Exhibit 6-1 Cost Report, Laboratory, June 1986

DIRECT COSTS	
Salaries	$10,000
Supplies	5,000
Other	5,000
TOTAL	$20,000
DEPRECIATION	
Building and Fixed Equipment	100
Major Movable Equipment	60
TOTAL	160
ALLOCATED COSTS	
Employee Benefits	150
Administration	500
Maintenance	250
Housekeeping	200
Laundry	100
TOTAL	1,200
TOTAL COSTS	$21,360
RELATIVE VALUE UNITS (RVU) PRODUCED	10,000
AVERAGE COST PER RVU	$ 2,136

given RVU may be higher or lower than the $2.00 calculated, which is the average value for all RVUs and not necessarily the cost for any specific unit.

Incorrect classification is a common problem in cost accounting. Costs are accumulated on a department or responsibility-center basis and may be direct or indirect with respect to that department. However, it can be misleading to say that the same set of direct costs is also direct with respect to the outputs of that department.

The major direct cost categories of most departments would include the following:

- salaries
- supplies
- other (usually fees and purchased services, such as utilities, dues, travel, and rents)

Indirect cost categories usually include

- depreciation
- employee benefits
- allocated costs of other departments

The concept of direct versus indirect cost may not appear to have much specific relevance to decision makers. To some extent this is true; however, the concept of direct versus indirect costs is pervasive. It influences both the definition and measurement of other alternative cost concepts that do have specific relevance.

Cost Behavior

Cost is also classified by the degree of variability in relation to output. The actual measurement of cost behavior is influenced by a department's classifications of cost, which provides the basis for categorizing costs as direct or indirect.

For our purposes, we can identify four major categories of costs that are classified according to their relationship to output:

1. variable
2. fixed
3. semifixed
4. semivariable

Variable costs change as output or volume changes in a constant, proportional manner. If output increases by ten percent, costs should also increase by ten percent; that is, there is some constant cost increment per unit of output. Figure 6-1 illustrates, graphically and mathematically, the concept of variable cost for the laboratory example of Exhibit 6-1. It is assumed that all supply costs in this case are variable. For each unit increase in RVUs, supply costs will increase by $.50.

Fixed costs do not change in response to changes in volume. They are a function of the passage of time, not output. Figure 6-2 illustrates fixed-cost behavior patterns for the depreciation costs of the laboratory example.

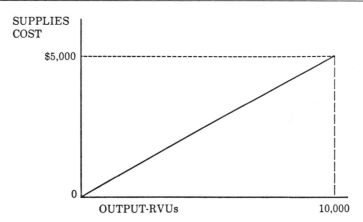

Note: Supplies cost = $.50 × number of RVUs.

Figure 6-1 Cost Behavior of Supplies Cost, Variable

Each month, irrespective of output levels, depreciation cost will be $160.

Semifixed, or step, costs do change with respect to changes in output, but they are not proportional. A semifixed cost might be considered variable or fixed—depending on the size of the steps relative to the range of volume under consideration. For example, in Figure 6-3, it is assumed that the salaries cost of the laboratory is semifixed. If the volume of output under consideration for a specific decision were between 6,000 and 8,000 RVUs, salary costs could be considered fixed at $9,000. Some semifixed costs may be considered variable for cost analysis purposes. For example, if smaller units of people could be employed instead of full-time equivalents (FTEs), such as on the basis of hours

generated by an available part-time pool, the size of the steps might be significantly smaller than 2,000 RVUs in our laboratory example. At the present, it is assumed that one additional FTE must be employed for every increment of 2,000 RVUs. Treating salary costs as variable in this situation might not be a bad procedure (see Figure 6-3).

Semivariable costs include elements of both fixed and variable costs. Utility costs are good examples. There may be some basic, fixed requirement per unit of time (month, year) regardless of volume—such as normal heating and lighting requirements. But there is also likely to be a direct, proportional relationship between volume and the amount of the utility cost. As volume increases, costs go up. Figure 6-4 il-

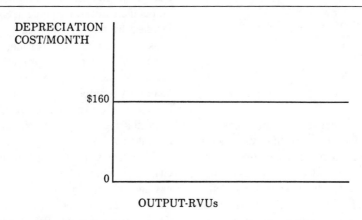

Note: Depreciation cost = $160 per month.

Figure 6-2 Cost Behavior of Depreciation, Fixed

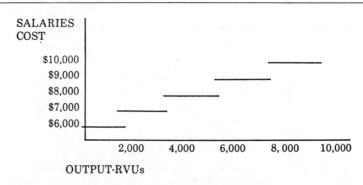

Note: Salary costs = $6,000 if RVUs are less than 2,000, $7,000 if RVUs are between 2,001 and 4,000, $8,000 if RVUs are between 4,001 and 6,000, $9,000 if RVUs are between 6,001 and 8,000, and $10,000 if RVUs are between 8,001 and 10,000.

Figure 6-3 Cost Behavior of Salary Costs, Semifixed

lustrates semivariable costs in our laboratory example.

In many situations, we do not focus on specific cost elements but aggregate several cost categories of interest. It is interesting to see what type of cost behavior pattern emerges when we do this. Figure 6-5 aggregates the four cost categories discussed earlier—supplies, depreciation, salaries, and other. A semivariable cost behavior pattern closely approximates the actual aggregated cost behavior pattern; this is true for many types of operations. Some very simple but useful methods for approximating this cost function are discussed under "Controllability."

Controllability

One of the primary purposes of gathering cost information is to aid the management control process. To facilitate evaluation of the management control process, costs must be assigned to individual responsibility centers, usually departments, where a designated manager is responsible for cost control. A natural question that arises is what proportion of the total costs charged to a department is the manager responsible for? The answer to this question requires that costs be separated into two categories: controllable costs and noncontrollable costs.

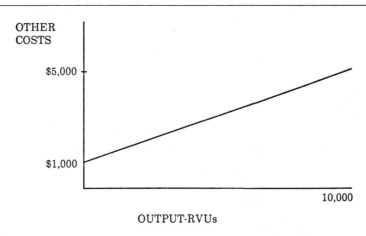

Note: Other costs = $1,000 per month + $.40 × RVUs.

Figure 6-4 Cost Behavior of Other Costs, Semivariable

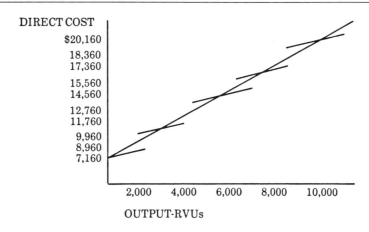

Note: Direct cost and depreciation = $7,160 per month + $1.30 × RVUs (approximation).

Figure 6-5 Cost Behavior of Aggregated Costs, Direct Cost, and Depreciation

Controllable costs can be influenced by a designated responsibility center or departmental manager within a defined control period. It is said that all costs are controllable by someone at some time. For example, the chief executive officer of a health care facility, through the authority granted to him by his governing board, is ultimately responsible for all costs.

The matrix of costs shown in Exhibit 6-2 categorizes the laboratory cost report data of Exhibit 6-1. All costs must fall into one of the six cells; however, it may be possible to categorize an aggregate cost category into more than one cell. In the laboratory example, other cost was viewed as semivariable, implying that part of the cost would be described as a direct variable cost ($4,000) and part as a direct fixed cost ($1,000).

There is a tendency in developing management control programs, especially in the health care industry, to use one of three approaches in designating controllable costs. First, controllable costs may be defined to be the total costs charged to the department; the department manager would view all costs in the above six categories as controllable. In our example, all $21,360 of cost would be viewed as controllable by the laboratory manager. In most normal situations, however, this grossly overstates the amount of cost actually controllable by a given departmental manager. The result of this overstatement has been negative in many situations. Department managers have rightfully viewed this basis of control as highly inequitable.

Second, controllable costs may be limited to those costs classified as direct. This system is

also not without fault; specifically, there may be fixed costs attributed directly to the department that should not be considered controllable. Rents on pieces of equipment, for example, may not be under the department manager's control. There may also be indirect costs, especially costs that are variable, that the department manager can control. For example, employee benefits may legitimately be the department manager's responsibility.

Third, in some situations, controllable costs may be defined as only those costs that are direct/variable. This limits costs that are controllable by the department manager to their lowest level. However, it excludes what could be a relatively large amount of cost influenced by the department manager. Failure to include the latter cost in the manager's control sphere may weaken management control.

Future Costs

Decision making involves selection among alternatives; it is a forward-looking process. Actual historical cost may be useful as a basis for projecting future costs, but it should not be used without adjustment unless it can be assumed that future conditions will be identical to past conditions.

A variety of concepts and definitions have been used in current discussion of costs for decision-making purposes. The following four types of costs appear to be basic to the process of selecting among alternative decisions:

Exhibit 6-2 Laboratory Cost Behavior Categorization

Traceability	Variable		Fixed		Semifixed		Total
Direct	Other Supplies	$4,000 5,000	Other	$1,000	Salaries	$10,000	
		$9,000		$1,000		$10,000	$20,000
Indirect	Employee Benefits Housekeeping	$150 $100	Depreciation Administration Housekeeping	$160 $500 $100	Maintenance Laundry	$250 $100	
		$250		$760		$350	$1,360
Totals		$9,250		$1,760		$10,350	$21,360

1. avoidable costs
2. sunk costs
3. incremental costs
4. opportunity costs

Avoidable Costs

Avoidable costs will be affected by the decision under consideration. Specifically, they are costs that can be eliminated or saved if an activity is discontinued; they will continue only if the activity is left unchanged. For example, if a hospital were considering curtailing its volume by 50 percent in response to cost-containment pressures, what would it save? The answer is those costs that are avoidable. In most situations, multiplication of current, average, and total cost per unit of output (patient days or admissions) by the projected change in output would overstate avoidable costs; a considerable proportion of the cost may be classified as sunk.

Sunk Costs

Sunk costs are unaffected by the decision under consideration. In the example above, large portions of cost—depreciation, administrative salaries, insurance, and others—are sunk or not avoidable in the proposed 50 percent reduction in volume.

The distinction between fixed and variable costs, on the one hand, and sunk and avoidable costs, on the other, is not perfect. Many costs classified as fixed may also be thought of as sunk, but some are not. For example, malpractice insurance premiums may be generally considered fixed cost, given an expected normal level of activity. However, if the institution is considering a drastic reduction in volume, malpractice premiums may not be entirely fixed.

Incremental Costs

Incremental costs are the changes in total cost resulting from various alternative courses of action. Avoidable costs may be thought of as a subset of incremental costs, but most people regard avoidable costs as the result of a comparison of cost in which one alternative is reduc-

tion in volume or discontinuation of some activity. Incremental costs usually arise in situations in which an alternative is an expansion of volume or the initiation of a new activity. For decisions involving only modest changes in output, incremental costs and variable costs may be used interchangeably. In most situations, however, incremental costs are more comprehensive. A decision to construct a surgi-center adjacent to a hospital would involve fixed and variable costs. Depreciation on the facility would be a fixed cost but it would be incremental to the decision to construct the surgi-center.

Opportunity Costs

Opportunity cost is the value foregone by using a resource in a particular way instead of in its next best alternative way. Assume that a nursing home is considering expanding its facility and would use land acquired 20 years ago. If the land had a historical cost of $1 million but a present market value of $10 million, what is the opportunity cost of the land? Practically everyone would agree that if sale of the land constituted the next best alternative, the opportunity cost would be $10 million, not $1 million. Alternatively, a hospital might consider converting part of its acute care facility into a skilled nursing facility because of a reduction in demand or obsolescence in the facility. The question arises, what is the value, or what would be the cost of the facility, to the skilled nursing facility operation? If there is no way that the facility can be renovated or if the facility is not needed for the provision of acute care, its opportunity cost may be zero. This could contrast sharply to the recorded historical cost of the facility.

COST MEASUREMENT

In this section, we examine the methods of cost measurement for two cost categories: (1) direct and indirect full cost and (2) variable and fixed cost. Both of these cost categories are useful in financial decisions, but the cost accounting system does not directly provide estimates for them.

Direct and Indirect Full Cost

In most cost accounting systems, costs are classified by department or responsibility center or by the object of expenditure. When costs are classified primarily along departmental lines, individual cost items are charged to the departments to which they are traceable. When costs are classified by object of expenditure, they may be identified as relating to supplies, salaries, rent, insurance, or some other category.

Departments in a health care facility can be classified generally as direct or indirect departments, depending on whether they provide services directly to the patient or not. Sometimes the terms *revenue* and *nonrevenue* are substituted for *direct* and *indirect*. In the hospital industry, the following breakdown is used in general-purpose financial statements.

Operating Expense Area	Type of Department
Nursing services area	Direct/revenue
Other professional services	Direct/revenue
General services	Indirect/nonrevenue
Fiscal services	Indirect/nonrevenue
Administrative services	Indirect/nonrevenue

Whatever the nomenclature used to describe the classification of departments, cost allocation is a fundamental need. The costs of the indirect, nonrevenue departments need to be allocated to the direct revenue departments for many decision-making purposes. For example, some payers reimburse on the basis of the full costs of direct departments and are interested in the cost of indirect departments only insofar as it affects the calculation of the direct departments' full costs. Pricing decisions need to be based on full costs, not just direct costs, if the costs of the indirect departments are to be covered equitably.

Equity is a key concept in allocating indirect department costs to direct departments. Ideally, the allocation should reflect as nearly as possible the actual cost incurred by the indirect department to provide services for a direct department. Department managers who receive cost reports showing indirect allocations are vitally interested in this equity principle, and for good reason. Even if indirect costs are not regarded as controllable by the department manager, the allocation of costs to a given direct department can have an important effect on a variety of management decisions. Pricing, expansion, or contraction of a department; the purchase of new equipment; and the salaries of department managers are all affected by the allocation of indirect costs.

Costs of indirect departments are in most cases not traceable to direct departments. If they were, they could be reassigned. In such cases, they must be allocated to the direct departments in some systematic and rational manner. In general, two allocation decisions must be made: (1) selection of the allocation basis and (2) selection of the method of cost apportionment.

Table 6-1 provides sample data for a cost allocation. In this example, there are four departments: two are indirect—laundry/linen and housekeeping—and two are direct—radiology and nursing. Pounds of laundry is the only allocation basis under consideration for the laundry and linen department. The housekeeping department can use one of two allocation bases, either

---

Table 6-1 Cost Allocation Example

Department	Direct Costs	Pounds of Laundry Used	Square Feet	Hours of Housekeeping Used
Laundry/Linen	$ 15,000	$ —	$ 50,000	$ 150
Housekeeping	30,000	5,000	—	—
Radiology	135,000	5,000	10,000	900
Nursing	270,000	90,000	140,000	1,950
Total	$450,000	$100,000	$200,000	$3,000

square feet of area served or hours of service actually worked.

In general, there are only three acceptable methods of cost allocation:

1. step-down
2. double-distribution
3. simultaneous-equations

Most health care facilities still use the step-down method of cost allocation. In this method, the indirect department that receives the least amount of service from other indirect departments and provides the most service to other departments allocates its cost first. A similar analysis follows to determine the order of cost allocation for each of the remaining indirect departments. This determination can be subjective to allow some flexibility, as we shall see shortly.

In the step-down allocation process illustrated below, laundry/linen allocates its cost first. Then, housekeeping allocates its direct cost, plus the allocated cost of laundry and linen, to the direct departments of radiology and nursing, based on the ratio of hours of housekeeping used by those departments. The allocation proportions are given in parentheses.

	Direct Costs	Laundry/Linen	Housekeeping	Total
Laundry/Linen	$ 15,000	$15,000		
Housekeeping	30,000	750 (.05)	$30,750	
Radiology	135,000	750 (.05)	9,711 (.3158)	$145,461
Nursing	270,000	13,500 (.90)	21,039 (.6842)	304,539
Total	$450,000	$15,000	$30,750	$450,000

The order of departmental allocation can be an important variable in a step-down method of cost allocation. Shown below is an alternative step-down cost allocation in which housekeeping allocates its cost first and precedes laundry/linen.

	Direct Costs	Housekeeping	Laundry/Linen	Total
Housekeeping	$ 30,000	$30,000		
Laundry/Linen	15,000	1,500 (.05)	$16,500	
Radiology	135,000	9,000 (.30)	868 (.053)	$144,868
Nursing	270,000	19,500 (.65)	15,632 (.947)	305,132
Total	$450,000	$30,000	$16,500	$450,000

The double-distribution method of cost allocation is just a refinement of the step-down method. Instead of closing the individual department after allocating its costs, it is kept open and receives the costs of other indirect departments. After one complete allocation sequence, the former departments are then closed, using the normal step-down method. The simultaneous-equations method of cost allocation is used in an attempt to be exact about the cost allocation amounts. A system of equations is established and mathematically correct allocations are computed. In the above example, if simultaneous equations had been used, the cost of radiology would be $145,075 and the cost of nursing would be $304,925.

Finally, it should be noted that using a different allocation base can create differences in cost allocation. For example, the use of square footage for housekeeping, instead of hours served, produces the following pattern of cost allocation when housekeeping allocates its cost first, using the step-down method:

	Direct Costs	Housekeeping	Laundry/Linen	Total
Housekeeping	$ 30,000	$30,000		
Laundry/Linen	15,000	7,500 (.25)	$22,500	
Radiology	135,000	1,500 (.05)	1,125 (.05)	$137,625
Nursing	270,000	21,000 (.70)	21,375 (.95)	312,375
Total	$450,000	$30,000	$22,500	$450,000

The important point in this discussion is that full cost is not as objective and exact a figure as one might normally think. Indirect costs can be allocated in a variety of ways that can create significant differences in full costs for given departments. This flexibility should be remembered when examining and interpreting full-cost data.

Variable and Fixed Cost

A very important and widely used cost concept is variability with respect to output. It is involved in determining for decision-making purposes such costs as avoidable, sunk, incremental, and controllable. However, accounting records do not directly yield this type of cost information. Instead, the costs are classified by department and by object of expenditure. Thus, in order to develop estimates of variable and fixed costs, the relevant data must be analyzed in some way.

Our discussion of cost concepts classified by variability with respect to output indicated that a semivariable cost pattern may be a good representation of many types of costs. A semivariable cost function is one that has both a fixed and variable element in it. A semivariable cost function often results when various types of costs are aggregated together.

Estimating Methods

Estimation of a semivariable cost function requires separation of the cost into variable and fixed components. A variety of methods, varying in complexity and accuracy, may be used. Three of the simplest methods are (1) visual-fit, (2) high-low, and (3) semi-averages.

To illustrate each of these methods, assume that we are trying to determine the labor cost function for the radiology department and we have the following six biweekly payroll data points:

Pay Period	Number of Films	Hours Worked
1	300	180 (low)
2	240	140 (low)
3	400	230 (high)
4	340	190 (high)
5	180	110 (lowest)
6	600	320 (highest)

In the visual-fit method of cost estimation, the above individual data points are plotted on graph paper. A straight line is then drawn through the points to provide the best fit. Visual fitting of data is a good first step in any method of cost estimation. Figure 6-6 shows a visual fitting of the above radiology data.

The high-low method is a simple technique that can be used to estimate the variable and fixed-cost coefficients of a semivariable cost function. The variable cost parameter is solved first. It equals the change in cost from the highest to the lowest data point, divided by the change in output. In the above radiology example, the variable *hours worked* would be calculated as follows:

$$\text{Variable Labor Hours/Film} = \frac{320 - 110}{600 - 180} = \frac{210}{420} = .50$$

The fixed-cost parameter may then be solved by subtracting the estimated variable cost (determined by multiplying the variable cost parameter estimate by output at the high level) from total cost. In our radiology example, fixed cost would equal

$$\begin{aligned} \text{Fixed labor hours/} \\ \text{Biweekly pay period} &= 320 - (.50 \times 600) \\ &= 320 - 300 = 20 \end{aligned}$$

Alternatively, it is possible to plot the high and low points and then draw a straight line through them.

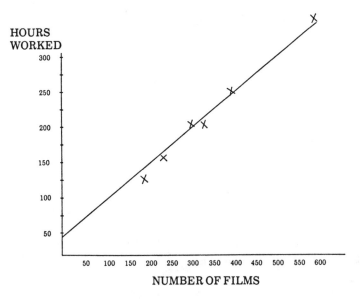

Figure 6-6 Visual Fitting of Radiology Data

The semi-averages method is very similar to the high-low method in terms of its mathematical solution. To derive the estimate of variable cost, the difference between the mean of the high-cost points and the mean of the low-cost points is divided by the change in output from the mean of the high-cost points to the mean of the low-cost points. In the radiology example, variable cost would be calculated as follows:

$$\text{Variable Labor Hours/Film}$$

$$= \dfrac{\dfrac{320 + 230 + 190}{3} - \dfrac{180 + 140 + 110}{3}}{\dfrac{600 + 400 + 340}{3} - \dfrac{300 + 240 + 180}{3}}$$

$$= \dfrac{246.67 - 143.33}{446.67 - 240.00} = .50$$

Fixed cost is solved in a manner identical to that used in the high-low method. In the radiology example, fixed cost would equal

Fixed labor hours/

Biweekly pay period
$$= 246.67 - (.50 \times 446.67) = 23.34$$

These three methods of estimating variable and fixed cost are highly simplistic. They are useful only in limited ways to provide a basis for further discussing and analyzing what the true cost behavioral pattern might be. However, in most situations a limited attempt, based on simplistic methods, to discover the underlying fixed/variable cost patterns, is better than no effort.

Data Checks

When any of the above methods are used, several data checks should be performed. First, the cost data being used to estimate the cost behavior pattern should be stated in a common dollar. If the wages paid for employees have changed dramatically from one year to the next, the use of unadjusted wage and salary data from the two years can create measurement problems. In our radiology example, we used a physical quantity measure of cost, namely, hours worked. A physical measure of cost should be used whenever possible.

Second, cost and output data should be matched; the figures for reported cost should relate to the activity of the period. In most situations, accounting records provide this type of relationship, based on the accrual principle of accounting. However, in some situations this may not happen; supply costs may be charged to a department when the items are purchased, not when they are used.

Third, the period of time during which a cost function is being estimated should be one of a stable technology and case mix. If the technology under consideration has changed dramatically during that period, there will be measurement problems.

BREAK-EVEN ANALYSIS

Certain techniques can be applied in analyzing the relationship between cost, volume, and profit. These techniques rely on categorizing costs as fixed and variable. They can serve as powerful management decision aids and may be valuable in a wide range of decisions. An understanding of these techniques is crucial for decision makers whose choices affect the financial results of health care facilities.

Profit in a health care facility is influenced by various factors, including

- rates
- volume
- variable cost
- fixed cost
- payer mix
- bad debts

The primary value of break-even analysis, or, as it is sometimes called, cost-volume-profit analysis, is its ability to quantify the relationships between the above factors and profit.

Traditional Applications

Break-even analysis has been used in industry for decades with a high degree of satisfaction. Its name comes from the solution to an equation that sets profit equal to zero and revenue equal to costs. To illustrate, assume that a hospital has the following financial information:

Variable cost per case	$1,000.00
Fixed cost per period	$100,000.00
Rate per case	$2,400.00

The break-even volume may be solved by dividing fixed costs by the contribution margin, which is the difference between rate and variable cost:

$$\text{Break-even volume in units} = \frac{\text{Fixed cost}}{\text{Rate} - \text{Variable cost}}$$

Thus, in our hospital example, the break-even volume would be

$$\text{Break-even volume in units} = \frac{\$100,000}{\$2,400 - \$1,000}$$
$$= 71.4 \text{ cases}$$

If volume exceeds 72 cases, the hospital will make a profit; but if volume goes below 71 cases it will incur a loss. Sometimes, a revenue-and-cost relationship is put into graphic form to illustrate profit at various levels. Such a presentation is referred to as a break-even chart. For our hospital example, a break-even chart is shown in Figure 6-7.

In many cases, some targeted level of net income or profit is desired. The break-even model is easily adapted to this purpose; the new break-even point would become

$$\text{Break-even volume in units} = \frac{\text{Fixed cost} + \text{net income}}{\text{Rate} - \text{Variable cost}}$$

In our example, assuming that a desired profit of $6,000 were required, the new break-even point would be

$$\text{Break-even volume in units} = \frac{\$100,000 + \$6,000}{\$1,400}$$
$$= 75.7 \text{ cases}$$

Multiple-Payer Model

Although break-even analysis is a powerful management tool, it cannot be employed in the health care industry without adaptation. The major revision required relates to the revenue function. The preceding discussion of break-even analysis assumed that there was only one payer or purchaser of services. That payer was assumed to pay a fixed price per unit of product. However, this situation does not exist in the health care industry, where there may be three or more major categories of payers. For our purposes, we will assume that there are three categories of payers:

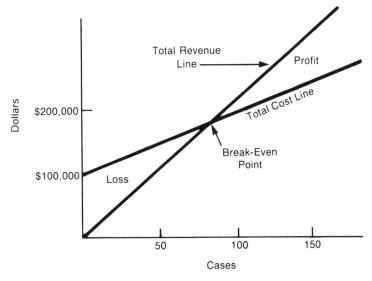

Figure 6-7 Break-Even Chart

1. cost payers (paying average cost of services provided)
2. fixed-price payers (paying an established fee per unit of service, for example, a fixed price per DRG)
3. charge payers (paying on the basis of internally set prices)

The break-even formula in these three payer situations can be generalized as follows:

Break-even volume in units =
$$\frac{(1 - CO)\, F + NI}{CH \times P_1 + FP \times P_E - (1 - CO)V}$$

This formula may look complex at first glance, but it is really very similar to the previous one-payer break-even formula. In fact, the above equation can be used in the one-payer situation and provides an identical result. To aid in our understanding of the formula, we should first define the individual variables:

V = Variable cost per unit of output
F = Fixed cost per period
NI = Targeted net income
P_1 = Internally set price that is paid by charge payers
P_E = Externally set price paid by fixed-price payers

CO = Proportion of cost payers
CH = Proportion of charge payers
FP = Proportion of fixed-price payers

Let us now examine each term in the equation:

- $(1 - CO)F$—This term represents the proportion of fixed cost (F) that is not paid by cost payers (CO). Cost payers are assumed to pay their proportionate share of fixed costs. This leaves the residual portion $(1 - CO)$ unpaid; it is included in the numerator as a financial requirement that must be covered before break-even takes place. If there were no cost payers, $(1 - CO)$ would be 1, and all of the fixed costs would be included. This is the case in traditional break-even analysis.

- NI—This term, targeted net income, is included as a financial requirement as in the traditional break-even formula. NI is not reduced by the cost payer portion because it is assumed that cost payers are not contributing toward meeting the net income requirement. Cost payers pay cost, nothing less and nothing more.

- $CH \times P_1$—This term represents the weighted price paid by charge payers.

When added to the next term $(FP \times P_E)$, we have a measure of the price paid by the two price-paying categories of customers—charge payers and fixed-price payers. It should be emphasized that P_1 represents the price received, not the charge made. For example, if 10 percent of the patients paid established charges of $2,400 per case and 20 percent paid 90 percent of established charges of $2,400 per case, the following values would result:

$$CH = .10 + .20 = .30$$
$$P_1 = (1.0 \times \$2,400) \times 1/3$$
$$+ (.90 \times \$2,400) \times 2/3 = \$2,240$$

- $FP \times P_E$—This term represents the weighted price paid by fixed price payers. The addition of this term to $CH \times P_1$ yields a measure of the price received by price-paying patients. The summation of the two terms can be compared with the rate term used in the traditional break-even formula. Again, there may be circumstances in which a subweighting may be necessary. For example, assume that Medicare pays $2,000 per case and that 40 percent of the cases are Medicare. Also assume that ten percent of the cases are from a health maintenance organization that pays $2,200 per case. The following values would result:

$$FP = .40 + .10 = .50$$
$$P_E = .8 \times \$2,000 \times .2 \times \$2,200 = \$2,040$$

- $(1 - CO)V$—This term represents the net variable cost that remains after reflecting the proportion paid by cost payers. Cost payers pay their share of both fixed and variable cost. If there were no cost payers, the entire value of the variable cost per unit would be subtracted to yield the contribution margin per unit.

To see that the traditional break-even formula is actually derived from our more general three-payer model, let us compute the break-even point using the data from the case example developed in our discussion of traditional break-even analysis:

Break-even volume in units =
$$\frac{(1 - 0) \times \$100,000 + \$6,000}{1.0 \times \$2,400 + 0 \times \$0 - (1 - 0) \times \$1,000}$$
$$= 75.7 \text{ cases}$$

Now having tested the accuracy of the three-payer break-even formula in a one-payer situation, let us expand the initial case example to a more realistic multiple-payer situation. The following data are assumed:

Payer Proportion	Payment Method
.20	pay average cost
.40	pay $2,000 per case (fixed price payer)
.10	pay $2,200 per case (fixed price payer)
.10	pay 100% of charges, $2,400 per case
.20	pay 90% of charges, $2,160 per case

Also assume that the variable cost is $1,000 per case and fixed costs are $100,000 per period. In addition the firm needs a profit of $6,000 to meet other financial requirements. The use of these data in our break-even model would produce the following result:

Break-even volume in cases =
$$\frac{(.8 \times \$100,000) + \$6,000}{(.3 \times \$2,240) + (.5 \times \$2,040) - (.8 \times \$1,000)}$$
$$= \frac{\$86,000}{\$892} = 96.413$$

To demonstrate the accuracy of the break-even formula, we can derive the following income statement for our case example, assuming 96.4 cases as the break-even volume:

Patient revenue

.20 × 96.4 × $2,037.34*	$ 39,279.92
.40 × 96.4 × $2,000.00	77,120.00
.10 × 96.4 × $2,200.00	21,208.00
.10 × 96.4 × $2,400.00	23,136.00
.20 × 96.4 × $2,160.00	41,644.80
Net patient revenue	$202,388.72
Fixed cost	100,000.00
Variable cost (96.4 × $1,000)	96,400.00
Net income	$ 5,988.72

*Average cost × ($100,000 + $96,400)/96.4 × $2,037.34

This income statement demonstrates that, at a volume of 96.4 patients, the firm's net income would be \$5,988.72. This value does not exactly match the targeted net income level of \$6,000.00 because of a small rounding error; the actual break-even volume was 96.413, not 96.4.

Special Applications

The break-even formula has many applications other than that of computing break-even points. Two specific applications are in (1) the computation of marginal profit of volume changes and (2) rate-setting analysis.

Computation of Marginal Profit of Volume Changes

In most business situations, executives are very concerned about the impact of volume changes upon operating profitability. At the beginning of a budget period, management may not be sure what its actual volumes will be, but it still needs to know how sensitive profit will be to possible swings in volume. If the payer mix is expected to remain constant, the following simple formula can be used to calculate the marginal changes in profit associated with volume swings:

Change in profit = Change in units × Profitability index

where

Profitability index = CH $(P_1 - V)$ + FP $(P_E - V)$

The profitability index remains constant and is simply multiplied by projected volume change to determine the profit change. Using our earlier case example, the profitability index would be

Profitability index = .3(\$2,240 − \$1,000)
　　　+ .5(\$2,040 − \$1,000) = \$892

The value for the profitability index is really the weighted contribution margin per unit of output. This fact is easily seen by comparing the value calculated above with that from our three-payer break-even example. The values are the same, \$892 in each case. This means that, for every one unit change in output, the profit increases by \$892. An increase of one unit will raise profit by \$892, and a decrease of one unit

will lower profit by \$892. A useful question to raise at this point is how large a reduction in volume can the firm experience before its profit falls to \$2,000? Using the preceding formula, the answer would be:

Change in profit = Volume change × Profitability index
(\$6,000 − \$2,000) = Volume change × \$892
Volume change = 4.48 cases

If volume falls by 4.48 cases, the firm's profit will fall to \$2,000. Further analysis could be used to portray other scenarios or to answer other what-if type questions. In each case, the resulting data could be displayed in a table or graph.

Rate-Setting Analysis

Rate setting is an extremely important activity for most health care organizations. Usually the objective is not profit maximization but rather fulfillment of financial requirements. In general, pricing services can be stated in the following conceptual terms:

Price = Average cost + Profit requirement
　　+ Loss on fixed-price patients

If Q represents total budgeted volume in units, we can use our earlier break-even model to develop the following pricing formula:

$$P_1 = AC + \frac{NI}{CH \times Q} + \frac{(AC - P_E) \times FP \times Q}{CH \times Q}$$

where

$$AC = \text{Average cost per unit} = \frac{F}{Q} + V$$

Again, it is useful to examine the individual terms in order to understand their conceptual relationships:

- AC—This term represents the average cost per unit. Average cost is the basis on which the firm marks up to establish a price that can meet its financial requirements.
- NI/(CH × Q)—This term divides the target net income (NI) by the number of charge-

paying units $(CH \times Q)$. This payment source generates the firm's profit. Internally set prices will not affect the amount of payment received from cost payers or fixed price payers.

- $(AC - P_E) \times (FP \times Q)/(CH \times Q)$—This term is complex but has a simple interpretation. The difference between average cost (AC) and the fixed price (P_E) represents an additional requirement that must be covered by the firm's charge-paying units. This difference per unit is then multiplied by total fixed-price payer units $(FP \times Q)$ to generate the total loss resulting from selling services to fixed price payers. Dividing by the number of charge payers $(CH \times Q)$ translates this loss into an additional pricing increment that must be recovered from the charge payers. It is important to note that, if the fixed price paid by fixed price payers exceeds average cost, this term will be negative. Prices to the charge payers could then be reduced because the fixed price payers would be making a positive contribution to the firm's profit requirement.

To test the validity of the pricing formula, let us apply it to the data in our earlier three-payer break-even example. Assume that the volume is 96.4 cases:

$$P_1 = \$2,037.34 + \frac{\$6,000}{.3 \times 96.4}$$
$$+ \frac{(\$2,037.34 - 2,040) \times .5 \times 96.4}{.3 \times 96.4}$$
$$= \$2,037.34 + \$207.47 - 4.43 = \$2,240.38$$

The required price as determined above, \$2,240.38, is approximately equal to the price established for charge payers, \$2,240. Again, a small discrepancy exists because of rounding errors.

It should be noted that \$2,240 is not the actual charge or price set per case. The actual posted charge is \$2,400. P_1 represents the net amount actually received. Because the firm had one category of payers who paid 90 percent of charges, the effective price realized was only \$2,240. When using this pricing formula to define hospi-

tal charges, the defined price must be increased to reflect write-offs due to discounts, bad debts, or charity care. The following general formula represents the markup requirement:

$$\text{Price} = P_1/(1 - \text{write-off proportion})$$

The write-off proportion is not based upon total revenue; it is based only on the revenue from charge payers. For example, in our case example, the charge payers represented 30 percent of total cases. Of that 30 percent, 10 percent paid 100 percent of charges and 20 percent paid 90 percent of charges. The write-off percentage is thus:

$$(1/3) \times (1.0 - 1.0) + (2/3) \times (1.0 - 0.9)$$
$$= .0667$$

Using this value to mark up the required net price of \$2,240 would yield \$2,400 (\$2,240/$[1 - .0667] = \$2,400$), which is the firm's established charge.

An important issue for many health care organizations concerns the maximization of profit per dollar of rate increase. In a number of states and regions, state regulations impose restraints upon a firm's ability to raise its rates. In addition, boards may wish to minimize rate increases in any given budgetary cycle.

The percentage of any price increase that will be realized as profit can be expressed as follows:

$$\begin{array}{c}\text{\% Price increase realized as profit}\\ = (\text{\% Charge payers}) \times (1 - \text{Write-off}\\ \text{proportion})\end{array}$$

Let us assume that a nursing home is interested in learning what effect a \$5.00 increase in its per diem would have on its profitability. Its present payer mix and write-off proportions are:

Payer Percentage	Payer Mode	Write-off Proportion
10%	Medicare—pays cost	.00
50%	Private payer—pays charges	.10
40%	Medicaid—pays fixed charge per diem	.00

Thus, a \$5.00 per diem increase would generate a 45 percent increase in profit, or \$2.25 per day:

$$50\% \times (1 - .10) = 45\%$$

SUMMARY

Cost accounting systems can be designed to provide different measures of cost for different decision-making purposes. This is a desirable characteristic, not an exercise in numbers playing. To understand what measure of cost is needed for a specific purpose, the decision maker must have some knowledge of the variety of alternative concepts of cost. The terms covered in this chapter should be useful in helping decision makers define their needs more precisely.

Break-even analysis presents management with a set of simple analytical tools to provide information about the effects of costs, volume, and prices upon profitability. In this chapter, we examined the application of several break-even models for health care providers with three categories of payers. Utilization of these models should help analysts understand the conceptual framework for improving profitability in their health care organizations.

Chapter 7

Estimating Cost Behavior

David K. Dennis
Associate Professor, School of Business and Administration
Duquesne University

In order to achieve cost planning and control, it is necessary to determine how costs change in relation to other measurable and controllable factors. Reliable cost estimates are usually the key to preparing accurate operating budgets, establishing standard costs, making pricing decisions, developing performance reports, and many other managerial activities.

In many cases, rule-of-thumb methods are used to estimate costs. These informal methods are sometimes formalized, perhaps in order to increase their credibility on a superficial level. An example of this is averaging two or more past years and then adding ten percent for inflation. Unfortunately, this rule-of-thumb approach does little to reflect the complex nature of cost behavior. As a result, it often produces estimates that do not reflect economic reality.

Lack of satisfaction with the results of informal procedures, combined with improved engineering, management, statistical, and accounting information system methods, has led to the development of improved techniques for analyzing cost behavior. These improved techniques are divided into two broad categories: (1) the historical cost method and (2) the engineering method. In the

historical cost method, cost behavior relationships are determined from an examination of costs and related activity (e.g., patient days) at different levels or volumes. The engineering method may be characterized as more introspective, because it looks at the detailed physical relationship of the inputs and outputs to the productive process.

THE HISTORICAL COST METHOD

Estimating costs usually entails using past accounting data obtained from the hospital's financial and cost records to calculate how the costs relate to the volume of services performed. For example, taking total costs and dividing them by total patient days gives us a cost per patient day. This is a most rudimentary estimation of the relationship between costs and patients served. It ignores many aspects of logical and meaningful cost estimation. Although such estimates may yield numbers that are significantly different from actual costs, many hospital and health care institutions still use them. They do so because it is simple and easy. However, they often lead to dysfunctional and inefficient decisions.

Total costs divided by total patient days yield an average of cost per patient day applicable *only*

This chapter is adapted from *Handbook of Health Care Accounting and Finance*, by W.O. Cleverley (Ed.) pp 149–167, Aspen Publishers, Inc., © 1982.

for that specific volume and mix of services. When this number is used to estimate total costs at other volume and service mix levels, it rarely gives a reasonable estimate. In an attempt to facilitate the estimation of costs, the calculation has been so oversimplified that many of the important cost relationships are not taken into account.

The most important cost relationships ignored are those parts of the total costs that are *fixed* and those that are *variable*. The straight calculation of costs per patient day assumes, quite unrealistically, that all costs are variable. There are other aspects ignored, including whether the cost function follows a straight line (linear); the amount and basis for allocated indirect costs (for example, from repairs and maintenance); and variability of labor and material.

It is important to note that these *estimates* of cost behavior are usually based on *past* records of costs, services, and activities, whereas almost all of the *uses* for these estimates relate to the *future*. Examples of the use of estimated costs include budget preparation; cost containment; prospective (as well as retrospective) reimbursement; capital budgets; refer or buy decisions (for example, CT scanners); and planned increase or decrease in service levels.

To the extent that estimated costs based on past data reveal understandable behavior patterns, they can help us come up with more reasonable details for future plans. Administrators and cost accountants should not, however, be lulled into thinking that these estimation techniques can predict the future. Cost estimation allows us to think in terms of what costs might be if other events (e.g., activity level, volume, skill levels, patient mix, length of stay) actually take place.

One more cautionary note: the historical costs obtained from the hospital's accounting records include many assumptions. Often, the so-called "actual" historical costs are a result of the use of accounting rules that have been arbitrarily selected from among many possible alternatives. When we estimate cost behavior we are really measuring past historical costs in a special way and using the results to help us predict expected future costs for decision-making purposes. The

result is an approximation that we hope will be good enough for the planned use. Generally, the simplest and least costly estimation technique is used (such as the scattergraph or the high-low technique). More complicated and more costly estimation techniques, such as multiple regression analysis, are used only when a closer approximation is desired and the increased benefit due to accuracy is not exceeded by the increased cost of the estimation technique.

THE ENGINEERING METHOD

The engineering method is based on a specific physical relationship between the *inputs* to some productive process and the observed *output* from that process. An example of this for radiology (x-rays taken of a patient) would be the measurement of all the physical inputs, such as x-ray technician's time and specific tasks; radiologist's time and specific tasks; amount and type of film used; developing costs; x-ray machine time and specific tasks; and power used (heat and electricity), plus a measurement of the output, such as a diagnosis based on the x-rays. Time and motion studies are often used as a part of this method, as are efficiency studies, where the input/output ratio is determined and either compared with a previously established standard or used to generate a new standard.

The productive process yields a certain physical output (e.g., x-rays read, patient days) that is based on some mix of materials, labor, and capital equipment. Total cost (comprised of materials and labor) can be estimated after the relationship between output (production) and input is determined. To do this, prices (material) and wages (labor) are assigned to the physical inputs. The result of this is still an estimate, because we do not know whether materials and labor will be used as efficiently next time.

This method works better for estimating direct costs such as materials, labor, and machine time, than for indirect costs of operation, such as costs of services and supervision, which are usually more difficult to estimate. Indirect costs are often common to several departments or include unidentifiable or unspecified time (e.g., slack time) that would allow output to increase or decrease without a change in the inputs. It also is possible that a small increase in output may cause a large increase in costs (inputs). The commonality of costs across several departments may make it possible to estimate pro rata cost inputs for each department's outputs.

The basic orientation of the engineering method is to look at the simplest elements of production, such as labor, utilities, materials, and how they relate to output. The focus is on what is actually done, rather than on costs. Of course, the engineering method and traditional accounting methods of estimating costs can be used together. That is, we can use the engineering method to determine the appropriate unit, department, or service that provides the most meaningful basis for estimating costs.

Work Analysis as a Basis for Cost Estimation

If the cost function is unknown because it is too complicated or because it is a new process, the best way to estimate the resource use, cost, and activity level is to use work analysis and design techniques developed by industrial engineers. This is often referred to as the *engineering method*. There is another somewhat intangible advantage to the engineering method. It is oriented toward the future activity rather than the past cost. It looks at cost prediction based on what costs should be. In theory it can be based on the most efficient means of achieving the desired service. If we want to estimate future cost behavior, it makes sense to use an approach that looks toward the future activity.

It often is impossible to estimate cost behavior using the traditional cost accounting techniques such as the high-low method or regression analysis. There are two situations. One relates to cost estimation based on historical costs where no clear pattern exists; the other, to completely new services that have no historical data. The first, and perhaps the most difficult to understand, occurs when little or no apparent relationship exists between costs and activity (e.g., cost of repairs and maintenance versus patient days). In some cases, there may even be an apparent

causal relationship between cost and activity (e.g., cost of nursing service versus patient days), yet regression analysis and other cost estimation techniques may not yield satisfactory results. The underlying relationship may be so complex that no reasonable cost-versus-activity estimation can adequately describe it.

The second situation in which the use of traditional cost estimation technique is difficult occurs whenever the health care institution considers adding a new department, procedure, or service. In these cases, historical data as to cost and activity level are not available. One relatively crude level of approximation that allows us to continue to use the accounting method can be obtained by "borrowing" data from other institutions or trade sources, or by using data from similar departments and services in our own institution. Even if such data are available, however, it is difficult to predict how well they would fit for the planned operation of the new department.

Principles of Work Analysis and Design

The principles of work analysis and design represent a systematic way of looking at all necessary details of a specific task (e.g., for passing medication to patients, the system of ordering, obtaining, and administering medication would be examined) in order to do the best job with the least money, effort, material, and time. These principles represent the general objectives and procedures used to study work systems. They are summarized as follows:

- Work systems should be studied by using a systematic procedure including

    1. identification and description of the work system
    2. determination of factors that affect the work system
    3. collection and analysis of data
    4. formulation of alternative systems
    5. selection of feasible systems
    6. testing
    7. installation

- All factors affecting the performance of the work system should be investigated, including

  1. raw materials
  2. process
  3. methods
  4. work places, tools, and equipment
  5. product design
  6. physical environment
  7. nonphysical environment

- The work system should be broken down into identifiable parts or subsystems to see if any part can be eliminated, combined, or simplified.[1]

Other aspects of work analysis and design principles include system design, layout, materials handling, and motion economy. System design is used to develop an overview of the work system (delivery of medical care) including the system's basic elements (nurses, doctors, supplies) and how they relate (e.g., the health care service provided by those nurses, doctors, and supplies).

Layout of physical facilities directly affects how work is performed. When considering a new department or building, management staff should plan the layout of the facilities according to details of the new work system. Even for established physical facilities, layout changes may be possible and result in improvements in the work system. Layout concerns not only the location of machines and equipment, but also the placement of materials, workers, and their movement.

Materials handling has to do with the movement and storage of medical supplies, pharmaceuticals, and laundry as they make their way through the work system. Labor costs of actual use and inspection of these items are usually less than the labor costs of handling and storage. Handling costs, and to a certain extent, storage costs, are generally considered to be unproductive, and are therefore costs that should be minimized.

Motion economy principles are used to develop work methods and equipment needed to do a task with the easiest characteristics of human movement. Characteristics of easy movement are simultaneous, symmetrical, natural, rhythmical, and habitual. These standardized movements also help us categorize work activity so that predictable costs can be established.

Work Analysis and Design Procedures

The procedure of work analysis and design is a systematic approach to

1. looking at the detail of the work system
2. looking at relevant factors
3. collecting and analyzing data
4. describing alternative systems
5. selecting the best alternative
6. testing the work system
7. installing it
8. setting performance standards [2]

The most important part of looking at the work system is to determine the function of the work. A work system as large and complex as a hospital must be broken down into components.

Hospital work systems simple enough to be studied may include the accounting department or the personnel department, each of which has fairly specific functions. Related functions of each department must also be shown. Sources of information that will help indicate those work systems that are in the most need of improvement and also indicate the actual cost and activity elements being used include employee complaints, cost accounting records, productivity indexes, environmental conditions, preliminary rough estimates of work distribution, and discussion groups.

Human Engineering

Human engineering focuses on the interaction between workers and machines and how to improve it. This breaks down into how a given task or job is performed, how performance can be made more efficient, and how performance can be made easier. Efficiency is a measure of the number of units of output per unit of input. Ease of performance, on the other hand, is a measure of how much difficulty or how much strain results from doing a task.

Many contributions to human engineering have come from such diverse fields as acoustics, anthropology, illumination engineering, physics, psychology, thermodynamics, and time and motion study. Human engineering takes into account factors such as the effects of noise, bone and muscle structure, light perception by the eye, basic concept of force, resistance and stability, body heat generated and radiated, and how fast and efficiently a person can make specified movements. Ergonomics is the term used to describe study and design of the man-machine interface.

The use of human engineering for hospitals and other health care institutions involves two steps. The first is to identify parts of the environment that impinge upon the worker. The second is to use the proper methods to construct the most productive, safe, and pleasant work environment possible.

For example, temperature, relative humidity, and air movement can have a direct and indirect effect on worker productivity. It has been well demonstrated that the number of mistakes per worker hour goes up as the temperature rises above 75°F. Therefore, the cost of errors and of the correction of errors should be budgeted for those areas of the hospital or times of the year when temperature control is not effective. Another factor that affects costs and performance is the amount of lighting provided. If illumination is too low, it may cause errors and accidents. Adequate lighting can increase output 10 to 20 percent. Recommended levels of illumination vary by area and task to be performed. It should be noted that the lighting costs include both fixed and variable components. This means that an estimation of costs cannot be made on a one-for-one basis using the recommended foot-candle levels for a work activity level. The fact that light may be required even when no work is being performed should be reflected as a part of fixed cost.

Cost of Safety Design and Management

With the continuing increase in safety requirements at the federal (particularly the Occupational Safety and Health Administration), state, and local levels, most administrators are aware that safety costs money. However, since safety usually does not directly increase productivity, it is often an area that is not considered to be of primary importance and one that is often overlooked for cost estimation purposes, except in the most obvious of cases. For example, the cost of a fire sprinkler system would not be ignored, but the cost of determining the safest way of operating a machine or of opening a door may well be overlooked. Even when the cost of the safest method of operation of a machine is considered, the training costs necessary to educate workers are often ignored.

One way to solve this is to make the safety program an integral part of the work analysis and design program. By training, the industrial engineer is most suited to consider the specific components of human movement, material requirements, and machine design (including doors) so that a thorough estimation of the cost of worker effort and training, material, and equipment can be made.

Function and Activity Analysis

This is another area in which industrial engineers can make a contribution to cost estimation. The emphasis here is on cost classification by identification of individual or work group *function* and *activity* or by tasks that are components of the function. Activities can then be subdivided into number and type of workers, machines, and processes.

Accurate cost estimation must be preceded by appropriate cost classification. This, in fact, is the premise of zero base budgeting. Costs must be analyzed by specific function, activity level, and task. Analysis based on the relationship of cost to department or section often results in arbitrary and inappropriate management resource allocation decisions, simply because the decision maker is not dealing with actual functions and tasks. For example, in order to control cost the administrator orders a 10 percent across-the-board cut in expenditures. There is a good chance that the administrator has absolutely no idea of what specific functions and tasks will be eliminated. In zero base budgeting, these functions and tasks are identified and ranked so that an informed decision can be made.

Activities related to purchasing, for example, may be performed by a separate department or by a group within the administrative department. But purchasing is also a function. The specific tasks that make up the purchasing function include writing specifications, checking prices, determining quantities, conducting open bidding, and searching for new supplies. If cost cuts are necessary, there are some activities in purchasing that are not as important as others. These should be cut first. Zero base budgeting based on function and activity analysis allows us to do this. The traditional 10 percent across-the-board cut does not.

One of the tools used in function and activity analysis is the work distribution chart. The work distribution chart breaks down activities into tasks, hours per week required, and name and position of the person performing the task.[3]

Sampling Studies

Sampling is a way of estimating the rate of occurrence of various activities. It is a statistical technique that allows us to look at a relatively small percentage of an activity or function and to calculate an estimate for the total activity or function. For example, assume that we want to determine the amount of idle versus productive time the nurses work. Using random observations of the nurses' work, based on a random numbers table, the amount of idle time and work time is recorded. If 10 percent of the nurses' work were observed, the idle and work time would be multiplied by 10 in order to estimate total idle and work time.

The alternative is to make a continuous time study. Continuous time studies have many disadvantages, including the fact that more than one person is required, that special training is necessary, that the observer is more likely to influence the behavior of those being observed, that stopwatches and other special equipment are required, that the observer can only study one activity, and most important that continuous study is much more costly.

A sampling study of use of nurses' time involving 4,576 observations was conducted at Johns Hopkins Hospital in 1961.[4] The categories were productive and nonproductive time. In addition, productive time was divided into five subcategories:

1. direct patient care—26.4 percent
2. indirect patient care—17.4 percent
3. paper work—11.5 percent
4. communication—13.7 percent
5. other—5.7 percent

Nonproductive time (meals, rest) was 25.4 percent.

A sampling study of nurses' time allows us to classify and assign appropriate costs for categories of productive and unproductive time. From a practical point, it is unlikely that an accounting system could provide the detailed information necessary to derive this classification. Even if the accounting system were detailed enough, the data would be of questionable accuracy, for nurses do many tasks and are too busy to record each category and increment of time they have worked. Sampling is a cost-efficient way of collecting data that are representative of what would be recorded if all activity was recorded.

Product Process Analysis

Product process analysis involves understanding how materials are used in order to complete a task or perform a service. The analysis includes:

- identification of the materials
- description of the materials (weight, volume, perishability, toxicity)
- location of inventory and use (storage room, refrigerator, operating room)
- breakdown of the process into operations, movements, delays, storages, and inspections
- time order of events
- equipment
- distances that materials are moved
- amount of time for each event
- quantity of material
- description of product flow

For the last step, description of product flow, work analysis uses symbols and arrows to describe the process in detail. This provides a detailed, comprehensive description of all materials, equipment, and processes used. It is therefore easy to use to compile costs or estimated total costs for a given product or service.

Paper Work Analysis

Paper work analysis can be viewed as part of product process analysis in which the product is the various forms used by the hospital. Since procedures performed with forms differ from those used with patients, slightly different techniques are used in paper work analysis. Some of the symbols used in the form process charts are used only to represent paper work *forms* and their unique process. For example, the symbol → means "removal of information from the form for use on another form or by another person." In addition to the special symbols, the form process chart is time sequence oriented. Paper work analysis can be applied to emergency room visits, admitting procedures, hospital medical records, pharmacy, payroll, and processing applicants for employment. In a sense, paper work adds to the cost without adding to the value. Paper work analysis helps to determine what is really needed and what can be eliminated to reduce cost. It also provides a basis for accurately estimating parts of paper work cost.

Worker Process Analysis

Whereas product and paper work analyses focus on what happens to inanimate objects, worker process analysis emphasizes what the worker does. It is the most important of the three process analyses, because in a hospital the activities and tasks are labor intensive. It is also the simplest type of analysis to make on workers. Worker process analysis is used when the worker moves from place to place. If the worker does not move from place to place, other techniques, such as motion and micromotion analysis, are more appropriate.

Process analysis provides methods for determining the specific procedures that an individual uses in a task and therefore can be used simply to improve the procedures used. As with the other engineering techniques, it also provides documentation of tasks needed to perform an activity and a function. It therefore provides a work-oriented basis for cost estimation.

Work System Layouts

Work system layouts generally are at an optimum when work system flows are minimized. There are two approaches to flow analysis. One is to look at the movement (flow) of the individual worker between work places (e.g., nurses' movement between nursing station and patient). The other is to look at flow of material between work places (e.g., medical supplies or even the patient). It also is desirable to minimize backtracking and bypassing; however, for some tasks, backtracking may be difficult to eliminate. Arrangement of work places to minimize flow when backtracking is inherent to the task also may be difficult.

One of the tools used in work system layout is *travel charting*. Distance traveled serves as a good basis in ranking alternative work place layouts. An example of a travel chart is shown in Figure 7-1.

In this example, movement occurs among all four work places, A, B, C, and D. Notice the frequency of movement and the relative degree of movement revealed by the travel chart. Movements from C to A and from D to A are prime candidates for reduction; however, if reducing the number of C to A or D to A trips results in a

		From			
		A	B	C	D
	A		10	20	30
To	B	4		7	1
	C	8	1		8
	D	2	6	3	

Figure 7-1 Travel Chart

large increase in travel between other points that more than offsets the reductions, the changes should not be made.

In this example all "trips" are treated as equal in time or cost. An additional refinement is to attach a specific cost for each trip. For example, the time to go from A to B might be one minute, while the time to go from D to C might be three minutes. This information, multiplied by the cost of the personnel involved, enables an estimation of total cost for all trips and cost of various partial trips. If the pattern and frequency of trips are changed, the use of work system layouts allows an easy calculation of the new estimated total cost.

Time Study and Standard Time

Work analysis can be used to help create efficient work systems. It helps to classify and estimate cost. However, on the implementation side, it also is necessary to plan, direct, and control the work system so that actual results are obtained from the work analysis and design program. If this is done, estimated cost, based on the work analysis and design, will be close to actual cost. The processes, equipment, and work places may be efficiently designed only for a given level of service. If the patient volume should drop, it may be difficult to adjust the processes, equipment, and work places to achieve efficient operation at the lower level. Thus, actual cost can vary dramatically from estimated cost if the critical underlying elements on which the estimated costs were calculated change. Time study and standard time help identify the underlying elements on which the cost is estimated.

Work measurement, and specifically *time study*, are techniques that measure the amount of time and the number of people required to accomplish a task under a given set of conditions. Their purpose is to develop standard times. Standard times have several uses. They permit more effective scheduling, setting of performance standards, and task assignments for members of a crew and make it possible to compare different methods of doing the same

task. They also permit the estimation of a standard cost based on the standard time, which in turn is based on a well-specified task or unit of work. Note that there is a difference between time study for work management (as used here) and the much more informal recording of time for work analysis.

Standard times also can be obtained by references developed by the method time measurement association (MTM). The tasks must first be broken down into standard work units. The standard time for these standard work units is then looked up in the standard time reference. Using standard time data to construct an overall standard time for a task is usually faster than doing a direct time study. It also can be used for work not yet performed. Some institutions develop their own elemental time data rather than using MTM standard time data because of the specialized nature of the tasks in their work places.

It is relatively simple to estimate total cost if the standard time units are known. The cost of each person performing each standard work unit is compiled and the total cost calculated. The advantage of standard time and work units is that it makes calculation of total cost relatively painless and also yields a cost number that can be used as an expected cost. These costs are based on well-established standards and can therefore be used in the budget for planning and control purposes.

ACCOUNTING ESTIMATES OF COST BEHAVIOR

Estimating the cost behavior of the health care facility's various expenditures is of crucial importance. There are two broad categories in which estimating cost behavior is important. First, it is necessary to collect information as to cost patterns (direct cost versus indirect cost and variable cost versus fixed cost) so that accurate cost classifications, budgets, and cost variances can be calculated. This, in turn, allows the decision maker to use these data in the day-to-day management of the health care facility.

Which costs, if any, will increase in the laboratory if patient load increases and the number of laboratory tests increases can be answered by using estimating techniques (such as high-low or regression analysis). These methods are used with cost classifications that describe in a common-sense way the different costs that the laboratory incurs.

Here we see the essence of estimating cost behavior: to determine as best as we can the way the cost changes in reference to changes in some important activity. The activity measure is usually volume (units of production, such as number of lab tests) or time oriented. Based on this estimating process, almost all costs fit into one of two categories: fixed costs that *do not* change with changes in volume, and variable costs that *do* change with changes in volume.

The other major use of estimated and classified cost behavior is to justify reimbursement, especially under prospective systems from third-party reimbursers. This, in turn, makes the estimating of cost even more important, since the setting of charges for those patients without a third-party payer is dependent on both the necessity to cover all costs associated with the individual patient (including fixed and variable, direct and indirect) and those costs not reimbursable by Blue Cross and Blue Shield, Medicare, and Medicaid. This includes bad debt allowance on patients without insurance, charity, malpractice insurance, courtesy discounts, and profit.[5]

Just as different concepts of cost are required for different decisions, the estimation of cost behavior often requires unique methodologies for cost measurement.[6] Cost data are reported by the cost accounting system. In the ideal case, the cost accounting system classifies and reports costs by products (outputs or services); by responsibility centers (departments or larger); or by both. However, the real world is quite another thing. This is especially so for health care facilities, where the "product" and/or the responsibility center are defined in such a way that the primary task, and thus the primary cost, are not easily identifiable.

Many secondary and service departments contribute to a given responsibility center or product. Examples include housekeeping, accounting, repairs and maintenance, and depreciation on the building. Many cost allocations have to be made before reaching the end designated as "patient service." The large number of cost allocations and the general complexity of the "product" provided to the patient are the reasons for the ambiguous nature of cost reports in many hospitals. The infamous "cost per patient day" is an example. It is often calculated as total costs tied to the activity measure, "patient days."

Even with limitations imposed by inadequate cost accounting systems and what may be inappropriate measures of activities (patient days), the proper use of techniques for estimating cost behavior can reveal some useful information. Generally, this information falls into one of two categories: the amount of the total cost that is variable (changes with the activity level) or the amount that is fixed.

In addition to estimating fixed and variable cost components and negotiating third-party reimbursement rates, cost behavior estimates can be used to

1. build a flexible budget
2. reach make or buy decisions
3. increase or decrease volume (add patients, add beds)
4. decide whether to make capital expenditures

Causal Models

The basic assumption of estimating cost, revenue, and activity relationships with causal models is that there exists some function that describes their relationships. Due to the ambiguity and arbitrary allocations that are a part of most hospital cost reporting systems, the direct relationship of cost and activity may not be apparent. Nevertheless, the relationship usually exists and can be estimated using the proper cost estimation techniques.

The type of relationship of the variables can be placed in one of three categories. In an *associative* relationship, the two variables, cost and activity, occur at a rate that can be specified. The *causal-static* (cause and effect) relationship analyzes current and past data for *cost* and *activity* relationships without making a statement about the effect of time. The *causal-dynamic* relationship makes predictions for the future as in a time series; that is, although the cost and activity variables had a certain relationship in the past, the time series prediction may specify a different relationship in the future based on the direction of change that is predicted for the cost and activity variables. Assumptions as to degree of causality are not necessarily related to the technique used to analyze the data.

Wheelwright and Clarke[7] collected information on forecasting methods used by 127 companies. The eight most commonly used methods included three qualitative methods: jury of executive opinion (used by 82 percent), sales force composite (74 percent), and customer expectations (57 percent). Of the five quantitative models, two were explanatory-regression analysis (76 percent) and econometric models (65 percent). The time series models were Box-Jenkins (40 percent); time series smoothing (75 percent); and index numbers, a type of decomposition model (67 percent). However, in a recent survey (1987) of a large number of hospitals, none reported using regression analysis of the high-low method. Most reported using judgment to estimate costs.

The results of the survey by Wheelwright and Clarke[8] show that regression analysis is used far more widely than any other quantitative technique. The only close competitors are the qualitative techniques, jury of executive opinion, which is used slightly more than regression analysis, and sales force composite, which is used slightly less.

Regression analysis is a popular choice because

1. most users have the technical ability to feel comfortable with it
2. its cost is reasonable
3. it is easy to use for cost, activity, and time-related prediction problems
4. it has good method characteristics such as accuracy and self-assessment statistics

Before discussing the regression analysis examples, we will discuss briefly some of the qualitative estimation techniques.

Qualitative Methods

Qualitative methods of forecasting continue to be used by many companies for three reasons. One, qualitative methods incorporate the decision maker's experience, analysis of the facts and intuition about the cost function, market, or service being considered. Two, qualitative methods require little or no training. Three, the process or method is understood by everyone.

There are two general types of qualitative methods. The more well known are basically surveys of opinion. Four of the better-known approaches to this qualitative method are

1. Delphi method
2. jury of executive opinion
3. sales force composite
4. customer expectations

The other types of qualitative methods include various approaches to structuring those phenomena, objects, costs, and activities being studied. Most of these techniques have been derived from quantitative *and* qualitative branches of mathematics. They often present a structure that can be used to organize variable relationships into a meaningful pattern. This structure usually takes a visual or graphic form.

Of the four better-known survey of opinion estimation techniques, the Delphi method is the best known, even though it is not widely used. It has two advantages over other qualitative methods. First, the members of the panel of experts being surveyed do not have to meet together. Thus, it avoids social pressures and personality biases. Second, the results can be shown as a range of values rather than a single (often misleading) point estimate.

The panel of experts usually includes five to fifteen members. They are polled by a panel coordinator, who compiles their initial responses. The summary of initial responses is then circulated to the individual panel members, who, in turn, are asked for another estimation in conjunction with an explanation as to why the individual panel member gave an estimate significantly different from 50 percent (the middle two quartiles) of the rest of the panel. This process is repeated several times, until a consensus has been reached.[9] The Delphi method is sometimes viewed as a more cumbersome variation of the jury of executive opinion method.

The other three methods of qualitative estimation, the jury of executive opinion, sales force composite, and customer expectations, all combine managerial judgments to arrive at a forecast. For the jury of executive opinion, the organization brings together executives from areas such as production, finance, marketing, purchasing, and staff operations in order to benefit the broad experience. The sales force composite is similar except that it uses salespeople and sales management and is more of a bottom-up approach. The customer expectations approach utilizes opinions of those outside the organization. With this approach, customers (doctors, patients) are asked what they expect their needs and requirements to be. This technique is difficult to use in markets where customers are numerous or not easily identified.

The second type of qualitative method includes the relevance tree method and time-independent methods. These methods help decision makers make estimates of variable relationships by providing or suggesting a basis structure that may be pertinent to the underlying variable relationships.

The relevance tree method was originally developed in decision theory as a quantitative technique. After the tree is developed, a panel of experts is asked to vote on each branch in order to determine the more important paths. It has been used to help determine what technological developments are necessary to reach long-range goals.[10] It also can be used to determine the likely costs necessary for a new process.

Quantitative Methods

The four quantitative methods of estimating cost behavior shown here are

1. the visual fit method (using a scattergraph)
2. the high-low method
3. simple regression analysis
4. multiple regression analysis [11]

The examples using these methods use an activity measure in the radiology department (x-rays taken) and the cost associated with that activity.

Regression analysis is the most widely used method in industries outside the health care field, and it is often used to estimate cost of activity relationships. Because the applicability of the tool is equally relevant to the health care field, we will discuss two examples of this type of application of regression analysis.

The examples shown include visual fit method, high-low method, simple regression analysis, and multiple regression analysis. An application of multiple regression analysis used as a time series forecast to predict volume of service is also discussed briefly. The first four examples are explanatory models in that they look only at cost versus activity relationships. The fifth example is a forecasting model that predicts the cost/revenue that might occur in the next accounting period.

Visual Fit. Visual fit is the easiest and quickest way to produce a straight line that approximates the cost behavior using a scattergraph. Simply plot the activity data (number of x-rays taken) on one side and cost data (total labor costs) on the other (Figure 7-2). Use a ruler to

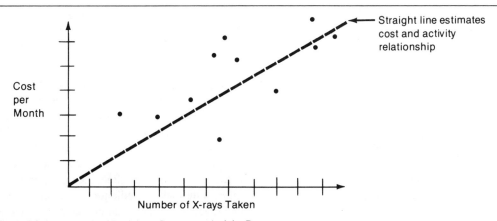

Figure 7-2 Scattergraph of Radiology Cost versus Activity Data

Table 7-1 X-rays Taken versus Labor Cost per Eight-Hour Shift

X = Number of x-rays taken on an eight-hour shift	Y = Total labor cost per eight-hour shift
120	$ 540
60	425
100	530
130	580
80	500
180	688
20	550
140	610
70	475
40	450
160	650

draw a straight line through the most points possible. Although this "quick and dirty" method can yield estimates of cost behavior that are accurate enough for many practical applications, it is not as objective or systematic as regression analysis. In addition, there is no documentation as to the specific data points considered, even though in theory all of the data points are considered.

High-Low Method. The high-low method is more objective than the visual fit method and documents the specific points used. Our example will use the data shown in Table 7-1, which show the activity in the radiology department as measured in number of x-rays taken versus the cost as measured by labor cost for an eight-hour shift. The data points (Table 7-1) for the highest cost and lowest cost are used to calculate the slope of the line. The slope of the line is interpreted as the variable cost per unit of activity. Calculation of the high-low method is illustrated in Figure 7-3.

High cost = $688   High activity = 180 x-rays
Low cost = $425   taken
                    Low activity = 60 x-rays
                                      taken

Variable rate
  = $\dfrac{\text{Changes in total cost}}{\text{Change in activity}}$

  = $\dfrac{\$688 - \$425}{180 - 60} = \dfrac{263}{120}$

  = $2.19 per x-ray taken

Fixed cost component = Total cost − variable
                                              cost

Fixed cost = $688 − ($2.19 × 180)
Fixed cost = $688 − $394.20
Fixed cost = $293.80

Therefore, we can state the total cost formula as:

Total cost = fixed cost + variable cost
Total cost = $293.80 + ($2.19 × number of
                              x-rays taken)

At 175 x-rays taken, the total cost is estimated as

Total cost = $293.80 + ($2.19 × 175)
Total cost = $677.05

While the high-low method offers more objectivity and documentation, it can give misleading results, as seen in Figure 7-4. This figure shows that a better estimate could have been achieved by using the visual fit method, which considers all points. In this example, the high-low method both overstates the variable cost and understates the fixed cost. Using the extreme points of cost makes the high-low method easy to use; however, it also causes the difficulty with this method since the extreme points often do not represent the normal cost function.

Simple Regression Analysis. Our first example looks at the cost and activity relationships in the radiology department of a hospital. Data for this example are presented in Table 7-1. Remember, even though regression analysis yields a relationship between two (or more) sets of data in the form of a straight line, the main purpose is to assist the task of prediction, decision making, and feedback.[12] The administrator can use one

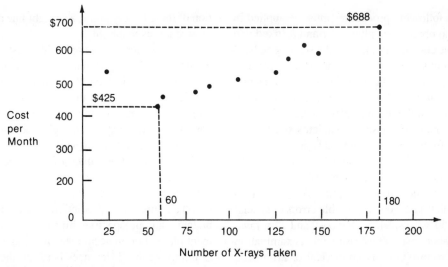

Figure 7-3 High-Low Method of Estimating Cost

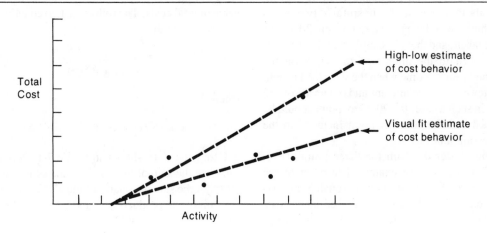

Figure 7-4 Scattergraph Showing High-Low Estimate versus Visual Fit Estimate

of the variables in a simple regression to predict the other variable and how far he or she might be off (probable error). For example, if the administrator knows the number of x-ray photographs taken, the relationship revealed by regression analysis will allow predictions of the cost of the x-rays. Actual costs can be compared with the estimate to find out how close the regression estimate is to actual.

The estimated cost function most often of interest is the total cost function, which is made up of fixed cost and variable cost:

Total cost (TC) = fixed cost (FC) + variable cost (VC)

where

FC = fixed dollar amount of cost is the same from month to month

VC = cost per unit of activity multiplied by the activity level for that month

Usually, these are restated as follows:

$$Y = a + bx$$

where

Y = total costs
a = fixed cost
b = variable cost per unit
x = number of units of activity
bx = total variable cost

The following procedures must be applied in order to obtain the values of *a* and *b* (fixed and variable costs). First, look at the scattergraph for data points that do not fit the general pattern. These points may be the result of unusual situations such as a strike or a local emergency, or they may be the result of clerical error. In either case, it may be advisable to delete extreme data points from the regression analysis.

The data shown in Table 7-1 give the radiologist labor cost (for each eight-hour shift sample) versus the activity in number of x-rays. Two data points stand out as possible errors or special cases: 60 x-rays, $425 labor cost; and 20 x-rays, $550 labor cost. Let us assume that examination of the records reveals no clerical or arithmetic error. Let us also assume that examination of the circumstances that produced each data point reveals that one of the hospital's two x-ray machines was being repaired when 20 x-rays were taken, and that the sample for the 60 x-rays was taken in the middle of the week on the midnight shift, a time when the workload is light and fewer x-ray technicians and others are on the job. In such a case, the 20 x-ray point should be deleted and the 60 x-ray point included in the regression analysis.

The scatter diagram for these points (Figure 7-3) also can be examined in order to see whether a straight line is a reasonable approximation of the relationship between labor costs and the number of x-rays taken. With the excep-

tion of the 20 x-ray point, a straight line appears to give a reasonable fit.

The next step is to apply the least squares method in order to pick the straight line that best describes the points on the scatter design. The (vertical) distance from the straight line to each point should be the minimum possible when compared with any other straight line that might be drawn. The object is to apply the least squares method to find the values of the constants *a* (fixed cost) and *b* (variable cost per unit) so that it will be possible to calculate y^* (total calculated costs) and use it as a prediction in our forecasts, budgets, and prospective third-party reimbursement plans. For an accurate estimation we want to minimize the differences between the actual cost and the estimated cost represented by the regression line $(y - y^*)^2$, where y is the observed value of total costs. The following two equations are used to do this:

$$\Sigma y = na + b\Sigma(x)$$
$$\Sigma(xy) = a\,\Sigma(x) + b\,\Sigma(x^2)$$

where

n = the number of observations (data points)

Using the data shown in Table 7-1 we can calculate the sum of the x's (Σx), the sum of the y's (Σy), the sum of squares of the x's (Σx^2), and the sum of the products of x and y (Σxy). These data are shown in Table 7-2.

Table 7-2 Computations for Least Squares Method

	X (no. of x-rays)	Y (actual total costs)	X²	XY
1	120	$540	14,400	$64,800
2	60	425	3,600	25,500
3	100	530	10,000	53,000
4	130	580	16,900	75,400
5	80	500	6,400	40,000
6	180	688	32,400	123,840
	20	550	*	*
7	140	610	19,600	85,400
8	70	475	4,900	33,250
9	40	450	1,600	18,000
10	160	650	25,600	104,000
	$\Sigma x = 1,080$	$\Sigma y = \$5,348$	$\Sigma x^2 = 135,400$	$\Sigma xy = \$623,190$

*Delete: nonrepresentative data point.

Substituting into the two simultaneous equations gives us:

$$5,348 = 10a + 1,080b \qquad (1)$$
$$623,190 = 1,080a + 135,400b \qquad (2)$$

Rearranging the simultaneous equations we obtain:

(multiplying the first equation by 108)

$$108 \times [5,348 = 10a + 1,080b]$$

$$577,584 = 1,080a + 116,640b$$

(subtract the second equation from the first to eliminate one [unknown] variable)

$$577,548 = 1080a + 116,640b$$

Subtract: $623,190 = 1080a + 135,400b$

| 45,606 | -0- | 18,994b |

$$b = \frac{45,606}{18,994}$$

$$b = \$2.401 \text{ estimated variable cost per x-ray}$$

(substituting b into one of the original equations)

$$5,348 = 10a + (1,080 \times \$2.401)$$

$$5,348 = 10a + 2,593.16$$

$$10a = 2,744.84$$

$$a = \$274.48 \text{ estimated fixed cost}$$

Substituting these amounts into the regression equation for a straight line ($y = a + bx$) we get:

$$y = \$274.48 + 2.401x$$

where y^* is the predicted of estimated total labor cost in the radiology department. We distinguish between y^*, the predicted value arrived at by use of the equation, and y, which is the actual total cost observed when we sample an eight-hour shift for x, the number of x-rays. For example, for $x = 100$, the equation predicts total labor costs of $y^* = \$274.48 + (\$2.401 \times 100)$ or $y = \$514.58$. Compare this with the actual cost observed when $x = 100$ (for one of the sample eight-hour shifts) of $y = \$530.00$. Because represented by $y^* = \$274.48 + \$2.401 \times x$, the prediction made by the line will always produce some error. For $x = 100$, the error is $y - y^*$ ($\$530.00 - \$514.58) = \$15.42$.

The important thing to remember is that the regression equation yields a line that is an average of the actual data points. By their very nature, averages rarely are as precise as the original observations, and they have all the other limitations averages have; that is, an average may include the influence of data points that should not have been included, especially if one hopes to find a line expressing "normal" relationships.

The question of how well the regression equation relates x (the number of x-rays) with y (cost) can be answered by calculating the coefficient of determination (r^2). In a general way, this is a measure of the extent to which the independent variable x relates to changes in the dependent variable y.

More precisely, the coefficient of determination (r^2) indicates the proportion of the variance $(y - y^*)^2$ that is explained by x. It is expressed as:

$$r^2 = 1 - \frac{\Sigma(y - y^*)^2}{\Sigma(y - \bar{y})^2}$$

where

$\bar{y}$ is the average of all y's

This really explains the *proportion* of the variation in total costs (y) that is accounted for by difference in the size of x (the number of x-rays taken per eight-hour shift). Needless to say, the higher (r^2) is the better the estimation of cost behavior calculated by the regression analysis.

Four assumptions must be satisfied in order to make valid inferences about the population (all labor costs in relationship to all levels of the number of x-rays) from the sample data (actual data observed):

1. Linearity exists between x and y; that is, their relationship is a straight line _____ $(y - y^*) = 0$ on average.
2. There is a uniform scatter of data points all along the regression line; that is, the standard deviation and variances are constant for all x.
3. The placement of any one data point on the scatter diagram is independent of any other point; that is, the costs are not "sticky" or serially correlated.
4. The points around the regression line are normally distributed.[13]

The first two assumptions, linearity and constant variance, can be checked by looking at the data on a scatter diagram. Because this step is often neglected, inappropriate data relationships are assumed. Two pressures are operating here. The first is the rush to analyze the data and produce a regression line for the cost/activity equation. This mechanical approach to data analysis can produce disastrous results. The second is the erroneous view that any data analysis procedure related to looking at a graph or diagram is somehow less meaningful than a list of numbers or an algebraic equation.

Serial correlation, which is the third assumption, can be a problem when the observed data are collected from successive time periods. Suppose that a sample is drawn from the eight-hour day shift for every Tuesday, Wednesday, and Thursday for two months. It is possible that the differences $(y - y^*)$ between the observed data point and that given by the regression equation are "artificially" correlated; that is, they are not independent. When this happens, the standard errors of the regression coefficients are underestimated, the sampling variance of the coefficients will be large, and the predictions of cost made from the regression equations will be more variable than is usually the case.[14] Understatement of the standard error is an especially seductive error, because it lulls the person doing the cost estimation into believing that the regression line is much better than it really is. Most computerized regression analysis programs contain tests that can be applied to check for linearity, constant variance, serial correlation, and normal distribution.

Multiple Regression. Simple regression analysis is the method of choice when only one variable, such as labor hours or number of x-rays, gives a good prediction of cost. However, there are many situations where a much better prediction can be made if two or more independent variables are used (x^1 = number of x-rays, x_2 = number of labor hours, x_3 = number of machine hours).[15] The typical linear multiple regression equation takes the form:

$$y = a + bx_1 + cx_2 + dx_3 + \dots n$$

where y is the variable to be predicted (for example, cost); x_1, x_2, and x_3 are the independent variables on which the prediction is based (such as labor hours, number of patients, number of hours open); a, b, c, and d are unknown constants; and n is what is left over (the net effect of all other factors including errors). Typical independent variables that can be used for cost predictions in the health care industry are included in Table 7-3.

Some of the independent variables in Table 7-3 will be used to show how multiple regression can be used for cost estimation and analysis. Although the details of multiple regression are beyond the scope of this chapter, the least squares method, as well as the other procedures used for simple regression analysis, are applicable. Many computer programs also are available for multiple regression analysis.

For an example, let us return to the radiology department and see how we might go about improving the estimation of total labor cost. Assume there are two x-ray machines: a large one and a smaller horizonal unit. Also assume there are two types of x-ray film: fast and extra fast. The following multiple regression can be stated:

$$y = a + bx_1 + cx_2 + dx_3 + ex_4$$

Table 7-3 Typical Independent Variables in the Health Care Industry for Use in Multiple Regression Analysis

Dependent (y)	Independent ($x_1 + x_2 + \dots + x_n$)
Cost	Labor hours
	Labor cost
	Machine hours
	Weight
	Dimension
	Temperature
	Patient age
	Diagnosis-related group
	Type of machine
	Type of labor
	Skilled nursing personnel
	Number of x-rays taken
	Number of laboratory tests
	Intensity of care classification
	Number of ancillary services required

where y = total costs, a = fixed cost, x_1 = the large x-ray machine hours, b = the cost per hour the large x-ray machine operates, x_2 = the small x-ray machine hours, c = the cost per hour the small x-ray machine operates, x_3 = the number of fast x-ray films, d = the cost per unit of fast x-ray films used, x_4 = the number of very fast x-ray films, and e = the cost per unit of very fast x-ray films used.

Other factors that might be included in this multiple regression equation include the following:

1. sizes of film
2. number of eight-hour shifts
3. number of board-certified radiologists, residents, and radiology technicians
4. number of patients rated as routine cases and number rated as severe cases (e.g., patients rated as severe take between 0 and 20 x-rays, while those rated as routine take between 0 and 4)

Forecasting with Multiple Regression Analysis. Some hospitals use multiple regression analysis to forecast volume of services for the revenue budget. This can be applied equally well to cost. A multiple regression model applied to data at St. Joseph Hospital in Lexington, Kentucky, used 47 variables initially. These 47 variables were related to patient days and could be analyzed over a 99-month period. These 47 variables were eventually reduced to 4 variables: year, month, patient days, and patient days two months ago. The final model, based on a multiple regression of the four variables, was selected from 1,023 difference models generated by the computer. It was significantly more accurate than either the simple regression model or the percentage change method.[16]

SUMMARY

There are two basic approaches to estimating cost behavior: the engineering method and the accounting method. The engineering method is more costly because it focuses on the details of a task, process, or activity, but it provides more normative costs. That is, the engineering method produces a better estimate of what costs should be, both for current activities and for new activities planned for the future. Because of this, the engineering method is intrinsically superior for budgeting purposes or whenever a best estimate of what the cost should be is important.

The accounting method uses past cost and activity relationships to estimate cost behavior. Because it is based on the costs that occurred rather than what costs should be, it may give less desirable data for budgeting and cost control purposes than the engineering method. However, if the cost and activity relationships are likely to remain the same as in the past and the actual costs incurred are assumed to be the costs that should have been incurred, then the accounting method may give acceptable results. Of course, an important consideration in favor of the accounting method is that it is generally considerably less expensive to use. The one exception to this is when a past data base does not exist or for various reasons is not usable.

When past data are available and are viewed as acceptable for estimating cost behavior, there are several techniques that yield a line or equation representing a line that describes the relationship between cost and activity. These include visual fit, high-low method, simple regression analysis, and multiple regression analysis. Multiple regression analysis often yields the most accurate equation describing the data.

NOTES

1. Edward A. Kazanian, *Work Analysis and Design for Hotels, Restaurants and Institutions* (Westport, Conn.: AVI Publishing Co., 1979), pp. 45–46.
2. Ibid., p. 27.
3. Ibid., pp. 123–30.
4. Ibid., p. 159.
5. William O. Cleverley, *Essentials of Hospital Finance* (Rockville, Md.: Aspen Publishers, Inc., 1978), p. 99.
6. Ibid., p. 82.
7. Steven C. Wheelwright and Darral G. Clarke, "Corporate Forecasting: Promise and Reality," *Harvard Business Review* (November–December 1976): pp. 40–64.

8. Ibid.

9. Doyle Z. Williams, Wig B. DeMoville, and Larry D. Franklin, "Costs and Forecasting," in *The Managerial and Cost Accountants Handbook*, ed. Homer A. Black and James Don Edwards (Homewood, Ill.: Dow-Jones-Irwin, 1979), p. 1221.

10. Ibid., pp. 1208–1209.

11. William O. Cleverley, "One Step Further—A Multi-Variable Flexible Budget," *Hospital Financial Management* (April 1976): 34–43.

12. Charles H. Horngren, *Cost Accounting—A Managerial Emphasis* (Englewood Cliffs, N.J.: Prentice-Hall, 1972), pp. 810–811.

13. Ibid., pp. 821–822.

14. Ibid., pp. 824–825.

15. Cleverley, "One Step Further," pp. 37–39.

16. Vincent W. Donlon, "Statistical Methods to Forecast Volume of Services for the Revenue Budget," *Hospital Financial Management* (April 1975): 38–47.

Chapter 8

Product Costing

William O. Cleverley
Professor, Graduate Program in Hospital and Health Services Management
The Ohio State University

Since the implementation of the prospective payment system, there has been a rapidly growing interest in cost accounting. The increased interest in developing sophisticated cost accounting systems is not limited to the hospital industry; it has infected all health care industry sectors. Most, if not all, of this interest is due to the establishment of fixed prices for services and to the increasing economic competition among health care providers.

A variety of terms have been used to describe the new methodology in cost accounting. Some refer to it as costing by diagnosis-related groups (DRGs), others call it standard costing, and still others refer to it as costing by product line or as product costing. For the purposes of this chapter, we shall use the term *product costing*. A product or product line is more generic, compared with the terms used in the other definitions. Also, the concept of product costing can be related to costing in other industries; most of the principles of product costing have been examined and debated for many years in the manufacturing sector. Thus, we do not have to reinvent the wheel in order to develop costing principles for the health care industry.

This chapter is reprinted from *Essentials of Health Care Finance*, 2nd ed., by W.O. Cleverley, pp. 225–241, Aspen Publishers, Inc., © 1986.

RELATIONSHIP TO PLANNING, BUDGETING, AND CONTROL

Cost information is of value only as it aids in the management decision-making process. Figure 8-1 presents a schematic that summarizes the planning-budgeting-control process in a business. Of special interest is the decision output of the planning process. The planning process should detail the products or product lines that the business will produce during the planning horizon.

Products and Product Lines

The terms *product* and *product line* seem fairly simple and easy to understand in most businesses. For example, a finished car is the product of the automobile company; individual types of cars may then be grouped to form product lines, such as the Chevrolet product line of General Motors.

Can this definition of a product be transported to the health care sector? Many individuals feel very strongly that products cannot be defined so easily in health care firms. The major dilemma seems to arise in the area of patients versus products. In short, is the product the patient, or is the product the individual services provided, such as lab tests, nursing care, and meals? In most situa-

```
      ┌─────────────┐
      │  Planning   │
      └─────────────┘
             │
             ▼
      ┌─────────────┐
      │  Product    │
      │  Lines      │
      └─────────────┘
             │
             ▼
      ┌─────────────┐
      │  Budgeting  │
      └─────────────┘
             │
             ▼
        ╭───────────╮
        │ Resource  │
        │Expectations│
        ╰───────────╯
             │
             ▼
      ┌─────────────┐
      │  Control    │
      └─────────────┘
             │
             ▼
        ╭───────────╮
        │ Corrective│
        │  Action   │
        ╰───────────╯
```

Figure 8-1 The Planning-Budgeting-Control Process

tions, we believe that the patient is the basic product of a health care firm. This means that the wide range of services provided to patients—such as nursing, prescriptions, and tests—are to be viewed as intermediate products, not final products. There is in fact little difference between this interpretation and that applied in most manufacturing settings. For example, automobile fenders are, on one hand, a final product; on the other, they are only an intermediate product in preparation of the final product, the completed automobile. Ultimately, it is the automobile that is sold to the public, not the fenders. In the same vein, it is the treated patient who generates revenue, not the individual service provided in isolation. Indeed, a hospital that provided only lab tests would not be a hospital but rather a laboratory. In short, it takes patients to be a health care provider.

Product lines represent an amalgamation of patients in a way that makes business sense. Sometimes people use the term *strategic business units* to refer to areas of activity that may stand alone. For our purpose, a product line is a unit of business activity that requires a go or no-go decision. For example, eliminating one DRG

is probably not possible, because that DRG may be linked to other DRGs within a clinical specialty area; it may be impossible to stop producing DRG 36 (retinal procedures) without also eliminating other DRGs, such as DRG 39 (lens procedure). Thus, in many cases, it is the clinical specialty, for example, ophthalmology, that defines the product line.

Budgeting and Resource Expectations

The budgeting phase of operations involves a translation of the product-line decisions reached earlier into a set of resource expectations. The primary purpose of this is twofold. First, management must assure itself that there will be sufficient funds flow to maintain financial solvency. Just as you and I must live within our financial means, so must any health care business entity. Second, the resulting budget serves as a basis for management control. If budget expectations are not realized, management must discover why not and take corrective actions. A budget or set of resource expectations can be thought of as a standard costing system. The budget represents management's expectations of how costs should behave, given a certain set of volume assumptions.

The key aspect of budgeting is the translation of product-line decisions into precise and specific sets of resource expectations. This involves five basic steps:

1. Define the volume of patients by case type to be treated in the budget period.
2. Define the standard treatment protocol by case type.
3. Define the required departmental volumes.
4. Define the standard cost profiles for departmental outputs.
5. Define the prices to be paid for resources.

The primary output of the budgeting process is a series of departmental budgets that spell out what costs should be during the coming budget period. Three separate sets of standards are involved in the development of these budgets (the three sets of standards are described later in the chapter).

Control and Corrective Action

The control phase of business operations monitors actual cost experience and compares it with budgetary expectations. If there are deviations from expectations, management analyzes the causes of the deviation. If the deviation is favorable, management may seek to make whatever created the variance a permanent part of operations. If the variance is unfavorable, action will be taken in an attempt to prevent a recurrence. Much of the control phase centers around the topic of variance analysis, which is explored in depth in Chapter 9.

THE COSTING PROCESS

Most firms, whether they are hospitals, nursing homes, or steel manufacturers, have fairly similar costing systems. In fact, in most cases, the similarities outweigh the differences. Figure 8-2 presents a schematic of the cost measurement process that exists in most businesses.

Valuation

Valuation has always been a thorny issue for accountants, one that has not been satisfactorily resolved even today. We need only to look at the current controversy over replacement costs versus historical costs to see the problem in full

bloom. Here, for discussion purposes, we have chosen to split the valuation process into two areas: (1) basis and (2) assignment over time. These two areas are not mutually exclusive; to some degree they overlap. However, both determine the total value of a resource that is used to cost a final product.

The valuation basis is the process by which a value is assigned to each and every resource transaction occurring between the entity being accounted for and another entity. In most situations this value is historical cost.

Having established a basis value for the resource transaction, there are two major types of situations in which that value will have to be assigned over time. First, the value may be expended prior to the actual reporting of expense. The best example of this is depreciation. Second, the expense may be recognized prior to an actual expenditure. Normal accruals such as wages and salaries are examples of this situation.

Allocation

The end result of the cost allocation process is to assign to direct departments all costs or values determined in the valuation phase of costing. Two phases of activity are involved in this assignment. First, all resource values to be recorded as expense in a given period are assigned or allocated to the direct and indirect departments as direct expenses. Second, once the ini-

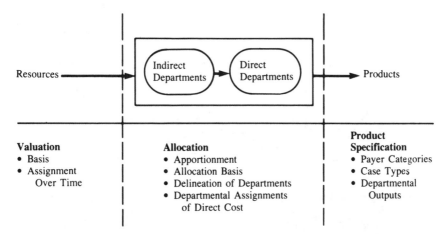

Figure 8-2 The Cost Measurement Process

tial cost assignment to individual departments has been made, a further allocation is required. In this phase the expenses of the indirect departments are assigned to the direct departments.

Using this framework for analysis, costing issues may be subcategorized. In the initial cost assignment phase, there appear to be two major action categories involved in the costing process: (1) assigning the cost to departments and (2) defining the indirect and direct departments.

In the first category, a situation may arise in which the departmental structure currently specified is not questioned, but some of the initial value assignments are. For example, premiums paid for malpractice insurance might be charged to the administration and general department, or they may be charged directly to the nursing and professional departments that are involved. In the second category, a situation may arise in which the existing departmental structure has to be revised. For example, the administration and general department may be split into several new departments, such as nonpatient telephones, data processing, purchasing, admitting, business office, and other.

In the second phase of cost allocation, the reassignment from indirect departments to direct departments, there are also two primary categories of action involved: (1) selection of the cost apportionment method and (2) selection of the appropriate allocation basis. With respect to the first category, cost apportionment methods—such as step-down, double-distribution, or simultaneous-equations—are simply mathematical algorithms that redistribute cost from existing indirect departments to direct departments, given defined allocation bases. An example of the second action category is the selection of square feet or hours worked for housekeeping as an appropriate allocation basis for an indirect department.

Product Specification

In most health care firms, there are two phases in the production (or treatment) process. The schematic in Figure 8-3 illustrates this process and also introduces a few new terms.

In Stage 1 of the production process, resources are acquired and consumed within departments to produce a product, defined as a service unit. Here, two points need to be emphasized. First, all departments have service units,

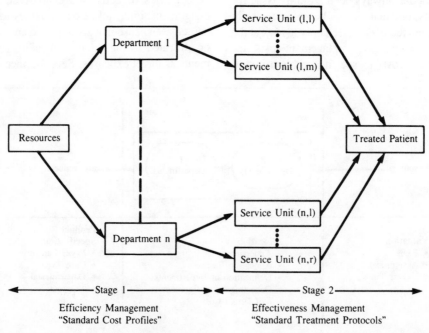

Figure 8-3 The Production Process for Health Care Firms

but not all departments have the same number of service units. For example, nursing may provide four levels of care: Acuity Levels 1, 2, 3, and 4. Laboratory, in contrast, may have a hundred or more separate service units that relate to the provision of specific tests. Second, not all service units can be directly associated with the delivery of patient care; some of the service units may be only indirectly associated with patient treatment. For example, housekeeping cleans laboratory areas, but there is no direct association between this function and patient treatment. However, the cleaning of a patient's room could be regarded as a service that is directly associated with a patient.

Stage 2 of the production process relates to the actual consumption of specific service units in the treatment of a patient. Much of the production process is managed by the physician. This is true regardless of the setting (hospital, nursing home, home health care firm, or clinic). The physician prescribes the specific service units that will be required to treat a given patient effectively.

The lack of management authority in this area complicates management's efforts to budget and control its costs. This is not meant to be a negative criticism of current health care delivery systems; all of us would prefer to have a qualified physician rather than a lay health care executive direct our care. Yet this is perhaps the area of greatest difference between health care firms and other business entities. Management at General Motors can decide which automobiles will have factory-installed air conditioning and tinted glass and which will not. In contrast, a hospital manager will have great difficulty in attempting to direct a physician to either prescribe or not prescribe a given procedure in the treatment of a patient.

Health care products to be costed may vary depending upon the specific decision under consideration. At one level, management may be interested in the cost of a specific service unit or departmental output. Prices for some service units, for example, for x-ray procedures, may have to be established, and to do that management must know the costs. In other situations, the cost of an individual treated patient or a grouping of treated patients may be desired. For example, management may wish to bid on a contract to provide home health services to a health maintenance organization (HMO). In this case, it is important for management to understand what the costs of treating HMO patients are likely to be. If the contract is signed, management then needs to determine the actual costs of treating the patients from the HMO in order to measure the overall profitability from that segment of the business. Alternatively, a grouping of patients by specialty may be necessary. A hospital may wish to know if it is losing money from treating a particular DRG entity or some grouping of DRGs, such as obstetrics.

STANDARD DEVELOPMENT

The key to successful product costing is management's ability to develop and maintain two systems: (1) a system of standard cost profiles and (2) a system of standard treatment protocols. The relationship between these two systems is shown in Figure 8-3. The link pin between them is the service unit (SU) concept. Specifically, management must know what it costs to produce an SU, and it must know what particular SUs are needed to treat a given patient.

Standard Cost Profiles

The standard cost profile (SCP) is not a new concept; it has been used in manufacturing cost accounting systems for many years. For our purposes, there are two key elements in an SCP: (1) the definition of the SU being costed and (2) the profile of resources required to produce the SU.

As noted earlier, the number of SUs in a given department may vary; some departments may have one, while others may have a hundred or more. If the number of SUs is very large, however, there may be an unacceptable level of costing detail involved to make the system feasible. In these situations, it may be useful to aggregate some of the SUs. For example, the laboratory may perform a thousand or more tests. In this situation, it may make sense to develop cost profiles for only the most commonly performed tests and to employ some arbitrary assignment method for the remaining noncommon tests.

The SU does not have to be a product or service that is directly performed for a patient. Many indirect departments do not provide services or products to the patient; instead, their products or services are consumed by other departments, both direct and indirect. However, many indirect departments have SUs that are directly provided to the patient. For example, dietary, often regarded as an indirect department, may not have revenue billed for its product to the patient. However, a meal furnished by it to a patient is an SU that is just as direct as a lab test or a chest x-ray. In a similar vein, housekeeping may provide cleaning for a patient's room that is, in effect, a direct service consumed by the patient.

Thus, SUs may be categorized as either direct or indirect. A direct SU is one that is associated with a given patient. An indirect SU is one provided to another department of the hospital, as opposed to a patient. The differentiation between direct and indirect SUs is important, not only in the development of standard cost profiles but also in the development of standard treatment protocols. Direct SUs must be identified when standard treatment protocols are defined, whereas indirect SUs need not be specifically identified, although some estimate of allocated cost is often required.

In the development of an SCP for a given SU, the following resource expense categories are listed: (1) direct expenses (labor, materials, and departmental overhead) and (2) allocated overhead. Ideally, the expense should also be categorized as variable or fixed. This distinction is particularly important in certain areas of management decision making, as pointed out in Chapter 6. Specifically, the differentiation between variable and fixed cost is critical to many incremental pricing and volume decisions. It is also important in flexible budgeting systems and management control. These topics are explored in greater depth in Chapters 9 and 14.

Table 8-1 presents an SCP for a regular patient meal in a dietary department. The total cost of providing one regular patient meal, or SU 181, is $2.50. The variable cost per meal is $1.30, and the average fixed cost per meal is $1.20.

In most situations, direct labor is the largest single expense category. In our dietary meal example, this is not true because the direct material cost, mostly raw food, is larger. It is possible, and in many cases desirable, to define direct labor costs by labor category. Thus, in our dietary meal example, we might provide separate listings for cooks, dietary aides, and dishwashers.

An important point here is the division of cost into fixed and variable quantities. Table 8-1 indicates that .05 unit of variable labor time is required per meal and .05 unit of fixed labor is required per meal. (In Chapter 6 we discussed several methods for splitting costs into fixed and variable elements.) The fixed cost assignment is an average based upon some expected level of volume. This is an important point to remember when developing SCPs; a decline in volume

Table 8-1 Standard Cost Profile for a Dietary/Regular Patient Meal, SU 181

Cost Category	Quantity Required Variable	Quantity Required Fixed	Unit Cost	Variable Cost	Average Fixed Cost	Average Total Cost
Direct labor	.05	.05	$6.00	$ .30	$ .30	$ .60
Direct materials	1.00	.00	1.00	1.00	.00	1.00
Department overhead	.00	1.00	.50	.00	.50	.50
Allocated costs						
Housekeeping	.00	.10	1.00	.00	.10	.10
Plant operation	.00	1.00	.10	.00	.10	.10
Administration	.00	.02	10.00	.00	.20	.20
Total				$1.30	$1.20	$2.50

below expected levels will raise the average cost of production.

The third column of Table 8-1 is unit cost. This represents management's best guess as to the cost or price of the resources to be used in the production process. Our dietary meal SCP indicates a price of $6 per unit of direct labor. This value reflects the expected wage per hour to be paid for direct labor in the dietary department. Again, it might be possible and desirable to further break out direct labor into specific job classifications. This usually permits better costing, but it does require more effort.

Any fringe benefit cost associated with labor should be included in the unit cost. For example, the average direct hourly wage in our dietary meal example might be $5 per hour, but fringe benefits may average 20 percent. In this case, the effective wage would be $6 per hour.

Departmental overhead consists of expenses that are directly charged to a department and do not represent either labor or materials. Common examples are equipment costs, travel allowances, expenses for outside purchased services, and cost of publications. Usually these items do not vary with level of activity or volume but remain fixed for the budgetary period. If this is the case, assignment to an SCP can be based on a simple average. For example, assume that our dietary department expects to provide 200,000 regular patient meals next year. Assume further that the department has been authorized to spend $100,000 in discretionary areas that constitute departmental overhead. The average cost per meal for these discretionary costs would be $.50 and would be fixed.

Allocated costs are probably the most difficult to assign in most situations. In our dietary example, we include only three allocated cost areas. This is probably a low figure; a number of other departments would most likely provide service to dietary and should properly be included in the SCP.

There are two major alternatives to the use of estimates of allocated costs in an SCP. First, individual costing studies could be performed, and services from one department to another could be recorded. This process may be expensive, however, and not worth the effort. For example, if separate meters were installed, utility costs could be associated with each user department. However, the installation of such meters is probably not an effective expenditure of funds; costing accuracy would not be improved enough to justify the extra expenditure.

The second alternative would be a simple averaging method. All overhead costs might be aggregated and apportioned to other departments on the basis of direct expenses, full-time equivalents (FTEs), or some other criterion. This method is relatively simple, but its accuracy would be suspect if significant variation in departmental utilization exists.

We believe that the best approach to costing is to identify all possible direct SUs. These SUs, which can be directly associated with a patient, are far more numerous than one would suspect. For example, a meal provided to a patient is a direct SU but is currently treated as an indirect product in most costing systems. Laundry and linen have certain SUs that are directly associated with a patient, such as clean sheets and gowns. Housekeeping provides direct services to patients when its personnel clean rooms. Administration and medical records also provide specific direct services to patients in the form of processed paper work and insurance forms. If such costs, currently regarded as indirect, were reclassified as direct, there would be a substantially lower level of indirect costs that would require allocation. This would improve the costing of patients, the health care product, and make the allocation of indirect costs less critical. Currently, indirect costs in many health care settings are in excess of 50 percent of total cost. With better identification of services or SUs, we believe that level could be reduced to 25 percent or less.

Standard Treatment Protocols

There is an analogy between a standard treatment protocol (STP) and a job order cost sheet used in industrial cost accounting. In a job order cost system, a separate cost sheet is completed for each specific job. This is necessary because each job is different from jobs performed in the past and jobs to be performed in the future. Automobile repairs are an excellent example of a job order cost system. A separate cost sheet is prepared for each job. That cost sheet then serves as the bill or invoice to the customer.

Health care firms also operate in a job-cost setting. Patient treatment may vary significantly across patients. The patient's bill may be thought of as a job order cost sheet in that it reflects the actual services provided during the course of the patient's treatment. Of course, not all of the services provided are shown in the patient's bill. For example, meals provided are rarely charged for as a separate item.

In a typical job order cost setting, standards may not always be applied. When you drop your car off for servicing, the dealer does not prepare a standard job order cost sheet. Dealers have no incentive to do this because they expect that customers will pay the actual costs of the service when they drop by to pick up their cars. If they do not, the dealer may take possession of the car as collateral.

In the past, a similar situation existed among health care firms; the client or patient would pay for the actual cost of services provided. Today this is no longer true for the majority of health care products. Today, most health care firms are paid a fixed fee or price regardless of the range of services provided. Medicare's DRG payment system is the most recent application of this type of payment philosophy.

Because the majority of health care revenue is derived from fixed price payers, we need to define specific STPs wherever possible. Ta-

ble 8-2 shows a hypothetical STP for DRG 208 (Disorder of Biliary Tract). (This STP is for illustrative purposes only; it should not be regarded as a realistic STP for DRG 208.)

In Table 8-2, STP costs are split into fixed and variable components. Thus, the STP requires 25 patient meals at a variable cost of $1.30 per meal and a fixed cost of $1.20 per meal. The basis for these data is the SCP (see Table 8-1). As noted earlier, this breakout into fixed and variable costs is extremely valuable for management in making its planning and control decisions. For example, if Medicare paid the hospital $1,400 for every DRG 208 treated, we would conclude that, at least in the short run, the hospital would be financially better off if it continued to treat DRG 208 cases, since the payment of $1,400 exceeds the variable cost of $1,014.50 and is therefore making a contribution to fixed costs.

Table 8-2 depicts two areas in which no actual quantity is specified: pharmacy prescriptions and other lab tests. In these instances, the total cost of the services is instead divided between fixed and variable costs. Because of the large number of products provided in each of these two areas, it would be impossible to develop an SCP for each product item. However, some of the heavier-volume lab tests or pharmacy prescriptions may be separately identified and costed; for example, lab CBC is listed as a separate SU.

Some of the items shown in Table 8-2 may not be reflected in a patient's bill. For example, pa-

---

Table 8-2 Standard Treatment Protocol for DRG 208 (Disorder of Biliary Tract)

Service Unit No.	Service Unit Name	Quantity	Variable Cost/Unit	Fixed Cost/Unit	Total Cost/Unit	Total Variable Cost	Total Fixed Cost	Total Cost
1	Admission process	1	$ 48.00	$52.00	$100.00	$ 48.00	$ 52.00	$ 100.00
7	Nursing care Level 1	1	80.00	40.00	120.00	80.00	40.00	120.00
8	Nursing care Level 2	7	85.00	45.00	130.00	595.00	315.00	910.00
9	Nursing care Level 3	1	110.00	45.00	155.00	110.00	45.00	155.00
29	Pharmacy prescriptions		38.00	19.00	57.00	38.00	19.00	57.00
38	Chest x-ray	1	12.00	8.00	20.00	12.00	8.00	20.00
46	Lab CBC	1	4.00	3.50	7.50	4.00	3.50	7.50
49	Other lab tests		85.00	55.00	140.00	85.00	55.00	140.00
57	Patient meals	25	1.30	1.20	2.50	32.50	30.00	62.50
65	Clean linen changes	5	.60	.50	1.10	3.00	2.50	5.50
93	Room preparation	1	7.00	3.00	10.00	7.00	3.00	10.00
	Total					$1,014.50	$573.00	$1,587.50

tient meals, clean linen changes, room preparation, and admission processing would not usually be listed in the bill. Also, separation of nursing care by acuity level may not be identified in the bill; many hospitals do not distinguish between levels of nursing in their pricing structures.

A final point to emphasize is that not all SUs will show up in an STP. Only those SUs that are classified as direct are listed. A direct SU is one that can be directly traced or associated with patient care. The costs associated with the provision of indirect SUs are allocated to the direct SUs. At the same time, the objective should be to create as many direct SUs as possible.

VARIANCE ANALYSIS

In general, given the systems of standards discussed above, four types of variances may be identified in the variance analysis phase of control:

1. price (rate)
2. efficiency
3. volume
4. intensity

The first three types of variances are a direct result of the development of the SCPs; they are the product of departmental activity. A rate or price variance is the difference between the price actually paid and the standard price multiplied by the actual quantity used:

Price variance =
(Actual price − Standard price) × Actual quantity

For example, assume that our dietary department of Table 8-1 produced 1,500 patient meals for the period in question. To produce these meals, it used 180 hours of labor and paid $6.25 per hour. In this case, the price or rate variance would be

$$(\$6.25 - \$6.00) \times 180 \text{ hours} = \$45.00$$

This variance would be unfavorable because the department paid $6.25 per hour when the expected rate was $6.00.

An efficiency variance reflects productivity in the production process. It is derived by multiplying the difference between actual quantity used and standard quantity by the standard price:

Efficiency variance = (Actual quantity
− Standard quantity) × Standard price

In our dietary example, the efficiency variance would be

$$(180 \text{ hours} - 155 \text{ hours}) \times \$6 = \$150$$

Standard labor is derived by multiplying the variable labor requirement of .05 by the number of meals produced, or 1,500. To this sum is added the budgeted fixed labor requirement of 80 hours (.05 × 1,600 meals). In our example, the department used 25 more hours of labor than had been expected. As a result, it incurred an unfavorable efficiency variable of $150.

The volume variance reflects differences between expected output and actual output. It is a factor to be considered in situations with fixed costs. If no fixed costs existed, the resources required per unit would be constant. This would mean that the cost per unit of production should be constant. For most situations, this is not a reasonable expectation; normally fixed costs are present.

The volume variance is derived by multiplying the expected average fixed cost per unit times the difference between budgeted volume and actual volume:

Volume variance = (Budgeted volume
− Actual volume) × Average fixed cost per unit

In the case of direct labor in our dietary example, the volume variance would be an unfavorable $30 ([1,600 meals − 1,500 meals] × $ .30).

Notice that in our example, the total of these variances equals the difference between actual costs incurred for direct labor and the standard cost of direct labor assigned to the SU, a patient meal:

Actual direct labor ($6.25 × 180 hours)	$ 1,125
Standard cost ($ .60 × 1,500 meals)	900
Total variance	$ 225
Price variance	$ 45.00
Efficiency variance	150.00
Volume variance	30.00
Total variance	$225.00

The intensity variance is the difference between the quantity of SUs actually required in treating a patient and the quantity called for in the STP. For example, if 20 meals were provided a patient categorized as DRG 208, there would be a favorable variance of five meals, given the STP data of Table 8-2.

Intensity variances are generically defined as follows:

Intensity variance =
(Actual SUs − Standard SUs) × Price per SU

Thus, in our example, the intensity variance for a patient with respect to meals would be a favorable $12.50 ([20 meals − 25 meals] × $2.50).

It may be useful to split intensity variances into fixed and variable elements. In our example, it is probably not fair to say that $12.50 was realized in savings because five fewer meals were delivered. Five times $1.30, the variable cost, may be a better reflection of short-term realized savings.

One final word on variance analysis: It is important to specify the party responsible for variances. This is, after all, part of the rationale for standard costing—to be able to take corrective action through individuals to correct unfavorable variances. In our example, three variances— price, efficiency, and volume—are distinguished in the department accounts. However, the department manager may not be responsible for all of this variation, especially in the volume area. Usually, department managers have little control over volume; they merely react to the volume of services requested from their departments.

The intensity variance can be largely associated with a given physician. Most of the SUs are of a medical nature, resulting from physician decisions regarding testing or length of stay. It may be very helpful, therefore, to accumulate intensity variances by physicians. Periodic discussions regarding these variations can be most useful to both the health care executive and the physician. Ideally, physicians should participate actively in the development of STPs.

SUMMARY

Product costing has become much more critical to health care executives today than it was prior to 1983. The emphasis on prospective prices and competitive discounting creates a real need to define costs. For health care purposes, the product is a treated patient. Various aggregations of patients may also be useful. For example, we may want to develop cost data by DRG, by clinical specialty, or by payer category.

To develop a standard cost system in a health care firm, two sets of standards must be defined. First, a series of SCPs must be developed for all SUs (intermediate departmental products) produced by the firm. This part of standard costing is analogous to that of most manufacturing systems. Second, a set of STPs must be defined for major patient treatment categories. These STPs must identify all the service units to be provided in the patient treatment. Physician involvement is critical in this area.

The purpose of standard costing is to make planning decisions, such as those involved in pricing and product mix, more precise and meaningful. Standard costing is also useful in making control decisions. Variance analysis is based on the existence of standard cost and the periodic accumulation of actual cost data. Timely analysis of variances can help management achieve desired results.

Chapter 9

Cost Variance Analysis

William O. Cleverley
Professor, Graduate Program in Hospital and Health Services Management
The Ohio State University

Cost variance analysis is of great potential importance to the health care industry. Successful utilization of cost variance analysis requires the existence of a sound system of standard setting, or budgeting, and a related system of cost accounting. Perhaps the major factor impeding the widespread adoption of more effective cost variance analysis in the health care industry has been the lack of interaction between it and our systems of cost accounting.

Cost accounting systems usually serve two basic informational needs. First, they supply data essential for product/service costing. Second, they provide information for managerial cost control activity. This second role is the major topic of this chapter.

COST CONTROL

The following conceptual model will be used to discuss the major alternatives to cost control in organizations:

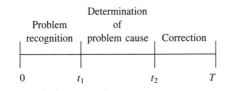

In general, there are three distinct time phases in an out-of-control situation:

1. recognition of problem (0 to t_1)
2. determination of problem cause (t_1 to t_2)
3. correction of problem (t_2 to T)

The unit of time used in the above representation may be minutes, hours, days, weeks, or even months. The important point is that, the longer the problem remains uncorrected (0 to T), the greater the cost to the organization.

The term *efficiency cost* is sometimes used to describe the total cost incurred by an organization from an out-of-control situation. Efficiency cost may be represented as follows:

$$\text{Efficiency cost} = T \times R \times P$$

where

T = total time units that the problem remains uncorrected
R = loss or cost per time unit
P = probability that the problem occurrence is correctable

The objective of management should be to minimize the efficiency cost in any given situation. In the accomplishment of this objective, two major alternatives are available to management: (1) the preventive approach and (2) the detection-correction (DC) approach.

This chapter is reprinted from *Essentials of Health Care Finance*, 2nd ed., by W.O. Cleverley, pp. 291–310, Aspen Publishers, Inc., © 1986.

In the preventive approach, management attempts to minimize the efficiency cost by minimizing the probability of a problem occurring (P). One of the major methods for reducing the value of P centers on staffing. Management attempts not only to hire the most competent individuals available but also to provide them with relevant training programs and materials to ensure consistently high levels of performance. The nature of the reward structure, both monetary and nonmonetary, also enters into this management strategy. The preventive approach is obviously employed by most organizations, but the emphasis on it is usually greater in small organizations. In these organizations, the control span is usually smaller and the evaluation of individual performance is more direct.

The DC approach seeks to minimize efficiency cost by minimizing the time that a problem remains uncorrected (T). This method is directly related to the effectiveness of variance analysis. Effective variance analysis should result in a reduction of both the recognition of problem phase (0 to t_1) and the determination of cause phase (t_1 to t_2). The actual correction phase (t_2 to T) rests primarily upon the effective motivation of management.

The development of cost variance analysis systems to reduce the recognition and determination phases usually involves the expenditure of funds. Prudent management dictates that the marginal expenditures of funds for system improvements be evaluated by their expected reductions in efficiency cost. For example, the frequency of reporting could be altered to reduce the problem recognition phase, or the number of cost areas reported could be increased to improve both recognition and determination times. However, these improvements are likely to result in increased cost and may not be justified. Areas of relatively small dollar expenditure or largely uncontrolled costs are thus not prime candidates for major system improvements.

INVESTIGATION OF VARIANCES

In the DC approach to cost control, cost variances are the clues that both signal a potential problem exists and suggest a possible cause. These variances are usually an integral part of any management-by-exception plan of operations. A decision to investigate a given variance is not an automatic occurrence. It involves some financial commitment by the organization and thus should be weighed carefully against the expected benefits. Unfortunately, management rarely knows whether any given variance is due to a random or noncontrollable cause, or to an underlying problem that is correctable or controllable.

Many organizations have developed rules to determine which variances will be investigated. Common examples of such rules are to investigate

- all variances that exceed an absolute dollar size (e.g., $500)
- all variances that exceed budgeted or standard values by some fixed percentage (e.g., 10 percent)
- all variances that have been unfavorable for a defined number of periods (e.g., three periods)
- some combination of the above

Actual specification of criteria values in the above rules is highly dependent upon management judgment and experience. A variance of $1,000 may be considered normal in some circumstances and abnormal in others.

At some point, management may wish to determine whether the historical criteria values should be changed. In that case, some method of testing whether the historical values are acceptable or not acceptable must be developed. In general, there are two possible theories that may be used to develop this information: (1) classical statistical theory and (2) decision theory.

Classical Statistical Theory

One of the most commonly employed means to determine which cost variances to investigate is the control chart. The control chart is often used to monitor a physical process by comparing output observations with predetermined tolerance limits. If actual observations fall between predetermined upper and lower control limits on the chart, the process is assumed to be in control.

Control charts can be established for determining when a cost variance should be investigated. The major assumption underlying the traditional development of control charts is that observed cost variances are distributed in accordance with a normal probability distribution. In a normal distribution, it can be anticipated that approximately 68.3 percent of the observations will fall within one standard deviation (σ) of the mean ($\bar{x}$), 95.5 percent will fall within two standard deviations ($\bar{x} \pm 2\sigma$), and 99.7 percent will fall within three standard deviations ($\bar{x} \pm 3\sigma$).

The control limits for any given variance will then be set at

$$\bar{x} \pm K\sigma$$

If the costs of investigation are high relative to the benefits in a given situation, then K may be set to a high value (e.g., 3.0). This will ensure that few investigations will be made and that some out-of-control situations may be continued. Conversely, if benefits are high relative to the costs of investigation, then lower values of K may be selected that will ensure that more investigations will be performed and that some individuals in control situations will be investigated.

To develop the control chart, the underlying distribution must be specified. An assumption that the distribution is normal means that the analyst must define both the mean ($\bar{x}$) and the standard deviation (σ). In most situations, this specification will result from an analysis of prior observations. To illustrate this process, assume that the following pattern of labor variances occurred during the 13 biweekly pay periods:

Pay Period	Variance (x_i)
1	800
2	400
3	− 500
4	− 100
5	200
6	− 700
7	500
8	− 300
9	− 200
10	300
11	200
12	− 200
13	− 400
	0

The mean ($\bar{x}$) of these observations is calculated as follows:

$$\bar{x} = \frac{\Sigma x_i}{n} = \frac{0}{13} = 0$$

An estimate of the standard deviation (s) is calculated as follows:

$$s = \sqrt{\frac{\Sigma(x_i - \bar{x})^2}{n-1}} = \$437.80$$

If the labor cost variances in this example are expected to follow a normal distribution in the future with $\bar{x} = 0$ and $\sigma = \$437.80$, control limits for investigation at the 95-percent level could be defined by multiplying the estimated standard deviation by two. The following control chart would result:

$$\bar{x} + 2\sigma = 875.60$$
$$\bar{x} = 0$$
$$\bar{x} - 2\sigma = -875.60$$

Any observation falling within the control limits would not be investigated, while variances falling outside the established limits would be investigated.

The major deficiency in the classical statistical approach is that it does not relate the expected costs of investigation and benefits with the probability that the variance signals are out of control. The control chart can signal when a situation is likely to be out of control, but it cannot directly evaluate whether an investigation is warranted.

Decision Theory

Decision theory provides a framework for directly integrating the probability of the system's being out of control and the costs and benefits of investigation into a definite decision rule. Central to this approach is the payoff table, which specifically considers costs and benefits. An example of a payoff table is presented below:

Actions	States In Control	Out of Control
Investigate	I	$I + C$
Do not investigate	O	L

where

I = cost of investigation
C = cost of correcting an out-of-control situation
L = cost of letting an out-of-control situation continue (expected loss)

The payoff table is a conceptualization of the actual decision evaluation process. It may be applied in any cost variance situation. The objective is to minimize the actual cost for a given situation. To accomplish this, estimates of the probabilities for the two states, in control and out-of-control, are required.

Assume that P denotes the probability that the system is in control and that $(1 - P)$ represents the probability that the system is out of control. The expected cost of the two courses of action can be defined as follows:

Expected cost of investigating = $(P \times I) + (1 - P)(I + C)$
= $I + (1 - P)C$

Expected cost of not investigating = $(P \times O) + (1 - P)L$
= $(1 - P)L$

By setting the two expected costs equal to each other, we can determine the value of P to which the decision maker is indifferent. Calculation of this break-even probability would be:

$$P^* = 1 - \frac{I}{L - C}$$

Evaluation of this formula provides a nice summarization of earlier comments concerning the costs and benefits of investigating variances. In situations of high investigation costs (I) and low net benefits ($L - C$), the critical value of P (P^*) becomes quite low. This, of course, means that, in order to justify an investigation, the probability that the system is actually in control (P) must be very low, or, alternatively, the probability that the system is actually out of control ($1 - P$) must be quite large.

To employ the decision theory model just described, the analyst must have estimates of I, C, L, and P. In most situations, there is a reasonable expectation that I and C will be relatively constant. These costs are usually directly related to the labor involved in the analysis. L, however, usually varies, depending upon the size of the

cost variance. In short, the loss depends upon the proportion of the variance to be saved in future periods and the number of periods over which the loss is expected to occur if the situation is not corrected.

The value of P is in many respects the most difficult of the parameter values to specify. Either objective or subjective approaches may be used. An objective method may be used to develop an estimated probability distribution for the system. If the underlying distribution is assumed to be normal, estimating the mean and standard deviation from prior observations will enable the analyst to specify the distribution from this estimated distribution. The probability of any given observation being in control (P) can then be defined.

Subjective estimates of P are possible on both an a priori and an ex post facto basis. A subjective normalized distribution of variances can be built in advance as a basis for the estimate. The analyst might ask department managers between which two values they would expect 50 percent of actual observations to fall. If the budget cost for labor in a department is \$4,000 per pay period, the department manager might specify that 50 percent of the time the manager would expect actual observations to fall between \$3,700 and \$4,300. Using this information, a normalized distribution could be defined as follows:

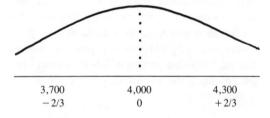

3,700	4,000	4,300
−2/3	0	+2/3

Subjective estimates of P may also be made after the fact and then related directly to the actual size of the cost variance. This assessment can then be related to a table of critical values of P necessary for an investigation decision of a given variance. This permits analysts to employ directly sensitivity analysis in their decisions. For example, assume that I is \$100 and that C is \$200. Assume further that L is equal to two times the absolute size of the variance. The following chart of critical values of *P* could then be defined:

Critical Value of *P*(*P**)	Size of Variance
0.50	$200
0.75	300
0.83	400
0.88	500
0.90	600

This chart is relatively straightforward. As the dollar size of the variance increases, the probability that the system is under control must increase to justify a ''do not investigate'' decision. For example, if a $600 variance occurred, the analyst must believe that there is at least a 90 percent probability that the system is under control.

VARIANCE ANALYSIS CALCULATIONS

Variance analysis is simply an examination of the deviation of an actual observation from a standard. For the purposes of this chapter, two types of standards for comparative purposes are used: (1) prior period values and (2) budgeted values. In each case, the objective of cost variance analysis is to explain why actual costs are different, either from budgeted values or from prior-period actual values. This objective is a very important element in the cost-control process in the organization.

Prior-Period Comparisons

Relevant Factors

An evaluation of the difference between current levels of cost and prior costs should suggest to management which factors have contributed to the change. In general, three major factors influence costs: (1) input prices, (2) productivity of inputs, and (3) output levels.

Input prices usually may be expected to increase over time. It is important, however, from management's perspective to evaluate what portion, if any, of that increase was controllable or avoidable. Rapidly increasing prices for some commodities may signal opportunities for resource substitutions, for example, by switching to a less expensive mix of labor or substituting one supply item for another. Measuring productivity has in fact become increasingly important in the health care industry as a result of the new emphasis on cost containment. One of the major difficulties in evaluating productivity, however, has been the changing nature of health care services. Comparison of productivity within a hospital for two time periods requires that the services in each period be identical. For example, a comparison of full-time equivalents (FTEs) per patient day in 1986 with FTEs per patient day of care in 1983 is meaningless unless a patient day of care in 1986 is identical to a patient day of care in 1983. Finally, changes in output levels also influence the level of costs. This influence may occur in two ways. First, the absolute level of output provided may affect the quantity of resources necessary to produce the output level. Second, service intensity may affect resource requirements. Any increase in the number of services required per unit of output will directly affect costs. For example, a change in the number of laboratory procedures performed per patient day of care will probably affect the total cost per patient day of care.

This discussion can be summarized in the following cost function:

$$\text{Total cost} = P \times \frac{I}{X} \times \frac{X}{Q} \times Q$$

where

P = input prices
I = physical quantities of inputs
X = services required per unit of output
Q = output level

In the above cost equation, P represents the effect of input prices, I/X represents the effect of productivity, X/Q represents the effect of service intensity, and Q represents the influence of output. Changes in cost can result from changes in any one of these four terms.

American Hospital Association Cost Indexes

A simple application of the preceding cost model was developed by the American Hospital

Association (AHA) in its attempts to explain better the factors causing the escalation in hospital costs. To accomplish this objective, the measure of output chosen was cost per adjusted patient day (APD). Cost per APD in any period (t) was defined as follows:

$$APD^t = \sum_{i=1}^{n} C_i^t X_i^t = C^t X^t$$

where

C_i^t = direct cost per unit of service (i) in period (t)
X_i^t = units of service (i) utilized in one patient day in period (t)
C^t = a 1 by n vector of C^t
X^t = an n by 1 vector of X^t

From this equation, two indexes that partition the causes of cost changes into two areas were derived as follows:

$$\frac{APD^t}{APD^o} = \frac{C^t X^t}{C^o X^o} = HCI \times HII$$

The hospital cost index (HCI) is defined as:

$$HCI = \frac{C^t X^o}{C^o X^o}$$

The HCI measures the change in cost attributed to both price increases and productivity changes. The other index, the hospital intensity index (HII), is defined as

$$HII = \frac{C^o X^t}{C^o X^o}$$

The HII measures the change in cost due to changes in service intensity.

To illustrate, these two indexes may be applied in the following cost comparison chart for a hospital.

During the three-year period, costs increased 44.7 percent [($29.45/$20.35) − 1], which is a rather sizable increase. However, a calculation of the two AHA indexes gives a somewhat different picture:

$$HCI = \frac{(\$2.50 \times 3.2) + (5.20 \times 3.1)}{(\$2.00 \times 3.2) + (4.50 \times 3.1)}$$

$$= \frac{\$24.12}{\$20.35} = 1.185$$

$$HII = \frac{(\$2.00 \times 4.5) + (4.50 \times 3.5)}{(\$2.00 \times 3.2) + (4.50 \times 3.1)}$$

$$= \frac{\$24.75}{\$20.35} = 1.216$$

Breaking down the increase in costs for the hospital would now yield the following:

Percentage increase due to cost increases	18.5%
Percentage increase due to intensity	21.6%
Joint cost and intensity	4.6%
Total increase	44.7%

Departmental Analysis of Variance

The preceding AHA indexes are very useful for analyzing cost changes at the total facility level. In such situations, a measure of output for the facility as a whole—such as patient days, admissions, discharges, visits, or enrollees—would be used. However, although this type of analysis may be very useful, it is also often desirable to analyze the reasons for cost changes at the departmental level. In general, the primary reason for a cost change at the departmental level between two time periods can be stated as a function of three factors:

1. changes in input prices
2. changes in input productivity (efficiency)
3. changes in departmental volume

	Lab Tests PD	Nursing Hours PD	Cost Per Lab Test	Cost Per Nursing Hour	Cost Per Patient Day (APD)
1983	3.2	3.1	$2.00	$4.50	$20.35
1986	4.5	3.5	2.50	5.20	29.45

The following variances can be calculated to compute the effects of these three factors:

Price variance =
(Present price − Old price) × Present quantity

Efficiency variance =
(Present quantity − Expected quantity at old productivity)
× Old price

Volume variance =
(Present volume − Old volume) ×
Old cost per unit

These formulas may be applied to the following laundry example. It is assumed that the laundry has only two inputs: soap and labor.

	1983	1986
Pounds of laundry	140,000	180,000
Units of soap	1,400	1,800
Soap units per pound of laundry	.01	.01
Price per soap unit	$ 40.00	$ 50.00
Productive hours worked	19,600	27,000
Productive hours per pound of laundry	.14	.15
Wage rate per productive hour	$ 5.25	$ 6.00
Total cost	$158,900	$252,000
Cost per pound	$ 1.135	$ 1.40

Price variances:
Soap = ($50.00 − $40.00) × 1,800 = $18,000 (Unfavorable)
Labor = ($6.00 − $5.25) × 27,000 = $20,250 (Unfavorable)

Efficiency variances:
Soap = [1,800 − (.01 × 180,000)] × $40.00 = 0
Labor = [27,000 − (.14 × 180,000)] × $5.25 = $9,450 (Unfavorable)

Volume variances:
Volume variance = (180,000 − 140,000) × $1.135 = $45,400 (Unfavorable)

With these calculations, the following chart can be generated to summarize the factors that created cost changes in the laundry department.

Causes of Laundry Department
Cost Change—1983 to 1986

	Dollars	Percentage Change
Increase in wages	$20,250	21.8
Increase in soap price	18,000	19.3
Decline in labor efficiency	9,450	10.1
Increase in volume	45,400	48.8
Total change in cost	$93,100	

The chart indicates that increased volume was the largest source of the total change in cost. It is often useful to factor this volume variance into two areas:

Intensity =
>   (Change in volume due to intensity difference)
>   × Old cost per unit

Pure volume =
>   (Change in volume due to change in overall service)
>   × Old cost per unit

Here, the intensity variance represents the change in volume due to increased intensity of service. For example, assume that, in 1986, 2.25 pounds of laundry were provided per patient day. The corresponding value for 1983 was 2.00 pounds per patient day. Also assume that total patient days were 70,000 in 1983 and 80,000 in 1986. The two volume variances would be:

Intensity variance =
>   [(2.25 − 2.00) × 80,000] × \$1.135 = \$22,700

Pure volume =
>   2.00 × (80,000 − 70,000) × \$1.135 = \$22,700

The system of cost variance analysis described above should be a useful framework in which to discuss factors causing changes in departmental costs. Aggregation of some resource categories will probably be both necessary and desirable. There would be little point in calculating price and efficiency variances for each of a hundred or more supply items. Only major supply categories should be examined. The supply items that are aggregated together could not be broken out in terms of individual price and efficiency variances because there would be no common input quantity measure. For example, the addition of numbers of pencils, sheets of paper, and boxes of paper clips would not produce a comparable unit of measure. For these smaller areas of supply or material costs, a simple change in cost per unit of departmental output may be just as informative as detailed price and efficiency variances.

VARIANCE ANALYSIS IN BUDGETARY SETTINGS

A final area in which variance analysis can be applied is in the operation of a formalized budgeting system. The presentation that follows assumes a budgeting system that is based upon a flexible model. This means that management must have identified in the budgetary process those elements of cost that are presumed to be fixed and those that are presumed to be variable. Although relatively few health care organizations employ flexible budgeting models at the present time, a trend toward their adoption is clearly visible. In this context, the variance analysis models examined here may be applied in any budgetary situation, fixed or flexible.

The cost equation for any given department may be represented as follows:

$$\text{Cost} = F + V \times Q$$

where

F = fixed costs
V = variable costs per unit of output
Q = output in units

The fixed and variable cost coefficients are the sum of many individual resource quantity and unit price products. These terms can be represented as follows:

$$F = I_f \times P_f$$
$$V = I_v \times P_v$$

where

I_f = physical units of fixed resources
P_f = price per unit of fixed resources
I_v = physical units of variable resources
P_v = price per unit of variable resources

In most budgeting situations, there are three levels of output or volume that are critical in cost variance analysis. The first is the actual level of volume produced in the budget reporting period. This level of activity is critical because, if management has established a set of expectations concerning how costs should behave, given changes in volume from budgeted levels, an adjustment to budgeted cost can be made.

The second critical level is that of budgeted or expected volume. It is upon this expected volume level that management establishes its commitments for resources, and therefore incurs cost. An unjustified faith in volume forecasts can lock management into a very sizable fixed-cost position, especially with respect to labor costs.

The third critical level is that of standard volume. Standard volume is equal to actual volume, unless there is some indication that not all of the output was necessary. For example, a utilization review committee may determine that a certain number of patient days were medically unnecessary or that some surgical procedures were not warranted. Alternatively, in some indirect departments, such as maintenance, it may be important to identify the difference between actual and standard, or necessary, output. The cost effect of these output decisions needs to be isolated and control directed at the individual(s) responsible.

The expected level of costs to be incurred at each of the three levels of volume (actual, budgeted, and standard) may be expressed as follows:

$$FB^a = F + V \times Q^a$$
$$FB^b = F + V \times Q^b$$
$$FB^s = F + V \times Q^s$$

where

FB^a = flexible budget at actual output level
FB^b = flexible budget at budgeted output level
FB^s = flexible budget at standard output level
Q^a = actual output
Q^b = budgeted output
Q^s = standard output

The major categories of variances can now be defined to explain the difference between actual cost (AC) and applied cost ($Q^s \times FB^b/Q^b$):

Variance Name	Definition	Cause
Spending	$(AC - FB^a)$	Price and efficiency
Utilization	$(Q^a - Q^s) \times (FB^b/Q^b)$	Excessive services
Volume	$(Q^b - Q^a) \times (F/Q^b)$	Difference from budgeted volume

For control purposes, it is important to break down the spending variance further into individual resource categories, and also to isolate the change due to price and efficiency factors. This will not only better isolate control for budget deviations but also improve the problem definition and determination phase times discussed earlier in the detection-correction approach to cost control. The spending variances are broken down as follows:

$$\text{Efficiency} = (I^a - I^b)\, P^b$$
$$\text{Price} = (P^a - P^b)\, I^a$$

where

I^a = actual physical units of resource
I^b = budgeted physical units of resource
P^a = actual price per unit of resource
P^b = budgeted price per unit of resource

With this background, we must now relate the structure we developed for standard costing in Chapter 8 to our analyses of budgetary variances. Two sets of standards are involved: (1) standard cost profiles (SCPs) and (2) standard treatment protocols (STPs). SCPs are developed at the departmental level. They reflect the quantity of resources that should be used and the prices that should be paid for those resources to produce a specific departmental output unit, defined as a service unit (SU). Below is a SCP for a nursing unit, with the SU defined as a patient day.

Using this chart, a standard variance analysis could be performed for any time period. For

Standard Cost Profile
Nursing Unit No. 6
Patient Day = Service Unit
Expected Patient Days = 630

Resource	Quantity Variable	Quantity Fixed	Unit Cost	Variable Cost	Average Fixed Cost	Average Total Cost
Head nurse	0.00	.30	$15.00	$ 0.00	$ 4.50	$ 4.50
RN	2.00	1.00	12.00	24.00	12.00	36.00
LPN	2.00	0.00	8.00	16.00	0.00	16.00
Aides	3.00	1.00	5.00	15.00	5.00	20.00
Supplies	2.00	0.00	2.20	4.40	0.00	4.40
Total				$59.40	$21.50	$80.90

example, the following data reflect actual experience in the most recent month:

Actual Month's Cost
Nursing Unit No. 6
Actual Patient Days = 600

Resource	Quantity Used	Unit Cost	Total Cost
Head nurse	180	$15.50	$ 2,790.00
RN	1,800	12.50	22,500.00
LPN	1,200	8.10	9,720.00
Aides	2,400	4.80	11,520.00
Supplies	1,300	2.40	3,120.00
Total			$49,650.00

In this example, the nursing unit would have incurred actual expenditures of $49,650 during the month. It would have charged to the treated patient its standard cost times the number of patient days:

Costs charged to patients = $48,540 = $80.90 × 600

The total variance to be accounted for would be the difference, or $1,110.00, which is an unfavorable variance. The individual variances that constitute this total are shown in the following calculations:

1. Spending variances
   • Efficiency variances $[(I^a - I^b)P^b]$
     a. Head nurse = $(180 - 189) \times \$15.00 = \$135.00$ (Favorable)
     b. RN = $(1,800 - 1,830) \times \$12.00 = \$360.00$ (Favorable)
     c. LPN = $(1,200 - 1,200) \times \$8.00 = 0$
     d. Aides = $(2,400 - 2,430) \times \$5.00 = \$150.00$ (Favorable)
     e. Supplies = $(1,300 - 1,200) \times \$2.20 = \$220.00$ (Unfavorable)
   • Price variances $[(P^a - P^b)I^a]$
     a. Head nurse = $(\$15.50 - \$15.00) \times 180 = \$90.00$ (Unfavorable)
     b. RN = $(\$12.50 - \$12.00) \times 1,800 = \$900.00$ (Unfavorable)
     c. LPN = $(\$8.10 - \$8.00) \times 1,200 = \$120.00$ (Unfavorable)

d. Aides = $(\$4.80 - \$5.00) \times 2,400 = \$480.00$ (Favorable)
e. Supplies = $(\$2.40 - \$2.20) \times 1,300 = \$260.00$ (Unfavorable)

2. Volume variance $[(Q^b - Q^a)(F/Q^b)]$
   • Volume variance = $(630 - 600) \times \$21.50 = \$645.00$ (Unfavorable)

Totaling up the above individual variances validates the accuracy of our calculations:

Price—Head nurse	$ 90.00 (Unfavorable)
Price—RN	900.00 (Unfavorable)
Price—LPN	120.00 (Unfavorable)
Price—Aides	480.00 (Favorable)
Price—Supplies	260.00 (Unfavorable)
Efficiency—Head nurse	135.00 (Favorable)
Efficiency—RN	360.00 (Favorable)
Efficiency—LPN	0.00
Efficiency—Aides	150.00 (Favorable)
Efficiency—Supplies	220.00 (Unfavorable)
Volume	645.00 (Unfavorable)
Total	$1,110.00 (Unfavorable)

A few further words about the calculation of the efficiency variances may be in order. The formula states that the difference between actual quantity (I^a) and budgeted quantity (I^b) is multiplied by budgeted price (P^b). The most difficult calculation is that for budgeted quantity. It represents the quantity of resource that should have been used at the actual level of output, or the sum of the budgeted fixed requirement plus the variable requirement at actual output (600 patient days). The chart on the following page shows the calculation of fixed and variable requirements for the individual resource categories.

The calculation for volume variance may also require some further explanation. This variance is simply the product of the difference between budgeted and actual volume ($Q^a - Q^b$) and the average fixed cost budgeted (F/Q^b). The average fixed cost, as calculated in the standard cost profile, amounted to $21.50. You will notice that, in our example, volume variance is unfavorable because actual volume of patient days (600) was less than budgeted patient days (630). Because actual volume was less than budgeted, average fixed cost per unit will rise. The reverse situation would have existed if actual volume had exceeded budgeted volume. In that situation, the volume variance would have been favorable.

1	2	3	4	5	6
		Budgeted		Budgeted	
	Average	Fixed		Variable	
Resource	Fixed	Requirement	Average Variable	Requirement	Total Requirements
Category	Requirement/Unit	(Col. 2 × 630)	Requirement/Unit	(Col. 4 × 600)	(Col. 3 + Col. 5)
Head nurse	.30	189	0.00	0	189
RN	1.00	630	2.00	1,200	1,830
LPN	0.00	0	2.00	1,200	1,200
Aides	1.00	630	3.00	1,800	2,430
Supplies	0.00	0	2.00	1,200	1,200

The third type of variance, utilization variance, results from a difference between actual volume and standard volume, or the quantity of volume actually needed. The measure of standard volume is generated from the STPs, which define how much output or how many SUs are required per treated patient type.

Let us generate a hypothetical set of data to apply to our nursing unit example. Assume that the patients treated in Nursing Unit No. 6 are all DRG 209 (major joint procedures) and are all associated with one physician, Dr. Mallard. Our STP for DRG 209 calls for a 14-day length of stay. A review of Dr. Mallard's patient records reveals that only 560 patient days of care should have been used (40 cases at 14 days per case). Dr. Mallard had 20 patients with lengths of stay greater than 14 days. These 20 patients accounted for an excess of 80 patient days.

Dr. Mallard also had 10 patients with shorter lengths of stay. These patients offset 40 days of the 80-day surplus. Thus, while 600 patient days of care were provided, only 560 should have been used. This creates an unfavorable utilization variance, calculated as the product of budgeted cost per unit and the difference between actual and standard volume. In our example of Nursing Unit No. 6, the utilization variance would be:

Utilization variance =
$(600 - 560) \times \$80.90 = \$3,236.00$ (Unfavorable)

This variance is not charged to the nursing department. It is charged to the manager of patient treatment, in this case Dr. Mallard.

Figure 9-1 depicts the flow of costs and the variances associated with each account.

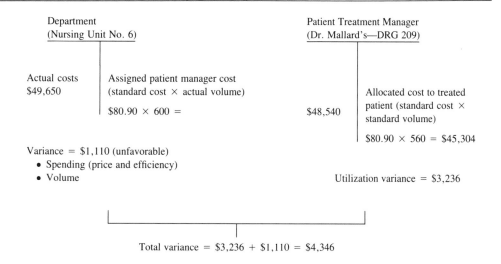

Figure 9-1 Cost Flow and Variance

This delineation of variances represents a very powerful analytical tool for analyzing cost variances from budgeted cost levels. The existence of a flexible budget model is not a prerequisite to its employment. The only real prerequisite is that major resource cost categories be separated into price and utilization components. Since effective cost control appears to be predicated on a separate analysis of price and utilization decisions, this does not seem too difficult a task, in view of the potential payoff. Finally, it should be noted that there is no requirement for a formalization of these variances into the budget reporting models. They can be calculated on an ad hoc basis to investigate and explain large cost variances.

SUMMARY

In general, within the framework for cost control, two approaches are possible: (1) preventive and (2) detection-correction. The detection-correction approach is usually based upon some system of variance analysis. From a decision-theory perspective, the investigation of a variance is based upon the cost of investigation, the probability that a correctable problem exists, the potential loss if the problem is not corrected, and the costs of problem correction. It may not always be possible to develop truly objective measures for these values, but sensitivity analysis may offer a useful aid in such situations.

Chapter 10

Costing Hospital Products

Kenneth F. Johnson
President, Strategic Healthcare Systems, Inc.

The changes that have occurred in the health care industry during the 1980s and the impact of these changes on hospitals have been dramatic. After 15 years the major payer, Medicare, significantly changed the rules of the game by switching from retrospective cost reimbursement to a prospective, fixed-price schedule for inpatients and some outpatients. During this period business organizations attempted to reduce their share of health care costs through managed care and ''managed cost'' arrangements such as health maintenance organizations (HMOs), preferred provider organizations (PPOs), and other competitive health plans.

Hospitals had become used to the idea that they were the dominate player. Now they have discovered new competitors in the marketplace. Not only must they compete with one another, they also must compete with a variety of free-standing clinics. The free-standing clinics, often initiated by members of the hospital's medical · staff, advertise lower prices and more ''user-friendly'' services.

These changes have placed new and more complex demands on hospital financial managers for more timely and accurate cost information. To be successful, today's health care managers must have an understanding of the basic concepts of cost accounting and how these concepts are applied in the health care setting.

Knowledge of the incremental and full costs of health care products is essential to attain enhanced fiscal viability through a more sophisticated and informed decision-making process.

COST ACCOUNTING WITHIN THE HOSPITAL ENVIRONMENT

Although management accounting systems are well established in other industries, they have only recently been given serious consideration within health care. Financial accounting systems are geared to producing information that satisfies external reporting requirements—reports to stockholders, lenders, regulatory agencies, and the like. The Medicare program has been the dominant influence on health care financial accounting. Management accounting systems, on the other hand, are designed to provide managers with current and accurate information upon which to base their decisions. A management accounting system, therefore, should have the flexibility to assemble and report information to meet the needs of the moment, which can change from day to day. To top it off, the flexibility of management accounting may be in conflict with the financial accounting requirement for consistency. The solution is to create a second set of books for the management accounting system.

An integral component of a management accounting system is cost accounting. Cost accounting includes classifying, allocating, recording, summarizing, and reporting current or prospective costs (or both) in terms of cost centers and products. To cost a product it must first be identified. Although the health care industry has avoided comparison with manufacturing, such comparisons can no longer be put aside. Recently the health care industry has recognized that hospitals have an identifiable product—a discharged patient. In any context, a product is the result of a process. In health care the process is patient care and the result is a discharged patient.

Hospitals have two levels of products: intermediate products, sometimes referred to as patient care units (PCUs), and final products. The final products are the individual cases or discharges and the intermediate products the treatments and procedures that are represented by billed charges within the patient accounting system. Case costs are an aggregation of intermediate product costs. This chapter focuses on costing of intermediate products.

Intermediate product costs should be determined in sufficient detail to provide management with the information required to carry out the planning, control, and evaluative functions. For example, if flexible budgeting is an objective, the procedure costing process should provide fixed and variable components for each identified cost element. A case-mix system may draw only upon summary costs, but having access to the detail will allow the flexibility to perform a variety of yet unforeseen demands for analysis.

Provided fixed and variable cost behavior patterns are reflected within the procedure costs, performance evaluation through variance analysis can become a byproduct of the budget process. The advantage of flexible budgeting is that the effects of variations from planned volume levels, which generally are beyond the control of the department head, can be removed. Departmental performance can then be evaluated appropriately on what is reasonably controllable at that level.

The use of intermediate product costs in the budgeting and pricing process is the subject of another chapter in this book.

NEW WINE IN OLD BOTTLES

To make the transition from traditional financial accounting systems to management accounting systems to support the decision-making process, it is necessary first to understand the fundamental differences in terminology. Terms that may have become familiar in the past may have taken on quite a different meaning within the context of management accounting.

Production versus Support Functions

Any production process, whether manufacturing widgets or treating patients, involves a variety of labor and material resources. For hospitals, the identification and control of resource consumption are critical if financial viability is to be maintained in the newly competitive prospective-payment environment. Traditionally, hospital cost centers have been classified as either revenue- or nonrevenue-producing. This distinction has little, if any, bearing on the patient care process or a hospital's organizational structure. When the patient care process is analyzed, it becomes apparent that a hospital does indeed have two distinct types of cost centers: those that are directly involved with the production of the final product and those that support the process. Thus, for a management accounting system, each hospital cost center should be classified as either a production function or a support function.

Although all revenue-producing cost centers are generally production functions, not all of the Medicare nonrevenue producers are support functions. It might seem like a small point, but nonrevenue-producing production functions such as admitting, patient billing, and medical records are directly involved in producing the discharge and may have varying unit costs based upon payer, length of stay, or other factors that should be considered when determining case costs. Eventually these factors could be important in bidding for a PPO's or HMO's business.

Cost Classification

Perhaps the most confusing inconsistency between management terminology and financial accounting terminology is the classification of costs. Under financial accounting, costs that are directly assigned through the general ledger to a cost center are classified as *direct costs* of the cost center; those that are allocated from non-revenue-producing cost centers are the *indirect costs* of the cost center. These definitions are appropriate if the objective is to determine costs at the cost center level. However, if the objective is to determine costs at a product level, more specificity is required. A cost accountant classifies product costs into three categories: direct costs, indirect costs, and overhead.

1. Direct costs are assigned directly to a cost center through the general ledger or are "reassigned" within a subsidiary ledger and can be directly traced to a specific product of that cost center. Direct labor relates to the time actually spent on patient care, e.g., in preparing a test.
2. Indirect costs are directly assigned to a cost center but cannot be traced to a specific product of that cost center. Indirect labor relates to the supervisory and administrative time spent by the department supervisor and the residual of the departmental labor time and dollars that are not accounted for as direct costs. Indirect costs are distributed to the cost center's products based upon direct labor hours or dollars, total direct costs, or some other appropriate basis.
3. Institutional overhead, or burden, is the term used by cost accountants to define costs assigned to a support function that cannot be directly traced to a production function or a specific product. During the cost-determination process, overhead costs are allocated to production functions using cost-finding techniques, and are then distributed to products using methodologies that are similar to those used to distribute indirect costs.

Cost Reassignment versus Allocation

Costs assigned directly to nonrevenue-producing cost centers have represented a significant portion of a hospital's total cost. Cost

allocation is an arbitrary process. If a lot of time and effort is to be expended in determining direct product costs, the advantage of directly reassigning support function costs to production functions should be apparent. For example, hospitals have allocated housekeeping costs to revenue-producing cost centers on the basis of square feet. This approach assumes that housekeeping costs are the same for every square foot in the hospital. Common sense says that this is not true. Production functions, for product costing, should be charged with their actual share of housekeeping costs.

In addition to the step-down cost-finding method, there are several other methods that may be used to charge production functions with the costs of support functions. Transfer pricing (intrainstitutional sales) can be used, either within the general ledger or a subsidiary management accounting ledger, to charge the production function and credit the support function for services rendered. This approach is used when measuring departmental profitability is an objective. Perhaps the most desirable approach is to reclassify the costs within a management ledger rather than disrupting the general ledger. This practice is common in other industries where a factory ledger is used to record the details required for management accounting. In either case the results will be the same: the indirect costs of production functions will increase and the overhead costs to be distributed will decrease.

Following the housekeeping example, management recognizes that it does not cost the same to clean a square foot in the laboratory as it does in the president's office, and transfers the housekeeping costs, on a work-order basis, to the appropriate cost centers. Is this appropriate for the general ledger? Maybe not. Consider the auditor's reaction or the impact on the responsibility-reporting systems. Use of a separate management accounting ledger starts to make more sense.

Cost Behavior

The distinction among direct, indirect, and overhead costs at the product level may seem unimportant; however, each of these cost types is controllable at different levels of responsibility and exhibits different behavior patterns. They will not change in a uniform manner over time or with volume changes. Cost behavior and cost control are often considered together. For years, the industry has regarded—and convinced most regulators—that because a significant part of a hospital's costs were fixed, they were not controllable. During the 1970s few in the health care industry would have believed that U.S. hospitals during the mid-1980s would be experiencing a 10 to 15 percent decrease in inpatient utilization concurrent with a modest increase in outpatient visits, while enjoying a stronger-than-ever bottom line. Hospitals reacted to declines in volume by recognizing, often subconsciously, the differences in short-term versus long-term cost behavior patterns as well as their long-term controllability.

The key to understanding and managing cost behavior is recognizing the appropriate *relevant range*. The term relevant range refers to either a period of time or a range of volume during which cost behavior is either stable or reasonably predictable. There are four basic cost behavior patterns readily identifiable within a hospital's cost structure.

1. Fixed costs are costs that are not expected to change over a specified relevant range. However, in the long run, these costs can be managed and controlled. Administrative salaries are generally fixed for a year's duration. If performance dictates, the governing board may well determine that an adjustment, up or down, is in order for the next year. Understanding fixed costs is particularly important if volume is not constant. Although as volume increases the cost per unit decreases, there will be a precipitous increase in the unit cost when the relevant range is exceeded.

2. Variable costs vary in direct relation to volume in a predictable manner. For example, a chest series requires two views and therefore two films. In this case, film is a variable cost even though only one film is required for some procedures and two or three for others. It is not necessary to have a one-to-one relationship for a cost to be

considered variable—only a consistent, predictable behavior.

3. Semivariable costs have both a fixed and a variable component. The behavior pattern reflects the fixed cost at lower volume levels and incremental increases thereafter. Utilities, with a fixed monthly rate and additional unit charges, are good examples of semivariable costs.

4. Step costs account for the largest share of hospital costs. The step-cost behavior pattern reflects normal staffing patterns by recognizing that some costs are "fixed" over relatively short relevant ranges. For example, consider the staffing plan for a routine nursing unit. The plan reflects differing levels of staffing for ranges of occupancy and treatment plans. The addition of one more occupied bed or a defined change in acuity units may cause the addition of a full-time equivalent and probably a changed staffing mix.

PROCEDURE COSTING OVERVIEW

Cost determination focuses on identifying costs at either the cost center or product level. Under Medicare cost reimbursement, hospital accountants became highly skilled at determining costs at the cost center level and developed sophisticated cost-finding methodologies. These skills must now be balanced with other skills that are more appropriate to product costing. The first critical step in this process is to identify the hospital's intermediate and final products. The final product is a collection of subproducts assembled under the direction of a "product designer," the physician. The final product is a case, and the subproduct comprises the procedures and services provided. Since each case is unique, i.e., has a different set of subproducts, the hospital's cost accounting system must recognize these different costs through the determination of detailed costs at the procedure level. Case cost determination is appropriately accomplished through the hospital's case-mix, or clinical management, system.

A hospital's procedure cost determination system should interface with the financial accounting systems and be integrated with the other components of the management accounting system. The interface capability is essential, since many of the base data used during cost determination are drawn from financial accounting sources. The procedure cost information developed through the cost-determination process, although interesting, is of no real value by itself. Procedure costs, however, are a basic ingredient of case-mix analysis, flexible budgets, and impact analysis through a modeling component.

There are seven basic steps to be accomplished to cost a hospital's final products.

1. Identify Final Products

Although a final product is a discharged patient, these are single events. Each case is unique. From a management perspective, cases need to be grouped into product lines that are meaningful for the particular audience: physicians, payers, patients, or managers. Medicare has imposed diagnosis-related groups (DRGs) on hospitals, but there are serious questions whether DRGs are valid for case management. A hospital's product lines should be defined in terms that are appropriate to their needs.

2. Identify Intermediate Products

In most cases intermediate products are the individual charge items included in a hospital's charge master. However, there are occasions when it is appropriate to group individual charges into intermediate products for costing. An example of such an occasion might be surgery. Many hospitals charge individually for each item included in a sterile surgical pack. The same pack could be used for several surgical procedures, making it appropriate to assemble the individual charge items into intermediate products for costing.

3. Identify Intermediate-Product Direct-Input Resources

There are a variety of resources used to produce intermediate products. The direct costs of an intermediate product should include only those resources that are directly traceable to the product and are readily quantified. The inclusion of insignificant resources as direct costs rather than indirect costs may cloud the cost structure unnecessarily.

4. Reassign and Allocate Support-Function Costs

The activities of support functions should be reviewed to determine whether costs can be discretely assigned to production functions. The object of cost reassignment is to reduce the size of the overhead pool of dollars allocated through arbitrary cost-finding methods to production functions. When all suitable costs have been reassigned, the remaining support-function costs should be allocated as overhead.

5. Determine Intermediate-Product Direct Costs

After a review of the production process used by a production function to produce intermediate products, determine the quantity of each identified input resource that is used. The aggregation of input unit quantities times their unit cost is the direct cost of the intermediate product.

6. Distribute to Intermediate Products Indirect and Overhead Costs

The direct costs of a cost center that are not accounted for as direct product costs are therefore indirect product costs. The total costs of intermediate products should include indirect product costs and allocated overhead. An indirect cost-distribution method for each type of cost should be selected that best suits the variability between products of that cost type. For example, supervision as an indirect cost seemingly would vary based on direct labor hours. A general rule for indirect cost distribution is when in doubt use either direct labor hours or total direct costs as the basis for indirect cost distribution.

7. Apply Intermediate-Product Costs to Final Products

Each final product represents an aggregation of intermediate products. Therefore, the cost of a final product is the sum of the intermediate-product costs. Since any product line defined for a hospital will not be 100 percent homogeneous, a resource-consumption profile should be developed for each product line. The resource-consumption profile may be a historical representation or a ''standard'' set of resources reasonably expected to be used in the case grouping. In either case there will be variances by the very nature of the final products—no two cases are the same. However inexact a resource-consumption profile may be, it is extremely useful for planning, budgeting, and obtaining an overall evaluation of performance.

Figure 10-1 represents a schematic presentation of the product-costing process.

INTERMEDIATE-PRODUCT COSTING STEPS

There are basic, common-sense steps to be followed when determining the costs of inter-

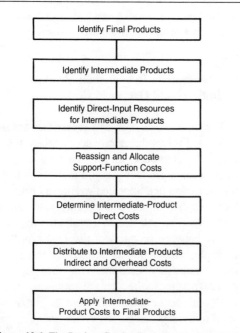

Identify Final Products

Identify Intermediate Products

Identify Direct-Input Resources for Intermediate Products

Reassign and Allocate Support-Function Costs

Determine Intermediate-Product Direct Costs

Distribute to Intermediate Products Indirect and Overhead Costs

Apply Intermediate-Product Costs to Final Products

Figure 10-1 The Product-Costing Process

mediate products. Most of the available computerized cost accounting/cost determination systems—for mainframe, minicomputers, or microcomputers—provide a vehicle to facilitate the process. The real work is done, however, outside the computer system. The cost-center personnel, much more familiar with the intermediate products and the processes employed than anyone else, should do the bulk of the work.

Although this might seem to be obvious, the cost-determination process cannot reasonably be applied simultaneously to all production functions without stretching resources; there should be prioritization of the tasks.

There are two factors to consider, the first of which is based upon need, such as which prices should be restructured. The second factor is the availability of data with which to facilitate the process. To get off to a fast start, the initial production function should be one that is easy to do. In addition, conducting a ''data source review'' in all departments should be considered. (What is uncovered may be a surprise, such as learning that some departments collect information that is neither shared nor made readily available to anyone outside the department.) A logical starting point might be with either a laboratory or radiology function. Most laboratories collect College of American Pathologists (CAP) units. A good laboratory manager will already know the differences between the published laboratory values and the actual time values of that laboratory. Since determining labor input is the most difficult step, initiating the process with the laboratory will provide a good head start. On the other hand, radiology has a clearly defined process and products with readily identifiable input resources. It is a toss-up, but either selection will provide a great sense of accomplishment due to sheer volume.

As the procedural steps are discussed in the following paragraphs, a case study, based upon medical records as a production function, is used to illustrate the process.

Case Facts

Coastal Community Hospital is an 80-bed acute care hospital located in a rural area approximately

35 miles from an urban center and about 20 minutes from another hospital of similar size. Coastal has experienced a significant increase in Medicare cases. However, George Brown, the administrator, is concerned that since some of the costs of nonrevenue-producing cost centers are not evenly distributed among payers, Medicare case-cost information may be understated. For example, he has noted that medical records has had to increase its staff because of the additional requirements of the Medicare program. With that in mind, George asked Jim Jones, Coastal's management accountant, to undertake a study to identify intermediate products for medical records and then determine the costs of each intermediate product.

Jim Jones proceeded to tackle the task given to him by his administrator by following the steps outlined in Figure 10-2.

Step 1: Identify the Costing Base Period and Review Source Data

Discussion. Cost determination can be based on historical or budgeted data, either on an annual basis or some other representative period. If the objective is to develop "standard costs," then budgeted data or historical data rolled forward should be used. Most cost determination systems allow the use of both historical and budgeted data, creating two sets of procedure

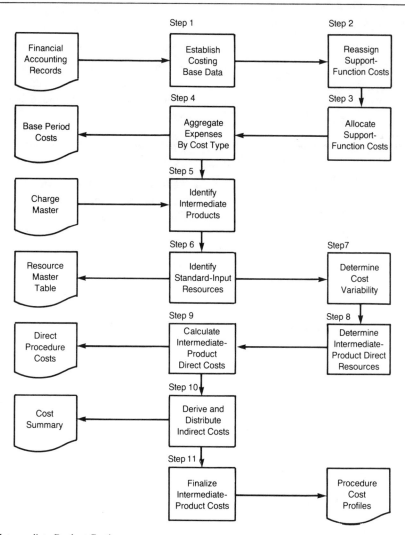

Figure 10-2 Intermediate-Product Costing

costs: actual and budgeted or standard costs. For the first pass, historical data may be the better choice since the available data tend to be more complete and to use this data will facilitate the verification of unit costs the first time around.

Typically the data sources will include the general ledger, patient accounting transaction registers, payroll records, fixed-asset records, and materials management files. Interfacing with these systems will eliminate unnecessary data input, reduce error rates, and facilitate updating detailed cost files.

Case Study. Since the fiscal year had just ended, Jim selected the most recent 12 months for the study. From the payroll department he obtained paid hours and average hourly rates for the three job classes within the medical records department:

Job Class	Description	Paid Hrs.	Avg. Rate
01	Supervisor	1,925	$12.03
02	Technician	9,998	7.41
06	Clerk	8,880	4.51

From general accounting he abstracted the year-end balances for the medical records accounts from the general ledger.

Step 2: Reassign Support-Function Costs to Production Functions

Discussion. There are instances when costs have been assigned through the financial accounting system to support functions that can be readily traced directly to specific production functions and, in some cases, specific products. Common examples can be found in the areas of employee benefits, depreciation of major movable equipment, and housekeeping. Employee benefits should be included as an indirect cost rather than allocated with the other general and administrative costs. The case for direct assignment of depreciation of major movable equipment is obvious; the argument for why housekeeping should be discretely costed was made previously. In any event, prior to cost determination, a complete review of all support-function cost categories should be undertaken to identify those costs that are appropriate for reassignment, with the appropriate adjustments made within the accounting subsidiary ledger.

Case Study. After reviewing the accounts and determining that both depreciation and employee benefits had been charged directly to medical records, Jim concluded that no reassignments were necessary.

Step 3: Allocate Remaining Support-Function Costs to Production Functions

Discussion. Without getting into a detailed discussion of the advantages and disadvantages of direct versus absorption costing, it is important to take this step, regardless of which costing procedure is chosen. If the user is interested in incremental costs and contribution margins, the

Account	Description	Amount
7180.01	Managers and supervisors	$ 23,158
7180.02	Technicians	74,085
7180.06	Clerks	40,085
7180.15	Employee benefits	24,720
7180.43	Department forms—laboratory	156
7180.46	Office supplies	5,600
7180.50	Other supplies	1,234
7180.60	Equipment repairs	2,945
7180.70	Depreciation—equipment	1,250
7180.89	Dues and subscriptions	1,146
7180.92	Travel	947
7180.93	Other expenses	17,866
	Total	$193,192

information can be extracted from a ''full cost'' file. However, if there is a need to determine the ''full cost'' of a procedure it will not be available unless overhead is allocated to production functions and distributed to procedures. Although the same cost allocation methodology (step-down) as used for Medicare can be employed for this purpose, it is suggested that the statistics, combinations, and sequence used for Medicare cost reporting be reviewed and revised to reflect reality. If the cost-determination system supports the maintenance of fixed/variable relationships of overhead cost components down to the procedure level, then these relationships should be determined prior to cost allocation.

Case Study. For this analysis Jim determined that only the direct costs of the medical records cost center should be used and the cost allocation step could be skipped in this case. However, Jim made a note that the intermediate-product costs developed through this study would require updating to include allocated overhead at a later date.

Step 4: Aggregate Expenses by Cost Type

Discussion. Most hospitals have set up a number of natural accounts to comply with external reporting requirements or to meet now forgotten needs. For cost determination (and perhaps for flexible budgeting), the detail recorded in the general ledger may be a distraction. Additionally, the classification of cost center expenses into uniform cost types simplifies cross-cost center comparisons.

Case Study. During other procedure-costing projects, Jim classified departmental direct costs into one of 12 cost types for reporting and the calculation and distribution of indirect costs. The standard-cost types included three for labor; two for supplies; and one each for equipment, facilities, professional fees, purchased services, other costs, employee benefits, and allocated overhead. Jim determined that of the twelve only seven applied to this project.

Jim mapped the medical records expenses to the identified cost types with the following results:

Technical labor	$ 74,085
Nontechnical labor	40,085
Department management	23,158
Supplies	6,990
Department equipment	4,195
Other costs	19,959
Fringe benefits	24,720
Total	$195,192

Step 5: Identify Intermediate Products and Establish Costing Priorities

Discussion. Typically, the intermediate products of a production function are well defined through the charge master used by patient accounting. If this is the case, the charge master should be reviewed for duplicate and/or redundant charges that should be mapped into intermediate products. If the production function is not a ''revenue-producing cost center,'' a study will be required to determine the appropriate intermediate products. As a general rule, intermediate products of ''nonrevenue-producing cost centers'' should be such that they relate to data already collected in the system.

Most hospital cost accounting literature discusses the 80/20 rule; all vendors point out that their systems provide the 80/20 capability. However, while it is true that 80 percent or more of a department's costs will be accounted for by 20 percent or less of the procedures, is it worth going to the trouble of calculating detailed costs for a handful of procedures and using a ratio of costs to charges (RCC) methodology to distribute costs to the remainder? The significance of this point will be left to the discussion of Step 10 below. At this point it is sufficient to say that once direct costs have been determined for the major procedures, it is simple to perform the remaining procedures. Above all, accuracy of procedure costs will not be hard to defend.

Case Study. Jim made a visit to medical records, where he found the manager eager to help with the study. Mary Roberts, the department head, quickly identified eight distinct medical records intermediate products based upon the current activities of the department. Each of the intermediate products could be identified and traced to a payer and/or patient type to alleviate problems in collecting volume data. The eight intermediate products and the "volume" obtained from the hospital's statistics for the cost-determination base period are given below.

Inpatient—Medicare	1,300
Inpatient—non-Medicare	2,500
Ambulatory surgery—Medicare	420
Ambulatory surgery—non-Medicare	720
Emergency room—Medicare	11,000
Emergency room—non-Medicare	13,400
Outpatient visit—Medicare	9,400
Outpatient visit—non-Medicare	8,700

Since there were so few intermediate products, Jim and Mary decided that the direct costs of each should be determined independently.

Step 6: Identify the Standard Direct Resources Used by the Cost Center

Discussion. Each department has its own bundle of input resources that go into producing its intermediate products. These resources can be classified by cost type, such as direct labor, supplies, purchased services, and equipment. Within each of the cost types are a variety of individual resource components, including labor classes and individual supply items. Only those resources that are significant, measurable, and can be traced to specific intermediate products should be listed. A resource master table, detailing the individual resource, will serve as a guide for the cost center staff when determining the direct costs of the intermediate products. Other resources will be considered as "bench stock" and treated as indirect costs of the intermediate products.

Case Study. Based upon his discussions with Mary, Jim knew that in addition to the three direct labor classes, there were only two other direct inputs: a medical records file folder at $.04 each and for Medicare inpatients an attestation label at $.10 a piece. Jim proceeded to enter the departmental expense information into the cost determination model and built the resource master table, which listed each of the resources used to produce the medical records "products."

The resource master table for medical records included the following information:

Resource	Unit Measure	Unit Cost
Technician	Minute	.1235
Clerk	Minute	.0752
Supervisor	Minute	.2005
Medical record folder	Piece	.0400
Attestation label	Piece	.1000

Step 7. Determine the Cost Variability of Each Cost Type

Discussion. Each cost type may have a different fixed/variable behavior pattern to be accounted for in the cost-determination process. Using the resource master table as a starting point, variability factors (or fixed factors if it is easier) should be determined for each identified cost type. By definition, direct costs are 100 percent variable. However, to consider that indirect costs are 100 percent fixed could prove fatal later on. Indirect costs are derived by subtracting direct costs from total costs. If total direct costs increase because of volume increases, it would be possible to have negative indirect costs. Therefore, it is necessary to determine what portion of the indirect costs will not change with volume increases or decreases.

Case Study. Jim and Mary reviewed the cost behavior patterns for each of the cost types appropriate to medical records and concluded that the entire amount was fixed for both departmental management and equipment. For the other accounts Mary estimated that the following amounts were fixed: $12,000 of the clerical, $2,500 of supplies, and $15,000 of the other costs. All of the remaining costs, Mary believed, varied in direct proportion to the volume of the department's activity as measured by the intermediate products.

Step 8: Determine the Direct-Resource Inputs for Each Studied Intermediate Product

Discussion. The "real work" of cost determination is completed during this step. The burden can be somewhat lessened, although at the expense of accuracy, if published weighted value units such as CAP units for laboratory and relative value units for radiology are used as a starting point. However, these units should be modified to reflect actual circumstances before using them. In the final analysis, there is no substitute for actual measurement of input units, which can be accomplished with time studies or activity analyses that are conducted with assistance from departmental personnel. Department managers generally have a thorough understanding of the department's activities. Consequently, taking advantage of this knowledge will speed up the process, lower staff resistance, and improve the credibility of the resulting unit costs at all levels of personnel.

Case Study. Jim and Mary decided that the medical records staff should record the time they spent on each case for the next two weeks. They would then review the information to test Mary's assumption that there is not a significant deviation from the average within each of the identified "products."

At the end of the two-week study period, Mary and Jim reviewed the data recorded by the medical records staff and concluded that there were in fact eight distinct products. Furthermore, Jim's quick review showed him that there was indeed a significant difference in cost between products. The direct-input data were aggregated.

Intermediate Products	Technician	Clerk	*Input Units* Manager	Folder	Label
Inpatient—Medicare	63	58	1	1	1
Inpatient—other	41	34	1	1	
Ambulatory surgery—Medicare	23	10		1	
Ambulatory surgery—other	18	5		1	
Emergency room—Medicare	9	6		1	
Emergency room—other	8	5		1	
Outpatient—Medicare	4	2		1	
Outpatient—other	3	2		1	

Step 9: Calculate the Direct Costs for Each Intermediate Product

Discussion. From this point on, most of the work is mechanical and, as such, lends itself to computerization. Direct costs are the product of multiplying input units by input unit costs for each resource component used in the procedure.

The variability factors are then applied, resulting in the calculation of the fixed and variable direct costs.

Case Study. Jim now had all the information he needed to calculate the direct costs of the eight medical records procedures and obtained the results shown below.

Intermediate Products	Labor	*Unit Costs* Supplies	Total
Inpatient—Medicare	12.34	.14	12.48
Inpatient—other	7.82	.04	7.86
Ambulatory surgery—Medicare	3.59	.04	3.63
Ambulatory surgery—other	2.60	.04	2.64
Emergency room—Medicare	1.56	.04	1.60
Emergency room—other	1.36	.04	1.40
Outpatient—Medicare	.64	.04	.68
Outpatient—other	.52	.04	.56

Step 10: Derive the Indirect Costs, by Cost Type, for the Cost Center and Distribute Them to the Intermediate Products

Discussion. Indirect costs, by definition, cannot be traced to procedures and they cannot be directly measured in terms of intermediate products during direct costing. They must, therefore, be derived by subtracting the accumulated direct costs, by cost type, from the total base-period costs for the cost type. Before continuing with costing, the distribution of dollars between direct and indirect costs for each cost type should be reviewed. If, for example, direct costs accounted for 95 percent of a labor cost type, there would be strong evidence that the direct costs were overstated.

Indirect cost types each have a different basis for distribution. For example, supervisory time relates more to direct labor hours than to total direct costs. There are several different distribution methodologies that are used by cost accountants, the most common of which are direct labor hours, direct labor cost, total direct cost, machine hours, volume, and price. The most suitable methodology should be selected for each labor resource component and nonlabor resource type, followed by calculation of appropriate factors and distribution of costs.

Case Study. The distribution of direct and indirect costs at the cost type level was about what Jim expected to see. The technicians had a relatively heavy direct cost percentage (80 percent) and the clerks were at 63-percent direct. Only a third of the total supply costs were accounted for as direct costs.

Cost Type	Direct	Indirect	Total
Technical labor	$58,900	$ 15,186	$ 74,085
Nontechnical labor	25,372	14,712	40,085
Department management	762	22,396	23,158
Supplies	2,028	4,962	6,990
Department equipment		4,195	4,195
Other costs		19,959	19,959
Fringe benefits		24,720	24,720
Total	$87,062	$106,130	$193,192

Jim decided to distribute indirect labor and supply costs to procedures using the cost type's direct cost as the basis and total direct costs for the remaining cost types.

Step 11: Calculate the Detailed Costs for Each Intermediate Product

Discussion. At this point, all of the necessary information has been assembled to calculate the fixed, variable, and total direct and indirect costs by resource type (overhead is a resource type) for each product. The job is done. The final mechanical step is to prepare the reports and pass the data to a case-mix system for costing final products.

Case Study. Having made all the calculations necessary to determine the costs for each of the eight medical records intermediate products, Jim prepared a detailed procedure cost profile for each intermediate product and the procedure cost summary.

SUMMARY

Hospital managers need timely and simultaneous access to data collected through traditional operating systems. This capability can be provided efficiently through an integrated strategic management information data base. The integrated strategic management information

	Direct	Indirect			Total Cost
		Variable	*Fixed*	*Total*	
Inpatient—Medicare	12.48	6.90	10.88	17.78	30.26
Inpatient—other	7.86	4.31	8.89	13.19	21.05
Ambulatory surgery—Medicare	3.63	2.10	1.21	3.31	6.94
Ambulatory surgery—other	2.64	1.56	.81	2.37	5.01
Emergency room—Medicare	1.60	.93	.62	1.55	3.15
Emergency room—other	1.40	.82	.54	1.36	2.74
Outpatient—Medicare	.68	.43	.27	.70	1.38
Outpatient—other	.56	.35	.24	.60	1.16

data base is the foundation of a hospital's decision-support system, which includes the functional capability to determine procedure and case costs, manage product lines, and develop and monitor operating budgets. Overlaying the decision-support system is the capability to develop and model a variety of ''what if'' analysis scenarios.

In the final analysis, decision-support systems are rapidly moving from the category of ''nice-to-have toys'' to the point where they are becoming necessary tools of the hospital manager's trade.

Timely and accurate procedure-cost data are more than a luxury—these data are essential as a basis for effective management. Procedure costs are the foundation of any decision-support system. The most difficult part of procedure costing is getting started. Once the process begins, it becomes easier and easier from procedure to procedure and production function to production function. The only other ''difficulty'' in the process is to remember that department personnel should be involved in the process from the outset. It will make the entire process run more smoothly and produce more accurate results.

Chapter 11

Human Resource Accounting

Jesse F. Dillard
Associate Professor of Accounting
The Ohio State University

Health care made tremendous advances during the 1970s and 1980s in both technology and delivery systems. At the same time, the governing agencies began to question the rising cost of health care.

The improved delivery systems and advanced technology have made the health care industry more dependent than ever upon highly trained, professional personnel. Many of these individuals are licensed and others are unionized. The professional patient-care team now includes physical therapists, occupational therapists, speech therapists, respiratory therapists, social workers, and dietitians.

These changes in the health care industry have created new challenges for the hospital administrator, the financial manager, and the human resources manager, as well as for the monitoring agencies. The financial statements of the average hospital show between 50 and 60 percent of the direct-expense budget being attributed to human resources. With hospital costs under constant scrutiny, and control threatened by the federal government and third-party payers, human resources management is critical. Unfortunately, there is currently no formal information system within health care facilities designed specifically for human resource management. This chapter reviews progress being made toward the development of a formal system for human resource accounting (HRA).

HRA has been defined as the "accounting for people as organization resources."[1] This accounting necessitates assigning quantitative values to the human component of an entity. Quantifying the value of human factors poses an interesting challenge that has stimulated numerous approaches. The proposed models that have resulted from the efforts generally focus on identifying and measuring the operational costs and benefits associated with the "human assets." The Work Institute of America has identified the goals of an HRA system:

- to furnish cost-value information for making decisions about acquiring, allocating, developing, and maintaining resources in order to attain cost-effective organizational benefits
- to allow managerial personnel to effectively monitor the use of human resources
- to provide a determination of assets control, (i.e., whether assets are conserved, depleted, or appreciated)
- to aid in the development of management principles by clarifying the financial consequences of various practices[2]

The following sections survey some of the proposed models and identify HRA techniques that are applicable to health care facilities.

HUMAN RESOURCE ACCOUNTING MODELS

The economic concept of human capital[3,4] is the theoretical basis for HRA. Simply stated, human capital refers to the stock or value of the future goods and services that are to accrue from the human components of an organization. The value of this human capital can be increased through investment in the human components (i.e., staff-development programs), and results can be measured as a rate of return on the incremental monetary investment. Thus, it is assumed that a cause-and-effect relationship exists between investments and rate of return (i.e., productivity of the staff member). HRA is concerned with evaluating and translating into dollars both the stock of human capital and the related periodic returns.

From a financial accounting perspective, the existence of human resources is not new. High employee productivity and morale, progressive management, and good customer relations have been recorded in the financial statements under the general heading of "goodwill." Specifically, Flamholtz states that "a major purpose of human resource accounting is to help managers to use an organization's human resources effectively and efficiently. Human resource accounting is intended to provide managers with information needed to acquire, develop, allocate, conserve, utilize, evaluate, and reward human resources."[5]

Some organizations, such as the R.G. Barry Corporation, have included HRA data in their annual reports;[6] however, because of the lack of generally accepted accounting principles, this information is primarily reported only in internal publications. The major obstacles are the lack of adequate measurement criteria and expert opinion against the appropriateness of considering human resources as "assets."[7] While it is generally accepted that well-trained, highly motivated personnel may be the most valuable asset possessed by an organization, there is little consensus as to how to place a dollar value on these resources. In addition, managers seem unwilling to acccept the additional accountability that comes with the implementation of an HRA system.[8]

If an organization's employees are to be viewed as an asset from an accounting standpoint, they should be measured as any other asset. An accounting definition of an asset is the "expected future economic benefits, the rights of which have been acquired by the enterprise as a result of some current or past transaction."[9] This definition requires that assets be acquired through a transaction and have future economic benefits. Some experts have argued human resources do meet these requirements. Human resources spending can be treated as an investment because the work force is regarded as the permanent property of the enterprise by its managers and its shareholders. Others contend that human resources do not meet these requirements because the enterprise does not have exclusive right to the future benefits of the services of the employees.[10] Consequently, either the traditional basis of accounting must be modified to accommodate human resources, or these assets must be measured by using something other than traditionally accepted accounting principles and be excluded from accounting reports.

Recently, some accountants have advocated that assets be defined as the gross future benefits, offset by a corresponding liability for the future cost associated with the benefit. This definition is consistent with the traditional economic concept of an asset. Both the net and gross concepts are compatible with valuing human resources and have been advocated by proponents of HRA.[11] Within this context, Lev and Schwartz[12] contend that the traditional balance sheet should contain the gross valuation of the organization's human capital on the asset side and the present value of the liability to pay wages and salaries on the liability side. They also state that these two values would, by definition, be equal.

An abundance of HRA models with vastly different approaches have been developed over the past 15 years. These models, which include both historical cost models and current valuation models, vary widely in complexity. The most critical problem in HRA remains that of developing an adequate means of measuring the value of human resources. An adequate HRA system depends on the environment of the organization (internal and external) and the users of the HRA system. Some managers may require detailed bottom-line monetary values for their human resources decisions while others may use turnover statistics (nonmonetary measures) for their human resources decisions. The use of either monetary or nonmonetary measures in human resources decisions depends on the decision-making and cognitive styles of the manager. Some managers' orientation is toward quantifiable and objectively determined measures of human resources, while other managers follow a more heuristic style in decision-making activities.[13] The manager must also determine whether to measure each employee as an individual or to consider groups of employees. The applicability of any type of HRA system within a given organization is dependent on management's needs and capabilities.

There are major differences in the human resource cost accounting (HRCA) models and human resource value accounting (HRVA) models. HRCA pertains to accounting for investments made by organizations in acquiring and developing human resources. This cost-based approach has an inherent attractiveness because it holds more closely to the conventional accounting methodology. This approach makes the implicit assumption that replacement value is accurately estimated by historical investment costs. HRVA proposes measuring the value of human resources in monetary terms without adhering to a historically based structure. Because of the complexities involved, efforts in HRVA tend to be difficult to implement, usually taking the form of conceptual proposals. The remaining portion of this section reviews two cost-based models and one current-valuation model, all of which may be applicable within health care organizations. These models are designed as attempts to implement HRA within the current accounting framework.

HUMAN RESOURCE COST ACCOUNTING

Managerial accounting uses the concept of cost in a variety of ways. Historical cost, acquisition cost, outlay cost, replacement cost, sunk cost, fixed and variable costs, marginal cost, and opportunity cost are some of the more frequent ways in which the term is used. Many of these cost concepts are applicable to human resources.

All costs may be conceived to have asset and expense components. An asset, as defined previously, is the portion of a cost that is expected to provide benefits during future accounting periods. An expense is the portion of a cost that has been consumed during the current accounting period. A basic accounting problem is the separation of the expense and asset elements of costs.

Two of the more important cost concepts in human resource accounting are historical cost and replacement cost. Historical, or original, cost refers to the actual forfeiture incurred to acquire or obtain a resource. Replacement cost refers to the sacrifice required to replace a resource presently owned or employed with one having the same future benefit or service potential. Outlay and imputed (direct and indirect) costs are components of the original and replacement cost concepts.

By identifying cost components, one may theoretically ascertain standards of anticipated human resource costs under predefined conditions. "Standard" human resource costs are usually established with respect to classifications of employees and functional accounts (i.e., x-ray technician, standard acquisition costs). These standards can facilitate improved management control. For example, this cost concept permits personnel management activities to be treated as a discretionary expense center or a profit center. As a profit center, the human resource function computes a transfer price, such as "cost per employee hired," that may be charged to other parts of the organization.

Historical Cost Model

Eric G. Flamholtz[14] has developed a model for the measurement of historical human resource costs that provides a structural framework for identification and classification of relevant costs (Figure 11-1).

Human resource acquisition costs generally include expenditures. Recruitment costs are incurred in identifying and attracting possible sources of human resources, both inside and out-

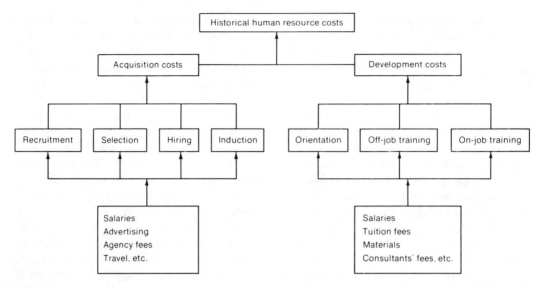

Figure 11-1 Model for Measurement of Human Resource Replacement Costs. *Source:* Reprinted from *Handbook of Cost Accounting* by S. Davidson and R. Weil (Eds.), with permission of McGraw-Hill, © 1978.

side an organization. These expenditures include recruiters' salaries, advertising costs, agency fees, travel, entertainment, and administrative expenses. Flamholtz suggests that all recruitment costs be allocated to the people actually hired. For example, if a newspaper advertisement is placed for one week at a cost of $1,000 and two people are hired, the allocation would be $500 per person. This allocation is independent of the number of interviews generated by the advertisement.

Selection costs are those costs incurred in evaluating and selecting potential employees. These costs vary, depending on the type of personnel (and level in the organization) being hired and the recruiting methods used. A trade-off often exists between the cost of recruitment and cost of selection. The use of mass media usually raises screening or selection costs. The use of agencies often reduces screening costs, but recruiting and selection expenses will be increased by agency fees.

Hiring and induction costs, from a practical viewpoint, may be considered as a single classification. These costs are incurred when bringing an individual into an organization and placing the person on the job. They include, for example, relocation expenses paid after the person has joined the organization. Induction costs may

also include "the cost of internal acquisition or replacement"[15] for a person who has been transferred from one position to another.

Development costs, as described by Flamholtz, refer to the sacrifice that must be incurred to train a person either to provide the level of performance normally expected from an individual in a given position or to enhance the individual's skills. Human resource development may be directed toward enhancing technical, administrative, or interpersonal skills.

Flamholtz's human resource cost accounting model includes three components of development costs: (1) orientation, (2) off-the-job training, and (3) on-the-job training.

Orientation costs are those associated with formal indoctrination and training. Orientation may be the process of becoming familiar with company policies, products, or facilities. It may range from simple instructions concerning how to do a repetitive job to highly specialized programs continuing over weeks, months, or perhaps years.[16]

Off-the-job training or education costs are generally incurred through development programs that are not directly connected with actual job performance. These programs may be the initial "break-in" training, advanced-technical training, or management-development programs.[17] Their duration can vary from a few hours to several years. Typical off-the-job training costs include the salaries of the trainers and trainees, tuition, meals, travel, facilities costs, consulting fees, and material.

On-the-job training costs refer to the cost of learning while on the job as opposed to during participation in formal training programs. The major direct cost of on-the-job training is the trainee's salary for the period that he or she is unproductive.[18] Subnormal productivity during the training process is an imputed cost. The imputed cost also includes the loss of performance of other people who are affected by the learning process.

To illustrate, suppose a health care facility hires an x-ray technician. This employee would be valued, or recorded on the company's books, as the sum total of the acquisition costs and development costs. Assume that acquisition costs, including travel and entertainment expenses, appropriately allocated portions of recruiters' salaries, advertising costs, and administrative expenses, total $2,500. Further, assume

that direct job development costs include the employee's salary during a formal orientation program and a three-week, off-the-job training course held by the local university, totaling $1,600. The cost of the university program is $650, and the allocated portion of the orientation program is $150. The total direct job-development costs are $2,400. Thus, using the historical human resource cost model, this employee is assigned a total "book" value of $4,900.

Replacement Cost Model

Human resource replacement cost, as previously defined, refers to the sacrifice required to replace a person presently employed in a given position with a substitute capable of rendering equivalent services. Flamholtz[19] has proposed an extension of his historical cost model as a replacement cost model. As shown in Figure 11-2, the replacement model includes separation costs, which are viewed as opportunity costs as well as the direct acquisition and development costs discussed above.

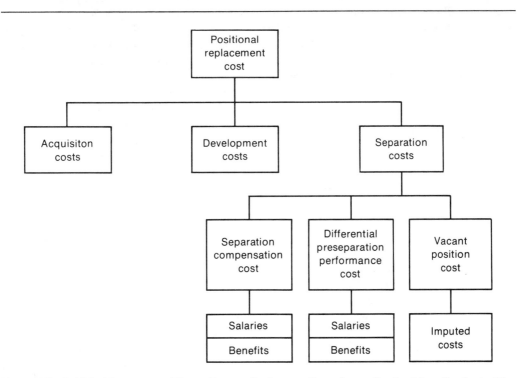

Figure 11-2 Model for Measurement of Human Resource Replacement Costs. *Source:* Reprinted from *Handbook of Cost Accounting* by S. Davidson and R. Weil (Eds.), with permission of McGraw-Hill, © 1978.

Separation costs are composed of three elements: (1) separation compensation, (2) differential-preseparation-performance costs, and (3) vacant position costs.

Separation compensation refers to severance pay. This may range from zero cost to required salary continuation for a year or more. Flamholtz suggests that average separation compensation costs be derived for a given position.

Differential-preseparation-performance cost reflects the cost of lost productivity prior to the individual's leaving the organization. Flamholtz recognizes that this may be difficult to measure but suggests that historical performance records may be useful.

Vacant position costs refer to indirect costs resulting from an unfilled position. These costs include loss in efficiency of remaining employees who are required to assume the responsibilities assigned to the unfilled position or loss of revenues if reduction in services is necessary.

To illustrate, assume that the x-ray technician described previously is valued by using the replacement cost model. The projected separation costs, say $4,000, would be added to the historical costs of acquisition and development, $4,900. Thus, under the replacement cost model the employee would be assigned a value of $8,900. This provides a quantitative benchmark for evaluating the administrator responsible for this employee.

HUMAN RESOURCE VALUE MODEL

Ogan,[20] relying heavily on the work of Flamholtz,[21,22] Lev and Schwartz,[23,24] and Morse,[25] proposed a detailed human resource value (HRV) model that incorporates important organizational and attitudinal components not included in the cost accounting model. As shown in Figure 11-3, this model presents many of the critical dimensions that determine the value of an organization's human resources. It also provides a means for determining the net present value of the human resources using what Ogan refers to as "certainty equivalents."

The model has two major components. The first is *net benefits,* which are defined as the difference between total costs incurred by the organization in training, developing, recruiting, and maintaining an employee and the total benefits accruing from employee's skills, ability, and motivation. The model indicates that these costs are a function of the organization's compensation and promotion policies, industry norms concerning these policies, the skill levels required, and the current market availability of these skills. The benefits comprise the "monetary value benefits potential" and the "individual performance index." The monetary value is a function of an employee's age, related useful life to the organization, and education level, as well as the standard industry wage rate for the position levels the employee is expected to hold.

The individual performance index comprises an efficiency index and a standard work index. The standard work index refers to the percentage of work time devoted directly to revenue-generating activities. The efficiency index reflects management's perceptions of an employee's expected job efficiency. This is a function of the employee's physical health and psychomotor ability as well as task complexity, related experience, and work motivation level.

The second major component in Ogan's model is the certainty factor. This factor is composed of two dimensions: the probability of continued employment and the probability of survival. The probability of survival is simply an actuarial estimate of the employee's chance for physical survival. The probability of continued employment is the result of expected total individual satisfaction and an individual equivocation index. Ogan defines the equivocation index as an individual's attitude toward change. It is seen to be a function of the employee's personality, marital status, family size, children's ages, and equity in a retirement pension plan.

Expected total individual satisfaction is a composite of expected internal individual satisfaction and expected external satisfaction. Internal satisfaction concerns employee satisfaction determinants within both the organization and the individual. Ogan postulates that internal satisfaction is a function of an inexplicable turnover component and an individual internal satisfaction index. Inexplicable turnover is viewed as

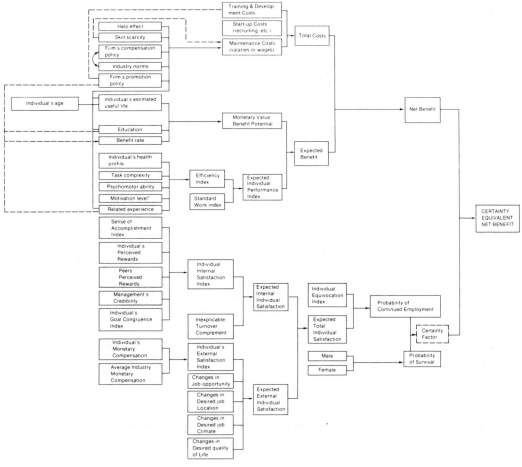

Legend:

→ Hypothesized determinant
--- Hypothesized intercept determinant
⋯→ Hypothesized possible determinant
— Hypothesized interrelationship

*A *caveat* because auto-correlation between the degree of satisfaction and motivation level is possible. In this respect, see Lyman W. Porter and Edward E. Lawler, III, *Managerial Attitudes and Performance* (Richard D. Irwin, Inc., 1968); —————, "The Effects of Performance on Job Satisfaction," *Industrial Relations* (1967): 20–27; L.L. Cummings and A.M. El Salmi, "Empirical Research on the Bases and Correlates of Managerial Motivation: A Review of the Literature," *Psychological Bulletin* (1968, 70): 127–141; and V. Vroom, *Work and Motivation* (Wiley, 1964).

Figure 11-3 Determination of Certainty-Equivalent Net Benefits. *Source:* Reprinted from *Accounting Review*, with permission of American Accounting Association, © April 1976.

the percentage of organizational turnover that cannot be attributed to any specific cause. The individual internal satisfaction index is composed of a set of attitudinal-type variables that have been shown to be important elements of employee satisfaction. These include an em-

ployee's sense of accomplishment, the perceived rewards resulting from accomplishments, the perceived equity of reward within the relevant work group, the perceived equity and credibility in management's implementation of the reward system, and the congruence of an employee's individual goals with those of the organization.

Expected external individual satisfaction concerns comparisons of an employee's current position with alternatives available outside the current organization. The dimensions of comparison include the employee's salary in relation to average industry compensation levels, alternative job opportunities, desirability of geographic location and climate, and the desired quality of life.

Ogan assumes that the model variables can be quantified and can be used to calculate current equivalent net benefits. The proposed model requires that this value for each employee be discounted to obtain a current valuation. These values are assumed over all employees in order to obtain the adjusted total net present value of the organization's human resources.

The HRV model is more detailed than the historical cost model or the replacement cost model. One of the critical components of the value model is the total cost incurred described by the replacement cost model. The x-ray technician's total cost was $8,900 under the replacement model. Under the HRV model, to these costs are added the expected salary to be paid to the employee for the useful work life, $200,000. Thus, the total costs associated with the x-ray technician are $208,900. These costs are subtracted from the expected benefit, which is determined by weighting the monetary value of the benefit potential by the individual performance index. For example, the monetary value is determined to be $500,000 and the performance index is 0.90. The expected benefit is $400,000 and the net benefit is $191,100. The net benefit is then adjusted by the certainty factor, say 0.80, to derive the certainty equivalent net benefit of $152,880.

GROUP INFLUENCES MODELS

The models discussed thus far have assigned a value of an individual employee. The value assigned to the human resources of an organization is the sum of these individual values. They do not incorporate the dynamics of group-interactive influences on the value of the organiza-

tion's human resources. Brummet[26] reviewed several models that do address these issues.

Likert[27] proposed a model designed to determine total productive efficiency in terms of group processes and subordinate terms of group processes and subordinate satisfaction. The group processes are assumed to be a function of peer leadership and organizational climate. Managerial leadership is seen as influencing all of these factors. Brummet[28] points out that if these factors can be measured and observed over time, they may be useful in predicting changes in productive efficiency. These changes could be used in assigning and revising the value of the organization's human resources.

Brummet summarized a method proposed by Brummet and Taylor for determining the changes in human resource values by considering interactive and group factors by deriving what they refer to as "a human resource value index." This index is calculated using an "interactive multiplier,"[29] individual performance ratio, and position contribution potential. The performance ratio represents the relationship between standard performance levels and current actual performance levels. The ratio is then multiplied by the position contribution potential. Brummet and Taylor suggest that salary ranges may be used as a measure of position contribution potential. The products of these two variables are summed over all employees. This sum is multiplied by the interactive multiplier, which measures interactive and group effects such as those specified by Likert.[30] As Brummet points out, this is the only model that explicitly includes individual, interactive, and group factors.[31]

For example, assume there are three x-ray technicians assigned to a work group. Their individual performance ratios are 0.9, 1.0, and 1.1, respectively, and their salaries are each $20,000. The salary is multiplied by the performance ratio and the products are summed, yielding $60,000. The interactive multiplier is determined to be 1.2, which reflects a positive contribution of the group and interactive factors, which is then multiplied times $60,000 to calculate a value index of $72,000 for the x-ray technician group. The total value of the human resources to the health care facility is the sum of the value index for all work groups.

APPLICATION OF HUMAN RESOURCE ACCOUNTING MODELS

The basic historical cost model proposes the capitalization and amortization of certain human resources costs. This is analogous to current, generally accepted accounting procedures for property, plant, and other physical resources. It requires capitalizing related costs identified in the prior section and not treating them as expenses, as is the current practice. HRCA employs routine expiration using an established amortization procedure. There are standard procedures for recording and writing off special losses such as unanticipated employee turnover, debilitating accident, or death. The culmination of this system would be reflected in standard reporting procedures that would facilitate issuing financial-type statements for both internal and external use.

The financial statements of the R.G. Barry Corporation, formerly an Ohio-based manufacturing firm (Table 11-1), illustrate how one company attempted to incorporate HRCA into its formal reporting system. Note that the human resource balance sheet contains only three additional accounts. The first is an asset account reflecting the "net investments in human resources." The second is a liability account reflecting the deferred income tax that resulted from treating all of the human resource expenses as period costs, thus deducting the full costs from taxable income. Probably the most controversial aspect of this system is including human resources value as part of the retained earnings. The income statement includes in net income the "net increase in human resource investment."

Implementing even this basic historical cost HRA system requires the resolution of some difficult questions. Where is the relevant information available and what is the appropriate level of aggregation? Should the accounting system be designed to collect and report on an individual employee level or would work groups or skill groups be adequate and less costly?

A basic premise of the model is that the full costs of human resources can be identified and measured. This requires that indirect costs be allocated to the human resources. As with any cost allocation scheme, the allocations tend to be somewhat arbitrary and inaccurate. However, they can prove to be very useful from both a planning and control perspective.

Once the allocation schemes have been established, the mechanism is in place for establishing standard costing for human resources. This would provide another dimension to the internal management control system. Managers could be held directly responsible for their human as well as physical resources.

HRCA presents special problems in adhering to accounting's matching principle. How are the costs, once determined, matched with the appropriate revenues? This requires addressing such issues as the effect of increased productivity and changing environmental factors.

As with other information systems, HRCA systems require continual reassessment. For example, the amortization policy must be revised to account for changes in the operating and work environment as well as changes in personnel and the personnel mix. Thus, there is a continual revision of the unamortized investment in human resources that affects the asset valuation shown on the balance sheet.

Convincing arguments can be made for implementing human resources systems that go beyond the historical cost basis. Several of the theoretical models set forth plausible alternatives with some form of current or replacement value being advocated. The arguments are analogous to those presented in defense of a total current value financial accounting system. Estimating current values for human resources may not be much more nebulous than obtaining current values for other assets. However, there have been few serious attempts made to implement the historical cost models, much less the more sophisticated HRA model.

MEASUREMENT OF HUMAN RESOURCES

The critical element in HRA, as in any accounting system, is the measurement of the desired component. In implementing any type of HRA system, management must decide which variables to measure. Some that might be rele-

Table 11-1 The Total Concept: Conventional and Human Resource Accounting

Balance Sheet

Assets	1972 Conventional and Human Resource	1972 Conventional Only
Total Current Assets	$16,408,620	$16,408,620
Net Property, Plant and Equipment	3,371,943	3,371,943
Excess of Purchase Price over Net Assets Acquired	1,288,454	1,288,454
Deferred Financing Costs	183,152	183,152
Net Investments in Human Resources	1,779,950	—
Other Assets	232,264	232,264
	$23,264,383	$21,484,433
Liabilities and Stockholders' Equity		
Total Current Liabilities	3,218,204	3,218,204
Long-Term Debt, Excluding Current Installments	7,285,000	7,285,000
Deferred Compensation	116,533	116,533
Deferred Federal Income Tax Based upon Full Tax Deduction for Human Resource Costs	889,975	—
Stockholders' Equity:		
Capital Stock	1,818,780	1,818,780
Additional Capital in Excess of Par Value	5,047,480	5,047,480
Retained Earnings:		
Financial	3,998,436	3,998,436
Human Resources	889,975	—
	$23,264,383	$21,484,433
STATEMENT OF INCOME		
Net Sales	$39,162,301	$39,162,301
Cost of Sales	25,667,737	25,667,737
Gross Profit	13,494,564	13,494,564
Selling, General, and Administrative Expenses	10,190,773	10,190,773
Operating Income	3,303,791	3,303,791
Interest Income	549,225	549,225
Income before Federal Income Taxes	2,754,566	2,754,566
Net Increase in Human Resource Investment	218,686	—
Adjusted Income before Federal Income Tax	2,973,252	2,754,566
Federal Income Taxes	1,414,343	1,305,000
Net Income	$ 1,558,909	$ 1,449,566

Source: R.G. Barry Corporation and Subsidiaries, *Annual Report*, 1972. Reprinted with permission.

vant are training received, turnover, absenteeism, job performance, patient satisfaction, or patient days. The selection depends on the objectives to be achieved by the system. For example, turnover could be used to evaluate the utilization and maintenance of unamortized human assets. However, the absolute turnover rates may be inappropriate, if some level of turnover is in fact desirable.

The historical cost model proposes that development costs represent a portion of the human resource value and thus should be used as a measure of its value. This has intuitive appeal. However, Lawler and Rhode[32] have pointed out several problems involved in using training costs. First, since people are personally capable of adding to their skills or productivity, their value can increase beyond that of their training and procurement costs. Second, individuals may experience an increase in their skill level due to personal experience independent of their work; such experiences can occur whether or not their employer has spent any money on training or development. Third, two individuals experiencing the same training may implement their training in different ways.

Another problem associated with human resource accounting is how, and if, the resource value should be written off. Physically and mentally, individuals grow and age at different rates. Organizations are also dynamic and require different skills at different times. A valuable employee today may be valueless tomorrow. Developing a means of writing off an individual's value presents another important measurement problem.

When evaluating and choosing appropriate measures, several desirable characteristics should be considered. The first is the validity of the measure. Is it measuring what it is supposed to measure as accurately and completely as possible? Further, all personnel who evaluate, or are being evaluated, by the measure must perceive it to be a legitimate representation of the desired phenomenon.

Second, can the measures be influenced by the people involved? This can be considered from two perspectives. If the manager being evaluated can manipulate the variable measure without regard to the underlying phenomena, then the measure is not useful. Further, the manager must have control over the human resource utilization upon which he or she is being evaluated, and efforts to properly manage this resource must be accurately reflected by the measure. In other words, measurement must be fair and objective.

Can the models presented earlier in this chapter meet these measurement criteria? The historical cost model meets the criteria of objectivity and accuracy. However, some might question its relevance in evaluating a dynamic and complex factor such as human resources. At best, it can be considered a first approximation. However, this may be adequate for practical purposes.

As the models become more realistic, they become more complex. Thus, relevance may be enhanced at the price of clearly definable, objec-

tive measures. For example, the HRV model requires some strong assumptions about internal rates of return and estimates of future benefits and costs. When the models include determinants of employee turnover such as intrinsic and extrinsic satisfaction, the problems of measurement validity and reliability increase by several orders of magnitude. Further, some of the models that propose productivity as the basic measurement unit may not work well in a health care facility because of the problems involved in establishing valid work standards.

EMPIRICAL SUPPORT

An HRA system is valuable if managers perceive the data presented as important and utilize them in their decision-making processes. Oliver and Flamholtz[33] present a study of the effect of human resource replacement cost numbers and the cognitive styles of decision makers on the layoff decisions of managers. The two dimensions of cognitive style addressed are tolerance for ambiguity and the relationship between decision style and information content (analytic or heuristic). The results show that human resource replacement cost numbers have information content for decision makers regardless of their cognitive characteristics, and the decision makers' confidence in the decisions increases when human resource replacement cost numbers are used.

The study by Harrell and Klick[34] of the promotion decisions of U.S. Air Force colonels shows monetary human assets measures have an advantage over nonmonetary measures in competing for a decision maker's attention. The decision by senior Air Force colonels on whether or not to promote captains to the rank of major differs when monetary measures of replacement cost (dollars) are presented instead of nonmonetary measures of replacement cost (months).

SUMMARY

This chapter has presented a brief review of HRA and has described various proposals of implementing such a system. The theoretical models that have been presented are designed primarily for private industrial organizations. However, human resource management is probably even more critical within the health care industry because of the increasingly vital role of highly skilled employees. The alternatives range from a strictly historical cost-based system to systems based on worker attitudes, group dynamics, and mortality tables. A practical, justifiable system from a cost-benefit perspective lies somewhere between these two extremes.

HRA provides management a clear, realistic picture of the human capital of the organization. It encourages management to use human capital to its best advantage in both the current and future periods. HRA will encourage better long-range planning and decision making. Upper-level management will become cognizant of how formal organizational policies and practices influence the human organization. Management will begin to clarify notions about monetary and psychological aspects of the human organization. The expanded information base will enhance the organization's efforts toward optimum amounts and mixes of human resources expenditures. Capital budgeting techniques can be implemented in making these resource allocation decisions.

Improving information will allow optimum employee skill mixes within work groups. This will also result in more realistic work standards for specific tasks, thereby establishing optimal rates of employee behavior. These standards facilitate the use of conventional cost accounting procedures for cost analysis and control. For example, managers can be evaluated on their ability to control conventional costs as well as human resources costs within their responsibility areas, thus providing a more complete evaluation. This method of evaluation can also result in a more accurate reward system. Further, the effectiveness and efficiency of the personnel department can be evaluated more accurately.

NOTES

1. Eric G. Flamholtz, *Human Resource Accounting* (Encino, Calif.: Dickenson, 1974), p. 3.

2. Rose DiCarlo, "Human Resource Accounting—A Synthesis," *Cost and Management* (July–August 1983): 57–60.

3. T.W. Schultz, "Investment in Human Capital," *American Economic Review* 51 (1969): 1–17.

4. L. Thurow, *Investment in Human Capital* (Belmont, Calif.: Wadsworth Publishing Co., 1970).

5. Flamholtz, *Human Resource Accounting*, p. 21.

6. Gordon Zacks, "People Are Capital Investments at R.G. Barry Corporation," *Management Accounting* (November 1971): 53–55.

7. DiCarlo, "Human Resource Accounting," p. 57–60.

8. Ibid.

9. Robert T. Sprouse and M. Moonitz, *A Tentative Set of Broad Accounting Principles for Business Enterprises* (New York: American Institute of Certified Public Accountants, 1967), p. 8.

10. DiCarlo, "Human Resource Accounting," p. 57–60.

11. Flamholtz, *Human Resource Accounting*.

12. Baruch Lev and Aba Schwartz, "On the Use of the Economic Concept of Human Capital in Financial Statements," *Accounting Review* (January 1971): 103–112.

13. Jan Oliver and Eric G. Flamholtz, "Human Resources Replacement Cost Numbers, Cognitive Information Processing and Personnel Decisions: A Laboratory Experiment," *Journal of Business Finance and Accounting* 5, no. 2 (1978): 137–57.

14. Eric G. Flamholtz, "Human Resource Accounting," in *Handbook of Cost Accounting*, eds. Sidney Davidson and Roman Weil (New York: McGraw-Hill Book Co., 1978), p. 26/12.

15. Flamholtz, *Human Resource Accounting*, 1974, p. 13.

16. Flamholtz, "Human Resource Accounting," 1978, p. 26/39.

17. Flamholtz, *Human Resource Accounting*, 1974, p. 26/13.

18. Flamholtz, "Human Resource Accounting," 1978, p. 26/39.

19. Flamholtz, *Human Resource Accounting*, 1974, p. 11.

20. Pekin Ogan, "A Human Resources Value Model for Professional Service Organizations," *Accounting Review* (April 1976): 319.

21. Eric G. Flamholtz, "A Model for Human Resource Valuation: A Stochastic Process with Service Rewards," *Accounting Review* (April 1971): 148–52.

22. Eric G. Flamholtz, "Toward a Theory of Human Resource Value in Formal Organizations," *Accounting Review* (October 1972): 666–78.

23. Lev and Schwartz, "On the Use of the Economic Concept," p. 103–12.

24. Baruch Lev and Aba Schwartz, "On the Use of the Economic Concept of Human Capital in Financial Statements: A Reply," *Accounting Review* (January 1972): 153–54.

25. Wayne Morse, "A Note on the Relationship between Human Assets and Human Capital," *Accounting Review* (July 1973): 589–93.

26. R. Lee Brummet, "Human Resource Accounting," in *Handbook of Modern Accounting*, 2nd ed., ed. Sidney Davidson and Roman Weil (New York: McGraw-Hill Book Co., 1977), pp. 37/12–37/20.

27. Rensis Likert, *The Human Organization: Its Management and Value* (New York: McGraw-Hill Book Co., 1967).

28. Brummet, "Human Resource Accounting," pp. 37/12–37/20.

29. R. Lee Brummet and Robert Taylor, *Human Resources Accounting—A Complete Model* (Chapel Hill, N.C.: University of North Carolina, 1974), p. 19.

30. Likert, *The Human Organization*.

31. Brummet, "Human Resource Accounting," p. 37/20.

32. Edward E. Lawler, III, and John Grant Rhode, *Information and Control in Organizations* (Pacific Palisades, Calif.: Goodyear, 1976), pp. 153–77.

33. Oliver and Flamholtz, "Human Resources Replacement Cost Numbers," pp. 137–57.

34. Adrian M. Harrell and Harold D. Klick, "Comparing the Impact of Monetary and Non-Monetary Human Asset Measures on Executive Decision Making," *Accounting, Organizations and Society* 5, no. 4 (1980): 393–400.

BIBLIOGRAPHY

American Accounting Association, Committee on Human Resources. "Accounting Report of the Committee on Human Resources Accounting." *Accounting Review* 47 (suppl.): 169–85.

———. "Report of the Committee on Accounting for Human Resources." *Accounting Review* 49 (suppl.): 114–24.

Brummet, R. Lee. "Accounting for Human Resources." *Journal of Accountancy* (December 1970): 62–66.

———. "Human Resource Accounting." In *Handbook of Modern Accounting*, edited by Sidney Davidson and Roman Weil, 2nd ed. New York: McGraw-Hill Book Co., 1977, 1–29.

Brummet, R. Lee, Eric G. Flamholtz, and William C. Pyle, eds. *Human Resource Accounting: Development and Implementation in Industry*. Ann Arbor, Mich.: Foundation for Research on Human Behavior, 1969.

DiCarlo, Rose, "Human Resource Accounting—A Synthesis." *Cost and Management* (July–August 1983): 57–60.

Flamholtz, Eric G. "A Model for Human Resource Valuation: A Stochastic Process with Service Rewards." *Accounting Review* (April 1971): 148–52.

———. "Toward a Theory of Human Resource Value in Formal Organizations." *Accounting Review* (October 1972): 666–78.

———. *Human Resource Accounting*. Encino, Calif.: Dickenson, 1974.

———. "Human Resource Accounting." In *Handbook of Cost Accounting*. Edited by Sidney Davidson and Roman Weil. New York: McGraw-Hill Book Co., 1978.

Gambling, Trevor. "A Systems Approach to Human Resource Accounting." *Accounting Review* (July 1974): 538–46.

Harrell, Adrian M., and Harold D. Klick. "Comparing the Impact of Monetary and Non-Monetary Human Asset Measures on Executive Decision Making." *Accounting, Organizations and Society* 5, no. 4 (1980): 393–400.

Heda, Shyam S., and Michael B. Shirk. "Human Resource Accounting System and Productivity Monitoring." *Hospital and Health Services Administration* (Fall 1979): 36–45.

Hekimian, James, and Curtis H. Jones. "Put People in Your Balance Sheet." *Harvard Business Review* (January–February 1967): 105–13.

Jurkus, Anthony F. "The Uncertainty Factor in Human Resources Accounting." *Personnel* (November–December 1979): 72–75.

Lawler, Edward E., III., and John Grant Rhode. *Information and Control in Organizations*. Pacific Palisades, Calif.: Goodyear, 1976.

Lev, Baruch, and Aba Schwartz. "On the Use of the Economic Concept of Human Capital in Financial Statements." *Accounting Review* (January 1971): 103–12.

———. "On the Use of the Economic Concept of Human Capital in Financial Statements: A Reply." *Accounting Review* (January 1972): 153–54.

Likert, Rensis. *The Human Organization: Its Management and Value*. New York: McGraw-Hill Book Co., 1967.

Macy, Barry A., and Philip H. Marvis. "A Methodology for Assessment of Quality of Work Life and Organizational Effectiveness in Behavioral-Economic Terms." *Administrative Science Quarterly* (June 1976): 212–26.

McKibbin, Richard C., and David M. Beck. "Labor Costs: Their Impact on Cost Control." *Hospital and Health Services Administration* (Summer 1979): 21–33.

Marvis, Philip H., and Edward E. Lawler, III. "Measuring the Financial Impact of Employee Attitudes." *Journal of Applied Psychology* 62: 1–8.

Morse, Wayne. "A Note on the Relationship between Human Assets and Human Capital." *Accounting Review* (July 1973): 589–93.

Myers, M. Scott, and Vincent S. Flowers. "A Framework for Measuring Human Assets." *California Management Review* (Summer 1974): 5–16.

Ogan, Pekin. "A Human Resources Value Model for Professional Service Organizations." *Accounting Review* (April 1976): 306–20.

Oliver, Jan, and Eric G. Flamholtz. "Human Resources Replacement Cost Numbers, Cognitive Information Processing and Personnel Decisions: A Laboratory Experiment." *Journal of Business Finance and Accounting* 5, no. 2 (1978): 137–57.

Schneider, Benjamin. *Staffing Organizations*. Santa Monica, Calif.: Goodyear, 1976.

Schultz, T.W. "Investment in Human Capital." *American Economic Review* 51 (1969): 1–17.

Scoville, Charles K. "Human Resource Development: Emerging Asset for Hospital Management." *Hospital and Health Services Administration* (Winter 1977): 22–36.

Sprouce, Robert T., and M. Moonitz. *A Tentative Set of Broad Accounting Principles for Business Enterprises*. New York: American Institute of Certified Public Accountants, 1962.

Steers, Richard M. "Problems in the Measurement of Organizational Effectiveness." *Administrative Science Quarterly* (December 1975): 546–58.

Thurow, L. *Investment in Human Capital*. Belmont, Calif.: Wadsworth Publishing Co., 1970.

Woodruff, R.L., Jr. "Human Resource Accounting." *Canadian Chartered Accountant* (September 1970): 156–61.

Zacks, Gordon. "People Are Capital Investments at R.G. Barry Corporation." *Management Accounting* (November 1971): 53–55.

Management Planning and Control

Chapter 12

Strategic Financial Planning

William O. Cleverley
Professor, Graduate Program in Hospital and Health Services Management
The Ohio State University

Is there a need to define corporate financial policy in a health care firm? If so, who should be responsible—the board of trustees, the chief executive officer, the chief financial officer, or some combination of these? How should the definition of financial policy be accomplished? What are the steps required?

These kinds of questions are only now beginning to surface in the health care industry. Finance and financial management have long been areas of concern, but their orientation has recently shifted. Reimbursement and payment system management have given way to financial planning. Survival tomorrow is no longer a guaranteed option. Health care firms must establish realistic and achievable financial plans that are consistent with their strategic plans. The primary purpose of this chapter is to help provide a basis for the very crucial task of financial policy formation in health care firms.

THE STRATEGIC PLANNING PROCESS

Most observers would probably agree that financial policy and financial planning should be

This chapter is reprinted from *Essentials of Health Care Finance*, 2nd ed., by W.O. Cleverley, pp. 155–181, Aspen Publishers, Inc., © 1986.

closely integrated within the strategic planning process. Understanding the strategic planning process is thus a first step in defining and developing financial policy and financial planning. It would be ideal if there were agreement among leading experts regarding the definition of strategic planning. But such is not the case. The literature on strategic planning is fairly recent; most of it has appeared since 1965. The application of strategic planning principles to the health care industry is even more recent; the bulk of the literature on such applications has been published since 1980.

One trend in health care strategic planning does appear clear, however: There is a definite movement away from "facilities planning" to a more market-oriented approach. Health care firms can no longer decide which services they want to deliver without assessing need or market. This requirement appears consistent with the concept of strategic planning as it is used in general industry. Indeed, as the business environments of the health care industry and general industry become more alike, strategic planning in the two areas should become increasingly similar.

Much of the literature that deals with the strategic planning process in business organizations appears to be concerned with two basic decision outcomes. First, a statement of mission and/or goals is required to provide guidance to the organization. Second, a set of programs or ac-

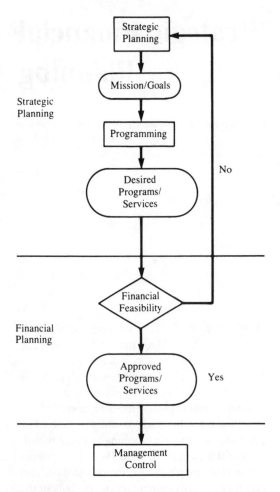

Figure 12-1 Integration of Strategic and Financial Planning

tivities to which the organization will commit resources during the planning period is defined.

Figure 12-1 shows the integration of the financial planning process with the strategic planning process. Financial planning is fashioned by the definition of programs and services and then assesses the financial feasibility of those programs and services. In many cases, a desired set of programs and services may not be financially feasible. This may cause a redefinition of the organization's mission and its desired programs and services. For example, a hospital may decide to change from a full-service hospital to a specialty hospital, or it may decide to drop specific clinical programs, such as pediatrics or obstetrics.

Three points concerning the integration of strategic and financial planning should be em-

phasized. First, both strategic planning and financial planning are the primary responsibility of the board of trustees. This does not exclude top management from the process, because management should be an active and participative member of the board. Second, strategic planning should precede financial planning. In some situations, the board may make strategic decisions based upon the availability of funding. While this may be fiscally conservative, it can often inhibit creative thinking. Third, the board should play an active, not a passive, role in the financial planning process. The board should not await word concerning the financial feasibility of its desired programs and services; it should actively provide guidelines for management and/or its consultants to use in developing the financial plan. Specifically, the board should establish key financial policy targets in three major areas:

1. growth rate
2. debt capacity
3. profitability objective (return on equity)

Financial Policy Targets

The term *financial feasibility* is often associated with an expensive study performed by a consulting firm in conjunction with the issue of debt. In such cases, the financial projections are so incredibly complex that few people profess to understand them, and even fewer actually do. In many people's minds, financial planning consists of a large number of mathematical relationships that can simulate future financial results, given certain key inputs. The validity of the projections is dependent upon the reliability of the mathematical relationships, or model, and upon the accuracy of the assumptions. Most financial feasibility studies developed in this way are never reviewed and never updated.

But conditions are changing, and changing very rapidly. A large number of health care firms are now beginning to develop formal strategic plans. They are beginning to redefine, or at least reconsider, their basic mission and to identify future market areas. It is increasingly clear that their financial plans and financial strategies must be integral parts of their overall strategic plan.

With the elimination of cost reimbursement and increased competition among health care providers, board members are beginning to insist on a greater role in financial policy making. Future financial viability is no longer a virtual certainty; some analysts predict that as many as one out of four existing hospitals will not survive.

Granted that health care board members and health care executives have an urgent need to understand financial policy and financial planning, can the requisite body of knowledge be conveyed in a manner that is capable of being understood? Must board members and executives remain passive observers in financial planning, or can they be given the means to establish key policy directives?

The simplest way to categorize and describe key financial relationships in a financial plan is through a balance sheet presentation. A financial plan can be thought of as a bridge between a current balance sheet and a balance sheet at some future date (see Figure 12-2). The bridge consists of three spans. First, the plan must specify what the *growth rate* and level of investment in assets should be at future dates. This span is directly linked to the strategic planning outcome that defines desired programs. Second, the plan must specify the *profitability rate* or the amount of equity financing that will be available. This span is dependent upon the definition and profit

rates of the desired programs. The third and final span involves the definition of *debt capacity*. Having defined required investment and available equity, the amount of debt is predetermined. However, the plan must assess both the desirability and the feasibility of the required debt levels. In short, does the organization want to assume that level of indebtedness, and can it meet the associated debt service requirements?

Requirements for Effective Financial Policy Making

The preceding discussion of the elements of financial planning and the three major target areas of financial policy suggests certain requirements for effective financial planning and policy making. The following ten requirements are of special importance.

1. The Accounting System Should Be Capable of Providing Data on Cost, Revenue, and Investment along Program Lines

Programs or "strategic business units" are the basic building blocks of any strategic plan. The financial plan must be developed on a basis consistent with the strategic plan. Unfortunately, present accounting systems are geared to provide data along responsibility center or departmental lines. For example, psychiatry may represent a program in the strategic plan, but the financial data on costs, investments, and revenues for the program may be intertwined with many departments, such as dietary, housekeeping, occupational therapy, and pharmacy. Still, this problem is not unique to the hospital and health care industry. Many organizations have programs that cut across departmental lines. In such cases, the financial data can be accumulated along programmatic lines, but some adjustments in cost and revenue assignments are necessary.

With the advent of the diagnosis-related groups (DRG) payment system, the hospital industry has been making major advancements in the accumulation of financial data in terms of DRG categories. It is now possible to define major programs or product lines in a hospital as consisting of a specific set of DRGs. For exam-

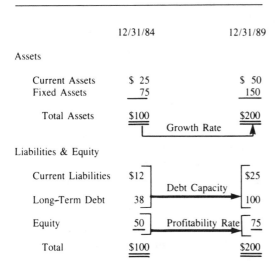

Figure 12-2 The Bridge Spans in Effective Financial Planning

ple, if obstetrics were a program, it might be defined as DRG 370 (Cesarean section with cord compression) to DRG 391 (normal newborns).

The important point to note here is that, although problems exist in obtaining financial data along program lines, they are not insurmountable. The health care industry is of course different from the automotive industry, but the differences do not necessarily imply greater difficulties.

2. No Growth Does Not Imply a Zero Growth Rate in Assets

The fact that no growth does not necessarily imply zero growth in assets is so obvious that it is often overlooked by many planning committees. Inflation will create investment needs that exceed present levels, even though the organization's strategic plan may call for program stabilization or an actual retrenchment. An annual rate of inflation equal to 7 percent means a doubling of investment values every ten years. For example, a hospital with assets of $25 million today should plan on being a $50-million-asset firm ten years from now. Just because the investment involved may not represent a real increase in value does not negate the need for a plan of finance that will generate $25 million in new equity and debt financing over the next ten years.

Over time, of course, expectations about future rates of inflation may change. The financial plan should reflect the best current thinking in this area. This may necessitate periodic changes in the financial plan. It is also important to recognize that there may be differences in investment inflation rates across programs. In some programs, such as oncology, where dramatic technology changes are likely to occur, a greater relative inflation rate may have to be assigned.

3. Working Capital Is a Major Element in Computing Total Future Asset Needs

In computing future investment needs, it is not uncommon to omit the working capital category. The majority of investment in any strategic plan is usually in bricks and mortar and equipment. However, working capital can still be a rather sizable component, accounting for 20 to 30 per-

cent of total investment in many health care firms.

The term *net working capital* is often used to describe the amount of permanent financing required to finance working capital or current assets. Net working capital is defined as current assets less current liabilities. It is important to remember this, since some current liability financing is automatic or unnegotiated. Just as inflation increases the dollar value of outstanding accounts receivable, it also increases wages or salaries payable and accounts payable. It is the net amount that must be financed. In Figure 12-2, the increase in net working capital was $12 ($25 − $13).

Working capital requirements vary by program. New programs usually have significant working capital requirements, whereas existing programs may experience only modest increases resulting from inflation. One of the primary causes for failure in new business ventures is often an inadequate amount of available working capital. New programs also may have significantly different working capital requirements. For example, a home health program may require little fixed investment in plant and equipment, but significant amounts of working capital may be required to finance a long collection cycle and initial development costs. Many firms that rushed into the development of home health agency (HHA) programs have become acutely aware of this problem.

If inadequate amounts of working capital are included in the financial plan, the entire plan may be jeopardized. For example, an unanticipated $2 million increase in receivables requires an immediate source of finance, such as the liquidation of investments. If those investments are essential to provide needed equity in a larger financing program, certain key investments may be delayed or cancelled in the future. A number of firms have had to reduce the scope of their strategic plans because of unanticipated demands for working capital.

4. Some Accumulation of Funds for Future Investment Is Critical to Long-Term Solvency

Saving for a rainy day has not been a policy practiced by many health care firms to any significant degree. As of 1984, the average hospital had approximately 37 percent of its replacement needs available in investments assuming 50 percent debt financing. This implies that the average hospital would need to borrow approximately 80 percent of its replacement needs. This level of debt financing may no longer be feasible in the hospital industry as lenders reassess the relative degree of risk involved.

It is critical that health care boards and management establish formal policies for retention of funds for future investment. Health care firms can no longer expect to finance all their investment needs with debt. They must set aside funds for investment to meet future needs in the same manner that pension plans are funded. An actuarially determined pension funding requirement is analogous to a board policy of replacement reserve funding. Yet, very few hospitals have seriously undertaken to set aside funds for future investment needs, which partially explains the dramatic growth in debt in the hospital industry.

5. A Formally Defined Debt Capacity Ceiling Should Be Established

Few health care firms have formally defined their firm's debt capacity or debt policy. This is in sharp contrast to most other industries. Without such a formally established debt policy, one of two unfavorable outcomes may result. First, debt may be viewed as the balancing variable in the financial plan. If a firm expects a $25 million increase in its investment and a $5 million increase in equity, $20 million of debt is required to make the strategic plan financially feasible. The firm will then try to arrange for $20 million of new debt financing. This is the situation in which many hospitals have found themselves. In such cases, additional debt could usually be obtained and adequate debt service could be demonstrated to lenders. Cost reimbursement had its advantages in that it could be used to provide payment for debt service costs. The strategic plan could remain unchanged, but a potential problem was that the debt to equity ratio might increase significantly.

Second, the balancing variable in the financial plan may shift to the investment side, but on an ex post facto basis. An approved financial plan may be unrealistic because the level of indebtedness required to finance the strategic plan exposes the hospital to excessive risks. Management may not realize this until the actual financing is needed. At that point, a scaling down of the programs specified in the strategic plan may be required. If a realistic debt capacity ceiling had been established earlier, existing funded programs might have been cancelled or cut back to make funds available for more desirable programs.

Debt capacity can be defined in a number of ways. It may be expressed as a ratio, such as a long-term debt to equity ratio, or it could be defined in terms of demonstrated debt service coverage. Whatever the method used, some limit on debt financing should be established. That limit should represent a balance between the organization's desire to avoid financial risk exposure and the investment needs of its strategic plan. Debt policy should be clearly and concisely established before the fact; it should not be an ad hoc result.

6. Return on Investment by Program Area Should Be an Important Criterion in Program Selection

The principle that return on investment by program area should govern program selection is related to the need for accounting data along product lines, as discussed above. In order to calculate return on investment along program lines, financial data on revenues, expenses, and investment must be available along program lines. Return on investment should be used as part of an overall system of program evaluation and selection.

Portfolio analysis is a buzz word that has been used lately to categorize programs in terms of market share and growth rate. Health care writers have applied the concept in the literature on health care planning and marketing. However, one difficulty with the application of portfolio analysis in the health care industry is in the selection of the dimensions for developing the portfolio matrix. In most portfolio matrixes, the dimensions used are market share and growth. Market share and growth are assumed to have an explicit relationship to cash flow. High market share is associated with high profitability and thus with good cash flow. High market growth is assumed to require cash flow for investment. For example, a program with a high market share and low growth is regarded as a "cash cow." It produces high cash flow but requires little cash flow for reinvestment, due to its low growth needs.

Here, we will employ a slight modification of the portfolio analysis paradigm, incorporating the dimension of profitability. Figure 12-3 illustrates the revised portfolio analysis matrix. Its two dimensions are (1) return on investment and (2) community need. Return on investment is used as the measure of profitability because it has the most direct tie to strategic and financial planning. Profit is merely new equity that can be used to finance new investment. Absolute levels of profit or cash flow mean little unless they are related to the underlying investment. For example, if Program A has profit of $100,000 and an investment of $2 million while Program B has profit of $50,000 and an investment of $100,000, which program is a better cash cow if both programs have low community need?

In our revised portfolio analysis matrix, community need replaces the traditional marketing dimensions of growth and market share. Community need may be difficult to measure quantitatively, but the concept appears closely aligned to the missions of most voluntary health care firms—firms that were usually formed to provide

health services to some reasonably well-defined market.

Figure 12-3 categorizes programs as "dogs," "cash cows," "stars," and "samaritans." With the exception of samaritans, these terms are identical to those used in the existing literature. An example of a samaritan program is one with a small or negative return on investment but a high community need. Thus, a hospital may provide a drug abuse program that loses money but meets a community need not met by any other health care provider. The program can continue if, and only if, the hospital has some stars or cash cows to subsidize the program's poor profitability. Dogs, that is, programs with low community need and low profit, should be considered in light of the resources they draw from potential samaritans. The new payment environment makes this kind of analysis mandatory.

7. Nonoperating Sources of Equity Should Be Included in the Financial Plan

In the preceding discussion of return on investment, we were concerned primarily with operating profitability. However, in most voluntary health care firms, nonoperating income can also be extremely important. In fact, in 1984, nonoperating revenue accounted for 30 percent of total reported net income in the hospital industry. If nonoperating income can be improved, a significant new source of funding will be available to help finance the strategic plan. This could mean either that a greater percentage of desired programs can be undertaken or that reduced levels of indebtedness are possible.

The investment portfolio of many health care firms is quite large. Funds are available for retirement plans, professional liability self-insurance plans, funded depreciation, bond funds, endowments, and other purposes. Thus, small increases in investment yields can create sizable increases in income. For example, a one percent improvement in the yield on invested pension funds may reduce annual pension expense by as much as ten percent. Clearly, hospital management should formally establish and incorporate target investment yields in its financial plans.

It should be noted that new equity can come from sources other than operating and non-

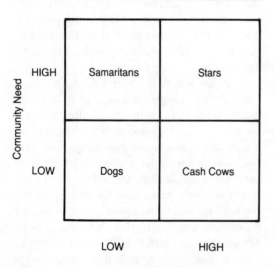

Figure 12-3 Revised Portfolio Analysis Matrix

operating income. Corporate restructuring arrangements can create proprietary subsidiaries that can issue stock. Joint venture relationships with medical staff and others can be used to finance plant assets. It is important that both board members and executives have a clear understanding of the possible alternatives available for raising new equity to finance the strategic plan. Raising new equity through stock or partnerships is no longer the exclusive domain of proprietary entities.

8. *The Financial Plan Must Be Integrated with the Management Control System*

The integration of the financial plan with the management control system is an obvious requirement, but it is often overlooked. Frequently, a large fee is paid to a consultant or enormous amounts of internal staff time are used to develop a financial plan that is never used.

Ideally, the financial plan is the basis for the annual budget. The key link between the budget and the financial plan should be the return on investment (ROI) targets specified in the financial plan. These ROI targets are critical to the long-run fulfillment of the strategic plan. Failure to achieve the targeted levels of profit will require revisions in the strategic plan.

Health care boards would not have to be involved in pricing debates if approved financial plans were available. In such situations, the profitability targets by program would already have been approved in the plans. The primary issues in the budgeting process should be the translation of profit targets by program lines to departmental lines via pricing allocations and the assessment of departmental operating efficiencies. Long, involved discussions about whether budgeted profit is too much or not enough should not be necessary.

9. *The Financial Plan Should Be Updated at Least Annually*

Management should have the most recent financial road map available at all times. Few people would plan a drive to San Francisco from Boston with a five-year-old road map, yet many organizations operate either with no long-range financial plan or with an outdated one. This can

be especially dangerous for health care firms at the present time, as the business environment continues to change rapidly. Today, financial plans based on cost reimbursement and minimal competition may be useless, or even misleading. In all financial plans, a careful reassessment of relative program profitability is periodically required, possibly prompting major revisions of the strategic plan. Knowing both where you are going and how you expect to get there is critical to survival in a competitive environment.

10. *The Financial Plan Is a Board Document and Should Be Formally Approved by the Board*

In many firms the financial plan, if it exists, is regarded as a management document. The board may be only mildly interested in reviewing it, and not interested at all in relating it to a strategic plan. This is rather strange behavior. Most boards would never dream of letting management operate without a board-approved annual budget for fear of failing to fulfill their board responsibilities. Yet planning for periods of time greater than one year is not regarded as important.

A recent hospital board meeting that followed a two-day strategic planning retreat illustrates this traditional perspective. During the retreat, strategic discussions about the future were held. The board and management agreed on a plan for the future that called for significant expansion into new market areas, such as long-term care. At the subsequent board meeting the chief executive officer and the chief finance officer presented the strategic plan and the related financial plan. The board members regarded approval of the financial plan as a waste of time. They did approve it, but in body only—not in spirit. Their rationale for apathy was clear. They could not foresee any problem with the financing. Most of them had been board members for a long time. Whenever money was needed in the past, they raised rates or borrowed. They could not see any reason to change this policy in the future. Behavior today would hopefully be different.

Fortunately, this kind of reaction is becoming less common. Board members today are beginning to realize that the financial plan and the strategic plan are integrally related. It is impossible to develop one without the other. Both are ultimately the responsibility of the board.

DEVELOPING THE FINANCIAL PLAN

In this section, we describe in some detail the steps involved in preparing a financial plan, using an actual case example. For our purposes, a financial plan may be defined as the bridge between two balance sheets. Here, we limit our attention to the financial plan as a projection of the balance sheet; discussion of methods used to project other financial statements, such as those involving income or cash flow, is beyond the scope of this chapter.

The Developmental Process

Four steps are involved in the development of a financial plan:

1. Assess financial position and prior growth patterns.
2. Define growth needs in total assets for the planning period.
3. Define acceptable level of debt, for both current and long-term categories.
4. Assess reasonableness of required growth rate in equity.

Assessment of Present Financial Position

The first step in the development of a financial plan is the assessment of present financial position. It is extremely important to determine the present financial health and position of the firm. Without such information, projections about future growth can be dangerous at best. In most situations, past performance is usually a good basis for projecting future performance. For example, a financial plan may call for a future growth rate in equity of 15 percent per year. If, however, the prior five-year period showed an average annual growth rate in equity of only 5 percent, there may be some doubt about the validity of the 15-percent assumption and thus about the reasonableness of the financial plan.

Three categories of financial information need to be assembled to assess present financial position:

1. prior financial statements for the past three to five years
2. compounded growth rates in individual balance sheet accounts
3. financial evaluation of the firm, using ratio analysis

To illustrate the application of this information in financial planning, the balance sheets presented in Exhibit 12-1 are used. These balance sheets provide information for ABC Medical Center for the years 1982 and 1987. The column at the far right identifies the average five-year compounded growth rate. This average rate of growth can be determined by using financial mathematics tables (see Chapter 11), by using a calculator with financial functions, or by solving the following equation:

$$(1 + i)^5 = \frac{1987 \text{ Value}}{1982 \text{ Value}}$$

where

i equals the average annual compounded rate of growth

The Exhibit 12-1 balance sheets are somewhat abbreviated but they provide sufficient information to illustrate the mechanics of financial planning. The data reveal some very interesting information about ABC's growth rate patterns. First, current assets have been growing at a much higher rate than other individual asset categories. During the past five years, the average rate of growth has been approximately 19 percent per year. This, of course, explains the very large increase in current assets. This finding is typical of most health care firms over the past decade. Current assets in general, and accounts receivable in particular, have experienced relatively high rates of growth; in projecting future growth rates, this should be kept in mind. Second, the growth rate in current liabilities is approximately equal to the growth rate in current assets. This finding is also very common and should be incorporated into the assumptions utilized in the financial plan. Third, ABC Medical Center has experienced a very large rate of growth in equity during the past five years. This is a very positive finding and lends support for the continuation of significant equity growth in the future.

Exhibit 12-1 Balance Sheets for ABC Medical Center

ABC Medical Center
Balance Sheets
(000s omitted)

	1982	1987	5-Year Growth Rate (percent)
Assets			
Cash	$ 161	$ 568	29
Accounts receivable	1,605	3,714	18
Inventories	211	102	−14
Other current assets	177	709	32
Total current assets	$ 2,154	$ 5,093	19
Replacement funds	4,981	7,705	9
Net fixed assets	9,789	12,245	5
Other	569	1,375	19
Total assets	$17,493	$26,418	9
Liabilities and Fund Balance			
Current liabilities	$ 1,079	$ 2,957	22
Long-term debt	10,070	7,330	−6
Deferred Medicare liability	456	1,285	23
Fund balance	5,888	14,846	20
Total liabilities and fund balance	$17,493	$26,418	9

Financial ratios for ABC Medical Center are presented in Exhibit 12-2. A review of these data provides us with a good assessment of both the firm's present financial position and its past financial trends. Among the significant findings that are likely to have a direct effect upon the firm's financial plan are the following:

- There was a large increase in days in accounts receivable over the past five years. This might cause us to assume that little real growth in days in accounts receivable will occur during the planning period. There might even be a slight reduction in days in accounts receivable during the period.
- The present average payment period has increased significantly during the past year. Future growth in current liability financing may not be as feasible, given the center's present position.
- The center's ability to assume additional long-term debt appears to be confirmed. Debt service coverage and times interest

earned ratios indicate good coverage of existing debt, and the present capital structure does not appear to be heavily leveraged relative to industry norms.
- The center's need for additional capital expenditures to renovate and replace its existing plant does not appear to be excessive. The center's present average age of plant ratio is only 6.35 years, which compares favorably with industry norms.
- The center's present replacement viability ratio is excellent. It has an unusually large amount of existing replacement funds that can be used to finance future capital needs.
- The center's operating profitability has been consistently above average. Its unusually high growth rate in equity is largely attributable to this factor.

Definition of Growth Rate of Assets

The preceding discussion of ABC Medical Center's financial position and prior growth pat-

Exhibit 12-2 Financial Ratios for ABC Medical Center

ABC Medical Center						
Financial Ratios (1982 – 1987)						
Liquidity	1982	1983	1984	1985	1986	1987
Current	1.996	2.091	2.067	2.037	2.398	1.722
Quick	1.636	1.758	1.775	1.775	2.137	1.448
Acid test	.149	.378	.159	.229	.229	.192
Days in patient receivable	54.335	48.849	50.832	55.615	61.979	63.207
Average payment period	40.092	38.624	33.671	38.145	35.012	53.901
Days' cash on hand	5.979	14.599	5.360	8.743	7.812	10.376
Capital structure						
Equity financing	.337	.392	.433	.472	.522	.561
Cash flow to debt	.127	.165	.191	.209	.227	.395
Long-term debt to equity	1.710	1.311	1.094	.893	.740	.493
Fixed asset financing	.982	.818	.805	.767	.752	.598
Times interest earned	3.255	2.888	2.688	2.937	3.577	5.027
Debt service coverage	2.508	3.343	3.275	3.574	4.284	5.573
Activity						
Total asset turnover	.629	.723	.829	.897	.909	.844
Fixed asset turnover	1.123	1.150	1.410	1.634	1.769	1.822
Current asset turnover	5.105	5.054	5.757	5.149	4.881	4.381
Inventory	52.106	55.146	68.646	70.208	75.006	78.932
Profitability						
Deductible	.121	.144	.122	.150	.142	.168
Markup	1.208	1.233	1.180	1.220	1.231	1.254
Operating margin	.060	.056	.038	.040	.058	.047
Nonoperating revenue	.222	.326	.482	.430	.319	.285
Reported income index	.892	.710	.749	.778	.647	.587
Return on total assets	.049	.060	.061	.063	.077	.107
Return on equity	.145	.152	.142	.133	.148	.191
Other						
Average age plant	6.361	5.798	5.632	5.952	6.064	6.350
Price level depreciation	1.710	1.640	1.675	1.672	1.638	1.605
Operating margin price-level adjusted	.028	.024	.004	.008	.025	.014
Reserve equity	.128	.079	.058	.030	.024	.000
Viability	1.036	.925	.939	.881	.628	.836
Replacement viability	.471	.943	1.042	1.051	1.079	1.236

terns gives us a good basis for defining future growth rates for individual asset categories. These growth rates must in turn be related to the center's strategic plan. Specifically, we must know what new programs and services the firm anticipates developing over the planning period, which is usually three to five years. These broad policy projections must be translated into specific financial requirements for future investment. Because of space constraints, we are not able to pursue this phase of the financial plan's development in the present context. It should be noted, however, that the projection of financial requirements for future investment is the key to successful financial plan development, in that it provides the link between strategic planning and financial planning.

In our case example, we assume a status quo model. In other words, the ABC Medical Center will attempt to maintain its present market share and position over the next five years with very little additional real growth into new market areas. This simplifies its projections and provides a basis for future plan modifications to take into account the impact of growth in new market areas.

One of the most important aspects of financial plan development is the assumption of a rate of inflation. In our economy, inflation is almost a given. It is assumed that assets will be replaced at values greater than original cost and that additional working capital will be required to meet operating needs. Financial projections are extremely sensitive to the assumed rate of inflation. In our example, we assume that the projected rate of inflation over the next five years (1987 to 1992) will be ten percent. This gives us a benchmark for the definition of specific growth rates in individual asset categories. These growth rates are summarized in the financial projections in Exhibit 12-3.

The following comments may be made on the individual growth rate projections in Exhibit 12-3:

• *Cash*. Cash was projected forward using an 11 percent growth rate, which is slightly higher than the assumed 10 percent inflation rate. This small increment above inflation was made because of the current weakness in operating cash position. The present day's cash on hand is slightly below the national average.

• *Accounts receivable*. The inflationary rate of ten percent was used to project accounts receivable. No increment above this rate was made because the current days in accounts receivable appear to be close to national norms. Therefore, the financial plan assumed that the present position would be maintained into the future. If ABC Medical Center's days in accounts

Exhibit 12-3 Projected Balance Sheet for ABC Medical Center

ABC Medical Center

Projected Balance Sheet
(000s omitted)

	Historical 1987	Projected 1992	Model Assumption
Assets			
Cash	$ 568	$ 957	11% Growth rate
Accounts receivable	3,714	5,981	10% Growth rate
Inventories	102	205	15% Growth rate
Other current assets	709	1,142	10% Growth rate
Total current assets	$ 5,093	$ 8,285	Summation
Replacement funds	7,705	9,834	5% Growth rate
Net fixed assets	12,245	20,634	11% Growth rate
Other	1,375	1,755	5% Growth rate
Total assets	$26,418	$40,508	Summation
Liabilities and Fund Balance			
Current liabilities	$ 2,957	$ 4,143	2:1 Current ratio
Long-term debt	7,330	12,380	60% of net fixed asets
Deferred Medicare liability	1,285	0	Elimination
Fund balance	14,846	23,985	Residual
Total liabilities and fund balance	$26,418	$40,508	Summation

receivable were much higher, for example 90 days, an argument might be made for using a rate lower than the inflationary rate.

- *Inventories.* Inventories were increased substantially above the current inflationary rate to 15 percent. Present levels of inventory appear to be slightly below national norms as measured by the inventory ratio. This, coupled with the decline in inventory values during the past five-year historical period, led us to increase our inventory levels. Note that the financial plan will not be very sensitive to alternative inventory projections because inventory accounts for such a small percentage of total investment.

- *Other current assets.* Other current assets were projected to increase at the inflationary rate. This estimate may be understated if the rate of increase in the future parallels prior growth rates. Note that the past five-year period showed a 32 percent annual growth rate.

- *Total current assets.* The value for current assets represents the summation of the individual elements that constitute current assets. The 1992 value of current assets represents a 10.2 percent compounded yearly growth rate.

- *Replacement funds.* A five percent rate was used to project replacement funds for the next five years. The rationale for using a rate that is significantly below the inflationary rate is based upon the present value of the replacement viability ratio. It is assumed that the center will begin to use some of these funds for replacement purposes and not expand its replacement reserves at the same rate it has in the past. The absolute level of funds will increase by approximately $2.1 million, but the relative level in terms of replacement needs will fall.

- *Net fixed assets.* A slight increment above the inflationary rate was used to project net fixed assets. Even though the current average age of plant ratio is slightly below the national norm, we are providing a small cushion for the hospital to expand into some areas that might require new investment.

- *Other assets.* A rate of five percent was used to project other assets. Much of the investment in this category will be amortized over the coming five-year period. Therefore, we have provided for only marginal real future growth.

- *Total assets.* Total assets, like current assets, are the result of summing the individual elements. The projected value of total assets ($40,508) represents an annual growth rate of 8.9 percent, which is slightly below the inflationary rate. This is the result of the low growth rates used to project replacement funds and, to a lesser degree, of the lower rate used to project other assets.

Definition of Acceptable Levels of Debt

The third step in the development of the financial plan is the definition of an acceptable debt policy. Debt should not be viewed as the balancing variable in a financial plan. That is, the financial plan should not project assets and equity and then balance the equation with debt. Sound financial policy requires that the board and management define in advance what their position is regarding the assumption of debt. Exhibit 12-3 projects the various categories of debt to 1992 and defines the assumption underlying the projections. The relevant projections and assumptions are delineated below:

- *Current liabilities.* Current liabilities are projected forward using a desired current ratio of 2 to 1. Since the projected current assets in 1992 are $8,285, the projected value for current liabilities would be one-half of that value, or $4,143. The current ratio of 2.000 represents a change from the 1987 ratio of 1.722. The assumption underlying the change is that the center will be relying upon current liability financing to a lesser degree than it is now. This means that the center will have to increase its equity financing in the planning period to replace the portion of current assets that is presently financed with current liabilities. If the center had used its present current ratio of

1.722 to project current liabilities in 1992, the projected value would have been $4,811 (rather than $4,143 as projected with a current ratio of 2.000). This means that the ABC Medical Center will have to generate approximately $670,000 in additional equity over the five-year planning period to replace the amount of current liability financing presently implied in its current ratio of 1.722.

- *Long-term debt.* ABC Medical Center is assumed to have a stated long-term debt policy of 60 percent debt financing of net fixed assets. This policy is consistent with its present fixed asset financing ratio of .598. To generate the 1992 long-term debt value, we simply multiply net fixed assets in 1992 by .60. The projected value for long-term debt in 1992 would therefore be $12,380. It is important to note that long-term debt does not usually change by constant increments each year. In most situations, a major financing will take place every five years or so. In our example, ABC Medical Center may do no long-term debt financing for the first three years of the financial plan and then borrow heavily in 1991. The target of 60-percent fixed asset financing simply provides it with an objective that it would like to see attained in the year 1992.

- *Deferred Medicare liability.* The deferred Medicare liability is projected to be zero in 1992. In other words, the balance will disappear as the method of payment for capital costs changes under the Medicare program. The present liability resulted from the use of accelerated depreciation and a gain on an advance bond refunding.

Assessment of the Reasonableness of the Required Equity Growth Rate

Determining whether the equity growth rate is reasonable is perhaps the most crucial step in the financial planning process. Defining the actual amount of required equity capital in the financial plan is relatively simple: Once the actual level of total assets has been projected and the entity's

debt policy has been defined, the level of required equity is the residual figure. In our example of ABC Medical Center, we can determine that it needs to have $23,985 in equity in 1992. That is the amount of equity needed to keep the balance sheet equation in balance. Anything less than that amount and the center will be forced either to reduce its level of total assets or to increase its level of debt.

The question of reasonableness in equity growth still remains, however. In our example, increasing the center's equity to $23,985 in 1992 translates into a 10.1-percent annual growth rate. Is this level of growth actually attainable?

The best way to assess the reasonableness of equity growth is to factor the growth rate into a number of specific areas that can be analyzed in terms of reasonableness. The following equation defines equity growth as a product of five factors:

$$\text{Equity growth rate} = \text{OM} \times \text{TAT} \times \frac{1}{\text{EF}} \times \frac{1}{\text{RII}} \times \frac{1}{\text{1-NOR}}$$

where

OM = operating margin ratio
TAT = total asset turnover ratio
EF = equity financing ratio
RII = reported income index ratio
NOR = nonoperating revenue ratio

By stating equity growth as a product of the five factors cited above, the analyst is better able to assess whether a required growth rate in equity is actually attainable. The best starting point is to examine the historical pattern of values for these five factors. Exhibit 12-4 provides the relevant data for ABC Medical Center.

Historically, ABC Medical Center has demonstrated a growth rate in equity that is far above the required growth rate of 10.1 percent called for in the financial plan. It has averaged approximately 20 percent per year in equity growth. The specific values for each of the five factors that determine equity growth show how this growth rate was accomplished. These data also serve as a basis for projecting into the future. The last column of Exhibit 12-4 provides details about ABC Medical Center's projected or targeted equity growth rate. The rationale for pro-

Exhibit 12-4 Equity Growth Rates for ABC Medical Center

	Historical Values					Target 1987– 1992
	1983	1984	1985	1986	1987	
Equity growth rate	21.7%	19.0%	17.2%	22.9%	16.8%	10.1%
Operating margin ratio	.056	.038	.040	.058	.047	.050
Total asset turnover ratio	.72	.82	.90	.91	.84	.76
Equity financing ratio	.39	.43	.47	.52	.56	.59
Nonoperating revenue ratio	.33	.48	.43	.32	.29	.25
Reported income index ratio	.71	.75	.78	.65	.59	.85

jecting the specific ratio values in this forecast is presented below:

- *Operating margin ratio.* The plan calls for an operating margin of 5.0 percent per year during the five-year planning period. This value is fairly consistent with prior values and represents a reasonable estimate of future levels of operating profitability. If the center had information to indicate that levels of competition might increase in the future, it might wish to reduce its operating margin projection. In this regard, it is useful to undertake a sensitivity analysis. For example, the effect of reducing the operating margin to 4.0 percent over the planning period would be to reduce the growth rate in equity to approximately 8.1 percent. Other scenarios could be tested to determine the effects upon the attainability of the targeted equity growth rate and thus the feasibility of the center's financial plan.

- *Total asset turnover ratio.* A small reduction in the value of the total asset turnover ratio from prior values is reflected in the forecast. The assumption for the reduction is based upon the prior trend, which has been declining over the past three years. The forecast calls for the total asset turnover ratio to be .76 in the five-year planning period, which is below the 1987 value of .84. Again, a sensitivity analysis could be performed to test the effects of possible changes upon equity growth. In situations calling for major capital replacement or ren-

ovation, total asset turnover ratios usually decline substantially. However, since ABC Medical Center does not anticipate major capital expenditures during the planning period, the lowered total asset turnover forecast appears to be reasonable, given prior trends.

- *Equity financing ratio.* Over the past five years, ABC Medical Center has shown a substantial increase in its level of equity financing. The percentage of assets financed with equity in 1987 was 56 percent, compared with only 39 percent in 1983. The projection calls for an equity financing ratio of .59 during the planning period. This value is consistent with the percentage of equity financing shown in the 1992 projected balance sheet in Exhibit 12-3. It reflects the slower rate of equity growth assumed in the initial financial plan for the ABC Medical Center.

- *Nonoperating revenue ratio.* The ratio of nonoperating revenue to net income has declined over the past four years for ABC Medical Center to a value of .29 in 1987. A value of .25 is projected during the planning period. This projection appears reasonable given the small increase in operating margin forecasted for the planning period. Note that the targeted operating margin is 5.0 percent, compared with 4.7 percent in 1987. Nonoperating revenue usually represents a smaller percentage of total net income when operating profits are increasing. In addition, investment income or replacement funds may decrease relatively, due to the lower growth rate used to project replacement funds.

- *Reported income index ratio.* The value projected for the reported income index ratio during the planning period is greater than in any period during the past five years. This is based on the conservative assumption that ABC Medical Center will be relying less on unreported income during the next five years than it has in the past. The rationale for this assumption is related to information that is not available in the data presented here, namely, that ABC Medical Center has benefited in the past from sizable levels of donor-restricted monies. The relative importance of these funds is decreasing, however, and the center is rapidly drawing on them for operating purposes. Though these funds will continue to exist in the planning period, the center believes that there will be a significant reduction in fund transfers during the next five years. This reduction is reflected in the increased value assumed for the reported income index ratio.

The individual values assumed for the five ratios that determine equity growth rate yield the projected rate of 10.1 percent

Equity growth rate =

$$.05 \times .76 + \frac{1}{.59} \times \frac{1}{(1-.25)} \times \frac{1}{.85}$$
$$= .101 \times 100 = 10.1\%$$

Comments and Conclusions

At this juncture in the planning process, alternative plans could be developed that would reflect different assumptions. For example, the ABC Medical Center might decide to expand its operations, embark upon a major renovation program, or change its debt policy. Each of these changes would require new sets of financial projections and new tests to determine if the required growth rate in equity were reasonable.

One final point should be made before we begin our discussion of the next stage, integrating the financial plan with the management con-

trol process. In most financial feasibility studies, the projection of funds flow and net income is extremely important; financial officers need to have very precise estimates of the flow of funds by period to plan their financing patterns. However, the financial planning process described here does not provide a basis for the projection of funds flow or net income. Our perspective has been more global; in this context, we have not concerned ourselves with the detail required for projecting funds flow. This does not mean, however, that our approach is inconsistent with a more detailed funds flow projection. In fact, the assumptions made in the ABC Medical Center's projected balance sheet would provide the basis for more detailed funds projections. The assumptions we have made concerning the factors that determine equity growth would also be integral to funds flow projections.

Finally, even though we have not projected revenues and expenses for the ABC Medical Center, we have specified, through our definition of the operating margin, the percentage of revenues that will be realized as income from operations. In this regard, it is useful to remember that a statement of revenues and expenses or net income provides detail about how a given change in equity was accomplished. The values specified in an equity growth model collectively provide the same data, but the approach described in this chapter is easier to understand and utilize. This is especially important as a basis for presentation to board members and executives who are interested in broad policy formulation and goal setting rather than the details of specific transactions.

**INTEGRATION OF THE
FINANCIAL PLAN WITH
MANAGEMENT CONTROL**

The development of a financial plan is a useless exercise unless that plan is integrated into the management control process. Management needs to know if the plan is being realized and, if it is not, what corrective action can be taken. In some cases, there is little that management can do. For example, assume that the entity has experienced an unusually large reduction in its operating margins, due to increased competition. In this case, perhaps the only course of action open to management is to revise its plan to reflect more accurately the current situation. Indeed it is important for management to assess the accuracy of its financial plan annually and to make appropriate changes in it as needed.

To integrate the financial plan with the management control process, some structure is needed. Financial ratios provide that structure. Figure 12-4 depicts detailed targets for the ABC Medical Center, reflecting its financial plan. In the figure, specific ratio values are delineated. The primary targets involve the five major ratios that together determine the center's equity growth rate. The secondary targets are concerned with additional data that can be used to monitor actual performance and detect possible problems.

To see how Figure 12-4 might be used in management control, let us assume that 1988 has just ended and the financial data essential to the calculation of the ratios are now available. ABC Medical Center's actual growth rate in equity for 1988 is assumed to be 8.7 percent, which represents an unfavorable variance from the required value of 10.1 percent. Actual values for the primary indicators are

	1988 Values
Operating margin ratio	.040
Total asset turnover ratio	.810
Equity financing ratio	.570
Nonoperating revenue ratio	.300
Reported income index ratio	.930

The major cause of the unfavorable variance in equity growth rate during 1988 is an unfavorable operating margin (.040 versus the .050 target) and an unfavorable reported income index (.930 versus the .850 target). The improvement in the nonoperating revenue ratio is the result of the reduction in operating profit.

We could also identify the cause of the unfavorable operating margin ratio by examining the values of the deductible ratio and the markup ratio. Let us assume that the markup ratio in 1988 was 1.20 and the deductible ratio was .17. This would narrow our attention to the markup ratio as the source of the problem. Upon

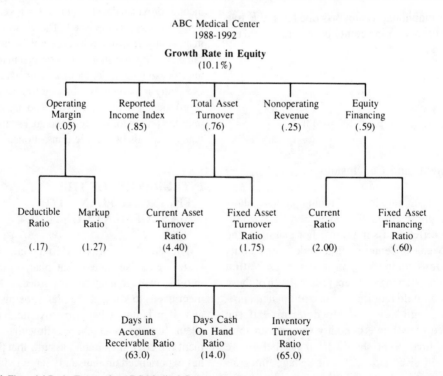

Figure 12-4 Financial Ratio Targets for ABC Medical Center

examination, we might learn that the primary reason for the unfavorable variation in the markup ratio was an unexpected increase in expenses. This situation may be correctable in future periods, putting the center back on track in terms of realizing its financial plan projections. However, it should be noted that because it did not realize a 10.1 percent growth rate in equity in the current year, it will need to plan on larger increases in the remaining four years. If it fails to realize growth rates in excess of 10.1 percent in future years, its financial projections will not be realized.

The reported income index value was also significantly above the projected value. This means that the center did not derive as much new equity from unreported sources as it had originally planned. If this trend continues, the center might be forced to change its initial assumptions and redefine its financial plan to reflect current circumstances.

The preceding framework for integrating management control and financial planning is reasonably concise and simple. It can be used by board members to assess more accurately the financial situation of their organization, and it provides a useful tool for communication by management. Finally, it relates directly to established financial planning targets and thus provides a structure for the delineation of secondary and tertiary targets, which may be particularly useful for lower levels of management.

SUMMARY

In the process of identifying the requirements for effective financial policy formulation in health care firms, it is especially important to relate the strategic plan to the financial plan. The financial plan should not be developed in isolation from strategic planning, nor should the strategic plan be developed in isolation from the financial plan. Both need to be developed together, reflecting in that context their individual requirements and assumptions. A strategic plan is not valid if it is not financially feasible, and a financial plan is of little value if it does not reflect the strategic decisions reached by management and the board.

A financial plan should be updated at least annually, projecting a forecast period of three to five years. Financial plans that are not updated stand a good chance of becoming invalid. The environment of health care delivery is changing, and a health care entity's financial plan must reflect the changes. In fact, a failure to update its financial plan can have disastrous consequences for an entity, leading perhaps to market share retrenchment or even financial failure.

Finally, financial plans should be integrated into the management control process. Financial ratios can be very useful in this regard. In particular, specific ratios can be usefully related to the key financial planning target of growth rate in equity.

Chapter 13

Analyzing Financial Statements

William O. Cleverley
Professor, Graduate Program in Hospital and Health Services Management
The Ohio State University

The major purpose of this chapter is to introduce some analytic tools for evaluating the financial condition of health care entities. Think for a moment how confusing and difficult it would be to reach any decisions on Omega Hospital's financial condition, as presented in Exhibits 2-1 through 2-5, without a key. Unless your training is in business or finance, the statements may look like a mass of endless numbers with little meaning. In short, there may be too much information in most financial statements to be digested easily by a general-purpose user.

An exhaustive list of people who might use general-purpose financial information would be difficult to prepare. Some of the potential users and their reasons for measuring financial condition are listed below:

- *boards of trustees*, to evaluate the solvency of their facilities and establish a framework for various decisions, such as those relating to investment, financing, and pricing

- *creditors*, to determine the amounts and terms of credit to be granted health care facilities and to evaluate the security of presently outstanding credit obligations

- *employee unions*, to evaluate the financial condition of a health care facility and its ability to meet increasing demands for higher wages; also to assess the capability of the facility to meet existing contractual relationships for deferred compensation programs, such as pension plans

- *department managers*, to understand better how operations and activities under their direct control contribute to the entity's overall financial position

- *rate regulation agencies*, to assess the adequacy of existing and proposed rates of a health care facility that is subject to rate review

- *grant-giving agencies* (public and private), to determine a grantee's ability to continue to provide services supported by a grant and to assess the need for additional funding

- *public*, to determine a community health care facility's financial condition and assess its need for rate increases and its use of prior funds to enhance and improve the delivery of health care services—as a basis for assessing the need for money in a fund drive.

This chapter is reprinted from *Essentials of Health Care Finance*, 2nd ed., by W.O. Cleverley, pp. 117–145, Aspen Publishers, Inc., © 1986.

RATIO ANALYSIS

The technique used to assess financial condition is financial ratio analysis—the examination of the relation of two pieces of financial information to obtain additional information. In this process, the new information is both easier to understand and usually more relevant than the unrelated, free-standing information found in general-purpose financial statements. For example, the values of fund balance and total assets may have little meaning when stated independently in a balance sheet. When the ratio of the two is taken, however, it indicates the proportion of assets that have been financed with sources other than debt.

Financial ratios are not another attempt by financial specialists to confuse and confound decision makers. Financial ratios have been empirically tested to determine their value in predicting business failure. The results to date have been quite impressive: financial ratios can, in fact, discern potential problems in financial condition even five years in advance of their emergence.

A sad fact is that much financial information is never really subjected to financial ratio analysis; the mass of figures just seems too voluminous ever to be synthesized. Decision makers tend to assume that, if the entity is breathing at the end of the year and is capable of publishing a financial statement, all must be well. If something goes wrong later, the accountant is blamed for not warning the decision makers. Sometimes the accountant *is* at fault. However, it is often the decision makers' fault for not analyzing and interpreting the financial information given to them in published financial statements.

The accounting profession was bombarded with criticism after the Penn Central collapse in 1970. To many it seemed that reporting standards must be too loose if the imminent financial collapse of a $7 billion business could not be determined from its financial statements. However, Paul Dasher, in the March–April 1972 issue of the *Financial Analyst's Journal*, showed that anyone who could apply normal financial ratios to published financial statements could have detected the impending failure. At the con-

clusion of this chapter, the reader should be able to examine selectively a few specific financial ratios to better assess the financial condition of a health care entity.

Meaningful ratio analysis relies heavily upon the existence of relevant, comparable data. Absolute values of ratios are usually more valuable than the underlying financial information, but they are even more valuable when they can be compared with existing standards. For example, the statement that a hospital earned three percent on its revenues in the previous year is useful, but a statement of the relationship of this three percent to some standard would be far more valuable.

Usually, the analysis of financial ratios involves two types of comparisons. Temporal comparison of ratios, the comparison of year-end ratios with prior year values, gives the analyst some idea of both trend and desirability. A projected financial ratio may similarly be compared with prior, actual values to test the validity of the projection and the desirability of the proposed plan of operation.

A second method of comparison uses industry averages as the relevant standards for comparison. The Financial Analysis Service (FAS), a comparative ratio service of the Healthcare Financial Management Association (HFMA), provides an excellent set of financial ratio averages for both hospitals and nursing homes.

For some time, the lack of uniformity in financial reporting has inhibited meaningful financial analysis in the health care industry. Specifically, the use of fund accounting has made it difficult to separate the financial effects of operations from the financial effects of other activities of the organization, such as those supported by endowment or grant monies. To some extent, this problem was solved with the publication of the American Institute of Certified Public Accountants' *Hospital Audit Guide* in 1972. This publication, though technically applicable only to audited hospital financial statements, has affected financial reporting of other health care entities. Its major feature is the requirement that funds be separated into restricted and unrestricted categories, as discussed in Chapter 2. In most situations, focusing the financial analysis on the unrestricted fund categories provides a better basis for evaluating actual health care operations.

Financial ratios can be classified into five major categories for the purposes of this chapter.

1. liquidity ratios
2. capital structure ratios
3. activity ratios
4. profitability ratios
5. other ratios

In the following discussion, individual ratios within each of these categories are defined with respect to their assessment of financial condition. The specific indicators described are a subset of the 29 ratios used in FAS. Additional information about FAS can be obtained by contacting HFMA in Oak Brook, Illinois. The financial statements of Willkram Hospital, shown in Exhibits 13-1 and 13-2, illustrate the discussion.

It may seem to some that undue emphasis is being placed on financial reporting and financial

Exhibit 13-1 Balance Sheet for Willkram Hospital

Willkram Hospital Balance Sheet, Unrestricted Funds, December 30, 1984 (with comparative figures for 1983) (000s omitted)

	December 31, 1984	December 31, 1983
Assets		
Current assets		
Cash and marketable securities	$ 119	$ 67
Accounts receivable	$ 6,600	$ 5,900
Less allowances and uncollectibles	868	753
Net accounts receivable	5,732	5,147
Inventories	682	578
Prepaid expenses	397	177
Due from restricted fund	396	232
Total current assets	$ 7,326	$ 6,201
Property, plant, and equipment		
Construction in progress	104	125
Property, plant, and equipment	43,070	40,763
	43,174	40,888
Allowances for depreciation	8,368	6,474
Total property, plant, and equipment	34,806	34,414
Other investments	1,360	1,193
Total assets	$43,492	$41,808
Liabilities and fund balance		
Current liabilities		
Accounts payable	$ 1,472	$ 1,265
Notes payable	0	250
Due to third party	310	188
Accrued expenses	708	611
Due to restricted funds	343	355
Total current liabilities	2,833	2,669
Long-term debt		
Mortgage payable	19,633	18,724
Total liabilities	22,466	21,393
Fund balance	21,026	20,415
Total liabilities and fund balance	$43,492	$41,808

analysis in the hospital sector. In terms of coverage in this chapter, this is true. However, ratios are general in nature and are just as relevant in other health care settings. For example, use of a current ratio that measures an entity's liquidity is valid and helpful not only for hospitals but also for nursing homes, health maintenance organizations (HMOs), outpatient clinics, and surgicenters. Furthermore, understanding the application of financial ratios in the relatively more complex hospital environment makes their application in other settings easier.

bilities. Liquidity is an important dimension in the assessment of financial condition. Most firms that experience financial problems do so because of a liquidity crisis; they are unable to pay current obligations as they become due. Measuring an entity's liquidity position is central to determining its financial condition. Other long-term factors, such as a poor accounts receivable collection policy, may explain a poor liquidity position, but the worsening of a liquidity position is usually the first clue that something more basic is wrong.

LIQUIDITY RATIOS

Liquidity is a term frequently used by business and financial people. It refers to the ability of a firm to meet its short-term maturing obligations. The more liquid a firm, the better it is able to meet its short-term obligations or current liabilities.

Current Ratio

One of the most widely used measures of liquidity is the current ratio, which equals

$$\frac{\text{Current assets}}{\text{Current liabilities}}$$

Exhibit 13-2 Statement of Revenue and Expense for Willkram Hospital

Willkram Hospital Statement of Revenue and Expense
Year Ended December 31, 1984
(with comparative figures for 1983)
(000s omitted)

	1984	1983
Patient service revenue	$31,824	$27,177
Allowances and uncollectible accounts	1,934	1,411
Net patient service revenue	29,890	25,766
Other operating revenue	1,421	1,150
Total operating revenue	31,311	26,916
Operating expenses		
Nursing services	9,306	7,364
Medical services	7,907	6,523
General services	5,285	5,271
Administrative services	3,683	2,780
Education and research	1,246	1,026
Depreciation	1,944	1,880
Interest	1,403	1,514
Total operating expenses	30,774	26,358
Net operating income	537	558
Nonoperating revenue	60	194
Excess of revenues over expenses	$ 597	$ 752

For Willkram Hospital, the current ratio values for 1984 and 1983 are as follows:

1984	1983
$\frac{7,326}{2,833} = 2.586$	$\frac{6,201}{2,669} = 2.323$

The higher the ratio value, the better the firm's ability to meet its current liabilities. A value commonly used in industry as a standard is 2.00; this means that two dollars of current assets

(assets expected to be realized in cash during the year) are available for each one dollar of current liabilities (obligations expected to require cash within the year). The 1984 FAS national median was 1.86. On both a trend and a standard-comparison basis, Willkram Hospital is in a favorable position (see Exhibit 13-3).

The current ratio is a basic measure that is widely used. However, if used alone, it does not tell the whole story. Some types of assets—cash and marketable securities, for example—are

Exhibit 13-3 Financial Ratio Analysis of Willkram Hospital

Ratio	1984	1983	FAS Median 1984	Trend	Standard
Liquidity					
Current	2.586	2.323	1.86	Favorable	Favorable
Quick	2.345	2.107	1.57	Favorable	Favorable
Acid test	.042	.025	.26	Favorable	Unfavorable
Days in accounts receivable	70.000	72.900	63.70	Favorable	Unfavorable
Days' cash on hand	1.510	.999	14.30	Favorable	Unfavorable
Average payment period	35.900	39.800	53.90	Favorable	Favorable
Capital structure					
Equity financing	.483	.488	.48	Unfavorable	Favorable
Long-term debt to equity	.934	.917	.71	Unfavorable	Unfavorable
Fixed asset financing	.564	.544	.62	Unfavorable	Favorable
Times interest earned	1.426	1.497	3.07	Unfavorable	Unfavorable
Debt service coverage	1.750	1.790	3.21	Unfavorable	Unfavorable
Cash flow to debt	.113	.123	.19	Unfavorable	Unfavorable
Activity					
Total asset turnover	.720	.644	.95	Favorable	Unfavorable
Fixed asset turnover	.900	.782	1.74	Favorable	Unfavorable
Current asset turnover	4.274	4.341	3.89	Unfavorable	Favorable
Average age of plant	4.300	3.440	6.87	Unfavorable	Favorable
Inventory turnover	45.910	46.570	69.70	Unfavorable	Unfavorable
Profitability					
Deductible	.061	.052	.183	Unfavorable	Favorable
Markup	1.080	1.067	1.265	Favorable	Unfavorable
Operating margin	.017	.021	.029	Unfavorable	Unfavorable
Operating margin price level adjusted	.001	.004	−.001	Unfavorable	Favorable
Return on total assets	.014	.018	.048	Unfavorable	Unfavorable
Nonoperating revenue	.101	.258	.310	Unfavorable	Unfavorable
Reported income index	.977	.641	.973	Unfavorable	Unfavorable
Other					
Restricted equity	0.000	0.000	.013	Neutral	Unfavorable
Replacement viability	.257	.298	.369	Unfavorable	Unfavorable

more liquid than accounts receivable or inventory. The current ratio does not account for these differences.

Quick Ratio

Another liquidity ratio, a refinement of the current ratio, is the quick ratio, which equals:

$$\frac{\text{Current assets less inventory}}{\text{Current liabilities}}$$

For Willkram Hospital, the quick ratio values for 1984 and 1983 are

1984	1983
$\frac{7,326 - 682}{2,833} = 2.345$	$\frac{6,201 - 578}{2,669} = 2.107$

As with the current ratio, the higher the value of this ratio, the better the firm's liquidity position. In industry, a value of 1.0 is often used. However, this value is too low for health care facilities because only a small amount of their current asset investment is carried in inventory. The 1984 FAS national median was 1.57. Thus, on both a trend and a standard-comparison basis, Willkram Hospital is in a favorable position with respect to quick ratio values.

In the quick ratio, the numerator is largely composed of cash and marketable securities, plus accounts receivable. These current assets are more liquid and make this a better test of liquidity compared with the current ratio. However, a key assumption is the liquidity of the accounts receivable. If they are not being collected quickly because of poor collection policies or delays in third-party payment processing, the quick ratio may not be a good measure of liquidity.

Acid Test Ratio

A refinement of the quick ratio is the acid test ratio, which equals

$$\frac{\text{Cash plus marketable securities}}{\text{Current liabilities}}$$

For Willkram Hospital, the acid test ratios for 1984 and 1983 are

1984	1983
$\frac{119}{2,833} = .042$	$\frac{67}{2,669} = .025$

Higher values again indicate more liquid resources available to meet current liabilities coming due. In this case, the liquid assets are limited to cash and marketable securities. Both these assets could be liquidated with little or no delay to pay maturing current liabilities. In both the quick and current ratios, there are categories of current assets that cannot be converted into cash without significant delays. The 1984 FAS median was .26. Willkram Hospital has a favorable trend but an unfavorable relationship to this standard value. In short, Willkram Hospital appears to be underinvested in highly liquid assets, like cash and marketable securities, but its trend over the two-year period is favorable.

Days in Patient Accounts Receivable Ratio

All three of the ratios discussed above—current, quick, and acid test—give indexes of the liquidity position of an entity. They do not, however, provide information as to *why* the current liquidity position exists, or what can be done to change it. In contrast, days in patient accounts receivable is a liquidity ratio that indicates the possible cause of a worsening liquidity position. It is simply ending net accounts receivable divided by an average day's revenue. Thus:

$$\frac{\text{Net patient accounts receivable}}{\text{Net patient revenue/365}}$$

For Willkram Hospital, days in accounts receivable for 1984 and 1983 are

1984	1983
$\frac{5,732}{\frac{29,890}{365}} = 70.0$	$\frac{5,147}{\frac{25,766}{365}} = 72.9$

Values for this ratio indicate the number of days in the average collection period. For example, Willkram Hospital in 1984 had 70.0 days outstanding in accounts receivable at the year end. This implies that it took the hospital 70.0 days on the average to turn its accounts receivable into cash. High values for this ratio could indicate problems in collection time that may be due to faulty collection policies and billing systems of the entity. However, a high value might also indicate that the underlying quality of the accounts receivable is poor, that is, their collectibility may be in doubt. This might imply that the write-off policy of the entity should be reexamined.

A good way to evaluate the collectibility of accounts receivable is to perform an aging of accounts receivable by payer. For example, let us assume that the following aging of Willkram Hospital's accounts receivable as of December 31, 1984, was performed.

Willkram Hospital
Aging of Accounts Receivable
December 31, 1984
(000s omitted)

	Gross	Self-Pay	Third-Party
Less than 30 days	$3,000	$ 800	$2,200
31–90 days	1,800	300	1,500
91–365 days	500	300	200
Over 365 days	1,300	700	600
Total	$6,600	$2,100	$4,500

The above aging of accounts receivable casts doubt on the collectibility of much of the $700,000 self-pay accounts receivable that is over one year past due. It might also raise a question of why $600,000 of third-party payer receivables over one year old are still outstanding. The answer could be a poor collection policy for payment by such third parties as Medicaid, or it may be due to an unresolved dispute between the provider and the payer over the amount actually due.

The 1984 FAS national median for days in patient accounts was 63.7 days. Willkram Hospital thus has a favorable trend in days in accounts receivable but an unfavorable comparison against the standard value. This could be part of the reason that Willkram's acid test ratio is low. For example, if the collection period were sped up by six days (the difference between Willkram's current collection period and the standard), an additional $491,000 in cash could be collected. If this potential cash balance were added to the present cash value of $119,000, the acid test ratio value would be raised to .215. This represents a 513 percent improvement over its current value.

Care must be exercised in using any of the liquidity ratios if seasonality is a factor. For example, if the dates for financial statement presentation occur during a slack period of the year, certain values of current assets may be understated and others overstated. In particular, the values of accounts receivable and inventory might be at their lowest point of the year, and the corresponding values of cash and marketable securities at their highest, or vice versa, giving a biased view of the liquidity position of the firm. In addition, standards vary by type of health care facility and region of the country. Clinics and HMOs can be expected to have significantly fewer days in accounts receivable than normal hospitals, while long-term care facilities may have significantly longer collection periods than normal hospitals. The collection period also depends heavily upon the composition of payers and their payment practices. Medicaid may pay on a prompt and timely basis in one state and yet be delinquent in another. The same holds true for Blue Cross and other major third-party payers.

Average Payment Period Ratio

Another index that provides information about causes of a worsening liquidity position is the average payment period ratio:

$$\frac{\text{Current liabilities}}{(\text{Total operating expenses} - \text{Depreciation})/365}$$

For Willkram Hospital, the values of this ratio for 1984 and 1983 are

$$\frac{2,833}{(30,774 - 1944)/365} = 35.9 \qquad \frac{2,669}{(26,358 - 1,880)/365} = 39.8$$

1984   1983

From a financial condition standpoint, low values of this ratio are better than higher values. Creditors often use a slight adaptation of this ratio:

$$\frac{\text{Accounts payable}}{\text{Purchases}/365}$$

If the data are available, both of the above average payment period ratios should be calculated. However, in the Willkram Hospital example, a separate listing of purchases for the year is not available.

The average payment period ratio indicates the length of time an entity takes to pay its obligations. The denominator, which is total expenses less depreciation divided by 365, provides an index of average daily cash expenses. (Remember, depreciation is a noncash expense). The numerator, current liabilities, represents obligations for expenditures during the coming year. Most normal supply items are expensed within the year in which they are purchased. The same is true of payroll expenses, which usually constitute the largest single element of accrued liabilities and expenses. A standard value for this ratio derived from the FAS sample is 53.9. On this basis, Willkram Hospital has both a favorable trend and standard-comparison evaluation.

Days' Cash on Hand Ratio

A final measure of liquidity is days' cash on hand:

$$\frac{\text{Cash} + \text{Marketable securities}}{(\text{Total operating expenses} - \text{Depreciation})/365}$$

For Willkram Hospital, the values of days' cash on hand for 1984 and 1983 are

$$\frac{119}{(30,774 - 1,944)/365} = 1.51 \qquad \frac{67}{(26,358 - 1,880)/365} = .999$$

1984   1983

Higher values of this ratio imply a more liquid position, other factors remaining constant. The ratio measures the number of days an entity could meet its average daily expenditures (as measured by the denominator) with existing liquid assets, namely cash and marketable securities. It is similar to the acid test ratio except that it uses a flow rather than stock concept. It attempts to define a maximum period of safety assuming the worst of all conditions, for example, no conversion of accounts receivable into cash.

The 1984 FAS national median for this ratio was 14.3 days. Using this value as the standard, Willkram Hospital is acutely underinvested in cash and marketable securities, although its trend is favorable. The value of this ratio in conjunction with the value of the acid test ratio strongly implies that Willkram Hospital should seriously consider increasing the amount of cash and marketable securities, especially marketable securities, that it carries. This is the only area where liquidity position is in drastic need of improvement.

It is useful to examine the value of the replacement viability ratio (see page 221) in situations of extremely low days' cash on hand. Sizable values for this ratio indicate the availability of funds that could be used for liquidity purposes. However, Willkram Hospital's values for replacement viability are low when compared with FAS standards, which dramatizes further the need for increases in cash.

CAPITAL STRUCTURE RATIOS

Capital structure ratios are useful in assessing the long-term solvency or liquidity of a firm. While the liquidity ratios just discussed are useful in detection of immediate solvency problems, the capital structure ratios are especially useful in longer-term assessment of financial condition. They are also valuable in detecting some short-term problems. Capital structure ratios are carefully evaluated by long-term creditors and bond-rating agencies to determine an entity's ability to increase its amounts of debt financing. In the past 20 years, the hospital and health care industries have radically increased their percentages of debt financing. This trend makes capital structure ratios vitally important to many individuals. Evaluation of these ratios may well determine the amount of credit available to the industry and thus directly affect its rate of growth.

Equity Financing Ratio

A basic capital structure ratio is the equity financing ratio:

$$\frac{\text{Fund balance}}{\text{Total assets}}$$

For Willkram Hospital the values for this ratio in 1984 and 1983 are

1984	1983
$\frac{21,026}{43,492} = .483$	$\frac{20,415}{41,808} = .488$

Higher values for this ratio are regarded as positive indicators of a sound financial condition, all other things being equal. After all, if an entity had zero debt or a fund-balance-to-total-assets ratio of 1.0, there would not be any possible claimants on the entity's assets and thus no fear of bankruptcy or insolvency. The ratio indicates the percentage of total assets that has been financed with sources other than debt. In industry, a value for this ratio of less than 50 percent can cause some alarm. In segments of the health care industry where there is greater stability in earnings, lower ratios may be permitted.

The 1984 FAS national median for the equity financing ratio was .48. Willkram Hospital is very close to this industry norm. Since it has such a high current ratio, we can infer that Willkram Hospital has a greater percentage of long-term debt financing. This will be discussed shortly.

Long-Term Debt to Equity Ratio

Another capital structure ratio used by many analysts is the long-term debt to equity ratio:

$$\frac{\text{Long-term debt}}{\text{Fund balance}}$$

For Willkram Hospital, the values for this ratio in 1984 and 1983 are

1984	1983
$\frac{19,633}{21,026} = .934$	$\frac{18,724}{20,415} = .917$

One deficiency of the equity financing ratio is that it includes short-term sources of debt financing, such as current liabilities. When assessing solvency and the ability to increase long-term financing, it is sometimes desirable to focus on "permanent capital." Permanent capital consists of sources of financing that are not temporary, including long-term debt and fund balance. Low values for the long-term debt to equity ratio indicate to creditors an entity's ability to carry additional long-term debt.

A value for this ratio used in general industry is 50 percent; that is, for every one dollar of long-term debt, two dollars should come from equity. In the health care industry this value may be higher, especially for hospitals. A value used by some investment bankers is 2.0. In other words they are willing to allow two dollars of long-term debt for every one dollar of equity. In part, this reflects the stability of the industry. It also reflects the relative difficulty in acquiring equity capital in a largely nonprofit industry.

The 1984 FAS national median for the long-term debt to equity ratio was .71. A comparison of Willkram Hospital's values with this standard yields both an unfavorable trend and standard-comparison evaluation. Willkram Hospital has utilized more long-term debt than the average hospital, and its future debt capacity may be limited.

Fixed Asset Financing Ratio

A capital structure ratio of special importance to the health care industry is the fixed asset financing ratio:

$$\frac{\text{Long-term debt}}{\text{Net fixed assets}}$$

For Willkram Hospital, the values for this ratio in 1984 and 1983 are

1984	1983
$\dfrac{19,633}{34,806} = .564$	$\dfrac{18,724}{34,414} = .544$

The fixed asset financing ratio is of special importance when the payment for capital costs is linked to cost-reimbursement formulas. In most cost payment plans, capital costs are limited to depreciation plus interest expense. The cash payment requirements would, however, consist of interest plus principal retirement. Remember debt principal is an expenditure, not an expense. In this situation, payments for depreciation expense would be needed to meet current and future debt principal payments. If depreciation expense were not of sufficient size to meet debt principal payments, the organization could experience some cash flow problems. In the fixed asset financing ratio, the numerator represents the total future debt principal payments, while the denominator represents a source of payment for debt principal, namely future reimbursable depreciation. As the value for the fixed asset financing ratio increases, the probability of cash flow problems may increase, especially if reimbursement of capital costs on a historical cost basis is a significant factor.

The 1984 FAS national median for the fixed asset financing ratio was .62. Values for Willkram Hospital compare favorably with this standard, but they do exhibit an unfavorable trend upward. Willkram Hospital does have a relatively young physical plant (see average age of plant ratio). This implies that it has probably completed a major renovation recently and will not require significant new long-term debt financing in the immediate future.

Times Interest Earned Ratio

A traditional capital structure ratio that attempts to measure the ability of an entity to meet its interest payment is the times interest earned ratio:

$$\frac{\text{Excess of revenues over expenses} + \text{Interest expense}}{\text{Interest expense}}$$

For Willkram Hospital, the values for this ratio in 1984 and 1983 are

1984	1983
$\dfrac{597 + 1,403}{1,403} = 1.426$	$\dfrac{752 + 1,514}{1,514} = 1.497$

Even though a firm has a very low percentage of debt financing, it may not be able to carry additional debt because its profitability cannot meet the increased interest payment. Repayment of interest expense is a very important consideration in long-term financing. Failure to meet interest payment requirements on a timely basis could result in the entire principal value of the loan becoming due. Meeting the fixed annual interest expense obligations is thus highly critical to solvency. The times interest earned ratio measures the extent to which earnings could slip and still not impair the entity's ability to repay its interest obligations. High values for this ratio are obviously preferable. An absolute minimum standard in general industry is 1.5. The 1984 FAS national median for the times interest earned ratio was 3.07. Compared with this standard, Willkram Hospital shows both an unfavorable trend evaluation and an unfavorable standards-comparison evaluation. Since this ratio indicates the ability to repay indebtedness, Willkram's low value could seriously impair its ability to acquire additional financing on favorable terms.

Debt Service Coverage Ratio

A commonly used capital structure ratio that measures the ability to pay both components of long-term indebtedness—interest and principal—is the debt service coverage ratio:

$$\frac{\begin{array}{c}\text{Excess of revenues over expenses}\\ + \text{ Depreciation} + \text{Interest}\end{array}}{\text{Principal payment} + \text{Interest expense}}$$

In the financial statements of Willkram Hospital that are available to us, the amount of principal repayments is missing, and thus there are no data to calculate values for this ratio. However, values for debt principal repayments in 1984 and

1983 can be identified in the footnotes to the financial statements (not reprinted here). Using these values, debt service coverage ratios for Willkram Hospital in 1984 and 1983 are

$$\underset{1984}{\frac{597 + 1,944 + 1,403}{850 + 1,403}} = 1.75 \qquad \underset{1983}{\frac{752 + 1,880 + 1,514}{800 + 1,514}} = 1.79$$

The debt service coverage ratio is a broader measure of debt repayment ability than the times interest earned ratio because it includes the second component of a debt obligation—the repayment of debt principal. The numerator of the debt service coverage ratio defines the funds available to meet debt service requirements of principal and interest. The ratio indicates the number of times that the debt service requirements can be met from existing funds. Higher ratios indicate that an entity is better able to meet its financing commitments.

A standard minimum debt service coverage ratio value used by investment bankers in the hospital industry is 1.5. The 1984 FAS national median for the debt service coverage ratio was 3.21. With this value as a standard, Willkram Hospital has both an unfavorable trend and an unfavorable standard-comparison evaluation.

Values for Willkram Hospital's debt service coverage ratio corroborate our earlier findings for the times interest earned ratio. The hospital is not in a good position to assume additional long-term debt. In fact, some debt service problems may arise in the future if values for both the times interest earned ratio and the debt service coverage ratio are not increased. Ultimately, increases in these ratios may be linked directly to improvements in profitability, especially operating margins, which are currently depressed.

Cash Flow to Debt Ratio

One of the best predictors of financial failure is the cash flow to debt ratio:

$$\frac{\text{Excess of revenues over expenses} + \text{Depreciation}}{\text{Current liabilities} + \text{Long-term debt}}$$

For Willkram Hospital, the values of the cash flow to debt ratio in 1984 and 1983 are

$$\underset{1984}{\frac{597 + 1.944}{2,833 + 19,633}} = .113 \qquad \underset{1983}{\frac{752 + 1,880}{2,669 + 18,724}} = .123$$

The cash flow to debt ratio has been found to be an excellent predictor of financial failure, even as much as five years in advance of such failure. The numerator, cash flow, can be thought of as the firm's source of total funds, excluding financing. The denominator, total debt, provides a measure of a major need for future funds, namely, debt retirement. A low value for this ratio often indicates a potential problem in meeting future debt payment requirements.

The 1984 FAS national median for the cash flow to total debt ratio was .19. Again Willkram Hospital demonstrates a potential problem in meeting future debt service requirements. Significant improvements in future profitability are urgently needed at this hospital.

ACTIVITY RATIOS

Activity or turnover ratios measure the relationship between revenue and assets. The numerator is always revenue; it may be thought of as a surrogate measure of output. The denominator is investment in some category of assets; it may be thought of as a measure of input. These ratios are also referred to as efficiency ratios, since efficiency ratios measure output to input. As noted in a later context, activity ratios also have a very important relationship to measures of profitability.

Total Asset Turnover Ratio

The most widely used activity ratio is the total asset turnover ratio:

$$\frac{\text{Total operating revenue}}{\text{Total assets}}$$

For Willkram Hospital, the values of the total asset turnover ratio in 1984 and 1983 are

$$\underset{1984}{\frac{31,311}{43,492}} = .720 \qquad \underset{1983}{\frac{26,916}{41,808}} = .644$$

A high value for this ratio implies that the entity's total investment is being used efficiently, that is, a large number of services are being provided to the community from a limited resource base. However, the ratio can be deceptive. For example, a facility that is relatively old, with most of its plant assets fully depreciated, is quite likely to show a high total asset turnover ratio. Yet it may not be nearly as efficient as a newer facility that has plant and equipment assets that are largely undepreciated.

A measure that may be used to evaluate partially the existence of this problem by detecting the age of a given physical plant is

$$\frac{\text{Allowance for depreciation}}{\text{Depreciation expense}} = \text{Average age of facility}$$

Using this measure for Willkram Hospital, the values for 1984 and 1983 are

1984	1983
$\frac{8,368}{1,944} = 4.30$	$\frac{6,474}{1,880} = 3.44$

The 1984 FAS national median for the average age of plant ratio was 6.87. Willkram Hospital is therefore operating a relatively young physical plant. This means that the costs of its physical assets are much more likely to be close to true current costs. We could therefore expect to see somewhat lower values for both the total asset turnover ratio and the fixed asset turnover ratio and not become too alarmed.

This is in fact the case for the total asset turnover ratio. The 1984 FAS national median for the total asset turnover ratio was .95. Willkram Hospital is significantly below this value, but it does exhibit a favorable trend. This is most likely attributable to the increasing age of the physical plant. As the facility ages, Willkram's total asset turnover will probably approach industry norms.

Fixed Asset Turnover Ratio

Another common turnover ratio is the fixed asset turnover ratio:

$$\frac{\text{Total operating revenue}}{\text{Net fixed assets}}$$

For Willkram Hospital, the values of the fixed asset turnover ratio in 1984 and 1983 are

1984	1983
$\frac{31,311}{34,806} = .900$	$\frac{26,916}{34,414} = .782$

The fixed asset turnover ratio is identical to the total asset turnover ratio, except that fixed assets, a specific subset of total assets, is substituted in the denominator. This substitution is an attempt to assess the relative efficiency of an individual category of assets. In fact, all the turnover ratios discussed subsequently are further segregations of various categories of assets.

Fixed assets are the number one investment in most health care entities. The fixed asset ratio can thus be of major importance in assessing the relative efficiency of plant investments. The 1984 FAS national median for the fixed asset turnover ratio was 1.74. Here, Willkram Hospital shows a favorable trend, but an unfavorable standard-comparison evaluation. As the facility becomes older, the value of its fixed asset turnover ratio will probably approach the standard value. In most situations, there are better ways to assess the efficiency of plant investment than by using this very simple ratio; for example, actual measures of utilization may be used. However, an aggregated measure of cost like that used in a fixed asset turnover ratio does provide important information with respect to output per dollar of investment.

Current Asset Turnover Ratio

The complement of the fixed asset turnover ratio is the current asset turnover ratio:

$$\frac{\text{Total operating revenue}}{\text{Current assets}}$$

For Willkram Hospital, the values of this ratio in 1984 and 1983 are

1984	1983

$$\frac{31,311}{7,326} = 4.274 \qquad \frac{26,916}{6,201} = 4.341$$

The current asset turnover ratio focuses on the relative efficiency of the investment in current assets with respect to the generation of revenue. The valuation of current assets is not subject to the same difficulties encountered in the measurement of fixed assets. The ratio is thus more comparable across facilities. The 1984 FAS national median for the current asset turnover ratio was 3.89. Willkram Hospital thus has a slightly unfavorable trend and a favorable standard-comparison evaluation with respect to this ratio.

Inventory Turnover Ratio

A refinement of the current asset turnover ratio is the inventory turnover ratio:

$$\frac{\text{Total operating revenue}}{\text{Inventory}}$$

For Willkram Hospital, the values of this ratio in 1984 and 1983 are

1984	1983

$$\frac{31,311}{682} = 45.91 \qquad \frac{26,916}{578} = 46.57$$

The inventory turnover ratio is a very important measure of financial condition in manufacturing and merchandising firms. A low value might imply an overstocking of items that are not selling. Conversely, a high value could indicate that inadequate inventory levels are reducing possible sales because of shortages. In service firms like health care facilities, inventory is of less importance. However, it still is a major category of current asset investment, and its relative efficiency is important. Using the 1984 FAS national median of 69.7, Willkram Hospital produces an unfavorable trend and an unfavorable standard-comparison evaluation. Given this situation, the hospital might do well to investigate its current level of inventory.

PROFITABILITY RATIOS

To talk of profit in a largely nonprofit industry appears to many to be a contradiction in terms. Yet few, if any, health care facilities can remain liquid and solvent if profits are held to zero. In such a situation, cash flow would not be sufficient to meet normal nonexpense cash flow requirements, such as repayment of debt principal and investment in additional fixed and current assets.

However, recognizing the basic need for profit is not the same thing as determining how much is needed. It is not healthy either for the public or for the health care entity if the entity's profitability is either too great or too small. Discussion of a need for profitability thus centers on a definition of financial requirements. Here we are concerned only with the interpretation of several commonly used financial ratios of profitability.

Deductible Ratio

A common profitability ratio in the health care industry that measures revenue write-offs is the deductible ratio:

$$\frac{\text{Deductions from gross patient revenue}}{\text{Gross patient revenue}}$$

For Willkram Hospital, the values of the deductible ratio in 1984 and 1983 are

1984	1983

$$\frac{1,934}{31,824} = .061 \qquad \frac{1,411}{27,177} = .052$$

The deductible ratio measures the proportion of gross patient service revenue that is not expected to be realized in cash. The major categories of deductions are contractual allowances, bad debts, charity care, and courtesy discounts. Ideally, it would be useful to break down the deductible ratio by major payer category. From a profitability perspective, increasing values of the deductible ratio are likely to result in declining profitability, simply because a larger percentage of the total revenue is not being collected. In addition, a large deductible ratio usually results in cross-subsidization between payer categories.

A high deductible ratio does not necessarily imply poor profitability. A hospital may react to high deductibles by raising its rates (high mark-up ratio) or by increasing its nonoperating sources of funding (high nonoperating revenue ratio or low reported income index ratio). In addition, a hospital should examine the specific causes of the current deductible situation. For example, it may be possible to improve the collection of self-pay accounts by making billing process changes, by instituting a bank financing policy, or by changing the hospital's policy on charity care. Contractual allowances may be reduced by improving reimbursement management. Whatever the ultimate solution(s), it is important to monitor the deductible ratio closely. Small changes in this ratio can have a very profound impact on overall hospital profitability.

The 1984 FAS national median for the deductible ratio was .183. Thus, relatively, Willkram Hospital has an unusually low deductible ratio. The average hospital write-offs are nearly three times the percentage of revenue that Willkram Hospital writes off. At first glance this may appear very positive. However, much of Willkram's low write-off is due to an extremely low markup. An increase in Willkram's rates to reflect its current costs would probably produce significantly higher deductibles, but it would also produce more operating profit, which is desperately needed by the hospital to improve its long-term solvency.

Markup Ratio

The markup ratio, used in conjunction with the deductible ratio, determines a firm's operating margin. The markup ratio is defined as

$$\frac{\text{Gross patient service revenue} + \text{Other operating revenue}}{\text{Operating expenses}}$$

For Willkram Hospital, the values of this ratio in 1984 and 1983 are

$$\begin{array}{cc} 1984 & 1983 \\ \dfrac{31,824 + 1,421}{30,774} = 1.080 & \dfrac{27,177 + 1,150}{26,358} = 1.067 \end{array}$$

The markup ratio defines the multiple by which rates are set above expenses. The numerator includes both patient service revenue and other operating revenue because the denominator, operating expense, is not usually divided by source of revenue. High values for the markup ratio imply higher rates or prices per dollar of expenses and a greater likelihood of a favorable profitability position. It should be recognized that the objective of most hospitals is not to maximize profit. Therefore, there are upper limits for markups.

As noted earlier, the markup ratio and the deductible ratio interact to determine the hospital's operating margin. High markup ratio values do not guarantee favorable profitability positions if they are associated with unfavorable deductible ratios. Markups are influenced by the age of the plant and the debt principal retirement schedule. Hospitals with relatively old plants and/or high debt service requirements may need to maintain relatively high markup ratios. In such situations, an average markup may not be enough to maintain hospital solvency. Finally, hospitals may also recognize the availability of nonoperating sources of income and choose to keep markups at relatively low values.

The 1984 FAS national median for the markup ratio was 1.265. Willkram Hospital's present rate structure is significantly lower than that of most hospitals. If its costs are not excessive, it should seriously explore the implementation of some sizable rate increases. At the present time, Willkram's poor operating margins are directly traceable to low markups.

Operating Margin Ratio

The most commonly cited measure of profitability is the operating margin ratio:

$$\frac{\text{Net operating income}}{\text{Total operating revenue}}$$

For Willkram Hospital, the values of this ratio in 1984 and 1983 are

1984	1983
$\dfrac{537}{31,311} = .017$	$\dfrac{558}{26,916} = .021$

From the entity's viewpoint, the higher the value of the ratio, the better its financial condition. In most situations, firms that have high profit margins are less likely to experience financial difficulties. A simple way to understand this ratio is to think of it as a measure of profit retained per dollar of sales. For example, in 1984 Willkram Hospital retained 1.7¢ of every revenue dollar as profit. The 1984 FAS national median for the operating margin ratio was .029. Thus, Willkram Hospital shows both an unfavorable trend and an unfavorable standard-comparison evaluation. As discussed earlier, Willkram's rate structure should be reexamined in light of a relatively low operating margin.

Operating Margin Price-Level Adjusted Ratio

It is often useful to adjust the operating margin ratio to reflect replacement cost depreciation. The operating margin price-level adjusted ratio does this:

$$\frac{\text{Total operating revenue} - \text{Operating expenses} + \text{Depreciation} - \text{Price-level depreciation}}{\text{Total operating revenue}}$$

For Willkram Hospital, the values for this ratio in 1984 and 1983 are

1983

$$\frac{26,916 - 26,358 + 1,880 - 2,322}{26,916} = .004$$

1984

$$\frac{31,311 - 30,774 + 1,944 - 2,455}{31,311} = .001$$

The operating margin price-level adjusted ratio is identical to the operating margin ratio

except that it substitutes price-level depreciation for depreciation expense reported on an unadjusted historical cost basis. The ratio defines the proportion of operating revenue net of deductions that is retained as income after deducting price-level adjusted depreciation. Though not totally accurate, this measure of operating profitability attempts to reflect the replacement costs of operating fixed assets in the calculation of the operating margin.

Values for this ratio that are below zero imply that the organization is not currently earning enough operating income to provide funds for the eventual replacement of its fixed assets. Future replacement needs may have to be met from an increased reliance on debt, if available, or from other equity sources, such as grants and contributions, if available. Values for this ratio that exceed zero are not to be interpreted as a guarantee of future fund availability for replacement. To the extent that increased working capital needs are financed with equity, an erosion of the replacement potential of the hospital will occur. Also, it should be remembered that the index used for price-level restatement is the Consumer Price Index for urban wage earners, which may understate the real replacement cost of the hospital.

The 1984 FAS national median for the operating margin price-level adjusted ratio was −.001. Willkram Hospital's ratio compares favorably with this value. Because of the relatively new physical plant at Willkram, operating profitability adjusted for replacement cost is much more favorable than unadjusted operating margins. Willkram is providing for replacement in its current price structure. However, it still needs sizable increases in operating profit to improve its debt service coverage capability.

Nonoperating Revenue Ratio

A profitability ratio that provides a means of analyzing the source of profit is the nonoperating revenue ratio:

$$\frac{\text{Nonoperating revenue}}{\text{Excess of revenues over expenses}}$$

For Willkram Hospital, the values for this ratio in 1984 and 1983 are

1984	1983
$\dfrac{60}{597} = .101$	$\dfrac{194}{752} = .258$

Depending on the individual situation, a high value for the nonoperating revenue ratio may be good or bad. A high value would indicate that a large percentage of total net income or excess of revenues over expenses was derived from sources other than operations. If the value is stable, it enhances the overall financial condition of the entity and provides a stable source of funding that could be used to meet temporary reversals in operations. However, a high value may also indicate a weak financial condition. For example, there are many health care facilities that are heavily dependent on nonoperating revenue sources to subsidize operations that, by themselves, are incapable of breaking even. If these sources are not guaranteed and exhibit a highly erratic pattern, the financial condition of the entity could be in jeopardy. The 1984 FAS national median for the nonoperating revenue ratio was .31. In the case of Willkram Hospital, comparison with the FAS median indicates significant room for improvement. There was a significant change in the proportion of income contributed by nonoperating revenue sources from 1983 to 1984. During this same period, net operating income was fairly stable. A longer-term trend analysis might reveal the importance of this change in nonoperating revenue. Given Willkram Hospital's low profitability ratio values, the sources of nonoperating revenue and their expected stability should be analyzed.

Return on Total Assets Ratio

A profitability ratio that measures the relationship of profit to investment is the return on total assets ratio:

$$\frac{\text{Excess of revenues over expenses}}{\text{Total assets}}$$

For Willkram Hospital, the values of this ratio in 1984 and 1983 are

1984	1983
$\dfrac{597}{43,492} = .014$	$\dfrac{752}{41,808} = .018$

The return on total asset ratio defines the amount of net income or excess of revenues over expenses earned per dollar of investment. This profitability measure includes both operating and nonoperating sources of income. It provides a measure of the return on capital invested in operations. Adequate levels of return are essential to the continued viability and replacement of hospital assets. In many situations, the return on total assets ratio is modified by using the excess of revenues over expenses before subtracting interest expense. The rationale for this adaptation is to separate the influence of financing decisions from operating results.

Values for this ratio are affected by the average age of the hospital's plant. A hospital operating with a relatively old and largely depreciated plant may have a very favorable return on assets ratio. However, because of near-term replacement needs, this favorable ratio value may be highly deceiving.

The return on total assets ratio is a function of the product of the total asset turnover ratio, the operating margin ratio, and the nonoperating revenue ratio:

$$\text{Return on total assets ratio} = \frac{\text{Total asset turnover ratio} \times \text{Operating margin ratio}}{1.0 - \text{Nonoperating revenue ratio}}$$

The return on total asset ratio can be increased by improving the total asset turnover ratio, the operating margin ratio, or the nonoperating revenue ratio. It is important to recognize that hospitals with relatively high average age-of-plant ratios should probably try to attain above-average values for the return on total assets ratio.

The 1984 FAS national median for the return on total assets ratio was .048. In light of this standard, Willkram Hospital has both an unfavorable trend and unfavorable standard-comparison evaluation. This is a direct result of its relatively poor position in all three of the ratios that combine to determine the return on total assets ratio—operating margin, total asset turnover, and nonoperating revenue.

Reported Income Index Ratio

Given the peculiar nature of fund accounting in the hospital and health care industry, another valuable profitability ratio is the reported income index ratio:

$$\frac{\text{Excess of revenue over expenses}}{\text{Change in fund balance}}$$

For Willkram Hospital, the values for this ratio in 1984 and 1983 are

1984	1983
$\dfrac{597}{21{,}026 - 20{,}415} = .977$	$\dfrac{752}{20{,}415 - 19{,}242} = .641$

As noted in Chapter 2, there are situations in which funds may be transferred to an unrestricted fund from a restricted fund and not be shown as income to the unrestricted fund. An important example of this is the purchase of fixed assets with dollars from a restricted plant replacement fund. The fixed assets purchased would be transferred to the unrestricted fund and shown as general plant property and equipment; a corresponding direct change or increase in fund balance of the unrestricted fund would also occur. This increase in fund balance is necessary if the basic accounting equation is to be kept in balance; assets must equal liabilities plus fund balance. If this situation occurs frequently, the financial condition of the entity is far more favorable than its profitability ratios would indicate. The ratio of excess of revenue over expenses to changes in fund balance is designed to determine to what extent such transactions are occurring. Values consistently, and significantly, less than 1.0 indicate that a very important unreported source of income is being used by the entity.

The 1984 FAS national median for the reported income index ratio was .973. In the case of Willkram Hospital, a significant input of unreported income occurred in fiscal year 1983; reported income or the excess of revenues over expenses accounted for only 64.1 percent of the total change in fund balance. A history of such situations could imply a much more favorable financial condition than current profitability ratios might indicate.

OTHER RATIOS

Two ratios do not fit neatly into the four categories discussed above. These ratios are nevertheless useful in providing additional information about the overall assessment of financial position.

Restricted Equity Ratio

To assess the availability of capital from third-party donor-restricted funds, the restricted equity ratio is often used:

$$\frac{\text{Total restricted fund balances}}{\text{Unrestricted fund balance}}$$

Willkram Hospital does not report any restricted funds in its balance sheet. This implies that values for both 1984 and 1983 would be zero.

High values for restricted equity ratios are usually desirable. An underlying assumption about the desirability of high restricted equity ratios is that the entity must already have adequate levels of unrestricted equity. This can be evaluated by analyzing the equity financing ratio. Restricted equity will usually improve hospital profitability in one of two ways. First, if the restricted equity is an endowment, it may provide a very stable flow of investment income that will be reported as nonoperating revenue. Second, if the restricted equity is for plant purposes, there will be future credits to the unrestricted fund balance.

Replacement Viability Ratio

To assess the feasibility of future plant replacement, the replacement viability ratio is frequently used:

$$\frac{\text{Restricted plant fund balance} + \text{Unrestricted investments}}{\text{Price-level-adjusted accumulated depreciation} \times 0.50}$$

For Willkram Hospital, the values for replacement viability in 1984 and 1983 are

1984	1983

$$\frac{0 + 1,360}{10,569 \times .50} = .257 \qquad \frac{0 + 1,193}{7,955 \times .50} = .298$$

The replacement viability ratio is used to measure the adequacy of current investments to meet replacement needs. The numerator, restricted plant fund balance plus unrestricted investments, is a measure of current funds available to meet potential replacement needs. The denominator is a measure of the present need. Price-level-adjusted accumulated depreciation is a measure of the current cost of fixed assets that has been written off as depreciation. It is not a perfect measure of a hospital's replacement need, but it gives a far better estimate than that produced by simply using unadjusted historical cost accumulated depreciation. Its value is multiplied by 0.50 to recognize that debt financing may be used, the assumption being that 50 percent of replacement needs will be financed with debt.

A standard value for the replacement viability ratio is 1.0. This implies a situation in which exactly enough funds are available for replacement needs. Values greater than 1.0 may indicate more than adequate levels of investment, while values less than 1.0 indicate deficiencies. Hospitals may adjust this ratio to reflect their own desired future financing patterns. This is done by multiplying the calculated replacement viability ratio as follows:

Adjusted replacement viability = Replacement viability
$$\times \frac{0.50}{\text{Expected proportion of equity financing}}$$

Willkram Hospital is significantly underinvested in relation to its potential replacement needs. Again, low profitability would appear to be the major cause for this problem. Unless Willkram adds significantly to its replacement reserves, it will be forced either to borrow a very large percentage of its future replacement cost or to reduce the size and scope of any renovation and replacement program. Either course would seriously jeopardize the hospital's long-term solvency.

SOME CAVEATS

In this chapter, we have demonstrated, through an examination of 26 separate financial ratios, the use of financial ratio analysis in the assessment of the financial condition of health care facilities. At this point, it is appropriate to add some general limitations that should be recognized when evaluating financial condition through financial ratio analysis.

Validity of Standards

The standards used in this chapter should be helpful in many health care settings. They are, however, of special importance in the hospital industry, since that is where they were derived. These ratios will vary by region of the country and time period. This implies that standards should be updated frequently. It also implies the importance of using adequate trend data. Financial ratios should be calculated over a minimum of five years if meaningful trends are to be discovered. The two-year comparisons developed in this chapter were used only to discuss basic methodology and are clearly inadequate. In this connection, participation in a financial service like HFMA's FAS is strongly encouraged.

Cost Valuation

The values reported in a balance sheet are usually stated at unadjusted historical cost. Though this valuation does have some advantages in terms of objectivity of reporting, it limits the utility of comparisons across facilities when inflation is a predominant factor. The need for adjustment of ratios that use balance sheet values, especially fixed asset values, cannot be overstated.

Projections

Financial ratio analysis uses historical data. It provides a picture of where the entity has been; it does not necessarily tell where it is going. Budgetary data are required for this purpose. The value of financial ratio analysis as a predictor rests on the assumption that past behavior validly indicates future behavior.

Accounting Alternatives

It should be recognized that there are available a number of acceptable accounting alternatives for measuring the financial effects of various transactions. The use of different accounting methods can create significantly different values for financial ratios, even when the underlying financial events are identical. There may even be situations in which differences in accounting methods impair the comparability of financial ratios across health care facilities or over time. Consistent use of a given set of accounting methods can help a health care facility avoid such comparability problems and should be encouraged.

Chapter 14

The Management Control Process

William O. Cleverley
Professor, Graduate Program in Hospital and Health Services Management
The Ohio State University

Twenty years ago, the word *budgeting* could not have been found in the vocabulary of many hospital managers and other health care facility administrators. Today, this is no longer true. Most hospitals and other health care facilities now develop and use budgets as an integral part of their overall management control process.

To a large extent, the attention being paid to budgeting by health care providers is attributable to changes in the environment. The recent adoption of prospective payment and the increasing price competition among health care providers have forced many health care firms to monitor and control costs with increasing care. Budgeting is of course a logical way for any business organization to control its costs. Indeed, other parties external to health care providers now require health care firms to prepare and submit budgets and other financial forecasts. For example, rate-setting agencies frequently require hospitals and other health care facilities to submit fairly detailed institutional budgets. The certificate of need (CON) also requires a projection of financial information for projects under review.

External forces thus have certainly stimulated the development of budgets in the health care industry, but most likely such budgets would

have been developed in any case. Hospitals and health care facilities have grown larger and more complex, in both organization and finances. And budgeting is imperative in organizations in which management authority is delegated to many individuals.

ESSENTIAL ELEMENTS

For our purposes, a budget is defined as a quantitative expression of a plan of action. It is an integral part of the overall management control process of an organization.

Anthony and Herzlinger[1] discuss management control in great detail. They define it as "a process by which managers assure that resources are obtained and used effectively and efficiently in the accomplishment of an organization's objectives."

Efficiency and Effectiveness

In the above definition, special emphasis is placed on attaining efficiency and effectiveness. In short, they determine the success or failure of management control.

These two terms have very precise meanings. Often individuals talk about the relative efficiency and effectiveness of their operations as if

This chapter is reprinted from *Essentials of Health Care Finance*, 2nd ed., by W.O. Cleverley, pp. 247–284, Aspen Publishers, Inc., © 1986.

efficiency and effectiveness were identical, or at least highly correlated. They are not identical, nor are they necessarily correlated. An operation may be effective without being efficient, and vice versa. A well-managed operation should ideally be both effective and efficient. Efficiency is easier to measure and its meaning is fairly well understood; efficiency is simply a relationship between outputs and inputs. For example, a cost per patient day of $110 is a measure of efficiency; it tells how many resources, or inputs, were used to provide one day of care, the measure of output.

Managers and other persons wishing to assess management in the health care industry are increasing their use of efficiency measures. In most situations, efficiency is measured by comparison with some standard. Several basic considerations should be understood if efficiency measures are to be used intelligently. First, output measures may not always be comparable. For example, comparing the costs per patient day of care in a 50-bed rural hospital with those in a 1,000-bed teaching hospital is not likely to be meaningful. A day of care in a teaching hospital typically entails more service. Second, cost measures may not be comparable or useful for the specific decision under consideration. For example, two operations may be identical, but one may be in a newer facility and thus would have a higher depreciation charge, or the two operations may account for costs differently: One hospital may use an accelerated depreciation method, such as the sum of the year's digits, while the other may use straight-line depreciation. Third, the cost concepts used may not be relevant to the decision under consideration. For example, a CON review to decide which of two hospitals should be permitted to build a 50-bed expansion will obviously consider cost. However, comparing the full costs of a day of care in each institution and selecting the lower one could produce bad results: for this specific decision, the full cost concept is wrong. Incremental or variable cost is the relevant cost concept in this case. The focus of interest is on what the future additional cost would be, not what the historical average cost was.

Effectiveness is concerned with the relationship between an organization's outputs and its objectives or goals. A health care facility's typical goals might include solvency, high quality of care, low cost of patient care, institutional harmony, and growth. Measuring effectiveness is more difficult than measuring efficiency for at least two reasons. First, defining the relationship between outputs and some goals may be difficult because many facilities' goals or objectives are not likely to be quantified. For example, exactly how does an alcoholism program contribute to quality of care? Still, objectives and goals can usually be stated more precisely in quantitative terms. In fact, they should be quantified to the greatest extent possible. In the alcoholism program example, quality scales, such as frequency of repeat visits or new patients treated, might be developed. Second, the output must usually be related to more than one organizational goal or objective. For example, solvency and reasonable cost are both legitimate objectives for a hospital. Yet continuing an emergency room operation might affect solvency negatively and at the same time positively affect patient treatment costs. How should decision makers weight these two criteria to determine an overall measure of effectiveness?

Control Unit

Most health care facilities have various responsibility centers over which management control is exercised. These centers are generally referred to as departments. Figure 14-1 presents an organizational chart of a hospital and its departments.

Usually the departments perform special functions that contribute to overall organizational goals, directly or indirectly. They receive resources or inputs and produce services or outputs:

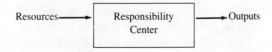

Responsibility centers are the focus of management control efforts. Emphasis is placed on the effectiveness and efficiency of their operations. Measurement problems occur when the responsibility structure is not identical to the

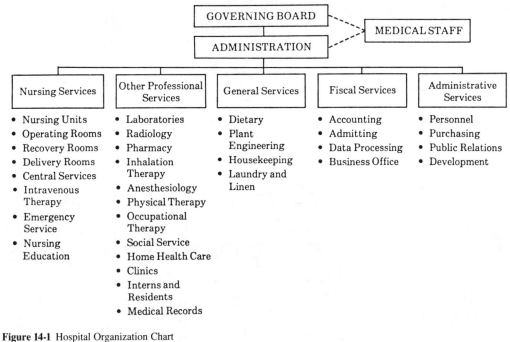

Figure 14-1 Hospital Organization Chart

program structure. Decision makers are frequently interested in a program's total cost. Yet in the case of a burn care program, for example, it is unlikely that all the resources used in the program will be assigned to it directly; the costs of medical support services—such as physical therapy, laboratory and radiology, as well as other general and administrative services—will not likely be contained in the burn care unit. Program lines typically run across responsibility center or departmental lines. This necessitates cost allocations for decisions that require program cost information. It should be remembered that where cost allocations are involved, the accuracy of the information as well as its comparability may be suspect. For example, one may be interested in the specific costs of a burn care program, but then find that those costs must be allocated from various departments or responsibility centers, such as laboratory, radiology, and housekeeping.

Responsibility centers vary greatly, depending upon the controlling organization. For a regulatory agency, the responsibility center might be an entire health care facility; for a health care facility manager, it may be an individual depart-ment; for a department manager, it may be a unit within the department. The only requirement is that a designated person be in charge of the identified responsibility center.

Phases of Management Control

Figure 14-2 illustrates the relationship of various phases of the management control process to each other and to the planning process. Management control relies on the existence of goals and objectives; without them, the structure and evaluation of the management control process is incomplete. Poor or no planning usually limits the value of management control. Effectiveness becomes impossible to assess without stated goals and objectives; in such cases, one can focus only on measuring and attaining efficiency. The organization can assess only whether it has produced outputs efficiently; it cannot evaluate the desirability of those outputs.

For the purposes of this discussion, we shall be concerned with the four phases of management control that Anthony and Herzlinger have identified in their work on management control:

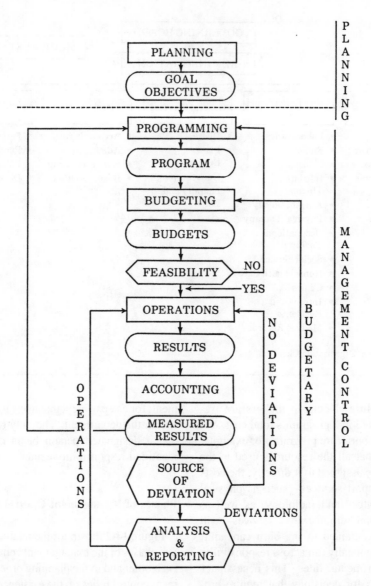

Figure 14-2 The Management Control Process

1. programming
2. budgeting
3. accounting
4. analysis and reporting[2]

Programming

Programming is the phase of management control that determines the nature and size of programs an organization will use to accomplish its stated goals and objectives. It is the first phase of the management control process and interrelates with planning. In some cases, the line

dividing the two activities may in fact be hard to draw. Programming is usually of intermediate length—three to five years. It lasts longer than budgeting, but is shorter than planning.

Programming decisions deal with new and existing programs. The methodology for programming is different in these two areas. Programming decisions for new programs involve capital investment or capital budget decision making (this process is examined more extensively in Chapter 18). The method for making programming decisions for existing programs is often referred to as zero-base review, or zero-base budgeting (this method is discussed later in this chapter).

To illustrate the programming process, assume that a stated objective of a hospital organization is to develop and implement a program of ambulatory care in the community. The decision makers in the programming phase of management control would take this stated objective and evaluate alternative programs to accomplish it, such as a surgi-center, an outpatient clinic, or a mobile health screening unit. After this analysis, a decision might be made to construct a ten-room surgi-center on a lot adjacent to the hospital. This would be a program decision.

Budgeting

Budgeting is the management control phase of primary interest. It was defined earlier as a quantitative expression of a plan of action. Budgets are usually stated in monetary terms and cover a period of one year.

The budgetary phase of management control follows the determination of programs in the programming phase. In many cases, no real review of existing programs is undertaken; the budgeting phase then may be based on a prior year's budget or on the actual results of existing programs. Proponents of zero-base budgeting have identified this practice as a major shortcoming.

The budgeting phase primarily translates program decisions into terms that are meaningful for responsibility centers. The decision to construct a ten-room surgi-center will affect the revenues and costs of other responsibility centers, such as laboratory, radiology, anesthesiology, and business office. The effects of program decisions thus must be carefully and accurately reflected in the budgets of each of the relevant responsibility centers.

Budgeting may also change programs. A more careful and accurate estimation of revenues and costs may prompt one to reevaluate prior programming decisions as financially unfeasible. For example, the proposed ten-room surgi-center may be shown, through budget analysis, to produce a significant operating loss. If the hospital cannot or will not subsidize this loss from other sources, the programming must be changed. The size of the surgi-center may be reduced from ten rooms to five to make the operation break even.

Accounting

Accounting is the third phase of the management control process. Once programs have been decided on and budgets developed for them along responsibility center lines, the operations begin. The accounting department accumulates and records information on both outputs and inputs during the operating phase.

It is important to note that cost information is provided along both program and responsibility center lines. Responsibility center cost information is used in the reporting and analysis phase to determine the degree of compliance with budget projections. Programmatic cost information is used to assess the desirability of continuing a given program at its present size and scope in the programming phase of management control.

Analysis and Reporting

The last phase of management control is analysis and reporting. In this phase, differences between actual costs and budgeted costs are analyzed to determine the probable cause of the deviations and are then reported to the individuals who can take corrective action. The method used in this phase is often referred to as variance analysis, which is discussed in greater detail in Chapter 9. Those doing the analysis and reporting rely heavily on the information provided from the accounting phase to break down the reported deviations into categories that suggest possible causes.

In general, there are three primary causes for differences between budgeted and actual costs:

1. Prices paid for inputs were different from budgeted prices.
2. Output level was higher or lower than budgeted.
3. Actual quantities of inputs used were different from budgeted levels.

Within each of these causal areas, the problem may arise from either budgeting or operations. A budgetary problem is usually not controllable;

no operating action can be taken to correct the situation. For example, the surgi-center may have budgeted for ten registered nurses (RNs) at $1,400 each per month. However, if there were no way to employ ten RNs at an average wage less than $1,500 per month, the budget would have to be adjusted to reflect the change in expectations. Alternatively, the problem may arise from operations and be controllable. Perhaps the nurses of the surgi-center are more experienced and better trained than expected. If this is true, and the mix of RNs originally budgeted is still regarded as appropriate, some action should be taken to change the actual mix over time.

THE BUDGETING PROCESS

Elements and Participants

Budgeting is regarded by many as the primary tool that health care facility managers can use to control costs in their organizations. The objectives of budgetary programs, as defined by the American Hospital Association, are fourfold:

1. to provide a written expression, in quantitative terms, of the policies and plans of the hospital
2. to provide a basis for the evaluation of financial performance in accordance with the plans
3. to provide a useful tool for the control of costs
4. to create cost awareness throughout the organization

The budgetary process encompasses a number of interrelated but separate budgets. Figure 14-3 provides a schematic representation of the budgetary process and the relationships between specific types of budgets.

The individuals and roles involved in the budgetary process may vary. In general, the following individuals or parties may be involved:

- governing board
- chief executive officer (CEO)
- controller

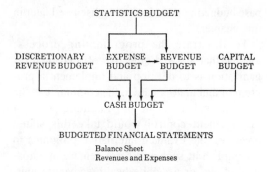

Figure 14-3 Integration of the Budgetary Process

- responsibility center managers
- budgetary committee

The governing board's involvement in the budgetary process is usually indirect. The board provides the goals, objectives, and approved programs that are used as the basis for budgetary development. In many cases, it formally approves the finalized budget, especially the cash budget and budget financial statements; these are critical in assessing financial condition, which is a primary responsibility of the board.

The CEO or administrator of the health care facility has overall responsibility for budgetary development. The budget is the administrator's tool in the overall program of management by exception, which enables the CEO to focus only on those areas where problems exist.

Controllers often serve as budget directors. Their primary function is facilitation: they are responsible for providing relevant data on costs and outputs and for providing budgetary forms that may be used in budget development. They are not responsible for either making or enforcing the budget.

Responsibility centers are the focal points of control. Managers of departments should be actively involved in developing budgets for their assigned areas of responsibility and are responsible for meeting the budgets developed for their areas.

Many large health care facilities use a special budgetary committee to aid in budget development and approval. Typically, this committee is comprised of several department managers, headed by the controller or administrator. A committee structure like this can help legitimize budgetary decisions that might appear arbitrary and capricious if made unilaterally by management.

Statistics Budget

Development of the statistics budget is the first step in budgeting. It provides the basis for subsequent development of the revenue and expense budgets. Together, these three budgets are sometimes referred to as the operating budget.

The objective of the statistics budget is to provide measures of work load or activity in each department or responsibility center for the coming budget period. There are three parts to this task:

1. controllable nature of output
2. responsibility for estimation
3. problems in estimation methodology

Controllable Nature of Output

Sales forecasts in many businesses reflect management's output expectations—how much of the business's product can be sold, given certain promotional efforts. There is some question about the extent to which health care facilities can determine their volume of service, at least within the usual budgetary period. Though, in the long run, through the development or discontinuation of certain programs, volume may be changed, most health care facilities implicitly assume in the development of their statistics budget that they cannot affect their overall volume during the coming budgetary period. Instead they assume that they will provide services to meet their actual demand. This leads to a reliance on past-period service levels to forecast demand. Assuming that demand patterns in the budget period will be similar to prior periods can, however, be a costly mistake. First, foreseeable but uncontrollable forces may dramatically alter service patterns. For example, retirement of key medical staff with no replacement could drastically reduce admissions. Second, the health care facility may in fact control service levels in the short run and do so in a way

that reduces costs. For example, a hospital may decide to use a preadmission testing program that reduces average length of stay in the hospital, thus reducing total volume and total cost.

Responsibility for Estimation

The second issue in the statistics budget is the assignment of responsibility for developing projected output or work-load indicators. Should department managers provide this information themselves, or should top management provide it to them? In some situations, department managers may tend to overstate demand. Overstatement of demand implies a greater need for resources within their own area and creates potential budgetary slack if anticipated volumes are not realized. The result of the information coming from top management may be the converse: understatement of demand may result in a lower total cost budget and eventually lower total actual costs. Negotiation thus often becomes necessary in determining demand for budgetary purposes.

Problems in Estimation Methodology

The last area of statistics budget development concerns problems of estimation. In most health care facilities, activity in departments depends on a limited number of key variables, such as patient days and outpatient visits.

Such indicators, measured for prior periods and applied through statistical analysis, can be used to project future departmental activity. The major problem becomes one of accurately forecasting values for the indicators.

The use of seasonal, weekly, and daily variations in volume poses an important estimation problem. Too often, yearly volume is assumed to be divided equally between the monthly periods throughout the year, even when that is clearly not the case. Recognition of seasonal, weekly, and daily patterns of variation in volume can in fact create significant opportunities for cost reduction, especially in labor staffing.

Finally, output at the departmental level is often multiple in nature. In fact, a department normally produces more than one type of output; for example, a laboratory may provide literally thousands of different tests. In such situations, a weighted unit of service is needed, such as the relative value units (RVUs) used in areas like laboratory and radiology. The need to use weighted unit measures in the statistics budget is especially important when the mix of services is expected to change. Assume that a hospital is rapidly increasing its volume in outpatient clinics. This expansion in volume will increase activity in many other departments, including pharmacy. If, in such a situation, the filling of an outpatient prescription requires significantly less effort than the filling of an inpatient prescription, the use of an unweighted activity measure for prescriptions could provide misleading information for budgetary control purposes. Far more labor than is actually needed might be budgeted.

Expense Budget

With estimates of activity for individual departments developed in the statistics budget, department managers can proceed to develop expense budgets for their areas of responsibility. Expense budgeting is the area of budgeting "where the rubber meets the road." Management cost control efforts are finally reflected in hard numbers that the departments must live with, in most cases for the budget period. Major categories of expense budgets at the departmental level include payroll, supplies, and other. In some situations, a budget for allocated costs from indirect departments may also be included, although this is usually not done by department managers.

In our discussion of expense budgeting, we shall focus on the following four issues of budgeting that are of general interest:

1. length of the budget period
2. flexible or forecast budgets
3. standards for price and quantity
4. allocation of indirect costs

Length of the Budget Period

Generally speaking, there are two alternative budget periods that may be used—*fixed* and *rolling*. Of the two, a fixed budget period is far more frequently used in the health care industry. A

fixed budget covers some defined time from a given budget date, usually one year. This contrasts with a rolling budget, in which the budget is periodically extended on a frequent basis, usually a month or a quarter. For example, in a rolling budget period with a monthly update, the entity would always have a budget of at least 11 months in front of it. The same is not true in a fixed budget, in which, at fiscal year end, there may only be one week or one month left.

A rolling budget has a number of advantages, but it requires more time and effort and therefore more cost. Among its major advantages are

- more realistic forecasts, which should improve management planning and control
- equalization of the work load of budget development over the entire year
- improved familiarity and understanding of budgets by department managers

Flexible or Forecast Budgets

The use of a flexible budget versus a forecast budget has received much discussion among health care financial people. At the present time, very few hospitals and other health care facilities use a formal system of flexible budgeting. However, flexible budgeting is a more sophisticated method of budgeting than typical forecast budgeting and is being adopted by more and more health care facilities as they become experienced in the budgetary process.

A flexible budget is a budget that adjusts targeted levels of costs for changes in volume. For example, the budget for a nursing unit operating at 95 percent occupancy would be different than the budget for that same unit operating at an 80 percent occupancy. A forecast budget, in contrast, would make no formal differentiation in the allowed budget between these two levels.

The difference between a forecast and a flexible budget is illustrated by the historical data and projected use levels for the laboratory presented in Table 14-1. The forecast levels of volume in RVUs for 1987 are identical to the actual volumes of 1986, except that a 10 percent growth factor is assumed. The departmental manager using this statistics budget must develop a budget for hours worked in 1987. A common

Table 14-1 Laboratory Productivity Data

| | 1986 Actual | | 1987 |
	Hours Worked	RVUs	Expected RVUs
January	2,825	5,700	6,270
February	2,700	5,200	5,720
March	2,900	6,000	6,600
April	2,875	5,900	6,490
May	2,825	5,700	6,270
June	2,700	5,200	5,720
July	2,750	5,400	5,940
August	2,625	4,900	5,390
September	2,725	5,300	5,830
October	2,750	5,400	5,940
November	2,750	5,400	5,940
December	2,775	5,500	6,050
Total	33,200	65,600	72,160

Note: 1986 average hours/RVU = $\dfrac{33,200}{65,600}$ = .5061

Table 14-2 Alternative Hours-Worked Budget for Laboratory

	Forecast Budget[a]	Flexible Budget[b]
January	3,043	2,967
February	3,043	2,830
March	3,043	3,050
April	3,043	3,022
May	3,043	2,967
June	3,043	2,830
July	3,043	2,885
August	3,043	2,747
September	3,043	2,857
October	3,043	2,885
November	3,043	2,885
December	3,043	2,912
Total	36,516	34,837

[a]$(.5061 \times 72,160)/12 = 3,043.35$
[b]January value = $(1,400) + (.25 \times 6,270)$

approach to this task is to assume that past work experience indicates future requirements. In this case, the average hours work required per RVU in 1986 was .5061. A common method for developing a forecast budget is to multiply this value of .5061 by the estimated total work load for the budget period, which is expected to be 72,160, and spread the total product equally over each of the 12 months. This is the forecast budget depicted in Table 14-2.

A major difference between a flexible and a forecast budget is that a flexible budget must recognize and incorporate underlying cost behavioral patterns. In this laboratory example, hours worked might be written as a function of RVUs:

$$\text{Hours worked} = (1,400 \text{ hours per month}) + (.25 \times \text{relative value units})$$

Applying this formula to the budgeted RVUs expected in 1987 yields the flexible budget presented in Table 14-2.

Two points should be made before concluding our discussion of flexible versus forecast budgeting. First, a flexible budget may be represented as a forecast budget for planning purposes. For example, in the laboratory problem of Table 14-2, the flexible budget would provide an estimated hours-worked requirement of 34,837 hours for 1987. However, in an actual control period evaluation, the flexible budget formula would be used. To illustrate, assume that the actual RVUs provided in January 1987 were 6,500 instead of the forecasted 6,270. Budgeted hours in the flexible budget would then not be 2,967, but 3,025:

$$1,400 + (.25 \times 6,500) = 3,025$$

This value would be compared with the actual hours worked, not the initially forecasted 2,967.

Second, dramatic differences in approved costs can result from the two methods. Recognizing the underlying cost behavioral patterns can change the estimated resource requirements approved in the budgetary process. In our laboratory example in Table 14-2, the forecast budget calls for 36,516 hours versus the flexible budget hours requirement of 34,837. The difference results from the method used to estimate hours worked. In a forecast budget method, the prior average hours per RVU relationship is used. In most situations, average hours or average cost should be greater than variable hours or variable cost. In departments with expanding volume, the estimated requirements for resources could be overstated. The converse may be true in departments with declining volume. In many cases, use of forecast budgeting methods is based on the incorporation of prior average cost relationships. Flexible budgeting methods do not make this error, since their use depends on explicit incorporation of cost behavioral patterns that distinctly recognize variable and fixed costs.

Standards for Price and Quantity

Earlier, three factors were identified that can create differences between budgeted and actual costs: volume, prices, and usage or efficiency. The use of flexible budgeting is an attempt to improve the recognition of deviations caused by changes in volume. The use of standards for prices and wage rates, coupled with standards for physical quantities of usage, is an attempt to improve the recognition of deviations from budget that result from prices and usage.

For example, assume that the flexible budget-hours requirement for the laboratory example is still hours worked = 1,400 + (.25 × RVUs). Assume further that the budget wage rate is $9 per hour and the actual RVUs for January 1987 were 6,500. Total payroll cost for hours worked (excluding vacations and sick pay) are assumed to be $31,000. If the actual hours worked were 3,100, the variance analysis report presented in Exhibit 14-1 would be applicable to the laboratory department.

The total unfavorable variance of $3,775 results from a $3,100 unfavorable price variance and a $675 unfavorable efficiency variance. Splitting the variance in this manner helps management quickly identify possible causes. For example, the $3,100 price variance may be due to a negotiated wage increase of $1 per hour. If this is the case, the department manager is clearly not responsible for the variance. If, however, the difference is due to an excessive use of overtime personnel or a more costly mix of labor, then the manager may be held responsible for the difference and should attempt to prevent the problem from occurring again. The unfavorable efficiency variance of $675 reflects excessive use of the labor input during the month in the amount of 75 hours. An explanation for this difference should be sought and steps taken to prevent its recurrence.

Standard costing techniques have been used in industry for many years as an integral part of management control. Although it is true that input and output relationships may not be as objective in the health care industry as they are in general industry, this does not imply that standard costing cannot be used. In fact, there are many areas of activity within a health care facility that have fairly precise input–output relationships—housekeeping, laundry and linen, laboratory, radiology, and many others. Standard costing can prove to be a very valuable tool for cost control in the health care industry, if properly applied (this topic is explored in greater detail in Chapter 9).

Allocation of Indirect Costs

There has probably been more internal strife in organizations over the allocation of indirect

---

Exhibit 14-1 Standard Cost Variance Analysis for Labor Costs, Laboratory, January 1987

1. Price variance = (Actual hours worked) × (Actual wage rate)
   − (Actual hours worked) × (Budgeted wage rate)
   = (3,100 × $10.00) − (3,100 × $9.00)
   = $3,100 [Unfavorable]

2. Efficiency variance = (Actual hours worked) × (Budgeted wage rate)
   − (Budgeted hours worked) × (Budgeted wage rate)
   = (3,100 × $9.00) − (3,025 × $9.00)
   = $675 [Unfavorable]

3. Total variance = $3,100 + $675 = $3,775 [Unfavorable]

Note: Actual wage rate = $31,000/3,100 = $10.00
   Budgeted wage rate = $9.00
   Actual hours worked = 3,100
   Budgeted hours worked = (1,400) + (.25 × 6,500) = 3,025

costs than over any other single budgetary issue. A comment often heard is, "Why was I charged $3,000 for housekeeping services last month when my department didn't use anywhere near that level of service?"

A strong case can in fact be made for not allocating indirect costs in budget variance reports. In most normal situations, the receiving department has little or no control over the costs of the servicing department. Allocation may thus raise questions that should not be raised. While it is true that indirect costs need to be allocated for some decision-making purposes, such as pricing, they are generally not needed for evaluating individual responsibility center management.

However, an equally strong argument can be made for including indirect costs in the budgets of benefiting departments. They are legitimate costs of the total operation, and department managers should be aware of them. If department managers can influence costs in indirect areas by their decisions, they should be held accountable for them. For example, maintenance, housekeeping, and other indirect costs can be influenced by the decisions of benefiting departments. Ideally, a charge for these indirect services should be established and levied against using departments, based on their use. Labeling the cost of indirect areas as totally uncontrollable can stimulate excessive and unnecessary use of indirect services and thus have a negative impact on the total cost control program in an organization.

Revenue Budget

The revenue budget can be set effectively only after the expense budget and the statistics budget have been developed. The not-for-profit nature of the health care industry demands that revenue be related to budgeted expenses. Moreover, some of the total revenue actually realized by a health care facility is directly determined by expenses because of the presence of cost reimbursement formulas.

Rate Setting

In this discussion of the revenue budget, we shall focus on only one aspect of revenue budget development—pricing or rate setting. Specifically, we shall illustrate through an additional example the rate-setting model discussed in Chapter 6.

Figure 14-4 illustrates the rate-setting model. Sources of information to define the variables of the model are identified. However, three parameters have no identified source:

1. desired profit
2. proportion of charge payer patients
3. proportion of charge payer patient revenue not collected

In many situations, departmental indicators for these three values are not available. Instead, institution-wide values or averages are substituted. In many cases, this may not be a bad approximation, but some serious inequities can result in departments where the relative proportions of inpatient and outpatient use differ greatly. Typically, departments with high outpatient use experience higher levels of charge reimbursement and higher levels of write-offs on that charge reimbursement, due to the reduced presence of insurance coverage for outpatient types of services. Furthermore, the charge payer patient reimbursement in inpatient areas may be commercial insurance, subject to smaller write-offs. The data illustrate this.

	Department 1	Department 2	Total
Desired profit	$ 500	$ 500	$ 1,000
Budgeted expense	$10,000	$10,000	$20,000
Estimated volume	100	100	—
Percentage bad debt	4%	20%	12%
Percentage charge payer patients	20%	60%	40%
Percentage bad debt on charge patients	20%	33%	30%

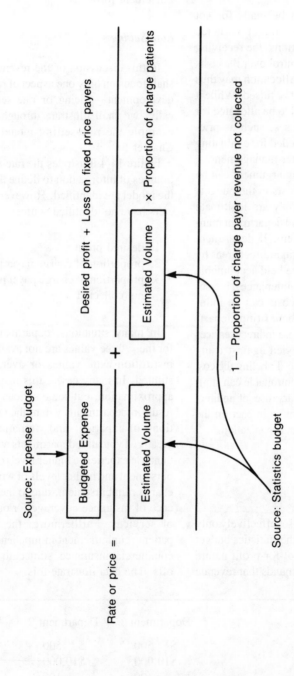

Note: The two source items indicate where values for budgeted expense and estimated volume may be found.

Figure 14-4 Rate Setting in the Revenue Budget

In most situations, separate figures for the percentage of write-offs on charge payer patients and the percentage of charge payers are not available on a departmental basis. Sometimes the best information available may be the percentage of bad debt write-offs on total revenue for the institution as a whole. In the example on page 235, a 4 percent write-off on 20 percent of the patients who pay charges in Department 1 implies that 20 percent of the charge patient revenue in that department is written off. The corresponding figure for Department 2 is 33 percent. Using these data, and substituting the total or aggregate values for the percentage write-offs on charge patients and the percentage of charge patients, the following rates would be established:

$$\text{Department 1 price} = \frac{\frac{\$10,000}{100} + \frac{\$500}{100 \times .4}}{1 - .30}$$
$$= \$160.71$$

$$\text{Department 2 price} = \frac{\frac{\$10,000}{100} + \frac{\$500}{100 \times .4}}{1 - .30}$$
$$= \$160.71$$

However, proper reflection of the departmental values would show the following rates:

$$\text{Department 1 price} = \frac{\frac{\$10,000}{100} + \frac{\$500}{100 \times .2}}{1 - .2}$$
$$= \$156.25$$

$$\text{Department 2 price} = \frac{\frac{\$10,000}{100} + \frac{\$500}{100 \times .6}}{1 - .33}$$
$$= \$161.69$$

In the former case, the use of aggregate or average values produces an inequitable pricing structure. The price for Department 1 was initially overstated, while the price for Department 2 was initially understated. If equity in rate setting is an objective, reliance on average values can prevent the development of an equitable rate structure along departmental lines. In many cases, the errors may be significant.

Desired Profit Levels

Determining a desired level of profit is not easy. In many cases, it is a subjective process, made to appear objective through the application of a quantitative profit requirement. For example, desired profit may be arbitrarily set at some percentage of budgeted expenses, such as two percent above expenses, or as a certain percentage of total investment. However, desired levels of profit can, in general, be stated as the difference between financial requirements and expenses:

Desired profit = Budgeted financial requirements − Budgeted expenses

Budgeted financial requirements are cash requirements that an equity must meet during the budget period. There are four elements that usually constitute total budgeted financial requirements:

1. budgeted expenses, excluding depreciation
2. requirements for debt principal payment
3. requirements for increases in working capital
4. requirements for capital expenditures

Budgeted expenses at the departmental level should include both direct and indirect (or allocated) expenses. Depreciation charges are excluded because depreciation is a noncash requirement expense.

Debt principal payments include only the principal portion of debt service due. In some cases, additional reserve requirements may be established, which may require additional funding. Interest expense is already included in budgeted expenses and should not be included in debt principal payments.

Working capital requirements were discussed earlier. The maintenance of necessary levels of inventory, accounts receivable, and precautionary cash balances requires an investment. Changes in the total level of this investment must be funded from cash, additional indebtedness, or a combination of the two. Planned financing of increases in working capital is a legitimate financial requirement.

Capital expenditure requirements may be of two types. First, actual capital expenditures may be made for approved projects. Those projects not financed with indebtedness require a cash investment. Second, prudent fiscal management requires that funds be set aside and invested to meet reasonable requirements for future capital expenditures. This amount should be related to the replacement cost depreciation of existing fixed assets.

Any loss incurred on fixed price payers, such as Medicare, must be added to the desired profit target. The amount of the loss would represent the projected difference between allocated costs or expenses and net revenue received from fixed price payers. If revenues exceed costs, the difference would be subtracted from the profit target. For example, if a firm received $5 million in revenue from Medicare and incurred $4.8 million in costs to provide care to Medicare patients, the difference of $200,000 would be subtracted from the desired profit target. The result would obviously be lower required rates or prices. (Chapter 6 provides more detail on price setting.)

How is the desired profit requirement allocated to individual departments? Usually it is just assigned on the basis of some percentage of budgeted expenses. If a hospital budgets $5 million in expenses and determines that $500,000 profit is required, each department might set its rates to recover 10 percent above its expenses. However, the importance of cost reimbursement and bad debts at the departmental level should also be considered.

Discretionary Revenue Budget and Capital Budget

Discretionary revenue may be important, especially for institutions with large endowments. A good management control system will have a budget for expected return on endowments. Variations from the expected level would then be investigated. In some cases, changes in investment management may be necessary.

Capital budgeting can give many health care managers a major control tool. It can significantly affect the level of cost. This is especially true when not only the initial capital costs associated with given capital expenditures but also the associated operating costs for salaries and supplies are considered. (The capital budgeting process is examined in detail in Chapter 9.)

The Cash Budget and Budgeted Financial Statements

The cash budget is management's best indicator of the organization's expected short-run solvency. It translates all of the above budgets into a statement of cash inflows and outflows. The cash budget is usually broken down by periods, such as months or quarters, within the total budget period. An example of a cash budget is shown in Table 14-3.

Departmental expense budgets, departmental revenue budgets, a discretionary revenue budget and a capital budget that do not provide a sufficient cash flow can necessitate major revisions. If the organization cannot or will not finance the deficits, changes must be made in the budgets to maintain the solvency of the organization. A poor cash budget could cause an increase in rates, a reduction in expenses, a reduction in capital expenditures, or many other changes. These changes and revisions must be made until the cash budget reflects a position of short-run solvency.

The two major financial statements that are developed on a budgetary basis are the balance sheet and the statement of revenue and expense. These two statements are indicators of both short- and long-run solvency; however, they are more important in assessing long-run solvency. Unfavorable projections in either statement might cause changes in any of the other budgets.

In short, the budgeted financial statements and the cash budget test the adequacy of the entire budgetary process. Budgets that result in an unfavorable financial position, as reflected by the budgeted financial statements and the cash budget, must be adjusted. Solvency is a goal that most organizations cannot sacrifice.

ZERO-BASE BUDGETING

Zero-base budgeting is a term that has recently gained publicity. It has been touted as management's most effective cost-containment tool. It has also been described as the biggest hoax of the century. The truth lies somewhere in the middle.

Zero-base budgeting or zero-base review, as some like to call it, is a way of looking at existing

Table 14-3 Cash Budget, Budget Year 1987

	1st Quarter			2nd Quarter	3rd Quarter	4th Quarter
	January	February	March			
Receipts from operations	$300,000	$310,000	$ 320,000	$1,000,000	$1,100,000	$1,100,000
Disbursements from operations	280,000	280,000	300,000	940,000	1,000,000	1,000,000
Cash available from operations	$ 20,000	$ 30,000	$ 20,000	$ 60,000	$ 100,000	$ 100,000
Other receipts						
Increase in mortgage payable				500,000		
Sale of fixed assets		20,000				
Unrestricted income—endowment	-0-		40,000	40,000	40,000	40,000
Total other receipts		$ 20,000	$ 40,000	$ 540,000	$ 40,000	$ 40,000
Other disbursements						
Mortgage payments			150,000		150,000	
Fixed asset purchase				480,000		
Funded depreciation			30,000	130,000	30,000	30,000
Total other disbursements	-0-	-0-	180,000	610,000	180,000	30,000
Net cash gain (loss)	$ 20,000	$ 50,000	$(120,000)	(10,000)	(40,000)	110,000
Beginning cash balance	100,000	120,000	170,000	50,000	40,000	-0-
Cumulative cash	$120,000	$170,000	$50,000	$40,000	$ -0-	$ 110,000
Desired level of cash	100,000	100,000	100,000	100,000	100,000	100,000
Cash above minimum needs (financing needs)	$ 20,000	$ 70,000	$ (50,000)	$ (60,000)	(100,000)	$ 10,000

programs. It is part of programming, but it focuses on existing programs instead of new programs. Zero-base budgeting assumes that no existing program is entitled to automatic approval. Many individuals have identified automatic approval with existing budgetary systems that are based on prior year expenditure levels.

Zero-base budgeting looks at the entire budget and determines the efficacy of the entire expenditure. It thus requires a tremendous effort and investment of time. It cannot be done well on an annual basis. This is why many refer to it as zero-base review instead of zero-base budgeting. Some individuals have suggested that a zero-base review of a given activity would be appropriate every five years.

Zero-base budgeting is a process of periodically reevaluating all programs and their associated levels of expenditures. Management decides the frequency of this reevaluation and may vary it from every year to every five years.

Although most decision makers agree with the concept of zero-base budgeting, in practice it poses two significant questions:

1. What arithmetic should be used in zero-base budgeting?
2. Who should be involved in the actual decision-making process?

In each case, the answers are important to the success or failure of the zero-base budget program. Yet there is still not complete agreement among experts regarding the answers.

In this section, we present what we believe to be the basis of the zero-base budgeting concept in terms of the above two questions. We shall illustrate our discussion with a case example of an actual application of the concept in the data-processing department of a hospital. In this example, significant savings were realized through the application of zero-base budgeting.

Arithmetic of the Zero-Base Budgeting Process

Nearly everyone would agree that cost benefit analysis should be the arithmetic of zero-base budgeting. There are two important issues

involved in the application of cost benefit analysis to zero-base budgeting programs: (1) Are the services that are presently provided being delivered in an efficient manner? (2) Are these services being delivered in an effective manner in terms of the organization's goals and objectives? A procedure for quantitatively answering these two questions involves seven sequential steps:

1. Define the outputs or services provided by the program/departmental area.
2. Determine the costs of these services or outputs.
3. Identify options for reducing the cost through changes in outputs or services.
4. Identify options for producing the services and outputs more efficiently.
5. Determine the cost savings associated with options identified in Steps 3 and 4.
6. Assess the risks, both qualitative and quantitative, associated with the identified options of Steps 3 and 4.
7. Select and implement those options with an acceptable cost/risk relationship.

Definition of Outputs

Table 14-4 lists outputs provided by the data processing department in our case example. Six basic functions or service areas are identified:

1. outpatient systems
2. inpatient systems
3. step-down
4. month-end
5. accounts payable
6. payroll

Determining the specific outputs of each of these areas, as shown in Table 14-4, is, in general, a useful procedure. Determining the basic factors involved in the establishment and maintenance of each department and program is a good first step in defining specific outputs.

Determination of Costs

The concept of cost that is most relevant in zero-base budgeting is avoidable cost. An attempt is made to discover what the costs of a department's services are now and what cost

Table 14-4 Data Processing Outputs and Costs

	Pages	Runs Per Year	Copies	Total Pages	Weighted Pages	$.0113/pg. Direct Supply Cost	$.2894/wtd. pg. cost Labor & Mach.	Total Cost	Cost Reductions
I. OUTPATIENT SYSTEM									
A. Outpatient Maintenance Report	2	365	4	2,920	1,460	$33.00	$422.49	$455.49	($8.25)
B. Outpatient Error Listing for Admissions	2	365	4	2,920	1,460	33.00	422.49	455.49	(8.25)
C. Outpatient Initial Edit Summary	1	365	4	1,460	730	16.50	211.24	227.74	(4.13)
1. Admissions Summary Total	1	365	4	1,460	730	16.50	211.24	227.74	(4.13)
2. Initial Cash Edit	1								
3. Additional Patients Added to Outpatient History		365	4	1,460	730	16.50	211.24	227.74	(4.13)
D. Daily Transaction Audit Report—Charges	11	365	4	16,060	8,030	181.48	2,323.69	2505.17	(45.37)
E. Outpatient Posting Control	40	365	4	58,400	29,200	659.92	8,449.78	9,189.70	(164.95)
F. Daily Revenue Report	42	365	4	61,320	30,660	692.92	8,872.27	9,565.19	(9,565.19)
G. Outpatient Billing Balance	4	365	4	5,840	2,920	65.99	844.98	910.27	(16.50)
H. Patients Transferred to AR/History File	5	365	4	7,300	3,650	82.49	1,056.22	1,138.71	(20.62)
I. Cash Receipts and Adjustments Report	3	365	4	4,380	2,190	49.49	633.73	683.22	
J. AR Transaction Audit	5	365	4	7,300	3,650	82.49	1,056.22	1,138.71	(12.37)
K. AR Error Listing	1	365	4	1,460	730	16.50	211.24	227.74	(20.62)
L. Self-Pay Patient Statement*	100	365	1	36,500	36,500	3,650.00	10,562.22	14,212.22	(4.13)
M. Revenue and Usage Statistics	42	365	2	30,660	30,660	346.46	8,872.27	9,218.73	
N. General Journal	3	12	2	72	72	.81	20.84	21.65	
O. Outpatient Edit Report	5	12	2	120	120	1.36	34.73	36.09	
P. Outpatient Activity Trial Balance	2,500	12	2	60,000	60,000	678.00	17,362.56	18,040.56	
Q. Outpatient Alpha Listing (Telephone)	800	52	4	166,400	83,200	1,880.32	24,076.08	25,906.00	(25,956.40)
R. Outpatient Alpha Listing (Balance)	800	52	4	166,400	83,200	1,880.32	24,076.08	25,956.40	(25,956.40)
II. INPATIENT SYSTEM									
A. Final Census Report	27	365	4	39,420	19,710	$445.45	$5,703.60	$6,149.05	($222.75)
B. Volunteer Alpha Listing	6	365	3	6,570	4,380	74.24	1,267.47	1,341.71	
C. Alphabetic Census	6	365	6	13,140	4,380	148.48	1,267.47	1,415.95	
D. Financial Class Census Report	10	365	2	7,300	7,300	82.49	2,112.44	2,194.93	(2,194.93)
E. Utilization Census	6	365	4	8,760	4,380	98.99	1,267.47	1,366.46	
F. Social Services Census	10	365	1	3,650	7,300	41.25	2,112.44	2,153.69	(50.00)
G. Statistical Census Reports	2	365	3	2,190	1,460	24.75	422.49	447.24	(447.24)
H. Clergy Listing	15	365	1	5,475	10,950	61.87	3,168.69	3,230.54	
I. Admission, Discharge and Transfer Report	4	365	8	11,680	2,920	131.98	844.98	976.96	

continues

Table 14-4 continued

	Pages	Runs Per Year	Copies	Total Pages	Weighted Pages	$.0113/pg. Direct Supply Cost	$.2894/wtd. pg. cost Labor & Mach.	Total Cost	Cost Reductions
J. Pap Smear Admissions Control Report	1	365	2	730	730	8.25	211.24	219.49	
K. Census by H-ICDA Code	7	365	2	5,110	5,110	57.74	1,478.71	1,536.45	
L. Daily Charge Transaction Error Listing	5	365	1	1,825	3,650	20.62	1,056.22	1,076.84	
M. Daily Transaction	44	365	1	16,060	32,120	181.48	9,294.76	9,476.24	
N. Daily Dialysis Report	1	365	2	730	730	8.25	211.24	219.49	
O. Inpatient Billing Balance	8	365	2	5,840	5,840	65.99	1,689.96	1,755.95	
P. Outpatient Billing Balance—Dialysis	2	365	2	1,460	1,460	16.50	422.49	438.99	
Q. Summary Patient Statement*	50	365	2	36,500	36,500	1,825.00	10,562.22	12,387.22	
R. Detail Patient Statement*	50	365	2	36,500	36,500	1,825.00	10,562.22	12,387.22	
S. Noncovered Charges	10	365	1	3,650	7,300	41.25	2,112.44	2,153.69	
T. New Accounts Receivable Report	3	365	2	2,190	2,190	24.75	633.73	658.48	
U. Cash Receipts and Adjustments	10	365	3	10,950	7,300	123.74	2,112.44	2,236.18	
V. AR Transaction Audit	10	365	2	7,300	7,300	82.49	2,112.44	2,194.93	
W. Daily Error Listing	3	365	2	2,190	2,190	24.75	633.73	658.48	
X. Schedule of Preadmission	3	365	2	2,190	2,190	24.75	633.73	658.48	
Y. Medicaid Review Census	2	365	2	1,460	1,460	16.50	422.49	438.99	
III. STEP-DOWN									
A. Step-Down Cost Center Description Table	2	12	2	48	48	$ .54	$ 13.89	$ 14.93	
B. Step-Down Allocations Master File	2	12	2	48	48	.54	13.89	14.43	
C. Step-Down Direct Expense Edit	2	12	2	48	48				
D. Step-Down Cost Allocation Statistics File	2	12	2	48	48	.54	13.89	14.93	
E. Step-Down Cost Allocation—Periodic	2	12	2	48	48	.54	13.89	14.93	
IV. MONTH-END									
A. Cumulative Monthly Statistical Census	1	12	2	24	24	.27	6.95	7.22	
B. Monthly Statistical Census by Day	1	12	2	24	24	.27	6.95	7.22	
C. Infection Control Report	1	12	2	24	24	.27	6.95	7.22	
D. Reimbursement Summary	1	12	2	24	24	.27	6.95	7.22	
E. Revenue and Usage Statistics	65	12	2	1,560	1,560	17.63	451.43	469.06	
F. Aged Accounts Receivable Summary	1	12	2	24	24	.27	6.95	7.22	
G. Detail Trial Balance	105	12	2	2,520	2,520	28.48	729.22	757.70	
H. In-House 21 Days Billing	25	12	2	600	600	6.78	173.63	180.41	
I. Dialysis Billing	89	12	2	2,136	2,136	24.14	618.11	642.25	
J. Zero Balance Roster	742	12	4	35,616	17,808	402.46	5,153.21	5,555.67	($5555.67)

K. Bad Debt Report	35	12	2	840	840	9.49	243.08	252.57
L. General Journal	5	12	2	120	120	1.36	34.73	36.09
V. ACCOUNTS PAYABLE SYSTEM								
A. Vendor Master Maintenance Report	2	156	2	624	624	7.05	180.57	187.62
B. AP Initial Edit Listing	1	156	2	312	312	3.53	90.29	93.82
C. AP Batch Proof	1	156	2	312	312	3.53	90.29	93.82
D. Cash Requirements Report	50	12	2	1,200	1,200	13.56	347.25	360.81
E. AP Monthly Reconciliation	30	12	2	720	720	8.14	208.35	216.49
F. AP Distribution	23	12	2	552	552	6.24	159.74	165.98
G. AP Trial Balance	50	12	2	1,200	1,200	13.56	347.25	360.81
H. Vendor Master Listing	2	12	2	48	48	.54	13.89	14.43
VI. PAYROLL								
A. Payroll Edit Summary								
1. Payroll Update Controls	1	104	2	208	208	$ 2.35	$ 60.19	$ 62.54
2. Payroll Master File Maintenance	10	104	2	2,080	2,080	23.50	601.90	625.40
B. Time Card Edit Report	60	52	4	12,480	6,240	141.02	1,805.71	1,946.73
C. Check Register	58	52	2	6,032	6,032	68.16	1,745.52	1,813.68
D. Department Benefits Statement	60	52	4	12,480	6,240	141.02	1,805.71	1,946.73
E. Labor Analysis Report	42	52	2	4,368	4,368	49.36	1,263.99	1,313.35
F. Payroll Journal Report	10	12	1	120	240	1.36	69.45	70.81
G. Quarterly 941 Report	27	4	2	216	216	2.44	62.51	64.95
H. W-2 Forms	1,091	1	1	1,091	2,182	12.33	631.42	643.75
I. Time Cards*	1,091	52	1	56,732	56,732	4,252.50	16,416.88	20,669.38 ($10,334.69)
J. Standard Payroll Checks*	1,091	52	1	56,732	56,732	3,373.65	16,416.88	19,710.53 (9,855.26)
K. Miscellaneous Reports								
1. Employee Longevity Report	10	12	2	240	240	2.70	69.45	72.15
2. YTD Earnings Report	1,091	4	2	8,728	8,728	98.68	2,525.67	2,524.29
3. Union Dues Paid	8	12	2	192	192	2.17	55.56	57.73
4. Estimated Yearly Budget Report by Status and by Grade	60	1	1	60	120	68	34.73	35.41
5. Sick Hour Control Report (not done)								
6. Prepaid Checks	20	104	1	2,080	2,080	138.76	601.90	740.66
7. LPN Listing	2	2	2	8	8	.09	2.31	2.40
8. Employee Address Labels (30/page)	30	2	1	60	60	.68	17.17	17.85
9. Century Club Membership Labels* (not done)								
				1,077,885	778,900	$24,702.00	$225,367.00	$250,069.00 ($90,138.00)

*Items for which supplies were directly costed.
Total pages for these items were 225,044 and total direct supply cost was $15,065.

would be incurred if those services were discontinued. In this context, the direct cost of the department is most useful. Indirect cost in most situations should be ignored because it is unavoidable. In our data processing case example, the three direct cost components are supply cost, labor and machine cost, and other. Of these three, only labor and machine cost and supply cost can be avoided, given a reduction in services.

The average supply cost per page was derived by dividing total supply cost, less supply cost that could be traced to a specific report, by the total number of pages, less pages associated with reports for which supply cost could be directly traced:

$$\text{Supply cost/Page} = \frac{\$24,702 - \$15,065}{1,077,885 - 225,044} = \$.0113$$

The six reports for which supply cost was directly traceable are

	System
1. self-pay patient statement	I-L
2. summary patient statement	II-Q
3. detail patient statement	II-R
4. time cards	VI-I
5. standard payroll checks	VI-J
6. prepaid checks	VI-K(6)

Labor and machine cost is divided by weighted pages to determine cost per weighted page. Weighted pages is an index that reflects the fact that little or no additional labor and machine cost is incurred for multiple copies of reports. The index uses a base report of two copies to provide the conversion. Thus, a four-copy report consisting of 3 pages would require 12 total pages, but it would be stated as a 6-page report when expressed in weighted pages. In certain situations, the index is modified to reflect a more realistic assessment of cost variation. In our data processing department, the labor and machine cost per weighted page was

$$\text{Labor and machine cost/Weighted page}$$
$$= \frac{\$225,367}{778,900} = \$.2894$$

Options for Modifying Output

Table 14-5 identifies 11 options for modifying the output of the data processing department. Typical output changes could occur through elimination of the service, reduction in the frequency of the service, reduction in the quality of service, or reduction in the amount of service. All of these types of changes, except reduction in quality, occurred in the data processing case example.

Options for Producing Services More Efficiently

Only after some determination of the need for services is made can efficiency be seriously examined. In our case example, there are no efficiency options identified. Yet the identifica-

Table 14-5 Options for Reducing Output in a Data Processing Department

Option	Risk	Savings
1. Reduce outpatient report copies I-A-K from four copies to three copies per day.	small	$ 314.48
2. Change usage demand on outpatient report I-F from daily to monthly.	small	9,251.02
3. Eliminate two copies of inpatient report II-A—Final census.	small	222.75
4. Discontinue inpatient report II-D—Financial class census.	small	2,194.93
5. Eliminate two copies of inpatient report II-E—Utilization census.	small	50.00
6. Eliminate outpatient report I-Q—Alpha listing with telephone number.	small	25,956.40
7. Eliminate outpatient report I-R—Alpha listing with balance.	small	25,956.40
8. Eliminate inpatient report II-G—Statistical census.	small	447.24
9. Eliminate zero balance roster report—Month end, Report II-J.	small	5,555.67
10. Pay biweekly rather than weekly; cut preparation and usage of time cards by 50%.	medium	10,334,69
11. Pay biweekly rather than weekly; reduce paychecks presentation and usage by 50%.	medium	9,855.26
Total estimated savings		$90,138.84

tion of improved ways to provide services is an important activity in efforts to minimize costs. In a complete zero-base review, efficiency should be considered.

Determination of Cost Savings

Table 14-5 also identifies the cost savings associated with the options for modifying the output of the data processing department. Avoidable cost is the cost concept that is used. The savings are limited to just supply costs when a report is not discontinued but only the number of copies is changed. When a report is discontinued or its frequency is reduced, then labor and machine costs are also reflected in the savings to be realized. Some may question whether significant labor and machine savings could be realized in changes this small. Since many costs of this type are step or semifixed, the actual incremental cost associated with a very slight reduction in volume may indeed be negligible. Still, in reviews of this type, where significant changes in work effort are envisioned, the average cost estimate may be a reasonable expectation of savings. In this example, total cost savings from the identified 11 options is projected to be approximately $90,000.

Risk Assessment

Risk is a function of two factors: the probability of an adverse consequence and the potential severity of that consequence. In most situations, both these factors are highly subjective. Nevertheless, some idea of risk, even subjectively determined, is necessary in the overall assessment of the option's desirability.

Management Decision Making

After concluding the above analysis, someone needs to make decisions concerning the specific options to be selected. This responsibility falls to those in the management structure who are involved in the zero-base review.

In general, with regard to management's participation in the decision-making process of a zero-base budgeting program, three major aspects must be considered:

1. In the case of general service or indirect departments, panels of managers from the using departments should be involved in identifying options for changes in outputs. These individuals have an obvious interest in and a need to know the changes that are likely to be made. In addition, their assessment of risk is important.
2. Individuals from the specific program area under evaluation should also be involved in the zero-base review. Their involvement is essential for two reasons: (1) In many cases, the best ideas for changes in output or methods of production will come from those who are intimately involved in the delivery of the product. (2) Participation of these individuals in the review process will help ensure cooperation in any decisions that are made.
3. Final decisions on options should be made by top management because it has a total perspective of the organization. Placing responsibility in lower level management may create problems of suboptimization.

SUMMARY

This chapter has focused specifically on budgeting and management control as practiced at the institutional or organizational level. The basic unit in management control is usually a department. However, the application of the principles of management control can be much broader. The control unit may be an entire hospital or region, and the controller may be a health system agency or a rate-setting organization. Even on this broad scale, the general principles of management control and budgeting discussed in this chapter are applicable.

NOTES

1. Robert Anthony and Herzlinger, *Management Control in Nonprofit Organizations* (Homewood, Ill.: Richard D. Irwin, 1976), pp. 16–23.

2. Ibid.

Chapter 15

Flexible Budgeting

J. Keith Deisenroth
Partner, Ernst & Whinney

David A. Hampshire
Senior Manager, Ernst & Whinney

Robert D. Roberts
President, Robert D. Roberts, Inc.

Health care is dynamic. External forces, in the form of regulatory agencies, technology, demographics, pricing, and competition, are effecting change, as are product mix, personnel turnover, medical staff changes, new sources of supplies, and other internal forces. Hospital management, in dealing with this changing industry, must utilize a variety of tools. One of the more important tools is the annual hospital budget, the topic of this chapter.

The first section of this chapter defines budgeting and the hospital environmental requirements for sound budgeting practice. Subsequently, the budgeting process is discussed with emphasis on the process required for flexible budgeting from a traditional and product-line perspective.

BUDGETING DEFINED

The hospital budget is the measurement tool to monitor the achievement of the planned objectives. Budgeting provides a means for positioning, organizing, communicating, and controlling the hospital's operational progress toward the plan, stated in dollar terms based upon anticipated outputs. The budget provides a mechanism for the evaluation of financial performance and controlling operations in accordance with the objectives, policies, and plans.

Formulating the hospital's annual operating budget actually involves the preparation of three basic budgets, which are operating, cash, and capital. While the focus of this discussion is the preparation of the operating budget, all three budgets provide information necessary for the annual budget.

The *operating budget* is a short-term plan (usually one year) based on estimated volumes of output that determine the projected operating expenses and operating revenues. The operating budget consists of the following three documents:

1. statistics budget: the accumulation of the necessary statistical data to drive the expense budget
2. expense budget: the conversion of statistical budget into anticipated dollar amounts of expense
3. revenue budget: the establishment of enough revenue to meet the financial requirements of the hospital

The *cash budget* is a projection of cash receipts, disbursements, and balances for a given future period of time. It is designed to assist in controlling the hospital's cash position. It enables management to predict the timing and amount of future cash flows, cash balances, and cash needs and surpluses, and to examine cost implications of cash decisions.

With the elimination of the federal government's periodic interim payment program and the increasing activity in insurance contracting, the cash budget is becoming increasingly important. The projection of cash flow will impact decisions regarding the third budget—the capital budget.

The *capital budget* is the schedule of capital expenditures, capital dispositions, and resources available for the budget period. In preparing this budget, decisions will be made based on the statement of cash flow developed above.

Through the preparation of these budgets, the hospital creates a tool for planning and controlling its operations toward the achievement of the financial requirements. When the budget process is properly administered and coordinated, the result is accurate information to support future decisions from both an operating perspective and a capital perspective.

Periodic analysis and comparison of actual operating results with the budget plan assist the organization in monitoring financial and operational progress against the plan and controlling the operating activities and related costs. The historical information gathered during this process contributes to the preparation of the budget for the next fiscal year.

While the annual budget is a powerful management tool for planning and controlling the operations of the hospital, there are two prerequisites for realizing its full benefits: a synergistic environment must exist, and certain fundamental requirements are necessary, as explained below.

FUNDAMENTAL REQUIREMENTS FOR SOUND BUDGETING

Policies and Objectives

The governing board's responsibility is to establish hospital goals and objectives. These objectives traditionally include

1. a mission statement
2. identification of community needs

3. patient care
4. education
5. research

These policies and objectives should be broadly defined and expressed in both short- and long-range time frames. Board members must differentiate between management of the day-to-day operations of the hospital and policy setting. Board members need to know what information to ask for and how to evaluate the information they receive. The board, in conjunction with the chief executive officer (CEO), must communicate the long-range plans for the hospital that will contribute to orderly growth. At the same time, it must identify short-range objectives that can be quantified for the next budgeting cycle. Long-range plans include responses to questions such as: What kind of patient mix will be served? Will patient load increase or decrease? What do patient mix and load estimates mean in terms of staffing? What will happen to prices over the next year?[1]

Unfortunately, board participation is often neglected in the budgeting process. In general terms, the board sees the budget for the first time when it is presented for approval by management. In many cases the budget is prepared by hospital administration with little or no input from department heads. Such a budget will never withstand the financial tests that lie ahead or be accepted by the specific departments. For flexible budgeting, without significant input and buy-in on the assumptions by department heads, the value of the information is lessened.

Organizational Adaptation and Communication

The budgeting process requires, at a minimum, an effective and operational organizational structure. This structure should clearly delineate the line of authority as it flows down from the governing board to the CEO, assistant administrators, department heads, and supervisory personnel. The complexities of today's health care delivery system make it impossible for one individual to manage the entire operation of a hospital. Delegation of duties and responsibilities is critical. Successful budgeting pro-cesses are the result of team efforts. Each person must know that he or she has the support of his or her immediate superior. If individuals are to be responsible for performance, each position within the organizational structure must possess the proper authority to achieve the assigned tasks and responsibilities.

Furthermore, the system must provide an effective means of communication. Information generated from within and outside the budgeting process and system must flow downward, up-ward, and laterally. The information must be both timely and accurate. The established chan-nels of communication will be the conduit for conveying plans and policies throughout the organization. All communications should be expressed in a comprehensible manner. The pur-pose of managerial communications is to support understanding by individuals as they achieve and maintain the cooperation needed to meet the hospital's goals.

Responsibility Accounting

The relationship between the planning and controlling functions and the assigned individual responsibilities within the organizational struc-ture is critical. In many respects, planning is based on historical data generated by the ac-counting system. Since control includes meas-uring actual results against plans and objectives,

> accounting can be defined as a "system
> . . . tailored to an organization so that
> costs are accumulated and reported by lev-els of responsibility within the organiza-tion. Each of these levels of responsibility
> is charged only with the costs for which it
> is responsible and over which it has con-trol. These levels of responsibility are
> called cost centers."[2]

A cost center may be defined as an activity or group of activities for which various costs may be directly identified and accumulated.

Department heads generally are held responsi-ble only for controllable costs, mainly salaries and supplies, that are subject to their direct con-trol. Administrative costs and depreciation are

referred to as noncontrollable costs. In most cases, department heads are never fully respon-sible for all direct costs; however, they are accountable for those direct costs over which they do exercise significant control.

The budgeting process should require a department head to offer and review the pro-jected direct costs to operate his or her depart-ment within a relevant range of volume. This action then justifies measuring that department head's performance against those projections. It is unjust to measure the department head's per-formance against the total departmental cost, unless the noncontrollable costs are properly identified and reported. If department heads are to be evaluated in an equitable manner, hospitals must develop a functionally classified chart of accounts. The *Chart of Accounts for Hospitals*, published by the American Hospital Associa-tion, provides a starting point for this endeavor and should be challenged for appropriateness for flexible budgeting and cost management.

Realistic Expectations

In budget planning, management must avoid both undue conservatism and unfounded opti-mism. The care with which budget goals and objectives are set for such items as revenue, expenses, capital expenditures, and cash flow is the determining factor in the future success of the budget process. The board's objectives and man-agement's specific budget goals should be real-istic. Budget goals must be related not only to specific deadlines but also to the external and internal environments in which the goals and objectives are to be realized. They must repre-sent a challenge both to the cost center as a whole and to the appropriate individuals. Goals should provide optimum motivation. Basically, the objectives should represent "expected actual," assuming that performance of hospital personnel will be efficient under the conditions that are expected to prevail.[3]

Statistical Data

A budget cannot be developed without ade-quate statistics. Statistics provide the necessary units of measure that serve as the basic building blocks in preparing the hospital's budget. For flexible budgets, the single most critical item is the definition of cost center statistics and their accumulation during the year. The elements of the statistical budget encompass occasions of service, work units, and relative value units (RVUs). Statistical data should readily be accumulated and reported by the hospital's transaction systems.

Historical statistical data may be analyzed to determine trends. In addition, consideration must be made for assumed changes in medical staff, hospital occupancy, intensity of service, and demographic changes in the community.

Product Definition

As the health care environment changes and with the advent of the fixed price-per-case reimbursement, hospital operations and planning will become more focused on products, that is, diagnosis-related groups or lines of service. The hospital budgeting process in turn will be driven by the forecasted volumes of product that will drive cost center volumes and expenses. To begin the budgeting process, hospitals need to define their lines of business, interact with the medical staff, and begin to build their assumptions through product definition.

Timeliness

Managing the hospital is a day-to-day decision-making process that necessitates continual assessment of the hospital's future. Budget planning and monthly reporting are best accomplished in a formal manner and on a definite timetable. The hospital therefore should have a budget manual and a budget calendar for the annual budget process and the monthly responsibility reporting.

Fiscal and Budget Periods

Conventional accounting requirements state that at certain specified time intervals (normally a year) hospital operations should be subjected to

an imaginary halt so that financial statements can be prepared. This imaginary halt enables the hospital to measure its profit or loss during the selected period and to assess its financial condition at the end of its fiscal year. The fiscal year may be a calendar year, some other designated 12-month period, or a 13-period year.

Once the hospital selects an appropriate fiscal year, it becomes the fiscal cycle used for measuring and evaluating the hospital's performance. This fiscal period should be maintained consistently in order for the hospital to perform comparative reporting and to evaluate trends. The budget process may be divided into two components: long-range and short-range plans. The long-range budget plan is typically more than one fiscal year and is usually broad and general; the short-term budget plan is generally prepared for a future one-year time period.

Reporting and Control Program

The hospital's budgeting system must provide timely, adequate, and accurate reporting of financial and statistical information. A timely basis in the health care industry is normally defined as 14 to 21 days subsequent to the end of the reporting period. A more optimum time frame would be 7 to 10 days. The reporting system should include both comprehensive formal accounting reports and performance measurement reports. The reports should compare budgetary costs to actual costs for the month and year to date. In addition, performance, productivity, and flexible budget reports should be distributed, and variances that exceed predetermined thresholds should be explained by department heads.

PREPARATION OF THE BUDGET

The ten basic activities involved in traditional hospital budget planning include the following:

1. Establish institutional and departmental goals and objectives.
2. Determine the budget calendar.
3. Distribute budget instructions, input forms, and hospitalwide inflation rates.

4. Obtain historical data on costs and volumes by accounting periods.
5. Analyze internal and external forces that could affect historical patterns.
6. Project the volume of activities (e.g., patient days, emergency room visits, admissions, surgeries) utilizing all of the above information.
7. Project expenses and revenues.
8. Determine the other capital needs (e.g., equipment, debt service, working capital).
9. Establish revenue and rates schedule, and net of reductions from revenue required to generate sufficient cash to cover the operating costs and capital needs.
10. Submit the budget to the board and others for final approval.

This process, which is the traditional approach to budgeting, results in a fixed, or static, budget. The fixed budget provides for specified amounts of expenditures and receipts that do not vary with activity levels. The reporting and control process is then a comparison of actual results of operation to this fixed budget. An overview of the total budgeting process is presented in Figure 15-1.

The activities that comprise the process of preparing a flexible budget are similar to the traditional process described; however, the flexible budget projects receipts and expenditures as a function of activity levels. The reporting and control process for the flexible budget compares actual results of operation to a budget that is appropriate for the actual level of activity experienced during the reporting period.

The process of preparing a product-line budget can be more likened to the approach used in manufacturing and where the demand and levels of output are first determined at the institutional level. For hospitals, this process starts by reviewing the plans of the members of the medical staff in terms of types of patients, quantities, and changes in treatment patterns. Subsequent to determining volumes of cases and treatment protocols, the departmental units of service can be determined and distributed to the department heads, and the rest of the budgeting process proceeds as illustrated in Figure 15-1.

Whatever type of budget is prepared (traditional, flexible, or product), a team effort is required to carry out a sound and productive budget process. Normally, coordination of the process and overall responsibility are assigned to an individual or to a committee. The individual may be the budget director or some other designated management team member.

A primary responsibility of the coordinator is to communicate to all personnel the importance of and reasons for the preparation of a budget. The budget process has a powerful impact on the entire staff. How the budget process is presented to the hospital personnel determines how it is received. The coordinator, therefore, needs to be both people-oriented and problem-oriented. The budget process should encourage participation from other levels within the organization (e.g., board, management, medical staff, individual departments). Their positive participation can be achieved as various programs are presented during the course of the year. These programs can be directed toward categories of personnel (e.g., management, supervisors) or along functional lines (e.g., radiology, nursing service).

Once the management philosophy is communicated, it is necessary to develop a budget manual. A good budget manual will serve as the framework for the budgeting process. It delineates the scope of the process and describes the pertinent duties and lines of authority. The manual gives examples of budget forms and reports, states the period of time to be covered, and describes approval procedures. The table of contents of a typical budget manual might read as follows:

- introduction
- goals and objectives
- budget calendar
- budget planning
- budget assumptions
- units of service
- staffing and payroll expenses
- nonsalary expenses
- capital budget
- revenue budget
- deductions from revenue
- operating budget
- performance reporting
- exhibits and appendixes

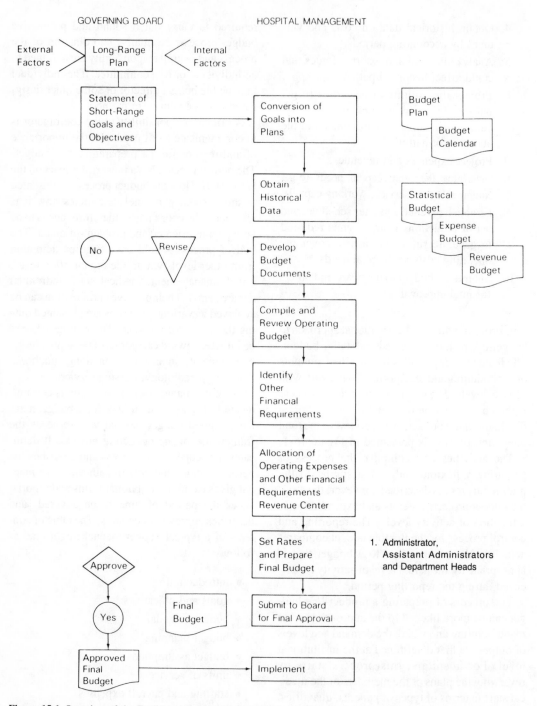

Figure 15-1 Overview of the Traditional Forecast Budget Preparation Process

To complete the budget on a timely basis, the coordinator also must make certain a budget calendar is prepared. The calendar (see Table 15-1) lists the significant tasks in the budget process, sets deadlines, and identifies those responsible for the completion.[4]

The budget calendar should be tailored to the needs of the individual hospital. For it to be effective, its goals must be realistic and its deadlines must be observed. Hence it is imperative that the coordinator allow adequate lead time for each task.

Table 15-1 Budget Calendar

Date	Participants	Purpose
August 15 to September 10	Budget director in staff relationship with medical staff, board members, and administrator	Prepare Statement of Assumptions after evaluating; medical staff projections of illnesses and diagnostic and therapeutic needs; department head recommendations; economic and population changes; introduction of new services and new methods of improving existing services; long-range capital plans; new developments in the health care field.
September 10	Governing board	Approve Statement of Assumptions, also goals and budget policies for the year.
September 12	Budget committee or administrator, budget director, and department heads	Review budget year objectives and specify general guidelines for attaining goals.
September 15	Budget director and department heads	Present Statement of Assumptions (i.e., anticipated general activity) for the budget year; distribute forms, schedules, and historical statistical data.
October 5 to October 10	Budget director and each department head individually	Review first draft of budget for purpose of giving technical assistance.
October 10 to October 20	Administrative management and departmental management	Review budget drafts; make and explain revisions.
October 20 to October 31	Budget director	Summarize department budgets into master budget.
November 1 to November 15	Budget committee or administrator, budget director, and administrative management	Review master budget; make and explain revisions. Make revised budget ready for review by governing board.
November 15 to November 30	Governing board, administrator, and controller	Review and approve or recommend for revision as necessary.
December 5 to December 15	Governing board, administrator, and controller	Review and approve, if not previously accomplished.
December 16	Department heads, administrator, and controller	Communicate final budget details to appropriate persons.
January 1	All personnel	Begin operations under budget.

Source: Reprinted from *Topics in Health Care Financing*, Vol. 5, No. 4, Aspen Publishers, Inc., © Summer 1979.

The groundwork for the budget program is completed once the coordinator has communicated the management philosophy and has developed or revised the budget manual and calendar. After the coordinator has received the goals and objectives developed by the board, the tasks of quantifying the goals and objectives begin. To do this, the coordinator must be certain those individuals involved in the process receive the necessary historical information and current assumptions needed to complete their individual budget tasks. During the course of budget preparation, the coordinator serves as the liaison and as a consultant to the various groups or individuals responsible for the different sections of the budget.

Budget Documents

The first document to be completed is the statistical budget. Its preparation involves

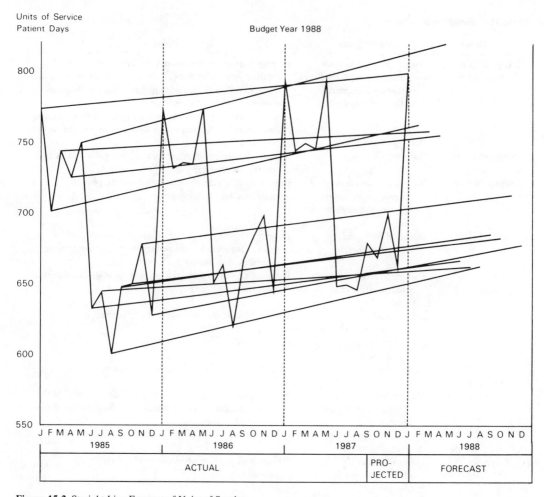

Figure 15-2 Straight-Line Forecast of Units of Service

accumulating statistical data (i.e., occasions of service, work units, and RVUs) by each cost center. Historically the department head has been responsible for gathering these data, and generally the tasks have been delegated to supervisory and clerical personnel. As the health care environment has changed, so have the data-accumulation systems. If the budget is to become a workable management tool, the unit of measure selected must relate directly to both activity and output of the cost center. Hospital procedures also should be developed that allow statistical data to be collected in an automated fashion that are accurate for both inpatients and outpatients. These procedures should be reviewed periodically and revised when appropriate.

There are a number of approaches to statistical forecasting. If computer capabilities are avail-

able, the hospital has available options such as regression analysis, exponential smoothing, moving average, and trend analysis. With the declining utilization rates and changes in product mix, the use of these approaches is limited to a certain extent. In addition, the use of these techniques requires skilled personnel.

Manual approaches are more time-consuming. The simplest manual approach entails plotting measures of activity on a graph and extending the trend line for future periods, following past trend lines as closely as possible. Figure 15-2 is an example of a straight-line forecast of units of service.[5]

The second document to be prepared is the expense budget. This involves converting the statistical budget into anticipated dollar expenses. The expense budget is segregated into two components: (1) salary and wage budget and (2) supplies and other nonsalary expenses. The salary and wage budget requires establishing staffing objectives and levels for each cost center. Methods that may be used for this purpose are

1. management-engineered standards
2. historical experience
3. experience of other hospitals

The nonsalary expenses are best forecast by

1. an understanding of accounting practices
2. knowledge of the relationship of expenses to the units of service
3. analysis of historical data
4. realistic estimates of vendor price increases
5. identification of technological and environmental changes

The forecast expenses must be reliable if the hospital's financial requirements are to be met. Expense records also must be maintained in a manner that clearly associates them with responsible cost centers. Expenses must be presented in enough detail to provide information needed for planning and control purposes.

The third document is the revenue budget. The hospital's financial objective is to generate enough net revenue to meet its financial requirements. Hospital revenues are normally generated from three sources: (1) patient revenues, (2) other operating revenues (i.e., activities incidental to patient services), and (3) nonoperating revenue (i.e., investment income, grants and donations, and endowments).

The revenue budget should cover the same time period established for the statistical and expense budgets.

In responsibility accounting, department heads are responsible only for the direct (controllable) costs. The indirect noncontrollable costs therefore must be allocated to the revenue-producing cost centers in order to determine full cost. As the health care environment evolves to one of fixed payments, the importance of fully allocating the noncontrollable costs diminishes. However, this allocation is achieved through

cost finding, a procedure done apart from, but in conjunction with, the regular accounting system and to the budgeting process. Cost-finding objectives are to provide full cost information for departmental rate setting, reimbursement, reporting, and managerial purposes.

In addition, deductions from revenue must be budgeted. These deductions are most commonly classified into four major groups:

1. bad debts
2. employee discounts, free services, policy deductions, and charity discounts
3. contractual allowances
4. third-party discounts

These calculations are normally subject to revision once the rate-setting evaluation process has been completed.

Once the operating budget is developed, reviewed, and accepted, the remainder of the budgeting activities can proceed quickly toward submission to the governing board for approval.

FLEXIBLE BUDGETING

In the above discussion of the budgeting process, the focus has been on the traditional approach to budgeting with some mention of a product-driven approach. How does the flexible budgeting process differ from the traditional approach?

The basic difference between the two is that the fixed budget is prepared at a given level of demand, and any shift in demand necessitates making changes at the point of origin (i.e., at the budget document preparation process). The flexible budget, on the other hand, develops a model for each department and permits management to evaluate how costs behave with changes in volume without having to revert to point of origin. For example, assume a hospital, in developing its budget, forecast 4,000 nursery room days at a cost of $120,000, but the hospital actually encountered 3,000 nursery days during the budget period at a cost of $150,000. Table 15-2 shows how the year-to-date line item would appear in a fixed budget report.

Table 15-2 Comparison of Budget Results of the Nursery Unit: Fixed Budget (3,000 Days)

	Actual	Budget	Variance Unfavorable
Nursery unit	$150,000	$120,000	$30,000

A comparison of this nature is virtually of no value, because to compare the cost of 3,000 actual days with the budget amount of 4,000 days is misleading because of the large fluctuation in volume. However, suppose the hospital, in preparing a flexible budget, had forecast the cost of the nursery as shown in Table 15-3. Using the flexible budget, a department head can develop budget figures for any level of activity within a relevant range that is actually experienced for that particular department. If, as stated in the example, the actual number of days was 3,000, the actual expense at that level of activity could be compared with budgeted expenses at the same level (Table 15-4). Since the hospital has determined the fixed and variable classifications as shown, the budgeted cost of 3,000 nursery days is merely the total of the fixed costs ($40,000) and variable costs at the level of activity (3,000 actual days × $80,000 ÷ 4,000 budgeted days), or $100,000 ($40,000 + $60,000).

The flexible budget, like the forecast budget, must provide in quantitive terms the plan of the

Table 15-3 Comparison of Budget Results of the Nursery Unit: Flexible Budget

	Estimated Level of Activity
Nursery unit	
Number of days	4,000
Fixed expenses	$ 40,000
Variable expenses	80,000
	$120,000

Table 15-4 Comparison of Budget Results of the Nursery Unit: Flexible Budget (3,000 Days)

	Actual	Budget	Variance Unfavorable
Nursery unit	$150,000	$100,000	$50,000

hospital, the basis for monitoring financial results, and the means of controlling costs. It is still essential that the same basic requirements of traditional budgeting be met. The flexible budget, however, also requires two additional activities:

1. First, it requires an analysis of cost behavior, that is, an analysis of how labor and other operating costs vary with changing workloads. Each expense element, labor, and supply must be analyzed to determine whether it is fixed, variable, or semivariable.
2. Second, standards must be set at a departmental level. These standards can be set by industrial engineering methods, historical analysis, or through the adoption of industrywide standards.

These activities in the flexible budgeting process are shown as boxes in Figure 15-3.

Cost Behavior

The preparation of a flexible budget requires an understanding of basic cost-behavior patterns. There are four basic cost-behavior patterns:

1. Fixed: costs do not change as the level of activity fluctuates.
2. Variable: costs vary in total more or less in direct proportion to volume.
3. Semivariable: costs vary in direct proportion to volume after a minimum level of activity has been reached.
4. Semifixed: Costs change with volume but not in direct proportion.

The relationships between cost and volume for the four cost-behavior patterns are illustrated in Figures 15-4 to 15-7. Fixed costs (Figure 15-4) bear no immediate relation to volume. Depreciation expense is an example of fixed cost. Costs that are variable increase/decrease with departmental volume (Figure 15-5). An example would be central supplies in relation to a nursing unit's patient days or the radiologist's

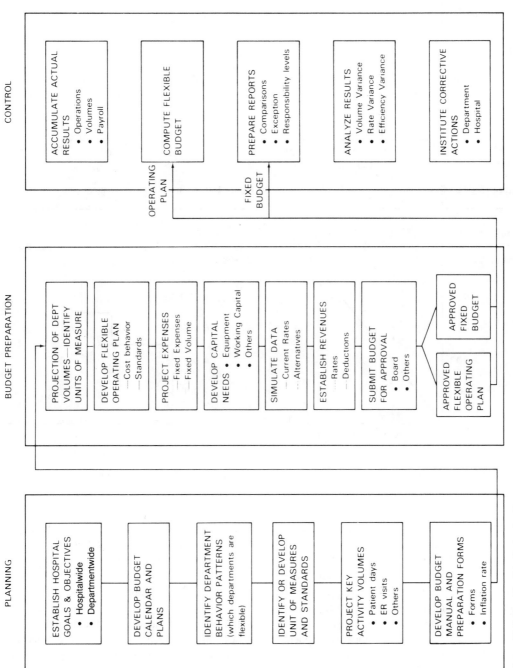

Figure 15-3 The Flexible Budgeting Process

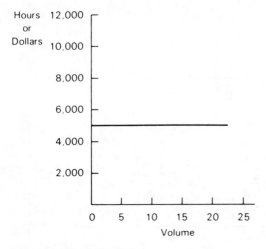

Figure 15-4 Fixed-Costs Pattern

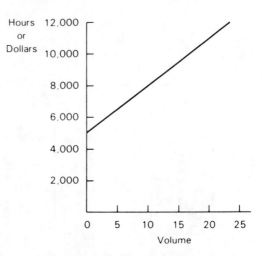

Figure 15-6 Semivariable-Costs Pattern

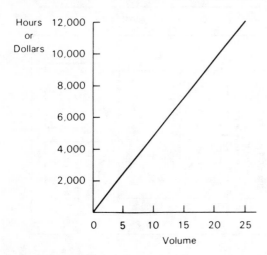

Figure 15-5 Variable-Costs Pattern

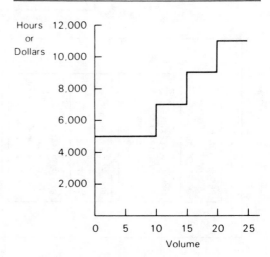

Figure 15-7 Semifixed-Costs Pattern

fee for service in relation to the number of services.

Semivariable costs, as shown in Figure 15-6, vary with volume once the volume exceeds a fixed level. An example of a semivariable cost is an intensive care nursing unit that requires a minimum of two nurses for one to four patients. An additional nurse is required for each additional two patients admitted to the unit. Semifixed costs, which are illustrated in Figure 15-7, include medical records, department supervision, and admissions. The difference between a semivariable and semifixed cost pattern depends to a large degree on the department's ability to manage or postpone work. For

example, an intensive care unit (ICU) cannot postpone adding staff when patient occupancy reaches a certain level. Therefore, the ICU is a variable or semivariable department. On the other hand, the medical records department is a semifixed cost department because it can manage its workload by shifting work to future periods. At some point the medical records workload cannot be shifted further and the staffing must be increased.

As a practical matter, costs may not behave in the way illustrated, and the real cost pattern may be a combination, as shown in Figure 15-8. It is for this reason that upper and lower volume limits are projected. One must determine how

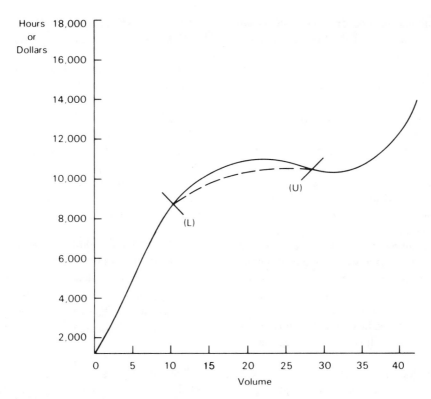

Figure 15-8 Realistic-Costs Pattern

each type of cost reacts within these limits, which are often referred to as the relevant range. Particular attention should be given to how costs behave between the lower limit (L) and the upper limit (U) of the relevant range.

Determining Department Cost Behaviors

The next step is to determine how cost behaves in each department in the hospital. What will be input to the flexible budgeting model?

There are no formulas for establishing which departments are fixed and which are variable nor do any laws dictate that certain operating costs, productive labor, supervision, or supplies always behave in a certain pattern. The cost-behavior patterns of departments differ from hospital to hospital because of items such as staffing levels, staffing mix, age of equipment, and physical layout. Furthermore, departments will also differ from one year to the next, and costs in departments providing similar services

in a hospital may behave differently. For example, an ICU's costs may vary quite differently with volume than those of a burn unit because of differences in size, occupancy, level of care, and so on. Therefore, to project future cost-behavior patterns, one must review past operations, project future activities, assess environmental changes, and use common sense.

Determining cost behavior generally involves three major steps:

1. Analyze the department's chart of accounts by account to determine the type of expense, the historical behavior, and the behavior by period and as volume levels change.
2. Review the unit of measure to determine whether it is an accurate measure of volume and related output.
3. Classify each type of operating expense into one of the four basic cost-behavior patterns.

An example of a department's budget work sheet developed from the hospital's chart of accounts is shown in Table 15-5. In this example, expenses are classified as fixed, variable, semifixed, or semivariable based on their behavior as it relates to the changes in volume. Although few costs are entirely fixed or 100 percent variable, a number of cost types can be classified within the reasonable volume range. All others must be assigned to the semivariable or semifixed group. Again, one must emphasize that such classifications generally should be made within a relevant range with upper and lower limits.

In the example, the chief technician's salary, clerical support salaries, nonmedical supplies, and equipment rentals are deemed to be fixed expenses that do not vary directly with volume fluctuations. However, because the salaries of the technicians, medical supplies, and the physicians' fees vary with volume, they are classified as variable.

In developing the laboratory's goals and objectives for this example, the department head noted that a clinical laboratory was to be opened beginning the first day of the budget year. Its weekly operation would require only one technician until volume reached 1,000 units of service per accounting period. Once the volume exceeded 1,000 units, a second technician from the main laboratory would be assigned during peak periods. The upper volume limit would not exceed 2,000 units per accounting period. Therefore, the labor costs of the clinical laboratories are classified as semivariable, as is evidenced during Period 5 of the budget year. Insurance expense also is designated semivariable because the policy requires a flat fee per month plus two cents per unit in excess of a predetermined amount.

Supervisory labor costs did change with volume, but not in direct proportion. The assumption developed regarding the relevant range is that if the volume exceeded 34,000 units in three accounting periods, a night supervisor will be required. Therefore, a night supervisor should be anticipated in the budget to the extent that it is expected that the average volume will exceed this figure.

PROJECTING THE LABOR HOURS AND COSTS

Sixty to seventy percent of hospital operating expenses are labor or labor-related. The labor cost in nursing departments can exceed 90 percent of the department's direct cost. Because labor costs represent a major expense item, and because they are difficult to budget and control, the single most important and time-consuming item in preparing the operating budget is labor. Therefore, the objectives of projecting labor hours and costs are

- to identify the skill level and work hours necessary to provide agreed-upon services
- to determine the labor costs, productive and nonproductive, to operate the department
- to provide a basis for the measurement of labor performance and control of labor costs

There are many acceptable methods of accomplishing these objectives. Differences in accounting systems, management philosophy, hospital size, and volume of services influence the method to be selected. In addition, the methods used in a department will depend on whether the labor costs are fixed, variable, semifixed, or semivariable and whether the labor costs are productive or nonproductive.

Projecting the Fixed Labor Hours and Costs

For the employees or job classifications determined to be fixed, projecting productive and nonproductive hours and the related costs is a rather straightforward clerical function. Table 5-6 illustrates a work sheet for estimating fixed labor hours and costs. The procedures for making such projections are as follows:

- Each employee or job classification code is listed.
- The nonproductive hours of each position are projected. Vacation and holiday time are represented as actual for current employees and estimated for new positions.

Table 15-5 Budget Work Sheet: "Most Likely" Results, Statistical Information, and Expenses

Department 2000   Volume Range: 29,000 to 45,000 Units

	1	2	3	4	5	6	7	8	9	10	11	12	Total
Volume-Activity													
Laboratory	34,000	32,000	34,000	35,000	38,000	40,000	37,000	40,000	41,000	39,000	41,000	36,000	447,000
Clinic laboratory	500	800	1,000	1,000	1,100	1,300	1,250	1,500	1,500	1,400	1,400	1,350	14,100
Total	34,500	32,800	35,000	36,000	39,100	41,300	38,250	41,500	42,500	40,400	42,400	37,350	461,100
Labor Hours													
Productive													
Chief technician	176	152	168	152	176	80	88	168	144	164	160	152	1,780
Supervisors	350	300	320	300	270	300	504	500	432	420	480	450	4,626
Technicians	7,083	6,667	7,083	7,292	7,917	8,333	7,708	8,333	8,542	8,125	8,542	7,500	93,125
Clinic technician													
Fixed	189	165	182	173	189	173	181	189	163	187	181	173	2,145
Variable					21	63	52	104	104	83	83	73	583
Clerical	460	380	450	460	460	380	420	470	376	424	450	480	5,210
	8,258	7,664	8,203	8,377	9,033	9,329	8,953	9,764	9,761	9,403	9,896	8,828	107,469
Nonproductive													
Chief technician	8	8	8	16	8	88	88	8	16	20	16	16	300
Supervisors	16	16	16	36	48	24	24	24	48	88	40	40	420
Technicians	921	867	921	948	1,029	1,083	1,002	1,083	1,110	1,056	1,110	975	12,105
Clinic technician													
Fixed	8	16	8	8	16	8	16	80	10	10	16	16	212
Variable					3	8	7	14	14	11	11	9	77
Clerical	20	20	100	40	20	100	20	30	24	16	40	60	490
	973	927	1,053	1,048	1,124	1,311	1,157	1,239	1,222	1,201	1,233	1,116	13,604
Total labor costs	9,231	8,591	9,256	9,425	10,157	10,640	10,110	11,003	10,983	10,604	11,129	9,944	121,073
Labor Costs													
Productive and nonproductive													
Chief technician	$ 2,000	2,000	2,000	2,000	2,000	2,000	2,000	2,000	2,120	2,120	2,120	2,120	$ 24,480
Supervisors	2,196	1,896	2,016	2,184	2,067	2,106	3,432	3,406	3,120	3,302	3,380	3,185	32,290
Technicians	40,724	38,333	40,724	46,119	50,070	52,701	48,750	52,701	54,022	51,386	54,022	47,435	576,987
Clinic technician	1,182	1,086	1,140	1,177	1,466	1,574	1,610	2,408	1,785	1,807	1,807	1,688	18,730
Clerical	2,239	1,866	2,566	2,332	2,239	2,240	2,176	2,472	1,978	2,176	2,423	2,670	27,377
Total labor costs	$48,341	45,181	48,446	53,812	57,842	60,621	57,968	62,987	63,025	60,791	63,752	57,098	$ 679,864
Other expenses													
Medical supplies	$ 3,623	3,444	3,675	3,780	4,106	4,336	4,208	4,565	4,675	4,444	4,664	4,109	$ 49,629
Nonmedical supplies	1,550	1,407	1,565	1,523	1,581	1,538	1,597	1,604	1,560	1,620	1,575	1,635	18,755
Equipment rental	1,000	1,000	1,000	1,000	1,000	1,000	1,200	1,200	1,200	1,200	1,200	1,200	13,200
Insurance	750	750	750	770	832	876	815	880	900	868	898	797	9,886
Professional fees	31,050	29,520	31,500	32,400	35,190	37,170	34,425	37,350	38,250	36,360	38,160	33,615	414,990
Total other	37,973	36,121	38,490	39,473	42,709	44,920	42,245	45,599	46,585	44,492	46,497	41,356	506,460
Total	$86,314	81,302	86,936	93,285	100,551	105,541	100,213	108,586	109,610	105,283	110,249	98,454	$1,186,324

Source: Reprinted from *Topics in Health Care Financing,* Vol. 5, No. 4, Aspen Publishers, Inc., © Summer 1979.

Table 15-6 Fixed Labor Work Sheet

Job Code	Position					Total Nonprod.	Total Avail. Hrs.	Prod. Hrs.	Over- time	Total Prod.	Current Rate($)	Comments	Allocation Code
001A	Chief technician	160	72	40	28	300	2,080	1,780		1,780	2.00	per month 6% increase at 9/1/89	(3)
009A	Office manager	80	72	40	8	200	2,080	1,880	200	2,080	5.00	per hr. 6% increase at 7/1/89	(2)
009B	Secretary	80	72	40	8	200	2,080	1,880	100	1,980	4.25	per hr. 6% increase at 7/1/89	(2)
009C	Clerk	40	36	8	6	90	1,040	950		950	4.00	per hr. 6% increase at 7/1/89	(2)
009D	Vacation relief						200	200		200	4.00	per hr. 6% increase at 7/1/89	(4)
	Total clerical (009)	200	180	88	22	490	5,400	4,910	300	5,210	4.665	(average)	

Allocation codes:
(1) Days in month
(2) Weekdays in month
(3) Per month
(4) Other
   Note: Table is mockup of actual work sheet.

Sick leave, education, and other leave are estimated based on prior experience and modified by current plans.

- The total nonproductive time is subtracted from the total available time of 2,080 hours (2,088 hours in a leap year) to arrive at the regular-pay productive hours.

- The paid overtime hours are estimated on prior experience and modified by current plans.

- The vacation hours and other leave time to be filled by another employee or temporary hire are estimated. Likewise, time chargeable to another department is subtracted from the department's budget.

- The current hourly rate for each job classification and the amount and date of expected increases are obtained. Premium pay, such as overtime, holiday, and shift differential can be included in the average hourly rate. The premium hours can also be budgeted separately and an hourly rate for each premium hour computed.

- All hours and costs are allocated to the appropriate accounting period. If an automated budgeting system is available, these calculations are automated.

The procedures outlined above are not all-inclusive and will vary by department and hospital.

Projecting the Variable Labor Hours and Costs

The method used to estimate the variable labor hours and costs depends upon the extent to which standard labor hours have been established and the presence of a cost management system. Many hospitals have developed detailed, engineered standards for determining productive and nonproductive time by skill level, procedure, or test as input into a cost management or productivity management system. Such standards are not necessary to begin flexible budgeting, but general standards of productivity, such as the nursing hours per patient day or number of procedures per productivity labor hour, are essential. Sophisticated standards can be introduced into the process over a period of time and will increase the accuracy and uses for the information. Given the lack of detailed standards, the following steps should be taken to project variable labor hours and costs:

- Determine whether previously developed general standards are still applicable.
- Determine the productive standard for the budget year.
- Determine the relationship between the productive standard and nonproductive time.
- Determine the average hourly rate(s) of pay.
- Allocate the labor hours and costs to the appropriate accounting period based on the volume projection.

Table 15-7 illustrates how variable labor hours and costs can be projected in developing a departmental budget. In this example, the productive standard is based on the actual productivity attained in the last half of the previous year, even though this level fell short of the ideal prescribed by an industrial engineer's study. Agreement on the productivity standard is the base for all other variable labor decisions and is the key to flexible budgeting and control. From this standard, the desired level of staffing, labor hours, and costs can be computed prospectively

Table 15-7 Variable-Hours Operating Plan

Department 2000	Productivity Standard (per Technician Hour)	Staff Mix		
		Full time (%)	Part Time (%)	Overtime (%)
Historical Data				
1977—Engineer study	5.0 units	70	20	10
1977—Actual	4.5 units	65	23	12
1978—Actual 1/1–6/30	4.5 units	70	20	10
1978—Actual 7/1–9/30	4.0 units	65	20	15
Budget Target, 1979				
Productive hours	4.8 units (or 12.5 minutes per unit)	65	25	10
Nonproductive hours				
Regular available			2,080	
Overtime			180	
Total			2,260	
Average nonproductive hours				
Vacation	112			
Holidays	72			
Sick	50			
Other	26			
Total	260		(260)	
Total productive hours			2,000	

Percent of nonproductive hours to productive hours = 13%.

Hourly Rate Computation

	Rate ($)		Mix (%)		Total ($)
Average full time	5.00	×	65	=	3.250
Average part time	4.50	×	25	=	1.125
Averge overtime	7.13	×	10	=	.713
Average hourly rate					5.088

Per union contract, hourly rate increased by 10% effective April 1, 1979.
Note: Table is mockup of actual work sheet.

for budget forecasts or retrospectively for control purposes. Therefore, care must be exercised in the determination of the productivity standard.

The productivity standard is somewhat determined by the skill level required to perform the task and the type of workers who usually perform the specified task. In Table 15-7, the assumption has been made that only laboratory technicians of equal skill level will be used. Differences in pay grade are adjusted by using an average wage rate for all technicians. However, greater flexibility in staffing can be provided by using a mixture of full-time and part-time technicians and overtime staffing during peak periods. The relationship of full-time, part-time, and overtime is noted in Table 15-7.

The productivity standard includes only the productive time. Each employee has paid nonproductive time such as vacation, holiday, and sick leave, and the hours and costs of such time must be computed. Table 15-7 illustrates how the relationship between the productive hours and the nonproductive hours can be computed.

The productive standard and the determined mix of full-time, part-time, and overtime hours are the basic ingredients necessary for projecting the variable labor hours and cost. An average rate of pay to staff the department in accordance with the above plan must then be computed. In most hospitals the budget director or accounting department assists the department head in arriving at an average rate of pay. Assuming that the proposed staffing plans do not vary greatly from the current staffing pattern, the current average rate can be used. This rate would be adjusted in the month that salary increases would be effective. The budget director can compute the amount and time of any wage adjustment.

This average pay rate is multiplied by the estimated number of productive and nonproductive hours to arrive at the cost. Many hospitals also include the cost of paid fringe benefits and payroll taxes in the average rate of pay as a method of budgeting for these costs. Other hospitals compute the fringe benefit costs separately as a direct expense to the department; still others include fringe benefits as an indirect overhead item.

Table 15-5 shows that the variable labor hours and costs have been spread to the various accounting periods based on the most likely volume of activity for each period. This is necessary for monthly performance reporting.

Semivariable Labor Hours and Costs

The semivariable labor hours and costs can be computed with the same techniques used to compute the fixed labor hours and the variable labor hours. The job codes determined to be fixed are budgeted in the same way as other fixed labor expenses. Those that are variable are projected in accordance with the techniques used in projecting variable labor. Table 15-8 illustrates how these computations might be made.

Semifixed Labor Hours and Costs

Semifixed labor hours and costs are computed by using the same techniques used for budgeting the fixed hours. The major problem is that the timing of the new hire, the labor rate of the nonproductive time earned, and similar factors must be estimated without knowing exactly when the volume of activity will warrant the additional staff.

Summary of Labor Costs

In these examples, all four basic types of cost-behavior patterns have been determined, together with the number of hours and estimated costs. This information can be used to establish the cost of the volume of activity and is the basis for comparing actual labor costs with the planned labor costs once actual volume is known. For example, in Period 6 of Table 15-5, the most likely volume of activity was estimated to be 41,300 and the labor costs were budgeted at $60,621. The actual results indicated that only 36,000 units were performed during the period. By having a flexible operating plan, the desired cost for 36,000 units ($53,812) can be computed and compared with the actual results. If a flexible operating plan had not been developed, the

Table 15-8 Semivariable Labor Work Sheet

Fixed Staff: Clinic Technician
Total hours available

Regular		2,080
Overtime		157
		2,237

Minus nonproductive hours

Vacation	80	
Holidays	72	
Sick	40	
Other	20	
Total	212	(212)

Total productive hours	2,025
Plus replacement hours	120
Total productive fixed hours	2,145

Total fixed hours (2,145 + 212) = 2,357

Rate: $6.00 per hour (effective April 1, 1979 rate $6.50 per hour.) Overtime included in base rate.

Variable Staff: Coverage from hospital laboratory—same productivity standard and hourly rate.
- Productivity standard   4.8 units/technician hour
- Nonproductive percentage   13%
- Rate $5.088
- Increase   10% (effective April 1, 1979).

Note: Table is mockup of actual work sheet.

Source: Reprinted from *Topics in Health Care Financing*, Vol. 5, No. 4, Aspen Publishers, Inc., © Summer 1979.

comparison of the actual results to the most likely results or to a fixed budget would produce a volume variance that would be difficult to analyze.

OTHER OPERATING COSTS

Other operating costs are projected in the same manner as are labor costs. Once a determination has been made that the costs are fixed, variable, semivariable, or semifixed, the department head and the budget director forecast the costs and determine when they will occur. The following questions should be asked for each cost-behavior pattern.

Fixed Cost

- What is the current cost rate?
- What increases or decreases in the cost rate can be expected? When are they likely to occur?
- How should the cost be allocated? (By number of days in the month? By number of weekdays? According to when paid or when accrued?)

Variable Cost

- What is the relationship of the cost of the unit of service?
- What is the current cost rate per unit of service?
- What increases or decreases can be expected in the cost rate? When might they occur?

Semifixed Cost

- At what volume of activity will the next increment of cost be incurred?
- What is the current cost rate?
- What increases or decreases can be expected? When might they occur?
- What will be the cost for the next volume increment?
- What increases or decreases can be expected in the incremental cost?
- How should the cost be allocated?

Semivariable Cost

- At what volume of activity will the variable cost become effective?
- What is the current cost rate of the fixed portion?
- What increases or decreases in the fixed portion can be expected? When will the changes occur?
- How should the fixed portion be allocated?

- What is the relationship of the variable cost portion to the unit of service?
- What is the current cost rate for the variable portion?
- What increases or decreases can be expected in the variable portion? When will they occur?

In Table 15-9, nonmedical supplies and equipment rental are fixed costs. Additional estimates and determinations revealed that the current costs for nonmedical supplies averaged $50 per day. It was expected that because of inflation the supply costs would increase 0.05 percent each month. The costs were to be allocated on the number of days in each month. The equipment rental contract was reviewed, and it was determined that the current rate of $1,000 per month would be in effect for the first six months, after which time the monthly rate would be $1,200. The rental cost will be allocated in accordance with the contract.

Medical supplies and physician fees were determined to behave in a variable manner. Currently, $0.10 of medical supplies were consumed for each unit of service, but the supplier indicated that there would be a 5-percent increase effective the first of the year and another 4.8-percent increase at midyear. Therefore, the medical supplies were to be budgeted at $0.105 per unit for the first six months and $0.11 per unit thereafter. Physicians' fees of $0.90 per unit would remain the same.

Only insurance expense was deemed to be semivariable. The policy required a flat fee of $750.00 per month and $0.02 for every unit over 35,000 per month. No increase in premiums was expected for the year. The cost should be allocated at $750.00 per month and $0.02 per unit over 35,000.

Table 15-5 illustrates that the labor costs and the other operating expenses have been allocated to the appropriate month and now represent a fixed budget based on the most likely results.

Table 15-9 Classification of Operating Expenses

Unit of Service—AX units
Volume Ranges:
  Laboratory—29,000 to 45,000 units
  Projected Clinic Laboratory—100 to 2,000 units

Chart of Accounts	Account No.	Fixed	Variable	Semivariable	Semifixed	Comments
Labor						
Chief technician	001	X				
Supervisors	002				X	Add night supervisor after 3 periods at 34,000 units or more
Technicians	005		X			4.8 units per technician hour
Clinic technician	006			X		1 unit to 1,000 units fixed, over 1,000, 4.8 units per technician hour
Clerical	009	X				
Supplies						
Medical	010		X			Current rate 10¢ per unit
Nonmedical	015	X				
Other						
Equipment rental	022	X				
Insurance	025			X		$750 per month, plus 2¢ for each unit over 35,000
Professional fees	030		X			$2.20 per unit

Note: Table is mockup of actual work sheet.

Source: Reprinted from Topics in Health Care Financing, Vol. 5, No. 4, Aspen Publishers, Inc., © Summer 1979.

Once the fixed budget and the flexible operating plan are established, the following steps should be performed:

- Summarize the budgets of all of the operating departments.
- Summarize all of the capital equipment budgets.
- Perform cost finding by allocating support and administrative service cost to the revenue-producing departments.
- Simulate various assumptions using the flexible operating plan and the fixed budget.

- Prepare cash flow analysis.
- Perform rate setting, including estimating the reductions of revenue (bad debts, charity, contractural adjustments).
- Submit the budget for approval.
- Assist the department heads in adjusting charge structures in accordance with the approved revenue budget.

The above duties are similar to those that must be completed in developing a traditional fixed budget, and the reader should study the process in more depth in other texts.

NOTES

1. R.E. Baker, *Budgeting Procedures for Hospitals* (Chicago: American Hospital Association, 1971), 6.

2. Hospital Financial Management Education Foundation (HFMEF), *The Budgeting Process* (Chicago: HFMEF, 1970), 10.

3. G.A. Welsh, *Budgeting: Profit Planning and Control* (Englewood Cliffs, N.J.: Prentice-Hall, Inc., 1971), 42–43.

4. Baker, *Budgeting Procedures*, 15.

5. California Hospital Association and California Chapters of Hospital Financing Management Association, *CHA/HFMA Budgeting Manual* (Sacramento: CHA/HFMA, 1978), 31.

Chapter 16

Revenue Budgeting and Product Pricing

Kenneth F. Johnson
President, Strategic Healthcare Systems, Inc.

INTRODUCTION

Before the implementation of Medicare's prospective payment system (PPS) and the adoption by other payers of global payment methodologies, revenue budgeting was relatively simple. Since over half of a hospital's revenue was from cost-reimbursed services, the most critical part of the process was determining total costs and the portions of those costs that were reimbursable. Pricing hospital services was equally streamlined. Payers either settled on their proportionate share of costs or paid the hospital on the basis of billed charges.

With PPS the focus of hospital pricing and billing has shifted from a la carte to global. Under a la carte pricing, each service, treatment, procedure, drug, or supply item provided to the patient is separately identified and included on the bill. Global pricing, on the other hand, aggregates all of the individual items charged for separately under the a la carte approach into a single price for the case based upon predetermined case definition criteria.

Global pricing methodologies are not new to hospitals. With the economic pressures of the 1930s, hospitals started charging for services based upon broadly defined diagnosis groupings or length of stay measures or both. As the economy improved in the 1940s, most hospitals

returned to a la carte pricing. However, a small group of hospitals in urban centers such as Cleveland retained the global structure through the use of all-inclusive rates based upon length of stay within clinical divisions.

During the mid-1970s, through an experimental program within three contained geographic areas, the federal government demonstrated an interest in all-inclusive rates as a means to contain its share of hospital cost increases. For a variety of political and economic reasons the project was dropped after only a couple of years. However, this study provided two observations that have a bearing on the current environment: there is price sensitivity in the health care market, and hospitals must expand their data-collection capabilities to operate within a global pricing system.

Global pricing has raised new concerns and intensified old ones with respect to revenue budgeting and product pricing. These concerns are revenue coverage of economic costs, definition of products, determination of costs of goods sold, and the constraints placed upon revenues and prices by the market in general and by regulatory bodies specifically.

These four basic concerns provide the basis for defining the budgeting and pricing process within the environment in which hospitals must now operate. This process (Figure 16-1) is more

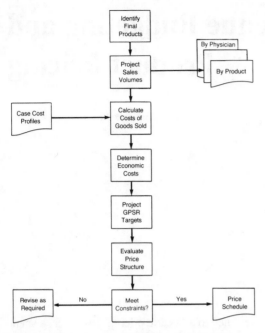

Figure 16-1 Revenue Budgeting within the Current Environment

comparable with the seven-step process followed by other industries than it was during the cost-based reimbursement era:

1. Identify the products to be provided during the budget period.
2. Project sales volumes by product, payer, and/or physician for the budget period.
3. Determine the cost of goods sold based upon projected sales volumes.
4. Ascertain the total economic costs sufficient to maintain the entity's fiscal viability during the budget period.
5. Calculate the gross patient service revenue (GPSR) required to cover the projected total economic needs.
6. Develop a price structure for final and intermediate products sufficient to generate the budgeted GPSR.
7. Test the price structure against internal and external constraints and modify the budget as required.

Within the remainder of this chapter those aspects of the process applicable to revenues and pricing will be expanded upon. The reader is

directed to other chapters of this handbook for additional discussions of topics related to budgeting and product costing.

DEFINING THE BASICS

Whether based upon cost reimbursement or prospective pricing, the basic objectives of the process have not changed. Through revenue budgeting a hospital determines what revenues are required to cover its anticipated economic costs for the budget period. Product pricing is the process that establishes the amounts to be charged for each "product" produced by the hospital to reach its budgeted revenue objective.

What has changed, however, is the means by which these ends are reached. There are several terms, such as *product, sales, cost of goods sold,* and *economic costs,* used within the brief descriptions of the seven basic budgeting/pricing steps that at first blush may appear to be inappropriate for the health care industry. These terms, more common to manufacturers, do have application within the health care lexicon and should be added to the health care manager's dictionary. The concepts that they represent have a direct bearing on the maintenance of an institution's fiscal viability in a competitive climate.

Product is a term that the health care industry has tried to avoid in the belief that health care providers render a service and thus do not produce a product. But hospitals and other providers do produce products. With the advent of Medicare's PPS and intensified competition among providers, the recognition of defined products has gained acceptance. The ultimate objective of the patient care process (services rendered to patients) is to discharge patients. Therefore, the hospital's final products are the discharged patients, or completed outpatient encounters. These final products can be identified readily through the patient accounting and case-mix systems and their revenues and costs quantified.

Sales are made by hospitals directly to the end user (patients) through independent contractors (physicians) or under a subcontracting arrangement (health maintenance organizations, preferred provider organizations, and so forth). In the past the availability of a service alone tended to generate demand. A hospital made known what services were available and the customer then "demanded" those services. With competitive pricing, hospitals have adopted more traditional marketing concepts and promote products and product lines that are more favorable to them. GPSR on a hospital's income statement is now considered to be more like a manufacturer's gross sales figure than it was under cost reimbursement. Likewise, contractual allowances are more comparable with sales discounts. (Bad debts have always been comparable—only their position within the income statement differs.)

Cost of goods sold reflects the aggregation of the direct, indirect, and overhead costs of the products sold during the period. This has been, and will continue to be, reflected in the hospital's income statement as "operating expense." The difference is in how the "cost of goods sold" figure is determined. Under cost reimbursement it was sufficient to focus cost accounting at the cost-center level. Cost reimbursement was based upon a pro rata share of allocated costs for revenue-producing cost centers, and a la carte billing caused these "revenue producers" to be considered as profit centers. Under global pricing methodologies, with the focus on case-based products and pricing, such as Medicare's diagnosis-related groups (DRGs), the cost of goods sold is the aggregation of the costs attributable to the products sold during the period. This should be the same as the total of all of the cost center costs. It is just derived in a more precise way.

Economic costs, traditionally referred to in the health care industry as "total financial requirements," were defined in 1979 by the American Hospital Association in the *Statement on Financial Requirements of Health Care Institutions and Services* as

> those resources that are not only necessary to meet current operating needs, but also sufficient to permit replacement of the physical plant when appropriate, education and research needs, all other needs necessary to the institutional provision of health care services that must be recognized and supported by all purchasers of care.

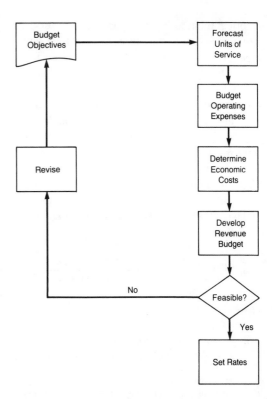

Figure 16-2 Revenue Budgeting Process Pre-PPS

In short, the economic cost for a hospital represents the sum of operating expenses and profit. Operating expenses are readily defined, and the approaches to developing an operating expense budget are discussed elsewhere in this handbook. It is through the generation of profits that an enterprise accumulates funds necessary to provide for those needs not accounted for as "operating expenses," such as capital replacement, changes in working capital needs, and maintainance of reserve funds.

THE BUDGETING/PRICING PROCESS

Traditionally, hospitals have budgeted GPSR after completing and aggregating the operating expense budgets for each cost center (Figure 16-2). The operating expense budgets were based on overall estimations of admissions and patient days for each of the major payers. Ancillary units of service were derived by using the historical relationship between ancillary service activities and either admissions or patient days depending on which had the best fit. This approach, although very crude, produced sufficiently accurate estimates of unit of service volume when the primary measure was at the charge level and volumes were relatively stable and predictable. The biggest task in the development of the revenue budget under this approach was to determine the deductions from revenue for the Medicare contractual allowance, other third-party differentials, and self-pay bad debts. Budgeted GPSR could then be determined using the following formula:

$$GPSR = \frac{(EC - OOR) - CP\%\,(AC - DC)}{(1 - CP\%) \times (1 - SPD\%)}$$

where

GPSR = gross patient service revenue,
EC = total economic costs,
OOR = other operating revenue (net),
AC = accounting costs,
DC = disallowed third-party costs,
CP% = cost payer revenue percentage, and
SPD% = deductions as a percentage of self-pay revenue.

The major difference between the traditional approach to revenue budgeting within an a la carte-oriented market and budgeting within the current product or case orientation is the starting point. The a la carte approach starts with budget objectives and forecasts of unit of service volumes. The new approach starts with product evaluations and sales forecasts.

Identify Final Products

A hospital's "final products" are represented by its discharged patients. Each case has a different set of characteristics based upon variables such as diagnosis, major procedures performed, severity of illness, and physician treatment protocols. For planning, budgeting, and management control, similar cases should be categorized into meaningful and definable products and product lines. The Medicare program has attempted to do this for hospitals through the DRG classification system. Cases are classified into DRGs based upon primary and secondary

diagnoses, major procedures, and, in some cases, the patient's age. Unfortunately, the Medicare DRG methodology does not include the condition of the patient during the stay. The severity of the patient's illness is considered to have a significant impact on the types and quantities of resources consumed in producing the product.

Although the DRG methodology, with or without severity modification, may be used to classify cases into products and product lines, an individualized classification system will provide a more meaningful case-mix management tool. The medical staff must have sufficient input during the development process to reflect properly the hospital's distinctive case-mix and treatment protocols.

Project Sales Volumes

There are three primary factors to be considered when projecting hospital discharges (sales): case classification (e.g., DRG), payer, and admitting physician. (Note that with increasing regularity the admitting and attending physicians are not the same. Therefore, case-mix records should have the provision to identify both. The admitting physician's data are used for forecasting and those of the attending physician to derive case management information.) Standard statistical forecasting tools, to account for growth, seasonal variations, and other independent factors, are appropriate for making these projections. However, as in any other industry, the statistical forecasts must be modified with solid doses of realism. A starting point would be to assume that each physician will retain the same case mix and volume after adjusting for retirements, new recruits, and other additions/deletions. Modifications to reflect product changes and shifts between payer are then entered. The result is a three-way forecast of sales for the budget period: by product, by payer, and by physician.

Calculate the Costs of Goods Sold for Projected Sales

Each of the hospital's products has a unique cost structure. Product or case costs are an accumulation of the intermediate product costs consumed during the patient's stay. The cost of each intermediate product, or procedure, should be developed through the hospital's cost accounting system and be available to the case-mix system. The procedure costs passed to the case-mix system should include the direct costs, fixed and variable indirect costs, and fixed and variable overhead for each intermediate product. The separation of variable costs is necessary to reflect properly the impact of volume changes.

If properly conceived, each case within a product, or case class, group will consume a relatively consistent set of resources represented by intermediate products. To determine the costs of goods sold for projected sales, a resource-consumption profile (RCP) should be constructed for each identified product. There are two basic ways that can be used to build these profiles. The first is to determine the historical average resource consumption for each product based upon actual case records. It is assumed that the hospital's case-mix system provides a linkage between information from medical records and the detailed charge data collected within the patient accounting system. The second approach is for the physicians involved with the product to develop a "standard" profile based upon their best judgment. It should be obvious that combining these approaches will achieve the best results. If the physicians are provided with a historical analysis based upon actual case-mix data, not only will they have an easier task and accomplish it more quickly, but they will also be able to observe instances where the actual treatment causes additional costs without impacting the outcome. This approach will invariably lead to changes in physician behavior and ultimately to lowering costs of cases that have an adverse effect on the quality of care.

The RCP includes the cost details and quantity of each intermediate product expected to be consumed to produce the final product. The costs of individual cases are determined within the case-mix system by applying the appropriate unit costs to the actual intermediate products consumed. The RCP is used as a standard to measure performance, to make "what if" evaluations, and to make projections for the budget and long-range plans. Since each of these uses assumes volume changes, it is essential that the case-mix

system have the capability to carry at least the five cost elements mentioned above (direct, indirect fixed and variable, and overhead fixed and variable). Under cost reimbursement, missed forecasts cost only 50 cents or less on the dollar; now they cost the whole dollar. Therefore, when developing the revenue budget the increases in variable costs have a direct bearing. If the competition understood the fixed/variable relationship better, its pricing might be "tighter" and thus draw business away.

Determine the Total Economic Costs for the Entity

A hospital's operating expense reflects a portion, albeit significant, of the total economic costs of the entity that must be recovered through GPSR. The composition of economic costs is represented by the formula in Exhibit 16-1. The methodology for budgeting each of these factors is slightly different, and also varies, from approaches that may have been employed previously by the hospital. The key is to make the best use of the expanded case and cost data sets now available.

- *Cost of goods sold.* Through the preceding step, the costs of goods sold are developed by applying intermediate-product standard costs to projected RCPs developed through the case-mix system. This process not only provides the costs by product but, when sorted by cost center, the projected cost of each of the hospital's production functions.

Exhibit 16-1 Economic Cost Formula

EC = (CGS − OOR − NOR) + (CA + BD) + P

Where
EC = Economic costs
CGS = Cost of goods sold
OOR = Other operating revenue
NOR = Nonoperating revenue (net)
CA = Contractual allowances and adjustments
BD = Bad debts
P = Profit

(A production function is any cost center within the hospital that has direct involvement with producing the final product. The remaining cost centers are considered support functions in that their mission is to support the activities of the production functions. The production function's costs represent the direct and indirect costs of the intermediate products they produce, and the support function's costs represent the product overhead costs. The reader is referred to Chapter 10 of this handbook for a more detailed discussion of these issues.)

- *Other operating revenue and nonoperating revenues.* These two budget categories are budgeted in the traditional way. However, if the concept of production and support functions replaces that of revenue and non-revenue-producing cost centers for management purposes, some categories that were previously classified as "other operating revenue" will now be considered as offsetting production or support-function revenue within the budget process.

- *Contractual allowances and adjustments.* Contractual allowances and adjustments are really sales discounts. The use of the term *contractual allowance* started with Medicare and cost reimbursement to account for the difference between billed charges and reimbursed costs. Now, with the absence of cost reimbursement, it is used to account for the difference between billed charges and the amount actually billed. Double talk? Yes! However, if it is required that there be a standard rate book for all intermediate products, an accounting will be required.

  The allowances and adjustments can be related directly to specific payers and, in some cases, specific benefit plans offered by payers. A good integrated case-mix system will facilitate the identification and quantification of these discounts, since the information is generally carried in the patient accounting system and can be retrieved from there. The various sales discount profiles are applied to the projected case mix by payer to arrive at the total budgeted amount for contractual allowances and adjustments.

- *Bad debts.* Bad debts can be budgeted using a similar approach. Historical bad debts for the self-pay portion of business are analyzed, adjusted for expected changes in economic conditions, and applied to projected self-pay sales. Using the case-mix data makes the task much easier, since not only are payers easily identified but so are the products with the higher propensity for bad debts.

Develop GPSR Targets

If the hospital's budgeted economic costs include each of the items detailed above, including profit requirements, total economic costs equal total GPSR. Application of the "gross-up" formula used prior to PPS, and discussed briefly above, is no longer necessary.

However, a new twist is added. As in other industries, it is not reasonable to assume that all products and product lines will be able to bear an equal share of the economic costs. Medicare, under PPS, pays what it considers to be the cost for each DRG. Other payers may well have their own DRG-like price schedules. Market constraints may dictate that other products be priced with smaller contribution margins. Therefore, gross revenue targets should be established separately for each product line. (A product line might include all of the products within a clinical specialty or other grouping with common market or clinical management characteristics.) When establishing these revenue targets, two factors should be considered. First, the product price should be sufficient to cover at least the variable costs required to produce the product. Cost accountants use the term *contribution margin* to define that portion of price that is available to contribute to the coverage of fixed costs and profit.

The second factor to consider is price/profit sensitivity. In other words, what will be the impact on profit of a dollar increase in price? It does not make any sense to price an inpatient product that is provided only to Medicare patients in excess of the DRG payment amount. Thus, if the Medicare business is a loser or marginal, the non-Medicare business still must pick up the tab for the short fall.

Evaluate the Adequacy of the Current Rate Structure

Even though more and more of a hospital's business is based upon global pricing methodologies, there will continue to be a need for a la carte pricing and billing for some time to come. Therefore, the same type of rate sensitivity analysis performed on the "final product" level should be performed on the "intermediate" product or charge level. This process is easier now than it was previously. The case-mix system and product RCPs will provide payer details for each intermediate product.

Determine That Prices Are within Defined Constraints

Pricing constraints are both internal and external. The external constraints are those imposed by regulatory bodies, payers, and the marketplace in general. If the regulatory and payer constraints are not adequately considered in the pricing process, a revenue shortfall will occur due to payer denials. Of equal importance are the market constraints. Ignoring these constraints may cause a decrease in sales volumes or an increase in bad debts. Market constraints fall into two general categories: economic conditions that influence collections, and prices charged by competitors. Given the increased sensitivity to prices in the health care market, charging more than a competitor for comparable products will drive away business. It should be noted that in this case comparability is in the eyes of the beholder.

Internal constraints are established by management, the governing board, or both. They may include minimum contribution margins and profit objectives.

CONCLUSION

Revenue budgeting and product pricing in hospitals have become more complex with the disappearance of retrospectively based cost reimbursement and the increased influence of competition in the health care marketplace. Hospitals have recognized that to succeed within the new operating environment, they must have access to more complete and current information about their products and the resources used to produce them. The availability of additional case-mix and cost data enables hospitals to employ more sophisticated methodologies in furthering their management objectives.

Chapter 17

Cash Flow Modeling

John F. Hill
Director of Finance, Benedictine Health System

INTRODUCTION

Effective corporate cash management involves two major activities: (1) maintaining sufficient cash on hand to meet day-to-day operating requirements and (2) maximizing earnings on cash balances available for investment. A proper balance between these two purposes needs to be struck, however. If too much cash is held for operations, then interest income will be foregone. On the other hand, too little cash on hand requires frequent juggling of investment portfolios. This may result in excessive transactions costs and can often force the liquidation of investments at a loss.

On a daily basis, cash flows are neither completely uncertain nor completely predictable. For example, payroll and related costs can be scheduled with considerable certainty for several months into the future. Many operating expenditures and, especially, cash receipts are more variable but can be forecast with varying levels of uncertainty. Thus, a model of future cash flows can be developed that will help establish the appropriate amounts of cash that should be retained for operations or available for investment.

The presence of third-party payers differentiates the health care industry from most other industries. Health care providers are not faced with an array of individual buyers whose payment patterns are stable statistically. Instead, individual clients are clustered into many payment sources. These sources are often subject to abrupt policy shifts, such as elimination of prospective interim payments for Medicare or funding delays and reductions for some state Medicaid programs.

A cash flow model is an integral part of an institution's cash management system. The model should incorporate scheduled and budgeted disbursements, a statistical pattern of receipts from patients and third-party payers, investment income, and projected account balances. Moreover, it must be able to respond to changes in payment policies of third-party payment sources.

COMPONENTS OF A CASH MANAGEMENT SYSTEM

Disbursements and Disbursement Control

Recurring and Scheduled Payments

Many types of expenses are known far in advance and can be scheduled for payment. Examples of such expenses are lease payments, maintenance contracts, interest and principal payments, and insurance installments. Certain other types of expenses are highly predictable and will vary only slightly from initial budgets or current projections. The best examples of these expenses are payroll and payroll-related items (taxes and benefits), which may comprise as much as 60 percent of total hospital expenses.

Many other expenses can be budgeted and known with certainty only when invoices have been received. These expense categories include such items as utilities, legal fees, supplies, and recruiting and travel expense. It is important to note that the magnitude and timing of these expenses become quite certain over a short planning horizon and are known with certainty upon receipt (and approval) of an invoice.

Ideally, an accounts payable system will provide most of the data required for the disbursement component of a cash flow modeling system. Recurring payments should be scheduled and approved invoices should also be given a date for payment. Over a short—say two-week—horizon, almost every disbursement should appear as a scheduled payment from the accounts payable system. Over a longer planning horizon, estimated payments based on updated budget figures would be used in the model.

Disbursement Strategies

Float represents the difference between a firm's book balance and its bank (collected) balance. It arises when a check is written to a supplier, for example, and is not immediately presented for payment from the issuing company's account. In fact, there generally will be a delay of several days because of the time required for the check to reach the supplier's bank (mail float) and the time required to clear the check through the Federal Reserve System (bank float). While the issuing firm will have credited its cash account when it disburses the check, it will actually have the use of the money for several days, until the check reaches the issuer's bank.

Strategies to maximize the net float available to a corporation should be part of every firm's cash management system. Techniques for increasing the bank float, such as remote disbursement systems and accelerating cash collections through lock box systems, are well known and readily susceptible to cost-benefit analysis. The estimation and management of float are facilitated by a cash flow modeling system. Once

lags have been estimated, alternative disbursement schedules can be developed and tested. The net float made available through these techniques can then be invested at a somewhat higher yield than might otherwise be possible.

Receipts

Many of the model building and statistical techniques of cash flow modeling have been developed to predict cash receipts to an organization. This is appropriate since, while disbursements generally follow an expense budget and can be controlled through the accounts payable system, accounts receivable represent services provided to a large number of disparate individuals and organizations. Payment patterns, therefore, may appear to take on a random character.

A variety of forecasting techniques have been employed to predict cash receipts. Generally, these fall into the following four categories:

1. subjective forecasts
2. econometric models
3. ad hoc forecasts
4. time series techniques

Subjective Forecasts

The value of these "seat-of-the-pants" projections should not be overlooked. Frequently the intuition of an experienced manager incorporates many of the factors that sophisticated statistical techniques try to capture. In many cases, such as an impending policy shift on the part of a major payer, a subjective forecast is more accurate since it does not depend explicitly on historical data. Of course, subjective forecasts should be compared with actual outcomes to see whether the forecaster has superior insight.

Econometric Models

The most familiar example of an econometric model is linear regression analysis. Methodologies have been developed to relate a dependent variable to one or more independent variables. This estimated relationship can then be used to predict the dependent variable based on predicted values for the independent variables. As a byproduct of the analysis, explicit estimates of the uncertainty of the forecast are obtained.

Although econometric models, and especially linear regression, are readily available to potential users, some care must be employed in their interpretation. First, the resultant formulas represent an estimate of some model that has been assumed to describe an underlying process. To the extent that the process has been mis-specified by the model, the formulas may not be an accurate description of the process and any forecasts derived from the formulas may be suspect. One needs to assess the reasonability of any model developed by purely statistical techniques.

Second, estimated regression models are based on historical data. While model equations can be developed from a relatively small set of data points, forecasts from such estimates will be more uncertain than if a large data base is employed. Furthermore, when an econometric model is developed, there is an underlying assumption that the relationships in the data base are stable. While there are techniques to compensate for structural changes in the historical data, one must be certain that they have been incorporated properly into the model. Given the rapid, recent changes in health care, this is particularly important in modeling patient receipts.

Third, using an econometric model to predict a dependent variable depends on using forecasts of the independent variables. If these forecasts are incorrect, the outcome of the model will be incorrect as well. Also, because econometric models are developed on a computer, there is a tendency to accept predicted values at their face value, without properly assessing other aspects of the model. Thus, a forecast of patient receipts over the next 12 months, for example, should not be accepted as a series of 12 values. Rather, it is a forecast of 12 ranges of values that become more dispersed and less certain over the forecast horizon.

Ad Hoc Forecasts

This category of forecasting techniques generally attempts to predict future values of a series of values, such as patient receipts, from their historical values. The most prominent of these models is exponential smoothing, which is basically an exponentially weighted moving average. Exponential smoothing models are fit to historical data by adjusting a number of parameters representing the "true" value, trend factors, and seasonal adjustments. By selecting the weighting factors appropriately, an exponential smoothing model can conform itself quickly to changes in the underlying process and fit the historical data quite well.

In applying an exponential smoothing model to make a forecast, however, one should be aware of several factors. First, estimating an exponential smoothing model requires quite a bit of historical data and, in general, several years are needed. In order to use exponential smoothing to predict daily cash receipts, many data points need to be gathered and processed.

Second, when the model is used to make a forecast, there is an implicit assumption that the underlying circumstances will be essentially the same in the future as they were in the historical estimation period. Finally, the model may forecast well in the near term, but, as with any forecast, future values become increasingly uncertain as the forecast horizon is expanded.

Time Series Techniques

This type of forecast uses a historical series of data to estimate a model for future values. The underlying assumption is that the actual values of the time series are an accurate manifestation of the underlying process. This is in contrast to an econometric model, which attempts to estimate the relationships for the underlying process itself. The most sophisticated time series techniques are referred to as "Box-Jenkins" models. These models are state-of-the-art but require considerable historical data to estimate, employ complicated computer algorithms, and, in making forecasts, rely on the assumption that the future will be similar to the past.

Decay Curve Analysis

Perhaps the most common way to develop forecasts of patient receipts is through the use of decay curves. These curves relate future collections to past billings and express the receipts as a

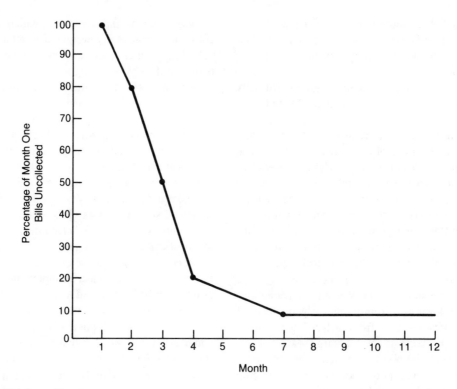

Figure 17-1 Decay Curve

percentage of prior billings. For example, 20 percent of billings may be paid within 30 days, 50 percent within 60 days, 80 percent within 90 days, and 95 percent within 120 days; the balance may be collected in the future or eventually become bad debts. Figure 17-1 depicts a sample decay curve.

Decay curve analysis has intuitive appeal, but implementing decay curves to forecast future daily receipts requires substantial data gathering and computation. Since patient bills may be outstanding a year after the initial bill has been sent out, it is necessary to follow the collection patterns of a significant sample of bills mailed on a given day throughout the course of an entire year. This must be repeated for daily billings over a substantial time period. Furthermore, in specifying the model it must be decided whether all payers—individual as well as third-party—should be aggregated or whether several classes of payers should be estimated separately.

Forecasts of daily receipts over some chosen horizon will depend on bills from previous days

together with projected billings in the immediate future. To see this, consider making a forecast of daily receipts over the next 60 days. Many of these receipts will be attributable to bills sent out over the preceding several months, but many others will come from bills mailed out over the next 60 days. It is apparent, therefore, that if the decay curve has been estimated with accuracy, near-term forecasts of daily receipts will be equally accurate, depending as they do on actual historical data. Needless to say, to ensure the continuing validity of a decay curve model, it must be re-estimated periodically.

Investments

An outcome of the cash flow modeling process is a forecast of daily net cash flows. Starting with the cash and investment balances at the beginning of the forecast period, one can determine how much cash the institution will have beyond its basic needs at any point in time.

These funds are available for investment until they are needed for operations or to be employed in a capital development program.

A carefully developed cash forecast will provide some confidence as to when cash will need to be available. From this forecast, it is possible to invest in securities that will mature when the cash is needed. The more accurate the forecast of cash requirements, the higher the yield on investments can be. For example, if the scheduled maturity of an investment were to occur before cash is actually required, then the investment would likely need to be rolled over into a short-term instrument, such as a money market fund, which probably will have a lower yield than the security that was redeemed. In the same way, if cash is required before a scheduled maturity, then the investment would have to be liquidated prematurely, again at a sacrifice in yield.

A conservative investment strategy, which avoids the risks outlined above, is to invest continually in the shortest-term investments possible; then cash will always be available to meet both operating and capital requirements, and there will never be a need to liquidate an investment prior to maturity. However, according to the usual structure of the yield curve (Figure 17-2), yields on investments increase with the time to their maturities. Thus, this conservative strategy sacrifices a great deal of potential investment income.

Rather than continually rolling over short-term money market funds, an investment manager could invest in government securities, such as treasury bills and notes; federal agency securities, including securities issued by the Federal National Mortgage Association (Fannie Mae) and the Government National Mortgage Association (Ginnie Mae); or in certificates of deposit issued by a credit-worthy bank. These instruments should satisfy the investment policy criteria of nearly every health care institution and provide greater returns than money market funds.

Reports

Many departments must cooperate to make a cash flow modeling system work properly. Timely information is required regarding accounts payable, accounts receivable, and current investments. Each of the departments responsible for these areas will have detailed reports for their own information and control purposes. However, a summary report should be available to the chief financial officer on a daily basis. An example of such a report is provided in Exhibit 17-1.

Information contained in the report consists of daily cash reports for a six-day period—the preceding business day through the four days following today's date. There is also a weekly projection for each of the next four weeks. Such reports can be adapted to the particular needs and operating style of an individual organization.

TYING THE SYSTEM TOGETHER

A cash flow modeling system interacts with many levels of an organization. It incorporates many matters of policy in developing its assumptions and, based on the outputs of the model, can help to refine those policies. At an operational level the system integrates information from many areas, requires access to substantial data-processing resources, and must be simple and accessible to its users so that simulation analysis can be conducted on a fairly routine basis.

As we have seen, the cash flow modeling system helps to determine how much cash can be diverted from the operating accounts into investments. In fact, this is often a policy decision and depends on what level of operating cash is desired to be maintained as a "safety stock." By analogy with traditional inventory theory, the

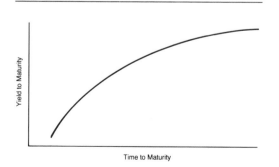

Figure 17-2 Yield Curve, Term Structure of Interest Rates

Exhibit 17-1 Daily Cash and Investment Report Summary (Dollars in Thousands): Friday, July 1, 1988

	Thursday 6/30/88	Friday 7/01/88	Tuesday 7/05/88	Wednesday 7/06/88	Thursday 7/07/88	Friday 7/08/88
Beginning Cash	$950	$965	$823	$768	$946	$818
Scheduled Sale of Investments	193	1,356	484	482	3,104	289
Total Cash Available	$1,143	$2,321	$1,307	$1,250	$4,050	$1,107
Operating Cash Requirements	178	(102)	(261)	(296)	(268)	(166)
Surplus (Deficit)	$965	$2,423	$1,568	$1,546	$4,318	$1,273
Scheduled Purchase of Investments		1,600	800	600	3,500	400
Ending Cash	$965	$823	$768	$946	$818	$873

	Week Ending 7/08/88	Week Ending 7/15/88	Week Ending 7/22/88	Week Ending 7/29/88
Beginning Cash	$823	$873	$889	$1,044
Scheduled Sale of Investments	4,359	4,011	6,136	3,168
Total Cash Available	$5,182	$4,884	$7,025	$4,212
Operating Cash Requirements	(991)	(205)	(1,219)	(195)
Surplus (Deficit)	$6,173	$5,089	$8,244	$4,407
Scheduled Purchase of Investments	5,300	4,200	7,200	3,500
Ending Cash	$873	$889	$1,044	$907

larger a safety stock required, the more uncertainty there is about future demands for cash. One of the benefits of a cash modeling system is that uncertainty can be reduced. This permits an institution to free up additional cash for investment at higher yields and improves overall financial performance.

In developing and implementing a cash modeling system a great deal of analysis will be performed on an institution's accounts receivable and accounts payable. As an example, it is likely that a seasonal pattern will emerge in accounts receivable, so that at certain times of the year bills may be paid more slowly than at others. The effect of this information is twofold: (1) seasonal fluctuations in common measures, such as days' sales outstanding, of accounts receivable can be anticipated and (2) the cash requirements that this may impose on the institution will be automatically incorporated into the cash flow model.

In a similar way, having access to a cash flow modeling system will enable experimentation with alternative disbursement strategies, so that accounts payable, by concentrating or spreading out disbursements, can increase the float available to the institution. Hence, the cash required to be maintained in operating balances will be reduced.

The actual implementation of a cash flow modeling system will require that an appropriate model—or models—be chosen to represent cash inflows and outflows. In practice, a number of forecasting techniques, selected from the categories described above, will be tried. Considerable creativity and experimentation are required to find the best model(s), and having access to computer-based statistical software is extremely important.

A cash flow modeling system requires the accumulation and analysis of a great deal of data. This is particularly important in developing and testing forecasting techniques. The ability to retrieve data from the institution's central computer data bases in a flexible format would help develop a robust and accurate model.

Finally, among the criteria for a successful implementation of a cash flow modeling system are that it not require the user to maintain a large and complex data base and that it encourage simulation and experimentation. Most of the models for making forecasts of future cash flows rely on relatively few parameters and data once they have been set up, so they meet the first criterion. As microcomputers have become more sophisticated in recent years, they are capable of running high-performance software. Moreover, their users have become increasingly accustomed to interacting with them. The ideal cash flow modeling system, therefore, will be used on a microcomputer, which would be able to accept data from the institution's central computer data bases.

SUMMARY

A cash flow modeling system is extremely valuable in conducting effective corporate cash management. It enables the corporation to monitor and predict operating cash needs with a greater degree of certainty than is possible with naive manual systems. While a great deal of resources will likely be involved in implementing a sophisticated cash modeling tool, the increasing accessibility of central computer data bases will alleviate much of the burden of gathering data. To be effective, a cash flow modeling system must encourage simulation and experimentation and should be updated at regular intervals, as its underlying structure and external environment change.

Chapter 18

Capital Budgeting

William O. Cleverley
Professor, Graduate Program in Hospital and Health Services Management
The Ohio State University

Capital budgeting falls in the programming phase of the management control process. Whereas zero-base budgeting or zero-base review can be thought of as the programming phase of management control concerned with old or existing programs, capital project analysis is the phase primarily concerned with new programs. Here, it is broadly defined to include the selection of investment projects.

Capital budgeting is an ongoing activity, but it is not usually summarized annually in the budget. The capital budget is the yearly estimate of resources that will be expended for new programs during the coming year. Capital budgeting may be thought of as less comprehensive and shorter-term than capital project analysis.

PARTICIPANTS IN THE ANALYTIC PROCESS

The capital decision-making process in the health care industry is complex for several reasons. First, the stated goals and objectives of a health care facility are likely to be more complex and less quantifiable than those of a for-profit firm in which profit is the major, if not exclusive,

This chapter is reprinted from *Topics in Health Care Financing*, Vol. 5, No. 4, Aspen Publishers, Inc., © Summer 1979.

goal. Second, the number of individuals involved in the process, either directly or indirectly, is likely to be greater in the health care industry than in most other industries. Figure 18-1 illustrates the relationships of various parties involved in the capital decision-making process of a health care facility.

External Participants

Financing Sources

The availability of external funding for many new programs is an important variable in the capital decision-making process. A variety of individual organizations are involved in the credit determination process, including investment bankers, bond rating agencies, bankers, and feasibility consultants. Many of these entities and their roles are discussed in Chapter 40. At this juncture, it is important to recognize that, collectively, these entities may influence the amount of money that can be borrowed and the terms of the borrowing and this can affect the nature and size of capital projects undertaken by a given health care facility.

Rate-Setting and Rate-Control Agencies

Many states have agencies that set and control the rates hospitals and other health care facilities can charge for services. The influence exerted by

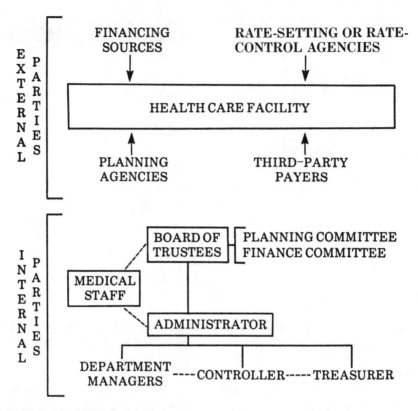

Figure 18-1 Capital Decision-Making Participants

rate-setting or rate-control organizations on capital decision making is indirect but is still extremely important. Control of rates can limit both short-term and long-term profitability. This control can reduce a health care facility's ability to repay indebtedness and thus limit its access to the capital markets. More directly, rate-setting organizations can limit the amount of money available for financing capital projects by reducing the amount of profits that may be retained. One of the major effects of rate control is to reduce significantly the level of capital expenditures by hospitals.

Third-Party Payers

Like rate-setting and rate-control agencies, third-party payers can indirectly influence the capital decision-making process. Through their reimbursement provisions, third-party payers can affect both capital expenditure levels and sources of financing. For example, many individuals feel that third-party cost reimbursement

provides a strong incentive for increased capital spending: in most situations, such cost reimbursement provides for the reimbursement of depreciation and interest expense, which may then be used to repay financial requirements associated with any indebtedness. As a result, the risk associated with hospital indebtedness is reduced. In the past, third-party cost reimbursement has favorably affected the availability of credit. Conversely, recent departures from cost reimbursement have had an adverse impact on credit availability.

Planning Agencies

In most states, state approval of capital expenditures is still required. In some areas, planning agencies at the local level initially review certificate of need applications. Their recommendations are then passed on to the state authority responsible for final approval or disapproval. An unfavorable decision by the state can be appealed in court.

Internal Participants

Board of Trustees

Ultimately, the board of trustees is responsible for the capital expenditure and capital financing program of the health care facility. However, in most situations, the board delegates this authority to management and special board committees. The board's major function should be to establish clearly defined goals and objectives. The statement of goals and objectives is a prerequisite to the programming phase of management control, which includes capital expenditure analysis. Without a clear statement of goals and objectives, capital expenditure programs cannot be adequately defined and analyzed.

Planning Committee

Many health care facility boards of trustees have established planning committees whose primary function is to define, analyze, and propose programs to help the organization attain its goals and objectives. These committees are specialized groups, within the board of trustees, that are directly involved in capital expenditure analysis.

Finance Committee

Some boards of trustees have also established finance committees that have authority in several key financial functional areas, including budgeting and capital financing. In the latter two areas, a finance committee may be involved with translating programs, perhaps identified by the planning committee, into financing requirements. These requirements may be operational or capital. The ensuring of adequate financing to meet program requirements is the financial committee's major responsibility. Many of the finance committee's budgetary functions are delegated to the controller and many of its capital financing functions to the treasurer.

Administration

The administration is responsible on a day-to-day basis for implementing approved capital expenditure programs and developing related financing plans. The administration must develop an organizational system that responds to the requests of department managers and medical staff for capital expenditures. Much of the authority vested in the administrator's position is delegated by the board of trustees. The administration may also seek board approval for its own programs.

Department Managers

Department managers make most of the internal requests for capital expenditure approval. In many health care facilities, formal systems for approving capital expenditures have been developed to receive, process, and answer departmental requests. The allocation of a limited capital budget to competing departmental areas is a difficult task for management. Careful definition of the criteria for capital decision making can help make this problem less political and more objective.

Medical Staff

Medical staff demands for capital expenditures are a problem unique to the health care industry. Medical staff members, in most situations, are not employees of the health care facility but rather use it to treat their private patients. Because of their ability to change a facility's use patterns dramatically and thus affect financial solvency, administrators listen to, and frequently honor, their wishes. Health care facilities are thus faced with strong pressure from individuals who have little financial interest in their organization and whose financial interest may in fact be contrary to that of the health care facility.

Controller

The controller facilitates capital expenditure approval. The controller is usually responsible for developing capital expenditure request forms and for assisting department managers in preparing their capital expenditure proposals. The controller usually serves as an analyst, assisting the administrator in allocating the budget to competing departmental areas. In many small health care facilities, the controller's function may be merged with that of the treasurer.

Treasurer

The treasurer is responsible for obtaining funds for both short- and long-term programs. The treasurer may work with the financial committee to negotiate for funds necessary to implement approved programs.

CLASSIFICATION OF CAPITAL EXPENDITURES

A capital expenditure is a commitment of resources that is expected to provide benefits over a reasonably long period of time, at least two or more years. Any system of management control must take into account the various types of capital expenditure. Different types raise different problems; they may require specific individuals to evaluate them or special methods of evaluation.

The more important classifications of capital expenditures are

- time period over which the investment occurs
- types of resources invested
- dollar amounts of capital expenditures
- types of benefits received

Time Period of Investment

Determining the amount of resources committed to a capital project depends heavily upon the definition of the time period. For example, how would you determine the capital expenditures needed by a project that had a very low initial investment cost but a significant investment cost in future years? Should just the initial capital expenditure be considered, or should total expenditures over the life of the project be considered? If the latter is the answer, is it appropriate just to add the total expenditures together, or should expenditures made in later years be weighted to reflect their lower present value? If so, at what discount rate? These are not simple questions to answer, but they are very important in evaluating capital projects.

A classic example of this type of problem in the health care industry is the initiation of pro-

grams that have been funded by grants. In many such situations, there appears to be little or no investment of capital expenditure, since the amounts are funded almost totally through the grants. The programs thus appear to be highly desirable. However, if there is a formal or informal commitment to continue the programs for a longer period of time, capital expenditures and additional operating funds for later periods may be required. In such cases, it is imperative that the grant-funded projects be classified separately and their long-run capital cost requirements be identified. The health care facility may very well not have a sufficient capital base to finance a program's continuation. Thus, granting agencies should assess the health care facility's financial capability to continue funded programs after the grant period expires.

Types of Resources Invested

When discussing capital expenditures, many individuals are apt to limit their attention to just the expenditure or resources invested in capital assets, that is, tangible fixed assets. This narrow focus has several shortcomings, however, and may result in ineffective capital expenditure decisions.

First, focusing on tangible fixed assets implies ownership, yet many health care facilities lease a significant percentage of their fixed assets, especially in the major movable equipment area. If a lease is not construed to be a capital expenditure, it may escape the normal review and approval system, that is, with regard to both the internal review and approval process and the review and approval process of a health system's agency. Lease payments should be considered as a capital expenditure. Furthermore, the contractual provisions of the lease should be considered in determining the total expenditure amount. Weight should be given to future payments or to the alternative purchase price of the asset.

Second, the capital costs of a capital expenditure are only one part of total cost; indeed, in the labor-intensive health care industry, capital costs may be just the tip of the iceberg. All of the operating costs associated with beginning and continuing a capital project should be considered. Programs with very low capital investment costs may not look as good when their operating costs are considered.

Life cycle costing is a method for estimating the cost of a capital project that reflects total costs, both operating and capital, over the project's estimated useful life. The life cycle cost of all contemplated programs should be considered—failure to do this can cause errors in the capital decision-making process, especially in the selection of alternative programs. Consider, for example, two alternative renal dialysis projects; both may have the same capacity, but one may have a significantly greater investment cost because it uses equipment requiring less monitoring and lower operating costs. Failure to consider the operating cost differences between these two projects may bias the decision in favor of the project with lower capital expenditures, and result in higher expenses in the long run.

Amount of the Expenditure

Different systems of control and evaluation are required for different-sized projects. It would not be economical to spend $500 in administrative time evaluating the purchase of a $100 calculator nor would it be wise to spend only $500 to evaluate a $25 million building program. Obviously control over capital expenditures should be conditioned by the total amount involved; and, if appropriate, the amount should be based on the total life cycle cost.

Controlling capital expenditures in most organizations, including health care facilities, typically follows one of three patterns:

1. approval required for all dollar-sized capital expenditures
2. approval required for all dollar-sized capital expenditures above a pre-established limit
3. no approval required for individual capital expenditure projects below a total budgeted amount

Retaining final approval of all capital expenditures lets management exert maximum control over the resource spending area. However, the cost of management time to develop and review expenditure proposals is high. In most organizations of any size, management review of all capital expenditure requests is not productive. However, some review is needed, so a limit must be established. For example, a given responsibility center or department need not submit any justification for individual capital expenditure projects requiring less than $200 in investment cost. In such cases, there is usually some formal or informal limitation on the total dollar size of the capital budget that will be available for small dollar capital expenditures. This prevents responsibility center managers from making excessive investments in capital expenditures that have no formalized reviewing system.

Another form of management control over capital expenditures is an absolute dollar limit; that is, any responsibility center manager may spend up to an authorized capital budget on any items in question. The real negotiation involves determining the size of the capital budget that will be available for individual departments. However, this system, while least costly in terms of review time, does not ensure that the capital expenditures actually made are necessarily in the best interests of the organization.

Types of Benefits

Depending upon the types of benefits envisioned for a capital expenditure, different systems of management control and evaluation may be necessary. For example, investment in a medical office building brings different benefits than investment in an alcoholic rehabilitation unit. Such differences make it inappropriate to rely exclusively on any one method of evaluating projects. This is important: *traditional methods of evaluating capital budgeting may not be appropriate in the health care industry*. Traditional methods evaluate only the financial aspects of a capital expenditure. However, projects in the health care industry may produce benefits that are far more important than a reduction in cost or an increase in profit.

The major categories of investment in which benefits may be differentially evaluated are

- operational continuance
- financial
- other

The first category of investment produces benefits that permit continuance of operations of the facility along present lines. Here, the governing board or management must usually make two decisions: (1) Are continued operations in the present form desirable? (In most cases the answer is affirmative.) (2) Which alternative investment project can achieve continued operations in the most desirable way (for example, with lowest cost, patient safety, and so on)? A classic example of this type of investment is one based on a licensure requirement for installation of a sprinkler system in a nursing home. Failure to make the investment may imply discontinuance of operations.

The second category of investment provides benefits that are largely financial, in terms of either reduced cost or increased profits to the organization. Many individuals may believe that these two are identical; that is, that reduced costs imply increased profits. However, as we will see, this may not be true if cost reimbursement for either operating or capital costs is present. The important point to remember is that if the major benefits are financial, traditional capital budgeting methods may be more appropriate.

The third category of investments is a catch-all category. Investments here would range from projects that activate major new medical areas, like outpatient or mental health services, to projects that improve employee working conditions, like employee gymnasiums. In this category, benefits may be harder to quantify and evaluate. Traditional capital budgeting methods may thus be appropriate only in the selection of least costly ways to provide designated services.

THE CAPITAL PROJECT DECISION-MAKING PROCESS

Making decisions on which capital projects will be undertaken is not an easy task. In many respects, this may represent the most difficult and important management decision area. The allocation of limited resources to specific project

areas will directly affect the efficiency and effectiveness, and ultimately the continued viability, of the organization.

For our purposes we can divide the capital decision-making process into four inter-related activities or stages:

1. generation of project information
2. evaluation of projects
3. decisions about which projects to fund
4. project implementation and reporting

Generation of Project Information

In this stage of the decision-making process, information is gathered that can later be analyzed and evaluated. This is an extremely important stage because inadequate or inaccurate information can lead to bad decision making. Specifically, there are six major categories of information that should be included in most capital expenditure proposals:

1. information on alternatives available
2. information on resources available
3. cost data
4. benefit data
5. data regarding prior performance
6. risk projection information

Alternatives Available

A major deficiency in many capital expenditure decisions is the failure to consider possible alternatives. Too many times, capital expenditures are presented on a "take it or leave it" basis; yet there usually are alternatives. For example, different manufacturers might be selected, different methods of financing could be used, or different boundaries in the scope of the project could be defined.

Resources Available

Capital expenditure decisions are not made in a vacuum. In most situations, there are constraints on the amount of available funding. This is the whole rationale behind capital expenditure decision making: Scarce resources must be allocated among a virtually unlimited number of investment opportunities. There is little question about the necessity of information concerning the availability of funding at the top level of management. However, there is some question about its importance at the departmental level. On one hand, a budgetary constraint may temper requests for capital expenditures. On the other hand, it may encourage a department manager to submit only those projects that are in the department's best interests. These may, in fact, conflict with the broader goals and objectives of the organization as a whole.

Cost Data

It goes without saying that cost information is an important variable in the decision-making process. In all cases, the life cycle costs of a project should be presented. Limiting cost information just to capital costs can be counterproductive.

Benefit Data

We can divide benefit data into two categories: quantitative and nonquantitative. It is believed by some that much of the benefit data in the health care industry is nonquantitative. To a large extent, quantitative data are viewed as synonymous with financial data. Since financial criteria are sometimes viewed as less important in the nonprofit health care industry, the assumption is that quantitative data are also less important. This is not true. Quantitative data can and should be used: Effective management control is predicated upon the use of numbers that relate to the organization's stated goals and objectives. It may not be easy to develop quantitative estimates of benefits, but it is not impossible. For example, assume that a hospital in an urban area opens a clinic in a medically underserved area. One of the stated goals for the clinic is the reduction of unnecessary use of the hospital's emergency room for nonurgent care. A realistic and quantifiable benefit of this project should be a numerical reduction in the use of the hospital's emergency room for nonurgent care by individuals from the clinic area. However, no quantitative assessments are either projected or reported; the only quantitative statistics used are those of a financial nature. The management control process in this situation is less valuable than it should have been.

Prior Performance

Information on prior operating results of projects proposed by responsibility center managers can be useful. A comparison of prior, actual results with forecast results can give a decision maker some idea of the manager's reliability in forecasting. In too many cases, project planners are likely to overstate a project's benefits if the project interests them. Review of prior performance can help a manager evaluate the accuracy of the projections.

Risk Projections

Nothing is certain in this world except death and taxes, especially when evaluating capital expenditure projects. It is important to ask "what if" questions. For example, how would costs and benefits change if volume changed? Volume of service is a key variable in most capital expenditure forecasts, and its effects should be understood. In some situations requiring projections for the highest, the lowest, and the most likely, projections of volume can help answer the questions. The same types of calculations can be made for other key factors, such as prices of key inputs and technological changes. This is an important area to understand because some capital expenditure projects are inherently more risky than others. Specifically, programs with extremely high proportions of fixed or sunk costs are far more sensitive to changes in volume than those with low percentages of fixed or sunk costs.

Evaluation of Projects

Although financial criteria are clearly not the only factors that should be evaluated in capital expenditure decisions, there are few, if any, capital expenditure decisions that can omit financial considerations. Our focus is on two prime financial criteria: solvency and cost.

Solvency

A project that cannot show a positive rate of return in the long run should be questioned. If implemented, such a program will need to be subsidized by some other existing program area. For example, should a hospital subsidize an outpatient clinic? If so, to what extent? This is the kind of policy and *financial* question the governing board of the organization needs to determine. The fairness of some patients subsidizing other patients is one of the basic qualitative issues in capital project analysis. Operation of an insolvent program can eventually threaten the solvency of the entire organization. Thus, organizations that plan to subsidize insolvent programs must be in good financial condition. Assessment of financial condition can only be done after the organization's financial statements are examined.

Cost

Cost is the second important financial concern. An organization needs to select the projects that contribute most to the attainment of its objectives, given resource constraints. This type of analysis is often called cost-benefit analysis. Benefits differ from project to project. In evaluating alternative programs, decision makers must weight those benefits according to their own preferences and then compare them with cost.

There is a second dimension to the cost criterion. All projects that are eventually selected should cost the least to provide the service. This type of evaluation is sometimes called cost-effectiveness analysis. Least cost should be defined as the present value of both operating and capital costs (methods for determining this are discussed later in the chapter).

Decisions about Which Projects To Fund

At this juncture of the capital expenditure decision-making process, it is time to make the decisions. In front of the decision makers is a list of possible projects that may be funded. Each project should represent the lowest cost of providing the desired service or output. In addition, various benefit data on each project should be described. These data should be consistent with the criteria that the decision makers used in their capital expenditure decision making.

To illustrate this process, assume that the governing board is deciding on how many, if any, of three proposed programs it will fund in the coming year. The three programs are a burn care unit, a hemodialysis unit, and a commercial laboratory. Assume further that the governing board has decided that there are only four criteria of importance to it:

1. solvency
2. incremental management time required
3. public image
4. medical staff approval

Since none of the three projects clearly dominates, it is not clear which, if any, should be funded. Thus, the decision makers must weight the criteria according to their own preferences and determine the overall ranking of the three projects. For example, one manager might weight solvency and management time very high, relative to public image and medical staff, and might thus select the commercial laboratory project. Another manager might weight medical staff and public image more heavily and thus select the hemodialysis or burn care unit project.

In the following example, the three projects can be ranked in terms of their relative standing on each of the four criteria.

	Project		
	Hemodialysis Unit	Burn Care Unit	Commercial Laboratory
Criteria			
Solvency	2	3	1
Management time	2	3	1
Public image	2	1	3
Medical staff	1	2	3

Project Implementation and Reporting

Most capital expenditure control systems are concerned primarily, if not exclusively, with analysis and evaluation prior to selection. However, a very real concern should be focused on whether the projected benefits are actually being realized as forecast. Without this feedback on the actual results of prior investments, the capital expenditure control system's feedback loop is not complete.

Here are some of the specific advantages of establishing a capital expenditure review program:

- Capital expenditure review could highlight differences between planned versus actual performance that may permit corrective action. If actual performance is never evaluated, corrective action may not be taken. This could mean that the projected benefits might never be realized.
- Use of a review process may result in more accurate estimates. If individuals realize that they will be held responsible for their estimates, they may tend to be more careful with their projections. This will ensure greater accuracy in forecast results.
- Forecasts by individuals with a continuous record of biased forecasts can be adjusted to reflect that bias. This should result in a better forecast of actual results.

JUSTIFICATION OF CAPITAL EXPENDITURES

In most health care organizations, there is a very formalized process for approval of a capital expenditure. Usually, this approval process is initiated by a department or responsibility center manager through the completion of a capital expenditure approval form. An example of a completed capital expenditure approval form is shown in Exhibit 18-1. Both the approval form and the approval process may vary among health care organizations, depending upon the nature of the management control process in each case.

The approval form in Exhibit 18-1 is in fact more comprehensive than that employed in most health care organizations. Thus, it provides a detailed summarization of the key aspects involved in capital expenditure approval:

- amount and type of expenditure
- attainment of key decision criteria
- detailed financial analysis

In most firms, small capital expenditures are usually not subjected to detailed analysis and do not require justification. For example, capital expenditures under $2,000 are not reviewed according to the instructions in Exhibit 18-1. This does not mean that a department has an unlimited capital expenditures budget if it spends less than $2,000 per item; the department is most likely subject to some overall level for small capital expenditures. For example, a department such as physical therapy might have an $8,000 limit on small capital expenditure items. No justification for capital expenditure items under $2,000 would be required if the aggregate limit of $8,000 is not violated.

Special recognition is also often given to replacement items. In the Exhibit 18-1 example, a replacement expenditure below $20,000 is not subject to review. The rationale for this higher limit relates to the operational continuance of capital expenditures. Replacement expenditures are often viewed as essential to the continuation of existing operations. They are therefore not as closely evaluated as expenditures for new pieces of equipment.

In any decision-making process, it is important to define carefully the criteria that will be used in the selection process. The example in Exhibit 18-1 has three categories of criteria:

1. need (management goals, hospital goals)
2. economic feasibility
3. acceptability (physicians, employees, community)

Most capital expenditure forms would probably ask for data in the area of economic or financial feasibility. The Exhibit 18-1 form provides data in other areas as well, and also includes a means for scoring the project. For the specific project being appraised, a raw score of

Exhibit 18-1 Completed Capital Expenditure Approval Form

APPRAISAL SHEET FOR
CAPITAL EXPENDITURE PROPOSALS

Department and # Surgery #818

Date of request for purchase 1/7/87

Summary description of item or package of items (attach original request for purchase)

IABP Model 10 with cardiac output computer and recorder (Intra Aortic Balloon

Pump)

Total capital expenditure, including training, renovation, and purchase of equipment (attach list) $19,500

Undepreciated value of equipment being replaced   0

  Total cost of implementation $19,500

Appraisal Instructions

Level I—Complete a Level I assessment for:
1. a new item having a total capital expenditure exceeding $2,000, or
2. a replacement item having a total capital expenditure exceeding $20,000, or
3. a proposed capital expenditure requiring an evaluation before a purchase (or lease) decision may be made.

Level II—Complete both a Level I and a Level II assessment for any proposed capital expenditure that:
1. exceeds $100,000, or
2. initiates or modifies the scope or type of health services rendered in the community and may require a certificate of need, or
3. requires a more extensive evaluation than offered by a Level I review.

Appraisal Outcome	By (initials)	Date	Priority Status
Request denied			
Request accepted & pending			
Request approved			

I. Level I Review—Complete the following assessment for any proposed capital expenditure requiring either a Level I or Level II review.

A. Need

1. Indicate whether the proposed capital expenditure contributes *directly* to the achievement of any of the following management goals (check those that apply)

    _____ Revenue

    _____ Hospital improvement study

    _____ Productivity

    ____X____ Quality assurance

    _____ Employee development

    _____ Management services consultant package

    _____ Other goal (specify) _____

2. Indicate whether the proposed capital expenditure contributes *directly* to the achievement of any of the following hospital goals (check one or more goals)

    ____X____ Patient care

    _____ Medical and allied health education

    ____X____ Community service

    _____ Cost containment

    ____X____ The leadership role

    _____ Clinical research

Exhibit 18-1 continued

3. Provide the following information on historical and projected utilization of items for the provision of patient care services. (See the Finance Department for assistance in completing this section.)

    a. For replacement items only:

        (1) Identify units of service, if any, provided through the utilization of existing equipment; the actual volume of services provided during the most recent year for which statistics are available; the current patient charge, if any, for these services; and the annual revenue realized.

Unit of Service	Historical Annual Volume	Patient Charge	Annual Revenue
1.			
2.			
3.			
4.			
Total	Units		$

        (2) Serial # of item _____

        (3) Fixed asset tag # _____

    b. For both new and replacement items:

        (1) Identify the units of service, if any, to be offered through acquisition of the proposed item and the estimated volume of services to be provided annually. If known, provide the proposed patient charge per unit of service.

Unit of Service	Estimated Annual Volume	Proposed Patient Charge
1. Ped. open heart	161	$459.16(Avg)
2.		
3.		
4.		

        (2) Identify any other services whose volume of utilization will be affected through acquisition of the proposed item.

        (3) Percentage of charge patients for department (from cost report) __93.1__

        (4) Estimated useful life of equipment: ____10____ years.

4. Document the reasons justifying the acquisition of the proposed capital expenditure, particularly as they relate to the achievement of hospital, departmental, and management goals and objectives.
We presently borrow General Hospital's Balloon Pumps 3 or 4 times per month. This is a life-saving device. Without it, some patients cannot survive open-heart surgery.

B. Economic feasibility
  1. Estimate any change in the annual operating costs associated with acquisition of this proposed capital expenditure. (See the Finance Department for assistance in completing this section.)

Exhibit 18-1 continued

	Change in Annual Operating Cost
Personnel	_____
Employee Benefits @ 23%	_____
Physician Cost	_____
Materials and Supplies	_____
Maintenance Contracts	_____
Insurance	_____
Other Depreciation	$1,950
Total Change in Annual Operating Cost	$1,950

Provide documentation in support of the above estimates.

2. Financial analysis (to be completed by Finance):

Estimated Cost to Purchase
IAPB Model 10 with Cardiac Output Computer

Cash Expenditure	Cost Reimbursement @ 26%	Net Cash (Disbursed) Received	Present Value @ 6%
$(19,500)	$ 507	$(18,993)	$(17,918)
	507	507	451
	507	507	426
	507	507	402
	507	507	379
	507	507	357
	507	507	337
	507	507	318
	507	507	300
	507	507	283
$(19,500)	$5,070	$(14,430)	$(14,665)
Total present value (cost)			$(14,665)

3. Space analysis:
   a. Change in the number of square feet of space required for item: N/A
   b. Is existing departmental space available for the item?
      (Circle one)   (Yes)   No
      If not, document plan for acquiring additional space.

C. Acceptability

1. Physician impact of the capital expenditure decision:

   a. What is the *scope* of any physician attitude change? (check one)
      _____ 1 No change. (skip to Section C–2)
      ____X____ 2 One or two physicians will be affected.
      _____ 3 The majority of the physicians in a hospital service will be affected.

   b. What is the *intensity* of the effect on physician attitude? (check two answers— one for acceptance and one for nonacceptance)
      Not accepted:
      _____ 4 The physicians affected will move their practices to other hospitals.
      ____X____ 3 The physicians affected will tend to reduce their practices at the hospital.
      _____ 2 The physicians affected, at the very least, will be disgruntled and will tend to discuss in the community and with other physicians the lack of the expenditure or project.

Exhibit 18-1 continued

> _____ 1 The physicians will be aware of the lack of support for the project and will be less likely to believe that the hospital is maintaining a proper level of patient care.
>
> _____ 0 No effect.

Accepted:

> _____ 0 No effect.
>
> _____ 1 The physicians affected will be aware of the expenditure or project and will be satisfied that the hospital is maintaining a high level of patient care.
>
> ___X___ 2 The physicians affected will be very impressed and will tend to discuss the expenditure or project favorably in the community and with other physicians.
>
> _____ 3 The physicians affected will tend to increase their practices moderately in the hospital.
>
> _____ 4 The physicians affected will move their practices to the hospital.

2. Employee impact of the capital expenditure decision:
   What is the effect on the attitude of hospital employees?
   (Check two answers—one for acceptance and one for nonacceptance.)

   Not accepted:

   > _____ 4 Major and widespread negative impact on employee morale and attitude toward the hospital.
   >
   > _____ 3 Widespread disappointment with the hospital and some general negative effect on the hospital's image among employees.
   >
   > ___X___ 2 Negative reaction from a limited group of employees (one or two departments).
   >
   > _____ 1 Limited reaction from a few employees.
   >
   > _____ 0 No effect.

   Accepted:

   > _____ 0 No effect.
   >
   > _____ 1 Limited reaction from a few employees.
   >
   > ___X___ 2 Positive reaction from a limited group of employees (one or two departments).
   >
   > _____ 3 Positive impact on nearly all employees.
   >
   > _____ 4 Major and widespread impact with long-term effect on employee attitude toward the hospital.

3. Community impact of the capital expenditure decision:
   What is the expected community impact?
   (Check the answers below which best describe the expected community impact; check one for acceptance and one for nonacceptance.)

   Not accepted:

   > _____ 4 Intense and widespread negative reaction in the community will result in a severe blow to the hospital's image.
   >
   > ___X___ 3 A widespread negative effect on the hospital's general image and reputation will result.
   >
   > _____ 1 The attitudes of relatively few people will be negatively affected.
   >
   > _____ 0 No effect.

   Accepted:

   > _____ 0 No effect.
   >
   > _____ 1 Relatively few people will be positively affected.
   >
   > _____ 2 Certain groups in the community will be favorably impressed.

Exhibit 18-1 continued

| | X | 3 | A widespread positive effect on the hospital's image and reputation will result. |
| | | 4 | Significant and widespread positive community reaction will contribute significantly to the hospital's general image and reputation. |

APPRAISAL SCORE SHEET FOR
CAPITAL EXPENDITURE PROPOSALS

	Assigned Value	Raw Score	Priority Instructions	Priority Score
A. Need evaluation				
1. If proposal directly contributes to one or more management goals (I–A–1)	+1	+1		
2. If proposal directly contributes to one or more hospital goals (I–A–2)	+1	+1		
(For Level II reviews only)				
3. Performance expectations (II–A–4)				
If negative or questionable	–1			
If positive	+1			
4. If certificate–of–need approval is necessary, but unlikely (II–A–5)	–3	___		___
			Enter positive raw score as	
Subtotal, need raw score		2	priority score.	2
B. Economic Evaluation				
1. If annual operating costs (including depreciation) are reduced (I–B–1–a)	+1			
2. Return on investment (I–B–2–a)				
If greater than 7.5%	+2			
If positive	0			
If negative	–2	–2		
3. If significant additional space is required (I–B–3)	–1			
(For Level II reviews only)				
4. If external financing is required (II–B–1)	–1	___		___
			Enter positive raw score as	
Subtotal, economic raw score		–2	priority score.	

Exhibit 18-1 continued

	Assigned Value	Raw Score	Priority Instructions	Priority Score
C. Acceptability Evaluation				
1. Physician attitude				
a. Scope (enter score for response to question I–C–1–A)	1 to 3	1	If scope score is greater than 2, enter raw score in priority score column.	
b. Intensity (add responses to question I–C–1–b)	0 to 8	5	If raw score exceeds 4, the excess is priority score.	1
2. Employee attitude (add responses to question I–C–2)	0 to 8	4	If raw score exceeds 4, the excess is priority score.	
3. Community attitude (add responses to question I–C–3)	0 to 8	6	If raw score exceeds 4, the excess is priority score.	2
Subtotal, acceptability raw score		16		3
Total Raw Score		16	Total priority score	5

Note: A capital expenditure proposal may be approved, disapproved, or deferred on the basis of an appraisal of the raw scores for need, economy, and acceptability, considered either independently or together. An approved capital expenditure proposal is ranked according to its priority score for future appropriation of capital expenditure funds.

16 and a priority score of 5 resulted. Different values could be obtained by changing the form's measures and their relative weightings.

The important point to recognize is that project selection usually involves the consideration of criteria other than financial. Failure to collect data on the attainment of those additional criteria for specific projects will often lead to more subjectivity in the process. Without such relevant data, individuals may make inferences that are not legitimate.

A key aspect of the capital expenditure approval process is the financial or economic feasibility of the project. In most capital expenditure forms, there is some summary statistic that measures the project's overall financial performance. In general, such measures are usually categorized as either discounted cash flow methods or nondiscounted cash flow methods. In the present discussion, we shall not be concerned with nondiscounted cash flow methods because they are usually regarded as less sophisticated than discounted cash flow methods.

DISCOUNTED CASH FLOW METHODS

In this section, we shall examine three discounted cash flow (DCF) methods that are relatively easy to understand and use:

1. net present value
2. profitability index
3. equivalent annual cost

Before examining these three methods, a word of caution is in order: In our view, the calculation of specific DCF measures is an important, but not a critical, phase of capital expenditure review. We strongly believe that the most important phase in the capital expenditure review process is the generation of quality project information. Specifically, the set of alternatives being considered must include the best ones; it does a firm little good to select the best five projects from a list of ten inferior ones. Beyond that, the validity of the forecast data is critical; small changes in projected volumes, rates, or costs can have profound effects on cash flow. Determination of possible changes in both these parameters is far more important than discussions over the appropriate discount rate or cost of capital.

Each of the above three DCF methods is based on a time value concept of money. Each is useful in evaluating a specific type of capital expenditure or capital financing alternative. Specifically, their areas of application are shown below.

Method of Evaluation	Area of Application
Net present value	Capital financing alternatives
Profitability index	Capital expenditures with financial benefits
Equivalent annual cost	Capital expenditures with nonfinancial benefits

Net Present Value

A net present value analysis is a very useful way to analyze alternative methods of capital financing. In most situations, the objective in such a situation is clear: the commodity being dealt with is money, and it is management's goal to minimize the cost of financing operations. (We shall consider shortly how this goal may conflict with solvency when the effects of cost reimbursement are considered.)

Net present value equals discounted cash inflows less discounted cash outflows. In a comparison of two alternative financing packages, the one with the highest net present value should be selected.

For example, assume that an asset can be financed with a 4-year annual $1,000 lease payment, or can be purchased outright for $2,800. Assume further that the discount rate is 10 percent, which may reflect either the borrowing cost or the investment rate, depending on which alternative is relevant. (We shall discuss the issue of an appropriate discount rate shortly.) The present value cost of the lease is $3,169. This amount is greater than the present value cost of the purchase, $2,800. With no consideration given to cost reimbursement, the purchase alternative is the lowest cost alternative method of financing.

However, for accuracy, the effects of cost reimbursement should be considered. Reimbursement of costs would mean that the facility would be entitled to reimbursement for depreciation if the asset were purchased, or entitled to the rent payment if the asset were leased. (Some third-party cost payers limit reimbursement on leases to depreciation and interest if the lease is treated as an installment purchase.) Assuming that straight-line depreciation is used and that 80 percent of capital expenses are reimbursed by third-party cost payers, the present value of the reimbursed cash inflow (using the discount factor from Appendix 18-A) would be as shown in the example below.

		Annual Reimbursement		Discount Factor		% of Cost Reimbursement		
Present value of reimbursed depreciation	=	$\dfrac{\$2,800}{4}$	×	3.170	×	.80	=	$1,775
Present value of reimbursed lease payments	=	$1,000	×	3.170	×	.80	=	$2,536

If the asset were purchased, the organization would pay out $2,800 immediately. For each of the next 4 years, it would be reimbursed for the noncash expense item of depreciation in the amount of $700 per year ($2,800/4). However, since only 80 percent of the patients are capital cost payers, only $560 per year would be received (.80 × $700). If the asset were leased, the organization would be permitted reimbursement of the lease payment in the amount of $1,000 per year. However, since only 80 percent of the patients are capital cost payers, only $800 (.80 × $1000) would be paid.

The net present value of the above two financing methods for considering cost reimbursement would be as in the following example.

	Present Value of Reimbursement (Cash Inflows)	Present Value of Payments (Cash Outflows)	Net Present Value
Net present value of purchase =	$1,775	− $2,800	= − $1,025
Net present value of lease =	$2,536	− $3,169	= − $633

In this case, cost reimbursement has changed the relative desirability of the two financing alternatives. If the organization's objective is cost minimization, the purchase alternative should be selected, since the present value of costs are lower under this alternative. If, however, the organization is primarily interested in solvency, the effect of cost reimbursement should be considered, and the lease alternative becomes the best financing package.

Profitability Index

The profitability index method of capital project evaluation is of primary importance in cases where the benefits of the projects are mostly financial, for example, a capital project that saves costs or expands revenue with a primary purpose of increased profits. In these situations, there is usually a constraint on the availability of funding. Thus, those projects with the highest rate of return per dollar of capital investment are the best candidates for selection. The profitability index attempts to compare rates of return. The numerator is the net present value of the project, and the denominator is the investment cost:

$$\text{Profitability index} = \frac{\text{Net present value}}{\text{Investment cost}}$$

To illustrate the use of this measure, let us assume that a hospital is considering an investment in a laundry shared with a group of neighboring hospitals. The initial investment cost is $10,000 for the purchase of new equipment and delivery trucks. Savings in operating costs are estimated to be $2,000 per year for the entire ten-year life of the project. If the discount rate is assumed to be 10 percent, the following calculations could be made, ignoring the effect of cost reimbursement and using the discount factors of Appendix 18-A.

$$\text{Present value of operating savings} = \$2,000 \times 6.145$$
$$= \$12,290$$

$$\text{Net present value} = \$12,290 - \$10,000 = \$2,290$$

$$\text{Profitability index} = \frac{\$2,290}{\$10,000} = .229$$

Values for profitability indexes that are greater than zero imply that the project is earning at a rate greater than the discount rate. Given no funding constraints, all projects with profitability indexes greater than zero should be funded. However, in most situations funding constraints do exist, and only a portion of those projects with profitability indexes greater than zero are actually accepted.

The above calculations give no consideration to the effects of cost reimbursement. If we assume that 80 percent of the facility's capital expenses are reimbursed and 20 percent of its operating expenses are reimbursed, then the following additional calculations must be made:

Present value of reimbursed depreciation

$$= \frac{\$10,000}{10} \times 6.145 \times .80 = \$4,916$$

Present value of lost reimbursement from operating savings
$$= \$2,000 \times 6.145 \times .20 = \$2,458$$

Net present value $= \$2,290 + \$4,916 - \$2,458 = \$4,748$

Profitability index $= \dfrac{\$4,748}{\$10,000} = .4748$

The above calculations require some clarification. We are adjusting the initially calculated net present value of $2,290 to reflect the effects of cost reimbursement. Depreciation is the first item to be considered. Since 80 percent of the facility's patients are on capital cost reimbursement formulas, it can expect to receive 80 percent of the annual depreciation charge of $1,000 ($10,000/10) or $800 per year as a reimbursement cash flow. The present value of this stream, $4,916, is added to the initial net present value of $2,290.

The second item to be considered is the operating savings. If the investment is undertaken, the facility can anticipate a yearly savings of $2,000 for the next 10 years. However, that savings will reduce its reimbursable costs by $2,000 annually, which means that 20 percent of that amount, or $400, will be lost annually in reimbursement. The present value of that loss for the 10 years is $2,458, which is subtracted from the initial net present value. The effect of cost reimbursement thus reduces increased costs associated with new programs, but it also reduces the cost savings associated with new programs.

The preceding example illustrates an important financial concept. Because some third-party payers still reimburse actual capital costs, a strong financial incentive exists for investment in projects that reduce operating costs. In the above example, the laundry facility's profitability index increased from .229 to .4748 when the effects of capital and operating cost reimbursement were considered.

Equivalent Annual Cost

Equivalent annual cost is of primary value in the selection of capital projects where alternatives exist. Usually these are capital expenditure projects that are classified as operational continuance or other. (The profitability index measure just discussed is used for projects in which the benefits are primarily financial in nature.)

Equivalent annual cost is the expected average cost, considering both capital and operating cost, over the life of the project. It is calculated by dividing the sum of the present value of operating costs over the life of the project and the present value of the investment cost by the discount factor for an annualized stream of equal payments (as derived from Appendix 18-A):

$$\text{Equivalent annual cost} = \frac{\substack{\text{Present value} \\ \text{of operating cost} + \text{Present value} \\ \text{of investment cost}}}{\text{Present value of annuity}}$$

To illustrate use of this measure, assume that an extended care facility must invest in a sprinkler system to maintain its license. After investigation, two alternatives are identified. One sprinkler system would require a $5,000 investment and an annual maintenance cost of $500 in each year of its estimated 10-year life. An alternative sprinkler system can be purchased for $10,000 and would require only $200 in maintenance cost each year of its estimated 20-year life. Ignoring cost reimbursement and assuming a discount factor of 10 percent, the calculations on the following page can be made.

From this analysis, it can be seen that the $5,000 sprinkler system would produce the lowest equivalent annual cost, $1,314 per year, compared with the $1,375 equivalent annual cost of the $10,000 system.

Two points should be made with respect to this analysis. First, the equivalent annual cost method permits comparison of two alternative projects with different lives. In this case, a 10-year life project was compared with a project with a 20-year life. There is an assumption here that the technology will not change and that in 10 years the relevant alternatives will still be the

Equivalent annual cost of $5,000 sprinkler system:

$$\text{Present value of operating costs} = \$500 \times 6.145 = \$3,073$$
$$\text{Present value of investment} = \$5,000$$

$$\text{Equivalent annual cost} = \frac{\$3,073 + \$5,000}{6.145} = \$1,314$$

Equivalent annual cost of $10,000 sprinkler system:

$$\text{Present value of operating costs} = \$200 \times 8.514 = \$1,703$$
$$\text{Present value of investment} = \$10,000$$

$$\text{Equivalent annual cost} = \frac{\$1,703 + \$10,000}{8.514} = \$1,375$$

two systems being analyzed. However, in situations of estimated rapid technology changes, some subjective weight should be given to projects of shorter duration. In the above example, this is no problem, since the project with the shorter life also has the lowest equivalent annual cost.

Second, equivalent annual cost is not identical to the reported or accounting cost. The annual reported accounting cost for the two alternatives would be the annual depreciation expenses plus the maintenance cost. Thus:

Accounting expense per year ($5,000 sprinker system)

$$= \frac{\$5,000}{10} + \$500 = \$1,000$$

Accounting expense per year ($10,000 sprinkler system)

$$= \frac{\$10,000}{20} + \$200 = \$700$$

Reliance on information like the above that does not incorporate the time value concept of money can produce misleading results, as it does in the above example. The second alternative is not the lowest cost alternative when the cost of capital is included. In this case, the savings of $5,000 in investment cost between the two systems can be used either to generate additional investment income or to reduce outstanding indebtedness. It is assumed that the appropriate discount rate for each of these two alternatives would be 10 percent.

Once again, the effects of cost reimbursement should be considered. In our example, we assume that 50 percent of the extended care facility's capital costs will be reimbursed and 10 percent of its operating costs will be reimbursed. The following adjustments result as calculated in the example given.

Equivalent annual cost of $5,000 sprinkler system:

$$\text{Present value of reimbursed operating costs} = \$500 \times 6.145 \times .10 = \$307.25$$

$$\text{Present value of reimbursed depreciation} = \frac{\$5,000}{10} \times 6.145 \times .50 = \$1,536.25$$

$$\text{Equivalent annual cost} = \$1,314 - \frac{(\$307.25 + \$1,536.25)}{6.145} = \$1,014$$

Equivalent annual cost of $10,000 sprinkler system:

$$\text{Present value of reimbursed operating costs} = \$200 \times 8.514 \times .10 = \$170.25$$

$$\text{Present value of reimbursed depreciation} = \frac{\$10,000}{20} \times 8.514 \times .50 = \$2,128.50$$

$$\text{Equivalent annual cost} = \$1,375 - \frac{(\$170.25 + \$2,128.50)}{8.514} = \$1,105$$

Again, some clarification of the calculations may be useful. To reflect the effect of cost reimbursement, consideration must be given to the reimbursement of reported expenses for the two alternative sprinkler systems. The reported expense items for both sprinkler systems are depreciation and maintenance costs, which are referred to as an operating cost. Depreciation for the $5,000 sprinkler system will be $500 per year ($500/10) and 50 percent of this amount, $250, will be reimbursed each year. The present value of the reimbursed depreciation ($250 × 6.145) is $1,536.25. Using the same procedure, the present value of reimbursed depreciation for the $10,000 sprinkler system is $2,128.50 ($250 × 8.514). In a similar fashion, the maintenance costs for the two sprinkler systems will also be reimbursed. For the $5,000 system, the annual $500 maintenance cost will yield $50 in new reimbursement (.10 × $500) per year. The present value of this reimbursement inflow is $307.25. Using the same calculations for the $10,000 sprinkler system yields a present value of $170.25. The present values of both reimbursed depreciation and maintenance costs are then annualized and subtracted from the initially calculated equivalent annual cost to derive new equivalent annual costs that reflect cost-reimbursement effects.

In this case, cost reimbursement did not change the decision. The lower-cost sprinker system, after consideration of the effects of reimbursement, is still the best alternative. In fact, the relative difference has increased.

SELECTION OF THE DISCOUNT RATE

In the three DCF methods just discussed, to specify the discount rate, we simply selected a number arbitrarily for each of our examples. In an actual case, however, the question of how to select the appropriate discount rate requires careful attention.

Before discussing methods of determining the appropriate discount rate, it may be useful to evaluate the role of the discount rate in project selection. A natural question at this point is: Would an alternative discount rate affect the list of capital projects selected? For example, if we used a discount rate of 10 percent and later learned that 12 percent should have been used, would our list of approved projects change? The answer is maybe. In some cases, alternative values for the discount rate would alter the relative ranking and therefore the desirability of particular projects.

Again, we believe that the definition of the discount rate is an important issue, but not a critical one—especially for health care organizations. This is true for several reasons. First, in the case of health care organizations, the financial criterion is not likely to be the only criterion. Other areas—such as need, quality of care, and teaching—may also be important. Second, a change in the relative ranking of projects is much more likely to result from an accurate forecast of cash flows than it is from an alternative discount rate. Efforts to improve forecasting would appear to be far more important than esoteric discussions over the relevancy of cost-of-capital alternatives.

In this context, we can examine three primary methods for defining a discount rate or the cost of capital for use in a DCF analysis:

1. cost of specific financing source
2. yield achievable on other investments
3. weighted cost of capital

The cost of a specific financing source is sometimes used as the discount rate. Usually, the identified financing source is debt. For example, if a hospital can borrow money at 11 percent in the revenue bond market, that rate would become its cost of capital or discount rate.

Another alternative is to use the yield rate possible on other investments. In many cases, this rate might be equal to the investment yield possible in the firm's security portfolio. For example, if the firm currently earned 13 percent on its security investments, then 13 percent would be its discount rate. This method, based on an opportunity cost concept, is relatively easy to understand.

The last alternative is to use the weighted cost of capital. This is the most widely discussed and used method of defining the discount rate. In its simplest form, it is calculated as:

Cost of capital = (% Debt × Cost of Debt) +

(% Equity × Cost of equity)

The advantage of this method is that it clearly represents the cost of capital to the firm. A major problem with its use, however, is the definition of the cost of equity capital. This is an especially difficult problem for nonprofit firms. How do you define the cost of equity capital? Detailed exploration of this issue and other aspects of discount rate selection are beyond the scope of the present discussion.

Readers who are interested in examining these topics in greater depth are referred to any good introductory finance textbook.

SUMMARY

The capital decision-making process in the health care industry is very complex, involving a great many independent decision makers. In this chapter, we examined the process and focused on methods for evaluating capital projects. Although capital expenditure decisions in the health care industry are not usually decided exclusively on the basis of financial criteria, most health care decision makers regard financial factors as important elements in the process. In that context, the three discounted cash flow methods we have examined can serve as useful tools in capital project analysis for health care facilities.

Appendix 18-A

Financial Mathematics Tables

Table 18-A-1 Future Value of $1.00 Received in *n* Periods

Period	2%	4%	5%	6%	8%	10%
1	1.0200	1.0400	1.0500	1.0600	1.0800	1.1000
2	1.0404	1.0816	1.1025	1.1236	1.1664	1.2100
3	1.0612	1.1249	1.1576	1.1910	1.2597	1.3310
4	1.0824	1.1699	1.2155	1.2625	1.3605	1.4641
5	1.1041	1.2167	1.2763	1.3382	1.4693	1.6105
6	1.1262	1.2653	1.3401	1.4185	1.5869	1.7716
7	1.1487	1.3159	1.4071	1.5036	1.7138	1.9488
8	1.1717	1.3686	1.4775	1.5938	1.8509	2.1436
9	1.1951	1.4233	1.5513	1.6895	1.9990	2.3589
10	1.2190	1.4802	1.6289	1.7908	2.1589	2.5938
11	1.2434	1.5395	1.7103	1.8983	2.3316	2.8532
12	1.2682	1.6010	1.7959	2.0122	2.5182	3.1385
13	1.2936	1.6651	1.8856	2.1329	2.7196	3.4524
14	1.3195	1.7317	1.9799	2.2609	2.9372	3.7976
15	1.3459	1.8009	2.0709	2.3966	3.1722	4.1774
16	1.3728	1.8730	2.1829	2.5404	3.4259	4.5951
17	1.4002	1.9479	2.2920	2.6928	3.7000	5.0545
18	1.4282	2.0258	2.4066	2.8543	3.9960	5.5600
19	1.4568	2.1068	2.5270	3.0256	4.3157	6.1160
20	1.4859	2.1911	2.6533	3.2071	4.6610	6.7276
30	1.8114	3.2434	4.3219	5.7435	10.0627	17.4495
40	2.2080	4.8010	7.0400	10.2857	21.7245	45.2597

Table 18-A-2 Present Value of $1.00 Due in n Periods

Period	4%	6%	8%	10%	12%	14%	16%	18%	20%	22%	24%	26%	28%	30%	40%
1	0.962	0.943	0.926	0.909	0.893	0.877	0.862	0.847	0.833	0.820	0.806	0.794	0.781	0.769	0.714
2	0.925	0.890	0.857	0.826	0.797	0.769	0.743	0.718	0.694	0.672	0.650	0.630	0.610	0.592	0.510
3	0.889	0.840	0.794	0.751	0.712	0.675	0.641	0.609	0.579	0.551	0.524	0.500	0.477	0.455	0.364
4	0.855	0.792	0.735	0.683	0.636	0.592	0.552	0.516	0.482	0.451	0.423	0.397	0.373	0.350	0.260
5	0.822	0.747	0.681	0.621	0.567	0.519	0.476	0.437	0.402	0.370	0.341	0.315	0.291	0.269	0.186
6	0.790	0.705	0.630	0.564	0.507	0.456	0.410	0.370	0.335	0.303	0.275	0.250	0.227	0.207	0.133
7	0.760	0.665	0.583	0.513	0.452	0.400	0.354	0.314	0.279	0.249	0.222	0.198	0.178	0.159	0.095
8	0.731	0.627	0.540	0.467	0.404	0.351	0.305	0.266	0.233	0.204	0.179	0.157	0.139	0.123	0.068
9	0.703	0.592	0.500	0.424	0.361	0.308	0.263	0.225	0.194	0.167	0.144	0.125	0.108	0.094	0.048
10	0.676	0.558	0.463	0.386	0.322	0.270	0.227	0.191	0.162	0.137	0.116	0.099	0.085	0.073	0.035
11	0.650	0.527	0.429	0.350	0.287	0.237	0.195	0.162	0.135	0.112	0.094	0.079	0.066	0.056	0.025
12	0.625	0.497	0.397	0.319	0.257	0.208	0.168	0.137	0.112	0.092	0.076	0.062	0.052	0.043	0.018
13	0.601	0.469	0.368	0.290	0.229	0.182	0.145	0.116	0.093	0.075	0.061	0.050	0.040	0.033	0.013
14	0.577	0.442	0.340	0.263	0.205	0.160	0.125	0.099	0.078	0.062	0.049	0.039	0.032	0.025	0.009
15	0.555	0.417	0.315	0.239	0.183	0.140	0.108	0.084	0.065	0.051	0.040	0.031	0.025	0.020	0.006
16	0.534	0.394	0.292	0.218	0.163	0.123	0.093	0.071	0.054	0.042	0.032	0.025	0.019	0.015	0.005
17	0.513	0.371	0.270	0.198	0.146	0.108	0.080	0.060	0.045	0.034	0.026	0.020	0.015	0.012	0.003
18	0.494	0.350	0.250	0.180	0.130	0.095	0.069	0.051	0.038	0.028	0.021	0.016	0.012	0.009	0.002
19	0.475	0.331	0.232	0.164	0.116	0.083	0.060	0.043	0.031	0.023	0.017	0.012	0.009	0.007	0.002
20	0.456	0.312	0.215	0.149	0.104	0.073	0.051	0.037	0.026	0.019	0.014	0.010	0.007	0.005	0.001
21	0.439	0.294	0.199	0.135	0.093	0.064	0.044	0.031	0.022	0.015	0.011	0.008	0.006	0.004	0.001
22	0.422	0.278	0.184	0.123	0.083	0.056	0.038	0.026	0.018	0.013	0.009	0.006	0.004	0.003	0.001
23	0.406	0.262	0.170	0.112	0.074	0.049	0.033	0.022	0.015	0.010	0.007	0.005	0.003	0.002	
24	0.390	0.247	0.158	0.102	0.066	0.043	0.028	0.019	0.013	0.008	0.006	0.004	0.003	0.002	
25	0.375	0.233	0.146	0.092	0.059	0.038	0.024	0.016	0.010	0.007	0.005	0.003	0.002	0.001	
26	0.361	0.220	0.135	0.084	0.053	0.033	0.021	0.014	0.009	0.006	0.004	0.002	0.002	0.001	
27	0.347	0.207	0.125	0.076	0.047	0.029	0.018	0.011	0.007	0.005	0.003	0.002	0.001	0.001	
28	0.333	0.196	0.116	0.069	0.042	0.026	0.016	0.010	0.006	0.004	0.002	0.002	0.001	0.001	
29	0.321	0.185	0.107	0.063	0.037	0.022	0.014	0.008	0.005	0.003	0.002	0.001	0.001	0.001	
30	0.308	0.174	0.099	0.057	0.033	0.020	0.012	0.007	0.004	0.003	0.002	0.001	0.001	0.001	
40	0.208	0.097	0.046	0.022	0.011	0.005	0.003	0.001	0.001						

Table 18-A-3 Future Value of $1.00 Received Each Period for *n* Periods

Period	2%	4%	5%	6%	8%	10%
1	1.0000	1.0000	1.0000	1.0000	1.0000	1.0000
2	2.0200	2.0400	2.0500	2.0600	2.0800	2.1000
3	3.0604	3.1216	3.1525	3.1836	3.2464	3.3100
4	4.1216	4.2465	4.3101	4.3746	4.5061	4.6410
5	5.2040	5.4163	5.5256	5.6371	5.8666	6.1051
6	6.3081	6.6330	6.8019	6.9753	7.3359	7.7156
7	7.4343	7.8983	8.1420	8.3938	8.9228	9.4872
8	8.5830	9.2142	9.5491	9.8975	10.6366	11.4360
9	9.7546	10.5828	11.0266	11.4913	12.4876	13.5796
10	10.9497	12.0061	12.5779	13.1808	14.4866	15.9376
11	12.1687	13.4864	14.2068	14.9716	16.6455	18.5314
12	13.4121	15.0258	15.9171	16.8699	18.9771	21.3846
13	14.6803	16.6268	17.7130	18.8821	21.4953	24.5231
14	15.9739	18.2919	19.5986	21.0151	24.2149	27.9755
15	17.2934	20.0236	21.5786	23.2760	27.1521	31.7731
16	18.6393	21.8245	23.6575	25.6725	30.3243	35.9503
17	20.0121	23.6975	25.8404	28.2129	33.7502	40.5456
18	21.4123	25.6454	28.1324	30.9057	37.4502	45.6001
19	22.8406	27.6712	30.5390	33.7600	41.4463	51.1601
20	24.2974	29.7781	33.0660	36.7856	45.7620	57.2761
30	40.5681	56.0849	66.4388	79.0582	113.2832	164.4962
40	60.4020	95.0255	120.7998	154.7620	259.0565	442.5974

Table 18-A-4 Present Value of $1.00 Received Each Period for n Periods

Period	4%	6%	8%	10%	12%	14%	16%	18%	20%	22%	24%	25%	26%	28%	30%	40%
1	0.962	0.943	0.926	0.909	0.893	0.877	0.862	0.847	0.833	0.820	0.806	0.800	0.794	0.781	0.769	0.714
2	1.886	1.833	1.783	1.736	1.690	1.647	1.605	1.566	1.528	1.492	1.457	1.440	1.424	1.392	1.361	1.224
3	2.775	2.673	2.577	2.487	2.402	2.322	2.246	2.174	2.106	2.042	1.981	1.952	1.923	1.868	1.816	1.589
4	3.630	3.465	3.312	3.170	3.037	2.914	2.798	2.690	2.589	2.494	2.404	2.362	2.320	2.241	2.166	1.849
5	4.452	4.212	3.993	3.791	3.605	3.433	3.274	3.127	2.991	2.864	2.745	2.689	2.635	2.532	2.436	2.035
6	5.242	4.917	4.623	4.355	4.111	3.889	3.685	3.498	3.326	3.167	3.020	2.951	2.885	2.759	2.643	2.168
7	6.002	5.582	5.206	4.868	4.564	4.288	4.039	3.812	3.605	3.416	3.242	3.161	3.083	2.937	2.802	2.263
8	6.733	6.210	5.747	5.335	4.968	4.639	4.344	4.078	3.837	3.619	3.421	3.329	3.241	3.076	2.925	2.331
9	7.435	6.802	6.247	5.759	5.328	4.946	4.607	4.303	4.031	3.786	3.566	3.463	3.366	3.184	3.019	2.379
10	8.111	7.360	6.710	6.145	5.650	5.216	4.833	4.494	4.192	3.923	3.682	3.571	3.465	3.269	3.092	2.414
11	8.760	7.887	7.139	6.495	5.988	5.453	5.029	4.656	4.327	4.035	3.776	3.656	3.544	3.335	3.147	2.438
12	9.385	8.384	7.536	6.814	6.194	5.660	5.197	4.793	4.439	4.127	3.851	3.725	3.606	3.387	3.190	2.456
13	9.986	8.853	7.904	7.103	6.424	5.842	5.342	4.910	4.533	4.203	3.912	3.780	3.656	3.427	3.223	2.468
14	10.563	9.295	8.244	7.367	6.628	6.002	5.468	5.008	4.611	4.265	3.962	3.824	3.695	3.459	3.249	2.477
15	11.118	9.712	8.559	7.606	6.811	6.142	5.575	5.092	4.675	4.315	4.001	3.859	3.726	3.483	3.268	2.484
16	11.652	10.106	8.851	7.824	6.974	6.265	5.669	5.162	4.730	4.357	4.033	3.887	3.751	3.503	3.283	2.489
17	12.166	10.477	9.122	8.022	7.120	6.373	5.749	5.222	4.775	4.391	4.059	3.910	3.771	3.518	3.295	2.492
18	12.659	10.828	9.372	8.201	7.250	6.467	5.818	5.273	4.812	4.419	4.080	3.928	3.786	3.529	3.304	2.494
19	13.134	11.158	9.604	8.365	7.366	6.550	5.877	5.316	4.844	4.442	4.097	3.942	3.799	3.539	3.311	2.496
20	13.590	11.470	9.818	8.514	7.469	6.623	5.929	5.353	4.870	4.460	4.110	3.954	3.808	3.546	3.316	2.497
21	14.029	11.764	10.017	8.649	7.562	6.687	5.973	5.384	4.891	4.476	4.121	3.963	3.816	3.551	3.320	2.498
22	14.451	12.042	10.201	8.772	7.645	6.743	6.011	5.410	4.909	4.488	4.130	3.970	3.822	3.556	3.323	2.498
23	14.857	12.303	10.371	8.883	7.718	6.792	6.044	5.432	4.925	4.499	4.137	3.976	3.827	3.559	3.325	2.499
24	15.247	12.550	10.529	8.985	7.784	6.835	6.073	5.451	4.937	4.507	4.143	3.981	3.831	3.562	3.327	2.499
25	15.622	12.783	10.675	9.077	7.843	6.873	6.097	5.467	4.948	4.514	4.147	3.985	3.834	3.564	3.329	2.499
26	15.983	13.003	10.810	9.161	7.896	6.906	6.118	5.480	4.956	4.520	4.151	3.988	3.837	3.566	3.330	2.500
27	16.330	13.211	10.935	9.237	7.943	6.935	6.136	5.492	4.964	4.525	4.154	3.990	3.839	3.567	3.331	2.500
28	16.663	13.406	11.051	9.307	7.984	6.961	6.152	5.502	4.970	4.528	4.157	3.992	3.840	3.568	3.331	2.500
29	16.984	13.591	11.158	9.370	8.022	6.983	6.166	5.510	4.975	4.531	4.159	3.994	3.841	3.569	3.332	2.500
30	17.292	13.765	11.258	9.427	8.055	7.003	6.177	5.517	4.979	4.534	4.160	3.995	3.842	3.569	3.332	2.500
40	19.793	15.046	11.925	9.779	8.244	7.105	6.234	5.548	4.997	4.544	4.166	3.999	3.846	3.571	3.333	2.500

Chapter 19

Zero-Base Budgeting

James D. Suver
Director, Programs in Health Administration
University of Colorado

INTRODUCTION

In previous chapters, the budgeting process has been introduced and various types of budgetary techniques have been discussed. Most of these chapters have addressed specific needs, i.e., capital budgeting, cash budgeting, etc. All serve a vital function in the organization's budgetary process. In this chapter, we continue this format with the introduction of the zero-base budgeting (ZBB) concept.

The ZBB concept consists of applying planning and control tools that the effective manager has probably used for a considerable length of time. Its primary strength lies in its systematic evaluation of inputs and outputs as part of the budgetary process. It is a bottom-up system in that the principal players are the line supervisors. It forces these supervisors to evaluate the activities they are performing and to determine whether these activities are cost effective. Basically, three major questions are answered:

1. Should the activity be performed at all?
2. What level of resources should the activity command?
3. Are there alternative ways to perform the same activity that are more cost effective?

The relationship between inputs and outputs is of vital concern to most health care managers.

Given scarce resources (inputs), the effective manager would like to maximize the benefits (outputs) received. For some activities, a definite relationship can be determined between inputs and outputs. For example, the amount of raw food prepared should result in a specified number of meals, or the amount of x-ray film should result in a specified number of exposures. Standards can be developed for these types of activities by knowledgeable individuals. Contrast this type of activity with the common support activities such as accounting, administration, housekeeping, and social service. The latter activities generally fall in the category of "managed" costs or discretionary cost centers. Discretionary cost centers do produce outputs; otherwise, they would or should not exist. The difficulty occurs in specifying the output as a function of input. Since output is difficult to quantify, most health care managers control the input side of the budget, i.e., the budgetary amount is negotiated based on the bargaining position of the various managers and on past experience.

It is in this area of managed costs that the ZBB process offers the most potential. Responsible managers are asked to support their budget requests based on activities performed. No level of budgeted amounts is taken for granted. Each area basically starts from the "ground up" and hence the name "zero-base budgeting" is derived.

HISTORY OF ZERO-BASE BUDGETING

Credit for the first ZBB attempt is generally given to Secretary of Agriculture Orville Freeman in 1964; however, it was not considered particularly successful. Texas Instruments was the first nongovernmental organization to apply successfully what is now called ZBB. The reporting of this success by Peter Pyhrr in the November–December 1970 issue of the *Harvard Business Review* led to its adoption by Governor Jimmy Carter in the state of Georgia. His election to the presidency in 1976 brought the ZBB system back to the federal government.

Many profit organizations and governmental units have tried ZBB and appear to have profited from the experience: Allied Van Lines; California Edison; the Playboy Club; Westinghouse; Xerox; the cities of Garland, Texas, and Wilmington, Delaware; a school district in Rochester, New York; and the state of Colorado. All have been reported as generally successful; however, this is not too surprising, since few people write about failures. Two exceptions should be noted: R.N. Anthony of the Harvard Business School posed some serious questions about the ZBB system,[1] and the author, together with Ray L. Brown, proposed a cautious approach to the adoption of the ZBB process.[2]

There have not been many published reports of successful implementation of the ZBB process in health care organizations. Arthur A. Kay III reported at the 1977 Hospital Financial Management Association Annual National Institute in Boulder, Colorado, in June 1977 on the application of ZBB techniques at Michael Reese Hospital and Medical Center in Chicago, Illinois. According to Kay, the technique offered considerable potential for future cost savings. Dean Grant and Bruce Fisher presented a detailed synopsis of how ZBB was applied at the Alexian Brothers Medical Center.[3] Again, considerable savings resulted from this application of ZBB.

This brief history of ZBB indicates that it can be applied successfully to health care organizations.

RELATIONSHIP OF ZBB TO TRADITIONAL BUDGETARY TECHNIQUES

The primary budgetary process used for the managed cost activities in most health care institutions is some form of incremental budgeting. Incremental budgeting generally implies that the current level of funding is used as a point of departure for negotiations on the new budget. Changes in activities, new requirements, and the impact of inflation are all considered a justification for changing the current funding levels. Additions and deletions from this current level are looked at as discrete activities to be considered. Negotiations focus on the changes and not on the major portion of the budget request. In the managed cost areas, this approach offers a workable solution because, as discussed earlier, the managed cost areas do not typically have identifiable input/output relationships. Generally, a "static" budget is developed for these kinds of activities, and input management is exercised. The activity manager is evaluated on how the inputs are expended, not on the output achieved except in an overall sense.

The ZBB process, on the other hand, concentrates on all activities to be performed, not just the changes. It requires the decision makers to identify the activities to be performed, the resources required, and the justification for various levels of activity and output. This concentration on all the activities instead of just the incremental changes offers a viable option to traditional methods. However, its strengths and weaknesses must be thoroughly understood if maximum benefits are to be achieved. The next section in this chapter concentrates on developing this understanding.

THE ZERO-BASE BUDGETING PROCESS

The ZBB process has three basic steps:

1. the development of activities to be performed into decision packages
2. the ranking of all decision packages in the organization
3. the allocation of resources based on the ranking process

These three steps will be developed in greater detail in the following pages; however, each organization should first evaluate how it fulfills the requirements discussed below.

Prerequisites to Implementation of a ZBB System

The successful implementation of a ZBB system requires that certain prerequisites exist before the process is initiated. These include

- a sound organizational structure
- an effective accounting system
- properly selected and properly motivated supervisors
- top management involvement and support
- a sufficient timetable

It should not come as a surprise that the preceding prerequisites would be the same for any effective budgeting system. Yet because of the "change" impact and the traumatic nature of a ZBB process, it could be stated that the five factors are even more important if a ZBB system is to be successful, as illustrated in the following paragraphs.

A Sound Organizational Structure

A ZBB system focuses on activities to be completed. In a health care institution, many activities are interrelated, and these relationships must be known if decisions are to be made about the scope of the activities to be performed. A clearly defined organizational structure can accomplish this goal by grouping activities into related areas and indicating who is responsible for completing these activities. If levels of authority and responsibility are not well defined, the institution is not a good candidate for the ZBB process.

An Effective Accounting System

A ZBB system requires considerable quantitative detail at the lower organizational levels in the institution. If the existing accounting system does not provide this detail in a timely and accurate fashion, many of the benefits expected

from the ZBB system will not be achieved. If only macrocompilation of data at the upper organizational levels is available, it is generally not effective to try to monitor activities through the ZBB process at lower levels in the organization. One must either develop a more detailed accounting system or managers must collect and compile their own data bases. The latter alternative is usually unsuccessful, and improvement of the accounting system should thus precede the implementation of a ZBB process.

Properly Selected and Properly Motivated Supervisors

People, not the budget system, achieve results. The ZBB process involves line managers to a much greater extent than any other budgeting system. Lower level supervisors can make or break a ZBB system because they are the key to preparing the budgeting requests, defining alternatives, and living with their commitments. Without such supervisors, a ZBB system is doomed to failure.

Top Management Involvement and Support

The successful implementation of a ZBB system requires that top management be involved and supportive from the initial stages. Because of the considerable effort that must be expended by all managers in the organization, there must be a commitment on the part of top management to use the results. Being aware of possible problem areas, allowing for resources to develop the ZBB process properly, and receiving frequent progress reports are vital aspects of top management involvement.

A Sufficient Timetable

The ZBB process requires managers to become more involved in their departments than ever before. Supervisors at all levels in the organization must make a determination of outputs for activities where none has existed before. Managers must ask themselves to justify fully all their activities for the first time and to list these activities by priority. They will be forced to make difficult choices. This requires formal training, formal guidance, a source of continuing expertise, and an understanding of the behavioral problems involved. Each organization, depending upon the development of its current budget system, will require different periods of time. However, even the most sophisticated organization will require at least a year before the effective date of the budget.

The Decision Package

The preceding prerequisites typically involve the entire hospital organization. However, the heart of an effective ZBB system is the determination of decision packages. A decision package should represent an activity that is the responsibility of a single manager. It should have measurable input and output characteristics that will enable management to make decisions about the package. This requires that either the formal reporting system or a well-established informal reporting system provide necessary information to prepare and evaluate the decision package.

The choice of what constitutes a decision package, the package's preparation, and its priorities must be determined by the individual supervisor. Top management levels and the controller staff can provide guidelines and formal instructions, but the choice must still remain with the preparing supervisor.

It must be stressed that there is no single correct method for determining the decision package size. Every organization, and indeed sections within the organization, will have different requirements. Two points should be stressed: (1) if the decision package is too large, i.e., contains too many activities and input resources, it will be difficult to evaluate properly; and (2) if it is too small, i.e., involves less than one full-time employee (FTE), there will be too many decision packages and too much paper work for effective preparation and ranking. Limits must be tailored to fit the needs of the organization, the existing accounting system, and the organizational structure.

Given the important nature of the decision package, top management must provide a formal structure for supervisors to use in preparing their own decision packages. Typically, this takes the nature of specified forms and funding limitations that must be used for preparing decision pack-

ages. For example, a decision package format should include information on

- the organizational entity of the decision package
- the description of the activity or activities
- the objective or purpose of the activity
- the resources required to accomplish the activity
- the output measurement factors
- the benefits accomplished by funding the activity
- the consequences of not funding the activity
- other incremental packages to accomplish the same activity
- the ranking of the decision package by the various reviewing levels

A sample form is shown in Exhibit 19-1. Some organizations also list alternative ways of performing the activity and the resources required. Usually the reasons for not selecting the alternative packages are also shown. It has been the author's experience that including alternative decision packages can lead to overly long decision packages, raise unnecessary questions, and complicate the preparation and reviewing process.

The other major guideline to be furnished by top management is the various levels of incremental funding that will be included in the decision package. If no guidelines are furnished, some supervisors may start at absolute zero levels of funding and prepare a new decision package for every $1,000 in increased funding, while others may assume that the current level of funding is the minimum level and proceed from there. It would be extremely difficult to properly evaluate and prioritize data derived so inconsistently.

In order to prevent this, top management should define numerous levels of funding for the decision packages. One technique is to identify four possible funding levels for consideration as decision packages. The first would be identified as a minimum level. If this amount of funding is not approved, the activity would cease to exist. The second level would be the current level of funding. Given inflationary pressures, this would usually result in a cut in activity levels.

Exhibit 19-1 Decision Package

1. Level of funding _____

2. Activity name and number_____ 3. Responsibility unit _____

4. Date_____ 5. Page_____ of_____

6. Prepared by_____ 7. Approved by_____

8. Description of activity:

9. Resources required (this package):

	Current Year	Proposed Budget	% Change
Personnel (FTE)			
Salaries			
Fringe			
Equipment			
Supplies			
Other			
Totals			

10. Measures of performance:

    Effectiveness

    Efficiency

11. Benefits of approval:

12. Impact of not funding:

Exhibit 19-1 continued

---

13. Other decision packages for this activity (attach details):

    1. Same dollar   Ranking_____

    2. Same effort   Ranking_____

    3. 120%   Ranking_____

---

14. Ranking of this decision package:

By preparing management level   Number_____ of_____ packages

By first reviewing management
level   Number_____ of_____ packages

By second reviewing management
level   Number_____ of_____ packages

Notes:

1. Level of funding for this activity (minimum, same dollars, same effort, or maximum).

2. Activity name and any identifying number used. Example: emergency room admitting #ER 1.

3. Name of cost center where activity is performed. Example: emergency room.

4. Date of preparation.

5. Number of pages in package.

6. Name of preparer of decision package.

7. Approval authority for this cost center.

8. Brief description of activity. Example: "This activity consists of admitting the patient into the health care system." Admitting documents would be prepared, patient history and nature of health problem determined, and appropriate health care personnel assigned.

9. The resources required for this package are determined for specific categories. Last year's budgeted amount would be compared with this package and the percent of change would be noted.

10. Activity measurements are typically divided into effectiveness and efficiency. Effectiveness measures include meeting hospital objectives for this activity. For the emergency room admitting activity this might include factors such as: (1) all patients desiring emergency room treatment will be admitted promptly and accurately; (2) proper health care personnel will be notified on a timely basis; (3) medical records will be prepared and maintained; and (4) proper collection procedures will be instituted. Efficiency measures would concentrate on establishing more specific measurement factors, such as: (1) no patient will wait more than 10 minutes to be admitted; (2) proper treatment will be started within

Exhibit 19-1 continued

> 20 minutes; (3) medical records will be prepared with no more than 5 percent errors; and (4) collections forms and procedures will be implemented no later than patient discharge from the emergency room.
> 11. This section should stress the benefits to be realized from approving this package. Example: "This level of activity will enable the organization to meet accreditation standards or provide minimum levels of care for emergency room patients."
> 12. This section should stress the impact of not funding this level of activity. Examples: "The hospital will not meet accreditation and/or legal requirements," or "all emergency room patients must be reported to the regular hospital admitting area for access to the health care system."
> 13. This section would list other packages developed for this activity and their ranking by the preparer.
> 14. This section would include data on how other reviewers ranked this package in relation to all other packages being reviewed.

The third level would be the current effort funding. At this level the funding required would represent the amount required to continue to perform the activity at existing levels. The final level would be considered a maximum package and would describe what level of activity would be accomplished if the current funding were increased by a certain percentage over the last budgeted amount. The maximum and minimum levels of funding should be established by top management during the planning period. For example, the minimum level might be established as 80 percent of last year's budgeted amount, with the maximum set at 120 percent. Some organizations use different colored paper for the different levels of funding to draw attention to and aid in the ranking and review process.

The last two levels of funding are important because both represent an increase in the budget. If they are not included, the ZBB process becomes a tool for budget cutting only and can have serious dysfunctional motivational aspects. The ZBB system should be used to allocate resources better. This usually results in a budget cut, but it does not always have to do so.

Types of Decision Packages

Decision packages fall into two major categories, those that define alternative methods of accomplishing the same activities and those that identify various incremental levels of funding to accomplish the same activity. This section will predominantly concentrate on the incremental funding packages; however, the instructions can easily be adapted to the mutually exclusive, or alternative type, of decision package.

Decision packages can be developed among various activity classifications. The important factor is the benefit to be received from performing the activity. The most common activity classification for decision packages is the cost center. This parameter is usually chosen because the accounting system and organizational structure support this classification. The capital investment decision is usually a natural classification for the ZBB process because it typically involves a separate decision on a project with identifiable costs and benefits. Other activity classifications are personnel decisions, programs or services provided, and cost reduction programs.

A major factor in selecting the type of decision package is the manner in which personnel requirements are determined. If a decision package is so small that it contains fractional FTEs or sharing of specific equipment, elimination of the activity would not normally result in a reduction in the resource cost. If the FTEs could be used in other activities, the decision package in a sense becomes a mutually exclusive type of package;

i.e., if the FTEs work in one package, they are unable to work in another. The proper size for a decision package is extremely subjective. What is proper for one organizational element may not be proper for another. Since there are no correct answers but only subjective estimates, the size of the decision package is primarily determined by experience and by trial and error.

Decision Packages and Measures of Performance

One of the more difficult tasks confronting the preparer of decision packages is determining what factors should be used to measure performance. Inherent in the ZBB process is a type of cost-benefit analysis. The costs are easily determined or at the least more explicitly stated. The benefits are much more elusive. In Exhibit 19-1, item 10 required the preparer to state measures of performance for two areas, effectiveness and efficiency. Effectiveness, as defined by Anthony and Dearden, usually relates to the accomplishment of some stated objective.[4] Efficiency, on the other hand, relates to an input/output relationship. Cost-benefit difficulties are primarily associated with this relationship.

The effectiveness criteria can be met in most areas by clearly stating the objective to be accomplished by a certain activity. For example, the objective of the admitting department would be to ensure the patient access to the health care delivery system. This could include subordinate objectives of obtaining proper verification of insurance, information concerning allergies, etc. An objective of the security section would be to provide adequate security for patients' and employees' valuables. The objectives that the activity seeks to provide should be stated in clear, nonambiguous terms. Many agencies will benefit from this activity whether or not they implement a ZBB system.

The next step, determining the output and the means of measuring it in relationship to the input required to accomplish it, can be much more difficult. Every activity must provide some benefits or it should not exist. The mere analysis of an activity can sometimes lead to its demise if no benefits are found to exist. In other cases, the benefits definitely exist but may be difficult to measure.

Once the benefits have been identified, the problem of measurement must be resolved. Anthony and Dearden approach the measurement problem by grouping output measurements into three categories: (1) results measures, (2) process measures, and (3) social indicators.[5]

A results measure expresses the output in terms that are related to the organization objectives, while a process measure relates to the activities being performed. For example, the output of an operating room could be measured in terms of successful operations accomplished, complications averted, etc. This would be a results measure of the objectives if the operating room were to provide timely, effective health care. If a process measure were to be designed, the number of operations performed, the type performed, etc., would be used. The basic difference between the two forms of measurement lies in the concept of measuring output. The process measurement indicates that the performance of the activities helps to meet the organization's objectives. The results measure is more restrictive.

For some decision packages, there may be a tendency to state the output in terms of social measures or in terms of quality of life. Although this type of output may appear to be the most appropriate for the activity being considered in the decision package, it is exceedingly difficult to quantify or to measure in terms of successful accomplishment. For example, an improvement in employee morale could be the major benefit from expenditures on parking security or additional cafeteria personnel. However, attempting to equate subjective estimates of improvements in morale with discrete expenditure levels is a difficult if not impossible task. Accordingly these types of packages should be kept to a minimum if the ZBB process is to be effective.

For most decision packages, there should be multiple measurement factors instead of a single index. Most activities are too complex to be clearly stated by one output measurement and in many cases, it can be dysfunctional to only measure one.

In determining output factors for measurement, some consideration should be given to making the measurement quantifiable. For example, the square footage of floor polished three times a week and the number of meals delivered within a specific time are measurable. The number of days elapsed before a bill is forwarded for collection can be measured, as can the number of minutes spent waiting for laboratory tests.

The output measurement of performance question is difficult but not impossible to resolve if the personnel involved in the ZBB process are realistic and knowledgeable about the activities being measured.

Sample Decision Packages

Based on the format developed in Exhibit 19-1, the sample decision packages in Exhibits 19-2 and 19-3 represent examples of some activities that could be included as decision packages. Each organization will have to tailor the type of decision package to meet its own requirements. The examples included here do indicate the level of detail and preparation that must precede the actual preparing of the decision package.

Ranking the Decision Packages

Once the decison packages have been prepared, they must be ranked. The ranking process involves prioritizing all the activities contained in the decision packages in terms of decreasing benefits to the hospital. Not only is this a subjective process, but it also can become a highly political issue. Supervisors are forced to evaluate the activities and decide which ones are more important than others. Although this ranking is done on all budgetary systems, the ZBB system tends to focus on microunits of analysis, and hence personalities can become more of a factor than when general cuts are made, as with an incremental system.

Although the ranking process is subjective in nature, it is important to develop a formal mechanical approach to reduce some of the behavioral conflicts that could occur. The initial step is to develop an identity system for the decision packages and the standardized format indicated earlier. A typical hospital organizational structure is shown in Exhibit 19-4.

By assigning a specific identification to each package, it can be easily traced through the ranking process. A decision package for the housekeeping supervisor would have the following identification: BBBA2-4. This would indicate that the decision package was developed for the support services area (B), is part of the housekeeping department (B), the package was prepared by the housekeeping supervisor (B), and this was an (A) activity, the second package out of four for the same (A) activity.

Exhibit 19-4 indicates that the housekeeping supervisor prepared decision packages for four activities: A, B, C, and D. Each of these activities had four decision packages, for a total of 16. The supervisor would then rank each of these packages 1 to 16 on the decision package form and the cumulative form shown in Exhibit 19-5.

The initial ranking by the department supervisor can be difficult but the supervisor should at least be familiar with the content of the decision package. This same familiarity does not usually exist as the decision packages flow upward through the organization.

In our sample hospital of Exhibit 19-4, the housekeeping department head must combine the decision packages of housekeeping and the initial supervisor's ranking of them with the decision packages from the laundry and linen supervisor and the personal quarters supervisor. Each will have selected his or her own number one decision package. The department head now has to rank 43 different packages and may not be familiar with all of the activities involved in them. This lack of familiarity can become even more of a problem as the rankings go higher in the organization; the support services assistant administrator, for example, must rank 85 decision packages. As discussed earlier in this chapter, the use of color coded decision packages that reflect different funding levels for decision packages may help the reviewer in the analysis. It can help identify if only minimum level packages are being funded, a factor that may have dysfunctional motivational impact on the preparers who may feel that there is no need to prepare any other level of funding.

One technique used to alleviate this problem is to establish a committee of the preparing supervisors under the direction of their immediate supervisors as the chairpersons. The preparing supervisors could answer questions about their

Exhibit 19-2 Sample Decision Package

---

1. General Hospital "Minimum Level Package" for Emergency Room

2. Activity name and number   Inventory Control ACEC 1 of 4

3. Responsibility unit   Emergency Room   4. Date   5 May 1980

5. Page 1 of 2   6. Prepared by J. Cooper   7. Approved by R. Brown

---

8. Description of activity:

Control of Inventory in Emergency Room. This includes ordering, monitoring stock levels, and controlling use of supplies. The FTE involved will draw needed ER supplies on a daily basis from central supply. Sufficient inventory will be maintained in the ER for evening and night shifts.

---

9. Resources required (this package):

	Current Year	*Proposed Budget*	*% Change*
Personnel (FTE)	2	1	100% decrease
Salaries	$30,000	$18,000	40% decrease
Fringe	3,000	1,800	40% decrease
Equipment	1,000	1,000	0
Supplies	100	125	25% increase
Other	100	50	50% decrease
Totals	$34,200	$20,975	38% decrease

---

10. Measures of performance:

Effectiveness

1. Medical supplies are on hand to meet emergency conditions on a 24-hour basis.

2. Routine medical supplies are available within normal quality of care standards.

Efficiency

1. No ER patient must wait more than 30 minutes for medical supplies.

2. Inventory costs will be no more than 125% of the level obtained from current level of funding or $9,000.

Exhibit 19-2 continued

---

11. Benefits of approval:

Inventory control will be maintained through application of inventory techniques by a trained specialist. Nurses will be available to provide assistance to physicians. Overall inventory dollar levels will be reduced.

---

12. Impact of not funding:

Nursing personnel will be required to control and order inventory. The investment in inventory is expected to increase by 50% due to inefficiencies and lost items. Due to nonavailability of proper supplies quality of care is anticipated to decrease.

---

13. Other decision packages for this activity:

1. Same dollar	Ranking	4–4
2. Same effort	Ranking	3–4
3. Enhanced	Ranking	2–4

---

14. Ranking of this decision package:

By preparing management level	Number __1__ of __13__ packages
By first reviewing management level	Number __8__ of __43__ packages
By second reviewing management level	Number __26__ of __175__ packages

---

own decision packages as the ranking process is started. Staff members from the controller's office could be asked to attend the meetings to become more familiar with the contents of the decision packages.

In our sample organization, supervisors A, B, and C would meet under the direction of department head B. There would be a total of 43 decision packages to review and rank. There are several suggested methods for accomplishing the ranking process. Each supervisor could first rank all packages from 1 to 43. Packages could be prioritized based on total votes received, with the lower totals representing the most desirable packages. This forces the supervisors to review all the packages before assigning a point total. While it may be feasible for 43 packages, it is probably not feasible for the 85 packages at the next management level.

Another technique would be to categorize the packages by specific classes, such as legal requirements, accreditation requirements, and community needs. Packages could then be ranked within these categories. A similar technique would be to separate each package into the various funding classes such as minimum level

Exhibit 19-3 Sample Decision Package

---

1. General Hospital "Same Effort" Package for Housekeeping

2. Activity name and number   Floor Maintenance BBCD 2 of 4

3. Responsibility unit   Housekeeping   4. Date   5 May 1980

5. Page 1 of 2   6. Prepared by J. Cooper   7. Approved by R. Brown

---

8. Description of activity:

   Specially trained floor care specialists on a year-round, regular basis will strip, seal, and wax floor areas of the institution at least once a year.

---

9. Resources required (this package):

	Current Year	*Proposed Budget*	*% Change*
Personnel (FTE)	0	2	not applicable
Salaries	Contracted out for $19,500	$13,520	
Fringe	0	1,352	
Equipment (depreciation)	0	500	
Supplies (wax, etc.)	0	2,300	
Other	0	0	
Totals	$19,500	$17,672	10% decrease

---

10. Measure of performance:

    Effectiveness
    1. Hospital floors meet health care standards for accreditation.
    2. Hospital floors are aesthetically acceptable.

    Efficiency
    1. 60,000 square feet of floors will be waxed once a year.
    2. 30,000 square feet of floors will be waxed twice a year.
    3. 10,000 square feet of floors will be waxed three times a year.

Exhibit 19-3 continued

---

11. Benefits of approval:

   Effective floor protection and an aesthetic environment without decreasing the present cleaning standards. The shift to internal cleaning will allow more control over the floor protection process and provide management flexibility in identifying problem floor space. Floor care responsibility will be placed on identifiable individuals who will be responsible for use of floor care supplies and maintenance of expensive equipment.

---

12. Impact of not funding:

   Present contract must be continued and negotiated at higher costs. No floor care would result in loss of floor protection, cleanliness requirements, and expensive replacement sooner than planned.

---

13. Other decision packages for this activity:

   None

---

14. Ranking of this decision package:

   By preparing management level   Number __7__ of __15__ packages

   By first reviewing management level   Number __38__ of __55__ packages

   By second reviewing management level   Number __48__ of __115__ packages

---

and maximum level. After the individual packages have been ranked within each category, trade-offs may be made between levels of funding to achieve the final ranking.

Some organizations establish cutoff points to facilitate the review process. For example, the preparing level in the organization would review and rank all decision packages. The next reviewing level would only have to review and rank 75 percent of the total packages; the third level, only 50 percent. Decision packages above the cutoff point would automatically be approved, and only those below the cutoff point would be subject to detailed review and ranking.

The adoption of a cutoff point can lead to some dysfunctional activities on the part of supervisors. For example, they could rank questionable decision packages higher, knowing they will probably not be reviewed thoroughly. They would rank the more desirable packages lower, knowing that upon review, such packages would probably be approved more readily. Another problem that can occur is the lack of incentive to prepare marginal packages properly if the preparers know they have little chance of funding.

All of the ranking techniques require a voting system. Each member could assign a rating on the package to indicate a value judgment of the

Exhibit 19-4 Typical Organizational Structure

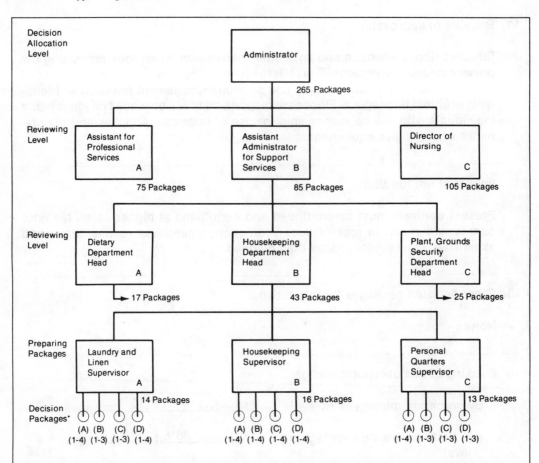

*Four incremental decision packages are the maximum shown for each activity, in keeping with the format developed earlier in the chapter. Some health care providers may have more or less, depending on their own requirements. Generally, four levels of funding are sufficient to provide suitable alternatives for performing the activity without creating unnecessary paper work. Flexibility in determining the level of funding should be allowed the supervisor if it is necessary to evaluate properly the activity; however, care should be exercised so that "nonstandard" decision packages are kept to a minimum.

need for the package similar to the following classifications:

1. essential for minimum levels of operation
2. necessary for effective operations
3. desirable
4. questionable value
5. not necessary at this time

Regardless of the technique used, the committee ranking technique should be approached with

some caution, since collusion between supervisors could be possible to obtain higher rankings for their favorite activities. They could effectively trade votes to freeze out noncolluding supervisors. One way to address the problem is to review and discuss individual rankings by package and to point out discrepancies in the rankings.

Once the final review has been completed, a priority ranking of all the activities to be performed by the organization will be available for

Exhibit 19-5 Decision Package Ranking

Organizational level _____	Number of packages _____
Date _____	Page _____ of _____
Prepared by _____	Next reviewing level _____

Ident. Number	Package Name and Number	Responsibility Unit	Type Package	Amount of Funding	Cumulative Funding	FTE	FTE Cum.	Comments
ADDC 1-4	Admitting	Emergency Room	Minimum	$25,000	$25,000	3	3	Legal Requirements
BBBA 1-4	Linens change	Housekeeping	Minimum	50,000	75,000	6	9	Accreditation Requirements
ADDC 2-4	Admitting	Emergency Room	Maximum	75,000	125,000*	6	12*	*2nd Admitting Package

*When another decision package from the same activity is ranked, the cumulative FTE and amounts must be adjusted to reflect incremental amounts.

the allocation decision. (See Exhibit 19-5.) The allocation decision involves the board of trustees and the administrator in the determination of the amount of resources available to fund activities for the next budget period. This determination should include estimating the revenues received from patient care, donations, grants, and non-operating income. Decisions on the priority ranking list would be funded until the cumulative resource requirements of the decision packages are equal to the total approved resource commitments. This becomes the budget for the organization. Decision packages or activities below the budget cutoff would not be funded. It is very important that the decisions on the activities to be funded be disseminated through the organization and that reasons be given wherever possible for not funding certain activities. Ideally, the unfunded decision packages provide a list of ready candidates if additional funding becomes available. Realistically, there would probably be another review and updating of the information in the decision packages before decisions can be made.

IMPLEMENTING ZERO-BASE BUDGETING

Preliminary Considerations

Before deciding to implement a ZBB system, an organization should carefully consider the following factors:

- What are the strengths and weaknesses of our current budgeting system?
- What do we expect from implementing a ZBB system?
- Do we have the necessary human resources to change the existing system successfully?
- Who will be the primary beneficiaries of the information generated by the ZBB process?
- How will the ZBB process mesh with other existing information systems?

The answers to these questions may help management decide whether to start the implementation process. For example, if an existing system is providing timely, useful management information, there will probably not be a need to install a ZBB system on a crisis basis. In fact, even the decision to implement a partial ZBB system could cause some motivational problems. The involved individuals may think they have failed. A thorough educational program is dictated under these circumstances.

A major weakness of most new systems is the tendency to promise too much. This has happened in many organizations. What does top management expect from a ZBB system? Expectations may include

- increasing top management's ability to allocate resources
- enabling all management levels to understand better the activities of the hospital
- creating more involvement by line supervisors in budget preparation
- providing for better evaluation of subordinate managers

These expectations will help focus on what should be included in the system and how best to design the decision packages. The answer to the third factor is particularly vital to the implementation question. Responsible, motivated, and properly trained supervisors are the prime requirement for a successful ZBB system. Identifying these requirements must be done early.

The question of who will use the information also can dictate the requirements. Will it be the third-party payers, government regulators, or the internal management?

Finally, the existing information systems provide other necessary data. Will the ZBB process infringe on their areas? Will it support or detract from their requirements? Must they also be changed if a ZBB system is implemented?

If these factors are carefully considered and evaluated, the odds of implementing a successful ZBB are greatly increased.

The Initial Steps

The decision to implement a ZBB system must start with top management. Although middle level supervisors may have the prime respon-sibility for implementing, operating, and monitoring the system, it must have the full support of the top administration. It is also vital that the top administrator must continually communicate this interest to all levels in the organization. One method that could be used is an initial letter from the administrator to all supervisors explaining why the ZBB process is being considered. There will usually be considerable fear and anxiety whenever a new system is being introduced. This must be recognized and alleviated as soon as possible.

Knowledge about the system and removal of uncertainties can do much to ease the behavioral problems. Early in the budget cycle, a ZBB committee should be formed to serve as a focal point for the collection and dissemination of information. The controller or associate administrator with fiscal responsibility may serve as chairperson of this committee. Other committee members should represent the medical staff, nursing administration, ancillary services, and support services. It might be appropriate to send some of the committee members to a formal training program on ZBB. The committee should also collect literature on ZBB that should be made available to supervisors in the hospital. (The bibliography included with this chapter would be a good place to start.)

After the committee members become knowledgeable about ZBB, they should prepare a formal manual of instructions on how ZBB will be implemented in the hospital. This should include forms adapted to meet the needs of the specific departments. It should be stressed that the ZBB process should be tailored to the specific institution. There are extremely few existing ZBB systems that can be directly applied to an institution.

While the manual is being prepared, it is useful to test the ZBB procedures in a selected department. This test could point out problem areas, unclear instructions, and potential behavioral problems. Training sessions could then be designed to correct these deficiencies. At this stage, the management information system and flow of accounting information should be analyzed to determine if the decision packages can be supported with adequate cost information. Since it usually takes considerable time to redesign an accounting system, the design of the decision package may need to be changed.

Top management interest

↓

Form ZBB committee
Obtain knowledge on the ZBB process

↓

Prepare formal instructions and procedures
Develop ZBB forms

↓

Selective test of ZBB procedures
Revise procedures
Evaluate appropriateness of ZBB for organization

↓

Decision to continue with implementation

↓

Select departments for ZBB process
Conduct training classes for supervisors

↓

Distribute ZBB instructions and forms

↓

Involve supervisors
Develop decision packages

↓

Rank decision packages
(preparing supervisors)

↓

Consolidate decision packages

↓

Rank all decision packages

↓

Develop final cutoff points for budget
Prepare in budget format

↓

Present budget to trustees
and decision makers

↓

Approve budget

↓

Disseminate approved budget to supervisors

↓

Implement budget

Figure 19-1 Summary of the Implementation Process

During this initial period, top management and the ZBB committee should decide in what areas the ZBB system should be implemented. Usually, it is better to apply ZBB on a selective basis rather than throughout the institution. The selective application will allow for improvements in the methodology, procedures, and training sessions.

The Design Phase

The ZBB process requires detailed involvement by supervisors at lower organizational levels in the hospital. These individuals may not even be familiar with the normal budget procedures. ZBB requires these supervisors to identify what they do, how they do it, and how to measure how well they are doing it. They will also be required to prioritize their activities. In most cases, considerable training and instruction will be necessary to obtain usable decision packages.

Sufficient time must be allowed during the design phase. One rule of thumb might be to double the normal budget preparation time allowed. Not allowing sufficient time can lead to a very dysfunctional attitude toward the ZBB system that may invariably result in failure. If the supervisors are not given the time and information to develop realistic and appropriate decision packages, the process not only will fail, but also can lead to improper decisions being made on erroneous data.

The Evaluation Phase

After the design of the ZBB system is completed, top management should evaluate it. This evaluation should answer the following questions:

- Is the ZBB system meeting the needs of the organization?
- Are there formal instructions available to answer questions about the system?
- Have the behavioral problems caused by the system been corrected?
- Do the benefits from the system exceed the costs?

If the answers to the above questions are positive, management should continue with the implementation process.

Figure 19-1 represents a step-by-step summary of the implementation process.

Pitfalls To Avoid in Implementing ZBB

- Lack of support from top management. As noted earlier, top management must support, be involved with, and use the ZBB system for resource allocation.
- Attempt to implement ZBB too soon. ZBB requires a considerable amount of time and effort. It cannot be rushed, and the initial effort will probably take at least 9 to 12 months of planning.
- Lack of proper training and instructions. A detailed, formal instruction manual is a necessity. Many supervisors will be experiencing their first exposure to the intricacies of the budget process. They need training before, during, and after the preparation of the decision packages.
- Complexities of procedures. There will be a tendency to create overly sophisticated forms and procedures. All the problems of the old system cannot be cured with one form. There will be time later to refine the system.
- Failure to reward those who increase efficiency by using the ZBB process. Supervisors who take the time to prepare the decision packages, assess alternatives properly, and propose new methods must be rewarded. Proper motivation is still the best way to effectiveness and efficiency. The reward system should not always be based on those who have the biggest budget.

BENEFITS AND LIMITATIONS OF A ZERO-BASE BUDGETING SYSTEM

Benefits

As discussed earlier in this chapter, a ZBB system has particular significance for the overhead areas of a health care provider. These areas typically contain most of the discretionary cost centers in which an input/output relationship is difficult to define. Compare the decision process involving the number of accountants to hire with the number of radiology lab technicians. The output of the lab technicians can usually be expressed in terms of the number of film processes, procedures accomplished, etc. What is the output of the accountants in the controller's office? Is it the number of reports? There are clearly many areas of the hospital or other health care providers where the output measurement problem exists. The ZBB system directly addresses the discretionary nature of overhead costs in the following processes:

- commitment
- communications
- coordination
- control
- personnel development

ZBB is basically a bottom-up budgeting approach. Supervisors at the cost center level in the organization must prepare the decision packages and they must be involved in the ranking process. In the preparation of the decision packages, alternative methods of accomplishing the activity itself must be examined. The supervisors at all levels in the organization must evaluate the cost effectiveness of the activities being performed.

Once the decision package has been prepared, reviewed, and prioritized, it becomes a commitment between the parties involved. The supervisors agree to accomplish the activities and management agrees to provide the necessary funding.

The bottom-up approach does not negate the importance of proper guidelines from top management. Top management must provide information on objectives and operational constraints for the coming budget year in clear, concise terms. This forces top management to sharpen its focus on where the organization is going and what the resources will be for the next year.

ZBB provides healthy interaction between the administrative staff and the cost center supervisors. Since most line supervisors will be unfamiliar with the intricacies of the budgeting process, the administrative staff must provide detailed instructions and be available for consultation during the preparation and implementation process. This close involvement enables all participants to understand better the problems and activities performed by each other. The successful implementation of a ZBB process should result in more effective communication among all levels of management in the health care organization.

The coordination process is vastly improved because individual supervisors should not eliminate or reduce activities that provide services or input of another cost center without coordination. For example, the decision by a dietary supervisor to reduce the meal service to specific times could have a decided impact on nursing scheduling for the various patient wards. The decision to reduce or change service provided by housekeeping, central supply, etc., could also have an impact in other areas of the organization. Because these impacts must be fully discussed during the decision package preparation and ranking process, overall coordination is improved. Thus, in many organizations, the significance of interdepartmental services has not been fully appreciated in the past. A ZBB system requires this knowledge and coordination.

The control process is also greatly enhanced by a ZBB system. The detail and specific information in the decision package provide the benchmark for evaluation and feedback for corrective action. Frequent comparison of actual results with approved decision packages can lead to timely information on possible problem areas and identify effective supervisors.

Finally, the training and personal development of the individuals involved in the process can be one of the most important outcomes of implementing a ZBB system. The preparation of decision packages, which involves estimating resources required and selecting output indicators, can be a valuable learning experience for the medically oriented supervisor. The ranking of activities requires that difficult choices be made at all organizational levels. Most organizations that have successfully implemented ZBB listed the learning factor as one of the significant benefits of the experience.

Limitations

ZBB, like most budgeting systems, has some inherent limitations and weaknesses. It requires considerable involvement by supervisors, who typically are not trained for this type of effort. It can be traumatic, dysfunctional, and a serious threat if not implemented properly. If the ZBB system is to be successfully implemented, it requires a long lead time, considerable training, and careful instructions.

There will be more expense and paper work associated with the implementation of a ZBB system. This can be especially true if a side-by-side approach with the existing system is considered. It takes time for top management to delineate objectives in enough detail for the supervisors to use. Perhaps more importantly, supervisors must establish output for areas in which experts are not in agreement. The limitations can be overcome, but the benefits must be compared with the costs. It has not been documented that ZBB is always an advantage.

After the Initial Year of Zero-Base Budgeting

The implementation year of the ZBB system requires the most effort and also promises the most benefits in terms of learning and resource allocation. After the first year, there is a difference of opinion as to whether it is necessary to perform a ZBB for every year.

The arguments for or against using ZBB every year primarily depend on the nature of the users' environment. In many health care institutions, the services provided do not change significantly from year to year. The preparation of decision packages is time consuming and involves considerable effort. Unless new services are offered, the supervisors may be content to submit the same decision packages as last year. A complete ZBB may only need to be prepared every three to four years.

The danger in not using ZBB every year primarily seems to be a return to incremental budgeting. One of the major reasons for implementing a ZBB system was the inadequacies of incremental budgeting.

Also, the periodic use of a ZBB process is very similar to a "sunset" review, which will be discussed in the next section. Basically, the choice of how often to use the ZBB process is dependent upon the dictates of management. No one option is best for all organizations under all conditions.

FUNCTIONAL VALUE ANALYSIS

The ZBB process offers the opportunity to review in depth the activities performed by the organization. Implementing a ZBB process may not be appropriate for every health care organization. An alternative budgeting technique that offers many of the same benefits is functional value analysis (FVA), developed by James E. Bennett and Jacques Krasny (see Chapter 20).

FVA does not require that each cost center in the organization prepare decision packages on all of its activities, but rather involves the establishment of a team effort to establish possible areas for analysis and cost savings. As Bennett and Krasny explain, total nonmedical expenses are broken down into cost centers with budgets of not more than $500,000. A full-time task force comprising senior management and technical staff assists the cost center manager in generating cost reduction proposals that must result in savings of 30 to 40 percent. These cost reduction programs are evaluated by all hospital managers who are affected by the proposals.

Senior managers finally decide which proposals will be implemented. The entire process usually takes four to six months according to Bennett and Krasny. By comparing the FVA approach to the ZBB process developed earlier in the chapter, the reader can determine which approach is best for the organization.

In summary, FVA can accomplish many of the improvements attributed to a ZBB system in the areas of commitment, communication, and coordination. It does not obtain the trade-offs that typically occur through the ZBB ranking process, and since it is not a continuing process some control benefits may not be obtained as "slack" creeps back into the annual budget.

OTHER MANAGEMENT TECHNIQUES

Some health care organizations will decide not to implement a ZBB system or FVA, yet still desire to obtain some of the benefits. The decision not to implement may be a political issue, a lack of trained personnel, or any of a multitude of organizational issues. Given these constraints, are there any other management techniques that will achieve similar results? The remainder of this section will focus on the following management systems:

- management by objectives
- operational auditing
- program budgeting
- "sunset" reviews

Management by Objectives (MBO)

In this management approach, both the supervisor and the subordinate manager agree on a common set of objectives: what is to be expected of each participant and what is to be used for performance measurement. If done properly, it can accomplish the involvement benefits achieved by ZBB. Like ZBB, it can take several years to properly train and motivate supervisors and subordinate managers to use MBO.

An effective MBO program requires the setting of specific individual goals instead of general group goals. This goal-setting process requires legitimate participation instead of activities that are directed one way, usually from the top down. Feedback is also a necessary condition for MBO to succeed. The feedback message should be clear, unambiguous, and timely.

MBO can achieve many of the same results as ZBB in terms of commitment, communication, and control. It does not usually achieve the same level of coordination that the ZBB ranking process can. It does involve a lengthy development period and top management involvement.

Operational Auditing (OA)

In contrast to MBO, OA usually focuses in greater depth on the cost and resource issues. OA typically involves an internal staff of trained auditors who visit an organization, perform in-depth analysis of activities performed and costs incurred, and prepare a written report to management. During the period of time of the audit, many of the benefits of the ZBB process can be achieved, i.e., communication, control, and coordination. OA, however, usually does not achieve any positive commitment, and this can quickly lead to a return to previous practices. Although it does not involve a lot of training for the individual supervisors, it does entail considerable expense in training the audit team. This technique is used successfully by the federal government with the General Accounting Office and the inspector general team of the various departments.

Program Budgeting (PB)

PB is actually a vital part of the ZBB process in that input and output analysis is performed for described activities. PB, as defined here, focuses more on the total programs rather than the organizatonal activities in the ZBB process. This, in turn, is a major weakness of PB because it does not contain the commitment from responsible supervisors. It does not foster responsibility for individual organizations unless the program is wholly completed within the one organization. It does require a defining of goals and objectives, determining the inputs and outputs of the program, and establishing means to measure results. An effective PB system can achieve communication and control objectives, but it is typically weak in terms of commitment and coordination.

"Sunset" Reviews

A "sunset" approach to budgeting for overhead areas involves establishing periodic in-depth reviews of all the activities performed by a certain cost center. This review can be accomplished by a team of experts in various disciplines, either from inside the organization or hired on a consulting basis. "Sunset" laws in various states require this approach to the evaluation of existing programs. Of the 27 states to adopt a "sunset" approach, mixed results have

been achieved, for very few activities have been eliminated. In addition, the cost of conducting "sunset" reviews has been much higher than anticipated. For example, Colorado reported that the audits of 13 agencies cost $216,300 for a savings of $11,000. "Sunset" reviews can be used to achieve some of the results expected from ZBB in terms of control or a review of all activities performed by the organization, but it cannot achieve the commitment, communication, or coordination benefits effectively.

SUMMARY

A ZBB system can provide an effective tool to allocate resources and make budget decisions. It offers an opportunity for all levels of management to become involved in the budgeting process and is probably one of the best budget training techniques available. After completing a ZBB cycle, every individual involved will have a more complete understanding of the organization than before. Assuming the ranking of decision packages is used to allocate resources, a more rational budget could not be adopted. However, the time and effort involved in implementing a ZBB process may be too traumatic and dysfunctional to the health care organization. FVA can achieve many of the same benefits that occur from ZBB. It can create fewer dysfunctional, motivational aspects because the involved personnel are part of a team effort and there is some positive feedback from being a select group.

The other techniques could be considered as viable options for those organizations that have limited or specialized resources. For example, PB may be a viable alternative for organizations that usually have short-run programs primarily done within one cost center. OA and "sunset" type reviews may be more appropriate for organizations that have strong internal auditing staffs and inexperienced supervisors.

Regardless of the system or technique selected, all should involve careful considerations of the benefits to be gained and the costs to be incurred. It may be better to maintain the status quo than to create unnecessary behavioral problems among key personnel.

NOTES

1. Robert N. Anthony, "Zero Base Budgeting is a Fraud," *The Wall Street Journal*, 27 April 1977, p. 2.

2. James D. Suver and Ray L. Brown, "Where Does Zero Base Budgeting Work?" *Harvard Business Review*, November–December 1977, pp. 76–84.

3. Dean Grant and Bruce Fisher, "The Alexian Brothers Medical Center," as quoted in Ray D. Dillon, *Zero Base*

Budgeting for Health Care Institutions (Rockville, Md.: Aspen Publishers, Inc., 1979), pp. 151–244.

4. R.N. Anthony and John Dearden, *Management Control Systems: Text and Cases*, 3rd ed. (Homewood, Ill.: Richard D. Irwin, 1976), p. 9.

5. Anthony and Dearden, *Management Control Systems*, pp. 685–686.

BIBLIOGRAPHY

Anthony, Robert N., and John Dearden. *Management Control Systems: Text and Cases*. 5th ed. Homewood, Ill.: Richard D. Irwin, Inc., 1984.

Anthony, Robert N., and David Young. *Management Control in Nonprofit Organizations*. 3rd ed. Homewood, Ill.: Richard D. Irwin, Inc., 1984.

Boehm, A.E. "Zero-Base Budgeting for Better Cost Control." *Dimensions of Health Services*, January 1978, pp. 36–37.

Broyles, R.W., and P. Manga. "Ranking: the Core of Zero Base Budgeting." *Dimensions of Health Services*, September 1979, pp. 16–17.

Calamari, F.A., G.M. Jezarian, and R. Wagner. "Zero-Base Budgeting: A Hospital Application." *Hospital Topics*, March–April, 1979, pp. 26–31.

Dillon, Ray D. *Zero Base Budgeting for Health Care Institutions*. Rockville, Md.: Aspen Publishers, Inc., 1979.

Dooskin, H.P. "Zero-Base Budgeting: A Plus for Management." *Association Society Manager*, January 1978, pp. 146–47.

Fan, D., and J. Bachtold. "Zero Base Budgeting in Social Services." *Dimensions of Health Services*, September 1979, pp. 28–29.

Farrell, M., and J. Eckert. "Zero-Based Budgeting in Nursing Education." *Nursing Outlook* 12 (1979): 792–5.

Goetz, J.F., Jr., and H.L. Smith. "Long-Term Care." *Health Service Administration Quarterly*, Summer 1979, pp. 139–48.

Hebert, Joseph L. *Experiences in Zero Base Budgeting*. Princeton, N.J.: Petrocelli Books, 1977.

Herzlinger, R.E. "Zero-Base Budgeting in the Federal Government: A Case Study." *Sloan Management Review*, Winter 1979, pp. 3–14.

Jessen, H., and J. Malcom. "Zero Base Budgeting in Medical Records." *Dimensions of Health Services*, September 1979, pp. 30–32.

Katz, E. "A Review of Zero Base Budgeting." *Dimensions of Health Services*, September 1979, p. 4.

Kaud, F.A. "The A to Z of Zero Base Budgeting." *Food Management*, May 1979, pp. 25–26.

Olson, M. "Zero-Based Budgeting in Food Service Departments of Health Care Facilities." *Journal of the American Dietetic Association* 74 (February 1979): pp. 146–48.

Otten, G.L. "Zero-Based Budgeting: Implications for Social Services?" *Administrative Social Worker*, Winter 1977, pp. 369–78.

Pattillo, James W. *Zero Base Budgeting: A Planning, Resource Allocation, and Control Tool*. New York: National Association of Accountants, 1977.

Pyhrr, Peter A. "Peter Pyhrr on Zero Base Budgeting" [interview by Patricia Rummer]. *Hospital Finance Management*, March 1979, pp. 32–33.

Read, D. "Zero Base Budgeting in Food Service." *Dimensions of Health Services*, June 1979, pp. 22–24.

Sargent, C.W. "Zero-Base Budgeting and the Library." *Bulletin of the Medical Library Association* 66 (January 1978); pp. 31–35.

Schick, Allen. "Zero Base Budgeting and Sunset: Redundancy or Symbiosis?" *Forum—The Bureaucrat*, Spring 1977, pp. 12–31.

Suver, James D., and Bruce R. Neumann. "Zero Base Budgeting." *Hospital and Health Care Administration*, Spring 1979, pp. 42–63.

Suver, James D., and Ray L. Brown. "Where Does Zero Base Budgeting Work?" *Harvard Business Review*, November–December 1977, pp. 76–84.

Thompson, G. Byron, and Peter Pyhrr. "Zero Base Budgeting: A New Skill for the Financial Manager." *Hospital Financial Management*, March 1979, pp. 26–33.

Vornbrock, J.G. "Should Hospitals Use Zero-Base Planning and Budgeting?" *Hospital Progress*, May 1979, pp. 69–70, 82.

Wood, G. "Zero Base Budgeting for a Psychiatric Hospital." *Dimensions of Health Services*, September 1979, pp. 18–20.

Chapter 20

Functional Value Analysis: A Technique for Reducing Hospital Overhead Costs

James E. Bennett
McKinsey and Company

Jacques Krasny
McKinsey and Company

Many administrators feel that the methodology suggested for functional value analysis (FVA) could beneficially be applied to many aspects of hospital administration beyond overhead functions. Some base their comments on their own experience in applying approaches similar to FVA to nonoverhead activities. Others—who have not yet used a similar technique—believe that FVA's discipline in methodology and in-depth participation of hospital personnel could produce results in areas such as radiology, laboratory, and nursing.

In the past several years, both policy makers and providers of service in the health care field in North America have increasingly faced the problem of balancing a seemingly infinite demand for care with limited financial resources. Hospital budgets—as the largest (50 percent) and fastest growing (13 to 15 percent annually) component of total health care costs—have felt the pressure most directly, particularly in Canada, where provincial governments have imposed stiff restric-

tions on growth in funds for existing activities and have cut back expenditures on new services.

While few American hospitals outside the Veterans Administration and military health systems may have yet felt the squeeze, the betting is that they soon enough will. For example, it is widely agreed that any move toward national health insurance must be accompanied by a vigorous cost containment program, which should include the prospective reimbursement of hospitals under a federally mandated scheme operated through commissions established by state legislation.

Thus, pressure on hospital budgets seems to be a matter of "when" rather than "whether." How, then, can hospital administrators in both Canada and the United States meet growing patient needs with increasingly less incremental money? Surely, before reducing individual services or taking steps to cut the overall utilization, an administrator should tackle nonmedical "overhead" costs, which typically account for 30 to 50 percent of the hospital's annual operating expenditures.

In this article we describe how to launch such an attack through FVA, a technique developed and proven in industry to achieve lasting 15 to 20 percent reductions in overheads. In FVA, total nonmedical expenses are broken down into cost centers with budgets of not more than

In the course of preparing this chapter, we solicited and received a great deal of valuable critique and inpi₁ from hospital and health care administrators. We gratefully acknowledge this assistance.

This chapter is reprinted from *Topics in Health Care Financing*, Vol. 3, No. 4, pp. 38–54, Aspen Publishers, Inc., © Summer 1977.

$500,000. A full-time task force assists the head of each such "unit" in going through a disciplined, analytical, and idea-generating process that must result in identification of a 30 to 40 percent saving. Cost reduction ideas are then evaluated by all managers who "consume" the unit's services, and finally, senior hospital management chooses the ones that will be implemented. From beginning to end, the process takes some four to six months.

In the remainder of this chapter we briefly outline why nonmedical costs should be top priority for attention and why FVA is likely to be successful. The article then describes how FVA is organized and carried out, and concludes with several questions to help administrators decide whether the technique is "right" for their hospitals.

OVERHEAD: FIRST TARGET FOR COST CONTAINMENT

As administrators are well aware, the most effective way to contain hospital costs is to cut back a particular service or reduce the overall utilization of the institution. Thus, significant savings can result if maternity services are eliminated or if the hours of outpatient clinics are substantially curtailed—provided that the hospital's manpower is reduced by the equivalent of most of the staff who worked in those areas. Similarly, a cooperative effort between the administrative and medical staffs to reduce average length of stay can produce substantial savings, but only if the freed-up beds are closed; otherwise, more patients will be admitted and total costs will *rise* due to the greater medical expenses incurred in the first days of a patient's stay.

Clearly, these types of actions most directly hurt the very individuals an institution is in business to serve: the patients in its community. Even if skillfully handled they are likely to arouse intense and emotional opposition from hospital employees—particularly the medical staff. Thus, it seems apparent that containing expenditures by eliminating services or reducing overall utilization should be pursued only after all other reasonable avenues have been exploited. Such an avenue is nonmedical costs, or what might be termed hospital "overhead."

Overhead is a substantial component of total operating expenditures. For example, an examination of the cost structure of 230 hospitals in Ontario shows that of the seven expense categories that make up more than three-quarters of costs, four are basically nonmedical: building operations, housekeeping, dietetics, and general administration (Figure 20-1). If the purely administrative components of nursing, laboratory, and radiology services were included, overhead in a large Canadian hospital could range from 30 percent to 50 percent of total operating expenditures. While the precise figures might vary in American hospitals, the proportions—excluding physicians' salaries—appear to be essentially similar.

Unlike other services, these overhead components—with the possible exception of dietetics—have little impact on the quantity and quality of *medical* care available to the institution's patients. Housekeeping may have some effect on a patient's comfort and convenience, but building operations and general administration seldom impinge on the patient during his or her stay in the hospital.

Then, if expenditures must be contained, these nonmedical, overhead costs should be the first place to look. Before taking the harsh step of cutting services, the prudent hospital administrator will ensure that the expenses of functions like housekeeping have been pruned to the limit.

FVA: AN EFFECTIVE TECHNIQUE

In undertaking the pruning job, the administrator has a range of choices. At the one extreme, he or she can wield a hatchet—for example, by requiring each overhead function to cut its budget by an arbitrarily decided percentage. While this approach may achieve results in a hurry, savings rarely last because the type and volume of work to be done do not really change; moreover, the wrong areas may be cut, genuine opportunities missed, and staff morale damaged in the process.

At the other extreme, the administrator and his or her immediate staff can undertake an exhaus-

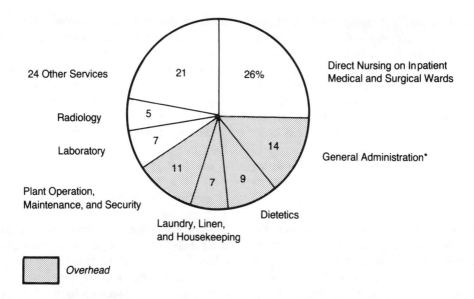

*In Canada, this category usually includes employee fringe benefits for the entire hospital. These would have to be allocated to other categories to reflect a fully accurate cost breakdown.

Figure 20-1 Ontario Public General and Allied Special Hospitals (Total Expenditures = 100 Percent)

tive review of all the work performed, and then modify some tasks or eliminate others. Although this might yield lasting savings, seldom is the necessary time available.

FVA is between these two extremes, but somewhat closer to the latter. Having been developed in private industry, FVA combines comprehensiveness with the sense of urgency imposed by the need to achieve rapid results. In the industrial context, the technique is a proven performer. More than 50 major companies in nearly every type of business have achieved lasting savings as high as 20 percent of overhead—which would be the equivalent of roughly $2 million annually in a large hospital with a $30 million operating budget.

Although FVA is not yet fully tested in hospitals, the features that have made it effective in industry point to success in the hospital context:

- Discipline: As will become clear later in this chapter, FVA is a systematic and carefully programmed review of *all* the activities and "end products" produced by overhead units within the scope of the examination. Thus, FVA enables management to overcome the fact that there are few

"big ticket" items that can result in easy cost reductions, and to come to grips with the countless individual tasks that together result in substantial overhead expense. Moreover, the disciplined review invariably reveals a high proportion of resources that are being devoted to comparatively unimportant tasks or are producing limited results.

- Involvement: FVA is carried out by the down-the-line professionals who actually run the operation. With guidance from a task force, they are the ones who identify the cost of each end product, and who generate ideas on how the same or better results can be achieved less expensively. Industry has found that this in-depth involvement leads to savings that last, both because changes are practical and because the people in charge are committed to implementing them. This should be particularly the case in the hospital setting, where much of the work is highly specialized and is managed by professionals who are suspicious—often rightfully—of attempts to intrude on their jurisdiction.

• Imagination: In carrying out FVA, down-the-line people are asked to identify savings opportunities that add up to a very challenging target—typically 40 percent of budget. Even though implementation generally goes no farther than half of this amount, managers and their subordinates are required to use all their ingenuity and imagination in generating ideas to meet the target. Through this process, a surprising number of innovative cost-cutting approaches typically result.

Although these features of FVA originated in engineering disciplines and were then adapted to private industry, hospital personnel clearly possess all the prerequisites for applying the technique: dedication to professionalism, ingenuity, and the willingness to work hard.

PHASE I: GETTING FVA UNDER WAY

If a hospital is persuaded that functional value analysis makes sense, how should it actually use the technique? To begin with, FVA—like any major management undertaking—requires careful advance planning to be successful. Thus, Phase I of the effort should be devoted to four preparatory steps:

1. deciding on the scope of the effort
2. organizing the FVA team
3. establishing the ground rules
4. developing communications and manpower programs

Deciding on Scope

The first step is to decide which parts of the hospital budget will be considered as overhead expense and will thus be included in the analysis. As a starting point, it seems reasonable that all of the "hotel" components of the hospital should be included: dietetics, housekeeping, and plant operations. General administration would also be a prime candidate, including some medical support activities such as records. At the judg-

ment of the executive director, the administrative component of the more directly medical functions such as nursing, laboratory, and radiology services might be involved as well. Indeed, the going-in premise should be that a unit ought to be included if it is more likely to benefit from a systematic self-examination of costs than to suffer from the inconvenience of undergoing the process.

Organizing the Team

The FVA "team" has three principal parts: unit managers, a task force, and a steering committee. Almost all of the members of this team are regular line management of the hospital who take on extra FVA functions for the duration of the process. In their FVA capacities these individuals direct, monitor, or actually carry out the generation and evaluation of cost reduction ideas. However, decisions as to what will be implemented and how it will be done are made by the normal chain of command of the institution. Figure 20-2 illustrates the way in which the relationships of the FVA team and line management interlock.

The unit managers—who spend from 5 to 40 percent of their time on FVA—are the most important component of the team. Because of their thorough knowledge of the operations of their units, they must be the ones to organize the cost data, generate the savings ideas, and take the lead in assessing their feasibility. As a selection criterion, each unit manager should be regarded as the obvious leader of the unit by his or her peers and subordinates, and should have 10 to 30 subordinates with a budget of not more than $500,000. The quality of the overall effort is primarily a factor of the quality of work done by these people.

Next, the full-time task force should be selected, with a rule of thumb being one task force member for every five to ten unit managers. In practical terms this will mean a task force of four to five people in a large hospital. The function of the task force members is first to tailor FVA to the specific needs of the institution. Then they must teach the necessary analytical techniques to the unit managers and, in a

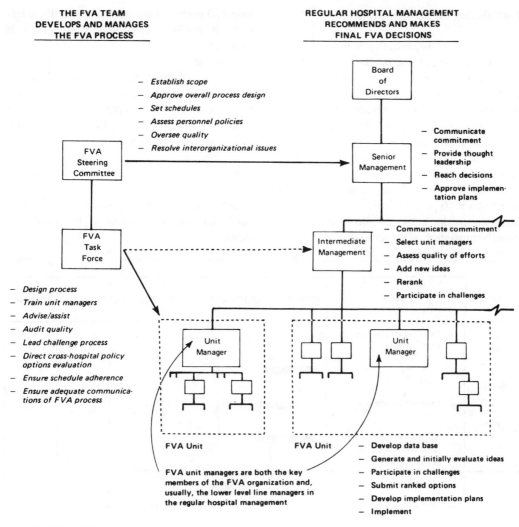

THE FVA TEAM DEVELOPS AND MANAGES THE FVA PROCESS

- Establish scope
- Approve overall process design
- Set schedules
- Assess personnel policies
- Oversee quality
- Resolve interorganizational issues

FVA Steering Committee

FVA Task Force

- Design process
- Train unit managers
- Advise/assist
- Audit quality
- Lead challenge process
- Direct cross-hospital policy options evaluation
- Ensure schedule adherence
- Ensure adequate communications of FVA process

REGULAR HOSPITAL MANAGEMENT RECOMMENDS AND MAKES FINAL FVA DECISIONS

Board of Directors

Senior Management

- Communicate commitment
- Provide thought leadership
- Reach decisions
- Approve implementation plans

Intermediate Management

- Communicate commitment
- Select unit managers
- Assess quality of efforts
- Add new ideas
- Rerank
- Participate in challenges

Unit Manager

Unit Manager

FVA Unit

FVA Unit

FVA unit managers are both the key members of the FVA organization and, usually, the lower level line managers in the regular hospital management

- Develop data base
- Generate and initially evaluate ideas
- Participate in challenges
- Submit ranked options
- Develop implementation plans
- Implement

Figure 20-2 The FVA Team

consultative capacity, assist them in carrying out the process. Finally, the task force maintains the discipline of FVA, by stressing adherence to deadlines and thoroughness of work. To ensure a balanced perspective in carrying out these functions, the task force might well include at least one physician and one senior nurse, in addition to administrative personnel.

Finally, a four- or five-member FVA steering committee and a chairman should be appointed from among the senior management of the hospital. This group is accountable to its colleagues as well as to the board of directors for the success of the overall program. In addition, it is charged with making any FVA process decisions—such

as which departments should or should not be included and how much time should be allowed for completion. In a large hospital, the FVA steering committee could be formulated in the same manner as most ad hoc project committees. In a smaller institution, the regular management group could, as a whole, take on this extra responsibility. The actual workload for this group is typically quite light—but it is an essential requirement for successful FVA.

The task force can and should effectively administer the program, but unless a high-level body actually "owns" and is responsible for FVA, there is a real risk of floundering and not getting the best possible results for the effort.

Establishing the Ground Rules

Once the FVA organization is in place, some ground rules for carrying out the analysis should be set. To begin with, each unit that will undergo FVA must be assigned a "stretch target"—that is, a percentage of its gross budget that becomes the target total of all its cost reduction ideas. As noted earlier, the purpose of this number is to stretch the thinking of unit managers and make sure that all good ideas are brought forward and discussed. The target that has usually been used in industry is 40 percent. In the hospital environment, this might be divided into 20 percent that could be implemented immediately, and an addi-

tional 20 percent that would substantially reduce the unit, but still permit it to continue its core functions.

In addition, because a key aspect of FVA is discipline, a rigorous timetable should be established for the completion of each of the analytical and decision-making steps that make up Phase II. Typically, the total FVA process takes four to six months (Figure 20-3). If necessary, it can either be done more quickly or can be extended to accommodate vacations or unusually heavy workloads. As in every other aspect of the process, the timing should be tailored to the needs and limitations of the individual hospital.

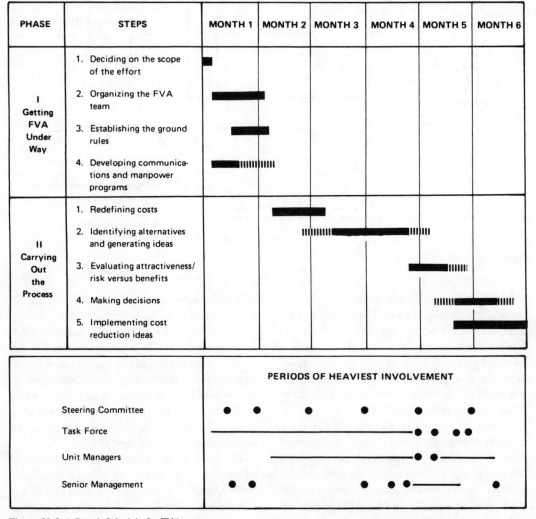

Figure 20-3 A Rough Schedule for FVA

Developing Communications and Manpower Programs

Before FVA is launched, hospital management should develop a communications program to protect the interests of the institution. For example, any senior administrative personnel and professional staff who were not part of the decision to undertake FVA should be sold on its needs and merits. In addition, the technique and timetable should be explained to the rest of the management and professional staff, and then management's intentions should be explained to union leaders—with the aim of gaining their understanding and, ideally, their cooperation. A complete communications program should also cover special interest groups, and should include contingency plans for explaining the effort to the community, should the need arise.

Perhaps the most critical preplanning step is the formulation of a manpower program. Because some two-thirds of hospital operating costs are personnel-related, achieving meaningful savings will at some point require manpower reductions. Given the relatively high turnover in many employee categories, it should be possible to capture most of these reductions in a reasonable time period through attrition. Nonetheless, it may be prudent to develop plans for reassigning personnel whose activities have been altered or eliminated, and it may be important to establish a program for accelerating attrition through such measures as special early retirement benefits. Further, in some hospitals, management might decide that the need for quick savings requires layoffs. If so, special severance benefits or relocation assistance may be needed. Whatever form the manpower program takes, however, management should think through the likely union reaction and prepare a labor relations strategy accordingly.

PHASE II: CARRYING OUT THE PROCESS

Once the appropriate groundwork has been laid, the hospital can get on with the job of carrying out the five main FVA steps that lead to lasting cost reductions:

1. redefining costs
2. generating cost reduction ideas
3. evaluating attractiveness—risk versus savings
4. making decisions
5. implementing ideas

While outside consultants can be invited to assist in all five steps, their role should be primarily one of guidance and quality control of the overall process. Indeed, the success of FVA depends on the extent to which the institution's own managers assume responsibility for the effort.

Redefining Costs

In the first step of the FVA analytical process, each unit manager carefully analyzes exactly what his or her unit produces or does for the other parts of the hospital and determines how much this costs.

Analysis of Function

The analysis begins with the development of a three-part "function tree" for each unit. As Figure 20-4 illustrates, a function tree should start with the basic missions of the unit. These are the reasons—usually few in number—that explain the "why" of the department. Some examples are "to provide clean linen," "to maintain hospital accounts," "to maintain building security," and "to maintain medical records." Stemming directly from the mission are activities—for example, the activities supporting the mission "to provide clean linen" might include

- collecting dirty linen
- inventorying linen stocks
- laundering dirty linen
- redistributing clean linen to wards and services
- purchasing new linen as required

The third element of a function tree is the end products and services of the unit, which can usually be stated as nouns or noun phrases. In some cases, they may be physical goods such as "clean linen" or "the clean linen inventory." In

MISSIONS   ACTIVITIES   END PRODUCTS

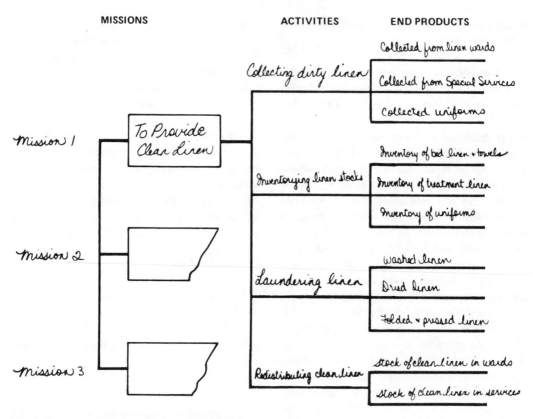

Figure 20-4 The FVA Function Tree—A Simplified Example

others, they may be more conceptual—for example, "tight building security" or "control of records." Once completed, the function tree provides a clear picture of what the particular unit is all about: a concise description of its missions, of its activities, and of the end products and services it produces.

Determining Cost of Operation

With this picture in hand, the unit manager goes on to determine how much his or her operation is costing the hospital—both in total and for each activity and end product or service. To determine the total, he or she first develops a "base line budget" for the unit. This budget should include the salaries and benefits of employees whose time is completely dedicated to the unit, as well as the cost of supplies the unit itself consumes. In addition, the base line budget must include an estimate of the resources indirectly used by the unit, such as the cost of floor

space, utilities, and general building services. Most American hospitals should find this allocation relatively straightforward, as they are accustomed to tracking indirect cost by service as a basis for determining patient charges. Although Canadian hospitals seldom assign indirect costs on this basis, the FVA task force and the unit managers should be able to develop rules of thumb that will enable at least an approximate allocation to be made without too much difficulty.

This approach will mean that the arithmetic total of the base line budgets of all FVA units will be substantially greater than their total current operating expenditures, because of double counting of some cost elements. For example, if base line budgets are developed properly, a dietetics department will include laundry as a cost of its meal service, while the housekeeping unit will show laundering expense as one of the elements in its base line budget. This method of double and frequently triple counting goes a long way toward helping the unit managers understand how much the services they provide actually cost the hospital. Also, the more angles from which a particular cost element is viewed, the greater are the chances of coming up with useful cost reduction ideas.

With the base line budget nailed down, the unit manager must then allocate it against all the end products he or she has defined. Because this is intended to be an exercise in judgment, rather than advanced accounting, accuracy of plus or minus 15 percent is quite acceptable. To avoid unnecessary detail, a useful rule of thumb is that no end product or service should be smaller than $2,000 or one-tenth of a man-year. The actual

allocation can be accomplished by creating a work sheet that arrays all the end products and services down one axis, and all the cost elements of the department (individual employees and nonpersonnel costs) across the other axis (Figure 20-5). This approach ensures that all the expenses of the unit are accounted for, and it also enables individuals to be involved in deciding how their own time is allocated to the various end products or services that are produced.

Generating Ideas

Once costs have been redefined for all units, the next step is to think about ways in which each

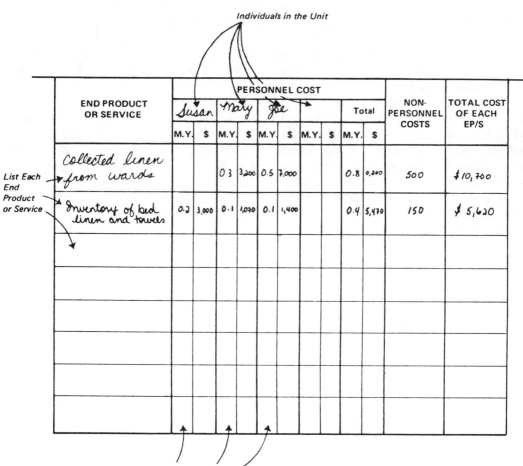

Individuals in the Unit

END PRODUCT OR SERVICE	PERSONNEL COST										NON-PERSONNEL COSTS	TOTAL COST OF EACH EP/S
	Susan		*Mary*		*Joe*				Total			
	M.Y.	$	M.Y.	$	M.Y.	$	M.Y.	$	M.Y.	$		
Collected linen from wards			0.3	3,200	0.5	7,000			0.8	10,200	500	$10,700
Inventory of bed linen and towels	0.2	3,000	0.1	1,070	0.1	1,400			0.4	5,470	150	$5,620

List Each End Product or Service

The Total of Any Person's Time Must Equal 1.0 M.Y.'s

Note: *M.Y.* = the fraction of the man-year spent on the end product
$ = the dollar value (based on salary plus fringes) of the time spent

Figure 20-5 FVA Resource Allocation Work Sheet—A Simplified Illustration

expense component could be reduced or eliminated. This second step is the heart of FVA, and
the overall effectiveness of the technique depends on how thoroughly and creatively it is
carried out. The key, of course, is to work with
the data base developed in the previous step—
which may already have generated a number of
likely opportunities.

Here, the task force plays a major role, as it
has the responsibility of designing for each unit
manager the best method of generating cost
reduction ideas. "Think sessions" are most frequently used in industry, but other methods—
such as consultation with peers in other hospitals—should be used as a supplement whenever
they seem likely to yield promising suggestions.

In any event, there should be at least one
"think session" for each unit manager. The
people who attend should be carefully chosen to
make sure that as many ideas as possible are
generated and discussed. At a minimum, this
would include the unit manager and his or her
one or two most trusted lieutenants. In addition,
at least one task force member should attend,
along with any expert either from within or outside the hospital who has something to contribute. For example, an individual from a hotel
chain might usefully participate in housekeep-
ing-related sessions, and someone from industry
who is familiar with scheduling techniques
might provide valuable input to cost reduction
ideas related to housekeeping and maintenance
schedules.

This work group should look at each end product or service of the unit in turn, and first consider each of the following possibilities to reduce
"demand" for the service:

- reduction in amount, frequency, or quality
- outright elimination
- combination with another activity
- deferral to a later point in time

In addition, consideration should be given to
automation (or deautomation), to having the
workload rebalanced, and to changing the work
flow entirely. For example, if "hospital security" is the end product being considered,
ideas might involve switching partially to electronic devices, closing or converting some doors

to "one way only," getting local police to patrol
hospital grounds regularly, asking the taxi dis-
patcher at the front door to perform some
security duties, arranging for volunteer groups to
perform some security functions, and so on.
Similarly, Figure 20-6 illustrates several ideas
that might be applicable to the end product "collected linen." Regardless of the end product or
service, all ideas should be considered no matter
how implausible they may seem at first. Frequently, those that are unthinkable on first examination can be modified to be more realistic,
and ultimately result in significant expense
reductions.

At this point in the FVA process, the predetermined "stretch target" becomes an important
element. The unit manager and his or her colleagues cannot declare peace on Step 2 until they
come up with cost reduction ideas, the total
value of which is equal to the target percentage
of their base line budget—usually the 40 percent. Again, while it is unlikely that this fraction
of any unit can or should be eliminated, every
attempt should be made to reach the figure, since
only with this challenge will every opportunity
be identified for examination. For this reason,
individual units should be given relief from the
target in only the most extenuating circumstances—and then only with the agreement of
the FVA steering committee.

Evaluating Attractiveness

In Step 3, line management—with the help of
the task force—evaluates the many ideas that
have been generated. In essence, for each idea
this means weighing up the potential dollar savings against the many kinds of risks involved.
First, an approximate (plus or minus 15 percent)
savings figure is put against the idea. Then, risk
is assessed in three stages: first, the types and
severity of consequences are considered; second, and independently, the probability of their
occurrence is estimated; and finally, these two
factors are combined to assess the total risk
incurred.

In assessing the severity of adverse consequences, the first consideration should, of
course, be any impact on the comfort or conve-

END PRODUCTS AND SERVICES	DOLLAR EXPENDITURE	ACTIVITY																		
		DEMAND REDUCTION						STREAMLINING								OTHER			
		REDUCE																	
		Amount	Frequency	Quality	Eliminate	Combine/substitute	Defer	Combine	Automate	De-automate	Balance workload	Change procedure or workflow	Increase skill level	Decrease skill level	Make or buy				
Collected linen	$10,700		1	2		3	4	5	6										

1. Collect linen only once per day.
2. Don't sort linen at the wards.
3. Collect linen and dirty dishes at the same time.
4. Collect linen only as new linen is needed and delivered.
5. Install linen sheets
6. Have ward orderly prepare linen for collection.

Figure 20-6 Idea Generation Work Sheet—A Simplified Illustration

nience of patients; for example, eliminating a snack may be felt to be a significant inconvenience. Beyond this, the effect on staff morale or professional competence must also be assessed. Finally, adverse consequences of a financial nature could be involved, in that a small saving could lead in the long term to a substantial net expense. When these types of consequences appear to be unacceptable, a unit manager should evaluate whether corrective action could be taken or the change reversed if the consequence were in fact to occur. Taking all these factors into account, then, he or she must rate the severity of risk of each idea as being slight, moderate, severe, or extreme.

Quite separate from the severity of an adverse consequence is the likelihood of its occurrence. For example, while eliminating one security guard might increase the risk of an extensive fire, the probability of such an event is relatively low. The unit manager must make a similar judgment as to the likelihood of occurrence of the adverse consequences he or she has identified for each idea, using three broad bands of probability: low (zero to 20 percent); medium (21 to 60 percent); or high (61 to 100 percent).

The assessments of both severity and probability are then combined by using a three-by-four matrix as illustrated in Figure 20-7. For ideas that fall into the high-risk category, the unit

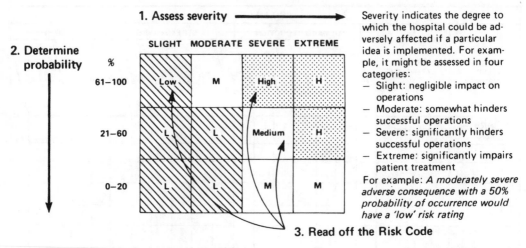

Figure 20-7 A Matrix for Determining the Risk of Ideas

manager should search for ways to reduce either the severity or likelihood—even if that means forgoing some portion of the potential savings.

Finally, this overall assessment of risk can be combined with the estimated potential savings to form an overall attractiveness score (Figure 20-8). In this way, each cost reduction opportunity can be ranked from the most attractive (high potential saving, low risk—Code A) to the least attractive (low saving, high risk—Code I). This overall attractiveness ranking permits the comparison of all the ideas from all the FVA units. For example, an A-rated idea from one part of the organization should be more attractive than a C-rated idea from another. A single form (Figure 20-9) is then used to summarize and describe the opportunity, to provide along with the attractiveness code a basis for decision by the FVA steering committee upon completion of Step 3 of the process.

Making Decisions

The next step in FVA involves verifying that the judgments made about potential dollar savings and risk levels are sound, and then deciding which ideas—of all those identified by the

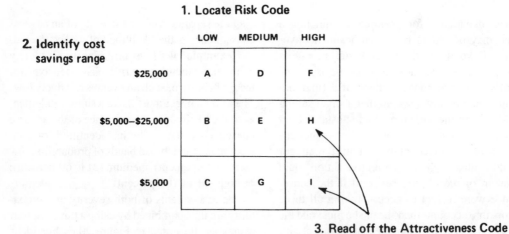

Figure 20-8 A Matrix for Determining the Attractiveness of Ideas

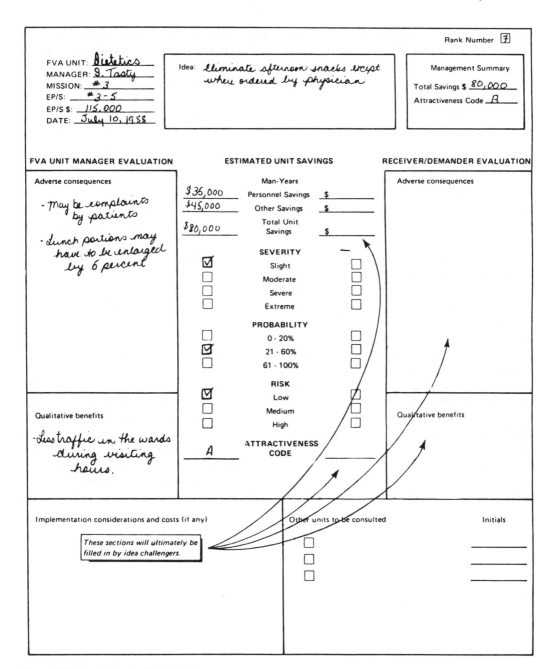

Figure 20-9 Cost-Reduction Idea Work Sheet

individual FVA units—should in fact be implemented.

To verify the judgments, every cost reduction opportunity that involves a change in a service performed for hospital personnel outside the unit in question should undergo a challenge process. That is, the other units or individuals in the hos-

pital who typically receive that service should have the chance to comment on the accuracy of the risk evaluation and to advise management of any aspects of a particular idea that have not been adequately considered. Opportunities that are internal to the unit submitting them (typically streamlining ideas) do not usually need this challenge, but it may be advisable nonetheless to obtain the reaction of the hospital's senior administrators in functions such as finance and personnel. In either event, the challenge process may well lead to changes in risk evaluations and savings estimates for individual cost reduction ideas.

With the analyses and recommendations of unit managers and the comments of the "challengers" in hand, senior management of the hospital decides which cost reduction opportunities will be implemented. They can elect to implement all those above a certain attractiveness level for every unit. Or they can seize the occasion to rethink the institution's overall priorities and substantially cut back one unit's budget (with, of course, a complete awareness of the risk involved) and increase that of another unit. Or they can make "reinvestment decisions" within a particular unit—taking suggested cost reduction moves and reinvesting the savings in another mission or activity within the same unit. No matter what course of action is finally decided upon, the FVA process should have ensured that it is based on a set of facts and analyses that reflects the realities of day-to-day operations.

Implementing Ideas

The final step of FVA is aimed at ensuring that the cost reduction ideas chosen by management are actually implemented and that estimated savings are in fact achieved. To begin with, management should ensure that every idea has one person assigned to its implementation. Generally, this assignment should be straightforward, since many ideas will have been generated by people who are well placed to carry them out. These individuals should be apprised of their responsibility and asked to develop an implementation plan describing how and when they will achieve the cost reduction objective. Periodic reviews to check progress are a useful forcing device for the individual, and also help to assure management that the projects are being carried out according to plan.

More broadly, a useful budgeting approach to facilitate implementation is the zero-base technique. In zero-base budgeting, managers develop and submit annual expense requests starting from a "zero" base, rather than from the previous year's expenses. Consequently, they must justify each cost component of their total resource package on its merits rather than merely arguing for a change from the previous year's costs. In practice, zero-base budgeting is much like Phase I of FVA and can become a natural extension of the FVA process. The real benefits of this new budgeting method are that costs are aligned to end products and the reason for a change in expenses, as it happens during FVA implementation and on a year-to-year basis, is easily observable.

WHETHER TO UNDERTAKE FVA

In summary, FVA is a two-phased process, each with a number of carefully programmed sequential steps. While in industry the technique has been proven effective in achieving lasting reductions in overhead expense, much time and work will be required of personnel of an individual hospital to achieve similar results. In addition, since staff reductions will be required at some point—even if achieved through attrition—FVA is a politically challenging exercise. Thus, a hospital probably ought not to undertake the process unless it can answer yes to at least two or three of the following quesions.

Strong Need To Contain Costs?

The basic motivation for FVA must be a strong need to cut or contain costs, as too much effort is involved to warrant using the technique as an intellectual exercise. Moreover, since most of the work is done by unit managers, they must know of and agree with the cost containment need. It is in the minds of these key people that tough questions such as "Do we really need this service at this level of quality?" and "How much is really being lost if we do away with that report?" must be answered. Frequently, FVA means they must recommend a reduction in their own department's size, responsibility, and possibly prestige. Obviously, to step up to this challenge, they must believe that the hospital really needs to cut costs.

Large Enough Hospital?

FVA, as described in this chapter, is a formal and complex process. A special organization is established, forms are designed, and a full-time task force is dedicated to the effort. Unless the institution is big enough to anticipate annually recurring savings that significantly outweigh the cost of the project, FVA is probably not warranted. As a rule of thumb, the full-blown effort is probably most appropriate in hospitals with annual operating budgets of $10 million or more, or where—using the norms noted earlier—the process could be expected to result in annual savings of at least $500,000.

FVA is flexible enough, however, to allow smaller institutions to gain some benefits from a modified version. With thoughtful adaptation, the five steps in Phase II could be collapsed into several intense working sessions or two or three small and geographically proximate hospitals could conduct a joint FVA program, sharing the full-time task force. Indeed, these hospitals should both expect and want to consider pooling and sharing some services (such as laundry), since this solution will almost inevitably be reached by a joint FVA task force. Yet another way for smaller hospitals to benefit is to wait until larger hospitals have completed FVA, and then explore the applicability of their cost reduction ideas.

Right Timing?

Some of the hospitals that are candidates for FVA have already undergone some of the more traditional types of cutbacks—"10 percent across-the-board" or "a freeze on all hiring." Often, this may mean that the workload is as heavy as ever but is assumed by fewer people. If this is the case, there is obviously a real danger of resentment and resistance to another cost

reduction effort, no matter how thoughtful. Because FVA relies primarily on the thoroughness and imagination of down-the-line hospital managers, this attitude can seriously jeopardize the success of the program, which may mean that the timing is not yet right. If no such past history exists, the main point to be made is that FVA, while it may be unpleasant, is still the most sensible approach to cost reduction. Obviously, it would be wise to ensure that this opinion is widely held if a program is to be undertaken.

Implementation Possible?

Properly done, FVA will develop new and imaginative approaches to cutting costs. However—as mentioned several times earlier—reductions will be required at some point to convert potential savings into "real" dollars. Consequently, FVA should not be undertaken unless it is likely that these reductions can, in fact, be accomplished. Where collective agreements or other legal restrictions limit the hospital's ability to let people go, these considerations must be part of the decision to conduct an FVA program. Where the decision is made to reduce staff only through attrition, management must determine whether cost reductions will be achieved quickly enough to meet budget restrictions.

Industry has long had to cope with the realities of overhead cost pressures, since expense containment is one of the main factors in competitiveness and profitability. While hospitals have always had to live within budgets of a sort, there has seldom been a great sense of urgency to contain operating expenditures. However, the urgency is coming as both public and private sources of funds are increasingly forcing hospitals to use incrementally less resources in meeting essentially unlimited patient demands. Thus, the question may no longer be whether to contain costs, as much as "What should we do?" and "When should we do it?" Functional value analysis aimed at nonmedical, overhead expense is a partial answer to the "how" question. Hospital management must answer the "when."

Chapter 21

Employee Incentive Systems

Frank G. Williams
Associate Professor, School of Health Administration and Policy
Arizona State University

Glenn Pearl
Research Assistant, School of Health Administration and Policy
Arizona State University

Employee incentive systems refer to methods and plans in which the compensation an individual employee or work group receives is determined by a contribution to productivity. In essence, the more workers and managers produce or accomplish, the more pay or other benefits they receive. The general purpose of employee incentive systems is thus to motivate the employee toward the goals of cost control, improved output, and creativity.

What motivates people? While there are perhaps many answers to this question, most employee incentives assume that motivation is created through positive reinforcement. The concept suggests that the correct reward, administered consistently and at the proper time for a specified behavior, will tend to encourage that behavior to be repeated. This is an important assumption, particularly in the health care field, where several groups hold claims to professional status. Professionals tend to be motivated by internalized rules of a particular profession. Part of the challenge in health care is to align professional imperatives with organizational fiscal or productivity goals.

The concept of incentives grew out of the scientific management movement of Frederick Taylor and others in the early 1900s, and it has been applied in various forms in industry for many years. Taylor utilized research and engineering studies to challenge and analyze traditional work methods to develop alternative processes to improve efficiency. Various pay plans based on output were also instituted as attempts to increase employee productivity, to make sure workers who produced were paid accordingly, and to give workers an incentive for performance.[1] Taylor believed that workers would share in the gains resulting from better work methods and their improved productivity, but employees came to resent scientific management. They saw it as a means for management to get workers to work harder for less.

The use of incentive systems in industry has become widespread and continues to gain supporters. In addition to pay-for-performance type schemes, there is increasing interest in employee involvement programs that seek to offer more interesting and rewarding work through job enrichment, job enlargement, and employee ownership. Several problems, however, inhibit the success of incentive programs, including employee resistance and an inability or reluctance in many cases to measure directly an individual's specific contribution to productivity. Another concern has been that incentives can lose their effect over time, as employees come to expect particular incentives as part of their basic compensation. Many other questions have arisen about whether incentive systems can respond effectively to the needs of today's employees.

A review of the literature reveals limited use of employee incentive systems in hospitals or other health care institutions, with most systems addressing the managerial level. Proponents of incentive systems have argued that this reflects a traditional lack of price competition in the health care field, but that the current prospective payment environment is perhaps creating more interest for incentive programs. Others, however, continue to argue that employee incentives are contrary to quality patient care and not suitable for application in a service industry where productivity and output remain difficult to define. The purpose of this chapter is to analyze employee incentive systems and their applicability to health care institutions.

INCENTIVE SYSTEM CHARACTERISTICS

Employee incentive systems are based on the premise that workers and managers will increase aspects of productivity over which they have control in order to obtain additional compensation. Incentive systems for workers are usually based on specific units of activity or output. They are used most often in situations where the work is routine, where standards are easy to establish, and where workers can directly affect their output. Management incentive programs are more general and tend to base rewards on accomplishment of organizational objectives. In the long run, incentives for managers may be the more effective, since these encourage a review of existing administrative systems and practices.[2]

Modern employee incentive systems emphasize the positive aspects of motivation. Positive rewards, rather than penalties, are used. In each system a standard related to productivity is established, and incentive pay or other reward is calculated according to how much the standard is exceeded.[3] At the same time, the base rate is paid even if the standard is not met. This base wage reduces a system's potential threat by assuring employees a minimum wage. Additionally, workers are not unduly penalized for events beyond their control, such as equipment failures.

When individuals or work groups consistently fail to meet or exceed standards, one should first examine the appropriateness of the standards. Has the situation changed? Are others performing adequately under similar conditions? If standards and conditions are found to be reasonable, employee training should be genuinely offered before personnel actions are applied. Employee incentive systems may help to identify unmotivated or incapable personnel, but these systems are not properly the means by which these employees are managed.

General Types of Systems

Employee incentives can be applied to individuals, to small work groups or teams, or to large groups or departments. Table 21-1 summarizes various types of incentive plans appropriate for individuals and groups, as discussed below.

Individual incentive systems at the worker level use standards developed through performance comparison and analysis, through time and motion studies, and through other work measurement techniques. Standards are determined either for the number of units produced in a given time period or for the time it takes to produce a particular unit. Standards must be specific, not estimates, and must be modified as work methods change. Inappropriate standards will lead to unwarranted pay levels and destroy the system's credibility.[4]

As compared with group incentives, individual incentives can be the stronger motivator, since employees receive all of the rewards resulting from their efforts. Bonuses are not shared with the rest of the team, and individual employees are not penalized by the lack of performance of others. On the other hand, individual incentives do not encourage employees to cooperate with others or to contribute to the total operation. Any effort that is not measured by the incentive system, such as stopping to assist a customer or fellow employee, is "counterproductive." It has also been argued that, when one has an economic

Table 21-1 General Types of Incentive Systems

Type	Description	Setting	Pros	Cons	Compensation
Individual Worker incentives	Specific standards to measure performance against; reduce absenteeism; solicit ideas; reduce errors	Worker's efforts isolated; output easy to measure	Individuals solely responsible for reward; no penalty for lack of performance by others	Does not encourage cooperation; attempts to beat system	Base + [(unit increase contribution to productivity) × (reward unit per increase)]
Managerial incentives	Bonuses or profit sharing	Manager unit's output identifiable	Encourages competi-tiveness	Short-term success dispro-portionately rewarded	Base + [(% award) × (excess $ contribution)]
Management by objectives (MBO)	Negotiate in advance specific standards	Manager unit's output identifiable	Fairness of foreknowledge of objectives; consideration of long-term goals	Difficult to determine appropriate objectives	May use worker or managerial-type incentives above
Group	Team tries to exceed predetermined goal	Longer, more complex tasks	Benefits from social interaction	Lack of cooperation between work groups	Base + [(unit increase contribution to productivity) × (reward unit per increase) × (predetermined % share of group reward)]
Profit-sharing	Often perquisites for tax advantages	For large groups	Encourages cooperation; group wins or loses together	Employee action not directly related to performance	Base + [(% award) × (excess $ contribution) × (predetermined % share of group reward)]
Scanlon plan	Labor savings; suggestion system	Generally small companies	Encourages cooperation; workers participate in decisions	Incentive may wear off in later years	Base + [(% award) × (reduction of total revenue paid for labor costs) × (predetermined % share of group reward)]
Rucker plan	Bonuses paid on improvements in revenue/cost ratio	Small to mid-size plants, mostly profitable; already good labor-management relations*	Encourages reductions in both labor and supply costs; cooperative effort	Percentage payoff greater from labor savings greater than equal reduction in material savings†	Base + [(base) × (value added/labor costs)]

continues

Table 21-1 continued

Type	Description	Setting	Pros	Cons	Compensation
Cost savings plans	Standard controllable costs established	Used more often in hospitals where reimbursement is based on cost	Savings may be shared with employees in a variety of ways; cost knowledge gained in plan development	Payments may occur to employees when profits are low†	Base + portion of savings from standard controllable costs
Improshare	Uses industrial engineering standards and actual work hours	Emphasis on working harder	Clear objectives	Lacks significant worker involvement*	[(Base) × (standard hours/actual hours)] per output unit
ESOP	Similar to profit sharing, except reward in company stock	Employees must be motivated through participation	Means of employee ownership; tax advantages for employees and company	May expose employer to dilution of control‡	Same as profit sharing. Base pay may also include stock
Complete and equal employee ownership	Each employee has one vote in decision making; strong emphasis on cooperation	Employees must be motivated through participation	Attempts to create process for improving quality of life	May take significant educational efforts	Hourly wages. Profit distribution determined by group

*Swinehart, "A Guide to More Productive Team Incentive Programs," *Personnel Journal*, July 1986, p. 114.
†Department of Health, Education and Welfare, "Employee Incentive Systems for Hospitals," Health Services and Mental Health Administration, 1972, pp. 13–14.
‡Siegal et al., "ESOPs—The Present and an Imperiled Future? *CPA Journal*, January 1986, pp. 20–22.

motive, the desire to get as much as possible leads to attempts to best the system through false reporting and manipulation of the time and motion studies.[5]

Individual employee incentive systems are most effective in situations where a worker's efforts are relatively isolated from those of others. Typically these are situations where the work is labor-intensive and relatively simple and straightforward, where output is easy to measure, where quantity is more critical than quality, and where a worker's pace is not affected by others. Individual incentive systems are common in piecework and sales. They have also been applied to reduce absenteeism, to solicit ideas and suggestions, and as bonuses for fewer errors.[6]

When applied to the management level, individual incentive systems are also more appropriate when the output or contribution to organizational objectives of a manager's unit can be identified separately. Individual manager incentive programs generally take the form of bonuses or profit sharing in situations in which a certain degree of competitiveness among managers is thought to be desirable. One researcher has determined that as organizations grow and diversify, the range and variability of possible bonus system payoffs increase, and bonuses become more closely tied to performance rather than position. However, this researcher has also noted that executive incentive compensation systems do not always properly balance payoffs for short- versus long-run performance or balance rewards for risk aversion versus risk taking.[7] For these and other reasons, greater utilization has been made of performance appraisal systems under management by objectives (MBO). The principle of MBO is that managers and their supervisors negotiate in advance specific, objective statements of what must be accomplished by a given date. Objectives are considered in light of long-run organizational goals so that the possible contradiction between successfully meeting individual objectives and unsuccessfully attaining organizational goals or objectives may be minimized. Managers know exactly what they are expected to achieve and are more likely to accept the subsequent determination of bonuses as being fair and equitable. Theoretically, the organization should be better off as well. Nevertheless, performance appraisal incentives under MBO are limited to the extent that one can identify appropriate long-term objectives and performance measures in advance.

One estimate claims that 75 percent or more of small- to mid-sized firms, other than hospitals, offer short-term incentives to senior management. Also, the greater the responsibility of the manager, the greater the incentive, as measured as a percentage of base salary.[8] On the international scene there is a growing trend for top-level multinational executives to be offered incentives based on performance. This trend has been instigated in part by increased competition in international business.[9]

With group or team employee incentive systems, an employee's basic compensation is supplemented in direct proportion to the extent that the productivity of the employee's team exceeds a predetermined goal. Group incentives are usually developed for longer, more complex tasks providing that, as with individual plans, the unit of production can be readily identified and measured.[10]

The trend in general industry and in health care has been a reduction in the number of employees under individual incentive plans and an increase in the utilization of group incentives. The primary reason seems to be that group incentives benefit from the social interaction and peer pressure within the work group, while workers on individual plans often restrict output because of the expected or experienced negative social and economic consequences for high productiv-

ity.[11] Employees who excel under individual incentive systems can become known as "rate busters" and are discouraged because of fears that management will set higher standards. Group incentives, however, provide a common goal that often contributes to team morale and mutual support. Employees not stimulated by the rewards of the incentive system itself may still be motivated by pressures from other group members who want the incentive.

The performance of workers under individual plans, as compared with group employee incentive systems, seems to vary according to the situation. Some evidence indicates that workers are more motivated by individual incentives to achieve if they perceive themselves as being top performers. In general, the effect of group incentive systems on performance seems to be related to such variables as the difficulty of the task; the importance of quality; and the group's characteristics, such as size and membership composition. Furthermore, as a group works together over a period of time, norms for minimum and maximum efforts for each person tend to become established.[12]

A second reason for the increased use of group rather than individual employee incentive systems is that group plans can be less costly to implement and administer. When utilizing group plans it is not necessary to develop, update, and monitor standards and performance levels for each employee. Group standards are also often easier to develop, since each individual's specific contribution to the unit of production need not be determined.

Third, there is some indication that group incentives will be in more widespread use as part of work redesign and organizational change programs.[13] Strategies for training and development that emphasize team building and communication more readily lend themselves to application of group incentives. Finally, it is suggested that "in today's complex and interdependent organization, teamwork and organizational cooperation are emphasized, rather than individual output, making direct individual rewards outside the sales function inappropriate."[14]

Group employee incentive systems in some organizations can be adversely affected by competition and lack of cooperation between work teams. Additionally, the complex nature of certain types of production and service industries makes it difficult to specify and measure output, even at the work unit level. In these situations, large group employee incentive systems are applied at the departmental or even institutional level. These plans usually base rewards on general measures of output, such as profit, sales, and costs, rather than on specific units of production or service.

Profit-sharing plans are the most common and well-known large group systems. Some of these plans offer fringe benefits such as insurance, pension plans, and other perquisites, instead of money, to obtain tax advantages for employees. Generally all full-time employees are covered under a profit-sharing plan after they have been with the company for a period of time, but some plans are limited to managers only. To ensure credibility, profits should be determined by an external audit, with incentives based on past profit data.

In addition to profit sharing there are other general types of large group plans, categorized as "labor savings." The Scanlon plan is considered somewhat unique in the way it encourages participation and includes psychological as well as monetary incentives. Employees are encouraged to be involved in decision making at all levels through participation in labor–management committees. These committees develop labor-saving suggestions that they may implement if investment requirements are minimal. More expensive and elaborate suggestions are referred to higher-level screening committees. The bonus paid to employees is based on the reduction in the percentage of total revenue that is paid for labor costs.[15]

The Scanlon plan differs from the typical suggestion system in that, to encourage cooperation, rewards are distributed to the entire group, rather than just to the individual with the original idea. The Scanlon plan also differs from profit-sharing plans in that in many profit-sharing systems workers may receive bonuses without having participated in the decision or activities that led to the increased profit. Savings are paid directly to employees, although typically a portion is held in reserve. Management usually retains the right to veto any suggestion or to limit

the suggestion committee's access to confidential information.[16] The Scanlon plan is purported to be the incentive system most compatible with labor unions, since it encourages communication of employee interests to management. The plan, in fact, takes its name from Joseph Scanlon, who was a union leader.

The "value-added" approach is exemplified by the Rucker plan. In its simplest form, value added is assumed to be the net increase in revenue, less material cost. Bonuses are based upon improvements in the ratio of value added (revenue-material cost) divided by labor costs for each production or service unit. For example, if the ratio improves 10 percent for a given period, employees receive a bonus equal to 10 percent of their base wages. The advantages of the Rucker plan are that it encourages reduction in both labor and supply costs through cooperative employee efforts, and automatically adjusts to changes in material price, price structure, and automation.[17]

The more general "cost-savings" plans have been used less in general industry than have other incentive approaches, but they have been significantly utilized in hospitals. In these plans, cost savings can be shared with employees in a variety of ways. Standards are established for material and labor costs for a given product or service mix. It is important that standards be set only for those costs that can be affected by employee action. These are referred to as "standard controllable costs."[18] Thus, cost-saving group employee incentive systems can be effective to the extent that workers believe their efforts make a difference and to the degree that costs can be identified specifically for each work group. Often one of the principal advantages attributed to implementing a cost-saving incentive plan, particularly in health care, is the knowledge that is gained concerning output, costs, and efficiency as the plan is developed.

Another form of an incentive system is the employee stock ownership plan (ESOP). Instead of paying out dollars as in profit-sharing plans, ESOPs pay with company stock. Unlike profit-sharing plans, ESOPs need not be positively and directly tied to profit. An employer "can tailor its contribution yearly to generate greater tax benefits in high income years or produce net operating losses in low income years. In addition, in light of the progressive bracket system, planning for tax bracket shifting can also be afforded by stock bonus plan ESOPs.'' There may also be tax advantages to the individual employee, similar to retirement benefits. In terms of incentive toward productivity, employees should be more motivated because of their participation in company ownership.[19]

Yet another form of employee motivation through participation consists of organizations in which all members have equal ownership rights. Such organizations stress collective decision making and general cooperation as a process for improving quality of life. The motivational factor is similar to that of ESOPs. Worker/owners are generally rewarded by a share of profits based on hours worked. The success of employee-owned organizations may be heavily dependent on sufficient orientation to the process of collective decision making and control, as workers may not be used to the idea and responsibility of being owners.[20]

Critical Issues

As noted earlier, employee incentive systems have not been universally accepted in business and industry. The particular characteristics of health care institutions that affect the feasibility of employee incentive systems are discussed later in this chapter, but it is important to note the major arguments for and against the use of incentive systems in general. The debate appears to center around three issues: (1) the relationship between incentives and motivation, (2) the financial impact of incentives with respect to wage and salary administration, and (3) the cost of implementation and maintenance.

Relationship between Incentives and Motivation

In discussing the relationship between incentives and motivation, it should first be remembered that the productivity of an employee is a function of the efficiency of the production process as well as the worker's performance. Efficiency is based on such factors as the level of

capital and technology, the characteristics of job design and operation, and management effectiveness. More specifically, productivity may be defined as the ratio of output to input. One author warns against equating efficiency with productivity. If, for example, the time it takes to do a task is reduced, efficiency has been achieved. However, if this reduction in task completion time is not accompanied by an increased output or decreased man hours, an increase in productivity has not occurred; rather, there is an increase in idle time.[21]

Employee incentive systems, which are designed to improve performance, are clearly no substitute for inadequate facilities, poor working conditions, or bad management. Incentives applied to poorly organized or poorly managed situations will only increase problem intensity and further encourage workers in their misdirected, and therefore counterproductive, efforts. Similarly, an employee's performance depends on capability as well as motivation. Obviously, incentives will lead to frustration and resistance when applied to individuals incapable of improved performance. Incentive plans can create significant expectations among employees, who say, "Now that you have made it worth my while to improve performance, show me how!" This challenge presents an opportunity to have employees participate in incentive systems, such as the Scanlon plan, to get their input on job and skill improvement. Unfortunately, there seems to be a natural tendency to view inadequate performance as being due to lack of motivation rather than to lack of employee training or low level of efficiency in the work process.

The debate concerning the relationship between incentive systems and motivation focuses primarily on what types of incentives really motivate managers and employees and whether these can be effectively controlled and paid out in some way by top management. The original, piece rate, individual employee incentive programs developed during the scientific management movement assumed money to be the prime motivator. This was a logical assumption in the early 1900s, since most nonagricultural workers were earning wages at the bare subsistence level. As wages and working conditions began to improve, however, it became evident that social and behavioral aspects were important to motivation. In Elton Mayo's now-famous "Hawthorne studies" at Western Electric, scientific management experiments were conducted to determine, among other things, the amount of lighting that would yield the best performance. Unexpectedly, the performance of the experimental work group improved, regardless of the light conditions. Employees responded positively to the attention they were getting in the experiments. Incentives offered to individuals in the Hawthorne studies also had less-than-anticipated effects on performance because work groups set informal production norms. Acceptance by fellow workers was more important than additional income in those situations.

Later work by Maslow resulted in the "hierarchy-of-need" theory. Maslow argued that a person's needs are in a hierarchy: physiological, security, social, esteem, and self-actualization. As the needs at one level are met, they become less important, and fulfilling those needs becomes less of a motivator. For example, money, which is used to meet one's physiological needs for food, clothing, and shelter, loses its incentive as these needs are met. Employees become more interested in security and social acceptance, according to this theory, as their income improves. When wages are high enough, there is even some evidence to indicate that employees will actually be motivated to work less. Sufficient income has been attained, and the rewards of less effort and even time off become more important.

Most incentive systems today are still based on the assumption that money is the prime motivator. However, as previously noted, group employee incentive systems also attempt to capitalize on the effects of interpersonal interaction, peer pressure, social acceptance, and the need for recognition by encouraging and rewarding team efforts. The issue is further complicated by society's tendency to measure esteem, success, and self-actualization in terms of wealth. Is money an incentive in itself, or a desired symbol of status and accomplishment? Many incentive programs offer merchandise, rather than cash, as rewards. Merchandise has more emotional appeal, greater visibility, and "awards people

beyond their 'comfort level,' the point at which they will not expend additional effort for incremental earnings."[22]

There have been many attempts to motivate employees by meeting their sociopsychological needs. These include programs that provide recognition; expand and enrich jobs to make work more meaningful and rewarding; and facilitate opportunities for training, advancement, team building, and organizational development. Problems arise, however, because of the difficulty in assessing and responding to each worker's needs in any systematic manner. Thus, employee incentive systems necessarily rely primarily on economic rewards, and the debate continues as to whether that is appropriate for today's worker.

The value of money as a motivator is also questioned by Herzberg's "two-factor" theory. Building on the work of Maslow, Herzberg classified motivational factors into "satisfiers" and "dissatisfiers." Satisfiers include such factors as responsibility, recognition, and the work itself, which Herzberg believed would positively motivate employees and managers. Dissatisfiers provide no positive motivation but produce only negative reactions when the individual perceives them to be inadequate. Dissatisfiers include such factors as company policy, working conditions, status, and salary.

The implication of Herzberg's research is seen when it is applied to employee merit incentive systems. Merit systems typically give certain employees an additional increase in salary for exceptional, meritorious performance when salaries are reviewed. However, when employees have been surveyed in various studies, nearly all have stated that they were above average, if not near the top, in their worth to the organization. Thus, those who receive merit pay feel that they have earned it and they are not especially motivated to perform better next year. On the other hand, except for those few who really do feel inferior, those not receiving merit pay become dissatisfied and are motivated to do less next year to balance their efforts with what they are paid. There are exceptions, of course, especially when merit awards are very large. Few systems, however, permit increases of sufficient magnitude to achieve motivation.[23]

Too often managers distribute merit money equally to avoid dissatisfaction and help offset inflationary pressures on employees. Nathan Winstanley, former manager of personnel planning at Xerox Corporation, joins many in concluding that most merit increases give little return and that "the time and effort saved by eliminating merit increase plans can be put where it can do more good, in training and development for example."[24] If merit incentive systems are to work, salary communications must be improved. Merit cannot be used as a substitute for inadequate salaries or poorly evaluated jobs, and merit bonuses must be significant and truly based on performance.[25]

Another aspect of the debate surrounding the relationship between incentives and motivation is the concept of "causal attribution." For an incentive to be an effective motivator, the employees must clearly see, understand, and appreciate the relationship between their efforts and the rewards received. The amount of the reward must depend on and be controllable by their behavior. The cause of the reward must be attributable to their performance, not to the machine's pace, the number of customers, or the manager's performance. As incentives are applied to larger and larger groups, causal attribution becomes more difficult. In profit sharing, for example, it is difficult for one worker to be motivated by believing that his or her performance will really make a difference in total profits and bonuses, especially when a change in the market or an investment decision will have much more impact.[26] For this reason, profit sharing is sometimes applied only at the management level.

A final concern about the relationship between incentives and motivation is that after a period of time employees may come to expect a reward, thereby causing it to lose its effectiveness. Incentives must be continually increased, some believe, to keep employees motivated. They argue that there should be no ceiling on earnings. In actual practice, however, there are practical limits on what any employee can achieve. Thus, the lack of a ceiling will ultimately encourage employees to find ways to "beat the system," once they reach practical performance limits. For this reason, one author suggests that ceilings

should be established, but that management should "buy back the increased productivity which employees innovate above the ceiling."[27] In theory, this places an emphasis on improving efficiency and not just on getting the most out of the incentive system itself. However, it still begs the question of whether incentives must continually be increased to maintain employee motivation.

Just as management can become concerned that employees will take incentives for granted, workers also may fear that the improved productivity levels will become expected. This year's achievement will become the standard for next year, when a new, more difficult target level will be established. Workers will be doing more for the same pay and no longer receiving a fair wage for their efforts as they see it, while management naturally attempts to contain costs and increase profit. This is a major argument of most labor unions that tend to resist employee incentive systems. Concerns by both labor and management as to who will ultimately benefit from incentives raise further questions about the long-run effect of employee incentive systems on motivation. Discussion of the issue is also complicated by studies that have found incentive systems to have a positive effect on motivation but a negative effect on job satisfaction. Even if satisfaction is not directly related to performance, other negative outcomes, such as high turnover and absenteeism, do result from low job satisfaction.[28]

The Financial Impact of Incentives

A second, less critical, issue concerning the viability of employee incentive systems is their financial impact, particularly with respect to programs in wage and salary administration. The purpose of these programs is to achieve equity in compensation. Each job is analyzed to assess its difficulty; the education, experience, and skills required; and its level of responsibility. The quantified result of this analysis is multiplied by a unit wage factor to determine the amount of pay. Real or apparent discrimination is avoided because wages and salaries are based on objective assessments of the job's value to the organization, rather than on subjective judgment of the capability of the person doing the job. Of course, even the best wage and salary programs must still be adjusted to reflect the supply and demand of personnel in the marketplace.

Contrary to some viewpoints, wage and salary administration is not necessarily incompatible with incentives. Quite frequently a salary or wage range is determined that allows a degree of adjustment based on performance. However, when employees come to view the incentive as a regular part of the wage, differing incentive amounts will result in apparent discrepancies in compensation levels between employees or work groups. Moreover, if employees perceive differences among individuals or departments concerning the effort or talent required to obtain an incentive reward, the credibility of the wage structure will be challenged. For example, it is common to award merit and bonus payments as a percentage of salary. Those with higher salaries receive larger bonuses, presumably because they are more important to the organization and thus had a larger role in achieving the productivity increase. Resulting variation in pay, however, will be greater than those suggested by wage and salary analysis. If a union exists, incentives will result in wage payments and employee outputs that differ from those negotiated in collective bargaining. One can conclude that, while employee incentive systems are not necessarily incompatible with wage and salary administration programs, inequities that exist in wage structures are likely to be exaggerated when incentives are applied. Thus, a larger, more refined, more frequently modified wage and salary administration program is required with the use of incentives than would otherwise be necessary.

The Cost of Incentive Systems

As one would suspect, the third issue critical to employee incentive systems is their cost. Typically, incentive systems cost more to implement than was anticipated because of the need for additional job evaluation, wage and salary administration, time and motion studies, and accounting.[29] After an employee incentive system has been successfully installed, it is always difficult to determine how much of the gain in performance was due to the system and how much was a result of the improved management practices that were required for implementation of the incentive program. Unfortunately, the little information that is available on the cost of employee incentive systems cannot be applied to other situations.

As noted, incentive systems assume the existence of an equitable wage structure, and it is debatable whether additional wage and salary administration costs should be included as part of the incentive system. However, job analysis and evaluation are also necessary to establish standard and target levels of performance. In service industries, such as health care in particular, a large, expensive effort is required to determine productivity and the contribution to it by specific employees or work groups. The standard of performance should be a ''fair day's work,'' which can only be determined by time and motion study or similar analysis.[30] Past performance may not be the level that is fair to expect. Management reporting costs will also increase, since cost and productivity data must be continually updated to reflect change in work processes, technology, and product or service mix. Accounting costs will increase simply because of the need to allocate costs more specifically and to keep track of each employee's production and corresponding incentive payments. As with other management programs of this type, employee incentive systems incur consulting and other implementation costs, as well as substantial cost for training, development, and communication to achieve employee understanding and acceptance.

In conclusion, support for employee incentive systems in industry varies because of widely different interpretations of costs and benefits and differences of opinion on the impact of situational variables such as the existence of a union, the nature of the production process, and employee resistance. The primary debate concerns what really motivates employees to perform and the nature and direction of the motivation that results from incentives. Differences in interpretation of costs and feasibility vary not only with the situation but also with the degree to which one assigns the costs of such management practices as wage and salary administration to the employee incentive program. Presumably, the results of employee incentive systems would speak for themselves, but, as we discuss in the next section, these results are inconclusive.

INDUSTRY EXPERIENCE

One estimate of the number of workers in the United States who are paid according to an incentive plan is around 30 percent;[31] another states 26 percent.[32] A survey by a consulting firm in conjunction with the American Institute of Industrial Engineers in 1977 reported that 44 percent of its responding companies utilized incentive plans, but the number of employees involved was not indicated. These results were compared with a study in 1959 that found 51 percent utilization, but the later study found more favorable attitudes toward incentive systems among managers. Thus, the 1977 study concluded "that there is no significant trend toward disenchantment with wage incentive."[33] Although other objective data are lacking, this survey does support the more subjective view of many authors that employee incentive systems are neither gaining nor declining in popularity to any significant extent.

The literature is generally limited to individual reports of successful employee incentive systems, with many authors taking the position that current problems with productivity in this country are due to a lack of incentive. One compensation consultant argues that incentive plans received a "deadening blow" in the 1940s, when the Internal Revenue Service (IRS) allowed the qualification of profit-sharing bonuses for retirement plans.[34] Bonuses not paid until retirement lose their incentive value. Another consultant takes the position that providing additional compensation in the form of benefits has reduced the effectiveness of incentives. Benefits are less directly related to performance by the employee, and workers profit from the expenditure only when they qualify to use a program benefit.[35]

Most of the positive reports of successful employee incentive systems in industry refer to large group applications, such as the Scanlon and Rucker plans, where the emphasis on labor's participation in decision making makes the pro-grams more acceptable to unions.[36] Of particular note is an article by Robert Schulhof, president of Rocky Mountain Data Systems, who reported in 1979 that after five years with the Scanlon plan profits increased to 11 percent on sales and 22 percent on assets, employee compensation increased 14 percent per year compounded, sales increased 16 percent per year, and turnover dropped 70 percent.[37] Rucker plans have been in place at Universal Cyclops Steel, Teledyne, and Amtrak.[38]

A more recent long-term success story reported in a case study suggested three factors of success: the plan was suggested by the union; success "in moving decision-making down to the shopfloor"; and commitment to employee involvement was sustained. The authors, however, indicate that few studies have been undertaken that assess the impact of productivity-sharing plans on organizational performance.[39] Another author warns against the possible disincentive of a Scanlon-type plan. When a plan is initially implemented, ideas and sound suggestions come quickly. As the plan gets on in years, however, the momentum of new suggestions may decrease, thus precipitating declining bonuses and presumably worker dissatisfaction. As a remedy, it is suggested that plans use more sophisticated ratios, so as not to penalize workers for prior years' successes. It is also suggested that plans be integrated as much as possible with existing suggestion and incentive structures.[40]

Since failures in implementation of employee incentive systems are generally not reported, their success rate is not known. Nevertheless, there are enough reported successes in the literature to make the case that incentive programs can be worthwhile, even if they serve only to stimulate better management and productivity analysis. While it is not feasible to list all of these possible experiences here, four are particularly worthy of note.

The first report is reviewed because of the magnitude of its results and because it is an example of an individual employee incentive system. In a plant of the Hoerner Waldorf Corporation, makers of corrugated shipping containers, most of the production processes involved individual workers operating a variety of machines. After the first 26 months of incentives, average output per employee increased 75 percent. After bonuses were paid, the net labor savings was 26 to 29 percent. And most significantly, the post-incentive periods averaged 58 percent greater efficiency as compared with industry standards.[41]

The second study offers insight into the importance of employee attitudes and values. At two separate plants of the Harwood Company, researchers gave psychological tests to employees in the respective shipping groups in order to determine why the company's incentive plan was successful in one plant but not in the other. After their tests the researchers were able to develop a model to predict productivity based on the different "psychological climates" of the two work groups. In both plants, the psychological conditions were the result of a great deal of work and effort on the part of management and a number of social scientists. They had succeeded in developing a positive attitude toward incentives in one situation, but had failed in the other.[42] In the discussion of the requirements for successful implementation of employee incentive systems later in this chapter, the reader must remember that success will be primarily contingent upon employee values and attitudes.

A third group incentive program is noted because of the unique situation in which it was applied. In 1973, a 20-month agreement was made between the city of Orange, California, and the Orange Police Association that provided for incentive payments if there was a reduction in four crimes: rape, robbery, burglary, and auto theft. During the first 7-month phase of the program, the decrease in reported crime was 17.6 percent. When the plan ended after 2 years, covered employees received a 3 percent pay increase, the maximum possible for reducing the crime rate for the entire period by 12.5 percent. Although robbery and auto theft actually increased during the period, these data were more than offset by reductions in rapes and burglaries to yield the net results.[43] It is interesting to speculate on tying incentives in health care institutions to improvements in health status.

In a fourth, more recent, example, Alamo Rent A Car has a "corporate policy of offering incentives to as many employees as possible. For example, car washers are paid a $1 bonus for every car washed. But that pool, shared by all car washers, is docked $2 for every complaint about a dirty car."[44] An incentive system for computer operations gives ten cents for every minute of "up time," and takes away ten dollars for "down time" from a bonus pool for operators. Operators may be penalized somewhat through faults not their own, such as equipment failure. The idea is for these workers to be motivated to get around all failures as quickly as possible.[45] Through a policy of aggressive use of incentive systems, Alamo may not have fine-tuned incentive relationships in regard to controllability, since workers may not be able to control mechanical breakdowns. In this case, however, incentives have motivated employees to increase the domain of controllability.

HEALTH CARE INDUSTRY EXPERIENCE

A review of wage incentive systems published in 1970 found very few descriptions of these systems actually in operation in U.S. hospitals or other health care institutions. The conclusion of that study that "wage incentives have not been extensively used in hospitals" remains valid today.[46] Since then there have been only a few additional reports. There has, however, been an increase in programs that reward individuals and committees for cost-saving ideas. Most of these programs are structured so that employees share in the institutions' cost savings through periodic cash or merchandise awards.[47]

Probably the most well-known application of employee incentives in health care is at Baptist Hospital in Pensacola, Florida. The hospital began to use incentives in the early 1960s, when it told employees they could go from a 48- to a 44-hour week and later, to a 40-hour week if they kept their output at the same level. On the average, departments met these objectives in less than a month. In 1965, incentives were formalized, first for the laundry department. Bonuses were paid for reductions in overtime and supplies. Success in this department led others to join. By 1970, the entire hospital was involved. Baptist Hospital reported convincing figures showing cost per admission to be consistently lower in recent years than comparable state and national averages, although these data were not adjusted for case mix.[48]

In 1970, Baptist Hospital expanded its incentive system into three separate programs to measure achievement in manpower utilization, supply utilization, and quality assurance. The manpower program compared actual man-hours used to standards based on engineering methods, past history, national comparisons, and detailed interviews. Standards were set for both a reward level, at which incentives begin, and a target level. "Dollars saved" is the number of hours worked below the reward level per patient day multiplied by the average hourly wage. A similar approach was used for supplies, with savings based on actual usage as compared with standard usage. Part of the total manpower and supply savings was paid to the department itself, while the rest is distributed to all employees to encourage cooperation. The quality assurance program relies on statistical sampling and audits of departmental activities to monitor quality and verify that there are no adverse effects from the incentives.[49] Although details were unavailable, a representative from the hospital indicates that a comprehensive incentive system is no longer in place. It is probably nevertheless safe to assume that the information acquired in running the incentive system in the past still contributes to management's comprehension, and thus decision control, of the organization.

Another often-reported employee incentive system in health care is the Memorial Employees' Retirement Incentive Fund, known as "MERIT," at Long Beach, California. After six months of employment, an employee may participate in the plan by investing between 2 and 10 percent of his or her salary. The hospital contributes to the fund according to relative efficiency percentage, total controllable expenses divided by operating revenues. The difference between the current percentage and that for a predetermined base period is then multiplied by the total payroll to determine the hospital's contribution to MERIT. During the first 12 years of the program, which began in 1962, the 800-bed hospital reported that its overall expense increase was 15.2 percent less than that experienced by the average community hospital.[50] Although quantitative data were unavailable, a representative of the hospital reported that the program is alive and well in the late 1980s. The interesting feature of the MERIT program is that its apparent success is contrary to the argument that incentive payments must be direct and paid immediately if they are to effect motivation.

More common are reports of incentive programs applied to just one or two departments within a hospital, where output can be more readily measured and perhaps where incentives are more acceptable. One such example is the Housekeeping Group Incentive Plan of Oak Ridge Tennessee Hospital of the United Methodist Church. This plan is unique because bonuses are paid for exceeding quality as well as efficiency standards. Equal payments are made to each employee when either quality or productivity standards are exceeded by the department as a whole. In 1975, after six years of operation, the hospital reported a savings of 11 percent of total departmental budget, with an increase in the quality averaging from 75 percent to 87 percent. A significant reduction in turnover was also reported.[51] Similarly, two other hospitals have stated they have achieved substantial productivity improvements when offering incentive pay to medical transcriptionists.[52,53]

While there are few reports of employee incentive systems in health care, especially since the early 1970s, it is interesting to note one rather unique approach. To reduce absenteeism, some hospitals play a game similar to bingo, except that the card is labeled "nurse." One number is drawn and posted each day. Each of the first five employees to complete a row wins $25. However, any person who is absent any full day during the month is ineligible. The programs appear to be successful.[54]

There is one report of a hospital incentive program that failed. Its administration concluded that a hospital that is efficient and appropriately staffed can do little to reduce costs and improve operations. This interesting conclusion was reached at Jewish Hospital of St. Louis after a one-year experiment in 1969. It was also argued that incentives work in industry because a backlog can be created, but in hospitals backlogs are not acceptable and therefore there is not the additional work to do in response to incentives.[55]

Finally, there is a more recent report of an incentive system that deserves note for at least two reasons: its targeting of physicians and its innovative conception of reward. The administration of Harford Memorial Hospital, Havre de Grace, Maryland, attempted to improve physician efficiency, as measured by standard practice patterns for the state. The reward for meeting criteria is reappointment to the medical staff. As a first step, the board of directors' bylaws were amended to include economic efficiency as a criterion for reappointment. Physicians are monitored by five screens, as follows: (1) average length of stay; (2) average charges per admission; (3) denials of admissions, days, and services as determined by existing utilization review programs; (4) bad debts; and finally (5) malpractice settlements in which physicians are codefendants with the hospital in actions resulting in significant claims. Physicians exceeding any two of the five screens are subjected to closer scrutiny to determine whether performance is inefficient. An additional review is made to determine whether there may be offsetting performance by the physician, including analysis of outpatient ancillary charges and evaluation of medical record documentation that potentially aids the hospital's reimbursement or cash flow.

After an initial negative reaction by the medical staff that resulted in a delay of the effective date for use of criteria for reappointment, the program was accepted by physicians. The year prior to first-year implementation, nine of 140 physicians were found inefficient. After the first year only three of those physicians were found inefficient, and only one did not make a dramatic improvement, although improvement was shown the next year. In addition, the efficient physicians became more efficient. Before the program, the hospital's case-mix adjusted length of stay was 8.3 percent above the state average. After the first year it was 2.5 percent below the state average. At year-end 1985, the hospital reported an average length of stay 9.1 percent below the state average. It appeared that all physicians would be receiving their reward of

medical staff reappointment when the effective date arrived in 1987.[56] It should be noted, however, that an incentive program tied into physician utilization may be in violation of a doctrine "known as the prohibition against the unlawful corporate practice of medicine."[57] Such incentive programs should therefore be pursued only under legal advisement.

FACTORS AFFECTING IMPLEMENTATION IN THE HEALTH CARE INDUSTRY

As previously discussed, the use of employee incentive systems is not widespread in the health care industry despite some apparent notable achievements. The purpose of this section is to examine some of the unique aspects of health care in order to assess the appropriateness of incentive programs in this industry.

Probably the most difficult challenge to implementing productivity incentives is to determine just what is meant by productivity, since the product of a health care facility is not easily defined or measured. As a result, the relationship between the process the incentive system is designed to reward and the outcome of the hospital or other institution is difficult to understand. Often the time and effort spent with a patient are unrelated to the quantity of patient care provided, regardless of how that output is measured.[58] Performance measurement is a problem in other service industries, but in health care there is a real question of whether the bottom line accurately reflects an institution's efficiency.

Another factor relative to employee incentive systems in health care is the special nature of quality. The quality of medical care is defined, in part, by the quantity and intensity of the service provided. Decreasing nursing hours per patient day, for example, may be the goal of an incentive program, as it was with the Baptist Hospital system previously described. However, in an earlier study by these authors, several administrators indicated that they would not be pleased if their nursing departments were significantly under budget (as adjusted for patient volume and intensity). The lower expenses for nursing would indicate to them that previously determined staffing, and therefore quality levels for patient care, had not been met. Most of the administrators surveyed also feared that since quality is hard to define or measure, employee incentive systems could make cost reduction, rather than efficiency, the primary objective.[59]

Physicians, nurses, and other health care personnel often view themselves in battle with administrators, regulators, and third-party payers who they believe are threatening the quality of patient care with controls, tight budgets, and incentives. Yet in most organizations the best services are provided by those who are the most efficient. Recognizing that much unnecessary expense is incurred in health care in the name of quality, it nevertheless must be recognized that the desire for optimum quality complicates the application of incentives to "work smarter, not harder" in the delivery of patient care.

The issues of productivity and quality brought forth another concern from hospital administrators in the authors' previous study. Successful incentive programs, it was argued, were indicative of inadequate budget preparation, a point similar to that set forth by the administration at Jewish Hospital in St. Louis, mentioned earlier. The budgeting process should set objectives and evaluate alternative means to these objectives. Incentives are appropriate for managers and participating employees at this point to encourage innovation in developing the most productive programs. However, once the most effective program has been selected and its costs accurately analyzed and allocated, there should not be any extra costs or resources to save through incentive systems. The argument continued that incentives to motivate employees to beat properly budgeted lean standards only encourage original cost estimates to be overestimated. It was the authors' recommendation that supervisors and department heads be rewarded for submitting lean budgets reflecting appropriate standards both of care and efficiency. Given the importance and elusiveness of quality, employees should be rewarded for achieving but not exceeding budgetary requirements. Hospital efficiency can best be achieved by rigorous budget preparation that stimulates planning and the

development of more effective means for patient care.[60]

Also related to the compatibility of incentive systems with quality and productivity goals is the complicated, interdependent nature of health care processes, particularly in hospitals. Since the objective of the hospital is to render individualized care and treatment directly to the client according to his or her specific needs and requirements, much of the work in the system cannot be mechanized, standardized, or planned. Work problems tend to be more variable, and work flow is more uneven. Variations in patient arrivals and emergencies create the need for standby, idle capacity that is difficult to express in terms of productivity.[61] One reason why many hospital administrators do not favor incentive programs is that expenditures theoretically under the control of a given department are often significantly affected by others, particularly physicians.[62]

With the introduction of prospective payment systems and diagnosis-related groups, managers may have better guidance and more power to implement incentive systems that require discrete outcomes for rewards. In particular, length of stay and charges for ancillary services affect costs significantly. An earlier example illustrated how physicians may be motivated to keep these variables in line if administration is bold enough to use staff privileges as an incentive. One author encourages hospitals to pay attention to a study conducted at Henry Ford Hospital, which found incentives effective for work subunits that reduced costs. It is recommended that incentives be used to enhance the cost-cutting measures of staff reductions, and better scheduling. That author suggests that such measures, including the introduction of incentive systems, are not just a good idea, but imperative under the current environment of prospective payment.[63]

In recent years, hospitals clearly have become more cost conscious. One suggested approach to this end is an introduction of product-line management into the hospital setting. Essential to the general idea of product-line management is that an organization functions as an inter-related collection of units, called strategic business units (SBUs). Properly speaking, an SBU is totally responsible for a distinct line of products or services, with responsibility for all costs, including capital expenditures, as well as revenues. Modifications of the SBU concept would include "cost centers," which are responsible for most variable costs, but not capital decisions or revenues.

While acknowledging limitations to product-line approaches to health care, one approach suggested is to develop product lines by using a marketing cube. The three planes of the cube are represented by market segments, such as consumer groups and geographic markets; clinical specialties, such as cardiology and obstetrics; and stages of production, such as prevention, diagnosis, or treatment. By extending these planes, with their divisions, through the cube, the cube becomes a block comprising individual cells. The idea is to identify clusters of cells for which it makes sense to establish a product (service) line. The concept is relatively new, and its use and impact in health care remain to be seen. It is estimated that perhaps 20 percent of Fortune 500 companies use some form of product-line management.[64] The potential application of incentives to a successfully identified product line should seem obvious. How far this concept may be carried in health care, again, remains to be seen.

A final factor affecting implementation of incentives in health care is the large number of employees who identify themselves as being professional. Their loyalty tends to be toward professional ideals, values, and standards, rather than to the organization. They do not respond to incentive systems that seem to insult their integrity with cash payment, put their professional identity at risk by equating them with "common" workers, or appear to be a threat to professional standards. "They prefer to make money by pushing up their salaries or fees, rather than by some payment by results method," according to one critic.[65]

In the early 1970s employee incentive systems in nonprofit hospitals faced a challenge from a different source, the IRS. The IRS was concerned about tax-exempt organizations that used cost-sharing plans to distribute what were in effect, profits, so it issued a prohibitive ruling.

Baptist Hospital in Pensacola, previously cited, spent two years in negotiation with the IRS to get its incentive program approved. Any standard based on departmental income or gross earnings had to be changed, and Baptist's approval applied only to its plan, not to any plan of other hospitals.[66] Although this issue can now be generally resolved, there still is a concern among many administrators that an incentive system can threaten a hospital's tax-exempt status. Obviously, this is another factor that must be taken into account in the design of an employee incentive system.

APPLICATION OF EMPLOYEE INCENTIVE SYSTEMS

Employee incentive systems are feasible in health care institutions, providing conditions are right and proper preparation is undertaken. Management and labor must really believe that incentives will work. Incentives are neither a game nor a management gimmick, and they must be consistent with a manager's style and philosophy to be successful.[67] Incentives will not be successful unless there is cost consciousness in the organization and an overall policy of rewards for performance.

Preparation begins with planning and the development of objectives. The incentive system should be designed to encourage employees at all levels to increase utilization of their time and effort, to make suggestions for methods improvement, and to accept more readily changes that improve efficiency.[68] The administrator must become an educated consumer of incentive systems to determine the one most appropriate for the organization's special characteristics. Most likely, the initial success of the program will depend on the chief executive officer's enthusiasm and support.[69] Employees should also be involved early in the program selection process to gain their acceptance and interest.

Generally, group incentive plans tend to be more appropriate for most health care employees because of the interdependency of patient care and the importance of cooperation. It is also easier to establish performance criteria at the department or service-unit level rather than at the individual level. Group incentives also alleviate the need to account for each individual's contribution to productivity. Additionally, a large group employee incentive system can be established to cover most or all employees from the beginning, if that is the desired strategy.[70] Others suggest starting with one department to test the plan and work out its problems, then build on the success throughout the organization.

Once an incentive program is selected, certain other questions should be addressed. Which employees will be eligible? Will supervisors or part-time employees be included? How long must employees wait to become eligible? (It is advisable to allow some waiting period in order to have an indication that the employee is relatively permanent and interested in the organization.) When and how will bonuses be paid? Should payments be in cash or set aside in a deferred distribution program?[71] The answers to these questions depend on the objectives of the program and employee interests.

A major requirement in the implementation of an employee incentive system is the development of productivity standards. In addition to determining accepted standards of performance, it is necessary to establish methods for measuring actual performance, means of comparing actual performance with standards, and a rule or formula for computing the incentive compensation. Standards can be either based on work study analysis within the specific organization or on industry norms that reflect what productivity should be. Historical standards are based on the previous performance of similar organizations as provided by statistics such as those of the hospital administrative studies of the American Hospital Association. Unfortunately, differences in hospital characteristics and reporting make such comparisons difficult. Subjective standards are the least desirable because they are based on "expert" opinion, or they are sometimes determined as a result of collective bargaining between management and labor.[72]

One consulting firm suggests that incentives for management be significant—that is, more significant than a salary increase—amounting to at least 12 percent to 20 percent of salary. The firm also stresses establishing clear relationships between organizational goals and objectives with specific performance measures. Hospital goals might include ensuring financially successful operations or high-quality patient care. The former may be measured by return on revenue, cost per patient day, or full-time employees per patient day, while the latter might be measured by infection rate, mortality rate, or number of lawsuits lost. It is recommended that no more than two qualitative and two quantitative goals be selected. This way a hospital is being specific about what it wants, and will better channel the efforts of its managers.[73]

Communication is important throughout the process of developing the incentive program, especially if the program is something management springs on the employees. "For a compensation system to be effective, employees must have information about the things for which they are compensated and the organization must have reliable and face valid measures to back up the system."[74] It is easy to get caught up in developing standards, measurements, procedures, and accounting systems, only to have the program fail because it was improperly presented to employees.

It should also be remembered that employee incentive systems are not static, yet too many managers are afraid to tamper with an outmoded program because of possible employee reaction. Incentive plans must be reviewed and updated regularly, normally about every two years.[75] Change can be difficult, but in an environment of fairness and equity in compensation, these regular improvements will maintain the system's credibility.

CONCLUSION

No one has yet found the universal answer on how to motivate. In fact, contemporary theory suggests that there is not one answer, but that each approach to motivation must be adapted to the situation. Employee incentive systems appear to be feasible and appropriate means for motivation in some organizations, if only as a catalyst for greater management involvement, but they are not for everyone. Nevertheless, the need to improve efficiency in health care delivery cannot be ignored.

No incentive system should be implemented without careful planning and preparation at the highest level. If the system is to succeed, the employees must want it.[76] Creating the appropriate climate and attitude and conducting the productivity analyses necessary for implementation probably achieve more results than the employee incentive systems themselves.

NOTES

1. Harold Koontz, Cyril O'Donnell, and Heinz Weirich, *Management*, 7th ed. (New York: McGraw-Hill Book Co., 1980), p. 41.

2. Charles J. Austin, "Wage Incentive Systems: A Review," *Hospital Progress*, April 1970, p. 37.

3. Department of Health, Education and Welfare (DHEW), "Employee Incentive Systems for Hospitals," Health Services and Mental Health Administration, 1972, p. 10.

4. Ibid., p. 9.

5. Edward Gross, "Incentives and the Structure of Organizational Motivation," *Hospital Administration* 16 (Summer 1971): 12.

6. Ron Zemke, "A Vote for Individual Incentive Plans," *Training/HRD* 16 (July 1979): A14.

7. Malcolm S. Salter, "Tailor Incentive Compensation to Strategy, *Harvard Business Review*, March/April 1973, pp. 94–95.

8. "Hospitals More Interested in Incentives," *Hospitals*, April 1, 1985, pp. 34, 36.

9. Brian J. Brooks, "Trends in International Executive Compensation," *Personnel*, May 1987, pp. 67–68, 70.

10. DHEW, "Employee Incentive Systems," pp. 10–11.

11. Manuel London and Greg R. Oldham, "A Comparison of Group and Individual Incentive Plans," *Academy of Management Journal* 20 (March 1977): 34.

12. Ibid., pp. 39–41.

13. Ibid., p. 34.

14. David P. Swinehart, "Compensation: A Guide to More Productive Team Incentive Programs," *Personnel Journal*, July 1986, p. 112.

15. DHEW, "Employee Incentive Systems," pp. 11–14.

16. Tom Quick, "Increasing Productivity with the Scanlon Plan," *Training/HRD* 16 (January 1979): 32.

17. DHEW, "Employee Incentive Systems," pp. 13–14.

18. Ibid., p. 13.

19. Andrew C. Siegel, Arthur A. Cohen, and Laurence I. Feibel, "ESOPs—The Present and an Imperiled Future?— Part I," *CPA Journal*, January 1986, pp. 14–22.

20. Virginia J. Vanderslice and Robert B. Leventhal, "Employee Participation: A Game Plan for the Real World," *Training and Development Journal*, February 1987, pp. 34–35.

21. Brian Channon, "Dispelling Productivity Myths," *Hospitals,* October 1, 1983, pp. 103–4.

22. Robert C. Eimers, George W. Blomgren, and Edward Gubman, "Money versus Merchandise: Which Is the Best Motivator—and the Best Incentive?" *Training/HRD* 16 (July 1979): A10.

23. Guy B. Arthur, "Money As a Motivator," *Southern Hospitals* (February 1971): 29.

24. Nathan B. Winstanley, "The Use of Performance Appraisal in Compensation Administration," *Conference Board Record* 12 (March 1975): 43–47.

25. C. Richard Farmer, "Merit Pay: Viable?" *Personnel* 55 (September/October 1978): pp. 57–63.

26. Gross, "Incentives and the Structure of Organizational Motivation," p. 11.

27. Mitchell Fein, "Restoring the Incentive to Wage Incentive Plans," *Conference Board Record* 9 (November 1972): 19–21.

28. Donald P. Schwab, "Conflicting Impacts of Pay on Employee Motivation and Satisfaction," *Personnel Journal*, March 1974, pp. 196–200.

29. Gross, "Incentives and the Structure of Organizational Motivation," p. 11.

30. DHEW, "Employee Incentive Systems," p. 31.

31. R. Michael Donovan, "Getting Your Incentive Plan under Control," *Industrial Management*, July–August 1978, p. 10.

32. Ron Zemke, "Sharing the Wealth: HRD's Role in Making Incentive Plans Work," *Training/HRD* 16 (January 1979): 31.

33. Robert S. Rice, "Survey of Work Measurement and Wage Incentives," *Industrial Engineering* 9 (July 1977): 18.

34. David J. Thomsen, "Compensation and Benefits," *Personnel Journal* 57 (October 1978): 538.

35. Samuel C. Walker, "Improving Cost and Motivational Effectiveness of Employee Benefit Plans," *Personnel Journal*, November 1977, p. 570.

36. Quick, "Increasing Productivity," p. 33.

37. Robert J. Schulhof, "Five Years with a Scanlon Plan," *Personnel Administrator* 24 (June 1979): 59.

38. Zemke, "Sharing the Wealth," p. 31.

39. Christopher S. Miller and Michael Schuster, "A Decade's Experience with the Scanlon Plan: A Case Study," *Journal of Occupational Behavior* 8 (1987): 168.

40. Swinehart, "A Guide," pp. 112–17.

41. Donald L. McManis and William G. Dick, "Monetary Incentives in Today's Industrial Setting," *Personnel Journal* 52 (May 1973): 387–92.

42. Cortlandt Cammann and Edward E. Lawler, III, "Employee Reactions to a Pay Incentive Plan," *Journal of Applied Psychology* 58, no. 2 (1973): 163–72.

43. Paul D. Staudohar, "An Experiment in Increasing Productivity of Police Service Employees," *Public Administration Review* 35 (September/October 1975): 518–22.

44. James Connolly, "Incentives Drive Alamo's MIS," *Computerworld*, April 27, 1987, p. 74.

45. Ibid.

46. Austin, "Wage Incentive Systems," pp. 38–40.

47. Anthony Rutigliano, "Incentive Plans Gaining in Cost Control Efforts," *Health Care Week* 2 (December 4, 1978): 12.

48. Pat N. Groner, "Employee Incentives," *Topics in Health Care Financing/Cost Containment* 3, no. 3 (1977): 81.

49. Ibid., pp. 68, 76.

50. William J. Loveday, "The Merit Plan: The Key to Productivity," *Osteopathic Hospitals*, May 1976, pp. 8–10.

51. J.R. Buchan and James S. Self, Jr., "Incentive Programs—Key to Productivity," *Southern Hospitals*, May 1975, pp. 11–13, 25.

52. Frank C. Grubbs, A. Charles Collier, and Rosemary Kirk, "Bonuses Spur Transcribers' Production," *Hospitals, JAHA* 46 (March 16, 1972): 83–85, 88.

53. Elsie L. Willis, "Incentive Pay for Medical Transcriptionists," *Medical Record News*, June 1976, pp. 40–43.

54. Edward Gross, "Incentives To Reduce Absenteeism," *Dimensions in Health Service* 55 (December 1978): 26.

55. Phillip Bassin, "Employee Incentive Program," *Hospitals, JAHA* 45 (May 16, 1971): 56–59.

56. Leonard E. Cantrell, Jr., and Jeffrey A. Flick, "Physician Efficiency and Reimbursement: A Case Study," *Hospital & Health Services Administration*, November/December 1986, pp. 43–50.

57. Carl Weissburg and Kenneth M. Stern, "Can Hospitals Reward Physicians for Reducing Unnecessary Utilization?" *FAH Review*, September/October 1985, pp. 45–46.

58. DHEW, "Employee Incentive Systems," p. 5.

59. Frank G. Williams and Dwight C. Anderson, "Cost Control Incentive Programs: Appropriate for Non-Profits?" *Hospital Financial Management* 32 (May 1978): 14.

60. Ibid., pp. 14–16.

61. Basil S. Georgopoulos, "Distinguishing Organizational Features of Hospitals," in *Health Services Management*, ed. Anthony R. Kovner and Duncan Neuhauser (Ann Arbor, Mich.: Health Administration Press, 1978), p. 50.

62. Williams and Anderson, "Cost Control Incentive Programs," p. 15.

63. Steven R. Eastaugh, "Improving Hospital Productivity under PPS: Managing Cost Reductions," *Hospital & Health Services Administration*, July/August 1985, pp. 97–111.

64. Martin F. Manning, "Product Line Management: Will It Work in Healthcare?" *Healthcare Financial Management*, January 1987, pp. 23–32.

65. Gross, "Incentives and the Structure of Organizational Motivation," pp. 17–18.

66. Pat N. Groner, *Cost Containment through Employee Incentives Program* (Rockville, Md.: Aspen Publishers, Inc., 1977), pp. 39–43.

67. Groner, "Employee Incentives," pp. 84–86.

68. Stanley M. Block, "Motivating Employees To Cut Costs," *Hospitals, JAHA* 45 (November 1, 1971): 51.

69. DHEW, "Employee Incentive Systems," pp. 36–37.

70. Robert S. Lund, "A Systems Approach to Employee Incentive Planning in Hospitals," *Hospital Financial Management* 24 (April 1970): p. 29.

71. Ibid.

72. DHEW, "Employee Incentive Systems," pp. 31–32.

73. The Croner Company, "Incentive Compensation: How To Inspire Your Management Team To Succeed," presented to the Western Conference of the American College of Healthcare Executives, November 1985.

74. Edward E. Lawler, III, and R.J. Bullock, "Pay and Organizational Change," *Personnel Administrator* 23 (May 1978): 33.

75. Donovan, "Getting Your Incentive Plan under Control," p. 10.

76. DHEW, "Employee Incentive Systems," p. 41.

BIBLIOGRAPHY

Alexander, Jeffrey, and Deal Chandler Brooks. "New Dimensions in Board-CEO Relations." *Trustee*, June 1986, pp. 24–27.

Arthur, Guy B. "Money as a Motivator." *Southern Hospitals*, February 1971, p. 29.

Austin, Charles J. "Wage Incentive Systems: A Review." *Hospital Progress*, April 1970, pp. 36–41.

Bassin, Phillip. "Employee Incentive Program." *Hospitals, JAHA* 45 (May 16, 1971): pp. 56–59.

"The Benefits of Gainsharing." *Small Business Report*, April 1987, p. 90.

Berman, Howard, and Henry Manning. "A Practical Approach to Incentives." *Hospital Financial Management*, March 1970, pp. 24–25.

Biggs, Dudley P. "Incentive Pay Plans Boost Managers' Performance." *Health Progress*, March 1987, pp. 60–62, 74.

Block, Stanley M. "Motivating Employees To Cut Costs." *Hospitals, JAHA* 45 (November 1, 1971): 51–55.

"Board Involvement Key to Incentive Comp Plans." *Hospitals*, April 16, 1985, pp. 58, 62.

Boyer, Vicki, and Alex M. Smith, Jr. "This Incentive Plan Improves the Care and Lowers the Cost." *Modern Hospitals*, September 1968, pp. 103, 105.

Brooks, Brian J. "Trends in International Executive Compensation." *Personnel*, May 1987, pp. 67–68, 70.

Browdy, Jerad D. "Tips for Tailoring an Incentive Compensation Plan to Your Employees' Needs." *Trustee*, July 1985, pp. 29–32.

Bruggen, Peter, and Stanford Bourne. "The Distinction Awards System in England and Wales 1980." *British Medical Journal* 284 (May 22, 1982): 1577–80.

Buchan, J.R., and James S. Self, Jr. "Incentive Programs Key to Productivity." *Southern Hospitals*, May 1975, pp. 11–13, 25.

Cammann, Cortlandt, and Edward E. Lawler, III. "Employee Reactions to a Pay Incentive Plan." *Journal of Applied Psychology* 58, no. 2 (1973): 163–72.

Cantrell, Leonard E., Jr., and Jeffrey A. Flick. "Physician Efficiency and Reimbursement: A Case Study," *Hospital & Health Services Administration*, November/December 1986, pp. 43–50.

Carner, Donald C. "Carner's Codes, Chapter 1: Your Compensation." *Hospital Forum* 25, no. 3: 45, 47–8, 51 passim.

Cecil-Wright, Jeremy. "How To Use Incentives." *Management Today*, January 1978, pp. 75–76, 108.

Channon, Brian. "Dispelling Productivity Myths." *Hospitals*, October 1, 1983, pp. 103–4, 106.

——. "Executive Incentive Plans for Hospitals." *Topics in Health Care Financing* 12 (Summer 1986): 27–38.

Cleverley, William O. "Management Incentive Systems and Economic Performance in Health Care Organizations." *HCM Review* 12 (Winter 1982): 7–14.

Coffin, Robert C. "Tailoring Incentive Bonus Plans for Special Situations." *Compensation Review* 7, no. 4 (1975): 16–30.

Collins, Linda I. "A Survey of Hospital Salaries." *Hospitals*, October 1, 1984, pp. 80–96.

"Compensation of Key Administrative Employees." *Topics in Health Care Financing* 7, no. 2 (1980): 59–67.

Connolly, James. "Incentives Drive Alamo's MIS." *Computerworld*, April 27, 1987, pp. 71, 79.

Copeman, George. "Sharing Profits by Incentives." *Management Today*, August 1978, pp. 55–57, 103–4.

The Croner Company. "Incentive Compensation: How To Inspire Your Management Team to Succeed." Presented to the Western Conference of the American College of Healthcare Executives, November 1985.

Cunningham, Robert M. "What Makes Workers Work?" *Hospitals, JAHA* 59 (May 1, 1979): 86–89.

Daly, Peter M. "Selecting and Designing a Group Incentive Plan." *Personnel Journal* 54 (1975): 322–3, 356.

Donovan, R. Michael. "Getting Your Incentive Plan under Control." *Industrial Management*, July–August 1978, pp. 10–11.

Doyel, Hoyt, and Thomas Riley. "Considerations in Developing Incentive Plans." *Management Review*, March 1987, pp. 34–37.

Dunn, Kenneth C.; Geoffrey B. Shields; and Joanne B. Stern. "The Dynamics of Leveraged Buy-Outs, Conversions, and Corporate Reorganization of Not-for-Profit Health Care Institutions." *Topics in Health Care Financing* 12 (Spring 1986): 19–35.

Eimers, Robert C., George W. Blomgren, and Edward Gubman. "Money versus Merchandise: Which Is the Best Motivator—and the Best Incentive?" *Training/HRD* 16 (July 1979): A10, A12.

Eastaugh, Steven R. "Improving Hospital Productivity under PPS: Managing Cost Reductions." *Hospital & Health Services Administration*, July/August 1985, pp. 97–111.

——. "Organization, Scheduling Are Main Keys to Improving Productivity in Hospitals." *FAH Review*, November/December 1985, pp. 61–63.

Eberhard, Michael J., Allen G. Herkimer, Jr., and Kenneth L. Uhi. "The HRU." *Hospital Financial Management*, February 1976, pp. 44–48.

Farmer, C. Richard. "Merit Pay: Viable?" *Personnel* 55 (September/October 1978): 57–63.

Fein, Mitchell. "Let's Return to MDW for Incentives." *Industrial Engineering* 11, no. 1: 34–37.

——. "Restoring the Incentive to Wage Incentive Plans." *Conference Board Record* 9 (November 1972): 17–21.

Fleishman, Raymond. "Human Resource Motivation." *Supervisor Nurse* 9 (November 1978): 57–60.

Fletcher, Donald J. "Managing for Profitable Productivity." *Purchasing* 72 (May 9, 1972): 31–34.

Fleuter, Douglas. "A Different Approach to Merit Increases." *Personnel Journal*, April 1979, pp. 225–26, 262.

Ford, Robert C., and Ronald Couture. "A Contingency Approach to Incentive Program Design." *Compensation Review* 10, no. 2: 34–42.

Galvin, Joseph Michael, Jr. "Not-for-Profits Should Restructure Deferred Compensation Plans." *Modern Healthcare*, March 27, 1987, p. 58.

Gehrman, Douglas B. "Techniques of Planning in Employee Relations." *Personnel Journal* 58 (November 1979): 761–70.

Goggin, Zane. "Two Sides of Gain Sharing." *Management Accounting*, October 1986, pp. 47–51.

Grant, Anthony. "How To Increase Job Motivation." *Dimensions in Health Service* 55 (March 1978): 8–10.

Gray, Robert D., and Charles C. Lindstrom. "Employees Are Made Partners in Cost Containment Efforts." *Hospitals*, May 1, 1981, pp. 45–46, 48.

Gregorich, Pauline. "Self-Appraisal Helps Improve Job Performance." *Hospitals, JAHA* 48 (August 1,1974): 71–76.

Groner, Pat N. *Cost Containment through Employee Incentives Program*. Rockville, Md.: Aspen Publishers, Inc., 1977.

———. "Employee Incentives." *Topics in Health Care Financing/Cost Containment* 3, no. 3 (1977): 63–86.

Gross, Edward. "Incentives and the Structure of Organizational Motivation." *Hospital Administration* 16 (Summer 1971): 8–20.

———. "Incentives To Reduce Absenteeism." *Dimensions in Health Service* 55 (December 1978): 26–27.

Grubbs, Frank C., A. Charles Collier, and Rosemary Kirk. "Bonuses Spur Transcribers' Production." *Hospitals, JAHA* 46 (March 16, 1972): 83–85, 88.

Guzzo, Richard A. "Types of Rewards, Cognitions, and Work Motivation." *Academy of Management Review* 4 (January 1979): 75–86.

Hamel, Pat. "Strategies for Exercising Incentive Stock Options after the Tax Reform Act of 1986." *CPA Journal*, June 1987, pp. 96–98.

Hardy, John W., Bryce B. Orton, and Weldon J. Moffit. "Bonus Systems Do Motivate." *Management Accounting*, November 1986, pp. 58–61.

Harris, Nelle, and James S. Self. "Productivity Incentives for Cost Control." *Executive Housekeeper* 19 (April 1972): 62, 64–65, 68.

Heese, Luke A. "Wage Incentives Eliminate 'Zombie Time.'" *Industrial Engineering*, October 1977, pp. 26–27.

Helling, Henry. "Base Salary and Incentive Compensation Practices in Not-for-Profit Organizations." *Compensation Review*, 4th quarter 1978, pp. 34–38.

Hendrickson, John P., and Joan E. Brophy. "Profit Sharing—Incentive for Efficiency." *Healthcare Financial Management* 38 (February 1984): 24–26.

Herrick, James D., and Steven H. Manning. "Monetary Incentive for Pharmacists To Control Drug Costs." *American Journal of Hospital Pharmacy* 42 (July 1985): 1527–32.

Hertzberg, Frederick, Bernard Mausner, and Barbara Block Snyderman. *The Motivation to Work.* 2nd ed. New York: John Wiley & Sons, Inc., 1959.

Holley, William H., Hubert S. Field, Nona J. Barnet, and the Department of Management, Auburn University, Auburn, Alabama. "Analyzing Performance Appraisal Systems: An Empirical Study." *Personnel Journal* 55 (September 1976): 457–59.

Homer, Carl G. "Methods of Hospital Use Control in Health Maintenance Organizations." *Health Care Management Review* 11 (Spring 1986): 15–23.

"Hospital Savings Mean Employee Earnings." *Health Services Manager*, December 1978, p. 8.

"Hospital Shows That It Cares about Costs." *Hospitals, JAHA,* December 1, 1978, pp. 46, 51.

"Hospitals More Interested in Incentives." *Hospitals,* April 1, 1985, pp. 34, 36.

Hranchak, William H. "Incentive Compensation and Benefits of Profit-Sharing Plans." *Topics in Health Care Financing* 12 (Fall 1985): 33–37.

Hubler, Myron J., Jr., and Thomas P. O'Neill. "Timing Inevitable Increases: A Monetary Incentive Program Could Cut Costs." *Hospital Financial Management* 35 (November 1981): 40–44.

Hudson, James I. "The Changing Character of Quality Assurance: Activities in Acute Care Hospitals." *Effective Health Care* 1, no. 2 (1983): 75–83.

Hughes, Elmer C. "Administrator's Participation: Key to Successful Incentive System." *Hospital Progress* 51 (July 1970): 75–77.

Jehring, J.J. "Back Talk." *Hospital Administration* 17 (Winter 1972): 5–7.

———. "The Effects on Productivity of Dropping Individual Incentives: A Case Study." *Personnel Journal* 45 (February 1986): 87–89.

Jolner, Carl, and John Hafer. "Reward Preferences of Nurses: A Marketing Concept Viewpoint." *Journal of Health Care Marketing* 3 (Spring 1983): 19–26.

Jones, Douglas T. "An Incentive Management Plan for Hospital-Based Physicians." *Journal of Medical Systems* 10, no. 1 (1986): 57–63.

Jordon, Douglas R., and Claudia J. Wyatt. "Financial Pressures Force Hospitals To Take a Second Look at Incentives." *Modern Healthcare,* July 1984, pp. 140, 142, 144.

Jydstrup, Ronald A. "Fringe Benefits for Hospitals." *Hospital Topics* 48 (May 1970): 39–46.

"Kaiser Permanente's 9,000 Striking Workers Voting Today on Pact." *Wall Street Journal,* 4 December 1986, p. 22.

Kelliher, Mathew E. "Managing Productivity, Performance, and Cost of Services." *Healthcare Financial Management,* September 1985, pp. 23–26, 28.

Kovner, Anthony R., and Duncan Neuhauser, eds. *Health Services Management: Readings and Commentary.* School of Public Health, University of Michigan. Ann Arbor: Health Administration Press, 1978.

Larcker, David F. "Short-Term Compensation Contracts and Executive Expenditure Decisions: The Case of Commercial Banks." *Journal of Financial and Quantitative Analysis* 22 (March 1987): 33–50.

Latham, Gary P., and Dennis L. Dossett. "Designing Incentive Plans for Unionized Employees: A Comparison of Continuous and Variable Ratio Reinforcement Schedules." *Personnel Psychology* 31, no. 1 (1978): 47–61.

Lawler, Edward E., III, and R.J. Bullock. "Pay and Organizational Change." *Personnel Administrator* 23 (May 1978): 32–36.

London, Manuel, and Greg R. Oldham. "Effects of Varying Goal Types and Incentive Systems on Performance and Satisfaction." *Academy of Management Journal* 19 (December 1976): 537–46.

———. "A Comparison of Group and Individual Incentive Plans." *Academy of Management Journal* 20 (March 1977): 34–41.

Longest, Beaufort B., Jr. "Productivity in the Provision of Hospital Services: A Challenge to the Management Community.'' *Academy of Management Review* 2 (July 1977): 475–83.

Louden, Teri. ''How To Select and Support the Hospital Sales Team.'' *Hospitals*, September 1, 1985, pp. 84–85.

Loveday, William J. ''The Merit Plan: The Key to Productivity.'' *Osteopathic Hospitals*, May 1976, p. 8–10.

Lund, Robert S. ''A Systems Approach to Employee Incentive Planning in Hospitals.'' *Hospital Financial Management* 24 (April 1970): 20–21, 28–29, 34.

Manning, Martin F. ''Product Line Management: Will It Work in Healthcare?'' *Healthcare Financial Management*, January 1987, pp. 23–32.

Markowich, M. Michael. ''Participatory Management Increases Motivation.'' *Hospitals, JAHA* 45 (September 1, 1971): 123–28.

Maslow, A.H. ''A Theory of Human Motivation.'' *Psychology Review*, July 1943, pp. 370–96.

Matheson, Stephen B., and Rose Marie Orens. ''Strategic Compensation: A Management Battle.'' *Mortgage Banking*, April 1987, pp. 109–18.

McAdams, Jerry. ''Rewarding Sales and Marketing Performance.'' *Management Review*, April 1987, pp. 33–38.

McManis, Donald L., and William G. Dick. ''Monetary Incentives in Today's Industrial Setting.'' *Personnel Journal* 52 (May 1973): 387–92.

Miller, Christopher S., and Michael Schuster. ''A Decade's Experience with the Scanlon Plan: A Case Study'' *Journal of Occupational Behavior* 8 (1987): 167–73.

Mitchell, F., K.I. Sams, and P.J. White. ''Directors' Reports on Employee Involvement.'' *Accountant's Magazine*, January/February 1986, pp. 30–31.

Mitchell, William G. ''Good Performance Rewarded in Cash.'' *Hospitals*, July 1980, p. 36–37.

Newald, Jane. ''Incentive Plans: ''Few 'Safe Harbors' from Abuse Laws.'' *Hospitals*, January 5, 1987, p. 50.

Nnadozie, Jonathan, and Reuban Edlar. ''Preference of Hospital Employees for Work-Related Outcomes.'' *Social Sciences and Medicine* 21, no. 6 (1985): 651–53.

Noll, Harland. ''How To Shape Incentive Plans for the Hospital's Top Executives.'' *Trustee*, August 1983, pp. 16–18.

O'Dell, Carla, and Jerry McAdams. ''The Revolution in Employee Rewards.'' *Management Review*, March 1987, pp. 30–33.

Pack, Jon W. ''Job Enrichment: How To Get Your Employees To Work for You.'' *Hospital Financial Management* 32 (November 1978): 27–28.

Patterson, Dennis J., and Kent A. Thompson. ''Product Line Management: Organization Makes the Difference.'' *Healthcare Financial Management*, February 1987, pp. 66–68, 70, 72.

Paynan, Steve W., and Michael McGregor. ''How To Implement a Proactive Incentive Plan.'' *Personnel Journal*, September 1976, pp. 460–62.

Peters, Tom. ''Rediscovering Productivity's 'Secret.''' *U.S. News & World Report*, February 17, 1986, p. 50.

Powills, Suzanne. ''Employees Audit Their Hospital Bills for Cash.'' *Hospitals*, October 20, 1986, p. 44.

Pozega, George. ''Hospital's Teamwork Incentive Plan Called 'Excellence in Service.''' *Hospital Topics* 49 (January 1971): 37–38.

Quick, Tom. ''Increasing Productivity with the Scanlon Plan.'' *Training/HRD* 16 (January 1979): 32–33.

Reed, Paul R., and Mark J. Kroll. ''Compensating the Red-Circle Employee.'' *Health Progress*, October 1985, pp. 39–41.

Reibstein, Larry. ''More Employers Link Incentives to Unit Results.'' *Wall Street Journal*. 10 April 1987, p. 25.

Rice, Robert S., Patton Consultants, Inc., and the American Institute of Industrial Engineers. ''Survey of Work Measurement and Wage Incentives.'' *Industrial Engineering* 9 (July 1977): 18–31.

Riffer, Joyce. ''Physician-Incentive Plans May Be Put on Hold.'' *Hospitals*, March 5, 1986, p. 80.

Riffer, Joyce. ''Incentive Plans Imperil Tax-Free Status, IRS Says.'' *Hospitals*, August 5, 1986, p. 59.

———. ''Physician-Income Guarantees May Jeopardize Tax-Exempt Status.'' *Hospitals*, December 20, 1986, p. 58.

Roethlisberger, F.J., and William J. Dickenson. *Management and the Worker*. Cambridge, Mass.: Harvard University Press, 1939.

Rosen, Robert M. ''IRS Won't Issue Private Letter Rulings on Some Types of Incentive Plans.'' *Modern Healthcare*, September 26, 1986, p. 56.

Rutigliano, Anthony. ''Incentive Plans Gaining in Cost Control Efforts.'' *Health Care Week* 2 (December 4, 1978): p. 12.

Salter, Malcolm S. ''Tailor Incentive Compensation to Strategy.'' *Harvard Business Review*, March/April 1973, pp. 94–102.

Scanolon, Burt K. ''Determinants of Job Satisfaction and Productivity.'' *Personnel Journal*, January 1976, pp. 12–14.

Schnee, Edward J., Walter A. Robins, and Connie L. Robins. ''Profit-Sharing Plans in Nonprofit Hospitals.'' *Nursing Management* 17 (February 1986): 24–27.

Schrieber, David E., and Stanley Sloan. ''An Occupational Analysis of Job Satisfaction in a Public Hospital.'' *Hospital Management* 108 (August 1969): 26–27, 30, 32.

Schulhof, Robert J. ''Five Years with a Scanlon Plan.'' *Personnel Administrator* 24 (June 1979): 55–63.

Schwab, Donald P. ''Conflicting Impacts of Pay on Employee Motivation and Satisfaction.'' *Personnel Journal*, March 1974, pp. 196–200.

Shahoda, Teri. ''Private Firms' Personnel Trends Warrant Mimicry.'' *Hospitals*, January 5, 1987.

Shyavitz, Linda, David Rosenbloom, and Lynn Conover. ''Financial Incentives for Middle Managers: Pilot Program in an Inner City, Municipal Teaching Hospital.'' *HCM Review* 10 (Summer 1985): 37–44.

Siegal, Andrew C., Arthur A. Cohen, and Laurence I. Feibel. "ESOPs—The Present and an Imperiled Future?—Part I," *CPA Journal*, January 1986, pp. 14, 16, 18, 20, 22.

Sihvon, W. Roy, and F.V. Gent. "Incentive Program at Niagara Improves Service, Costs." *Hospital Administration in Canada*, February 1970, pp. 22–24, 54, 56.

Silber, Mark B. "Motivating Hospital Employees To Identify with Their Work." *Hospital Programs* 53 (April 1972): 62–64.

Sims, Calvin. "Hospital Chain Sells 104 Units." *New York Times*, 1 June 1987, pp. D1, D10.

Sims, Henry P., Jr., and Andrew Szilagyi. "Leaders Reward Behavior and Subordinate Satisfaction and Performance." *Organizational Behavior and Human Performance* 14 (1975): 426–38.

Smith, Elizabeth A., and Gerald F. Gude. "Reevaluation of the Scanlon Plan as a Motivational Technique." *Personnel Journal* 50 (December 1971): 916–19, 923.

Smith, Howard L., David J. Ottensmeyer, and Derick P. Pasternak. "Physician Incentive Compensation in Group Practice: A Review with Suggestions for Improvement." *Health Care Management Review* 9 (Winter 1984): 41–49.

Smith, Judson. "How Cash Incentives Help Change Attitudes." *Training/HRD*, July 1979, A11.

Staudohar, Paul D. "An Experiment in Increasing Productivity of Police Service Employees." *Public Administration Review* 35 (September/October 1975): 518–22.

Stephens, Ted A., and Wayne A. Burroughs. "An Application of Operant Conditioning to Absenteeism in a Hospital Setting." *Journal of Applied Psychology* 64, no. 4 (1978): 518–21.

Swinehart, David P. "Compensation: A Guide to More Productive Team Incentive Programs." *Personnel Journal*, July 1986, pp. 112–14, 116–17.

Tang, Roger Y.W., Gail Bowser, and R.L. Williams. "Designing an Effective Executive Incentive Plan." *CMA Magazine*, May/June 1987, pp. 32–37.

Thomsen, David J. "Compensation and Benefits." *Personnel Journal* 57 (October 1978): 538, 540.

Ulsafer-Van Lanen, Jane. "Lateral Promotion Keeps Skilled Nurses in Direct Patient Care." *Hospitals*, March 1, 1981, pp. 87–90.

Umiker, William O. "Exploding Some Myths about Merit Pay." *Medical Laboratory Observer*, August 1984, pp. 59–60.

U.S. Department of Health, Education, and Welfare. *Employee Incentive Systems for Hospitals*. Washington: Health Services and Mental Health Administration, 1972.

Vanderslice, Virginia J., and Robert B. Leventhal. "Employee Participation: A Game Plan for the Real World." *Training and Development Journal*, February 1987, pp. 34–35.

Vestal, Anne J. "Developing an Incentive Program." *Hospital Topics* 48 (January 1970): 55–58.

Vestal, Anne J. "How an Incentive Program Based on a Team Concept Was Developed." *Hospital Topics* 48 (February 1970): 71–74, 80–82.

Walker, Samuel C. "Improving Cost and Motivational Effectiveness of Employee Benefit Plans." *Personnel Journal*, November 1977, pp. 570–72.

Weaver, Charles N., and Sandra L. Holmes. "What Hospital Employees Value Most." *Hospital Progress*, January 1979, pp. 60–62, 64.

Weisman, Carol S. "Recruit from Within: Hospital Nurse Retention in the 1980s." *Journal of Nursing Administration*, May 1982, pp. 24–31.

Weissburg, Carl, and Kenneth M. Stern. "Can Hospitals Reward Physicians for Reducing Unnecessary Utilization?" *FAH Review*, September/October 1985, pp. 45–46.

Whitted, Gary S., and Charles M. Ewell. "A Survey of Hospitals' Management Incentive Programs: What Will Motivate the Motivators?" *Hospitals* 58 (March 1, 1984): 90, 92, 94.

Wildt, Albert R., Clyde E. Harris, and James D. Parker. "Assessing the Impact of Sales-Force Contests: An Application." *Journal of Business Research* 15 (1987): 145–55.

Williams, Frank G., and Dwight C. Anderson. "Cost Control Incentive Programs: Appropriate for Non-Profits?" *Hospital Financial Management* 32 (May 1978): 14–17.

Willis, Elsie L. "Incentive Pay for Medical Transcriptionists." *Medical Record News*, June 1976, pp. 40–43.

Winstanley, Nathan B. "The Use of Performance Appraisal in Compensation Administration." *Conference Board Record* 12 (March 1975): 43–47.

Wolfe, Arthur V., and Kent J. Wolfe. "Results-Oriented Compensation-Benefit to Hospitals and Employees." *Hospital Topics*, May/June 1978, pp. 21–26.

Woolf, Donald A. "Measuring Job Satisfaction." *Hospitals, JAHA*, November 1, 1970, pp. 82–87.

Zemke, Ron. "Sharing the Wealth: HRD's Role in Making Incentive Plans Work." *Training/HRD* 16 (January 1979): 30–31, 34–35.

———. "A Vote for Individual Incentive Plans." *Training/HRD* 16 (July 1979): A14.

Chapter 22

Internal Auditing Services

Seth Allcorn
Administrator, Department of Medicine
Strong Memorial Hospital

Jerome R. Gardner
Vice President, Audit Services
Oklahoma Health Care Corporation

INTRODUCTION

Internal auditing has become an accepted contributor to the operating efficiency and effectiveness of modern health care delivery. This chapter outlines the growing role of internal auditing services in health care delivery organizations. The vastly increased operating complexity that health care administrators must manage demands that internal auditors respond with corresponding increases in responsibility, scope of work, and skills. The development of complicated corporate structures and affiliations has required internal auditors to review a wide variety of groups and activities: foundations, contracts, construction, joint ventures, lien and bond applications, participation in health maintenance organizations and preferred provider organizations, purchases of real estate, services and products not directly related to health care delivery, home health care agencies, and financial and control analyses of organizations being considered for purchase.

Internal auditing now makes its optimum contribution by participating in the design, development, implementation, and monitoring of hospitalwide and corporatewi systems and programs. This participation includes evaluating and making recommendations about the following:

- the soundness and adequacy of accounting, financial, and operating systems and internal control, and operational effectiveness
- the compliance of employees and management with established hospital and corporate policies and procedures, and the degree to which hospital and corporate goals and objectives are achieved by individuals, departments, and programs
- the adequacy and reliability of all management information
- the accountability and safeguarding of hospital and corporate assets
- the degree to which the activities of managers, employees, departments, and programs are integrated in a compatible manner that provides for the maximum achievement of the hospital's or corporation's mission[1]

Achieving these goals makes internal auditors major contributors to overseeing the operations of their institutions. Internal auditors must now have competencies in areas as diverse as industrial engineering; large-scale computer applications; and the use of desk top computers, including specially designed software, data bases, and spread sheets. Recommendations for change made by internal auditors must be well informed and developed in a manner upon which top management will act. This is a challenge for internal auditors when the health care delivery operating environment of economics, competition, technology, politics, social influences, laws, regulations, limited resources, constant change, interdepartmental conflict, and human nature is taken into consideration. It is this complexity that makes effective internal auditing an immense challenge and of immense value. The challenge and the value added are gained by uncovering inefficiencies and ineffectiveness; unnecessary operating risks; poor management and internal controls; missed income-generating opportunities; and poorly designed, poorly implemented, and cost-ineffective systems and programs that must be brought to management's attention without provoking defensiveness. Internal auditors of the future will not be internal auditors of the past but rather valuable members of a hospital or corporate management team—providers of internal auditing services.

THE ROLE OF INTERNAL AUDITING IN MANAGING HEALTH CARE DELIVERY ORGANIZATIONS

Good management begins when governing boards and their presidents, chief executive officers (CEOs), and hospital directors agree upon a mission statement and plan, organize, staff, and direct the administrative affairs of a health care delivery organization. The performance of these management functions has been viewed as the prerequisite of management and internal control. The complexity of modern health care delivery organizations, however, has forced recognition that management and internal control should be developed as an integral part of planning, organizing, staffing, and directing.[2] Management and internal control can no longer be considered the last steps in the management process. As a result, internal auditors should have an active role in management decision making regarding the development and implementation of new programs and management systems, and the reassessment and redesign of existing ones.

Internal auditors make valuable contributions to the management of health care delivery organizations. Internal auditors who actively participate in the overall administration of health care delivery organizations can ensure that a solid foundation is developed for managerial and internal control. Management control encompasses six basic steps to which internal auditors can contribute.[3] First, the governing board and the corporate president or hospital director must state the health care delivery organization's mission. Similarly, mission statements should be developed for programs and systems, including internal auditing. It must be clear what is expected. The development of mission statements facilitates the creation of goals and objectives that, when met, will fulfill the missions. These goals must, in turn, be clearly communicated to departments, programs, and employees. Internal auditors can make valuable contributions to these management activities by seeking clarification of the mission statement, goals, and objectives based on their broad and in-depth understanding of the functioning of the institution. In particular, internal auditors will be able to spot gaps and inconsistencies in goals and objectives that may eventually compromise management and internal control.

The second step is the development of measurable standards of performance against which performance is evaluated. Internal auditors will be especially effective at assessing the measurability of standards that are set based on their detailed knowledge of existing information systems. Standards should not be developed that either cannot be measured or for which sufficient information cannot be gathered for assessment.

Third, the performance of individuals, groups, programs, and systems must be measured and compared with performance standards, goals, and objectives. Internal auditors, having contributed to the development of measurable objectives and suitable performance standards, can contribute to designing the means for documenting work accomplished that will permit comparison with standards and objectives.

Fourth, performance deviations both above and below standards, goals, and objectives must be analyzed. Internal auditors can contribute to developing analyses based on their extensive knowledge of the organization.

Fifth, corrective actions must be selected and implemented. Internal auditors understand the broad nature of operating problems and the many interactions a planned solution may have with other programs and systems. Internal auditors can make insightful contributions to the selection and implementation of solutions to problems.

Finally, corrective action, once taken, must be monitored to determine whether the outcome is a positive one. Internal auditors can have an active role in developing and carrying out the needed monitoring.

In sum, good management and internal control do not just happen; they must be planned and developed to meet the needs of the institution. Internal auditors can be invaluable in developing and refining management and internal controls as well as adjusting them to the realities of day-to-day operations.

The inclusion of internal auditors in the design, development, and implementation of business systems potentially compromises the objectivity of internal auditors.[4] The possibility of compromise must be acknowledged. However, the increasing levels of professionalism and size of internal auditing staffs buffer the threat of compromise in favor of internal auditors realizing their fullest potential by participating in "front-end" management decision making. The development of policies and procedures is management's responsibility, one that should be enhanced by internal auditing.

Internal auditors, while contributing to the overall management and operation of health care delivery organizations, will remain the final authority on internal control. Internal control involves developing carefully designed systems of checks and balances intended to minimize human error and eliminate fraud and embezzlement. Good internal controls should be found everywhere in hospitals and related enterprises. For example, an internal control to avoid errors is batch control in electronic data processing or a system for ensuring that the receipt of a specimen at a pathology laboratory requires a timely report to be issued and a charge generated for the correct patient. An example of an internal control that prevents embezzlement and fraud is the sharing of responsibility for cash receipts. One person may account for all cash received, while a second applies the receipts to patient accounts, and a third reconciles bank statements and compares cash-received reports with payment applications. Once these types of internal control are implemented, they need to be reviewed only periodically unless a change in organization occurs. While internal controls do not need to be subjected to frequent reviews, management must be certain that employees are complying with the internal control procedures. This level of review falls upon internal auditors in their roles of financial and compliance auditing.

Good internal controls and internal auditing of financial matters and employee compliance directly benefit health care delivery organizations in a second manner. Hospitals receive regular visits from certified public accountants (CPAs), auditors from third-party payers, and regulatory agencies. Hospitals that have good internal controls and an active internal auditing service lose less time and have less disruption when audited by CPAs. This can save as much as 20 percent of the audit fee and considerable staff time when seeking solutions to problems that are uncovered.[5] Similarly, good internal controls and vigorous internal auditing can minimize a hospital's exposure to time-consuming audit processes and negative findings from Medicare, other third-party payers, and regulatory agencies that can lead to fiscal penalties.

DEVELOPING INTERNAL AUDITING SERVICES

Developing a good internal auditing service requires the commitment of the governing board and the CEO or hospital director.[6] This commitment may involve reviewing available literature, requesting assistance from a public accounting firm, contacting the local chapter of the Institute of Internal Auditors, surveying other hospitals as to their experience, contracting with consultants who specialize in developing internal auditing services, and contacting the Healthcare Internal

Audit Group and the Health Care Financial Management Association. Those responsible for developing internal auditing services should avail themselves of these resources. Regardless of the approach used, board members, CEOs, and hospital directors must be prepared to provide internal auditing a level of independence that does not exist for other departments, and then be willing to stand behind internal auditors who uncover major problems that often arouse the antagonism of managers, program directors, and employees.[7] Internal auditors lacking dependable support of the board, CEO, or director will eventually suffer poor morale and will avoid raising controversial issues.[8] In addition to receiving adequate support, internal auditors may find support from auditees by using task forces that include staff from the department involved as well as individuals from other departments. Ideally, managers should seek out the services of internal auditing to improve the performance and internal control of their departments.

Internal auditing must be provided a clearly written charter detailing its autonomy and scope of operations. The *Standards for the Professional Practice of Internal Auditing* developed by the Institute of Internal Auditors should be consulted when writing the charter and developing the service as a whole.

Before discussing the selection of staff for the internal auditing service, the possibility of contracting for internal auditing services should be considered. Large hospitals that have fully developed internal auditing services may market their services to other hospitals and physicians. Hospitals and other health care delivery organizations that do not have internal auditing capabilities may want to explore contracting for internal auditing services from a nearby institution that has an established internal auditing service.

The Career Connection

In the past, health care internal auditing has often been viewed as good training for stepping into management. This occurred when internal auditing was given a low priority in health care delivery organizations and correspondingly marginal salaries and career-development opportunities. Today this is no longer uniformly the case. Many health care delivery organizations have acknowledged the important contribution that internal auditing services can make by according directors of internal auditing vice-presidential status. This change has created opportunities for career development. Greater participation in management decision making has also made the internal auditor's role more fulfilling. Executive-level status has also required auditors to participate in community activities as representatives of their institution. The development of public relations and people skills has become critical for internal auditors who aspire to executive roles. Health care internal auditing is a career choice that merits consideration. Recruiters and directors of internal auditing services no longer need to feel defensive when filling internal auditing positions. Individuals should be sought who see health care internal auditing as a challenging and important career opportunity.

ORGANIZING INTERNAL AUDITING

Internal auditing services raise two questions about organization: First, where should internal auditing be located within a health care delivery organization? Second, how should the service organize its staff and resources to be most effective? Regarding organizational placement, it is generally agreed that internal auditing services should report directly to the CEO and indirectly to the governing board. The CEO should ensure that internal auditing is free of influences from other executives and departments. This will involve separate budgets, performance reviews, and records. The CEO must not permit those staffing the service to feel compromised by, in effect, being held directly accountable by others whom they audit. The indirect reporting relationship to the governing board should include providing copies of all audit reports to the board's audit committee, acquiring board approval for audit schedules, and accepting direction from the board.

The organization of the internal auditing service staff and resources can range from relatively simple arrangements for one individual or a small staff to more complicated arrangements in the case of a larger staff with many different responsibilities. Another aspect of organization is the development of audit schedules, operating procedures, and standards performance. Audit schedules should be developed with the planning cycle of the organization in mind. For example, if an organization has developed a five-year plan, it is recommended that internal auditing develop a five-year plan for scheduling internal audits.[9] Careful planning of where, what, how long, and how frequently to audit ensures the best coverage of all departments. Written operating procedures should be developed to direct the routine aspects of work. The degree of detail that is suitable will depend on the size and complexity of the service. Once developed, written procedures should be approved by the CEO and governing board. Typical procedures might include accounting for time on the job, projecting time budgets and progress reports, notifying areas to be audited, requesting additional clerical support or computer time, accounting for expense reporting, ensuring records retention, and evaluating performance, to list but a few of the more common aspects of operations that are usually rendered into written procedures. In many cases the hospital's or organization's procedures manual will cover many of these points. Performance standards should be developed that detail management expectations for the service as a whole and the individual performance of auditors. The standards should be explicit and permit meaningful evaluations.

Good internal auditing services do not just happen; they must be thoughtfully developed. Those responsible for the service must ensure that internal auditing has proper autonomy and authority and is properly organized to carry out its mission. Progressive and insightful thinking must be in evidence, regarding not only the present but also the future.

EXPANDING INTERNAL AUDITING SERVICES

Modern health care internal auditors can offer services that are not directly related to the performance of management, operational, and financial and compliance audits. The expanded role of internal auditors in management decision making has been discussed. Internal auditors are also now making contributions to in-house education, generating income by marketing their services to other health care delivery organizations, and participating in the administration of such areas as quality assurance.

Internal auditors can provide valuable in-house training. Internal auditors can train employees on a wide range of topics: cost control, cash control, control of computer operations, control of risks, improving efficiency, developing goals and objectives, assessing performance, and recognizing and solving problems. Internal auditors can also provide discussions of topics such as the impact of legal and contractual obligations on operations, and the activities of CPAs and auditors from third-party payers. Specialized training can be provided in areas such as accounts receivable management, inventory management, review of construction contracts, oversight of construction projects, analyses of financial statements and reports, and design consideration for management information systems.

The marketing of internal auditing services to other health care providers creates an income-generating possibility that can change internal auditing into a revenue center. Services marketed to nearby health care institutions and physician medical groups not only provide income but also enhance the experience of internal auditors who, as a result, will work more effectively in-house.

Closely related to marketing, internal auditing offers hospitals an effective means of developing bonding relationships with physicians. Bonding is becoming more important in the ever-present competition for admitting and referring physicians. Hospitals that want to offer services to affiliated physicians and medical groups should find a thorough internal audit the best means of assessing the types of services needed. Rather than try to market services that physicians may see little advantage in having, services can be offered based on insightful and documented analyses of a physician's or medical group's operations.

Internal auditors are also participating in the administration of hospital programs such as quality assurance with the advent of the nurse auditor. Additional departments, areas, and programs may benefit from internal audit participation when, for example, dealing with deficiencies relative to regulations of the Joint Commission of Accreditation of Healthcare Organizations, reviews by third parties, cost reduction and control programs, visitor and employee safety, and utilization review.

INTERNAL AUDITING METHODS

Health care internal auditing encompasses management, operational, and financial and compliance auditing. Each method contributes to the comprehensive assessment of an organization's performance.

Before discussing internal auditing methods, several points should be highlighted. The reader should be aware that, while each type of audit is approached separately, all three are inter-related. Substantial problems in one of the three areas can compromise the other two.[10] Internal auditors are aware that these compromises occur and deal with them by expanding the scope of their audits. This inter-relatedness makes management's support of internal auditors essential as their audit programs and findings route them through an organization's operations. Internal auditing's contribution must not be compromised by restrictions. In particular, internal auditors must have unrestricted access to all records of any kind.

Management Auditing

Management auditing involves appraising the performance of management at all levels in the organization. If managers do not accomplish their duties, it is virtually impossible to develop sound operations at lower levels in the organization. Management auditing is also important to governing board members, who should have a good idea of how well managed their institution is but who usually lack the time and often the expertise to find out. Internal auditors can be depended on to provide to governing boards comprehensive and informed analyses of man-

agement's performance. Health care internal auditors must be prepared to evaluate how well managers carry out their functions of planning, organizing, staffing, directing, and controlling.[11]

Auditing Management Planning

Planning is an ongoing, forward-looking, reasoned, orderly, realistic, and systematic commitment to action.[12] Planning should coordinate the work of organizational members, sections, divisions, departments, and programs. There are a number of common planning pitfalls that should be avoided.

- Upper levels of management must express a sincere and active interest in planning and provide leadership and direction. Internal auditors must be alert for instances where indifference undermines planning by lower levels of the organization.
- Rigidly centralized planning should be avoided. Top-down planning often leads to plans tailored to the desires and beliefs of top management that may not reflect the true needs of departments and operating subdivisions. Internal auditors should be alert for the contributions of lower organizational levels to planning.
- Internal auditors should thoroughly review the forecasts and information upon which planning is based. Poor forecasts and incomplete or misleading information can result in distorted and unrealistic planning.
- Internal auditors should try to assess whether planning tends to optimize or whether it is too conservative, aggressive, or overly optimistic. Beyond optimizing, planning should show innovation.
- Planning should not become an expensive, overly thorough activity nor should it appear to be accepted as a routine function. Internal auditors must be aware of tendencies in these directions and be alert for signs that planning produces inflexibilities in meeting operating needs.

Internal auditors should not only be aware of problems with planning but also be able to spot instances where planning is proceeding well. Planning should, in addition to providing direction to a health care delivery organization's operations, coordinate activities at all levels, provide suitable resources for departments, and demonstrate an ability by management to cope with problems encountered by even the best of plans.

Auditing Management Organization

Good organization is essential for complex health care delivery organizations. Internal auditors must be watchful for instances where management has not effectively organized activities and inter-relationships involving authority, responsibility, and work. Poor organization often presents symptoms that appear as though they are the root problem when ultimately they are not. Organizational problems may take many forms.[13]

- Well-documented organizational charts, supported by detailed position descriptions, should be available. Internal auditors should examine these materials to determine how accurately they reflect current conditions and to assess the appropriateness of the organization depicted.
- Internal auditors will want to compare the current organization with the institution's goals and objectives to ensure that there are no obvious incompatibilities. Other factors that should be considered are whether the organizational scheme is compatible with the administration's leadership style and whether the staff is aware of and basically agrees with the structure.[14]
- The roles of all levels of management should be examined with regard to the amount and means of their contribution to the formation of the overall organizational scheme.
- Internal auditors should be able to discern that the organizational structure has been able to adapt to change, has been able to attract and retain good managers, has provided for good morale, and has minimized conflict and unnecessary duplication.
- Conversely, auditors should not find instances where poor organization has re-

sulted in frequent changes, poor accountability, and slow decision making and where management has tolerated mediocre performance.[15]

Auditing management's organization of the institution is a challenge. Internal auditors will have to gather information from many sources and will have to be insightful when identifying causes of problems. Internal auditors must assure themselves and the governing board that their institution is held together by a comprehensive organizational scheme that promotes operating efficiency.

Auditing Management Staffing

Staffing an organization with good employees is no minor achievement. Internal auditors will seldom find that an entire organization has achieved optimum staffing; however, there must be an ongoing effort to try to achieve this elusive goal, and there must be evidence that a framework of good personnel administration exists. Auditing staffing involves evaluating a number of areas:[16]

- A comprehensive, up-to-date, and legally correct set of personnel administration policies and procedures should be in place. It should be clear that these policies have been disseminated to all those who need to rely on them and that those who use them understand how to apply them in their work. The policies and procedures should also be explicit enough that they are not left open to a great deal of interpretation.
- The personnel department's effectiveness at recruiting, wage and salary administration, and training should be evaluated. Internal auditors will have many questions to answer. Has the institution been consistently short of qualified staff? Are there viable pools of applicants from which to select? Do recruiting policies and procedures comply with the law and are they followed? Are applicant credentials, licensing, education, and references consistently checked and verified? Is there an exit interview program? What is learned from it? Is employee turnover high?

- The institution's fringe benefit program should be reviewed for its competitiveness. Areas such as employee health and safety should be included.
- Performance evaluation is traditionally a difficult program to carry out in a meaningful way. However, having acknowledged the difficulty, internal auditors should review the process of performance evaluation as it occurs at all levels and in all areas of the institution.

Personnel administration is reviewed implicitly as part of all audits. Operating problems that are uncovered may often lead internal auditors to reflect about the adequacy of and performance of employees.

Auditing Management Direction

Good managers are effective leaders, motivators, counselors, and teachers. Managers invest a considerable amount of their time fulfilling these responsibilities. Evaluating the ability of managers to direct the work of others requires internal auditors to have a good understanding of the literature on organizational behavior, leadership, and motivation and how it applies to a variety of situations. In particular, internal auditors must be prepared to understand the meaning of comments made to them about managers and other employees.

When problems are found, managers must be encouraged to reassess their style and methods of directing. Interventions by personnel trainers and consultants may be appropriate. Internal auditors should not avoid dealing with issues related to directing. There are a number of aspects of human behavior in organizations to which internal auditors should be attentive.

- Coalitions of employees may develop around a particular issue, such as their handling by a supervisor. When it is apparent that a number of people who interact with each other share in common the same concern, regardless of whether it is appropriate or accurately reflects reality, productivity is disrupted and a better understanding of the various points of views and issues should be developed.

- Employees who are inhibited in what they say and, by extension, think may be feeling cornered and perhaps coerced by management. Negative employee attitudes and beliefs that are verbalized should be challenged to find out what lies behind them. Closely related is whether communication is encouraged by management. Are there suggestion award and complaint programs? Is top management open to receiving employee input and responsive when that input is received?
- Employees who are overly zealous about teamwork and avoiding problems may be suppressing unresolved conflicts that, if surfaced, may be threatening but may offer improved group and organizational performance.
- The presence of a rigidly adhered to hierarchy of positions and authority may be the result of a manager who defends against the development of operating problems by avoiding errors and sources of problems in the first place. Over-control has negative consequences. Internal auditors should be attentive to instances where employees and work seem overly controlled.
- Internal auditors will be exposed to many managers in their work. Some may espouse unenlightened management theories and practices or espouse enlightened theories and practice but not in fact follow through on them. Internal auditors should be attentive to what they hear and do not hear in this regard and be objective in evaluating content and meaning.

Auditing Management Control

Managers must monitor performance, compare results to plans, and implement change as needed. Thoughtfully designed management controls can require a minimum of time to maintain and need not be unduly restrictive.[17,18] Managers should have timely, accurate, and representative information about departmental and organizational performance. Internal auditors should become experts at appraising management's control processes. There are a number of checkpoints that internal auditors should keep in mind:

- Managers must establish and communicate clear and measurable performance standards. The standards themselves must be appraised as to their adequacy. Internal auditors should be aware that average managers will very likely perpetuate mediocre performance by setting average standards.

- All management information should be validated as timely, accurate, and representative. There are numerous problems, both intentional and unintentional, that can result in faulty and misleading information. No information system is immune to at least some of the problems, and most systems are susceptible to many.[19] Validation involves following information from its origin to its ultimate user. Auditors will want to be certain the right people receive the information, while others who are not involved do not. Auditors will want to determine whether enough information is generated or possibly too much. The means used for generating the information should be as accurate and efficient as possible. In this regard, computer applications should be reviewed. Reporting formats should be examined as to whether they present the information in the most concise, comprehensible manner.[20] Reports that rely on quantitative information should do more than report quantities: they should interpret them. Last, internal auditors will want to know what managers do with the reports they receive.

- Members of management must be able to demonstrate that they are actively using information they receive. After all, it is managers who are responsible for the operations of their departments and it is they who are to be held accountable. Are deviations being routinely spotted, analyzed, and reacted to?

- Management must be effective in taking corrective action. A review of a current or recent operating problem and its resolution may be in order.

Internal auditors can make swift and substantial contributions during their reviews of management controls and management information. An important additional area of management control is internal control, which will be dealt with more thoroughly when financial and compliance auditing are discussed. It will suffice to say good internal controls should be found everywhere in an organization. Lack of or excessive use of internal controls should quickly attract the auditor's attention.

Operations Auditing

A second important internal auditing method that complements management auditing is operations auditing. Operations auditing has gradually expanded in scope to include the entire organization. The greater the comprehensiveness of operations auditing, the greater is its potential to improve operating efficiency and effectiveness.

The nature of operations auditing is best described by explaining the four basic steps of an operations audit: planning the audit, examining and evaluating information, communicating results, and follow-up.

Planning the Audit

There are four steps for planning an operations audit. First, background information on the type of department should be reviewed and material pertaining directly to the department's operations read and analyzed. Part of this background should include reviews of regulations and standards from regulatory agencies and flow charting the more complex administrative and operating aspects of the department. Second, the auditor should develop a set of preliminary objectives for the audit and define its scope.[21] This step should be reviewed by the director of internal auditing (if there is one), the CEO, and the manager of the department in question to ensure that all pertinent operating questions, problems, and issues are included in the audit in a suitable manner. It is hoped that allowing the department manager to discuss the scope and objectives will assure the manager's good will and also help educate the manager concerning internal auditing. Third, the internal auditor should become familiar with the department's goals, objectives, organization, staffing, management information system, and standards for performance.[22] A walk-through of the department with the manager is advisable. During the walk-through, the auditor can observe the space the department occupies, how it is equipped, the nature of the work performed, and activities of employees. The auditor may observe crowding, broken or unused equipment, and safety hazards, and gain an idea of how employees do their work. The walk-through also provides an opportunity to meet key employees who may have to be contacted during the audit. The fourth step of planning is to prepare an audit program that states the audit's scope and objectives and all the detailed audit steps that will be performed.

Examining and Evaluating Information

The audit program is the framework for gathering facts and processing them into meaningful information. As data are gathered the auditor will enter findings on work sheets designed to facilitate data entry and interpretation. During this process the internal auditor must be certain to acquire sufficient, competent, relevant, and useful information. It must be sufficient in the sense that it is factual, adequate, and convincing; competent in the sense of reliable, best, and most timely; and relevant in the sense of supporting findings and recommendations. It should also be complete, accurate, and representative. Good documentation of findings and supporting recommendations is critical to the auditor's credibility.

The single most important problem in gathering information is the auditor's loss of objectivity.[23] An internal auditor who becomes biased tends to develop information that supports the auditor's own point of view and exclude information to the contrary. A second pitfall in gathering information occurs when the auditor is presented with a plausible but not easily verifiable explanation of why a problem exists or is presented with new information or problems that, if dealt with, will detract from completing the audit as planned. While these types of information cannot be ignored, internal auditors should not deviate from the audit program unless there is a compelling reason to do so. The new information may be incorporated in the next

audit or explored as part of a separate study. Other problems may be encountered regarding the preparation of recommendations. Internal auditors should avoid the temptation to compete with the manager to originate the best idea. Internal auditors must not feel that they are always right and management is wrong. Although it is easy to slip into this mode of behavior, it is definitely not the best method of fulfilling internal auditing's role in the organization's overall mission.

Internal auditors, to ensure that no unexpected information or response will be forthcoming from the department's management, should discuss all findings and recommendations with the department manager and encourage him or her to criticize the findings and recommendations before the report is submitted to the CEO and governing board.[24]

Communicating Results

Internal auditors should be able to communicate at two levels—informal and formal. Internal auditors should informally discuss findings, interpretations of information, and recommendations with department managers to acquire a better idea of the department's operations, to test their understanding, and to gain management's support in implementing some of the auditor's ideas. If a problem has an immediate consequence, quick corrective action is required and informal communication is in order. Another important use of informal communication is to permit the department manager to comment on the preliminary draft of the audit report. The internal auditor must make every effort to gain management's support and uncover areas of disagreement prior to issuing the formal report. The internal auditor must also be adept at preparing interesting formal reports that management will act on. Much of what is reported is critical in nature. Praise should be included when merited, which may include discussion of finely designed and operated systems or changes made that solved prior problems or responded to prior audit findings. Care must be taken to develop a thorough record-keeping system for maintaining audit reports and documentation; this system will form the basis of a valuable reservoir of knowledge for future audits.

Follow-Up

Internal auditors should ensure that changes that have been agreed to are implemented and that they work. After a reasonable time, the auditor should make a brief follow-up visit to verify implementation and, if appropriate, appraise the effectiveness of the changes. Follow-up should also include review of the effectiveness of the audit program that was used and the time budget that was allotted. Both may be improved upon based on experience.

The nature of operations auditing is varied and complex. Internal auditors must appraise the operations of all departments on a regular basis to ensure that they are operating at maximum efficiency and effectiveness and making their planned contribution to the organization's mission.

CONDUCTING OPERATIONS AUDITS

Operations audits can improve the performance of any department, function or program.[25] The audit checkpoints that follow can usually be applied to all operations audits. The reader should also be aware that audit checkpoints discussed under the heading of a particular department, function, or program may often be applied equally well in audits of other departments, functions, or programs.

Organization and Internal Control

- To whom does the administrator of the department report? Is this the right person? How often are reports made, and in what form? Are the reports clear, accurate, representative, and timely?
- How is the department organized? Is there an organizational chart? Does it provide for good internal control? Are areas of authority and responsibility clearly indicated? Is it

centralized or decentralized, and to what advantage?
- How is the department's work coordinated with that of the rest of the organization? Are the interdepartmental relationships clear and satisfactory?
- What internal controls are used? Do they accomplish their purpose economically?
- What records are generated by the department? Do the records facilitate management control and promote accomplishing work efficiently?

Policies and Procedures

- Are departmental policies and procedures in writing? Who prepared them? Were they approved by the governing board? Are they followed?
- Are the policies and procedures complete and current? Are they adequate? Do they provide for efficient and effective routine aspects of patient care and work performance?
- Are departmental policies and procedures consistent with those of the organization?
- Are there too many or too few policies and procedures? Are there procedures for handling all routine decisions? How are nonroutine decisions made?
- Have all policies and procedures been communicated to employees? Are employees aware of the policies and procedures?

Goals, Objectives, and Planning

- Have clear goals and objectives been established for the department? Are they in writing?
- Are the goals and objectives measurable and achievable? Are they in harmony with those of the organization?
- Are plans committed to writing? Is there sufficient planning? How is departmental planning integrated with the overall planning process of the organization?

Staffing

- Are employee interviewing and screening procedures adequate?
- Are employees properly certified?
- What provisions are made for training?
- Are employees routinely moved about when there is not enough available work to keep everyone fully employed? How are absences backed up?
- Are there adequate job descriptions? Are there adequate productivity and quality measures?
- How good is employee morale? What is the employee turnover rate? How are breaks and absences handled? What is their impact on internal control?
- Is the area staffed with proper numbers of employees who are qualified and capable of performing at expected levels?

Facilities

- Does the department's location contribute to accomplishing its goals?
- Is the department adequately equipped? Is the equipment modern and in good operating order?
- Does the department have good communications systems? In particular, is there effective use of telephone communication capabilities?
- Is there enough space for employees and patients? Do the existing amount and arrangement of space promote efficiency?
- Is the environment of the area safe? Does it promote efficiency? Is it clean, well-lighted, and temperature-controlled?
- What security measures exist to safeguard the space, equipment, employees, and patients?

These lists of common audit checkpoints should be referred to every time an operations audit program is being prepared. To illustrate their use, some of these points will be referred to

in the audit checklists for departments and programs that follow.

Operations Auditing of Patient Care Areas

The reader is reminded that the impact of findings of management audits will affect findings generated by operations audits. Good management is a prerequisite for excellent performance by individuals, departments, and programs.

An operations audit begins with an analysis of operating and policy manuals and supplemental written instructions for the department. The analysis should determine the accuracy, adequacy, completeness, and soundness of the procedures. There are a great many considerations involved in performing the appraisal. Below are checkpoints that may be used to begin to analyze systems, procedures, and operations of patient care departments. It should be noted that the third step after an operations audit is to verify whether employees are complying with the instructions and policies (financial and compliance auditing).

Admitting and Discharge Policies, Procedures, and Operations

- Are patients with certain types of illnesses not admitted?
- What is the policy for emergency admissions? What priority do they have over other admissions, and how is the privilege protected from abuses?
- What liability release forms are required?
- What patient classification system exists, and does it describe adequately the various patient groups?
- Are patients routinely segregated by type of admitting diagnosis?
- What policy is used to admit charity patients, and how does the hospital control its charity load?
- What is the policy on requiring advance deposits from patients without third-party payer coverage?

- What is the screening process for determining patient ability to pay, for acquiring financial information, and for verifying insurance coverage? How are advance payments handled?
- How are patients handled for readmission when they have outstanding balances?
- What is the policy for discounts on hospital bills?
- Is the admitting office located in one area under one supervisor or decentralized to other buildings and areas under several supervisors? Is the form of organization effective?
- To whom do the supervisors of admissions report?
- What authority and responsibilities do the supervisors have?
- Is the organizational pattern documented, and do all employees know and understand it?
- What provision is there for coordinating other hospital operations with admissions?
- Do adequate job descriptions exist for all employee positions? Does each position serve the goal of competent and efficient admissions work? Do employees know their jobs?
- What provision is there for monitoring employee turnover, absenteeism, and overtime? How are staff shortages managed? Are temporary employees used, or do persons from other departments fill in temporarily?
- What provisions exist for orientation of new employees, training, performance evaluation, wage and salary administration, and staff benefits?
- Do employees appear motivated? Do they identify with the hospital's goals?
- What provisions exist for employee feedback?
- Where is the admissions office located in relation to the lobby, main entrances, emergency room, medical records, the business and cashier's offices, and patient and physician traffic patterns?

- Is there sufficient space to provide patient privacy during interviews, and has adequate space been assigned for waiting areas, toilets, equipment, records storage, and personnel?
- Are operating conditions safe and comfortable, and do they encourage good employee performance? Is the area clean, climate-controlled, nicely decorated and furnished, and well lighted? Are there enough clearly marked exits and sufficient aisle space?
- Is the admissions office equipped properly with business machines, copy machines, and telephones?
- Does the area facilitate a normal flow of operation?
- Is there a system of preregistering elective patients and, if so, do the forms and instructions sent to patients provide enough information for the hospital and the individuals?
- Is the current census known at all times, and are available beds well controlled?
- Do admitting forms provide complete information for all hospital business systems? What is the distribution of the forms?
- How are patients' clothes and valuables safeguarded and returned?
- Is there an effort to control workload by staggering patient arrival times?
- Are patients received with warmth and courtesy? What provisions exist for patient and family feedback regarding treatment by staff?
- How are patients escorted to the wards, and what forms and records accompany them?
- What care-related activities come under admissions' responsibility? What routine tests are part of the admitting process? Is admissions responsible for notifying the attending physician of the patient's arrival?
- Are physicians kept informed of bed occupancy levels?
- Does admissions compile daily and weekly statistics on all activities?
- Who has the authority to discharge or transfer a patient, and how is admissions informed?

- Is adequate attention paid to patient dignity and convenience? Do patients have to wait regularly for transportation or have to sit waiting for extended periods of time for ancillary services or processing in often-uncomfortable hospital gowns?

- Are relatives informed as early as possible of a patient's discharge and is transportation home arranged for the patient? Who is responsible for being certain the patient can make the trip home safely?

- Who is responsible for seeing that the patient has received proper health care instructions and drugs if needed? What is the procedure for follow-up appointments as an outpatient?

- What control procedures exist for the patient's medical record and other records and reports?

Good admitting and discharge policies, procedures, and personnel can offer patients a positive experience during their hospitalization. Every effort should be expended to ensure that this occurs. Internal auditors might consider "blueprinting" (a term borrowed from marketing) patient visits to their institution. This involves observing and recording all steps a patient encounters during a visit—inpatient or outpatient. Many good observations can be developed by using this technique.

Ancillary Services Policies and Procedures

Most patients will receive diagnostic tests and various types of therapy. Patients can quickly judge services that appear to be ineffective or inefficient. Every effort should be made to ensure that laboratories and therapeutic areas of the hospital are performing their work in a professional manner. Below are audit checkpoints that may be used to form the basis for auditing hospital ancillary services.

- What procedures have been established to ensure that tests, procedures, and therapies are performed by licensed and qualified staff?

- What are the procedures for ensuring that the correct service is performed on time and

properly? What procedures exist to ensure that patients do not receive a service not ordered by the physician?

- Are the results of test procedures and therapy reported promptly and in a manner that is controlled so as to make sure the physician receives the information?

- Are test results and films retained in an orderly manner? Have record-retention schedules been prepared, and are they followed?

- Do the various laboratories maintain logbooks that provide positive control over specimens and patients? Do the laboratories adequately control all processing, and do the controls ensure processing on a timely basis?

- How are drugs controlled on the wards? Do medical records reveal instances of patients receiving drugs not ordered or of patients being billed for drugs not administered?

- Is it clear to all ward and laboratory personnel and physicians how services are to be requested and reported?

- Are personnel friendly and courteous to patients? Do patients frequently complain about the quality of care?

- What system is used to transport patients to and from testing and therapy? Does it provide for prompt pickup and delivery?

- Do the laboratories and therapy areas coordinate the times patients will be called for tests? Do the ancillary service areas frequently schedule their work at the same time, making it difficult to get patients to all appointments?

Medical Records Management and Control

Proper management of medical records is important for the operation of hospitals. Balances must be achieved between absolute control of medical records and accessibility to physicians, house staff, students, and other health care providers. Other important aspects of medical records management are keeping the records up to date and accurate, and ensuring that the records provide clear documentation of services rendered that have been billed. Audit checkpoints that may form the basis of the creation of an operations audit program are listed.

- What procedures exist to ensure that medical records are complete and support the patient billings? Does the system get the job done effectively and with minimum delays? How is it monitored?
- What group is responsible for the management of the medical records department? Are the group members qualified to supervise the department, and do they actively manage the medical records systems and procedures?
- Are medical records personnel qualified for their jobs? Are there training and continuing education programs for staff?
- Does medical records have an operating manual? Is it up to date and complete? Are the procedures adequate?
- Are the physical facilities and equipment of the medical records department adequate? Is comfortable space provided for department personnel and for physicians who come to review or complete patient records?
- How are medical records filed? Do procedures facilitate accurate filing and quick retrieval?
- Who is allowed access to the records, and how is this enforced? Are there specific standing orders on the release of information on patients?
- How are medical records protected from loss and destruction?
- What reports are compiled routinely by medical records? Are there enough or too many? Do the right people receive them?
- In general, do the physicians and ward personnel believe that medical records management and control procedures are satisfactory?

Outpatient Department

Internal auditors must assure the hospital's administration that outpatients receive prompt, courteous, and professional service. The outpatient department (OPD) can be an important contributor to a hospital's income and public image,

and every effort should be made to be certain that the department is fulfilling its planned role. This is especially important with the much greater emphasis being placed upon outpatient services such as ambulatory surgery. Below are audit checkpoints generally applicable to outpatient departments.

- Who is responsible for managing the OPD? Is ambulatory surgery managed by the OPD staff? What is the organization of the business system used by the clinics?
- Who decides policy for the OPD, and what are the policies?
- Is there an operating manual? If so, is it up to date and complete?
- How is the OPD staffed? How are the physicians selected? How is the support staff selected? Are staffing arrangements planned for flexibility to meet varying patient loads?
- What reports does the OPD prepare, and what is their distribution?
- What is the fee schedule for the department and the doctors? How are charges determined?
- Are patients routinely followed up when they fail to complete prescribed treatments and make return visits? How are charges determined?
- How good are the physical facilities? Is the equipment modern and in good repair? Is there enough space for patients and staff, and is the area comfortable?
- Is there good access to therapeutic and diagnostic laboratories from the OPD, and are patients handled promptly and courteously? Are test results returned promptly to the OPD?
- To what extent does the OPD earn its way? How are deficits, if any, made up?

Many of the audit checkpoints listed for inpatients and outpatients are interchangeable.

Emergency Room

The operation of emergency rooms and new trauma centers can be exceedingly expensive, inefficient, and disruptive to a hospital's routine flow of patients. Internal auditors must be especially sensitive to the unique needs of emergency health care areas, for they probably never will achieve a level of operation that may be regarded as optimal. Operating systems and procedures to be effective must be unobtrusive, and regrettably it may not be possible to control all phases of all activities. Below are audit checkpoints to guide internal auditors who perform operations audits of emergency room care.

- How closely does the emergency room work with the OPD? Does the emergency room carry a large subacute patient care load that should be handled routinely by the OPD?
- Are emergency room personnel assigned additional duties when the demand for emergency services is low? If so, with what result?
- How are charges determined and accumulated? In particular, are all supply and equipment usages accounted for after emergency care has been delivered?
- Is the emergency room properly stocked with drugs and supplies and is it well equipped?
- Where is the emergency room located? Does it provide easy access to unloading facilities for ambulances and walk-in patients and to other areas of the hospital such as the OPD, diagnostic labs, medical records, and admissions?
- Are emergency room personnel properly qualified and certified for such service?
- What is the emergency room policy for extending care outside the hospital for accident victims, disasters, cardiac failure, and maternity cases? Who decides emergency room policy?
- Does revenue generated by the emergency room support its operation?
- What are the policies for providing information to journalists and for controlling access to patients and their records?
- What are the procedures for protecting evidence for victims of crimes such as rape and assault? How are injured criminals handled and, in particular, those with gunshot wounds?

Internal auditors must assure themselves that the emergency medical care facility accomplishes its goals.

Pharmacy

Hospital outpatient and inpatient pharmacies are important contributors to patient care and hospital revenues. Pharmacies should have clearly stated goals and well-developed operating systems and procedures. Below are audit checkpoints that provide the basis of an operations audit.

- Do hospital policies and procedures provide control measures that prevent members of the medical staff from abusing the privilege of writing prescriptions for narcotics and other drugs? What is the policy on outpatient prescription refills?
- What procedures are used to control inventories of drugs, and who is responsible for taking inventory? What procedures exist for disposal of expired drugs? What policies exist on approval of stocking new drugs and controlling brand proliferation? What policies have been developed to manage experimental drugs?
- What are the procedures for returning unused drugs to the pharmacy? Is unit dosage in use and is it effective? How are patient accounts credited for returned drugs? Is the process of return and crediting efficient, and does it minimize the number of credits to be made? How are returned drugs handled?
- What is the hospital's policy for pricing drugs? Are the pharmacy's prices in line with those of other community pharmacies? What method is used to price individual products? Are employees permitted discounts? Are late charges held to a minimum?
- What provisions are there for emergency drugs for the wards and emergency room? How are they controlled?
- Is the pharmacy conveniently located for outpatients? Is there a comfortable waiting area? Have satellite pharmacies been developed and with what effect?

- What drugs and solutions are manufactured by the pharmacy? How is the production process controlled? Is up-to-date equipment used, and are all processes efficient? Are solutions spot-checked for contamination?

- What are the procedures for cleaning the pharmacy? Who performs the routine janitorial work? Is the work performed in a manner that avoids contaminating drug inventories? How are drugs safeguarded from maintenance and housekeeping personnel who may have routine access to the pharmacy?

- What agreements, if any, exist with other pharmacies in the community for emergency prescription service?

- What are the procedures for handling cash receipts? What types of reports on activities are prepared? How many are prepared? How often? Who receives them? Do the reports fairly represent the pharmacy's performance?

OPERATIONS AUDITING OF SUPPORT SERVICES

Hospital support services have an important secondary impact on patient care. Smoothly operating support services often go unnoticed; however, if operating problems develop, the dependence of the patient care areas upon the support services becomes obvious. Hospitals have many common support services as well as unique ones. Below are operations audit checkpoints that cover six diverse departments and emphasize the flexible nature of operations auditing.

Auditing Safety and Security

Hospital administrators must be assured that their institution is safe for patients, visitors, and employees and that the assets of the hospital as well as the possessions of all those in the hospital are safeguarded. Internal auditors will want to find the answers to many operating questions, such as the following:

- What written procedures exist for safety and security? Are they complete and do they comply with existing city and state laws and regulations?

- Who is responsible for safety and security? Does the existing organization aid in achieving safety and security goals?

- What are the hospital's plans for evacuation in the event of fire or other disaster? What procedures exist for keeping track of patients as they are moved about within the hospital?

- Does the hospital require that patients, visitors, and employees complete accident reports?

- Are there safety training programs, including fire-fighting training? Is there a program of regular inspection for safety hazards?

- How does the hospital control access to all buildings and all rooms? Does the plan succeed, and is it followed?

- What are the procedures for reporting loss of, damage to, or theft of property of the hospital, patients, visitors, and employees? Are they effective?

- How safe are the hospital's grounds and parking lots? Are they properly lighted and patrolled? Is there an escort service for employees, visitors, and patients if requested?

- Does the hospital have an active program of crime prevention? Are keys to rooms carefully controlled? Are pieces of equipment engraved with control numbers? Are supplies carefully monitored with attention directed to drugs, syringes, and other items of value to drug addicts?

- Are hospital security personnel properly trained, equipped, and supervised? Are there enough personnel?

Auditing Personnel Administration

Hospitals must be properly and completely staffed in order to fulfill their mission. Personnel departments perform many vital functions. They provide effective recruiting, employee orientation, labor relations, handling of terminations and grievances, wage and salary administration, and employee training. They must maintain a system of employee evaluations and records. Hospitals with large personnel departments may have only some of these functions audited at any one time, whereas hospitals with small personnel departments may receive a comprehensive operational audit. Regardless of the exact approach, many of the audit checkpoints below will be of value in constructing personnel operations audit programs.[26,27]

- Have the organization, authority, and responsibilities of the personnel department been defined? Have policies been written, and are they complete and up to date?[28]
- Are all members of the personnel department's staff qualified for their jobs? Are there enough staff, space, and equipment?
- What is the attitude of the hospital's administration toward personnel management, organized labor, wage and salary administration, training programs, and all other phases of personnel administration? Is the administration supportive and prepared to provide the resources required by personnel management programs?
- What reports does personnel generate routinely? For example, what is the hospital's turnover rate? Is the rate broken down by job title and location? What is the average time required for recruiting for various job titles? How much training is needed?
- Are all jobs properly described? Are wages and salaries set with skill levels in mind? Do employees believe that the hospital's wages, salaries, and fringe benefits are acceptable? How do they compare with those offered by other nearby hospitals and industries? How are staffing levels determined, and by whom?
- How actively does the personnel department recruit nurses, technicians, secretaries, and clerks? How are applicants interviewed and screened? Who is responsible for making the employment decision?
- How active a role does the personnel department have in maintaining and improving employee morale? Are employees allowed to offer complaints and suggestions?

How does the administration respond to employee feedback? Does the hospital have a news publication that is distributed to all employees?

- How adequate are training, orientation, employee evaluation, and personnel record management programs? Are there adequate procedures and are they followed?
- Are employee attitudes surveyed and, if so, with what result? Has top management been responsive to real or perceived employee needs and wants?
- What role does the personnel department play in forecasting needs and in preparing plans to meet them?

Auditing Public Relations

As the public has become progressively more interested in health care costs, quality of service, and availability, hospital administrators have had to improve their ability to "tell the hospital's story." A second important aspect of public relations is the development of a positive image of the hospital as reflected by the employees and perceived by the public. Hospital administrators are responsible for developing a positive image within the hospital through internal marketing measures and training programs such as patient relations. Internal auditors will find an operational review of hospital public relations a challenge. Beyond using the audit checkpoints provided below, internal auditors will want to be certain to review literature in public relations in general and as applied to hospitals.

- How is the function organized and staffed? What policies and procedures have been established and by whom? Are they in writing?
- Have goals been established and standards set to measure performance where possible? Are the standards in fact measurable?
- Are the goals of the program compatible with those of the hospital? What provisions are there for reviewing public relations goals and hospital goals to ensure that they will continue to be complementary?

- What patterns of communication have been established between top management and public relations personnel? Are the patterns adequate? Do they provide for accurate and timely information?

- Is there overall planning for public relations, internal marketing, and employee training?

- Have contingency plans been prepared and agreed upon for handling unusual events such as negative media coverage or special-interest groups?

- What provision has been made for feedback from the public and employees? Is the information acted on?

- Are files maintained of clippings from newspapers and journals? Are they used to generate new ideas for presenting the hospital's health care delivery story?

- What efforts are made to improve employee attitudes toward patient care and the hospital? How effective are the existing methods of communicating with employees?

- Is the general atmosphere of the hospital indicative of an effective public relations attitude on the part of the administration?

Auditing Hospital Purchasing

Hospitals can benefit greatly from an effectively run purchasing department. The purchasing department will usually be subjected to more than one internal auditing technique. In addition to operations audits, financial and compliance audits are necessary. These methods may be applied at the same time or separately. A great deal of literature is available to the internal auditor on auditing purchasing departments. Below are many of the more important audit checkpoints to be used:

- How is the purchasing department organized? Is it staffed adequately with qualified employees? Are its systems and procedures documented? Are they adequate? Is purchasing independent of receiving and accounts payable?

- Are the purchasing department and its operations organized to promote efficient and effective processing of orders? How does the volume of orders and their dollar value correspond with staffing and paper-processing costs?

- What procedures exist for authorizing purchases? Are they adequate and are they followed? Has the administration defined the purchasing department's powers and responsibilities, and does it have effective means for controlling the department?

- Are purchasing's facilities adequate? Is there adequate space for receiving and interviewing vendors? Are there adequate records and forms? How are they safeguarded from loss?

- Does the purchasing department provide leadership in keeping the hospital stocked at reasonable levels at minimum costs and with few supply outages? Does the hospital participate in group purchasing? Are competitive bids used? Are new vendors sought? Are orders submitted so as to take advantage of quantity discounts? What controls exist over product proliferation?

- Does the purchasing department exhibit a service orientation to other hospital departments? If purchasing is completely centralized, how do units such as pathology, pharmacy, and central supply view the purchasing department's functioning? Are communications good?

- What reports does purchasing routinely prepare and what is their distribution? Are the reports timely and accurate and do they provide meaningful management information? Do the reports reveal the cost effectiveness of the purchasing department?

- What procedures exist for emergency ordering? Is the privilege used frequently, and if so, why?

- Do written purchasing policies exist and have they been communicated to all hospital personnel directly and indirectly related to the function? Are there policies for vendors and have they been communicated? Do the policies cover points such as purchases for employees, gifts from vendors, relationships with departments, receiving, and accounts payable? Do the policies help ensure a high level of integrity by all concerned?

- Do the internal checks on the purchasing department provide good control of paper work, orders, bids, discounts, vendors, and reorder points? Do the controls operate efficiently? What actions are taken to resolve problems, such as duplicate orders unmatched with receiving reports and damaged or otherwise unacceptable goods? Does purchasing learn from its problems with vendors and other departments? From its own problems?

Auditing Electronic Data Processing

A well-run electronic data-processing (EDP) system in a hospital can make tremendous improvements in all aspects of the hospital's operations. However, hospitals with poorly planned, organized, staffed, and controlled data-processing systems may actually be in worse condition than if all systems were manual. The field of internal auditing is meeting the challenge of effectively auditing EDP capabilities, and hospital internal auditors will find considerable assistance in the literature. Below are many of the more important audit checkpoints that must be included in an operations audit of hospital data processing:

- How is the data-processing area staffed? Are the director and staff properly qualified? Are training programs adequate? Has data processing planned for effective use of commercially available computer software packages?
- Does the data-processing function provide the hospital's administration with timely, accurate, and useful information that effectively and efficiently supports the decision-making process? How are microcomputer applications supported? How is user training handled? Is best advantage taken by management of desk top computing capabilities?

- Do systems that have been implemented actually perform in the manner planned? How do the actual costs and benefits compare with the plan? Are differences carefully isolated and evaluated? Are the differences the result of poor planning, poor performance, or both?
- What is the relationship between the data processing department and the rest of the hospital? Is it independent or does it report to another department? (It is recommended that the data-processing function report directly to the hospital director.)
- EDP requires the design of very complicated systems and procedures. Is there adequate documentation that is accurate and up to date? This is a frequent problem area that, if neglected, produces negative consequences. How are various duties segregated among employees? How is access to computers, data, and operating systems controlled? What advantage is taken of security codes? What provision is made for backing up data? What plans exist to recover from central processing unit and storage disk failures? How is overall utilization monitored and controlled?
- Have clear goals and objectives been established for data processing? Have standards of performance been set and communicated? Are the standards measurable? A function this complicated and expensive and that has such a broad impact requires a thorough, continuing, management oversight process.
- Is there sufficient short-term and long-range planning? (Planning covers the entire range of operations, from improving schedules and utilization, to preparing for major changes in hospital operations, to implementing new programs, to replacing existing hardware and software as new technology in health care and computers emerges.)
- What reports are prepared routinely for top management on data-processing operations? Are they accurate and of use? Do they enable management to evaluate and control the function?

- Is top management able to communicate effectively with EDP personnel? Do administrators understand EDP, and do they contribute actively to the planning, design, and evaluation of data-processing systems? Does top management appear to be uninformed about computers and their operation and generally avoid dealing with EDP personnel?

- Has adequate attention been given to the dehumanizing effects of computerization on patients and employees?

Auditing Hospital Laundry Facilities

Hospitals generate a considerable amount of laundry and it must be handled economically. Hospitals with their own laundries should be subjected to thorough operations audits. Below are a number of operations audit checkpoints for laundries.

- Is the laundry room adequately staffed? Does labor turnover disrupt operations?

- What is the laundry room's safety record? How many injuries have been reported? Are there any obvious safety hazards? Is the laundry room clean, adequately lighted, and ventilated?

- Are the employees supervised properly? Does the laundry room manager report to management on operations? Does the manager communicate freely with all hospital areas that generate laundry?

- How well is the laundry room equipped? Is the equipment in good operating condition? Who is responsible for maintaining it?

- How are inventory records of linen in storerooms and in circulation maintained? How often is it inventoried? What is the expected life of linen in service? What costs are associated with repair and replacement? Is there an adequate amount of inventory, too little, or too much?

- How is laundry processed? How is contaminated, stained, and infected linen wasted? Are detergents suited to water hardness, and do they contribute to pollution? What is the usual processing time required to have linen back in service?

- How do operating costs compare with those of commercial laundry room services? Is accurate cost information available for comparison? Are utilities used by the laundry room metered separately?

- How is laundry transported? How are soiled items delivered to the laundry room? How is contaminated laundry marked and separated from regular laundry? What records are kept of laundry received and delivered?

- How is damaged linen detected and repaired? Is there a sewing room for repairs? What other services are offered by the sewing room? Is the sewing room equipped properly?

- What is the overall quality of the laundry room's service? Do nursing personnel believe the laundry service is good?

AUDITING HOSPITAL PROGRAMS

Hospitals have many programs that are not in the form of departments. These programs can have a considerable impact on the hospital's missions and they must be reviewed to ensure that they are making their maximum contribution to the hospital. Depending on the nature of the program, internal auditors may have occasion to use all internal auditing techniques (management auditing, operations auditing, and financial and compliance auditing) at some time during the review. Two common hospital programs are discussed below. The concepts and techniques incorporated in the audit checkpoints provided can, however, form the basis for reviewing other programs.

Cost Containment Programs

Internal auditors should inform the governing board and the hospital director of the extent to which the hospital is controlling its costs. A good cost containment program will share many of its attributes with others. Below are audit checkpoints that are applicable to cost containment programs. Internal auditors should be certain to review literature on cost containment and tailor their review to the unique qualities of their hospital.

- Who is responsible for the hospital's cost containment program? Has a committee been formed? If so, what are its composition, goals, and powers? Are its operating procedures written down?
- Have clear, attainable, and measurable goals been selected for all hospital areas? Are they consistent with the institution's goals? Do cost containment policies complement overall operating policies?
- Are the efforts of the cost containment program directed properly? Has the overall direction of the program been to cut costs wherever possible, rather than to prepare a process of meaningful cost effectiveness studies leading to well-planned decisions on expenditures?
- How thorough is the committee's work? Are in-depth cost-finding studies made that identify all expenses? Are the costs broken down further on a range from "fixed" to "variable?" Are utilization studies performed where necessary?
- Does top management support the program? What reports and recommendations are received from the cost containment program? What actions result?
- Does the committee exhibit originality and resourcefulness in dealing with cost containment problems? Does the committee request several alternative proposals for dealing with particular problems of departments so as to make more informed decisions? Creativity and resourcefulness are essential to the program's success.
- What specific areas have been reviewed since the program's inception? Have shared services been analyzed to avoid unnecessary duplications among local hospitals? What services are shared: laundry, purchasing, food service, computer, microfilming? Have ambulatory and outpatient services

been reviewed for increases in such areas as outpatient surgery or hemodialysis? Have staffing levels been analyzed and put under continuing supervision? Are job descriptions, organizational charts, and operating statistics requested before approving new positions or refilling existing positions?

- Have cost-containing incentive systems been implemented to encourage all employees to spot potential areas for savings? Are employees motivated to improve their own performances? Are performance incentive systems directed at individuals, teams, and larger groups? What efforts have been made to make physicians more cost-conscious?
- Have advanced financial control systems been implemented, and do they effectively identify costs for all areas? How is this information used by the committee? How are length of stay and consumption of ancillary services and supplies monitored to control costs?
- Has the committee dealt effectively with obvious areas where cost savings can be achieved? Has the pharmacy's inventory been examined to reduce inventories, have computer services been examined for improved and reduced utilization, have the cafeteria's costs and revenues been analyzed, and have all opportunities for marketing the hospital's services been explored?

Infection Control Programs

While infection control is the responsibility of physicians and nurses, internal auditors can contribute to making the program as effective as possible by evaluating the administrative aspects of the program. Below are a number of audit checkpoints that may be used to review the administration of infection control programs.

- What are the goals of the hospital's infection control program? What precautions are taken for preventing harm to patients? Does the infection control program also include employees, visitors, and the community?

- What objectives have been established? Do they include the means for gathering data on the incidence of infection, effective reporting of infection occurrence ratios that are higher than normal, remedial and preventive actions, review and evaluation of antibiotic usages, and education?
- Has an infection control committee been formed? Is it chaired by the hospital epidemiologist in a large hospital or by physician knowledge of infection control in a small hospital? Does it have a heterogeneous membership, including infection control officers and representatives of nursing, pharmacy, microbiology, surgery, housekeeping, dietary, and the emergency room?
- Has the committee carefully documented the methodology to be used to monitor infections and the use of drugs? This is essential not only for purposes of management but also for the scientific aspects of infection control that require data to be gathered in a consistent manner over long periods. In particular, have the methods for reviewing infection reports, for inspecting equipment, for reporting, and for record keeping been established clearly?
- Is there an effective program of infection control education? Does it cover all pertinent areas and employees?
- To what extent do physicians and nurses cooperate by reporting infections? Are infections reported only on a cyclical basis after periodic pressures are brought by the infection control committee? (Lack of cooperation will result in unreliable data.)
- Does the hospital employ a full-time or part-time infection control nurse? (The position generally is regarded as full-time for hospitals of 400 beds or more.) Infection control nurses often are made necessary because of noncooperation by physicians and nurses.
- How are data processed and reported? Is EDP available?
- What documentation is maintained on corrective actions by physicians and departments? When is it necessary to confront a physician or department on poor health care

practices? Is the action documented carefully to ensure that an accurate record is created for future reference? When corrective action is necessary, are the positive educational, rather than punitive, aspects stressed?
- How does the hospital's record compare with national averages? What legal actions are pending on infections acquired while in the hospital?

Conclusions

Operations auditing is a flexible auditing method that should not have a restricted scope. The independent and systematic review of all hospital departments, functions, and programs can benefit hospitals in many ways. Members of the governing boards of hospitals and hospital directors must be certain that internal auditors are uninhibited in their work and receive their clear support. There is no other hospital management function that can yield the breadth and depth of management and operations review that internal auditing can.

FINANCIAL AND COMPLIANCE AUDITING

Financial and compliance auditing was the first auditing method used by internal auditors, and it remained so until the 1940s. Financial auditing deals with evaluating how hospital accounting, assets, receipts and disbursements, payroll, billing, and other elements of fiscal operations are controlled. Compliance auditing involves determining whether employees follow written policies, systems, and procedures that constitute the controls. A third aspect of financial and compliance auditing is preventing fraud. Internal auditors are not responsible for preventing most types of fraud and illegal activities in a hospital. Internal auditors can have a proactive role in preventing fraud in such areas as relationships with vendors, which should be analyzed for historical trends and accounts payable. In most other areas of operations, internal auditors, by performing their audits with due care, enhance the possibility of their uncovering fraud or illegal acts that may have occurred. Responsibility for fraud and other illegal behavior must rest on the management of the hospital and its departments.

Many of the more common financial and compliance auditing areas are discussed below. The focus of the audit checkpoint lists is much narrower. Financial and compliance auditing methods have a limited scope and therefore potentially contribute less to improving hospital operating effectiveness and efficiency than the methods described above. However, hospitals with poor internal control systems and procedures and employee compliance can benefit a great deal from these audits.

Auditing Accounts Payable

Good accounts payable systems provide prompt, authorized, and accurate payment to vendors for materials received. Below are audit checkpoints that internal auditors should consider in developing a financial and compliance audit program of accounts payable.

- What procedures are used to control accounts payable? Are requests for purchases entered into the purchasing system at the earliest possible time? Is there a controlling ledger? Are only purchase transactions recorded? How does the system control against double payments? Are the address files in the accounts payable system controlled that control for payments to unauthorized vendors?
- What is the frequency with which payments are made to vendors? Is there a period of accumulation before preparing a check to pay multiple invoices, or are many small checks issued?
- When the person authorized to approve disbursements signs the checks or vouchers, is supporting documentation available for review? Are receiving notices provided? Have all invoice prices, extensions, and footings been checked for accuracy? Are checks ever made out to employees or cash? Who mails the checks? Are freight charges

that were agreed to or bid billed? Do they seem excessive? Are purchase order dates prior to those of invoices? Are the billing addresses and shipping addresses the same? Have vendors insisted upon cash on delivery?

- Are vendor discounts taken advantage of? Are they paid near the last day of the discount's availability so as to permit the hospital use of the funds a few additional days?
- How are credit memos handled? Do they become the responsibility of the accounting department? How are orders and payments controlled on blanket authorizations? How are advance payments controlled?
- Are all accounts paid within vendor time limits? This will require preparing a schedule that ages accounts payable. Are delinquent accounts reviewed and resolved?
- Is there a significant number of deficiencies in accounts payable? If so, the auditor should consider confirming a sample of all vendors, regardless of whether or not hospital records indicate an active accounts payable balance. What impact have new procedures such as electronic invoicing had upon control and processing? If in use, are there adequate audit and paper trails?
- How are records of requisitions, orders, vouchers, and disbursements maintained? What is their retention period? Are they cross-referenced so as to permit inquiries by vendor, purchase order, or disbursement?
- What organizational relationships exist among purchasing, receiving, accounting, and check signing? Are they independent of each other? What are the paper flows to and from each area, and what are their responsibilities? For example, which area receives invoices—purchasing or accounting? Are procedures used in conformance with the governing board's guidelines? Are good internal controls evident in each department, or are many functions performed by a few persons in some departments?
- Are vendors evaluated for their performance by purchasing, receiving, accounting, and the utilizing department (see Exhibit 22-1)? Are vendor questionnaires

Exhibit 22-1 Vendor Performance Evaluation

Dear

_____ is one of several vendors who have submitted written proposals (bids) to render services for the hospital, and has given your name as a reference.

We would appreciate returning to us, at your earliest convenience, your rating estimate of:

	Poor	Fair	Good	Excellent
Professional aptitude				
Quality of work/product				
Cooperation in working with employees/management				
Attitude				
Knowledge of service/product				
Completion timeliness				
Billing timeliness and accuracy				
Would you use the services/products again?				

Yes   No

_____
Signature

All information will be held in strict confidence.
Additional information: _____

Thanking you for your cooperation.

used by internal auditing to solicit information about the purchasing function's processes such as bidding and ease of access (Exhibit 22-2)?

Many of these audit checkpoints can be applied to other types of payables such as travel expenses, financing through loans and notes, and insurance payments.

Auditing Accounts Receivable

Good internal control is a necessity for the management of accounts receivable. Internal controls guard against fraud and errors and ensure complete management control. Poor internal controls can quickly result in serious operating problems. The outcome of most of these problems will be the loss of funds to the hospital. Below are audit checkpoints for the

financial and compliance auditing of accounts receivable.

- What policies have been developed to deal with decisions on credit, referrals of patient accounts to collection agencies, indigent patient care, lawsuits, and bad debts? Are they reasonable and are they followed? Who is authorized to approve these decisions? Is the performance of collection agencies monitored? Are bad debts reconciled annually with collection agencies? Is it appropriate to segregate bad debts by type, such as emergency room, outpatient, and inpatient? If more than one collection agency is used to control for performance, do the agencies receive a representative cross-section of accounts or does one receive older or more difficult accounts to collect? Are personnel responsible for approving credit denied access to cash? What policies and procedures exist for un-

Exhibit 22-2 Evaluation of Hospital Performance Report

VENDOR AND/OR MFG. NAME _____ Date _____

For each of the characteristics listed below, please rate the hospital from 1 to 5—one (1) being the best, five (5) being the worst.	PURCHASING	ACCOUNTING	RECEIVING	*USING DEPT.	COMMENTS
Ability to take maximum cash discounts allowed (if applicable)					
Ability to take maximum volume discounts (if applicable)					
Adherence to bidding process					
Allows equal representation of product line					
Appeal mechanism (if applicable)					
Credit/return/breakage handling					
Encourages competition					
Handling of back orders					
Knowledge of product line					
Maintains fair business dealing practices					
Maintains prescribed par levels (if applicable)					
Overall cost effectiveness/efficiency					
Payment processing (within contract terms)					
Problem solving					
Procurement ability					
Professional appearance					
Professional attitude					
Receiving/stocking ability					
Telephone courtesy					
Total					

Estimated Annual Purchases

$ _____   Vendor Control Number _____

How would you rate these departments compared to their counterparts at other area hospitals? _____

_____

What are your recommendations on areas that we can possibly improve? Please be specific. _____

_____

Performance report completed by: _____ Title _____ Date _____

*Please indicate using department(s) _____

　*Information provided here will be kept confidential. Please return to applied payments? How are unposted payments applied? How often is the unapplied payment-holding account reconciled?

- Does the organization of the accounts receivable section, credit department, cashier, and collection department promote good internal control? Are employees of these sections restricted from working in the other areas, even during lunch breaks and absences? How are records safeguarded from unauthorized access? What provisions are there for controlling, sharing, or lending records?

- What type of controlling account or ledger is used for accounts receivable? Are accounts receivable reconciled on a regular basis?

- Do the types, size, and aging of accounts receivable and bad debt write-offs resemble local and national averages?

- How are cash receipts posted to individual accounts? Are they reconciled to total receipts? What internal controls have been developed to prevent employees' posting payments to their own accounts and accounts of family members and friends?

- In what form are patient accounts maintained? What detail is available on charges and payments? How often are electronic billing systems purged? What backup is maintained?

- How often and in what manner are charges posted? What internal controls exist that ensure that all charges are posted and posted correctly? Are there many late charges? Is a complete bill available to the patient at the time of discharge? How are returned bills handled? Is there an excessive number?

- How are credit balances controlled? What are the policies and procedures for refunding credit balances to the patient? Who authorizes the refunds? Are there enough credit balances to affect reporting of accounts receivable materially? If so, credit balances should be placed in a separate account.

- What reports are prepaid routinely, and what is their distribution? Are all excep-

tions reported? Are accounts receivable aging schedules prepared that cover aging by date of discharge, by date of last payment, and by area of payment responsibility, starting with the discharge date? What reports are prepared on unapplied payments?

- Is confirmation of accounts receivable performed? This may be a standard step of the CPA firm's annual audit. This process will help determine whether patients' payments have been applied properly to their accounts.

Auditing Payroll

Payroll expenses are the largest single expenditure of hospitals. A good payroll system must meet requirements imposed by labor and tax laws and by the hospital's operating procedures. In order to achieve a smooth level of operation, there must be well-thought-out systems and procedures and internal controls. Internal auditors will need to examine the audit checkpoints below.

- What records are used to control payroll? How are pay scales checked for accuracy? How are payroll calculations checked, including computation of overtime, holiday pay, bonuses, pay differentials, and on-call time? How is overtime authorized? How are payroll advances requested and approved? How and for how long are records retained? How are payroll deductions authorized and reported to employees? What records are used to document employees' receipt of pay?

- How are payroll checking accounts controlled? Are they regularly reconciled by employees other than those in payroll? Are payroll employees properly bonded? Does the hospital use multiple payroll checking accounts to save time on reconciliations? Multiple accounts will allow reconciliations of individual payroll periods.

- What internal controls are in evidence? Are the various payroll steps distributed among employees? Are employees rotated on jobs on a regular basis? What provisions are there to avoid using employees of one department to fill in for absences or lunch hours in other departments, and thus permit possible tampering with records? Are blank payroll checks safeguarded? Are checks prenumbered? Who is responsible for approving or signing the payroll and the checks? Do the steps taken by the person in charge guard effectively against error and fraud?

- What is the procedure for distributing payroll checks and cash? How are employees identified? How are unclaimed payroll checks and payments handled? Does a department other than payroll resolve the exceptions? What procedures exist for mailing out income tax statements? Does the procedure secure the statements from tampering? Who is responsible for mailing checks and statements? How are returned checks and statements handled?

- Who is responsible for authorizing hiring, pay scales, and overtime? Are there sufficient records on employees to document hiring levels and raises? What forms must newly hired employees complete? Are W-4 forms completed regularly? How is citizenship established?

- What types of time records are kept? Are they accurate? How are time card calculations verified and reverified? Do supervisors monitor employees closely to make sure times reported are correct? Reporting should be regularly audited to ensure against managers or employees padding the payroll. How is overtime approved and verified? How is it managed? What records are maintained for vacations, personal time off, floating holidays, compensatory time off, and sick leave? How are changes in name and leaves of absence handled? How are payroll deductions verified? Are they regularly reconciled with employee authorizations? How are they authorized and documented? Are W-2 forms updated annually? Are social security numbers checked for accuracy?

- Do the payroll systems and procedures appear to be efficient and do they accomplish the function at a minimum of cost? Do they promote accuracy? Does the system handle emergency payroll situations effectively?

- Are payroll distributions made on time? Are all time records and other documents received on schedule from all departments? What EDP applications exist? What provisions have been made to direct electronic deposits to banks? How effectively are direct deposits controlled?

- How is the confidentiality of the payroll records safeguarded? Do payroll employees avoid discussing records with others? Are records disposed of in a manner that safeguards confidentiality?

- What reports and analyses are prepared routinely of payroll matters and what is their distribution? Are quarterly tax reports prepared and deposits made on time?

Auditing Cash Receipts

It is most important to control cash effectively, for it is the most vulnerable hospital asset. Hospitals deal with large sums of money paid in person or by mail. Beyond safeguarding cash, there must be a well-documented process of accounting for it and applying it to patient accounts. Below are a number of important financial and compliance auditing checkpoints.

- Is the custody of cash separate from those responsible for cash receipt records and reporting? Cashiers must be responsible only for receiving cash, not accounting for it. Are all employees properly bonded? How are new employees screened?

- Is a minimum number of employees involved with handling cash? How are absences and lunch hours covered?

- Is cash received centrally? If not, are remote locations properly staffed, equipped, and controlled? Is cash adequately protected physically? For example, do security guards escort employees carrying cash receipts from the cafeteria to the cashier's office? Are daily deposits made intact? Is maximum advantage taken of interest-earning opportunities?

- Are employees required to rotate jobs and to take vacations?

- If the hospital routinely cashes checks, is an imprest fund used? Are the procedures associated with the fund followed closely?

- Are mail payments from individuals and third-party payers opened and listed by personnel other than those of the cashier's office, accounting, and the business office? Are reports of the mail receipts provided to persons who can check the amounts deposited? Are checks restrictively endorsed at once? Do all payments come to a central location? If not, what systems are used to ensure that receipts reach the appropriate office? How rapidly do payments get posted to patient accounts? Has a separate account for unapplied payments been established? If so, how is it managed?

- Are cash registers used for over-the-counter payments? Is the cash drawer balanced against the internal tape? Are prenumbered receipts used? What provision is there for multiple cashiers? Are cash draw-downs used to keep cash draw balances at a minimum? Are spot cash counts performed?

- Is the bank deposit slip returned to somewhere other than the cashier's office or accounting? Is an armored car service used to transfer cash? Are deposits timely?

- How are cash receipts for interest, dividends, sale of scrap, rents, and all other nonpatient revenues handled? Are they reported separately from patient fee revenue?

- Does the institution receive payments for physicians and other health care professionals not paid by the hospital?

Auditing Uncollectible Patient Accounts

Hospitals that have poor systems and procedures for controlling delinquent patient ac-

counts will experience unnecessary losses of collections and will have financial statements that are unrepresentative. A good financial and compliance audit may uncover many problems, ranging from poor collection efforts to poor admitting policies. Below are audit checkpoints that should be incorporated in a review of uncollectible patient accounts.

- Are accounts that are written off as bad debts adequately documented as to all efforts at collection? Are all policies and procedures followed? How rigorous are they? Do they permit an unnecessarily high level of uncollected accounts to be written off? Is an attorney used when appropriate? Were the policies approved by the governing board? Have patients been adequately counseled or referred to social service agencies in the event they may qualify for Medicaid or other charity services?

- Are bad debt write-offs authorized by a person who exercises control over the process?

- How are bad debts reported and accounted for? How are the records maintained, and for how long? Are bad debts reported to collection agency reporting networks and other credit-verifying agencies?

- Is a sample of bad debts confirmed to ensure that collection efforts are rigorous?

- Are uncollected accounts referred to a collection agency? Are these referrals controlled by a separate account? Are they segregated by inpatient, outpatient, emergency department, and other pertinent revenue centers? How are patients notified of the status of their accounts? Are accounts organized by surname or address to help determine abuses by particular individuals or families?

- Is the collection agency making a reasonable effort on all accounts, or does it concentrate on the easier ones? What percentage of accounts is collected? It is important to distribute all types of accounts to multiple agencies to ensure that performance comparisons are representative. What impact does the collection agency's efforts have on community relations? How and how often are collection agency balances reconciled to hospital balances for the agencies?

- What has been learned from the hospital's uncollectible accounts experience? Is there an indication that policies and procedures need to be changed? Are bad debts confirmed periodically with collection agency records to ensure that payments were posted properly?
- What impact does the hospital's screening procedure have on uncollectible accounts? Does the screening include verification of insurance coverage and credit? Are copayment obligations discussed? Does the hospital have adequate financial counseling for patients?
- Are the credit, collections, and counseling areas adequately staffed by qualified personnel?
- What is the hospital's policy on patients who return for care with account balances owed from prior visits?

Auditing Inventories of Supplies and Equipment

Hospitals have large sums invested in equipment and supply inventories. Good systems and procedures are required to maintain proper control of these inventories. Hospitals can save money by properly managing these inventories and being ready to document losses for insurance coverage should the need arise. Internal auditors must verify whether the hospital has achieved maximum control at a minimum cost. Below are audit checkpoints that should be included in the audit.

- Does the hospital have a central receiving area that checks in all supplies and equipment? Is central receiving independent of purchasing, accounting, and ordering departments? Are copies of receiving slips given to the person approving disbursements? What control exists over free sam-

ples of drugs and supplies? How are narcotics controlled, and does the control meet federal standards? Consideration should be given to designating an individual who is responsible for rigorously monitoring controlled substances, including spot-checking supplies and reviewing Drug Enforcement Agency reconciliations. It is recommended that billing records be compared with drug administration notes in medical records to verify that all drugs paid for were consumed.

- Are perpetual inventory records maintained on all major classes of supplies by personnel other than those in the storeroom? Are EDP applications appropriate?
- Have inventory reorder points been established for all supplies? Are the reorder amounts reasonable? Do they take advantage of quantity discounts? How often do stock outages occur? How are supplies that are received checked in?
- What controls exist over the total number and types of supplies stocked? Is there an unwarranted proliferation of items? Is there stock on hand that no longer is used? Are turnover ratios periodically performed? How are floor stocks controlled?
- What are the procedures for receiving and distributing supplies? What documents are used? Do the procedures require proper authorization? How are inventories controlled after working hours? Is adequate information provided to permit the storeroom to bill the right patient or department? What is the procedure for pricing?
- How often are physical inventories taken? What are the procedures for taking the inventory? Who supervises the process? Are spot checks made of the accuracy of counts by disinterested employees or internal auditors? Are pricing schedules checked? Who may authorize a change in perpetual inventory records? How are shortages and overages reported, and to whom? Is consumption of supplies analyzed by the calculation turnover ratios?
- How are supplies stored? Is there enough space that is properly climate-controlled and free from spoilage by water or pests? Is

the area clean? Are supplies stored in an orderly manner? What condition are the supplies in? Are supplies with limited shelf lives rotated carefully to ensure that none expires before use? How are supplies secured from theft and fire? How are returned supplies and overorders handled? How are credits handled?

- Is there adequate documentation on purchases of equipment? Are warranties, maintenance agreements, and leases controlled adequately?

- How is the equipment controlled? What dollar value of materiality has been set for inventorial equipment? How are items like gas cylinders, wheelchairs, and loanable equipment controlled? Are inventory numbers assigned to individual pieces of equipment and affixed securely? Is bar coding utilized? How often is equipment inventoried (preferably annually)? What procedures are followed, and who supervises the process? If lists of equipment are generated to be located, employees responsible for taking the inventory should also be encouraged to report equipment not found on the list. Is it clear which departments and managers are responsible for equipment? How are gains and losses of equipment managed and analyzed?

- What are the hospital's policies on equipment depreciation? Is depreciation properly claimed on equipment?

Auditing Patient Billing

Patient billing systems may be manual or automated, or they may involve a combination of both techniques. Regardless of the specific system used, it must achieve timely and accurate compilation of patient expenses. Internal auditors should be very thorough when reviewing billing systems, for a small percentage of error can amount to large revenue losses for the hospital. Below are checkpoints that should be incorporated in the overall program of hospital billing.

- Do the medical reports support the charges to patients? Are there records or reports for all laboratory tests, and are there physician and technician notes for all professional services rendered and billed? How secure is the medical record from loss and damage?

- How are business records maintained? Is the system economical, and does it promote accuracy and efficiency? What use is made of microfilm/fiche? What records retention schedules have been prepared? Are they reasonable? Are records retrieved quickly when requested? How secure are the records from damage, loss, and search by unauthorized personnel?

- Are patient billings reviewed routinely for obvious problems and errors? Are there numerous late charges? Do they vary by location, such as inpatient and outpatient? Do review and audit efforts contribute to reduced claims rejections, requests for additional information, and audits by third-party payers? If concurrent chart review is used, how effective is it in terms of expediting patient care, assuring complete and timely medical records, and minimizing patient inquiries about their bills?

- What procedures are used to determine hospital charges? How often are charges adjusted and new ones added? How effectively is the hospital's charge master maintained? Who may enter changes and how are changes authorized? How are manual and electronic adjustments controlled? Who may authorize adjustments and what documentation is created to accompany adjustments? Are there adequate cost-finding studies? Do charges comply with contracted amounts and discounts?

- Are charges compiled by revenue centers so as to permit comparisons with operating costs? How are costs and revenues managed relative to diagnosis-related groups (DRGs)?

- What controls are used to ensure that all chargeable supplies and services are billed to the patient? How are electronic order and charge entry systems controlled? Are inventories of supplies controlled to permit accounting for sales and unexplained shrinkages? Are billing system forms designed carefully and, when appropriate, controlled by prenumbering? What methods are used in batching and batch control? How are in-house (unposted charges) accounts controlled? Do they vary by location, such as inpatient or outpatient? How many additional days of receivables do they represent?

- What are the procedures for computing, checking, and entering contractual adjustments on patient accounts?

- What is the procedure for billing the room charges to the patient? Is the record used to prepare the billing reliable? Does the procedure allow for instances such as a patient transfer to an intensive care unit and return to the ward the same day?

- Does the billing system provide for adequate detailed and summary reporting? Are detailed reports of all charges sorted in a manner to permit inquiry? Do summary reports provide information useful to controlling DRGs? Are data available by DRG per physician? Are resource utilization trends available by DRG and physician? What use is made of them?

- Is there a continuing system for auditing at least a sample of medical records for supporting documentation for charges? This is an especially important process for hospitals that have large patient populations with Medicare and Medicaid coverage.

CONCLUSION

Internal auditors must be certain that the hospital's administration has provided the hospital with fiscal systems and procedures that offer a maximum of internal control and employee compliance at minimal cost. Internal auditors will be constantly challenged to find better ways of accomplishing this goal.

NOTES

1. Douglas R. Carmichael and John J. Willingham, *Perspectives in Auditing* (New York: McGraw Hill Book Co., 1979), pp. 356–75.

2. Donald H. Taylor and G.W. Glezen, *Auditing: Integrated Concepts and Procedures* (New York: John Wiley & Sons, Inc., 1985), pp. 113–35.

3. Michael J. Barrett and David L. Nich, *Effective Health Care Internal Auditing* (Rockville, Md.: Aspen Publishers, Inc., 1986), p. 17.

4. Lawrence Sawyer, *The Practice of Modern Internal Auditing* (Orlando, Fla.: The Institute of Internal Auditors, Inc., 1973), pp. 77–97.

5. E.H. Fly, "Cut Your Auditing Costs by Auditing," *Hospital Financial Management*, December 1968, p. 13.

6. Barrett and Nich, *Effective Health Care*, pp. 43–46.

7. Howard F. Stettler, *Auditing Principles* (Englewood Cliffs, N.J.: Prentice-Hall, Inc., 1977), pp. 452–75.

8. Barrett and Nich, *Effective Health Care*, pp. 85–99.

9. John J. Willingham and Douglas R. Carmichael, *Auditing Concepts and Methods* (New York: McGraw-Hill Book Co., 1979), pp. 115–44.

10. Jack C. Robertson and Frederick G. Davis, *Auditing* (Plano, Tex.: Business Publications, Inc., 1985), pp. 197–98.

11. Stettler, *Auditing Principles*, pp. 54–80.

12. Roy A. Lindberg and Theodore Cohn, *Operations Auditing* (New York: American Management Association, 1979), p. 56.

13. Institute of Internal Auditors, "The Internal Auditor's Review of Organizational Control," *Research Committee Report 18*, Institute of Internal Auditors, Inc., p. 12.

14. Victor Z. Brink, James A. Cashin, and Herbert Witt, *Modern Internal Auditing: An Operational Approach* (New York: Ronald Press Co., 1973), p. 50.

15. Lindberg and Cohn, *Operations Auditing*, p. 79.

16. Rockwell Schulz and Alton C. Johnson, *Management of Hospitals* (New York: McGraw-Hill Book Co., 1976), p. 203.

17. Addison C. Bennett, ed., *Improving the Effectiveness of Hospital Management* (New York: Preston Anglearn Publishing Co., 1972), p. 105.

18. J.G. Morfin, "The Function of Control and Internal Control," *Internal Auditor*, February 1973, p. 42.

19. Bennett, *Improving the Effectiveness*, pp. 112–16.

20. Robertson and Davis, *Auditing*, pp. 317–57.

21. Brink, Cashin, and Witt, *Modern Internal Auditing*, p. 100.

22. Bradford Cadmus, *Operational Auditing Handbook* (New York: Institute of Internal Auditors, Inc., 1964), p. 25.

23. Taylor and Glezen, *Auditing: Integrated Concepts*, pp. 39–52.

24. Fly, "Cut Your Auditing Costs," p. 14.

25. Seth Allcorn, *Internal Auditing for Hospitals* (Rockville, Md.: Aspen Publishers, Inc., 1979).

26. Brink, Cashin, and Witt, *Modern Internal Auditing*, pp. 320–24.

27. Dale L. Flesher, *Operations Auditing in Hospitals* (Lexington, Mass.: Lexington Books, 1976), p. 79.

28. B.J. Hall, *Auditing the Modern Hospital* (Englewood Cliffs, N.J.: Prentice-Hall, Inc., 1977), p. 200.

BIBLIOGRAPHY

Allcorn, Seth. *Internal Auditing for Hospitals*. Rockville, Md.: Aspen Publishers, Inc., 1979.

Barrett, Michael J., and David L. Nich. *Effective Health Care Internal Auditing*. Rockville, Md.: Aspen Publishers, Inc., 1986.

Brink, Victor Z., James A. Cashin, and Herbert Witt. *Modern Internal Auditing: An Operational Approach*. New York: Ronald Press Co., 1973.

Carmichael, Douglas R., and John J. Willingham. *Perspectives in Auditing*. New York: McGraw-Hill Book Co., 1979.

Flesher, Dale L. *Operations Auditing in Hospitals*. Lexington, Mass.: Lexington Books, 1976.

Hall, B.J. *Auditing the Modern Hospital*. Englewood Cliffs, N.J.: Prentice-Hall, Inc., 1977.

Lindberg, Roy A., and Theodore Cohn. *Operations Auditing*. New York: American Management Association, 1979.

Robertson, Jack C., and Frederick G. Davis. *Auditing*. Plano, Tex.: Business Publications, Inc., 1985.

Sawyer, Lawrence B. *The Practice of Modern Internal Auditing*. Orlando, Fla.: The Institute of Internal Auditors, Inc., 1973.

———. *The Manager and the Modern Internal Auditor*. New York: American Management Association, 1979.

Stettler, Howard F. *Auditing Principles*. Englewood Cliffs, N.J.: Prentice-Hall, Inc., 1977.

Taylor, Donald H., and G.W. Glezen. *Auditing: Integrated Concepts and Procedures*. New York: John Wiley & Sons, Inc., 1985.

Willingham, John J., and Douglas R. Carmichael. *Auditing Concepts and Methods*. New York: McGraw-Hill Book Co., 1979.

Chapter 23

Loss Prevention

Norman Jaspan
President, Norman Jaspan Associates, Inc.

Walter Nagel
Vice President, Norman Jaspan Associates, Inc.

Theft—along with ever-increasing wages; high professional salaries; the use of more sophisticated equipment and complicated collection procedures requiring more clerical staff; and the skyrocketing cost of energy, surgical supplies and food products—is a major factor contributing to spiraling health care costs. Theft may even drain hospital assets more than waste. Certainly, if all types of manipulations and conflict of interest arrangements are included under the category of "theft," the losses through waste cannot compete with those generated by theft.

PREVENTABLE VERSUS NONPREVENTABLE THEFT

In the health care industry, as in other areas of the business world, the term "theft" can be categorized in various ways. For practical purposes, perhaps the most realistic approach would distinguish between preventable theft and theft for which there is no realistic remedy. This is an important distinction because if administration invests a monumental amount of energy, payroll hours, and equipment in coping with petty pilferage, which is very difficult to deter, the amount of energy left to attack the more compli-

cated forms of dishonesty is severely reduced. Many categories of theft do lend themselves to curtailment by realistic control measures.

If statistical measurements were possible, researchers would probably find that in hospitals the largest losses from theft occur in the procurement process. Construction jobs—a never-ending activity in most medium and large hospitals—offer the most opportunity for fraud. Overpricing through rigged bids and padded invoices to finance kickback arrangements are notorious practices nationwide. Hospitals may be among the hardest hit victims of theft of this type.

The purchase of staple supply items such as food products, linen, paper goods, plastic goods, and chemicals offers temptation along similar lines. The maintenance and engineering departments in any health care institution are infinitely more vulnerable to theft in this area than are equivalent departments in industrial plants.

Theft in the procurement process requires a certain amount of enterprise, but it is the least risky of the various categories of theft because it does not involve actual removal of materials from the health care institution. In total dollar value it undoubtedly exceeds losses due to simple theft—picking up materials and walking out with them or loading them onto a vehicle.

Theft ranges from petty pilferage of small quantities of office and general supplies taken for

This chapter is from *Topics in Health Care Financing*, Vol. 5, No. 2, Aspen Publishers, Inc., © Winter 1978.

personal use to large-scale removal of materials and equipment. Large-scale removal of materials can be accomplished by individuals or through collusive action between employees of the health care institution and outsiders for joint disposal at a profit. The varieties are endless.

Petty pilferage can amount to infinitely larger total quantities in hospitals than in most other establishments, yet it is essentially not preventable. The patient who when discharged packs two clean sheets and four pillowcases into a suitcase can rarely be intercepted and searched. The aide who furnishes an apartment with linens and silverware taken from the hospital has virtually no chance of getting caught. All hospitals sustain losses as a result of employees consuming food in or taking it out of the institution.

Organized, planned, and repeated large-scale theft perpetrated through manipulations or collusive removal deserves the highest priority in devising realistic methods of curtailment. Practical deterrents must be established, reducing the opportunities for theft and increasing the risk of disclosure.

COMPUTER FRAUD

In some respects, the danger of intrusion into a hospital data-processing system is somewhat greater than the average risk of intrusion into a typical industrial installation. Hospital computers entail the same risks as most standard computer installations in the business world. In addition, they include features that are peculiar to hospitals alone.

Medical Records

The main item in this category is computerized patient records. It used to require a good deal of knowledge and just as much daring to enter a medical records department unauthorized and search through the manual files to find the records for a specific patient. Once found, these records could be easily copied, at least in the past 20–30 years, since dry office copying was invented and became popular. However, such an enterprise was never sure of success, and it was always risky in terms of someone's being caught searching through the files without authorization.

We are, of course, referring to activities connected with malpractice suits directed at the hospital or a doctor, where the lawyers involved would appreciate having direct evidence from the medical records concerning their case. We have no statistics about the frequency of such incidents, but we can argue theoretically that under a totally computerized medical records system it is conceivably easier to extract information than it was under manual filing. No matter what safeguards are in place in the form of highly confidential entry codes, the variety of personnel who have specific entry authority has to be considerable in a hospital operation. Once entry is successful, computer systems facilitate extraction of the desired information.

The coding system should prevent unauthorized people from gaining information in such a fashion. The problem is the consistent turnover of the equipment, requiring enormous, never-ending tasks for the programmers. In introducing such changeovers, no matter in what area of hospital operation—and most of them affect medical records—the problem of preventing unauthorized entry very often is at the bottom of the priority list. The practical coding alternatives are never the same in any two institutions, even among those using identical equipment. However, even without changing the equipment, every change in programming affecting medical records in any way has the potential of weakening the control over unauthorized access.

To address that problem, all the administration can do is make a specific team of people responsible for putting each programming change under a magnifying glass and examining it from the exclusive standpoint of unauthorized accessibility to the information. That team essentially should consist of the assistant administrator to whom medical records reports and the manager of data processing. Also, the risk manager in many cases would be a better candidate than the security director because, if the risk manager has a legal background, he or she is more likely to be better qualified to develop an above-average working knowledge of computer programming techniques than is a security director, whose background may be in the investigative field.

Inventory Control

Another area where the risk of intrusion can be higher in hospitals than in typical industrial enterprises is inventory control. Many supply items used in hospital operations are purchased by a central purchasing department and are centrally stocked in a warehouse operation, usually referred to as general stores. With varying degrees of success, the general stores items are controlled by a computerized perpetual inventory, with replenishment based on minimum/maximum calculations.

Many supply items that are easily marketable and therefore substantially vulnerable to theft are stocked in these general storerooms. They arrive from the receiving dock, are placed on shelves, and are pulled on the basis of departmental requisitions or on rotating refill procedures. Theoretically, the perpetual inventory usually reported on daily printouts should show a balance on hand identical with the quantity on the shelf. As it is well known, that goal is rarely achieved because of innumerable, unavoidable errors in counting, posting, stocking, and order picking. It is said that, if a perpetual inventory shows on-hand balances that are on the average 95 percent accurate, an excellent result has been obtained.

As we will point out further in our discussion of the receiving process, many general storerooms are located adjacent to the receiving dock or very close by; furthermore, the receiving staff is very often recruited from the general stores staff for easy interchangeability in case of shifting workloads and absenteeism. Therefore, the same staff member who unloads the truck and creates the receiving record that is posted as incoming inventory may also be the order filler who picks the item based on requisitions or stock rotation rules. Under this configuration—which we encountered in a large number of hospitals, perhaps even the majority—it is very tempting for employees to camouflage their thefts by computer fraud. They may have a choice of either reducing the quantities reported as received and posted to the perpetual inventory, or to increase the posted quantities picked in filling the requisitions from the nursing stations and all of the other hospital departments. One reason why this type of computer fraud is easier and more likely to occur in hospitals than in industrial or wholesale warehousing operations is the ready interchangeability of personnel; other factors are the frequent turnover of low-paid help and the very large variety of items in storage, some of them moving in and out with great speed. While we are not claiming that computer fraud to conceal theft is a feature unique to hospitals, it is normally easier to perpetrate in a hospital than in a standard commercial or industrial warehousing operation.

Payroll

One of the most profitable targets for fraud can be a computerized payroll operation. Payroll fraud can range all the way from relatively insignificant overtime padding or payments for unexcused absenteeism to carrying nonexistent persons on the payroll. These activities are often referred to as the "ghost-on-the-payroll" syndrome. A disloyal department head may carry a totally fictitious person on the payroll if he or she feels it can be undetected, even with a fictitious social security number; or he or she can carry an actual existing person on the payroll, using the legitimate social security number. In that case, the department head will have to have an arrangement with the person whom he or she carries fraudulently as an employee. In many operations, such as industrial plants with a lot of shift work and part-time help, the favorite method may be to continue someone who has been laid off for a few more days or weeks. This is relatively easy if a supervisor is assigned the responsibility of handing out the pay, particularly when the pay is given out in cash. What has changed with the advent of computerized payrolls is the speed with which the paychecks are created. A payroll that includes a large percentage of unskilled workers, particularly those subject to heavy turnover, is easier to pad with ghosts than is a payroll that consists mostly of skilled workers and has little turnover.

Hospitals notoriously require a substantial supply of unskilled labor, from dishwashers to orderlies to cleaning crews. It is an impossible task for the personnel department of a 1,000-bed hospital with 4,000–5,000 employees to screen every payroll for the legitimacy of each name. To overcome the burden of such a voluminous effort, some computerized payroll systems can attack the problem with exception reports showing every new hiring, every separation, every transfer, and every promotion. In industry, this sometimes offers a manageable way of detecting and discouraging computer fraud on the payroll. In outfits such as hospitals, which employ great numbers of part-timers and contingents, no mechanical control is possible.

There is one rule that should be mandatory: the person who posts the working hours for payroll purposes must never be allowed to collect or distribute the paychecks.

Of course, knowledgeable auditors know that W-2 forms that are returned at year-end because they are not deliverable deserve scrutiny as leads to possible payroll abuses.

Fictitious Invoices

The most lucrative type of computer fraud may be abuse of the purchasing and disbursement system. The classical method is setting up a fictitious vendor and subsequently putting through fictitious invoices supported by fictitious packing slips and receiving records. This, in fact, does not necessarily qualify as a type of fraud unique to computerized accounts payable systems. There is ample evidence that this type of fraud was not infrequent when checks were made by accounting machines, manually typed, or when those systems were replaced by conventional IBM punch cards. The difference again is that a computerized disbursement system is a rapid-fire operation controlled by harsh batching deadlines, so that the invoice-processing operation itself permits little time even to glance at the documentation to detect signs of dubious legitimacy. The fictitious vendor would be set up upon request by the same purchasing agent who requests all of the legitimate vendor introduc-

tions; therefore it would not be easy for data processing, when receiving such a request, to subject it to the type of scrutiny that would detect and discourage fraud.

The temptation for setting up fictitious vendors is intensified in institutions with weak receiving departments. We will refer to this at various points of our discussion. We can summarize our viewpoint by stating that, when the accounting department cannot reliably identify the legitimacy of the receiving record, computer fraud, by setting up fictitious vendors, will be a realistic danger. The activities under such circumstances will surface only if the perpetrators become greedy and keep increasing the dollar amounts collected by fictitious invoices so that someone, even without looking, will suddenly become suspicious and explore the matter further.

Certainly, it is not defensible for the administration to depend upon chance. On the contrary, an aggressive policy addressing the problem of fictitious vendors and fictitious invoices should be high on the priority list in any fraud and theft-prevention program. The first order of business has to be directed at accounts payable. Every effort must be made to assure that accounts payable is so staffed that deadlines can be met without such pressures that make it impossible for the staff to scrutinize the documentation for validity. However, even if this is achieved, it is rarely an achievement of any permanence. Sooner or later personnel will turn over or there will be a merger of several control functions without allowing for extra payroll hours; or there will be a replacement of experienced personnel with untrained personnel. In short, any arrangement allowing the accounts payable department to function as an adequate auditor addressing its scrutiny to all of the documents flowing through the payment process is bound to be subject to rising and falling pressures. For that reason, one of the most vital functions of the loss-prevention team is to keep a watchful eye on the documents crossing the accounts payable desks. If the hospital permits a budget for a special internal auditor who reports directly to the president or the senior administrator and who is in charge of the overall loss-prevention effort, this should be one of his or her highest priority targets.

Mailing Lists

A type of computer intrusion to which credit card companies and department stores are particularly sensitive, although hospitals occasionally experience it, is the surreptitious generation of mailing lists. There have been incidents of photographic services recruiting data-processing employees in hospitals to develop lists of names of the parents of newborn babies—a relatively harmless case of conflict of interest. We learned of one unsuccessful attempt by a funeral parlor to solicit the names of deceased patients.

Night Shifts

The most vulnerable period in which illicit intrusion for any of the above purposes is easier than during regular working hours is the Sunday afternoon and nighttime shifts, when many computer installations are thinly staffed—sometimes by only a single operator. In scrutinizing each change in the program, the effectiveness of the access codes has to be probed with specific concentration on those periods when isolated computer operators are working unobserved during odd hours.

Access Control

For control of physical access to the data-processing installation, it is always advisable to choose the most tamper-proof lockup devices available. One frequently used device is the push-button lock, but a better device is a magnetic card key entry lock. Here there is a choice of a simple, inexpensive installation in which the card key does nothing more than release the lock. A better and more costly installation is one in which each opening is recorded in the computer by the employee's identification number plus time and date. In that case, a daily printout can be screened to see who entered and when.

Lockup devices do not prevent the authorized operator from admitting someone else. Once there are suspicions of undesirable entries, for whatever purpose, the entry control can be strengthened by training a closed-circuit TV camera on the entry area. It would have to be a videotape camera, triggered whenever the door is opened. As hospitals are occasionally targets for secluded social gatherings, such as marijuana parties, for example, it is advisable to protect the computer room more than any other area from such gatherings; they could occasionally develop into high-spirited vandalism from which the computer installation should be protected.

THEFT IN PURCHASING

The degree of decentralization of purchasing varies among hospitals. The food service manager or chief dietitian in most cases is virtually autonomous in purchasing perishable food, including meat products. The chief pharmacist is usually autonomous in purchasing drugs, including commercial nonprescription drugs. Maintenance is often autonomous in purchasing materials and equipment.

Effect of Centralization

Many institutions have unsuccessfully attempted to centralize these purchasing functions. Incompetent or dishonest practices by these autonomous departments often result in a frantic attempt to throw the entire burden of these purchasing activities on already overloaded purchasing agents and their inadequate staffs. Many people believe that merely requiring the countersignature of the purchasing agent on purchase orders, for example, will prevent or minimize the number of overpriced purchases, inflated invoices, or fraudulent payments. In reality, mere centralization usually creates horrendous communications bottlenecks without necessarily improving the quality or integrity of the purchasing process.

Even for those materials that are theoretically purchased centrally by the purchasing department, the purchasing agent usually exercises little authority. Departments such as central sterile supply and x-ray, and numerous laboratories and research facilities may stipulate a specific manufacturer or supplier, along with the price, of a product when submitting their requisitions, leaving the purchasing agent little room for obtaining competitive bids. The backlog of orders to be processed usually means the agent will gratefully accept all the preparatory work done by the requisitioning departments. Thus, even though the purchase order is eventually signed by the purchasing agent, the requisitioning departments are virtually autonomous, no less so than officially autonomous departments such as dietary, maintenance, or pharmacy.

Under such purchasing arrangements, the person negotiating with a vendor or placing an order for the payment of a commission or kickback in one form or another has few obstacles. It is immaterial whether payment is made in cash, in the form of a percentage of the purchase price or in kind by the delivery of favors or certain commodities. Invariably such a payment is financed by inflating the invoice—by increasing the price of the invoice, by overbilling on the quantity or, in the case of food products, for example, by skimping on the quality.

Purchasing general storage items, which are purchased on a minimum/maximum inventory control basis, usually involves the purchasing department. These items are often contracted on a yearly basis, and both the purchasing agent and the specific using department jointly negotiate the order. The order may be subject to the countersignature of an administration official who actively compares prices, preventing the purchasing agent or the department staff from arranging a kickback from the supplier and having it financed by inflating the invoice.

Purchases Most Vulnerable to Theft

The purchases most vulnerable to theft are those ordered autonomously by a staff member of a department. These orders may be placed formally in writing or informally over the telephone. Shipments received by the department that placed the order are also very vulnerable to theft. Again these situations prevail in the dietary, maintenance, and pharmacy departments.

Under such an arrangement no fictitious price inflation is necessary. The department that places the order receives the shipment and con-

firms the accuracy of the quantities received. Overstating the quantity is all that is needed. In some instances the same person who places the order receives the shipment, making out whatever receiving document is acceptable to propel the vendor's invoice into the payment process. It is immaterial whether this receiving document is a copy of a purchase order, an individual receiving slip, a form developed by the hospital itself, or simply the packing list issued by the vendor and accompanying the shipment, signed or initialed and dated by the person who placed the order.

Informal purchasing and receiving methods involving only one person are not infrequent. Under these circumstances, it is hard to resist making an arrangement for a vendor kickback or commission payment at the expense of the institution. But even if some lower-ranking employee, such as a dietary stockroom attendant, a tool crib attendant, or a clerk in the pharmacy, is responsible for receiving orders, it is often easy for higher-ranking employees to steal. They can influence lower-ranking personnel by threatening to fire them or by offering them a share in the profits. They can then convince the receivers to make only a casual check of incoming shipments and to see that discrepancies are ignored so that the inflated invoice can be easily processed for payment.

Prevention

This type of manipulative theft involving no physical movement of stolen merchandise is less easy to perpetrate when storeroom items are automatically replenished. Where there is an established minimum/maximum or reorder point method, unexplainable shortages or startling out-of-stock conditions sooner or later will bring such manipulations to someone's attention. Such evidence is never conclusive. The shortages can be the result of miscounts, unrecorded requisitions, undocumented withdrawals, pilferage from the shelves, misplaced stock, or faulty minimum/maximum calculations. Nevertheless there is at least an indicator that something is wrong if specific items repeatedly show up short on the shelves. Also, for specific individual purchases originating in individual departments through itemized requisitions, the opportunities for collusive arrangements between requisitioner and vendor or between purchasing agent and vendor are less tempting and certainly less lucrative.

For these purchases, inflating the price is usually the only feasible method of financing a kickback. Manipulating the quantities by overstating the packing slip and the invoice for isolated shipments going into a specific department is more difficult to achieve. Therefore, by and large, the danger of dishonest manipulations in connection with individual purchases made by or for the various laboratories, x-ray department, operating room, intensive care units, or central surgical supply is less significant than for repetitive quantity purchases.

THEFT IN RECEIVING AND INVOICE PAYMENT

The receiving process is an area where the problem of dishonesty is critical. Yet in many, if not most, health care institutions, the potential for theft in receiving is ignored.

Although the receiving process deserves the most attention, it is too often given the lowest priority when protecting the hospital's assets. Many institutions invest enormous amounts of dollars, energy, and payroll hours in protecting their employees and clients. Massive reports are accumulated on stolen wallets, lost dentures, slashed tires, stolen bicycles, and molesting of nurses. But the receiving operation is being given the scantiest attention. It is provided the most miserly facilities, the least competent help, and the poorest form of supervision.

This imbalance may be motivated by the lack of glamour that a receiving dock radiates. Wealthy donors certainly prefer their names to appear on a plaque over the x-ray department or kidney dialysis unit rather than over a receiving dock.

The processes of document control and matchup may be another reason for the inattention to potential theft in receiving. Document

control and document matchup are tedious and uninspiring tasks. People responsible for these tasks may have a tendency of skimming through them, with the result that the documentation is not checked thoroughly, and the opportunity for dishonesty is increased. Whatever the reasons, administrators should realize the seriousness of theft in the receiving process.

The Problem

Overworked, incompetent, or disgruntled receivers may easily be the victims of dishonest drivers. Some drivers simply do not deliver to the hospital all the goods that were ordered. If the receivers fail to notice the shortage, the drivers keep the rest of the shipment, selling it to another buyer for their own profit. If the receivers detect the shortage, the drivers may offer them a bribe or an actual share in the proceeds from the resale. Since drivers often dispose of part of their shipments before they even arrive at the hospital, they are rarely caught in possession of stolen goods, making this form of theft infinitely less risky than the actual removal of stolen materials from the institution.

Collusive theft arranged between receiver and driver is particularly tempting with repetitive deliveries of easily marketable items. In health care institutions these items include food products (particularly meats and expensive canned goods); linen; bulk paper products; and widely used chemicals. The selection of easily marketable items, of course, varies according to geographic location of the institution and fluctuating market conditions.

Cause

Dishonesty in the receiving process is caused by a combination of factors: weak accountability, low reliability, inadequate personnel and facilities, and lack of documentation.

Weak Accountability

In many institutions the receiving process is so decentralized—more so than the purchasing process—that supervision and accountability of the individual receiving areas are completely impossible. Receivers rarely report directly to an assistant administrator or comparable official who is in no way connected with the purchasing process itself. More often than not they report to the storekeeper or in fact are members of the general stores staff. Sometimes they report directly or indirectly to the purchasing agent. This may be a grievous mistake; many receivers are unskilled and are among the lowest-paid employees in the hospital. They may be more likely to yield to the temptation of stealing to supplement their incomes.

Yet often the receiver's signature is actually the equivalent of a signature on a bank check; sometimes reduced to a mere scribbled initial, it authorizes payment of an invoice that may total as much as $3,000.

Since receivers are usually overworked, they have little motivation for developing any degree of loyalty to the institution and are easily tempted to sign the receipt of a shipment without accurate accountability. Thus the payment of vendors' invoices is the responsibility of a person who is extremely likely to steal from the institution. This problem is serious enough in the case of a neutral, independent receiving department; it is infinitely worse when the same department that autonomously places a purchase order receives the shipment.

This potentially dangerous situation is not unusual. Quite the contrary: it is common to the majority of health care institutions.

Low Reliability

While the degree of competence in and accountability of the receiving process may vary, as does the degree of autonomy in purchasing, the level of reliability is usually low in most institutions. This low reliability level is exemplified by the structural problems encountered in the receiving process. Only in recent years during major expansion projects have major hospitals provided adequate receiving dock facilities with supporting office space and staging areas. In the majority of institutions, space for receiving is inadequate, with single docks often serving institutions with several hundred beds. In

many cases a simple alley with no proper unloading facilities serves for receiving of most materials. Inadequate facilities interfere with reliable operation and increase the chance for theft.

Dual Receiving Accountability—A Solution

The principle of dual receiving accountability as a prerequisite for invoice payment is the most powerful device for protecting against buyer/vendor collusion and driver/receiver collusion.

Method

The accounts payable department should be required to receive two separate pieces of documentary evidence proving that the shipment has arrived as stipulated by the purchase order, the packing slip, and the invoice. The first evidence of receipt should be generated by the receiver on the dock who actually assists in or witnesses the unloading of the shipment. The second evidence should be provided by the final recipient. This can be in general stores, central supply, the dietary stockroom, the pharmacy, or any one of the laboratories and various other supporting departments receiving individual shipments.

The tools for implementing dual accountability can vary in many ways. There can be two different receiving copies of the purchase orders. Requisitions can have specific copies to serve as receiving documents. Separate receiving documents can be developed, for example, with the original being filled in and signed by the dock receiver while the duplicate accompanies the shipment to its destination. The duplicate is filled in and dispatched to accounts payable, where a matching process takes place.

Implementation

Many complexities can make the implementation of dual accountability quite difficult. Within a large institution the identical system and paper work flow will not be practical for all divisions. Variations will have to be devised and exceptions will have to be authorized. The problems may be similar, but the solutions are never the same.

However, by establishing a solidly enforced dual receiving operation, successfully implemented by an alert accounts payable matching process, the institution will curtail two of the major avenues of fraud and theft draining the funds of the institution.

THEFT IN CONSTRUCTION

On municipal and state-financed construction projects, budgeted funds are frequently exhausted when the projects are barely half completed; some of the funds are lost due to inflation but most of them disappear into the pockets of public officials on various levels. It is not unusual for a visitor being shown a recently completed plant or office building to be told, "This impressive structure cost $112 million, one-third of which was lost to graft."

To a lesser degree the pattern is similar with privately financed construction. Hospital construction, mostly financed through a combination of public appropriations, bond issues, and private donations, approaches more closely the graft pattern experienced with municipal and state-financed projects. Realistic comparisons are impossible to make; suffice it to say that temptation for graft in hospital construction is enormous.

Conflict of Interest

Virtually every phase of a construction project lends itself to brazen conflict-of-interest manipulations. The project engineers can make bid-rigging arrangements with any number of subcontractors, such as electricians, pipe fitters, truckers, and equipment renters. They can easily pad invoices for building materials or arrange for short deliveries of such items as cement, lumber, piping, sheet rock, wiring, etc. Padding of construction payrolls is a common method of stealing, with foremen working sometimes on their own, sometimes in collusion with other crew members. Sometimes the same worker is paid as a full-time employee by several different subcontractors; in this case the pay may go to the project engineer or may be split with the work-

ers. Engineers may also receive pay for "ghosts on the payroll," nonexistent people or people who have long been retired.

Need for More Control

Many of these practices are not peculiar to the construction business, but the construction business offers greater temptation and easier success at smaller risk. In spite of that fact, the administrative staff and finance divisions in the hospital field rarely exercise aggressive and watchful control over the activities of the construction teams. Frequently the architectural firms in charge of the project are asked to furnish a coordinator to function as general watchdog. However, this person primarily concentrates on the quality of building materials, compliance with local codes, meeting completion deadlines, and battling with vendors to meet delivery schedules. Rarely is such a coordinator expected to expend a great deal of time and energy scrutinizing the validity of bids, receiving records, payroll records, vendors' invoices, etc.

To be sure, there are exceptions, pertaining mostly to major construction projects such as those involving the erection of a complete new hospital complex. Here it is frequently arranged to have an assistant administrator, plus an accountant, assigned on a full-time basis to probe into the total range of activities of the construction engineers and all the subcontractors.

In medium-size construction jobs—major renovation, the addition of a new wing, the construction of new departments designed to house modern equipment—these watchdog exercises are usually absent. In these projects the administration and the finance division of the health care institution must at the point of inception set up an active mechanism for monitoring the bidding process, checking various phases of completion, and verifying vendors' and subcontractors' invoices.

In summary, financing of the project and disbursement of funds should not be dependent exclusively on the judgment and approval of the same personnel who are involved in the original negotiations and who are responsible for the execution of the project. If the engineers in charge of a major project are dishonest, a massive effort on the part of the security investigators and financial auditors is needed to uncover or thwart diversions of funds.

THEFT IN ENGINEERING AND MAINTENANCE

Tools and maintenance materials are some of the items most frequently stolen from health care facilities. Many mechanics and maintenance and repair personnel work in the evenings and during weekends when there are fewer health care staff on duty in the institution. It is not difficult for them to steal equipment and materials without being observed.

Equipment Theft

In hospital complexes with a campus-type layout, where numerous buildings are scattered over several city blocks, maintenance materials and tools are frequently transferred from one building to another on a daily basis. At some institutions, the maintenance department, including tool cribs and storage facilities, is located in a separate building. In such situations the only way to prevent massive disappearance of tools and equipment is through a rigid system of documentation of materials requisitioned, specifically those charged to an individual work order.

As outlined previously, the greatest opportunity for diversion of maintenance material exists in the requisitioning, purchasing, and receiving process. Next, the transfer of materials from building to building offers the greatest opportunity. These types of losses are impossible to curtail altogether, but the procedures for storage, inventory control, and issuance control can limit the opportunities drastically.

Payroll Fraud

Another area of substantial drain on hospital funds is the maintenance payroll. Since maintenance personnel, skilled and unskilled, often have to work for prolonged periods of time in outlying buildings, away from the foreman, it is difficult for even the most loyal and most efficient foreman to keep strict control over the staff. As a result, there is a constant risk of staff disappearing for periods of time to perform moonlighting jobs elsewhere while on hospital time. The most serious loss in this area stems from staff completing jobs on overtime which were not completed during regular daytime hours because crew members were moonlighting.

Only rigid detailed scrutiny by the chief of maintenance of hours spent on individual work orders can narrow the chances of substantial loss through this type of payroll fraud.

Abuse of Professional Privilege

Finally there is the pattern of abuse of executive and professional privilege. When maintenance staff members, including the leader, are dishonest, they soon give in to requests from administrators, physicians, and innumerable department heads. They may first make small repairs in the private homes of executives and professionals. Next they may agree to minor construction for these professionals—all on hospital time and with hospital tools and equipment. In some institutions these abuses have been minor; in others they have assumed startling proportions before being uncovered.

THEFT IN DIETARY SERVICE

Food

Petty Pilferage

In terms of petty pilferage, food is the most diversified target in any hospital, with much food being dishonestly consumed on the premises. This type of pilferage may be relatively harmless, resulting in little or no loss to the hospital, particularly when employees eat food left on patients' trays. Attempts to curtail this type of eating on the premises for contamination reasons usually are without success. In spite of attempts at locking up food supplies in the kitchen, employees can pilfer food by invading the kitchen's storerooms and the pantries on the inpatient floors. This usually occurs at night. It is the guards and maintenance and housekeeping personnel who are often the biggest offenders, since they are in charge of submaster keys that allow access to these areas.

Organized Pilferage

Some food pilferage involving eating on the premises is more organized. In large cities, hospital employees, particularly the unskilled employees of the dietary department, have on occasion brought in whole families from their neighborhoods to feed them in deserted corridors or hidden stockroom corners of the hospital.

The hospital's guard force is not sufficient to resolve this problem. Sometimes the guard force itself is guilty of petty food pilferage and will ignore these pilferings. Only in a hospital with successful perimeter control will it be possible to intercept this type of theft. This would involve guard coverage at all accessible entrances and a capacity for challenging identifications, checking visitor passes, and distinguishing legitimate employees from intruders.

Moreover, when intruders are challenged and politely evicted, their compatriots on the hospital payroll may conceal food on their persons and carry it out to their families and neighbors instead.

Priorities for Preventive Measures

However, even in the inner-city hospitals where such activities can assume sizable proportions, the total volume of pilfered food is rarely enough to raise the food cost per patient per day significantly. Therefore, if the buildings lend themselves to easy concealment and the traffic is essentially uncontrollable, as in most campus-type institutions, it is usually a waste of energy to cope with this type of theft.

Highest priority should be given to diversion of food in quantity. To curtail this type of theft there is only one principal method—lockup—to achieve very limited accessibility. High-priced items such as meats and poultry, canned fish, coffee, and any packaged foods that are highly desirable and easily concealed must be locked in freezers, coolers, stockrooms, or cages where only the personnel assigned to these areas have access. Specifically, nighttime lockup must be very strict, with hardware not keyed to submasters available to nondietary personnel. Personnel who allow access to unauthorized persons must be subject to severe disciplinary action.

As in most such procedures, it is easy to make the rules; finding ways of enforcing them is the problem. Enforcement depends upon the supervisory structure and, most importantly, on the loyalty of supervisory personnel. If supervisory staff want to avoid conflict, they will turn their backs on these types of infringements. In that case, the losses from concealed thefts can be quite substantial.

The biggest losses always result from collusive actions between requisitioner and vendor or between receiver and driver. The most vulnerable items are those that are both purchased and received by the dietary department. In most hospitals this applies to all perishable foods, including the most high-priced products such as meat, poultry, and fish. But even shipments of lettuce and other produce have been known to be received short, with drivers pilfering and selling them to the taverns around town and splitting the proceeds with the receiver. For that reason, it is indefensible to have a process where the payment of an invoice for food products requires only the signature of a dietary employee. The principle of dual accountability in receiving, difficult as it is to accomplish in many institutions, is always a step in the right direction.

Nonfood Supplies

Nonfood supplies used in dietary operations are also subject to pilferage. Most institutions have experienced the disappearance of silverware in great quantities in spite of the fact that lockup in cages or closets has been initiated.

Since pilferage of silver in small quantities by patients, visitors, nursing staff, and kitchen help has always been difficult to detect and prevent, the majority of institutions changed over to plastic or paper utensils. Still the vast variety of disposable plastic and paper products is an attractive staple item. Drivers often have a lucrative market for these items, as well as other paper products received in large quantities. These items are not easily diverted within the dietary department itself, since in most institutions nonfood supplies come in through the general receiving process and the general storeroom. So it is in the receiving process that dual accountability should be instituted to protect against diversion.

THEFT IN GENERAL STORES

The most serious flaw in a majority of general stores operations is the fact that the staff doubles as receivers on the dock. In fact, in many hospitals the general stockroom is located adjacent to or immediately beneath the receiving dock so that receivers, upon unloading a shipment, can transfer the cartons easily into the general storeroom. Because storeroom personnel alternate working as receivers, frequently the same person who functions as the dock receiver also eventually places the shipment on the storage shelves. This situation offers the most powerful incentive for a receiver to go into collusion with a driver to steal goods.

Hospitals should separate receiving from both general storage and purchasing. There is nothing wrong with having all three report to the same assistant administrator, but they should be independent functions so that none of the three can easily cover up for the shortcuts or manipulative activities of any of the others.

Such a separation is easily accomplished in a large institution. It is more difficult in a small health care facility where the number of staff is significantly smaller. Even where a compromise cannot be reached, the mere awareness of the risks inherent in these overlapping functions will present an obstacle to pilferage that could otherwise snowball into mass diversion.

Requisitioning Systems

Most departments order their supplies from general stores through the use of "laundry lists" by product classification. In smaller hospitals, the same person who receives, signs for, and stocks the merchandise also serves as the dispensing agent distributing the same items to departments and nursing stations. Realizing that most areas, especially nursing stations, never count the items in the supply cart, dispensers can cover by devious short-order filling methods any shortage resulting from collusion with drivers in the receiving process.

Supervisors of general stores departments are usually so busy handling special telephone requests or emergency run-outs that they are unable to perform even a 10 percent random spot check of departmental delivery carts. To compound the problem, in certain hospitals computer chargeouts to departments are grouped as a total dollar figure at the end of the accounting month. No department manager can associate a dollar figure with the material received in the department. Also, if a delivery copy is not left with the recipient department, even though charges may be broken down by category, it becomes an exercise in frustration to try to associate every item delivered a month previous to the computer printout.

Naturally, it would be preferable for items to be counted and checked off against the requisition at the recipient department or nursing station. A unit clerk could handle these duties. The recipient department should receive a copy of the requisition and know what it is being charged for. Whether chargeouts are processed through key punching or cathode ray tube (CRT) input techniques, the systems basically remain the same. The most important factor is that the computer should be programmed to classify and code charges, in both quantities and dollar figures. These figures can then be compared with budget allowances and to bed occupancy from month to month.

Par Stock and Cart Replacement Systems

Many hospitals have been experimenting with two methods of general stores distribution—par stock and cart replacement. However, these systems may be causing the proliferation of dishonest actions by general stores personnel. Par stock and cart replacement are both under the control of the person delivering the merchandise, who refills to the par level and itemizes the amount of merchandise stocked. For cart replacement, the filled cart is left and the partially used cart taken away. Thus deliverers have the perfect opportunity to manipulate stock replenishment figures to their own benefit.

Another problem at nursing stations is that nurses sometimes fear running out of critical items. When ordering or having merchandise delivered, they may take supplies and hoard them in a supply area. In one hospital, three nursing stations on one floor were found to have more stock on hand of several items (central sterile and general stores materials) than the rest of the hospital and the storeroom combined. In another hospital, where storeroom facilities had not kept pace with hospital growth, large quantities of supplies, including disposable hypodermic needles and syringes, were found in elevator corridors.

Although the dollar value of these items may be insignificant, disposable needles and syringes offer the greatest marketability, and any large quantities of these items should be kept in central locked areas. If central storage space is not available for other items, heavy wire mesh cages might suffice until permanent storage space is allocated.

Before installing a par stock or cart replacement system, administration should clearly define the logistics of such a move. Items selected for either of these systems should fall into the category of disposable stock items or certain sterile kits, or nonchargeables to patients. Take-home types of supplies should be limited. Where possible, random checking of replacements or stock remaining in returned carts should be initiated by nursing administration or storeroom supervision. Also, to prevent hoarding of supplies, nursing and storeroom supervisors should make inspection tours at least once a month and ensure that overages are returned to stock.

LINEN THEFT

Not only do all people use sheets and pillowcases in their homes, but linen, if it is in good condition (particularly factory new) is very marketable. Linen has even been accepted as currency in the dope traffic market. One heroin addict was told exactly where to find linen in a certain hospital. He was told, ''You come back with one sheet or three pillowcases, and I'll give you a fix.''

Prevention

As with pilferage of many other hospital materials, linen theft in small quantities is difficult to prevent. The general target in safeguarding linen can be easily defined, however. Linen, wherever possible, should be stored so that only personnel who have access to it as part of their actual duties can pilfer it. Linen supplies in stock should be made inaccessible to a large crew of stock people and order fillers by being kept under lock and key. The keys must not be submastered. In fact, where possible, access to unused linen storage would be best protected by a dual keying operation where no one individual in possession of one key can have access to the stock.

The difficulties in protecting linen in transit are numerous. Expensive experiments and failures have been endless. Locked linen carts have not succeeded in preventing pilferage. The frames bend, the doors jam, and the keys are lost. Moreover, when the patient census changes, the cart does not have enough space and linen is piled up on top. The linen on top of the cart is inviting to potential thieves.

Zipped plastic or canvas covers, even padlocked at one end, have been more successful. At least they have brought about an obstacle to the temptation to rifle the carts in elevators, on elevator landings, and in corridors.

On patient care floors, nursing staff no longer wear linen closet keys around their necks as they did before World War II. The linen cart has increasingly replaced the lockable linen closet. A well-designed inpatient floor would have a closable, preferably lockable alcove to house the linen cart where it at least can be protected from easy access at night. The linen closet most vulnerable to theft is the one without lockup hardware at the far end of a deserted corridor.

Positioning the closet or linen cart alcove directly facing the nursing station is the best way to deter pilferage. In this way, even during thinly staffed hours, the linen is within a reasonable line of vision of the nursing staff. This is the most practical and reasonably enforceable method of protecting linen from pilferage by people walking through the hospital corridors (patients, visitors, professional staff, housekeeping staff, and intruders).

In summary, there is no one prescription for curing dishonest actions. Some of the measures are self-defeating. For example, keeping the supply of linen very low to correspond with bed occupancy on each floor in theory would limit the quantities of linen accessible to patients and visitors, thereby eliminating the temptation for theft and reducing the losses. In practice, more often than not these tactics have resulted in massive hoarding by the staff, with nurses tucking linen away in a variety of closets and corners, including patient rooms. Thus limiting accessibility quickly results in increased accessibility and consequently increased losses.

Recent Developments Affect Exposure to Theft

Recent developments have influenced the level of linen exposure to theft. Automated transportation (the use of conveyors, lifts and cart ejection mechanisms) certainly will reduce exposure in transit. But the actual degree of exposure will depend upon the immediacy with which the fresh linen arriving by automated means is picked up at its destination and safely stored away.

The use of commercial or cooperative laundries serving numerous health care institutions also changes the pattern of exposure. Trucks hauling soiled linen in one direction and bringing back clean linen offer a new dimension. Soiled linen is not a significant target of theft. But diversion of clean linen involving truck drivers in transit can amount to substantial losses. Control by weighing, the prevalent method of keeping track of linen, is notoriously unreliable due to delays in the turnaround (caused by equipment breakdowns, labor problems, etc.). Locking or sealing trucks at the point of departure is not

feasible when trucks make frequent pickups and deliveries.

Locking or sealing of individual hampers or carts wheeled onto the truck, however, is a workable protective measure. It makes it necessary for the driver to be in collusion either with a loader at the laundry or the unloader at the hospital before the linen can be successfully diverted. Seal number accountability or custody of the keys to the hampers is a tedious task, yet often worth the effort to prevent massive losses while trucking clean linen.

THEFT OF SURGICAL SUPPLIES

Surgical instruments and medical supplies do not normally offer a target for massive diversion. Even petty pilferage is rarely significant in this area in terms of total quantities, and most of it is not preventable. Disappearing thermometers can amount to a substantial loss over a long period, but stolen bandages, adhesive tapes, gauze bandages, pins, and needles will never amount to more than a negligible fraction of the total expenditure for surgical supplies. The notorious loss of stethoscopes and ophthalmoscopes at the end of the residents' term usually is substantial, but it occurs once a year and again is not completely preventable.

In central surgical supply itself scissors may be the one major target. Most staff who work in these departments have little use for other surgical instruments. There have been occasions where a connection was established between an employee in the central supply room and a privately owned surgical supply house, but those incidents are infrequent.

THEFT IN HOUSEKEEPING

In most hospitals, housekeeping supplies and equipment are purchased centrally and stocked in general storage. The numerous cleaning fluids and paper products used by housekeeping crews are rarely a prevalent target for mass diversion. Petty theft is easily accomplished, but there is a good chance that waste is a greater source of loss in the housekeeping department than pilferage.

The difficulty of supervising a cleaning crew that is widely dispersed throughout the hospital or health care institution aggravates the waste problem. Even fresh linen is not safe, since instead of walking some distance to the housekeeping closet for a supply of rags the housekeeping crew often picks up towels and pillowcases to wipe walls, etc.

Cleaning equipment is occasionally removed, particularly in a campus-type hospital where control of car and truck traffic is difficult to achieve. Usually, however, all the floor polishers and vacuum cleaners stolen do not represent a very substantial loss.

The biggest risk with the housekeeping crew is their exposure to other supplies and equipment. Cleaners, sweepers, and polishers often work in deserted departments where office equipment, microscopes, and other items are easily accessible. Trash disposal offers the housekeeping staff the biggest opportunity for concealing and eventually removing valuable equipment. Without concealment in the trash, removal of heavy equipment is usually too difficult and too risky. For that reason trash compacting equipment is one of the best investments not only for efficient trash disposal, but also for narrowing the chance of valuable equipment and supplies being concealed in huge trash disposal units.

EQUIPMENT THEFT

Office equipment is infinitely more vulnerable to theft than medical equipment. Late-model electric typewriters and dictation machines bring a very high price, sometimes as much as 60 percent of the prevailing retail price, when sold to "fences." Microscopes are practically the only lab equipment that has a considerable attraction, but they are rarely stolen for financial profit. More often they are taken by employees or intruders who want them for personal use. There is no significant market offering a worthwhile price for second-hand medical equipment, at least not for the type of equipment that can be carried from the premises.

Under these circumstances a health care facility is well advised to expend the greatest effort in protecting its office equipment. The nuisance of such protection is considerable. Bolting down or chaining typewriters, calculators, or dictation machines makes it difficult to move them around or make repairs. Often the most concentrated effort to avoid theft will be fruitless. According to a celebrated story, an administrator's private secretary flatly refused to continue working if her new electric typewriter was bolted down or chained. The administrator was adamant; the secretary resigned. The typewriter was chained and bolted down, but it was stolen within 24 hours. Certain machines and equipment are so lucrative that thieves may use powerful steel-cutting equipment to remove them.

The lesson learned from incidents of this type is that while the bolting or lockup of office equipment is essential, it is not enough to protect the equipment. If it is practical, traffic in and out of the hospital should be controlled through effective guard coverage and package or equipment transports should be monitored. The guard force should also aggressively challenge personnel suspected of stealing. Rigid measures like these are usually called for in urban institutions. They are less essential in rural or suburban environments.

THEFT OF DISPERSED STORAGE ITEMS

Petty Pilferage

Patient care areas are notorious sites for storing a large variety of items, many of them useful to almost everybody—pencils and paper clips, aspirin, bandages, and various surgical supplies. Although petty pilferage is unavoidable, the total loss even over a long period of time represents a small percentage of the entire outlay for supplies in any health facility. There is no profit in locking up pencils and paper clips and issuing them out on request because the nuisance and the payroll cost of such issuance far outweigh any amount of losses that could conceivably occur. These items are usually not removed in quantity.

The best method of protecting the supplies should be the same as applied to linen. Storage facilities, whether they are desk drawers, wall closets, or cabinets, should be within the circumference of the nursing station if at all possible. Indeed, this principle is usually applied to new inpatient areas. If this is not possible, attempts should be made to have these basic supplies stored in closets across from the nursing station, so that the storage areas are within reasonable line of sight of the staff.

Nightly Lockups

On floors that are very thinly staffed at nighttime, it would be a good measure to provide for lockup of the storage facilities when the day shift goes off duty. That will require a supervisory effort to enforce compliance, which is going to be successful only where the nursing staff is pliable and willing. Where there is friction, a spirit of mild rebellion, or heavy turnover, those lockup rules cannot be enforced.

In hospitals that maintain ward managers or unit clerks whose exclusive duty is administrative, such lockup rules are more easily enforced. Still they require the cooperation of the nursing staff on the evening and night shifts. In summary, a major effort is not called for in this area because even without protection the losses of the numerous miscellaneous items on the floors never reach catastrophic proportions.

Accessibility

In any outpatient clinic or emergency room, standard surgical supplies have to be within easy reach, virtually in every treatment area. This in itself will contradict any attempts at making accessibility difficult. Lockup will prove unnecessary. Under the circumstances the wisest approach to these patient areas is to consider all supplies expendable and written off whether used judiciously, wasted, or pilfered.

THEFT IN PHARMACY

Like a cashier's booth, a pharmacy in these days of lucrative narcotics traffic is vulnerable to theft not only by employees but by violent intruders. Holdups and burglaries may not be very frequent, but they do occur and their success is essentially dependent upon the precautions in existence.

Pharmacy thefts have spread with the proliferation of satellite pharmacies, a definite trend in hospital construction and renovation. While the unit-dose system may have reduced the total volume of critical drugs in accessible patient care areas, concentration of the drugs has spread with the dispersion of satellites. There are more targets for holdups and burglaries. Pharmacists themselves also are exposed to greater temptation to steal since they usually attend the satellite pharmacies alone with no supervision or surveillance, and therefore no restraint. Yet it can be argued that a pharmacist working in close proximity to numerous other pharmacists in a central installation is in as easy a position to pocket high-priced drugs, critical hypnotics, and narcotics as a pharmacist who attends a satellite alone.

Safeguards

In large installations there is usually a back door leading to a deserted corridor where the drug shipments arrive. These areas are highly vulnerable to theft. To protect against collusive removal of drugs in quantity, as well as against holdups and burglaries, a wide range of measures are available. These range from panic buttons and bulletproof teller windows to videotape television cameras, conventional burglar alarms, and sophisticated intrusion detectors. These measures are costly in hospitals with no previous alarm installation or central security control room where these installations can be monitored. But a compromise, such as monitoring these alarms in the switchboard room, is better than leaving the pharmacists entirely to their own devices.

In the central pharmacy it is also essential to protect the receiving process from theft. Dual verification prior to payment of the manufacturer's and distributor's invoices is vital. At the same time steps must be taken to prevent messengers or delivery staff from removing quantities of drugs and pharmaceutical products from the pharmacy. Therefore, an alarm and television surveillance installation is sometimes an advisable step.

Purchasing Process

Even with these protective measures, the purchasing process remains vulnerable. Substantial losses may continue for a long time without being discovered if the pharmacy director or whoever is responsible for purchasing is in collusion with vendors or manipulates to supply privately owned drug stores from hospital stock. This is particularly true if the stock is diverted in the receiving process. Such activities are not infrequent.

But even with a strong purchasing department, to exercise meaningful control over the procurement of drugs is a difficult task. It is more difficult than having purchasing exercise control over dietary or maintenance procurement. The trend of automating staple drug purchases is likely to prove a step in the right direction, not only improving the efficiency and reducing payroll cost, but also narrowing the risks.

THEFT IN X-RAY

X-ray does not usually present one of the major theft problems since the only marketable product is the film. There have been incidents where x-ray technicians sold film to x-ray outfits in business for themselves, but these incidents have been sporadic. Film storage requires refrigeration, and good lockup is usually easy to combine with refrigeration. Consequently, quantities of easily accessible x-ray film are usually limited.

A more frequent problem is the fraudulent use of x-ray equipment and film by hospital technicians working in collusion with physicians. This is a practice which is peculiar to inner-city rather than suburban or rural hospitals.

The opportunities for theft vary with work schedules. Where x-ray departments work around the clock, only one or two technicians frequently staff evening, night, and weekend shifts. Theft activities are virtually impossible to prevent in these situations. However, they are not as prevalent as moonlighting by the maintenance staff. Still, hospital administrators should be alert to the potential problem.

PAYROLL THEFT

Petty payroll fraud is most prevalent among those hospital workers who are the most difficult to supervise. They are the employees who are widely dispersed throughout the institution, such as the materials handlers, orderlies, the cleaning crew, and the maintenance staff.

Time Clock Fraud

Punching the time clock for someone who is absent, who arrives late or departs early is one of the most common forms of payroll fraud. A more serious form is when an employee deliberately avoids work during regular working hours and stays overtime to get the needed work done. A combination of excessive lenience or relative incompetence of supervisors condones or encourages these practices.

The most effective means of coping with the first of these problems is a centralized time clock installation. The time clock should be strategically placed at a designated employee entrance, permanently attended by the guard force. The guards would be responsible for seeing that no one punches the clock for anybody else. While this approach is widely applied in industry, few hospitals have been able to implement it. One of the main reasons is the wide dispersion of buildings in campus-type hospitals. Another reason is that hiring a guard exclusively to watch an employee exit is rarely a profitable investment. In fact the cost for hiring a guard will probably never reduce payroll fraud sufficiently to make it a defensible expense.

Under the circumstances, it is understandable that most hospital administrations will be satisfied with the compromise of depending exclusively on supervision, limited as it may be, to curtail the type of abuses described.

Abuse by Supervisory Staff

The most damaging payroll fraud in industry, in construction, and perhaps in hospitals is usually perpetrated by the supervisory staff themselves. These people may receive pay for "ghosts" on the payroll—nonexistent or retired employees. Employees who have quit may continue to receive their pay and split it with their former supervisors. Any variety of schemes can work.

Effective Prevention

A most effective method of uncovering and thereby preventing this type of fraud is to conduct unpredictable pay distribution tests by independent auditors. Due to ever-changing shift patterns, these payouts are not always easy to perform. Usually they are resorted to only if the administration's suspicion is aroused. This is a mistake. Certain departments that are notoriously vulnerable to payroll padding fraud would best be exposed to unpredictable payouts from time to time. They are costly, they are a nuisance, and they can cause employee friction, but they are usually worth these risks.

CASH THEFT

One of the easiest areas of the hospital to steal from is the cashiering unit. If not monitored, cashiers may pocket money, or people walking by an unattended unit may be tempted to steal.

Protecting the Cashiering Unit

Measures for protecting cashiering units vary according to factors such as

- the ratio of cash versus checks collected at the unit during a given day or weekend

- guard and/or police response time, especially in rural areas
- the location of the cashiering unit within the hospital
- the location and size of the hospital (for example, security measures for a 1,000-bed hospital situated in the midst of a declining urban neighborhood will differ from those applied to a 300-bed hospital servicing middle- and high-income families in an established rural community)
- the attitudes of administration in maintaining community relations and image of friendliness in rural areas
- the number of ancillary services performed by cashiering units: cashing employees' personal or payroll checks; in some smaller hospitals, distributing payroll checks; in other hospitals, maintaining vault service for patients' valuables; and collecting and balancing of funds from cafeterias, gift shops, vending machines, and parking lots.

Location of the Unit

Various factors affect the placement of cashiering units, including types of services offered at the hospital, number of buildings composing the hospital complex, its geographic location, and patient convenience. Hospital administrators may select one main cashier, two or three primary cashiering units, or a combination of one main cashier and several satellite stations spread throughout various buildings and serving individual departments such as obstetrics or extended care facilities.

In one hospital complex, for example, a satellite cashiering unit was designed to serve the admitting office, the business office, patient services, medical records, and the discharge office for each 100-bed floor. In addition, a main cashiering unit was expected to remain for some time to serve the older part of the hospital complex.

The cashiering unit usually adjoins a business office, a financial office, or the admissions office. Minimum precautions should be to keep the door between the cashier and those other offices locked at all times. When used, the door should automatically close, with a lockset provided for keyed entry only from the outer office. A small window in the door and a low-voltage bell and buzzer can be provided to enable recognition by the cashier before allowing authorized personnel to enter the area.

More sophisticated arrangements may be necessary if the cashier's door is in an area traversed by the public, such as an admissions office or a hospital corridor. The door should then be alarmed or made inaccessible to unauthorized personnel 24 hours a day. Entry or exiting equipment can be controlled through a shunt key or magnetic card key. After it has been opened legally, the door should automatically return to the alarmed or inaccessible mode and return to a closed position.

At each of the cashiering positions, the minimum protection that should be provided is a "panic button" or holdup alarm that can be foot, knee, or hand operated. This alarm should be silent and should annunciate by both a light and a bell or buzzer at a different location in the hospital. The alarm should be relayed (preferably automatically or by telephone) to a local law enforcement agency. In all cases, even if the guard force is armed, the relay should be made to police authorities. The police are usually much better equipped to handle these situations than a guard force empowered only with the rights of "citizen's arrest." The cashier should be taught to comply with the burglar's request, not to try to be a hero, but at the same time follow the prescribed routine for activating the alarm.

One of the problems found in several hospitals is that relief cashiers are not properly trained, and are not even advised of the location and operation of the panic alarm.

In high-crime areas, an additional piece of equipment that might be considered is a videotape closed-circuit television (CCTV) camera mounted behind the cashiers and trained on the cashiering locations. The camera could be triggered simultaneously by the activation of the panic alarm. The videotape would be useful later for identification purposes.

The Dangers of the "Friendly" Atmosphere

The "friendly" atmosphere prevalent in rural areas and middle- and high-income locales often

dictates the physical arrangement at cashiering offices. However, this may be dangerous. It is easy for would-be burglars, with or without weapons, to jump over low cashier counters, get behind the cashiers preventing them from using the panic alarm, and force them to open the till; the burglars then jump back over the counter before the cashiers can take any action.

In other hospitals, modern cashiering offices may contain CRTs, printers, and other small items such as digital calculators, electric typewriters, and adding machines. Some cashiering locations are in open areas or corridors, leaving electronic equipment open to sabotage or vandalism, and other items free to be stolen.

The "friendly-atmosphere" hospital faces a dilemma of trying to retain its attitude in dealing with the community. Depending on the small amount of cash accumulated and low number of ancillary services rendered by the cashiers, a compromised security solution must be reached. For daytime protection, a panic button would have to suffice. For nighttime protection, a roll-up grill could be designed to enclose the cashiering location, or the cashiering function could be made a separate room removed from a main corridor with a doored entrance. Lockup protection should at least include a padlock for the roll-up grill and a lock for the door of the room. In this case all monies must be collected in a vault, away from the cashiering office. In one case, where neither a rollup grill nor a separate room could possibly be designed or constructed, enclosures had to be designed for nighttime protection of the CRT and printer.

Naturally, small equipment such as digital calculators should be placed in locked drawers or cabinets, while items like electronic typewriters in open areas should be bolted to desks.

Security in Urban Hospitals

In urban hospitals, main cashiering locations should be protected by bullet-proof glass with small pass-through windows. Some hospital administrators argue against this concept by pointing out that even banks in large cities are not constructed in this manner. But many banks have armed guards on duty, and expensive videotape CCTV cameras. Urban hospitals should consider protective devices such as the following:

- controlled entrance to the cashiering office, which is protected by alarm 24 hours a day and which has limited access
- a bullet-proof glass enclosure with small pass-through windows
- a panic button at each cashiering location tied into the hospital alarm system, if any, and simultaneous relay to local police authorities
- an optional videotape camera triggered by an alarm condition when the cashier uses the panic (or holdup) button
- a commercial night depository safe that has an outside opening constructed through either a reinforced wall or a cut-out slot in the bullet-proof glass, if collections are made from other hospital departments after hours or on weekends when the cashiering office may not be staffed

Systems Security

Main Cashier

Without detailing cashiering systems, monies collected for deposits, discharge payments, and so forth, one important rule should be imposed on cashiering functions. Through modern advanced systems technology, cashiers may be equipped with electronic means such as a CRT to view the customer account status. The cashier's function would be to collect the monies owed to the hospital at the time of discharge. Whether the receipt is electronically printed or manually written by the cashier, it should be fully able to be audited and numerically controlled. This applies to all payments by cash, checks, or charge card, whether they are processed through a cash register or collected in a cash box.

Most hospitals are on a 9- to 15-day cycle for final billing (except for terminal billing, which might be immediate). Whether the system is manual or data processed or a modern CRT approach is used, the cashier should not possess the means manually to remove a patient account from the file by keypunching or by access coding. The cashier should act only as the collection agent and should not be able to feed information into the patients' account system. This input to

the system should be accomplished by another person in the control division of the hospital.

Most other hospital functions that use cash registers fall into one general category, including cafeterias (employee and/or public), the outpatient department, pharmacies, gift shops, coffee shops, and garage facilities.

Cafeteria

Of course, the most complicated type of cashiering is in the general employee cafeteria, which serves visitors, volunteers, and medical staff. Visitors might pay a slight additional surcharge, volunteers may receive discount or no-charge meals, and medical staff may receive free late-night dinners. Discounts may occur with meal coupons, paper punch cards, passes, or sign-out sheets. Whatever the system, the recipient of the discounted or free meal rarely watches what the cashier rings into the register. The cashier could benefit easily by ringing lower rates and having the recipient sign for a larger total or punching a higher total on the meal ticket. On a sign-out sheet, the cashier could insert a false name and employee identification number.

The best defense against this type of theft (besides eliminating all uncontrolled free or discounted meals) is to constantly test cashiers to be sure they are ringing and collecting the right amount for each item. This testing can be performed by an outside specialized service that employs professional "shoppers" familiar with cashiering practices, or by hospital security personnel trained in "shopping" techniques. This will ensure against direct theft from the cashiering unit, but it will not prevent cashiers from charging friends less than they should for meals.

In one hospital studied, two registers were used for each of two cafeteria lines. One register was used as a "pre-ring," the other register was used for collecting money and making change. They were supposed to balance but never did. The imbalance was due to the number of "walkouts" between the first and second registers. There was a large condiments table between the registers, allowing access (and an unplanned egress route) to items like salt, pepper, and ketchup. The access route was supposed to be used for people who had forgotten to take these items on their trays while they were in line waiting to go to the second register position. Some employees or visitors found it very easy to slip past the second register while the cashier was concentrating on making change.

The condiments table was subsequently installed behind the cashier, and the cashiering position moved up. In other hospitals, sections of railings have been added, keeping people in a line toward the cashier, along with a one-way turnstile at the entranceway to block exiting there.

Register Thefts

The walkouts are usually minimal, compared with the different techniques used by cashiers for helping themselves to funds of $10 to $20 a day. Though some hospitals have modern registers and divide food or other types of sales by classification (in cafeterias—juice, meat, vegetables, and dessert; or in gift shops—candy, cards, and toys), most hospital registers have two classes, namely item plus sales tax if any. More sophisticated registers have separate drawers or separate keys for individual cashiers who are then responsible for their own tills.

Whether in a food service operation or other hospital cashiering area, or whether a simple or sophisticated type of register is used, the biggest mistake made by hospitals is to allow the cashier to have both keys needed to operate the register. The first key unlocks the mechanism for register operation and gives total readings for money and number of transactions. (This is usually termed an "A" total, or if two or more different drawers or separate cashier operating keys, there can be "B," "C," and "D" totals.) The second key produces totals, either by cashier or classification, and resets all totals back to zero. This is commonly termed the "Z" total or "Zed" total.

When a simple type of register is used, as in most hospitals, if the cashier has control of both keys, the hospital is probably losing money. For example: a cashier starts at breakfast, rings up about $20 worth of sales, "Zeds" out the register, removes that part of the detail tape, takes out the $20 and starts to ring all over. In a large hospital, this would go unnoticed. Since caf-

eterias are part of food service, the cost of the cafeteria is partially hidden in the cost of patient meals per day.

In smaller cashiering areas, such as a gift shop, shortages might be revealed by losses discovered by physical inventories. However, if the gift shop is combined with a coffee shop that does not maintain its own inventory and is serviced by the dietary department, there is still room for the cashier to pocket some of the proceeds.

In both of these examples and other similar situations, the financial division rather than departmental personnel should obtain "Zed" totals and reset registers. The financial division should retain the second keys to the register(s) and should be the only ones able to zero out the registers and obtain the final readings. In single drawer registers used by more than one cashier during a day, separate cash tills (banks) can be provided for each cashier. If registers are to be reset only once a day, balancing by cashier can still be achieved. Here are two examples:

1. Cashier I started breakfast with zero totals and a $30 cash bank. By the end of breakfast, she had rung up $147.15 worth of sales and performed 172 transactions using her first key. The "A" total then gave this information on the detail tape that could be read through the window of the register.
2. Cashier II started lunch with a $40 cash bank. He rang in his sales, ending up with $1,248.42 and 862 transactions on the "A" key.

The balancing could be accomplished as shown in Table 23-1.

The simple example in Table 23-1 includes typical imbalancing factors of an overage of one dollar and a shortage of ten cents. Cashiers who balance exactly to the penny every day are not only a rarity but should be watched since they may be "skimming," with a cover-up of an exact balance. A cashier repeatedly producing shortages should also be the subject of "shopping" routines by security personnel. Naturally, where coupons or stamps are used, the balance sheet would be more complicated and would have to be designed to accommodate the different items used in lieu of cash.

Table 23-1 Balancing by Cashier for Registers that Are Reset Only Once a Day

	Cashier I	Cashier II
a. Cash on Hand	$177.05	$1,289.47
b. Cash Bank	$ 30.00	$ 40.00
c. Difference (a − b)	$147.05	$1,249.47
d. Ending Register Reading	$147.15	$1,395.57
e. Starting Register Reading	$ 0.00	$ 147.15
f. Sales (d − e)	$147.15	$1,248.42
g. Over +/ Short ( )	$ (.10)	$ +1.05
h. Final Transaction Reading	172	862
i. Starting Transaction Reading	0	172
j. Total Transactions (h − i)	172	690

Garage Cashiering

Garage cash registers do not use the type of system described above. In fact, the registers in most cases do not reset to zero. Usually the registers are programmed (or reprogrammed as necessary) to charge a set rate based on the time used for parking. As an example:

- ½ hour, $.75
- 1 hour, $1.50
- 2 hours, $2.25
- 3 hours or more, $3.00

Usually the garage cashier hits a classification key, which automatically adds single charges to cash totals already in the register and advances the transaction reading. Incoming parking tickets are stamped with a transaction number either by the cashier or by a device that automatically dispenses parking tickets. Most automatic parking ticket-dispensing devices are activated by a vehicle pressuring a metal plate in a garage entrance lane. The driver of the vehicle must pull the ticket from the dispenser to raise a toll gate, thus allowing the vehicle to enter the parking lot.

At the end of the day, total charges should balance with the cash in the garage register. The total number of transactions accumulated in the register should be checked against the number of parking tickets turned in and also balanced against the number of tickets originally issued by the cashier or the automatic ticket dispenser.

One of the major problems in garage cashiering is the issuance of ''complimentary'' parking tickets. Administration should develop a system where the issuance of complimentary parking tickets is carefully monitored. Right of issuance of complimentary parking tickets should be limited to a few select administrative-level personnel.

People visiting the hospital are sometimes cheated by garage cashiers. After visiting someone in the hospital, drivers may be upset and in a highly emotional state. Realizing that these drivers are less likely to count their change, some garage cashiers shortchange them; the cashier may give the driver change for $10 when he or she actually received a $20 bill.

Like main and satellite cashiering units, garages should be shopped frequently to find out if cashiers are taking funds from visitors in this manner.

THEFT IN ANCILLARY CHARGES

Though some hospitals have an all-inclusive rate for patient care, Medicare, Medicaid, or other third-party plans usually require a separate listing of ancillary charges. Also, certain services such as x-ray, cardiac, and respiratory may be excluded from the all-inclusive rate. In some hospitals these types of departments are established as private corporations and process their own charges. Depending on the data-processing facilities at the hospital and arrangements made with these departments, charges to patients can be processed through the hospital's computer, an outside service organization, or manually by the department itself. Therefore, whether the hospital charges for each item separately or operates on a full-inclusive or partial-inclusive rate, ancillary charges usually have to be billed to the proper patient or processed through the internal accounting system.

Patient Accounts

Most hospitals today have some type of computer system for patient accounts. The older systems use a charge card type of patient identification, which includes the patient's name and number (sequential city or state number, as required); the name of the physician; and other pertinent information. Ancillary charges are processed by imprinting the patient identification onto an ancillary charge form. The forms are then keypunched and entered into the computer. The more sophisticated systems employ CRTs at the nursing stations for entering patient information. In other cases, charges for special items are "precharged" and retained in computer memory until the second entry at the nursing station removes the precharge and transfers the amount with coding to the patient's account. In most cases, services are charged to patients when administered.

CRTs

Administration should not assume that it will capture all ancillary charges by the use of CRTs. The medical staff may accidentally forget to charge a patient, or a nurse purposely fail to enter a charge for a patient who is a friend or relative.

Administrators tend to assume incorrectly that in the newer systems using CRTs the patient identification number (with a check digit) ensures that the proper patient is charged and that if departmental charge codes and dollar amounts are programmed correctly the right charge is billed. The CRT cannot ensure that certain charges, such as those for monitors and defibrillators, go to the appropriate patient. Equipment, such as monitors and defibrillators, is moved from patient to patient, and often the wrong patient is charged for these services. The

cardiology or biomedical engineering departments must be responsible for issuance and control of equipment.

Unbillable Charges

Some years ago, a study was conducted in a large hospital (more than 1,000 beds) that used a charge plate, imprinter, and keypunch system. For a 10-day period, it was found that 3,427 charges were not billable for one or more of the following reasons:

- 127 plates contained incorrect serial numbers
- in 2,032 cases, charge plates were not used or the plate impressions were poor
- 44 charges were not priced
- 1,345 charges were not coded

Projecting the data from the above sampling, it was estimated that about $2.5 million per year was not being charged, of which 20 percent or $500,000 would have been billable to patients or third-party insurers.

Other Problems

This same hospital suffered from other problems concerning bad debts accumulated through emergency room charges, mix-ups in clinic patients or private patients registering through the emergency room, late submissions to Medicare for visiting nurse service, and unbilled outpatient charges (i.e., dental, oral surgery and ophthalmology). Each of these problems relating to unbilled charges had to be handled separately, and rules had to be set up to ensure the timely processing of correct forms and patient identifications for billing purposes.

It is a mistake to assume that computers will perform all the audit functions. Some computers can do this if their programs include audit trails and control functions. However, it is important to realize that computer programs can only translate information supplied into the system by people.

THEFT IN BILLING AND COLLECTION

The billing and collection process in hospitals and other health care institutions has become so complex that it is a favorite topic of discussion among journalists, the media, and hospital consultants. All the advance admitting preparations, the automated charge methods, and the computerization have done little to reduce the monstrous proportion of errors and the staggering load of patient complaints and claims adjustments.

Collection

The potential for fraud in the collection process may be small in comparison with other areas in the hospital, but when such fraud is successfully perpetrated over a period of time, it can substantially drain the hospital's assets.

There have been cases of massive collusion between collection personnel within the hospital and collection agencies. Perfectly collectable accounts are sometimes declared uncollectable. They are then handed over to an agency and collected in full. A portion may be deposited with the hospital with the remainder being divided between the in-house collection personnel and the collection agency.

Billing

With ever-increasing coverage by third-party carriers, the opportunities for theft in the billing and collection process may gradually diminish. However, the opportunity for theft will always be great when the entire billing process is suffering from a staggering load of unresolved receivable balances. The less up-to-date the legitimate billing and collection processes are, the easier the defalcations will be.

Preventing theft in this area is difficult. Billing systems vary, as do the loopholes and the opportunities for fraud. Suffice it to say that eager attention to legitimate billing and collection processes is not enough. Alertness to potential fraud is essential. The total system of checks and balances, internal audit methods, and investigative techniques has to be geared to the problem.

PERSONAL PROPERTY THEFT

All hospitals are easy targets for purse snatchers and wallet thieves. Personnel are usually more frequent victims of this type of theft than are patients. Employees are often careless about leaving pocketbooks in easily accessible places. Patients sometimes fall asleep with their pocketbooks at the foot of the bed. Other employees, particularly the professional staff, often hang up their jackets with their wallets inside, making them easily available to the potential thief.

Employees' Goods

Lockup Facilities

Some administrators believe that if staff and patients do not have enough sense to protect their personal property, personal property theft should not be the hospital's concern. This position is not entirely justified. Personal property theft can be avoided only with the provision of lockup facilities. For example, unless the nursing staff has reasonably adequate storage space in lockers, cabinets, or desk drawers that are lockable or located in constantly attended areas, no degree of care and alertness will prevent theft.

Alertness

In addition to ample lockup facilities for staff and for patients, the hospital should encourage a general alertness to the risks of theft. In inpatient areas where there is a ward manager, this is relatively easy to achieve. The ward manager can tour the inpatient area every day, picking out exposed purses and jackets containing wallets, finding their owners and pointing out to them the available lockup facilities. In this way a general awareness of potential theft situations can be gradually built up. Since this type of inspection requires entering the patients' rooms, the guard force cannot be responsible for this task. Also, since it requires frequent disciplinary warnings, particularly addressed to student nurses and nurses' aides, the nursing department's administrative staff should be responsible for this method. If no ward managers or unit clerks can assume this function, there is no choice but to have the charge nurse delegate the function to someone else on the staff.

Inspections

Frequently repeated inspections should also be maintained in offices and supporting departments, such as laboratories, treatment areas, outpatient clinics, and emergency rooms. Inspection is not a very time-consuming task, and it can be very effective in reducing massive theft of personal property.

Patients' Goods

Safes for patients' valuables substantially reduce the risk of theft of patients' belongings in most institutions. However, patients may at first refuse to turn in their valuables, surrendering them only before going to surgery. When this happens, jewelry and dentures may be temporarily locked up in nurses' desks or even in the narcotics cabinet, and are exposed to theft. A better method, although a considerable burden to the staff, would be to dispatch these personal belongings to the valuables safe as the patient goes into surgery. Although this problem plagues most hospitals, it rarely assumes monumental proportions. However, it is better to formalize a safeguarding procedure rather than entrusting personal property to the nursing staff.

PARKING LOT THEFT

Parked cars seem to be an ever-increasing target of vandalism and theft. Incidences of car vandalism and theft increase at night and occur more frequently in covered parking garages that have many levels. Slashed tires, stolen spare tires, and stolen CB radios are the most frequent incidents, but the highest-priority problems involving covered garages and parking lots not adjacent to the hospital include purse snatching, mugging, and rape.

Effective curtailment of these combined risks is possible, although quite costly. The best approach is a combination of steady patrolling,

preferably motorized, and massive CCTV surveillance. Each institution should decide whether to apply the major portion of the available budget to one method or to divide it equally between both. The decision will depend on existing traffic patterns, the overall organization of the security department, the size of the guard force, the variety of its other duties, and, most importantly, the existence of a central security control center that is properly staffed and capable of effective monitoring and dispatching. The pattern will not be the same in any two institutions. The variations in risks among urban, suburban, and rural institutions will also play a major part in these decisions.

PERIMETER TRAFFIC AND EMPLOYEE THEFT

The ease with which theft of larger pieces of equipment and sizable quantities of supplies can be curtailed varies. One factor determining this is the level of existent protection of the perimeter of individual buildings or the total complex. Modern hospitals consisting of one major single structure are easier to protect than huge campus-type facilities consisting of innumerable buildings, some completely separate, others connected by tunnels and bridges. Some campus-type installations covering several city blocks lend themselves to effective fencing; others do not.

Methods of Prevention

Controlling Traffic

It should be difficult for people entering or leaving the institution, especially employees, to carry stolen equipment or supplies out of the building. Controlling pedestrian traffic is not impossible but is usually very costly. It is also time-consuming and may affect the attitude of hospital personnel. Costly measures may include a centrally monitored burglary-type alarm system, a carefully planned and rigidly enforced lockup schedule, and strategic guard coverage of all unlocked exits.

Channeling of different types of traffic through different entrances and exits is also an excellent method. Ideally, no staff members should enter or leave by the same exit reserved for patients and visitors. Entering or exiting vendors, salespeople, delivery people, contractors, and service personnel should not be allowed to mingle with patients and visitors; rather they should be routed through a permanently guarded entrance where they can be identified, scrutinized, and properly directed. No pedestrian traffic of any kind should be permitted to cross receiving docks, trash docks, morgue exits, or truck gates.

These thorny problems often defy solutions even if ample budgetary funds are available and the administration is determined to attack the problems aggressively. All hospitals must sometimes compromise in traffic regulations.

Alarm Systems

In general, an elaborate perimeter alarm system, where every fire exit door is wired into a central monitor, is justified only in urban institutions. Urban hospitals usually have to allocate a massive budget for guards who are needed primarily for an escorting service, and for controlling incoming and outgoing pedestrian traffic.

Visitor Passes

Although a visitor traffic policy is one of the cornerstones of pedestrian traffic control, visitor passes have been abolished in many institutions, even in some inner-city hospitals. Attempts at rigid visitor pass enforcement continue, even in some rural hospitals. Drastic structural variations, which have become the fashion in recent years, have made visitor control close to impossible in some institutions. This is especially true when outpatient services (treatment areas and private physicians' offices) intermingle with inpatient areas. Thus coping with intruders has become the task of a patrolling guard force, aided by ward managers and the nursing staff.

Compromise

The recent trend is to combine numerous health care services with hospital facilities. By increasing the complexity and size of these facilities, this trend undermines most practical chances

for their realistic protection. Although theft cannot be totally cured in these situations, administrators can seek enlightened compromise to minimize theft opportunities.

RESPONSIBILITY FOR PROCEDURAL SECURITY

It is usually a mistake to place the primary responsibility for preventing loss of hospital assets on the security director, captain of the guards, or a similar individual. A capable security chief or captain of the guards can make essential contributions in the area of perimeter protection; internal lockup effectiveness; traffic control in all its dimensions; and investigative activities, including contact with law enforcement agencies. However, the most competent security chiefs, whether they enter the hospital field with a police background or other law enforcement experience, cannot with any degree of effectiveness assume the responsibility for the numerous loss prevention problems involving systems and procedures. These limitations must be realized, without detracting from their strong and essential contribution.

The responsibility for procedural security must be assumed by a person well versed in the problems of materials handling, paper work documentation, and accounting procedures. In a medium-sized or small hospital, the controller would be the logical choice. However, controllers are "desk-bound" accountants, with little knowledge of materials handling, truck traffic, receiving operations, and distribution methods.

The Assistant Administrator

The ultimate choice therefore should be an assistant administrator whose talent, exposure, and interest permit the merging of procedural accountability problems with physical security problems in arriving at overall solutions protecting the assets of the hospital.

Rarely does one person possess the talents and the experience that would allow accepting total responsibility for all phases of loss prevention, procedural as well as physical. Hospitals with at least 750 beds usually have an industrial engineering staff or a systems and procedures department. Often these are the people best suited for assuming a comprehensive responsibility for loss prevention programs. But they will require strong efforts at coordination.

Committees

The establishment of a committee can be an excellent approach to coordinating industrial engineering staff or systems and procedures staff. The committee, for example, could consist of the controller, an industrial engineer and the security director. This can be successful if the committee representation is strong and reacts to changing situations with great speed. However, the committee approach can also be a stumbling block if it has a tendency to generate procrastination rather than action.

Internal Audits

One of the essential tools in enforcing even the simplest loss prevention rules is an aggressive internal audit program. The controller, whether participating in writing the procedures and setting the policies or not, must take responsibility for using the internal audit effort as an enforcement tool. This is essential in all areas of procedural security, such as receiving accountability, cash accountability, the distribution of supplies, and enforcement of billing and collection rules. An aggressive internal audit staff can even expand into the areas of physical security by organizing tests and spot-check inspections, checking on the performance of the guard force, verifying the effectiveness of perimeter protection measures and night lockup, and verifying the protection of vulnerable office equipment.

Controller's Role

No matter how broad the responsibilities of the security chief, and regardless of who in the administration has the ultimate loss prevention responsibility, the controller has to take an active part in the vast majority of the loss prevention measures. This active part must include influencing the procedures and the policies as they are

generated, and using the audit staff as the most effective potential enforcement tool.

In smaller hospitals, where the budget does not permit a sizable audit staff, the same principle should prevail. But in practice, controllers in small hospitals, with the help of external auditors under contract, will have to function as internal auditors would in larger institutions.

The Role of the Board of Trustees

The ultimate responsibility for the operation of a health care institution is being increasingly placed on the shoulders of trustees or members of the board of directors. No longer is it up to the individual trustee to decide whether to participate actively in the affairs of the hospital. Trustees are expected to assume not only some of the responsibility for the financial soundness of the institution but also for the overall quality of medical care and for the level of compliance with the vast variety of federal, state, and local regulations.

This trend is bound to extend to the problems of loss prevention and the protection of the hospital's assets and thus to the total package of physical and procedural accountability measures. An administrator who takes charge of security, loss prevention, and overall accountability for the hospital's assets may appoint one of the trustees to share this responsibility. If this happens, the trustee may be required to present the board with monthly reports on progress achieved, major failures that recently came to light, policy decisions to be submitted for approval, and ongoing procedural work directed at loss prevention. In this fashion, the board of trustees will become a sounding board, or better still, an active participant and perhaps an aggressive monitor of the administration's activities in the overall field of loss prevention and protection of the hospital's assets.

CONCLUSION: A TOTAL APPROACH TO LOSS PREVENTION

A comprehensive security program must encompass the two basic facets of security: physical and procedural.

Physical security involves protecting the facility against intrusion from without and diversion from within. It involves the integration of a large variety of protective measures such as control of the facility's perimeter, alarm installations, lockup techniques, electronic surveillance, and traffic control. It must include a clear definition of the guard force, including its safety duties.

Procedural security must be an integral part of standard operating procedures. It should include specific accountability controls directed at all procurement functions, the flow of hospital supplies, receiving, storage, and distribution. It also has to address storage and the risks in finance management, such as cash defalcations, patient accounts, and payroll fraud.

The key to success for all security measures is their enforceability. Any rules requiring an enormous effort to enforce will eventually collapse under their own weight.

THE INVENTORY OF EXPOSURE

One of the best approaches to developing a comprehensive, practical loss prevention program is the "inventory of exposure" method. It starts out with distinguishing the two principal types of dishonest action: petty pilferage perpetrated by employees, visitors, or intruders and large-scale theft or fraud committed through collusion among deliverers, receivers, material handlers, maintenance personnel, janitorial staff, as well as among department heads, purchasing agents and vendors, engineers and contractors, and business office staff and collection agencies. The inventory of exposure must begin with a realistic assessment of the relative risks and potential losses in the various categories of theft or fraud.

Then comes the attack on the individual targets of vulnerability, such as

- the procurement process
- the receiving operation
- storage areas
- distribution of supplies
- laboratory equipment

- offices, treatment rooms, and maintenance shops

Specific attention must also be paid to opportunities for loss in certain areas of financial activity. These possibilities include

- vendor collusion
- contractor collusion
- credit agency collusion
- payroll fraud
- expense account abuse

SCOPE OF SECURITY PROGRAM

In terms of scope, the inventory of exposure should avoid drastic, long-range recommendations. Every effort should be made to shape the corrective measures in such a way that they can be worked in with the existing procedures. Major upheavals, controversial policies, and backbreaking training efforts should be avoided. Appropriate corrective measures might include

- procedural revisions in materials handling, documentation, and paper flow
- personnel policy revisions affecting pedestrian traffic, locker usage, key distribution, and selective access rules
- revision of loading dock activities and trucking patterns
- regulations in filing and distribution of information

Traffic

In developing a comprehensive security program, the health care facility must include

- charting of anticipated patterns of traffic by both vehicles and pedestrians
- control of truck traffic directly connected with the security program, including the receiving and loading docks
- close attention to traffic involving contractors and their employees

- monitoring of traffic according to strictly defined rules
- curtailment of employee pilferage by channeling, if possible, all employees entering or leaving the building through an opening that serves employees exclusively
- placement of time clocks and locker rooms in strategic locations, making it more difficult or inconvenient for employees to avoid a designated and guarded exit
- separation, if possible, of employee parking lots from the hospital by a fence.

Internal Security

The system of internal security chosen by a hospital should be based on selective inaccessability, i.e., the vulnerability of specific equipment and materials.

Key Custody

An integral part of the security program is a clearly defined set of regulations governing the issuance of individual keys, submaster, master, and grand master keys. The system must include a method of authorization for key issuance and an easily enforceable procedure for retrieving keys.

Alarm Systems

In designing an alarm system, planners must weigh the wide variety of choices, basing decisions on relative levels of risk, external and internal.

Guard Coverage

The best-trained and best-organized guard force will at most provide only a fraction of required security in any hospital. The guard force should be considered only one part of the total security program. Guard duties and guard coverage must be designed so that they do not constitute the exclusive security measure in any one area.

Any fixed guard post, whether covering an employee exit or a truck gate, should be so designed as to cover additional duties simultaneously. Such duties may involve the monitoring of a string of CCTV screens, the operation of a public address communication system, or the operation of a remote control gate connected to the guard station. Giving a guard such added responsibilities not only makes the payroll investment economical, it also tends to help the guard stay alert.

BASIC GUIDELINES

In summary, when instituting a total loss-prevention program, the basic guidelines must call for

- low-cost, easily enforceable measures permitting rapid implementation and requiring minimum training
- highly practical solutions, combining procedural accountability with physical security measures
- close teamwork, encouragement of critical dissent, persuasion instead of pressure
- substantial staff acceptance of the program
- clearly written proposals so that the report can serve as a ready implementation tool

The following hospital security questionnaire (Appendix 23-A) may assist administrators in evaluating their hospital's vulnerability as a first step in planning an effective loss-prevention program.

Appendix 23-A

Hospital Questionnaire:
Security and Loss Prevention

Targets	This questionnaire is submitted for two purposes:
	1. To focus on most critical topics
	2. To gather information for establishing current nationwide patterns

Hospital Name		Address	

Hospital Data	Urban _____	Suburban _____	Rural _____
	No. of beds _____	Compact structure _____	Multiple bldgs. _____
	Teaching hospital _____	Dispersed satellite clinics _____	

Administration	
	Does the board take active part in loss prevention?
	Yes _____ No _____
	Does an auditor, responsible for loss prevention, report
	to the board? _____
	to the president? _____
	to the administrator? _____
	Does each associate or assistant administrator share responsibility for security and loss prevention?
	Yes _____ No _____

Purchasing	Which departments are almost autonomous in purchasing their supplies? Dietary _____ Maintenance _____ Pharmacy _____ OR _____ X-ray _____ Central Supply _____ Labs _____ Laundry _____ Housekeeping _____ Are purchase orders computerized? Yes _____ No _____
Receiving	Which departments listed above do their own receiving, directly from vendors?

Payment of Invoices

What supports a vendor's invoice?

	Keyed-in Receiving Report	Packing Slip	Written Receiving Record	PO Copy
Received at Central Dock				
Received by Department				

Construction	Are competitive bids from contractors mandatory?
	For all construction _____ For projects over $_____
	What documentation is required for contractors' invoices?
	      for labor _____
	      for materials _____
	      for equipment rental _____
	Whose approval will authorize payment?
	Chief engineer _____ Chief of maintenance _____
	Administrator (associate or assistant) _____
	Does an auditor participate in decisions on
	Bidding specs _____ Making awards _____ Incremental payments _____

Drugs	Is unit-dose system in place? Partially _____ Fully _____ Not at all _____ If system is in place, are medications not given to patients returned to pharmacy? _____ Are pharmacy and nursing staff tested for addiction? Yes _____ No _____
Food	Are food deliveries subject to double-receiving verification? Perishables _____ Dry food _____ Are high-priced food products accessible to total dietary staff? _____ Only to chefs and dietitians? _____

Inventory	Are volume deliveries of paper goods, plastic goods, medical-surgical supplies, linen, x-ray film subject to double-receiving verification? Describe _____

Stores

Easy access versus reliable lockup

Storage areas	Accessible to roving guards, janitors, aides, maintenance people, construction crews	Reliable lockup
General stores		
Central supply		
Dietary		
Pharmacy		
Linen		
Maintenance		
Laboratories		
X-ray		
Accounting		

Distribution

Supply categories	Manual by carts, hampers flat trucks, baskets	Mechanical		
		Dumbwaiters	Conveyors	Automated Lifts
General supplies				
Surgical supplies				
Meals				
Drugs				
Prescriptions				
Linen				

Is par stock in place for linen? _____
Medical-surgical supplies? _____
General supplies? _____

Inpatient floors	Risky exposure versus reasonable protection

Open storage			
Supply categories	Dispersed	Part of nursing station	Reliable lockup
Surgical supplies			
General supplies			
Linen			
Nonprescription drugs			
Purses, wallets— nursing staff			

Holdup risks	Are cash and drugs protected by holdup devices?

	Panic alarms	TV surveillance
Main cashier		
Satellite cashiers		
Main pharmacy		
Satellite pharmacies		
Cafeteria cashiers		
Vending machines		
Gift shop		
Garage cashiers		

Parking	What protection is available against theft, vandalism, or personal attack in parking lots and garages?

	Guard patrols	Audio surveillance	TV surveillance	Panic alarms
Open lots				
Covered garages				

Equipment	Are electric typewriters, desk top computers, word processors bolted down?	Yes _____	No _____
	Are tape recorders, projectors locked up?	Yes _____	No _____
	Will guards intercept employees or intruders departing with such equipment?	Yes _____	No _____
Computers	Are medical records computerized? _____ Are access codes and passwords reviewed and revised periodically? _____ Is entrance to computer rooms electronically controlled? _____		
Security devices	Does the hospital rely heavily on CCTV? _____ Intrusion alarms? _____ Door contact alarms? _____ Guard coverage-fixed posts? _____ Patrols? _____		
Action history	Describe the most potent recent measures taken attacking specific loss prevention or security measures:		
Comments	Personal comments, suggestions, possible avenues to pursue:		

Name _____ Title _____

Mailing address _____

_____

Chapter 24

Mergers and Acquisitions: Process and Valuation Fundamentals

Edward A. Grant
Partner and Health Care Industry Group Leader
Arthur Andersen & Co.

The purpose of this chapter is to provide readers an overview of the merger and acquisition (M&A) process in the health care industry and the fundamental concepts involved in valuation. The chapter is organized in the following manner: First, there is a brief discussion of the recent M&A environment in the health care industry. Following that, there is a discussion of the M&A due diligence process. After the M&A due diligence process, there is a discussion of the fundamentals of valuation followed by a summary of related other significant points to consider in a merger or acquisition.

CURRENT MERGER AND ACQUISITION ENVIRONMENT

The health care industry continues to undergo a great deal of change in its business and economic environment. Provider payment mechanisms are changing significantly, characterized by general reductions in governmental payment structures and significant increases in the proportion of services that are rendered under fixed or contracted payments. In addition, because of significantly decreased provider utilization and fixed or decreased payments, the hospital market has become extraordinarily competitive in a very short period. As the competition heightens and providers turn to price cutting as a means for

protecting or gaining market share, overall provider margins and related cash flows from operations will erode significantly. The combination of decreased margins and excess capacity in the industry has greatly increased the activity and the search for affiliations and alliances to protect providers' positions in this suddenly hostile marketplace. As the health care industry will continue to undergo distress and proceed through this consolidation process, the level of activity of M&As will also continue to grow.

MERGER AND ACQUISITION PROCESS

In pursuing an acquisition or merger, it is important for a health care provider first to clearly understand the business purpose of the transaction. The strategic fit and strategic value of the M&A candidate are the key matters to be determined. Certain questions must be addressed in this regard. For example, what is the objective of the M&A? Typical objectives include the following:

- maintain or improve competitive position
- protect market share
- expand service lines (i.e., specialty hospital)
- provide alternative delivery mechanisms

- enhance profitability
- achieve economies of scale
- expand outpatient services
- expand geographic service

Clearly defining the objective of the M&A, however, only partially achieves the determination of the business purpose. The related question that must be addressed is that of conformity or fit with the organization's strategy or mission. Relevance to organizational mission may take on several dimensions. For example, the literal objectives or statements of the mission must be supportive. However, other unstated or subtle aspects—including religious or faith-based affiliations, ethical considerations, and community service and needs—may be significant in given situations, and therefore need to be considered and understood relative to the mission before proceeding with the M&A. As part of this determination of business purpose, it is highly recommended that, for any M&A initiative, the business purpose be reduced to writing and that key board and management individuals be agreed upon and supportive of the stated purpose before proceeding. The breadth of circulation and the concurrence necessary are dependent upon the nature and magnitude of the M&A being evaluated and the board and management style of the acquirer.

Due Diligence

A major undertaking of an M&A process is that of the due diligence or purchase investigation (PI). The purpose of a PI is to conduct an evaluation and generate recommendations that address the viability and propriety of the acquisition. A PI should develop and focus on the relevant issues to be addressed in M&A negotiations and postacquisition integration. In addition, it should provide a broad understanding of the M&A candidate and its operations. Finally, the PI should provide a uniform, disciplined approach to evaluate the M&A while minimizing the risk of overlooking significant issues or problems.

The PI should be carried out by the acquisition team. An acquisition team should be a relatively

structured, small yet qualified, flexible, task force. This team should have the charge of conducting a rapid, efficient, accurate, and complete analysis, following the methodology necessary to meet the requirements of the company's acquisition planning process. This acquisition team should include the representation of executive management, legal counsel, finance, and, depending upon the nature and magnitude of the M&A candidate, other appropriate representation such as medical staff, governance, engineering, risk management, and tax consultants. This task force may consist entirely of "in-house" members if the required skills are present in the organization. However, where this is not the case or where the qualified individuals do not have the time available, the necessary expertise should be acquired for the project. M&As represent significant risk transactions, and anything that can be done to reduce this risk is highly desirable. Another recommendation regarding the task force is that the executive who will have direct management responsibility for the acquisition, if completed, should chair the task force and be responsible for its final report. This is a key concept in assigning management responsibility and related accountability for the new entity operations to that individual responsible for the conduct of the M&A process. In addition, depending upon the nature and magnitude of the acquisition, a board and top management steering committee may be appropriate.

As in most other conventional management areas, the information to be gathered by the task force should be identified in an M&A PI plan. The plan, as developed and agreed upon by the task force members and approved by the board (if appropriate), should include responsible individuals, due dates, and regularly scheduled meetings leading to the conclusion of the effort. Included in Exhibit 24-1 is a list of information to be considered for gathering under the due diligence process. This checklist, while not exhaustive, suggests many of the areas that may be important to a given health care M&A.

In discussing the particulars of the due diligence effort, two observations are necessary. First of all, a confidentiality agreement should be signed by the parties before undertaking the due diligence. This is necessary in order to protect

Exhibit 24-1 Merger and Acquisition Due Diligence/Purchase Investigation Checklist

A. Organizational data
   1. Key management people and their backgrounds/intentions
   2. Bylaws, articles of incorporation
   3. Licenses, inspection reports
   4. Joint Commission reports, IRS rulings

B. Financial data
   1. Audited financial statements (three years)
   2. Monthly financials (current year)
   3. Lease agreements
   4. Debt agreements
   5. Official statements for debt offerings
   6. Management letter from auditors
   7. Tax returns (three years)
   8. Revenue agents' reports
   9. Accounts receivable analysis
   10. Tax effects

C. Operational data
   1. Budgets
   2. Recent feasibility studies
   3. Hospital-based physician contracts
   4. Strategic plan
   5. Long-range plan
   6. Marketing plan
   7. Facilities plan
   8. Capital budget

D. Personnel data
   1. Personnel handbook
   2. Employee retirement, profit-sharing, and other benefit plan agreements
   3. Current wage and salary structure and payroll data
   4. FTEs by department
   5. Actuarial reports
   6. Pension plan audited financial statements
   7. Union contracts
   8. Management incentive plan and deferred compensation plans
   9. Key members of management and contracts
   10. Board members
   11. Personnel turnover experience
   12. EEOC and OSHA reports

E. Marketing/products/local market data
   1. Population data and projections
   2. Socioeconomic data
   3. Patient origin data (county or zip code)
   4. Primary and secondary service areas
   5. Major competition and related statistical data, including services provided, patient days, medical staffs, bed complement, occupancy level, affiliations, proximity, ownership, and expansion

F. Legal matters/risk management
   1. Listing of all asserted and unasserted claims and related reserves
   2. Listing and description of all lawsuits that the hospital has been a party to in last five years
   3. Insurance policies in force and historical coverage, including general and professional liability, fire and extended coverage, fidelity bonds, workers' compensation, etc., and other contracts, agreements, etc.
   4. Antitrust matters (Sherman, Clayton, FTCA, Hart-Scott-Rodino, state law)
   5. CON, licensure, third-party contracts
   6. Debt agreements, covenants, restrictions
   7. Restricted and endowment funds

Exhibit 24-1 continued

G. Third-party/fixed-rate payers
   1. All third-party cost reports for past two years and copies of most recent adjustment reports and PPS calculations
   2. Copies of all third-party payment contracts, including HMO, PPO, physician
   3. Copy of rate authority regulations, state or local
   4. Determination of all open matters, pending issues, etc.
   5. Hill-Burton obligation
   6. Medicare depreciation recapture
   7. Good will treatment

H. Site visits/physical properties
   1. Date of facility construction and descriptions and dates of subsequent additions and renovations
   2. Review for binding commitments that would restrict future additions or renovations
   3. Zoning restrictions, changes, noncompliance
   4. Floor plans
   5. Copies of space leases (either lessor or lessee)
   6. Physical facilities' condition and future investment necessary
   7. Building code compliance, noncompliance

I. Medical data
   1. Current medical staff profile, including age, specialty, location, and number of discharges for the past three years
   2. List of physicians occupying related medical office buildings
   3. Recent or expected changes in medical staff
   4. Medical school/teaching affiliations
   5. Medical staff contracts

competitive data, technical know-how, and any other information that is of a confidential nature and should be protected via written agreement.

The second observation is that, typically, by the time parties enter into a due diligence effort, a letter of intent (LOI) has been executed. The terms and conditions of an LOI should be viewed as being contractually binding, as would any other written agreement. Therefore, no terms should be placed in the LOI that the organization cannot abide by; accordingly, once included in an executed LOI, all provisions should be strictly abided by. Although some or all terms or provisions may be specifically identified as being nonbinding, clearly, legal counsel should participate in the drafting of the LOI.

As can be seen in Exhibit 24-1, the broad categories that are included under the purchase information gathering are organizational data, financial data, operational data, personnel data, marketing/products/local market data, legal matters/risk management, third-party/fixed-rate contracts, site visits/physical properties, and medical data. Gathering and understanding data

with respect to each of the above areas requires the involvement of knowledgeable and experienced professionals. An M&A process that has reasonable prospects for success requires a thorough and competent PI.

The areas that are reflected in the due diligence listing may have particular significance or importance in any given acquisition, and therefore should be carefully evaluated and pursued based upon the M&A's facts and circumstances. However, some areas should be highlighted as follows.

Under financial data, existing debt agreements should be very closely scrutinized early on. The terms and provisions of these agreements may dictate aspects of financial ratios, acquisition structure, asset transfers, debt service coverage, and advanced refunding or defeasance provisions. Any of these aspects may have significant effects on acquisition value, structure, and business planning for the transaction. In addition, under financial data, revenue agent reports and tax exposures should be carefully analyzed and evaluated by competent experts.

Depending upon filing positions taken and the manner in which provisions are booked, significant unrecorded contingent liabilities may exist. As many health care providers that historically have had only tax-exempt operations diversify into taxable activities, issues may arise with respect to inurement and unrelated business income. Also, under financial data, accounts receivable should be carefully analyzed if significant. In some instances, accounts receivable may represent an underperforming asset that may be readily convertible, in part, to cash, given proper attention and performance from the business office. However, in other situations, accounts receivable may be overvalued and not fully realizable and, therefore, may significantly impact an entity's future cash requirements and value as compared with amounts recorded on the books and records.

Under personnel data, several points need to be emphasized. First of all, any personnel handbook that is widely distributed to employees should be carefully reviewed and evaluated. Employee handbooks may, in some circumstances, have the binding effect of a contractual agreement, and an acquirer should understand the obligations with respect to the work force that it may be undertaking prior to executing the transaction. Second, wage, salary, and benefit structures should be carefully reviewed, particularly if the entities and operations are geographically proximate or are to become integrated. If the latter is the case, likely the compensation structures will be conformed among existing and target entities and operations. Based on experience, the tendency is to adjust the lower compensation base up rather than reduce the higher base. Therefore, the cost of conforming to the higher scale should be fully recognized in any financial projections prepared. A final area to focus on under personnel data is that of pension plans. This generally requires a significant level of expertise as pension obligations almost invariably require relatively complex actuarial calculations and determinations. Understanding the plan's benefits, projected benefit obligation, actuarial assumptions, funding status, assets at fair market value, and the plan benefits is of extreme importance. Actuarial analyses may

determine that there is a significant unrecorded asset that may be accessed or, conversely, a significant unrecorded obligation that must be funded.

The importance of the legal and risk management investigation also cannot be overemphasized. Particularly for acquisitions that involve providers of health care services, the potential for professional liability claims is great. The first two steps in understanding the professional liability exposure are (1) gaining a very thorough understanding of the facts surrounding all asserted and unasserted claims and related reserves and (2) obtaining a very good analysis of insurance policies by year and by layer, remaining coverage and the related companies. The insurers themselves are of extreme importance. The due diligence effort should evaluate the financial strength and viability of the insurers and their ultimate ability to provide the coverage in force if called upon. Certainly another key area under legal matters is that of existing contracts and agreements. They should be reviewed as to terms, provisions, and potential impacts on post-transaction plans. Depending upon the nature of the transaction, these may very well become agreements of the successor entity. Legal counsel's involvement in this area is a necessity.

Another area in the PI review is that of third-party/fixed-rate payers. Two areas of particular significance to this are that of fixed-rate contractual agreements and third-party exposures. Under fixed-rate agreements, many health maintenance organizations and preferred provider organizations contract with providers for fixed-rate care for given populations or for admissions on a per-day basis or on a capitation basis. Any obligations entered into under these arrangements should be carefully evaluated and reflected in the financial feasibility studies or projections that are prepared. Furthermore, third-party exposures with respect to potential payments required on filed positions as compared with final settlements should be analyzed and understood. There continues to be a significant decrease in settlement or cost reporting exposures due to the prospective payment system and other conversions of cost based to fixed-rate payment mechanisms.

However, because of the long tail on the resolution of some issues, there may remain significant contingent liabilities or assets that should be considered in the due diligence effort. In addition, depending upon the nature of the transaction and the type of entity involved, there may be significant Medicare impacts due to the recapture of previously allowed depreciation or potential benefits from an allowable on disposal of provider facilities.

Under the site visits/physical properties area, a number of matters must be emphasized. If hard assets, "bricks and mortar," are being acquired, then a review by a qualified engineer is a necessity. The review should include a determination or estimation of the expenditures necessary to bring the facility up to the standard that the acquirer would require. Furthermore, and in some instances of greater importance, there is the need to understand current building code compliance or noncompliance and any effects that may take place upon a change of ownership with respect to enforcement of the current building code or grandfathering of a previous code. In some localities, a sale will automatically trigger the requirement that buildings be brought up to current code before the transaction can be completed.

A final comment under the due diligence deals with that of the medical staff. For the acquisition of an entity whose revenues are dependent upon admissions or upon medical staff relations, understanding the complement of the medical professionals and their working relations is of the highest importance. This cannot be overemphasized, including understanding the impact of the proposed transaction on that of future working relationships. Postacquisition results can be catastrophic if this area is not properly understood or attended to.

Deal Structure

The third major area under the M&A process is that of structuring the deal. Under a merger scenario, a merger of exempt organizations is a somewhat unusual transaction. This is because exempts are not "owned" in the commercial sense of a stock or taxable corporation. Exempts are owned by the citizens of the state in which they are incorporated and, therefore, a merger is determined or established via control. The manner in which exempt control is typically achieved is through the corporate bylaws and, in particular, the voting of the "exempt" corporate membership. In some instances, for example, one exempt corporation will be the sole member of another. As a result, the transfer of control for merger purposes of two exempts can be an extremely sensitive process involving voluntary relinquishment or sharing of control. This voluntary relinquishment may also involve issues of differing missions, faith-based origins, operating philosophies, and communities served, among others. As a result, the chemistry, the good faith, and a good-quality working relationship are absolutely essential to the successful merger of two or more exempt organizations. Also, as often is the case, absent economic distress, it may not be possible to achieve the governance perspective necessary for the voluntary relinquishment of control.

The merger of taxable corporations, while potentially involving great technical complexity, may be more achievable simply as a result of the differing ownership and economic interests as contrasted with those of the exempt organizations. The merger of taxable corporations is achieved via the exchange of shares of stock, meeting specified criteria. However, to achieve a tax-free "reorganization," extremely involved aspects of the tax code relative to such transactions must be fully understood and complied with. Because of the highly technical and complex nature of these tax considerations, as well as their continually changing nature, they are outside the scope of this chapter. Suffice it to say, if the tax status of the transaction is significant to the transaction itself, competent tax professionals must be consulted. In some instances, it will be prudent to obtain an advance letter ruling from the Internal Revenue Service if the nontaxable nature of the transaction is significant to the transaction.

Whereas the mergers of either taxable or exempt organizations often are complex and difficult endeavors, purchases typically are more simple and straightforward transactions. However, there are some limitations. For example, while an exempt corporation may purchase a taxable corporation, a taxable corporation may not purchase an exempt corporation. In addition, while an exempt organization cannot sell its exempt status, it may sell its assets and operations to another exempt corporation or to a taxable entity, and thereby achieve nearly the same result as selling the entire organization, although not conveying the tax status. While a taxable corporation may acquire both the assets and operations of an exempt organization, these assets and operations lose their exempt character once they are acquired by a taxable business. A taxable business may structure a purchase in the form of an asset purchase, a stock purchase, or acquisition of assets and assumption of liabilities. When acquiring the stock or when assuming all of the liabilities of an organization, any unrecorded liabilities or contingent liabilities related to preacquisition operations would be included and would therefore be obligations of the new postentity transaction. This concept is the same for merging organizations. Once merged, the organizations share common assets and liabilities, including all obligations disclosed or undisclosed. This points up the necessity of doing a thorough and competent due diligence in order to understand fully an entity's obligations and liabilities, contingent or otherwise, that may be borne upon the completion of the transaction.

Planned Transaction Review

A final observation with respect to the process of health care business combinations is made with respect to planned transaction reviews. The planned transaction review is a comparison of the actual results achieved versus those planned when authorization was sought and received for completing the transaction. Planned transaction reviews should take place on a regular basis with reporting of the results going to the same level of the organization (chief executive officer and board) as was required to approve entering into the transaction. This process of regularly scheduled comparisons of planned versus actual results for this type of transaction helps achieve the appropriate level of management responsibility and accountability for a business combination in a manner similar to that that is in place for most other management activities.

FUNDAMENTALS OF VALUATION

The structures of health care business combinations take on as many different forms as there are transactions themselves. However, one common question arises in virtually all health care business combinations. That question is "What is the value of the respective parties?"

Regardless of whether cash consideration is involved in a business combination or the combination is a merger of two entities with similar faith origins, inevitably, somewhere in the process, the question will be raised as to what is the value of the entity or of the operations or the assets being merged or acquired. For a transaction involving cash or other consideration, it is obvious why this question must be asked and correctly answered. It is less obvious for a transaction or merger of exempt organizations where control, and not cash consideration, is exchanged. However, valuation may be of equal or even greater significance to exempt transactions. For example, in acquisitions involving publicly traded entities where there is a daily market for the company's shares, there is a readily available starting point for determining value. While premiums above the traded share price are assigned for acquisitions almost without exception, the presumption can be made that a reasonably informed market value has been established as a point to begin determining the final price.

In the case of exempt health care provider mergers where there is no established market, determination of value can be a very significant aspect of the business combination. This determination of value will assist in arriving at a fair price for disposal of exempt assets or operations, determination of control represented by number of board seats, the power of appointment or ratification of board nominees, and the other manifestations of control in exempt organizations. In fact, the inability to determine relative values and to resolve the related proportion of control issues often prevents the successful completion of exempt provider mergers.

A number of different methods of valuation are seen in the health care industry today. Examples include a multiple of earnings, a pay back period in number of years, and comparison of asking price with net worth as reflected by net book value. While these methods may yield interesting results, they are generally of limited use in appraising value in business combinations. There are three methods that do have what might be termed general acceptance among professional appraisers and economists. These methods are (1) comparative market transactions, (2) reproduction or replacement cost, and (3) the free cash flow or income approach. What do each of these methodologies mean and how can they be used? Each has its own merits and deficiencies, and these will be described. Even among these three commonly practiced methodologies, only one has what is considered an underlying economic basis for establishing fair market value. That method is the free cash flow model. When sophisticated financial analysts, whether working for investment bankers or for large publicly traded companies, make a determination of business value for acquisition pricing purposes, it is almost invariably based upon the free cash flow methodology. Free cash flow is by far the method of choice for pricing the major business combinations today. On the other hand, comparative market transactions and reproduction or replacement cost methodologies are usually at least considered in a pricing or a determination of value exercise and may bring important information to the table when making pricing decisions.

Comparative Market Transactions

The underlying concept of comparative market transactions is that similar transactions should yield similar pricing. Therefore, if comparable market transactions can be identified, those prices can then be used to determine the value of the business combination being considered. As one can imagine, this methodology involves a great deal of investigation when looking for those purchases of health care properties or operations similar to that being considered. For example, hospital acquisitions are fre-

quently publicized and the total purchase price publicly disclosed. Typical comparisons made among such transactions are average costs per bed or other such comparables. There are a great number of sources for these "comparable transactions." Sources include trade publications, business libraries, Securities and Exchange Commission filings, appraisal firms, investment bankers, and public accounting firms. In addition, there are a limited number of service bureaus that accumulate merger and acquisition data and can sort their data base by industry, period, type of transactions, etc., for a reasonable fee. Even when available, however, comparative market transactions should be approached with a great deal of caution. It is rare that truly comparable transactions can be identified. In recent hospital acquisitions, there is a wide range of prices paid per bed. Does this mean that errors were made with respect to pricing? That is, of course, not the case. More likely, the pricing was determined based upon the underlying economic value or projected free cash flow of the hospital rather than upon the number of beds. But this does serve to demonstrate the types of problems that can be encountered when searching for comparative market transactions. Also, a transaction may be identified that on the surface appears to be quite comparable. For example, hospitals with very similar competitive payer mixes in communities with comparable demographics and similar competitive positions with respect to neighboring hospitals and perhaps even similar results from operations may yield very different purchase prices upon acquisition. Why should this be? One possible answer is that other liabilities and assets in the transactions may have impacted the purchase price. There may be the assumption of the hospital's liabilities by the purchaser in one instance and by the seller in the other. There may be significant other nonoperating assets being acquired in one transaction, such as excess cash and investments or undeveloped land or properties not used in operations with a significant market value. There may also be assets such as excess pension plan assets or underperforming accounts receivable that can be readily turned into cash by the purchaser, thereby increasing the price that the purchaser is willing to pay.

Factors such as these and others may significantly influence a purchaser's or seller's price and, therefore, may make a transaction totally dissimilar that on the surface appears to be very similar. Ultimately, though, market value is established by the price one party is willing to pay and another is willing to sell. As can be seen by innumerable examples, errors are made in pricing acquisitions across industries all the time. If relied upon too heavily, "comparative market transactions" that are priced in error will in turn lead to other pricing errors. Comparisons such as these, however, are not intended to represent an independent evidence of value but, rather, one of the considerations in determining value. While it is true that comparable market transactions should be approached with great care, they often will represent a very useful "sanity check." This type of check may be extremely helpful in identifying pricing errors. It may help identify errors in free cash flow pricing or other methodologies used for establishing price. When comparative market transactions lead to the conclusion that proposed pricing is out of line or against trends of the industry, further investigation is indicated before establishing a final transaction price.

Reproduction or Replacement Cost

Reproduction or replacement is an estimate of value based upon the cost to reproduce or replace the "bricks and mortar," less a factor for accumulated depreciation. This theory assumes that a productive facility will not be worth more than its cost of replacement. There are a number of sources that can be called upon for estimating a value by this methodology. Property casualty insurance appraisers, real estate firms, and general appraisal firms, among others, are familiar with and use this type of methodology daily. In addition, however, if one has data about the health care facility in question, such as year of construction, square footage, construction grade, location, or original cost, a reproduction or replacement cost can be calculated. This, again, would entail researching business libraries in order to find the construction indexes and/or insurance tables that will translate the above

information to an estimated current replacement cost.

Similar to the use of the comparable market transactions, reproduction or replacement cost rarely will be used as the sole determinant of market value, but rather as a further sanity check. While reproduction cost is useful in understanding the cost of reproducing a similar facility today, there are many other significant factors contributing to value that it does not capture. For example, the start-up costs of establishing business to the point that it is currently operating is not reflected. These values may be also in the form of the good will established with the market served. In addition, the location of the facility may be particularly valuable in terms of the demographics or competitive business of the health care market. These and other determinants of value are not captured by the replacement methodology. The major flaw with reproduction or replacement cost is that, while it reflects the value of the productive facility, it captures nothing else. There are, of course, a variety of other very significant factors that will influence the cash flow yielded from operations beyond the hard assets themselves. A valuation based upon only the reproduction cost could be significantly in error. However, where hard productive assets are involved in the acquisition, going through the exercise of determining reproduction or replacement cost is desirable. Once again, this methodology can provide an important checkpoint to see if other valuation methodologies have produced a reasonable value.

Clearly, both comparative market transactions and reproduction or replacement cost methodologies for determining value have significant conceptual and practical limitations. On the other hand, when properly developed, the free cash flow model yields a fully economic justifiable value.

Free Cash Flow

The economic fair value of a health care entity as determined by the free cash flow model is a function of the expected return on the assets and operations, the timing of the expected return, and the risk or certainty of the return. In order to understand the free cash flow valuation model, each of these respective elements must be understood.

The first element is that of the return on the acquired assets. The return on the acquired assets is, simply stated, the cash yields from the operations that are not required to be reinvested or retained in the business and are therefore available for other purposes. Free cash flow or cash yield is defined as the cash generated by operations excluding interest expense and net of taxes, and after the reinvestment in operating productive capacity and working capital necessary to sustain future cash yields (see Exhibit 24-2).

The purpose of excluding the impact of net interest expense from the pro formas is to separate the financing decision from the investment decision. The free cash flow model is intended to arrive at valuation for pricing purposes. The manner in which the investment is capitalized should not affect this pricing and, therefore, interest expense, a direct result of the capitalization, must be excluded. The investment decision does reflect the capitalization and related costs through the discount rate utilized. The discount rate, generally representing the cost of capital, includes the interest costs associated with intended borrowings, as will be demonstrated. As is further discussed under the cost of capital (Appendix 24-A), the cost of capital reflects the costs and proportions of the elements making up an entity's capitalization. As debt capital is one component or element of this capitalization, the associated interest expense, or "cost" of that component of capital, is included in this total "cost of capital." Capitalization provides a cash fund available for the entity's investment purposes. This investment activity may take the form of new product development costs, a factory, start-up costs of a new business, or it may represent the acquisition of an existing business (an M&A). Regardless, the investment, exclusive of any capital costs, must generate a return sufficient to recover the costs of the entity's capitalization (cost of capital) in order for the investment to be economically justified. Therefore, to include interest expense in the investment decision pro formas would result in mixing the financing or capitalization decision

Exhibit 24-2 Free Cash Flow

Not-for-Profit Entities

Earnings before Interest
Add Noncash Expenses

= Cash Flow from Operations
Less Investment (Increase in Plant and Net Working Capital)

= Free Cash Flow

For-Profit Entities

Earnings before Interest, Tax Effected
Add Noncash Expenses

= Cash Flow Generated from Operations
Less Investment (Increase in Plant and Net Working Capital)

= Free Cash Flow

---

with the investment decision, clearly an undesirable outcome.

How is this cash yield or free cash flow determined? Expected cash flow is based upon a financial feasibility study or financial projection. Naturally, all the cautions and caveats that are attendant to a financial projection in the health care industry under any circumstances apply when considering the cash yield for valuation or pricing determinations. An extended discussion of the risks attendant to financial projections for the health care industry in general could be included at this point; however, that is beyond the scope of this chapter. Rather, the care, prudence, and due diligence that should be undertaken in preparing the financial pro formas when attempting to determine a value are extremely important.

The second element of determining value is that of the timing of the expected return. This, too, is a product of the financial projections or pro formas. With respect to the timing aspect of valuation, a number of observations are appropriate. A rule of thumb for these pro formas is that they should continue for a period of not less than five years but no more than ten. The reason for this is that in a period of less than five years it is less likely that the annual cash yield has "normalized." At the other end of the range, however, in going beyond ten years the projected cash yield from operations is so far into the future that it is difficult to derive reliable numbers. Such great changes take place in the health care industry and its economic environment in much shorter periods, as has been the experience, that long-term assumptions are suspect. The pro formas should extend for a period such that the final year of the projection represents the expected ongoing annual rate of free cash flow generated by operations into the future.

The third primary element of the free cash flow model is that of the risk or certainty of the return. This risk or certainty is represented by the discount rate to be applied to the future free cash yield generated by operations in order to bring those cash flows to a present value of today. Theoretically, a cost of capital can be calculated for any business enterprise. In practice, though, to attempt to determine this discount rate with great precision may be a futile exercise (see Appendix 24-A regarding cost of capital). This is a result of a number of factors, such as the fact that the cost of the elements of a cost of capital change daily as capital markets change, the fact that when working with exempt enterprises there is not a good approximation available for the cost of exempt equity capital, and the fact that the specific industry or entity risk beyond that of an equity premium is difficult or impossible to measure under many circumstances. On the other hand, a reasonable discount rate often can be estimated without extraordinary effort. In general, a reasonable proxy for a discount rate is the cost of capital of the health care enterprise, representing the business risk that should be reflected in the valuation model. For a recommended approach for estimating this discount rate, see Appendix 24-A.

Some general rules are important with respect to this discount rate. First, the discount rate should not, under any circumstances, be less than the long-term borrowing rate for the enterprise. If there is such an inversion, too high a value will be assigned to future cash flows due to an inappropriately low risk being assigned to the "equity investment" in the health care business. A second rule of thumb is that the discount rate

or cost of capital should be that of the selling entity and not that of the purchasing entity. The risk assigned to the free cash yield from the future operations should be the risk of those operations purchased and generating the cash flow, not the risk of the entity that is acquiring those operations.

Another important aspect of the free cash flow valuation model is that of the residual value. The purpose of determining a residual value is to reflect the value of the continued generation of free cash flows beyond the pro forma period. The residual value or terminal cash flow value is based on the assumption that the final-year cash yield generated by the entity will continue indefinitely. The cash flows for the pro forma years had been valued based upon the discount rate (or cost of capital) factor necessary to determine the value today of one dollar received in that pro forma year. However, if by the final year of pro formas the free cash flows have stabilized and are expected to continue at that level indefinitely, the value of those cash flows beyond the pro forma periods must be calculated. The calculation is made by simply dividing the final-year free cash flow by the discount rate and in turn multiplying the results by the present value factor for the first year beyond the pro forma period (see Exhibit 24-3). Dividing by the discount rate has the effect of yielding the present value of a one-dollar annuity into perpetuity. Multiplying by the present value factor of the discount rate for the first year beyond the pro forma periods has the effect of bringing the value of that annuity that begins in year $n + 1$ (n being the number of pro forma years) to the present or today. Given the correct discount rate and terminal cash flow, this calculation will result in the proper economic value assigned to the business results generated beyond the pro forma period.

Once the free cash flow value is determined, there remain some final adjustments necessary to arrive at a price. First, any excess cash and investments, excluded of course from the pro forma free cash flow, should be added at fair market value. Excess cash and investments mean liquid funds, cash, or cash equivalents not required to operate the business. As these would be transferred to the acquirer after the transaction, these excess funds should be added to the purchase price. To the extent added to the purchase price, these funds are immediately recovered by the purchaser after the transaction is completed.

Second, debt outstanding, at fair market value, should be subtracted. Once again, while excluded from the free cash flow pro forma, debt will have a "pass-through" effect in the transaction and therefore no net price impact after the entire transaction is completed. The significance of "fair market value" is that the debt may bear a fixed interest rate different from what current market conditions would dictate for a similar credit and maturity. If the interest rate is higher than current market conditions, this debt is more expensive and will reduce the purchase price by an amount greater than the face amount of indebtedness. Conversely, if the debt bears a below-market rate, the debt is less costly and will reduce the purchase price by less than the face amount.

A simple case example of a free cash flow hospital valuation is included as Exhibit 24-4.

Exhibit 24-3 Residual Value

"TERMINAL" CASH FLOWS
(FINAL-YEAR FREE CASH FLOW
DIVIDED BY
DISCOUNT RATE)
MULTIPLIED BY
PRESENT VALUE FACTOR
EQUALS
RESIDUAL VALUE

OR

Residual Value = (FYCF (a) ÷ DR (b)) × PVF (c)

(a) FYCF = final-year free cash flow, assumed to be representative of cash flows generated for years beyond pro forma indefinitely
(b) DR = discount rate or cost of capital used in calculating present values
(c) PVF = present value factor or the value of $1 to be received the first year beyond the pro forma period (the year that the "annuity" of residual cash flows commence) at the cost of capital or discount rate

Note: See Exhibit 24-4 for an example calculation.

Other Valuation Considerations

In addition to these basic elements of a free cash flow value model, there are some other important aspects to be considered for developing a price.

- Given the uncertainty inherent in any pro forma and in any discount rate, it is prudent to include a sensitivity analysis. A sensitivity analysis should reflect moving key assumptions or variables within reasonable ranges in either a favorable or unfavorable direction to demonstrate the impact on cash flows and the related valuation. This is desirable in order for management to understand the range of values that may result given operating results different from those projected.

- The seller in any M&A, health care or otherwise, will have more knowledge regarding the assets and operations being sold than the purchaser. This puts the seller at a significant advantage when establishing a purchase price. The corollary of that observation is that the seller, having more intimate knowledge of the business entity and its value, will not sell at a price offered below the intrinsic value but will sell when the price offered is above the intrinsic value.

- The valuation methodologies described above are not necessarily appropriate to fix a purchase price. Rather, they should be used in the development of a purchase price. These methodologies should be an extremely useful tool to management in helping understand the performance that the acquisition must achieve in order to make an acquisition price economically justified.

- In considering or pursuing an M&A transaction, it should be fully understood that these are risk transactions. Management should fully acknowledge this and approach these transactions in a manner that best minimizes and manages that risk.

- The final caveat is that conveyed via the classic observation from Warren Buffett,

Exhibit 24-4 Free Cash Flow Case Study: Example of Calculating the "Total Value" of a Hospital Using the "Free Cash Flow" Valuation Methodology

FACTS:

1. **Condensed Balance Sheet ($ in 1000s)**

Net Working Capital	$ 35,000
Fixed Assets, Net	68,000
Excess Cash & Investments (@ FMV)	19,000
Long-Term Debt (@ FMV)	(10,000)
Net Worth	$112,000

2. **Agreed-Upon Pro Forma Profit and Loss and Other Data ($ in 1000s)**

Year	1	2	3	4	5
Net Revenues	$120,000	$125,000	$125,000	$137,000	$140,000
Cash Expenses	94,000	95,000	96,000	99,000	104,000
Interest	1,000	1,000	2,000	2,000	3,000
Depreciation	11,000	11,000	14,000	15,000	16,000
Net Income	$ 14,000	$ 18,000	$ 13,000	$ 21,000	$ 17,000
Annual Investment in Working Capital	$ 2,000	$ -0-	$ 1,000	$ 3,000	$ 2,000
Plant	$ 8,000	$ 18,000	$ 11,000	$ 17,000	$ 19,000

3. **Cost of Capital is 12%**

4. **Year 5 Cash Flow Represents Future Expected Annual Cash Flow**

5. **What Is "Total Value" of the Hospital?**

Answer

1. **Free Cash Flow ($ in 1000s)(a)**

Year	1	2	3	4	5
Net Income	$14,000	$18,000	$13,000	$21,000	$17,000
Interest	1,000	1,000	2,000	2,000	3,000
Depreciation	11,000	11,000	14,000	15,000	16,000
Working Capital	(2,000)	-0-	(1,000)	(3,000)	(2,000)
Plant	(8,000)	(18,000)	(11,000)	(17,000)	(19,000)
	$ 16,000	$ 12,000	$ 17,000	$ 18,000	$ 15,000
Present Value Factor (b)	× .893	× .797	× .712	× .636	× .567
	$14,288	$9,564	$12,104	$11,448	$ 8,505
Total					$55,909

(a) Derived from facts.
(b) Present value of $1 in year *n* at 12% discount rate.

Exhibit 24-4 continued

---

2. **Residual Value ($ in 1000s)**

Terminal Cash Flow	$ 15,000 (a)
Discount Rate	÷ 0.12 (b)
	$ 125,000
Present Value Factor	× 0.507 (c)
	$ 63,375

(a) Final-year cash flow, expected annually in future.
(b) Calculation derives value of an annuity into perpetuity at a 12% discount rate.
(c) Present value of $1 in year 6, the first year beyond the pro forma period, when the ''annuity'' of the terminal cash flow begins, at a 12% discount rate.

3. **Total Value ($ in 1000s)**

Present Value Future Cash Flows	$ 55,909 (a)
Residual Value	63,375 (b)
Excess Cash & Investments	19,000 (c)
Long-Term Debt	(10,000)(c)
Total Value	$128,284

(a) From Answer 1.
(b) From Answer 2.
(c) From Facts.

Conclusion: Given the above facts, the total value of the hospital is $128,284,000 using the ''free cash flow'' valuation methodology.

---

chairman of Berkshire Hathaway, as he once observed in an annual report: ''Managerial intellect wilted in competition with managerial adrenalin. The thrill of the chase blinded pursuers to the consequences of the catch.'' While mergers and acquisitions can be very significant transactions to the furtherance of a given provider's mission, they should be viewed with all of the management discipline and will necessary to walk away from the contemplated transaction if the merger or acquisition does not properly achieve the organization's objectives. The completion of the deal should never become the primary purpose of the business combination.

OTHER SIGNIFICANT MATTERS

There are a number of key issues, problems, and caveats that should be carefully considered in any health care merger or acquisition. First, there must be a great deal of sensitivity and discretion with respect to medical staff relations. Resistance of any level manifested by the medical staff may have significant impacts on contemplated transactions. Medical staff concerns should be thoroughly understood and appropriately addressed before they become issues that affect the success of the business combination. A second factor is that of compatibility of organizations. This compatibility may be represented by management chemistry, systems integration, employee compensation levels, and physician contracts. The effects of significant or irreconcilable differences should be fully understood and correctly reflected in the business combination planning process and the projected financial performance. Another area that can, in some situations, be terminal to a proposed business combination is that of union contracts. The presence of a union in one entity and not the other, and binding agreements with respect to work force security and compensation levels, among others, may significantly impact organizational plans and flexibility and should be fully understood and reflected in the planning process. Contingent liabilities, whether they be professional liability claims, commitments, tax assessments, or other asserted or unasserted claims, should be fully understood and considered in a realistic manner. Finally, contractual obligations to be assumed should be fully understood and carefully evaluated.

On the other hand, great rewards may accrue to an organization that successfully plans and completes a business combination. While there is significant risk associated with this potential reward, this risk may, in part, be managed through the thoughtful incorporation of the following key success factors.

First, organizations should stick to businesses that they know when considering a business combination. The risk is great enough in acquiring a business in management's own industry without compounding that risk by acquiring a business in an industry that management does not know. Second, the business combination team should be a small, knowledgeable, competent task force, including that individual who will have the executive management responsibility for the new organization's operations after completing the transaction. The proper skills, knowledge, and experience on that team will go a great deal of the way to bringing the risk to an acceptable level in a business combination. Third, the M&A team should execute faithfully the M&A plan. The team should do its homework and pay attention to the details. There must be a significant amount of discipline and rigor in the execution of the business combination plan if the inherent risks are to be managed properly. Fourth, and finally, if the pre-established business combination goals or "hurdles" are not met, management should be prepared and have the discipline to walk away from the transaction. An organization must not become so enthralled with the contemplated transaction that it allows itself to be led to an unreasonable or inappropriate transaction structure or price.

CONCLUSION

Business combinations are a fact of life in the health care industry. Furthermore, their frequency and magnitude are increasing and will continue to increase as the industry undergoes economic distress and related consolidation. As business combinations represent significant risk transactions, the greater the management knowledge, preparation, and discipline reflected in the planning and execution of the transactions, the greater the likelihood of its ultimate success. The desired outcome of this chapter is that it will provide a meaningful basis upon which to approach the inevitable activities and risks that are attendant to an industry undergoing consolidation. This chapter should represent a basic and key resource to the prepared health care financial professional.

Appendix 24-A

Cost of Capital

Cost of capital represents the rate of return required to compensate the sources of capital for debt or equity investment. A weighted average cost of capital is simply the weighting of the debt and equity costs of capital target proportions of the business entity. Debt cost of capital is relatively easily determined, as this represents the current borrowing rate for the business or credit risk that the business represents. Although this will change daily as interest rates and capital markets move, comparably rated recent debt issues for most health care concerns can usually be identified. However, the cost of equity capital is another matter.

The cost of equity capital is viewed as the return, as measured by dividends and capital appreciation, required for equity capital. A number of significant problems arise in this regard in the health care industry. First, there is not a comparable "return" on investment (contributions and retained earnings) for exempt providers, a significant part of the total industry. Second, while publicly traded health care providers (HCA, Humana, and others) have "determinable" costs of equity capital, these are very different economic entities from the local tax-exempt community hospital and, therefore, their cost of equity capital will not be truly "comparable."

Theoretically, though, the cost of equity capital is calculated as follows:

$$\text{Equity cost of capital} = \text{Risk-free rate} + (\text{market risk premium} \times beta)$$

The risk-free rate is typically viewed as the U.S. Treasury securities rate. This changes at each Treasury-bill auction or daily. The equity risk premium is the return above the risk-free rate required by equity investors. One study of the total Standard and Poor 500 index for the period 1925–1979 found this to be approximately 5.9 percent. However, this too changes daily as the market moves, and differing periods or differing pools of stocks will yield differing market or equity risk premiums. The *beta* represents the risk of an individual investment relative to the total market risk premium. This is measured by the covariability of the individual investment return compared with the total market. For New York Stock Exchange companies, this is routinely calculated and reported by investment banking firms. For health care businesses that are not publicly traded, the *beta* is not readily determinable. However, the *beta* for the health care proprietary chains may be a useful approximation. Likely, given the economic magnitude and maturity of the proprietaries, the *beta* for most community health care providers should not be less than the proprietary *beta*.

Given the following facts:

Risk-free rate	7.0%
Equity risk premium	5.9%
Beta	1.055
Debt capital	10.5%
Debt/equity ratio	45/55

456

The cost of capital can be calculated as follows:

Equity cost of capital = 7.0% + (5.9% × 1.055)
Equity cost of capital = 7.0% + 6.2245%
Equity cost of capital = 13.2245%
Cost of capital   = (13.2245% × 0.55) + (10.5% × 0.45)
Cost of capital   = 7.273475% + 4.725%
Cost of capital   = 11.998475%
            or
Cost of capital   = 12%

While precisely calculating a cost of capital for a given health care business may not be feasible, the above exercise can yield a usable approximation and should provide a better answer than using incremental borrowing costs or investment returns as a cost of capital.

Tax Administration

Chapter 25

Tax Planning for Unrelated Business Income

Diane Cornwell
Partner, Arthur Andersen & Co.

Now more than ever, unrelated business income (UBI) tax planning must be considered by all tax-exempt organizations. In many cases, the activity generating the income, which is arguably unrelated, may be documented and operationally restructured in a manner that falls within a UBI exception or demonstrates that the activity is actually related to the organization's exempt purpose.

The Internal Revenue Code (IRC) sections governing the taxation of UBI are

- 511, which imposes tax on UBI (as defined in Section 512) of exempt organizations, defines organizations subject to the tax, and prescribes tax rates
- 512, which defines unrelated business taxable income from unrelated trades or businesses (as defined in Section 513) and sets forth modifications that apply in determining the amount of income subject to tax
- 513, which defines unrelated trade or business
- 514, which defines unrelated debt-financed income subject to UBI tax and sets forth rules for calculating the amount of such income that is taxable

This chapter is reprinted from *Topics in Health Care Financing*, Vol. 14, No. 4, pp. 15–21, Aspen Publishers, Inc., © Summer 1988.

BASIC DEFINITIONS

Unrelated Trade or Business

Generally, an exempt organization is engaged in an unrelated trade or business when that trade or business is regularly carried on and is not substantially related to accomplishing the exempt purposes of the organization. The term trade or business includes any activity carried on for the production of income from the sale of goods or the performance of services. If an activity is not competitive in nature, it generally will not be treated as a trade or business. Several court cases in the 1970s attempted to clarify activities that constitute an unrelated trade or business.[1,2]

The IRC provides that an activity does not lose its identity as a trade or business because it is carried on within a larger group of similar activities or other endeavors that may or may not be related to the exempt purposes of the organization. However, the fact that the overall activity is related does not protect each part within the activity.

For example, if a hospital pharmacy sells pharmaceutical supplies to the general public, the Internal Revenue Service (IRS) position is that the sales, even if only a small part of the hospital's total pharmacy sales, constitute a separate trade or business. It is only this unrelated portion of the pharmacy sales that would be subject to tax as UBI. However, in some cases, the courts have exempted pharmacy sales to the general public from the tax on UBI.[3,4]

Regularly Carried On

A regularly carried on business operates with the frequency and regularity of comparable commercial activities of nonexempt organizations.[5] For example, a sandwich stand operated by a hospital auxiliary for two weeks at a state fair would not be a regularly carried on business, but the operation of a commercial parking lot one day a week may be treated as such.

Substantially Related

The use of net income from business activities for charitable purposes does not have any bearing on whether the income is subject to tax. That an activity furnishes funds used to accomplish the exempt purpose of an organization is not a sufficient criterion to make it a related activity.

IRS regulations provide that an activity must contribute importantly to the accomplishment of the exempt purposes, as determined by the facts and circumstances involved.[6] The IRS views the exempt purpose of hospitals as providing health care services to patients. Determining whether individuals are patients of the hospital is the key to whether the IRS will view the activity as related.

Revenue Ruling 68-376 describes the situations that qualify a person as a patient and not a member of the general public.[7] A patient is defined as a person who is

- admitted to a hospital as an inpatient
- receiving general or emergency diagnostic, therapeutic, or preventive health services from outpatient facilities at the hospital
- directly referred to the hospital's outpatient facilities by his or her private physician for specific diagnostic or treatment procedures
- refilling a prescription written during the course of treatment as a past patient of the hospital

- receiving medical services as part of a hospital-administered home care program
- receiving medical care and services in a hospital-affiliated extended care facility

Because new technology and innovative planning result in new modes of health care delivery, the definition of a hospital patient is constantly changing. In the case of *Carle Foundation v. U.S.*,[8] the U.S. Court of Appeals for the Seventh Circuit reversed a lower court decision. The court held that sales by an exempt hospital pharmacy—part of a complex that included both an exempt hospital and a nonexempt clinic—to the clinic and patients of the clinic were unrelated because the sales were not for the hospital patients' convenience. The court held that the clinic patients were not hospital patients merely because the clinic did some outpatient testing for the hospital.

Subsequent cases have outlined exceptions to the *Carle Foundation* rule imposing UBI for outpatient sales and testing. Exceptions recognized by the courts include a rural exception (sole provider hospital in a small rural community),[9] teaching function exception (testing associated with teaching hospital),[10] and technologically advanced service exception (high-technology laboratory facility with unique facilities).

Another area of particular significance involves the sale of services by affiliated tax-exempt organizations to "patients" of related tax-exempt organizations within a reorganized health system. In one instance, the IRS reviewed the implementation of a reorganization by the hospital into a multicorporate system. The IRS ruled that the hospital's sale of pharmacy, laboratory, radiology, or other ancillary medical services to patients of related tax-exempt organizations within the system would be treated as sales to patients of the hospital and would not constitute UBI.[11]

SALE OF NONPATIENT SERVICES TO OTHER INSTITUTIONS

One factor that seems to influence the IRS's decision on whether nonpatient service (e.g., personnel, data processing) income constitutes UBI is the relationship between the organization providing the service and the recipient organization. The provision of such services to affiliated organizations is more likely to be considered "related" to the organization's exempt purpose. In contrast, the provision of services to an unrelated organization (taxable or tax-exempt) is more likely to result in a finding of UBI.

An exception to this general principle is found in IRC Section 513(e), which provides specific rules under which tax-exempt hospitals can render certain services to other tax-exempt or governmental hospitals and not recognize UBI. To come within the scope of Section 513(e), five basic requirements must be satisfied:

1. The services provided to the other organizations must be one or more of the services listed in Section 501(e)(1): data processing, purchasing, warehousing, billing and collection, food, clinical (including radiology), industrial engineering, laboratory, printing, communications, record center, and personnel (including selection, testing, training, and education) services. Laundry services are not included.
2. The services must be rendered to exempt hospitals that have an exempt purpose of providing medical care, hospital care, medical education, or research.
3. The services must be provided solely to hospitals that have facilities to serve not more than 100 inpatients.
4. Such services must further the exempt purpose of the recipient hospital.
5. The services must be provided at a fee or cost that does not exceed the actual cost of providing the services, including straight-line depreciation and a reasonable return on capital.

As a general rule, the services listed in Section 501(e)(1)(A) would be considered an unrelated trade or business when provided by a tax-exempt hospital even if provided to another hospital. Section 513(e) carves out a limited exception to this general rule. The exception does not apply to services not listed in Section 501(e)(1)(A), including laundry services.

GENERAL EXCEPTIONS TO THE RULE

A trade or business regularly carried on but not substantially related to the accomplishment of the organization's exempt purposes may escape taxation if it meets one of the following exceptions:

- a trade or business in which substantially all work is performed for the organization with volunteer labor (e.g., the operation of a retail store by an exempt orphanage where substantially all the work is performed by volunteers without compensation)
- a trade or business carried on primarily for the convenience of members, students, patients, or employees (e.g., the sale of drugs by a hospital pharmacy to employees)
- a trade or business that involves selling merchandise received by the organization as a gift or contribution (e.g., the operation of a hospital thrift shop where the merchandise being sold was donated)

PASSIVE INCOME MODIFICATIONS

Income that is passive in nature is not derived from competition with commercial enterprises and generally is not taxed. The types of passive income generally excluded are dividends, interest, annuities, royalties, and rents from real property. If passive income is earned from debt-financed property, all or a portion may be subject to tax.

Rent from real property is generally not subject to tax. On the other hand, rent from personal property is generally considered UBI. U.S. Treasury-issued regulations outline the situations in which rents will be considered UBI. Rents from real property based on gross receipts or sales are treated as passive and, therefore, are excluded from UBI unless based on the profits of the person renting the property.

One increasingly important provision in today's multientity structures is IRC Section 512(b)(13). It provides that exempt organizations cannot avoid UBI on rents, interest, or royalties under the passive income modification (1) if received from a taxable or tax-exempt controlled organization (80 percent owned or controlled) and (2) if that organization was formed to operate a taxable trade or business where a deduction is taken for the rents, interest, or royalties paid to the exempt parent organization. This may apply even though the controlled organization realized no immediate tax benefit from the deduction due to an operating loss. Rules for calculating this income are covered by Section 512(b)(13) and related regulations.

RULES GOVERNING DEBT-FINANCED INCOME AND PROPERTY

Passive income (rents from real property, dividends, and interest) is not subject to tax unless the property generating the income is debt financed, in which case the percentage of the gross income included as UBI is computed by dividing the average debt outstanding by the average amount of adjusted basis of the property for the taxable year. The same debt-to-basis ratio is used to compute the deduction amount allowed in determining the UBI. Only the straight-line method is allowable in computing depreciation expense for debt-financed property.

A portion of the capital gain or loss from the sale of debt-financed property is also included in UBI. The capital gain or loss is multiplied by the debt-to-basis ratio to determine the amount to be included in determining the UBI. To prevent an exempt organization from decreasing its presale debt to reduce the amount of taxable gain, the debt-to-basis ratio is based on the highest amount of acquisition indebtedness on the property during the 12-month period preceding the date of disposition. One remaining planning opportunity to shelter the gain from tax may be to retire the debt at least one year and one day before the sale of the property.

Debt-financed property includes any property held to produce income that was acquired with acquisition indebtedness, with certain exceptions. These exceptions include property used for purposes related to the organization's exempt purposes and property to the extent its income is already taxed as UBI.

One alternative for real property acquired with acquisition indebtedness is the neighborhood land rule. To qualify for this exception, the property must be located in the neighborhood of other property owned and used by the organization for exempt purposes. The organization must also acquire the property with the principal purpose of using it for exempt purposes within 10 years. This rule applies only to structures on the land when it is purchased and only if the intended use of the land requires that the structures be demolished.

Debt-financed property must be income producing and purchased with acquisition indebtedness. In general, acquisition indebtedness is determined on a property-by-property basis, and will exist whenever the indebtedness was incurred in acquiring or improving the property, or would not have been incurred "but for" the acquisition or improvement of such property. If indebtedness is incurred following the acquisition or improvement of the property, it will not constitute acquisition indebtedness unless its incurrence was "reasonably foreseeable" at the time of the acquisition or improvement.

If a mortgaged property is acquired by bequest or devise, the debt secured by the mortgage will not be treated as acquisition indebtedness for ten years following the time an organization receives the property. In certain situations, if an organization acquires property by gift subject to a mortgage, the debt secured by the mortgage will not be treated as acquisition indebtedness for ten years following the gift.

COMPUTING AND REPORTING UBI

UBI is reported annually on IRS Form 990-T, Exempt Organizations Business Income Tax Return, on or before the 15th day of the fifth month after the close of the taxable year. Form 990-T must be filed if the exempt organization has gross income from unrelated sources in excess of $1,000. An organization not meeting this threshold amount should consider filing Form 990-T if the unrelated activities produce a taxable loss. This will establish and document the loss for future reporting years.

If an organization does not report questionable activities on Form 990-T, it should disclose the income-producing activity and the gross receipts from the activity on the information return, Form 990. If this is done in good faith, the statute of limitations should begin to run when Form 990 is filed. If all the necessary facts are not disclosed, the statute of limitations does not begin because Form 990-T was never filed as required.

The expenses incurred by an exempt organization in operating an unrelated business generally are deductible if they are expenses normally deductible by a for-profit enterprise and are directly connected to the unrelated trade or business. If facilities and personnel are used for exempt and nonexempt purposes, a reasonable allocation has to be made between the two uses. For example, labor costs for employees working part time on an unrelated activity could be based on time spent. A federal court of appeals case stated that allocating dual expenses based on gross revenues from related and unrelated activities is reasonable.[12]

General, administrative, and other overhead expenses (including supervisory wages, accounting expenses, rent, and utilities) should also be allocated on a reasonable basis. Under current law, the allocation of allowable expenses for tax purposes need not agree with allocations utilized on cost reports, financial reports, and so forth. Exempt organizations should accumulate supporting data and document the logic on which the allocation of all indirect costs is based. If gross income is derived from an unrelated activity that exploits an exempt activity, such as advertising in an exempt organization's related periodical, special rules limit the amount of allowable deductions.

A tax-exempt corporation is taxed on UBI at the same rates as a taxable corporation, and a tax-exempt trust is taxed at the same rates as a taxable trust. Additionally, the alternative minimum tax applies to organizations subject to tax under IRC Section 511 with respect to items of tax preference that enter into the computation of taxable UBI. UBI—from profits and losses—is aggregated for each exempt organization. Net operating losses are allowed, as is a specific deduction up to $1,000, in computing the amount of income subject to tax. The specific deduction is not allowed in computing a net operating loss.

By highlighting the community benefits generated by the activity, by providing a clear description of how the activity is related to the organization's exempt purpose, and by distinguishing the organization's activities from similar activities conducted by for-profit organizations (e.g., charity care), the organization may be able to minimize taxes that might otherwise be due. It is therefore essential that tax-exempt organizations carefully consider tax planning strategies for UBI.

NOTES

1. *Greene County Medical Society Foundation v. U.S.*, 345 F. Supp. 900 (W.D. Mo. 1972).

2. *Clarence LaBelle Post No. 217 v. U.S.*, 580 F.2d 270 (8th Cir. 1978).

3. *Hi-Plains Hospital v. U.S.*, 670 F.2d 528, USCA 5 (1982).

4. *St. Luke's Hospital of Kansas City v. U.S.*, 494 F. Supp. 85 (W.D. Mo. 1980).

5. Treas. Reg. §1.513-1(c).

6. Idem. §1.513-1(d).

7. Rev. Rul. 68-376, 1968-2 CB 246.

8. *Carle Foundation v. U.S.*, 611 F.2d 1192 (7th Cir. 1979).

9. *Hi-Plains Hospital v. U.S.*, 670 F.2d 528 (5th Cir. 1982).

10. *St. Luke's Hospital* supra note 10.494 F. Supp. 85.

11. IRS Private Lett. Rul. 8512093.

12. *Disabled American Veterans v. U.S.*, 704 F.2d 1570 (1983).

Chapter 26

Physician Recruitment/Retention Programs

Donna Daugherty
Consultant, Arthur Andersen & Co.

Physician recruiting/retention programs have become a primary focus for health care entities. Payors are putting increased pressure on hospitals to reduce length of stay, thereby reducing the need for hospital beds. Additional pressure is present to switch to performing procedures from an inpatient basis to an outpatient basis. New methods of delivery have brought about new, alternative organizations designed to provide managed care. As a result, exempt hospitals have found themselves competing for quality physicians with other exempt hospitals, for-profit entities, and entities that provide other alternative methods of health care delivery. Hospitals have been forced to remain competitive by offering recruitment incentives to attract and retain qualified physicians to their medical staffs.

The first advantage for the hospital of a properly structured recruiting program is the development of a stronger referral base. Additional advantages are the ability to expand or preserve market share, expand medical staff coverage in areas that are underserved or in new areas selected for expansion, increase the hospital's ability to compete with other health care deliverers, permit more efficient use of facilities, and prevent physicians from competing either through the provision of services or through their affiliation wtih competitive entities.

Physicians are viewing recruitment/retention programs as ways of shifting risks of establishing new programs or practices away from themselves and onto the hospitals. Hospitals, in many cases, assume the risks of the development of new practices. Additionally, physicians are looking for ways to supplement their income levels either through new patient referrals or equity interests in health-related activities.

In structuring recruitment/retention programs, the hospital should begin by conducting a physician market need study to determine overall hospital and community needs. The hospital should be able to show a valid business purpose for instituting a recruitment program.

No one individual factor should be used in structuring the program. The hospital should review its demographic data, community support, and current medical staff composition before beginning negotiations with any physician. The overall recruitment plan should be discussed with hospital upper management and the board of directors to ensure their support and their awareness of all policies and procedures. All contracts should have a reasonable number of reviews and approval steps to ensure their compliance with all operational, medical, tax, and legal considerations.

TAX CONSIDERATIONS

Why the concern? Everyone asks why the concern with regard to physician contracts. Why not do whatever it takes to attract and retain physicians? Corporations have always offered recruitment bonuses and salary incentives to their employees. Why not just follow their example? Just what is the problem with physician recruitment/retention plans? In order to answer this last question, it is important to understand the rationale of a tax-exempt entity and the issue of inurement.

An entity receives its tax exemption by qualifying under Section 501(a) of the Internal Revenue Code. Hospitals obtain their exemption from Section 501(c)(3), which exempts organizations operated for charitable, religious, or educational purposes. Additionally, this code section dictates that no part of the net earnings of the entity can *inure* to the benefit of any shareholder or individual. Private shareholders or individuals are persons having a personal and private interest in the activities of the organization.

The regulations, which describe and outline code sections, state that in order for an organization to qualify as a 501(c)(3) organization, it must be organized and operated exclusively for one or more exempt purposes. They further state that an organization is not operated exclusively for one or more exempt purposes if its net earnings inure in whole or part to the benefit of private shareholders or individuals. The regulations go on to state that an organization must demonstrate that it is not organized or operated to benefit private interests such as "designated individuals, the creator or his family, shareholders of the organization, or persons controlled, directly or indirectly, by such private interests."[1]

The Internal Revenue Service (IRS) has unquestionably recognized that a hospital, which is established for the promotion of health, is a charitable activity. The IRS has also stated that physicians qualify as a private interest, since they "are persons who have a personal and private interest in the activities of the Hospital."[2] General Counsel Memorandum (GCM) 39670 expanded on this definition and stated that all persons who perform services for an organization have a personal and private interest and therefore possess the requisite relationship necessary to find private benefit or inurement.

In light of this relationship, how do hospitals contract with physicians in recruitment/retention programs? Hospitals must show that all transactions with related parties, in this case physicians, are at arm's length and are based on reasonable compensation or fair market value. Additionally, they must be able to show that the benefits received by the physicians are incidental to the overall benefits received by the hospital and community at large.

REASONABLE COMPENSATION

The IRS in GCM 39498 recognized that exempt entities must offer incentives to attract qualified physicians to provide quality health care. While a GCM is an answer to an IRS reviewer's question and not binding on the IRS, the IRS usually follows the position taken. In reviewing physician contracts, the IRS takes a hard look at individual facts and circumstances to determine whether inurement is present.

It is important to note that in GCM 39498 the IRS recognized a hospital's need to offer a one-time recruitment bonus that would not be contingent on services to be rendered, but rather based on the need for a certain type of physician within a community. These recruitment incentives include moving expenses of households and medical practices, loans or loan guarantees, and/or assistance in establishing medical practices, such as tenant finish-out, discounted rents, and office and administrative services. In this GCM, the hospital guaranteed a physician's annual income for a period of two years. The physician was under no obligation to repay any of the guarantee unless the amounts earned during the two-year period were in excess of the guarantee. The physician was also required to perform certain educational services as well as provide services in the hospital's emergency room.

The IRS stated that "the Hospital's proposed revised guaranteed minimum annual income contract must be examined to determine the effect, if any, on the Hospital's exclusive pursuit of its charitable purpose. We [IRS] view the question of subsidies under the Hospital's physician recruitment program to be essentially a question of whether a given compensation arrangement comports with the requirements of exemption."[3] The hospital, in this case, could not show that all of the benefits paid to the physician would fall under "reasonable compensation." The hospital had not put a ceiling on the total dollar value of the incentive offered.

The IRS recognized certain factors that should be taken into account in determining "reasonable compensation." Some of the factors the IRS recognized are the competitive marketplace and the physician's reluctance to relocate to a given area. Other factors that should be considered are physician responsibilities and qualifications, the physician's contribution to the hospital's exempt purpose, the hospital's size, and the physician's time devoted to the hospital's needs. The GCM does not state per se that all guarantees of a physician's salary are a violation of its exempt purpose. Rather, it states that all incentives, whether in cash or kind, must be considered, with each case being reviewed on its individual facts and circumstances. The GCM stressed that all transactions should be between unrelated parties and at arm's length.

GCM 39598 reviewed a physician recruitment transaction that was conducted through a subsidiary organization, a medical office building. In this case, a separate tax-exempt organization was created to master-lease a medical office building from a group of physicians. The subsidiary then subleased the space back to the same physicians for use in their private practices at a rental rate below its original lease rate. The exempt entity provided billing, collection, secretarial, and nursing services. Over a three-year period, the new tax-exempt subsidiary generated significant financial losses. In actuality, the new tax-exempt subsidiary absorbed losses, both operationally and on the costs associated with unleased space. These losses should have been recognized by the physicians, that is, the actual owners of the medical office building. The tax-exempt affiliate lost its tax-exempt status, since it could not show that the transaction resulted in an overall community benefit. Additionally, the IRS reviewed the effect that the above transaction would have on all affiliated tax-exempt entities, including the hospital. Although in this case the IRS did not pierce the corporate veil, it reserves the right to do so when the facts and circumstances warrant.

Two key points came out of this GCM. The IRS expanded on the concept that private benefit must be incidental in both a qualitative and quantitative sense. In order to be incidental in a qualitative sense, the benefit must be a necessary concomitant of the activity that benefits the public at large, that is, the activity can be accomplished only by benefiting certain private individuals. To be incidental in a quantitative sense, the private benefit must not be substantial after considering the overall public benefit conferred by the activity.[4]

The qualitative aspects include the ability to show other nonquantifiable components for recruiting/retention of the physician. Physicians are viewed as related parties to hospitals and other tax-exempt entities, and therefore the exempt entity should be able to show that the deal was not structured to be a conduit for the channeling of funds to the physicians.

In reviewing the quantitative aspects, certain considerations must be questioned. It is important to document the fair market value of the service, property, or space being provided; the dollar value of all of the benefits to the physicians; and, most important, the dollar value of all of the benefits to the community. In this case, the hospital could not show that the transaction was structured at fair market value and that the physician benefits were not incidental to the benefits received by the community as a whole.

The second key point outlined was the IRS' position regarding its ability to pierce the corporate veil. The IRS has stated that an affiliate entity must be organized for a bona fide purpose of its own and not a mere sham or instrumentality of the parent. A bona fide purpose can be shown through a valid business purpose. Additionally, the parent organization should not have day-to-day control of the subsidiary. The affiliate entity should not be structured to operate merely as a department of the parent. The subsidiary should be able to show that it is separate and distinct from the hospital. It should have its own board meetings, books and records, bank accounts, separate employees, and separate officers and administrators.

GCM 39646 clarifies GCM 39598 with regard to the IRS's ability to pierce the corporate veil when an organization has a multitiered structure. This GCM states that if funds merely pass through one tax-exempt entity to another, and an inurement situation exists, the exemption status of both organizations can be affected. A hospital cannot insulate itself from an inurement charge simply by setting up and funding a new tax exempt entity. (While the GCM does not deal with a taxable/tax-exempt situation, care should be taken since the IRS could easily apply the same logic.)

DOCUMENTATION AND EVALUATION

The first goal in the development of a recruitment/retention plan should be the identification of the overall business plan. Once a business plan has been developed, the hospital should begin to identify the types of incentives it will provide and what the impact and risks of each incentive will be.

All incentives should be identified and quantified. Direct incentives should be valued based on their cost. Indirect costs should be documented and, where possible, quantified. The hospital should show, where possible, the additional benefit of a physician within a certain subspecialty. It is important not to structure an arrangement strictly on a physician's ability to refer patients.

All duties, responsibilities, qualifications, and restrictions of both parties should be addressed and identified. Appropriate monitoring and follow-up procedures should be established. Regular reporting of contract status should be made to upper management and/or the board as appropriate.

TYPES OF SUBSIDIES

Relocation Expenses

Relocation expenses are expenses related to the payment or reimbursement of moving expenses associated with moving the physician's personal belongings as well as his or her office practice. Relocation expenses should be limited to actual expenses of moving his or her household and office belongings and expenses for setting up a residence and office in the new loca-

tion. All payments should be documented to show reasonableness.

Rental Subsidies

The IRS has, through numerous GCM and private letter rulings, allowed a tax-exempt entity to offer rental subsidies to physicians to induce them to affiliate with the exempt's medical office buildings. Hospitals have shown the benefit of filling their medical office buildings with medical personnel who will be available to serve their patients.

Rental subsidies should be short-term in nature. Subsidies should be tied to rental agreements that are negotiated at arm's length and are for a period of time that will help to show the community benefit derived.

Leasehold Improvements

Leasehold improvements or tenant finish-out allowances are also used to attract physicians to related medical office buildings. All tenant allowances should be tied to a long-term contract and be required to be repaid if the contract is terminated without cause by the physician.

Loans or Loan Guarantees

All loans and loan guarantees (guaranteeing of a loan by the hospital at a bank or other financial institution) should be shown to be for the community benefit. Interest should be charged on all loans and based on market conditions. All loans should be adequately secured and shown to be a good investment for the hospital.

The IRS has clarified that a loan does not have to go into default in order for inurement to be present. The potential for inurement is enough for the IRS to revoke the tax-exempt status of an exempt entity. Therefore, loan guarantees should be properly structured in order to ensure that the IRS does not deem these guarantees as inurement. Hospitals should require adequate security to offset any potential losses. The hospital should charge a loan-guarantee fee based on market conditions and degree of risk.

Income Subsidies and Guarantees

Income subsidies are amounts guaranteed to a physician based on the income the physician generates in private practice. These subsidies can be structured under two alternatives. Under the first, the subsidy is structured as a loan, and the physician is required to reimburse the hospital for all amounts advanced. In many cases, interest accumulates on the subsidy. In the second case, the hospital's subsidy to the physician is treated as compensation and is not required to be repaid.

The IRS has stressed that in order to avoid the inurement concerns, the subsidies should be structured as loans with interest based on fair market value. The loans should be structured to include a cap on the maximum amount allowed to be paid by the exempt entity, and the loans preferably should be for a period not to exceed two years. This maximum amount should be used in determining whether the overall recruitment/retention package is reasonable.

OTHER CONSIDERATIONS

Medicare Fraud and Abuse

Contracting with physicians to provide medical services through a physician recruitment/retention program can create Medicare fraud and abuse problems. Fraud and abuse occur when an individual solicits, offers, or pays a physician any type of remuneration, either directly or indirectly, in cash or in kind, for referring a patient. As stated earlier, the IRS requires an organization to quantify all of the components of the recruitment/retention program. Most hospitals, as part of this process, quantify expected admissions. It is very important that at no time does the hospital state or imply that the contract is being offered and is contingent upon the physician's admitting his or her patients to the hospital. This would include ensuring that no covenants of the contract include the provision that the physician cannot admit patients at other institutions.

Violations of Medicare's fraud and abuse provisions can be detected many ways. The most common methods are through complaints by current or past employees or physicians, complaints by disgruntled competitors, or through audits of unrelated areas. Both the hospital and the physician can be subject to penalties and criminal conviction if found guilty. Violations carry fines of up to $25,000, imprisonment up to 5 years, or both.

The Medicare Catastrophic Act of 1988 contains a provision that requires the Inspector General of Health and Human Services to issue regulations regarding safe harbors for payment provisions that would not be considered criminal offenses under the Medicare fraud and abuse statutes. The Inspector General has issued proposed regulations with the final regulations due out tentatively by August 1989. Safe harbors are provided for in the area of physician recruitment, referral services, and sales of physician practices.

Antitrust

Care should be taken to ensure that any physician recruitment/retention program is consistent with federal and state antitrust laws. The program/contract should be carefully written to ensure that competitors cannot charge the hospital with price fixing, maintaining exclusively of a program or service, restraint of trade, or contracting to divide or allocate a specific market or service. As with Medicare fraud and abuse, violations are usually detected by disgruntled competitors, either hospitals or physicians.

Annual Reports and Filings

Once a hospital has determined that the physician has been paid compensation, it must determine whether the parties involved have an employer/employee relationship or whether the physician is acting as an independent contractor. All components of the recruitment package should be reviewed and, where appropriate, properly reported to the IRS and/or state reporting agency. Examples of filing requirements include Form W-2 or 1099, state Federal Unemployment Tax Act (FUTA) tax forms, and proper reporting on Form 990, if appropriate.

Corporate Practice of Medicine and Other State Laws

All applicable state laws and statutes should be reviewed prior to contract negotiations in order to ensure compliance. Some states have an active corporate practice of medicine statute that prohibits any organization from providing the unlicensed practice of medicine. At minimum, all medically related decisions must be made by qualified physicians.

Reimbursement Issues

An analysis of reimbursement considerations should be made prior to ratifying a physician contract. Medicare reimbursement limitations may apply when a hospital contracts with a physician for the provision of services. The reimbursement structure may vary depending on whether the physician is an employee or independent contractor or is based in-house or in a free-standing practice.

SUMMARY

In summary, all nonprofit hospitals should have or develop a policy regarding physician recruitment and retention plans. The policy should address all potential areas of risk regarding physician contracts.

A hospital should document all of the quantitative and qualitative reasons for entering into a contract. This documentation should outline the benefits to the community and to the organization, including how the transaction aids in furthering its exempt status. All benefits to the physician should be acknowledged and documented. Additionally, the hospital should show that the contract is the result of arm's length negotiations, and that the *overall* compensation package is reasonable.

The IRS will not issue an advance ruling as to whether compensation is reasonable.[5] Therefore, it is extremely important for the hospital to develop documentation that is as specific and extensive as possible. Legal and/or tax opinions may be advisable on certain proposed arrangements in order to minimize exposure areas.

NOTES

1. Section 1.501(c)(3)-1(d)(1)(ii) of Internal Revenue Code of 1986.

2. General Counsel Memorandum (GCM) 39498, January 28, 1986.

3. GCM 39498, January 28, 1986.

4. GCM 39598, December 8, 1986.

5. Revenue Procedure 87-3, Section 3.01(7)1987-1 C.B. 523.

Chapter 27

Joint Ventures: Benefits and Pitfalls

Dawson Taylor
Partner, Arthur Andersen & Co.

The health care industry has already experienced the first wave of significant joint venture activity. In the wake of the initial onslaught it is estimated that nearly 70 percent of hospital joint ventures are headed for failure.[1] These failures are attributed to a variety of factors, including lack of experienced management, "catch-up"-oriented planning, insufficient investigation of the market, and, in some cases, overreliance on tax aspects to create good economics.

Industry observers have noted that any joint venture activity that relies solely on tax benefits as its economic mainstay is a candidate for failure.[2] Despite the outcry of health care industry commentators against tax-motivated deals, the tax aspects of joint venture activities will continue to be an important factor in the overall economics of any health care venture.

Recent legislation has significantly changed the tax economics of many joint venture arrangements, particularly those that are capital intensive in nature. The Internal Revenue Service (IRS) has also been active in exercising its interpretive function in areas of concern to exempt health care providers, including the propriety of a tax-exempt organization acting as a general partner in joint venture activities and the continuing exempt status of exempt health care venturers.

TYPICAL FORMS OF JOINT VENTURES

Joint ventures can take a variety of forms, including partnerships, leases, service contracts, and corporations. They are often formed between tax-exempt hospitals and taxable partners (e.g., physicians), combining the financial strengths and managerial skills of the hospitals with the specialized medical skills of the physicians.

Some of the various forms of joint ventures are summarized below. While the accompanying illustrations focus on a joint venture between a hospital and a group of radiologists, the principles may be applied to virtually any joint venture.

- *Partnerships*: A hospital can form a joint venture with a group of radiologists to provide magnetic resonance imaging services to patients. The venture might take the form of a partnership, as shown in Figure 27-1, wherein the hospital and the radiologists share ownership of the equipment through the joint venture, which bills a service charge to the patient. The radiologists bill their professional fees directly to the patients.

This chapter is reprinted from *Topics in Health Care Financing*, Vol. 14, No. 4, pp. 47–52, Aspen Publishers, Inc., © Summer 1988.

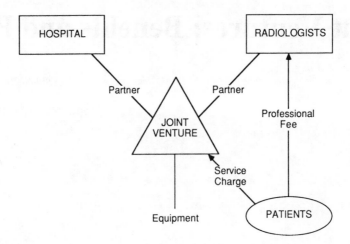

Figure 27-1 Partnerships

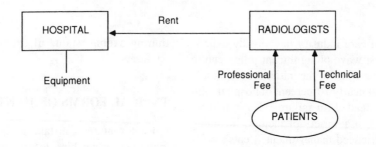

Figure 27-2 Leases

- *Leases*: Alternatively, the hospital might purchase the equipment itself and lease it to the radiologists. This joint venture structure is shown in Figure 27-2.
- *Service contract*: Under a service contract, a hospital might provide technical and administrative personnel to operate equipment owned by the radiologists. This arrangement is illustrated in Figure 27-3.
- *Corporation*: For reasons of legal liability or other business considerations, the hospital and the physicians may choose to operate the joint venture in the corporate form, as shown in Figure 27-4.

In addition to the above examples, there are many other ways to structure joint ventures. This flexibility enables the participants to select a structure that is custom tailored to their particular needs.

EFFECTS OF TAX REFORM

Tax reform has had a dramatic effect on hospital-physician joint ventures due to the extension of depreciable lives of property, the elimination of capital gains benefits, the repeal of the investment tax credit, and limits on passive losses. Joint ventures not involving taxable participants have not been significantly affected by tax reform.

Depreciation

While accelerated cost recovery system depreciation was designed primarily to provide an investment incentive, the new rules are designed to reflect depreciation more evenly over the economic or useful lives of particular assets. Although deductions are still accelerated compared with pre-1981

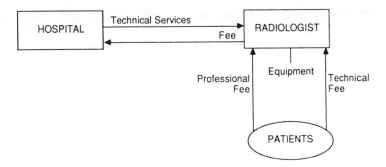

Figure 27-3 Service Contracts

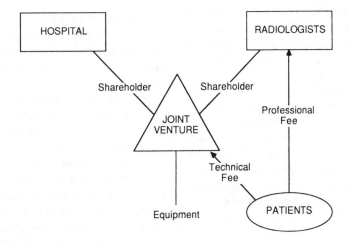

Figure 27-4 Corporate Form

law, the new recovery period for nonresidential real property of 31.5 years is 66 percent longer than the depreciable life allowed under the pretax reform provisions. For medical equipment, tax depreciation continues to be relatively generous. (Tax practitioners will need to consider also the effects of Internal Revenue Code Section 168(h), which deals with the tax-exempt use of property.)

Capital Gains

The elimination of capital gains is perhaps even more significant. Previously, in typical real estate ventures, a large portion of the expected return for the equity investor came from appreciation in the value of the property. Furthermore, the ability to claim depreciation deductions at ordinary income rates and to recover those

deductions at capital gains rates was very important in shielding the equity investor from taxation on inflationary, as opposed to real, gains. The elimination of preferential treatment for capital gains puts a much greater emphasis on current return and inflation risk, and real estate may become less attractive to investors.

Investment Tax Credit

Tax reform also repealed the investment tax credit (ITC), which had served as a source of financing for many joint ventures. In general, assets placed in service after December 31, 1985, are not eligible for any ITC. This change, perhaps more than any other, reflects the congressional desire to remove direct tax incentives for investment in machinery and equipment. The repeal of ITC will be likely to cause investors to focus on the pretax rate of return from investments in equipment.

Passive Losses

"Passive activity" limitations will have a major impact on individual physicians and professional corporations participating in health care joint ventures. The concept of the new passive activity limitations is deceptively simple. According to Section 501 of the Tax Reform Act of 1986, the tax attributes (i.e., income, deductions, and credits) of a taxpayer's passive activities are segregated from those of other taxable activities. Income and loss within each of the resulting categories may be netted, but any aggregate net loss from passive activities cannot be used to offset net income from other sources, and tax credits arising from passive activities can be used only to reduce the tax attributable to passive activity income. In other words, a physician may not use losses from a limited partnership to offset income earned from the practice of medicine.

STRUCTURING NEW JOINT VENTURES

In the past, a limited partnership was a popular structure for attracting new physicians to medical office buildings (MOBs). Since the passive loss rules severely restrict the ability of an individual investor to use losses from a limited partnership interest, thoughtful consideration should be given to using the condominium format for structuring an MOB joint venture. Under the condominium format, the physician's ownership of the building is integrated with his or her medical practice, thus avoiding the negative effect of the passive loss limitations. Of course the legal and operational aspects of condominiums differ from partnerships and need to be carefully evaluated along with the tax aspects.

Since the restrictions on benefits of leases of property to tax-exempt organizations do not apply to high-technology medical equipment or certain short-term leases, the use of lease financ-

ing, funded by physicians, may be attractive in some circumstances.

Additionally, consideration should be given by hospitals to the creation of partnerships that would generate passive income. Such partnerships will be attractive to physician investors who will seek passive income to permit the use of passive losses from prior tax-oriented investments.

PROTECTING TAX-EXEMPT STATUS

A number of pressures in today's environment may cause tax-exempt hospitals to enter into arrangements that may threaten their exempt status. One potential threat is inurement, since exempt hospitals may feel the need to provide added financial incentives to attract new physicians who are willing to share joint venture risks and to admit patients to hospital facilities.

The IRS has recognized that certain transactions entered into in furtherance of exempt purpose may result in the receipt of "incidental" benefit by private persons, without jeopardizing an organization's tax-exempt status.[3] In the view of the IRS, a private benefit is incidental only when it is secondary to demonstrable public benefit and necessary to the achievement of the public goals of the exempt entity.

Potential sources of more than "incidental" benefit include joint venture deals that allow participation by individuals considered to be "insiders" of the exempt organization; stop loss, loan, or other types of operating guarantees by the exempt partner; and operating deficit coverage arrangements. Other sources are non–fair-market value rental arrangements; unreasonable compensation arrangements; and loans whose provisions for market interest, security, payment terms, and provisions in the case of default indicate that unreasonable benefits are being conferred upon private individuals.

When an exempt organization serves as a general partner in a limited partnership, it may face a conflict between its fiduciary obligation to maximize the profits of the partnership and its statutory obligation to operate exclusively for charitable purposes. In a recent General Counsel Memorandum, the IRS indicated that exempt organizations would not necessarily jeopardize their exempt status by serving as general partners, but that the facts of each case would be carefully evaluated.[4] Further, the Counsel stated that efforts to avoid inurement by limiting the liability of the exempt organization could create other issues, such as the classification of the entity as a partnership.

If a contemplated transaction presents a risk of inurement, the use of a taxable participant may provide limited protection to the exempt status of the sponsoring organization. Many consultants routinely recommend the use of taxable subsidiaries where inurement is an issue. While this approach may be helpful, the inurement insulation provided by the taxable corporation is limited where an exempt organization provides funds to the taxable venturer or its unrelated partners.

Since the issue is whether the exempt organization is operated exclusively for exempt purposes or whether any of its earnings inure to private individuals, it is irrelevant whether it deals directly in the venture or creates a corporate veil through a separate entity. If the exempt entity funds a taxable corporation that is providing private benefits, the resulting inurement may be attributed back to the exempt entity.[5] In addition, if inurement exists at the subsidiary level, investment in the subsidiary may be in contravention of the shareholder's exempt purpose.

The same principle would apply if an exempt subsidiary were used to protect the exempt parent. As with the taxable subsidiary, a certain amount of insulation is achieved but the degree of insulation cannot be quantified, and is probably nominal. Any participation by an exempt entity in a joint venture calls for careful evaluation of all the relationships and economic factors in the arrangement.

Despite the effects of tax reform, joint ventures should continue to serve as alternative financing sources for hospitals, and the trend toward providing care in less acute settings should present additional opportunities for joint ventures. By exercising effective management of economically sound ventures and attending to the important tax aspects, a hospital will be better positioned for profitability in the new age of competition.

NOTES

1. K. Sandrick, "Joint Ventures: Why Do 7 Out of 10 Fail?" *Hospitals* 60, no. 24 (1986): 40–44.

2. K. Kaufman, M. Hall, and D. Higgins, "Joint Ventures Revisited: We're All in This Together." *Healthcare Financial Management* 40, no. 3 (1986): 24–30, 32.

3. General Counsel Memorandum (GCM) 39498, April 24, 1986.

4. GCM 39546, August 15, 1986.

5. GCM 39646, June 30, 1987.

Chapter 28

Employer Executive Compensation and Benefits after the Tax Reform Act of 1986

Andrew E. Zuckerman
Attorney, Sanders, Schnabel, and Brandenburg

William H. Hranchak
Manager, Arthur Andersen & Co.

As tax-exempt hospitals strive to obtain and retain qualified personnel, they must develop compensation packages that fit the needs of the institution and individual employees. Compensation planning for administrative and medical personnel overlap, particularly where physicians are classified as employees for tax purposes. These tax rules continue to be restrictive in many areas. However, a hospital can be creative in developing compensation packages that provide incentive to employees while remaining cost effective for the hospital. Careful consideration of the tax implications of compensation plans can help hospitals reduce unanticipated tax problems.

The Tax Reform Act of 1986 (1986 Act) has had a major impact on employee benefits, in many instances broadening plan coverage and possibly increasing benefit levels and, therefore, costs. Unfortunately, the 1986 Act significantly restricted the ability of tax-exempt organizations to offer their employees deferred compensation. The vast majority of changes to these programs became effective in 1989, so the time for review and analysis is now.

This chapter is reprinted from *Topics in Health Care Financing*, Vol. 14, No. 4, pp. 61–72, Aspen Publishers, Inc., © Summer 1988.

INCENTIVE COMPENSATION

The hospital industry continues to use incentive compensation to a great degree because it effectively increases employee productivity and reduces costs. In an industry faced with increased competition for revenue and capital, incentive compensation is an especially valuable tool, particularly for executive and midlevel management employees.[1]

To date, few exempt hospitals have implemented incentive compensation arrangements, for a number of reasons.[2,3] Historically, the prevalent attitude among trustees and management has been that incentive compensation is inconsistent with the charitable mission of an exempt hospital. Only recently have competitive concerns and tax law changes focused attention on the benefits of and need for such arrangements. Even where the need has been identified and the philosophical objections reconciled, a significant deterrent has existed in the possible adverse impact that incentive compensation might have on a hospital's exempt status. This concern is warranted because the Internal Revenue Service (IRS) has occasionally taken the position that incentive compensation constitutes prohibited inurement of an organization's net earnings in violation of its exempt status. Although recent developments indicate that the

IRS and Congress are relaxing this position, planning for such compensation arrangements deserves careful attention by exempt hospitals.

Incentive compensation (also called contingent or variable compensation) is remuneration that is tied to specific employer objectives and is paid to an employee in place of or, more frequently, in addition to base salary and fringe benefits. Incentive compensation ranges from the bonus voted by the trustees for the chief executive officer after a "good year" to the adoption of a formalized profit-sharing plan covering all hospital employees. These arrangements take on a variety of characteristics depending on what basis the awards are determined (e.g., formula versus discretionary), the manner of payment (e.g., current versus deferred), and the number and classification of employees covered by the arrangement (e.g., management only versus all employees).

The IRS Position

While the IRS has expressed concern over various types of incentive compensation, it has focused attention on arrangements based on a percentage of the organization's income.[4] The position set forth by the IRS states that percentage-of-income arrangements will not jeopardize a hospital's exempt status ". . .provided the specialist (1) does not control the hospital, (2) enters into an agreement with the hospital that was negotiated at arm's length, and (3) receives an amount for services rendered that is reasonable in terms of the responsibilities and activities assumed under the contract."[5]

Until very recently, when taxpayers requested approval of percentage-of-income arrangements, the IRS responded that such arrangements were inherently inconsistent with an exempt organization's charitable purpose and that the establishment of such a plan would jeopardize the organization's tax-exempt status. An internal IRS memorandum, written in February 1980 and released in May 1983, indicated that the IRS had reconsidered its position, at least with respect to "qualified plans." The memorandum concluded that such an arrangement did not necessarily jeopardize tax-exempt status if it were "properly conceived and administered."[6] A plan would satisfy this requirement if it met the standards and limitations established for qualified employee benefit plans under the Employee Retirement Income Security Act of 1974 (ERISA, Pub. L. No. 93-406) and the Internal Revenue Code (IRC). The 1986 Act ultimately provided congressional approval for profit-sharing–type plans.

An IRS training manual indicates that although contingent compensation arrangements are not "*per se* improper," the determination of whether inurement exists would be based on the facts and circumstances similar to those mentioned above, while the ". . . facts and circumstances should not reflect a significant incentive for the executive to promote his own interests at the expense of the charitable endeavors of his exempt employer."[7]

Another recent internal IRS memorandum stated that profit-sharing–type incentive compensation plans covering a broad base of employees would not affect the organization's tax-exempt status. One example provided in the memorandum permitted management personnel to participate in the arrangement.[8] In a more recent private letter ruling (unpublished at the time this chapter was drafted), the IRS approved an incentive compensation plan not based on profits that covered only management employees where the award was "reasonable." Thus, certain nonqualified plans currently being considered by tax-exempt organizations will be acceptable to the IRS.

Although the IRS warns taxpayers and its own agents that private letter rulings may not be used as precedent, those rulings are generally indicative of the IRS's current position. However, because of IRS concerns, hospitals planning to establish any incentive compensation plan should consider obtaining their own ruling. At the minimum, hospitals should consult a tax adviser familiar with exempt organizations and related issues.

Reasonable Compensation

An employee's compensation may jeopardize a hospital's tax-exempt status if it is determined to be "unreasonable." To determine whether an employee's compensation is reasonable, all components of compensation—including incentive amounts—are aggregated. Compensation satisfies the reasonableness requirement if the amount is reasonable in relation to the services being rendered. Even if this test is met, the compensation must be made in consideration of services rendered and not as a gift or a distribution equivalent to a dividend.

To determine whether compensation is reasonable for services rendered, the courts generally consider what position is held; what hours are worked; what duties are performed; how important the employee is to the success of the organization; whether the employee's salary is comparable with the salaries of similar employees for similar services; and what the organization's size is as indicated by revenue, volume, or capital value, as well as business and general economic conditions.

DEFERRED COMPENSATION

Deferred compensation plans are among the most valuable compensation tools available to employers of high-income individuals. These plans allow employees to temporarily exclude from gross income a portion of their annual earnings by crediting or paying that portion into a plan while postponing taxation of the deferred income until payments are made to the employees. This is an especially advantageous tax planning tool for individuals who expect their retirement income to be substantially lower than their current income. Employees can save taxes to the extent that they can defer current compensation to lower-income retirement years.

Not all deferred compensation arrangements are tax-exempt and some arrangements allow employees and employers more favorable tax treatment than others. A hospital should carefully analyze the attributes of the three basic deferred compensation arrangements currently being used by health care institutions: nonqualified plans, qualified plans (as discussed below), and Section 403(b) plans.

NONQUALIFIED PLANS

It is often difficult or impossible to provide similar benefits to all classes of hospital employ-

ees. An employer can select those employees to be covered under a nonqualified plan, with tax deferral benefits available to participating employees; however, the employer generally is not allowed a tax deduction until the deferred income is actually paid to the employee. This is obviously not a detriment to an exempt hospital. The two fundamental types of nonqualified plans are funded and unfunded.

Funded Plans

A funded plan often takes the form of employer or employee contributions to an independent trust or insurance company. Alternatively, the hospital could use the funds to purchase a nonqualified annuity contract with the employee as the beneficiary. Because the deferred income would be an asset beyond the control of the hospital, the employee would be sure that the hospital's creditors or trustee in bankruptcy could not reach the funds. This advantage is not available if the nonqualified plan is unfunded. However, like qualified plans, funded nonqualified plans can be subject to onerous ERISA requirements.

The primary objective of deferred compensation plans is to defer taxation of a portion of the employee's income. As a general rule, an employee is taxed on income paid to a trust, or paid to purchase annuity premiums, at the time of the payment, unless the employee's right to the deferred income is subject to substantial risk of forfeiture (SRF). IRC Section 83 addresses whether a SRF exists. If an employee's rights to deferred compensation are subject to that type of risk, the amount paid in the current year will escape tax. When the risk disappears, the value of the employee's interest in the trust or annuity contract will be taxed to the employee, whether or not it is distributed to that individual. Typically, the deferred income is paid to the employee as it is vested.

One method commonly used to ensure the existence of a SRF is to mandate that employees work for the employer-hospital for a given number of years before their rights become vested. This can tie a key employee to a hospital in addition to providing a gradual taxation of the deferred compensation. If the employee leaves before becoming completely vested, the un-vested amount is forfeited.

Unfunded Plans

In the case of unfunded plans, no funds are contributed or paid to an outside party but instead are reflected as a hospital liability. Such plans can provide that a balance accrues interest until withdrawal.

An unfunded, nonqualified retirement plan has few of the attributes of its funded counter-part. Under an unfunded plan, the employee receives an unsecured nonnegotiable contract right—the hospital's promise to pay the deferred portion of the employee's income in later years. Unfunded assets must still be subject to the claims of the hospital's general creditors. How-ever, the IRS has ruled privately that a plan will be considered unfunded even if a trust is estab-lished, as long as it is subject to the employer's judgment and bankruptcy creditors.[9,10] This area permits employees to use deferred compen-sation trusts (Rabbi trusts) while obtaining a degree of assurance that their deferred income cannot be withdrawn by an action of their employer.[11]

Such arrangements can provide for immediate vesting and still result in tax deferral as long as the employee generally cannot demand and receive any specified portion of his or her deferred compensation. The key to the timing of the taxation of deferred compensation is the moment at which the employee obtains control over the deferred income.

Because the unfunded, nonqualified retire-ment plan is not subject to the complicated SRF rules under Section 83, these arrangements nor-mally are more flexible than funded plans. Employees must be aware that they exchange some measure of security for the advantage of having nonforfeitable rights to their deferred income.

The 1986 Act restricted the ability of employ-ees of tax-exempt entities to defer compensation through unfunded arrangements by extending the rules and limitations of IRC Section 457, which formerly applied only to government entities such as government and district hospi-tals, to all tax-exempt entities for amounts deferred under plans set up after 1986. Conse-quently, deferrals by an executive with respect to a given taxable year are limited to the lesser of one-third of the employee's annual compensa-tion or $7,500. The limitation must also be reduced dollar for dollar by any amounts contrib-uted to a Section 403(b) annuity or 401(k) plan.

Tax-Sheltered Annuities

Hospitals and similar tax-exempt institutions have a uniquely advantageous retirement plan alternative: the tax-sheltered annuity under IRC Section 403(b). Most organizations qualifying as exempt under IRC Section 501(c)(3) are eligible to use a 403(b) plan. State, county, local, and city hospitals may not be eligible for such plans because they are generally not 501(c)(3) organizations.

The primary tax advantage of a 403(b) plan is that a portion of the employee's income can be deferred; invested funds are allowed to grow untaxed until withdrawal during retirement. Before 1989, 403(b) plans that permitted indi-viduals to make pretax contributions by reducing their pay (salary reduction) did not have to cover all hospital employees and could be used solely for key administrative employees. For years beginning after 1988, 403(b) plans must generally satisfy the same coverage and nondiscrimina-tion rules applicable to qualified retirement plans, including those for matching employer contributions.

This plan can be financed through a salary reduction program under which the participating employee either agrees to a salary reduction or foregoes a salary increase; the amount of reduc-tion or the future increase is contributed to the 403(b) plan. Beginning in 1989, the opportunity to make salary reduction contributions of a mini-mum of $200 was made available to all employ-ees if executives made such an election.

Contribution Limits

Salary reduction contributions to a 403(b) plan generally are limited to the lesser of (1) a formula (20 percent of annual compensation

Table 28-1 Congressional Offset Rules

If any combination of 401(k) and 403(b) salary reduction equals	then	Maximum 457 deferral equals
$ 0		$7,500
$2,000		5,500
4,000		3,500
6,000		1,500
7,000 [max. 401(k)]		500
8,000 [e.g., $7,000 401 (k) and $1,000 403 (b)]		0
9,500 [e.g., $7,000 401 (k) and $2,500 403 (b)]		0

times years of service) minus prior excludable contributions, (2) 25 percent of the employee's compensation, or (3) $9,500 (reduced by the 1986 Act from $30,000). In some cases, a hospital can make certain elections that allow contributions in excess of these amounts. In practice, some hospitals have not monitored the pre-1986 limitations and are now experiencing problems on examinations by the IRS. Although the salary reduction limit has been reduced from $30,000 to $9,500, through 1988 the employer may make employer contributions to a plan on behalf of the employee of the difference between the employee's salary reduction contribution and $30,000 (subject to a 25-percent-of-compensation limitation).

Interaction of Executive Deferral Arrangements

As stated above, individuals may defer varying amounts of income depending on the arrangement selected. However, to prevent excess deferrals by any executive, Congress has provided for offset rules, which are illustrated in Table 28-1.

QUALIFIED RETIREMENT PLANS

These plans continue to play a significant role in the employee benefit package. The major attributes of qualified retirement or pension plans are the following:

- the benefits of the plan must be generally available to all employees
- all contributions are made to a properly established tax-exempt trust
- employer contributions generally are currently deductible
- employees are taxed only when the income is withdrawn
- generally, income the trust earns on the funds contributed will not be taxed because it is tax exempt
- advantageous tax provisions come into play at retirement, including a special five-year averaging provision

The special tax benefits afforded qualified retirement plans come with corresponding costs. Profit-sharing, retirement, or pension plans must meet ERISA requirements to be classified as qualified.

In the 1986 Act, Congress extensively modified the rules for these arrangements. Numerous technical changes broaden the numbers of rank-and-file employees who must be covered by these plans and ensure that highly compensated individuals do not receive plan benefits out of proportion to those of rank-and-file employees. Virtually all qualified plans will have to be amended to meet these new rules generally effective in 1989.

Nondiscrimination Requirements

The area of major change pertaining to qualified retirement plans is nondiscrimination. These changes include

- new rules for matching employer contributions (effective 1987)
- tighter rules for the integration of plans with Social Security
- more rapid minimum vesting standards
- modifications to the minimum coverage requirements
- new minimum participation requirements

Monitoring these plans is suggested to ensure that the discrimination rules are satisfied. This will increase the costs of maintaining a plan.

Profit-Sharing Plans

Over the years there has been much controversy over whether a tax-exempt organization could maintain a qualified profit-sharing plan. Profit-sharing plans are popular becuase they provide the flexibility of not requiring a contribution in an unprofitable year and incur relatively lower administrative cost when compared with other qualified retirement arrangements. Congress, in the 1986 Act, resolved the controversy by creating a new category of profit-sharing retirement plans called "discretionary contribution plans." An employer may now maintain a plan with the same features of a profit-sharing plan without the profit element. Tax-exempt organizations are specifically permitted to maintain these arrangements.

Cash or Deferred Arrangements

Under cash or deferred arrangements, often called 401(k) plans, employees may take a salary reduction or forego a salary increase and have that amount contributed to a qualified plan. Beginning in 1987, employees may electively defer a maximum of $7,000 per year, subject to special discrimination and offset rules discussed above. Tax-exempt organizations may not maintain 401(k) plans unless they were adopted by July 1, 1986.

Pension Plans

Pension plans are the last major category of retirement plans. These arrangements require annual contributions by the employer, notwithstanding the employer's revenues, which can limit an employer's flexibility. There are also increased administrative costs due to actuarial determinations and Pension Benefit Guaranty Corporation insurance premiums for certain types of pension plans.

Contributions to a qualified, defined-contribution plan (i.e., profit-sharing and discretionary plans) generally are limited to the lesser of $30,000 or 25 percent of the employee's compensation. Defined-benefit pension plans might have higher contribution limits because benefits of up to $90,000 per year may be funded. The cost of covering an entire hospital with a qualified plan using the maximum permissible contribution limits can be prohibitive.

Many employers with overfunded pension plans have been terminating them to recapture excess plan assets. The 10 percent excise tax on these reversions, designed to discourage reversions, does not generally apply to tax-exempt organizations.

Reorganization Considerations

Before reorganizing, a hospital must review the effect of reorganization on existing and proposed retirement plans. Often a reorganization can alter the mix of employees covered under a qualified plan. This alteration may cause a plan to lose its qualified status if the change causes the highly compensated to be covered in greater numbers or with better benefits than the non-highly compensated.

The benefits of a qualified plan must be generally available to all employees. In the case of a group of commonly owned and controlled organizations, the benefits of one corporation's qualified plan generally must be provided to the employees of each corporation. Similar requirements may come into play in the case of organizations that are only affiliated with each other in rendering services, depending on the degree of the affiliation. These relationships may arise in the joint ventures that hospitals are currently entering. If proper planning is not initiated, it could result in the disqualification of the joint venturer's qualified plans.

EMPLOYEE FRINGE BENEFITS

Hospitals are in a unique position to provide a variety of fringe benefits to hospital employees that are unavailable to independent contractors and incorporated physicians. Hospital-paid employee benefits usually include insurance, parking, sick and vacation leave, time off for professional development, and pension or similar retirement plans.[12]

Congress wanted to make many employee benefit programs more equitable toward rank-and-file employees by applying tighter nondiscrimination rules to these programs. The 1986 Act, therefore, applies complex new and revised nondiscrimintion rules to insurance-type fringe benefit plans. These rules, as explained below, could require increased employee coverage and benefits, thus increasing the cost of those benefits to employers.

Paid Insurance

Hospital-paid insurance coverage can take a variety of forms. One of the most common is group term life insurance. Under such policies, the cost of the first $50,000 of coverage is not included in the employee's gross income. The cost of coverage in excess of $50,000 is deemed income to the employee as determined under an IRS table. Many insurance companies offer programs that include permanent insurance coverage as part of the group insurance arrangement. Hospital employees have to include as income the cost of permanent hospital-paid coverage. An exempt hospital may want to consider a split-dollar insurance program, under which the hospital pays premiums on whole life coverage for key employees and retains the cash surrender value of the insurance contract. The employees, or their designated beneficiaries, own the insurance coverage in excess of the cash surrender value.

Another common insurance benefit is partial or complete payment of premiums on group medical insurance policies. These plans vary among hospitals, with some institutions now self-insuring inpatient hospital expenses for their employees. If properly structured, these plans need not result in any taxable income to the employees. Disability insurance programs also are available on a group basis, generally at much lower rates than could be obtained on an individual basis.

Financial Counseling

Today, employers frequently pay part or all of the financial counseling costs for their executives. Financial counseling may include tax return preparation and planning, family tax planning, cash forecasting, analysis and review of insurance coverage, and investment counseling. This service reduces the financial concerns of key employees and promotes more effective utilization of their time. The IRS requires that financial counseling fees paid by an employer for the benefit of its employees be included in the employee's gross income, subject to withholding. Such fees for tax planning or investment counseling are deductible by the employee to the extent that they exceed 2 percent of adjusted gross income when combined with other miscellaneous deductions.

Cafeteria Plans

Cafeteria plans are employee benefit plans under which a participant may choose between benefits consisting of cash and nontaxable fringe benefits. The nontaxable benefits include group term life insurance, accident and health benefits, and dependent care assistance programs.

Cafeteria plans allow employees to select benefits that best fit their needs and prevent the hospital from having to fund for all employee benefits that may be desirable to only a few. The noncash benefits are not subject to federal income tax or Social Security tax, resulting in increased take-home pay for the employees and reduced payroll taxes for the hospital. This program can be installed by converting a portion of the employees' present taxable salaries to nontaxable benefit payments.

If the plan discriminates in favor of key employees, those employees will be required to include the benefits in gross income. Therefore, the cafeteria plan should be available to all employees, not just key personnel.

Below-Market Interest Rate Loans

The high cost of borrowing makes the interest-free or below-market rate loan a significant fringe benefit. The individual is allowed to borrow hospital capital to use as equity for the purchase of a home, tax shelters, or other investments.

The IRS perceives interest-free and below-market rate loans as two separate transactions. First, the hospital transfers compensation to the employee equal to the interest value of the loan. Second, the employee pays the hospital an amount equal to the annual interest on the loan. The way these imputed amounts of income and expense must be recognized by the employee depends on the terms of the loan. For example, if $30,000 is loaned interest free to a newly recruited employee and is repayable on demand, and if the controlling IRS interest rate is 12 percent for a given year, the employee would have received compensation of $3,600 and an equal interest expense that year. However, before adopting such an arrangement, state charitable trust law should be reviewed for possible restrictions.

Other Employee Benefit Provisions

Many employers provide company-owned cars to employees who must drive in connection with business. However, the employee must report as compensation, or reimburse the employer for, any personal use, including travel to and from work. Although certain exceptions exist, records generally must be maintained to substantiate the business portion of employee use. The tax effects and recordkeeping burden on both the employee and employer differ depending on the method used.

Among other employee benefit provisions are the following;

- *Educational assistance plans*. The income exclusion for benefits from these plans depends on the employee's position and the type of education.
- *Employee awards*. All employee awards are now generally treated as taxable compensation. However, certain employee achievement awards (other than cash and gift certificates) may be excluded from an employee's income. Another exception

applies to gold watches presented on retirement.
- *Dependent care assistance*. For tax years beginning after December 31, 1986, the exclusion for dependent care assistance is limited to $5,000 a year for a married couple filing jointly or $2,500 for a married individual filing separately.

Nondiscrimination Rules

To encourage increased employee participation and benefits, the 1986 Act provides complex nondiscrimination rules for most fringe benefits that may greatly increase the administrative and benefit costs to employers. The new rules cover fully insured health benefits that never before were subject to nondiscrimination requirements.

The 1986 Act affects group term life insurance plans, accident plans, health benefit plans, dependent care assistance programs, and cafeteria plans. Under the 1986 Act, if a benefit discriminates in favor of highly compensated employees, these employees are generally taxed only on the discriminatory portion of the otherwise tax-free benefit. In the case of discriminatory accident or health benefits, the amount imputed to highly compensated employees is the value of the employer-provided coverage in excess of the nondiscriminatory coverage. In the case of a discriminatory group term life insurance plan, the amount imputed is based on the higher of the cost of coverage or the amount contained in existing Treasury Department regulations.

LEASED EMPLOYEES

It has become increasingly popular for organizations to "lease" employees to reduce administrative and benefit expenses. Although Congress realized that leasing employees to perform the duties of what ordinarily would be full-time employees is a valid business method, it was not believed to be equitable or fair if the primary motivation was to avoid providing these individuals with employee benefits. The 1986 legislation revised rules added by the Tax Equity and Fiscal Responsibility Act of 1982 that treat a leased employee who performs services for another person (the recipient) as the recipient's employee for determining whether the discrimination rules for qualified plans and other employee benefits are satisfied. If the leased employee causes the recipient's plan not to satisfy the discrimination rules, he or she may have to be covered under the recipient's plan. A safe harbor exists for retirement plan purposes if the leasing organization maintains a generous money purchase pension plan and not more than 20 percent of the recipient's employees are leased.

SUMMARY

As tax-exempt providers focus more on financial results, knowledge of what and how executive compensation and employee benefits can be used to achieve their goals will increase. There is already much discussion (and some early experimentation) regarding incentive measures that can meet the difficult dual test of motivating key employees without jeopardizing an institution's continued tax-exempt status. Careful analysis and documentation of the public benefits will significantly increase the chances for success.

NOTES

1. Arthur Andersen & Co. and American College of Hospital Administrators, *Healthcare in the 1990s: Trends and Strategies* (Chicago: Arthur Andersen & Co. and ACHA, 1984).

2. B.S. Cole, "Executive Pay Raises Slim Again, but They Stay Ahead of Inflation," *Modern Healthcare* 14, no. 14 (1984): 140–41.

3. L.I. Collins, "A Survey of Hospital Salaries," *Hospitals* 58, no. 21 (1984): 80–84, 91.

4. R.S. Bromberg, "The Effect of Tax Policy on the Delivery and Cost of Healthcare," *Taxes* 53, no. 8 (1975): 452–78.

5. *Exempt Organization Handbook*, IRM 7751, Internal Revenue Manual 4 (CCH) ¶382.41, pp. 20587–20589 (1982).

6. General Counsel Memorandum (GCM) 38283, February 15, 1980.

7. U.S. Department of the Treasury, Exempt Organization Continuing Professional Education Technical Instruction Program, No. TPDS 89093 (1-87), p. 46.

8. GCM 39674, June 17, 1987.

9. Private Lett. Rul. 8325100.

10. Private Lett. Rul. 8329070.

11. Private Lett. Rul. 8634031.

12. Arthur Andersen & Co., *Study of Reimbursement and Practice Arrangements of Provider-Based Physicians* (Chicago: Arthur Andersen & Co., 1977).

Chapter 29

Charitable Giving

Gary Zmrhal
Partner, Arthur Andersen & Co.

INTRODUCTION

Charitable giving is a big business in the United States. In 1986, $87 billion was donated to charitable organizations, representing a 9 percent increase over the previous year. Only 14 percent (approximately $12.26 billion) of these donations were received by health care institutions.[1] A much smaller amount went specifically to hospitals.

The escalating cost of providing quality health care and the increasing difficulty of fully recovering these costs from third-party payers are making hospitals more dependent on charitable contributions to remain solvent, fund research, and pay for otherwise uncompensated care. Hospital executives and board members who can discuss with potential donors the tax economics of charitable giving are better able to increase donations. Careful planning can result in properly structured donations that reduce donor-paid taxes, increase the donor's personal cash flow, and increase contributions to the hospital. This should remain true even though the Tax Reform Act of 1986 increased the after-tax cost of private philanthropy.

BASIC RULES OF CHARITABLE GIVING

The amount of tax deduction allowed for charitable contributions depends on the type of organization to which the donation is made, the type of property contributed, and the use of the donated property by the charity.

Qualified Gifts

A transfer of money or other property to a hospital is not always a tax-deductible contribution. Qualified gifts must meet certain qualifications.

- If the hospital provides something of commensurate value in return for the contribution, no deduction is allowed to the donor.[2]
- A gift must be complete and irrevocable.[3]
- If a hospital receives a gift that requires an event precedent to the gift's becoming effective, the gift yields a current tax deduction to the donor only in the limited case of deferred gifts discussed below.[4]
- No deduction is allowed for a gift of services to the hospital no matter how valuable those services may be.[5–7]
- A tax deduction is allowed for the gift of an income interest to a hospital only if the transfer is made in trust.[8]

Qualified Donees

Tax deductions are permitted only for gifts to organizations having a charitable purpose as specified in Internal Revenue Code (IRC) Section 501(c). Deductions limited to 50 percent of an individual's adjusted gross income are permitted for gifts to hospitals as well as to churches, schools, government entities, organizations that receive a substantial part of their revenue from the general public (public charities), and certain private foundations.[9] For other charitable organizations, primarily private (nonoperating) foundations, the 1984 Tax Reform Act established a deductible limit of 30 percent of the donor's adjusted gross income. That Act retained the 20 percent limitation for all gifts of capital gain property to private foundations.[10]

Limitations

The percentage limitation is determined by a percentage of an individual's adjusted gross income and refers to the maximum contribution deduction allowed in a given taxable year. For example, the 50 percent limitation generally applies only to cash gifts. In addition to the 20 percent and 50 percent limitations, a special 30 percent limitation applies, except to private nonoperating foundations, to contributions of long-term capital gain property.[11] Such 30 percent contributions may qualify for the 50 percent limitation if the donor elects to reduce the deductible contribution by 100 percent of the long-term gain that would have resulted had the property been sold.[12] Contributions made by corporations are limited to 10 percent of the taxpayer's taxable income.[13]

Deductions for contributions of ordinary income property must be reduced by the amount of any gain that would not have been long-term capital gain, including depreciation recapture, had the donor sold the property at fair market value.[14] For taxpayers engaged in a trade or business, inventory items acquired during the year may be charitably donated and charged to cost of goods sold to avoid percentage limitations on contributions.[15]

Additional rules are provided in IRC Section 170(e)(3) for certain contributions of inventory and other property by certain corporations. Under these provisions, corporations may receive an increased percentage limitation resulting in an increased contribution deduction for the donation of inventory and depreciable or real property used in trade or business by the donor provided that the donee's use of the property is related to the exempt purposes of the donee organization and the property is to be used solely for the care of the ill, the needy, or infants. Thus, contributions of pharmaceuticals by a drug manufacturer to a hospital may result in a contribution deduction greater than the cost of the donated inventory. Contributions of computer hardware, although not as directly related to the exempt activities, might also be eligible for increased contribution deductions that exceed the established percentage limitations.

Carryovers

Contributions made to hospitals and other 50 percent organizations that exceed 50 percent of the taxpayer's adjusted gross income may be carried over and deducted in the five succeeding tax years.[16] Donations subject to the 30 percent limitation that exceed 30 percent of adjusted gross income may likewise be carried over and deducted (subject to the same 30 percent limitation) in the five succeeding tax years.[17] As of 1984, gifts to private, nonoperating foundations are subject to a five-year carryover provision.[18]

CURRENT GIVING

Two general types of charitable contributions may be made to a hospital: *current*, or outright, contributions in which the transfer of the property to the hospital is completed in the same year the tax deduction is claimed, and *deferred* gifts that result in a current income tax deduction to the donor even though the hospital must await some future event before receiving the property.

Current contributions usually consist of cash but may include appreciated property such as stock or real estate. The donor receives an income tax deduction in the year of the donation and typically will pay a reduced estate tax by removing the property from his or her estate. The hospital benefits immediately by receiving the property for its own use.

Cash donations are probably the most common type of outright gift made to health care organizations. The donation is complete upon receipt of the check or cash by the donee hospital, and the donor's canceled check and receipt are sufficient documentation to substantiate the deduction.

Although more complex, gifts of property may offer substantial tax benefits to the prospective donor. With a gift of property, the deductible amount to the donor may be the fair market value of the property at the date of the gift or the cost (or basis) of the property in the hands of the donor. For contributions of long-term capital gain property made after August 15, 1986, the amount of otherwise untaxed appreciation will constitute a tax preference item for alternative minimum tax purposes.[19]

Valuing gifts of property is more difficult. Listed securities are valued at the average of their high and low quotations of the day of the gift.[20] The Internal Revenue Service (IRS) imposes appraisal and reporting requirements if the amount claimed as a charitable deduction exceeds $5,000 for any single item, and $10,000 for stock that is not publicly traded. These requirements apply to charitable deductions claimed by an individual, a closely held corporation, a personal service organization, a partnership, or a S corporation.

The donor must obtain and retain a written appraisal by a qualified appraiser for the property contributed and must attach a signed appraisal summary, with the appraiser's tax identification number, to the return in which the deduction is first claimed. The appraisal must be received by the donor before the due date, including extensions, of the return in which the deduction is claimed. Regulations require additional information to be furnished by the donor, including the cost and acquisition date of the donated property. These provisions are effective for contributions made after 1984.[21]

In addition, if a donee hospital sells, exchanges, or otherwise transfers certain donated property within two years of the receipt thereof, the hospital must furnish an information report to the IRS providing certain information concerning the donated property disposed of and the name (and identification number) of the donor of that property.[22]

Although the IRS imposes penalties for overvaluations of charitable donations, it may waive the penalty for good-faith valuations having a reasonable basis.[23]

Since the donor is generally not required to recognize any taxable gain on the transfer of appreciated property,[24-29] it is usually more advantageous for the donor to give the hospital the appreciated property intact than for the donor to sell the property and then donate the proceeds to the hospital. The following demonstrates these two alternatives (also see Figure 29-1).

A donor in the 28 percent tax bracket owns stock with a $12,000 market value. The donor's basis (cost of purchase) in the stock is $2,000, and he or she has pledged $10,000 to the hospital. If the donor contributes $10,000 of stock in the hospital to satisfy his or her pledge, he or she retains $2,000 of the stock. The hospital receives $10,000 of stock, immediately sells it, and converts it to cash. Because the hospital is tax-exempt, it does not pay tax on the gain inherent in the stock, and the IRS receives nothing from the transaction.

Conversely, if the donor sells all of the stock, the donor owes tax of $2,800 ($10,000 × 28%) on the gain inherent in the stock. The hospital receives only $9,200 and the individual has nothing left over.

While the IRS benefits from the sale of stock before contribution, the charity loses $800. If the taxpayer does not wish to retain the $2,000, he or she can give it to the charity, so the charity receives the $12,000 worth of stock. Still, no taxes would have to be paid.

Because losses are not recognized on the contribution of property,[30] a prospective donor having property with an inherent loss should sell the property to receive a tax benefit and then contribute the proceeds of the sale to the hospital.

Frequently, a donor transfers property to a hospital to sell in return for the cash proceeds. If the donor engages in the negotiations, the IRS may argue that the transaction benefits the donor, in which case the donor would be taxed on the gain realized on the sale.[31,32]

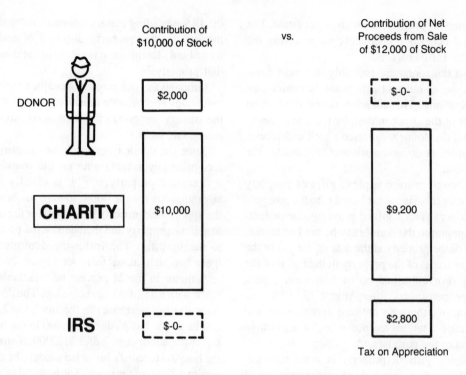

Figure 29-1 Advantage of Intact Transfer of Property. *Source:* © Arthur Andersen & Co.

DEFERRED GIVING

In deferred giving, a donor receives an immediate tax deduction for the transfer of a future interest in property, although the actual transfer is consummated in the future. Unlike a current gift, which yields a current deduction equal to the fair market value of the property, a deferred gift's value is divided into two parts—typically an income interest that the donor retains in the form of annuity and a remainder interest that passes to the hospital in the future.

The present value of the remainder interest determines the donor's current contribution deduction. The older the income beneficiary, the less the anticipated annuity income and the greater the value of the contribution deduction.

Based on the income tax regulations, if a 50-year-old taxpayer contributes property to a hospital and retains a 10 percent income interest, he or she could expect to receive 85 percent of the value of the property as an annuity. The remaining 15 percent of the present value would pass to the hospital on the donor's death. An 80-year-

old taxpayer, on the other hand, could expect to receive only 44 percent of the property value as the income interest, with the remaining 56 percent passing to the hospital. Thus, on a $100,000 charitable remainder contribution through a qualified trust, the 50-year-old taxpayer would receive a $15,000 deduction, while the 80-year-old taxpayer would receive a $56,000 deduction.

Procedures for structuring deferred gifts are complex. Current law provides that no charitable contribution deduction will be allowed for income, estate, or gift tax purposes for the value of a remainder interest unless transferred in trust[33] or unless the remainder interest is in a personal residence or a farm.[34]

In a charitable remainder trust, a donor contributes property in trust for the benefit of a hospital and appoints a local bank or other party as trustee. The trustee pays trust income to the donor or other beneficiary the donor may name. On the death of the income beneficiary, the remainder interest of the property left in the trust is distributed by the trustee to the hospital (Figure 29-2). The IRC provides that three types of

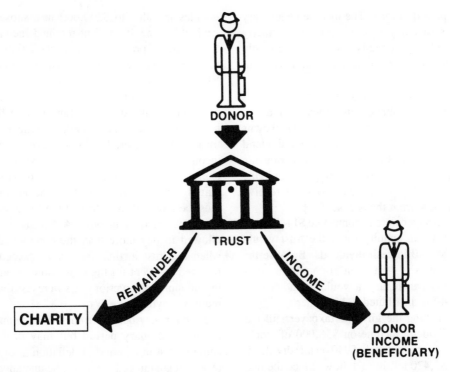

Figure 29-2 Charitable Remainder Trust. *Source:* © Arthur Andersen & Co.

trusts may be used to contribute a remainder interest in property to hospitals and other charitable organizations.

Charitable Remainder Annuity Trust

A taxpayer donor creates a charitable annuity trust by transferring property to the trust and reserving an annuity for his or her lifetime, for the joint lives of taxpayer and spouse, for the life of another, or for a specified number of years. The retained income interest is fixed at the time of the gift to a percentage of the property value at the time of the gift.[35] For example, if a donor contributed $100,000 to a hospital through the use of an annuity trust and retained a 6 percent income interest, he or she would receive an annuity from the trust of $6,000 each year until death without regard to the annual value of the trust property. At the time of death of the income beneficiary, the trust would be liquidated and the property would go to the hospital.

To qualify, a charitable annuity trust must meet certain requirements:

- The trust must pay a fixed sum to at least one noncharitable beneficiary, who must be living at the time the trust is created.

- The amount paid cannot be less than 5 percent of the initial net fair market value of the contributed property.

- The fixed sum must be payable, at least annually, either for a term of years (but not for more than 20) or for the life or lives of the noncharitable beneficiary or beneficiaries.

- On the death of the income (or noncharitable) beneficiaries, the trust corpus must be transferred to or for the use of a qualified charitable organization or retained by the trust for such use.

- No additional contributions to an annuity trust are permitted after the initial contribution.[36–38]

The principal advantage of an annuity trust is that the donor receives an immediate tax benefit from the charitable deduction for a portion of the amount placed in trust. The income beneficiary continues to enjoy income from the property contributed. The annuity income is generally taxable to the income beneficiary in the year of receipt.

For example, assume that a taxpayer pays $8,640 in 1988 to support his 70-year-old father. The son is in the 28 percent tax bracket and owns $200,000 of stock that pays an annual dividend of 6 percent ($12,000). Between the income tax on the dividend ($3,360) and the payment to the father ($8,640), the taxpayer does not receive any cash flow from this stock.

If the taxpayer were to contribute $144,000 of the stock to an annuity trust, the trust would receive $8,640 in cash dividends. Because the trust receives a deduction for amounts distributed to a beneficiary, it would pay no taxes if the $8,640 is distributed to his father.

After making the gift, the taxpayer still has $3,360 dividend income on $56,000 of stock, pays tax of approximately $940 on this dividend, and has $2,420 left in cash flow. Since the taxpayer had zero after-tax cash flow before the gift, he has realized a $2,420 increased cash flow after the gift. In the year of the gift, the taxpayer will realize an income tax savings of approximately $25,680 from deducting the charitable contribution to the trust and will also have used a portion of his or her unified gift and estate tax credit. However, the donor has also parted with $144,000 of stock previously held.

Charitable Remainder Unitrust

The principal difference between an annuity trust and a unitrust lies in the computation of the annual annuity. With an annuity trust, the annual income interest is based on the value of the property on the date of the gift. With a unitrust, the retained income interest is a fixed percentage of the property's annually determined value[39] (Exhibit 29-1).

For example, if a donor contributes $100,000 to a hospital through the use of a unitrust and retains a 10 percent income interest, the annuity in the first year would be $10,000, the same as it would be with an annuity trust. If the property

doubles in value to $200,000 in a subsequent year, the same 10 percent retained income interest would produce an annuity payment of $20,000 from the unitrust, while remaining at $10,000 from the annuity trust.

Although a unitrust generally must pay a fixed percentage of the annual net fair market value of its assets to the noncharitable beneficiary, the trust can be structured to distribute only the trust income amount received in a year when the income is less than the payment ordinarily required.[40,41] An annuity trust, on the other hand, must be required to distribute the fixed amount regardless of trust income. A unitrust may be allowed to pay more than the contractual rate when the trust income for a year exceeds the required payment for the year to the extent that the amounts paid in prior years were less than the required payments.

A donor may benefit from a variable annuity in an inflationary period but may prefer an annuity trust in a period of deflation in order to receive a guaranteed income. The annual valuation requirement of the unitrust could present a recurring problem when the trust is funded with assets that are difficult or expensive to value, such as the stock of a closely held corporation or mineral interests.

A donor may fund an annuity trust or a unitrust with tax-exempt securities that would pass to the hospital on the donor's death. As long as the trust holds the securities, the annual annuity income distributed to the beneficiary would be tax-free.

Since annual valuations are required to determine the annuity amount, additional contributions to a unitrust are permitted. As noted above, contributions subsequent to the initial funding of an annuity trust are prohibited.

Pooled Income Fund

Hospitals should consider the benefits of pooled income funds, which colleges and universities have utilized to great advantage for years. A pooled income fund is an investment fund maintained by a tax-exempt organization that receives contributions from many donors who retain life income interests in the property

Exhibit 29-1 Key Differences between an Annuity Trust and a Unitrust

ANNUITY TRUST	vs.	UNITRUST
• Property Valued on the Date It Is Placed in the Trust • Annuity Fixed		• Property Valued Annually • Annuity Varies

ANNUITY BASED ON PROPERTY VALUE

they have contributed. When a beneficiary dies, his or her pro rata share of the trust assets is distributed to the hospital, but the trust remains in existence for the remaining beneficiaries and future donors. A pooled income trust is depicted graphically in Figure 29-3.

To qualify, a pooled income trust must meet the following criteria:

- The donor must transfer an irrevocable remainder interest in property to or for the use of an organization qualifying for the 50 percent charitable deduction and retain an income interest for the life of one or more beneficiaries.
- The property transferred must be commingled with property transferred by other donors.
- The trust may receive only amounts received from gifts that meet the requirements for pooled income funds.
- The trust must be controlled by the exempt organization for which the remainder interest is contributed and cannot have a donor or a beneficiary of an income interest as a trustee.
- The income received each year by the income beneficiary must be determined by the rate of return earned by the trust for that year.[42,43]

A principal advantage of the pooled income fund is that it allows hospitals to receive deferred contributions that otherwise would be too small to establish a separate unitrust or annuity trust. The pooled income fund also gives the donor

access to the professional investment skills of the fund's managers. A donor concerned with ensuring that the corpus of the remainder trust will pass intact to the charitable beneficiary may prefer a pooled income fund for making a gift, since the fund generally distributes only the income and does not invade the corpus to make distributions to the income beneficiaries.

One disadvantage of a pooled income fund is that it cannot be used to secure tax-exempt income for the beneficiary, as it is prohibited from investing in tax-exempt securities. Also, a donor cannot retain an income interest for a term of years because a lifetime interest must be retained.

Personal Residence or Farm

The Tax Reform Act of 1969 specified provisions for tax deductions resulting from the charitable contribution of a remainder interest in a personal residence or a farm.[44] The regulations provide that while the interest must be in a personal residence, it does not have to be the donor's principal residence.[45] Vacation homes may qualify for this type of contribution deduction. Farms are defined as land and improvements used for the production of crops, fruit, or agricultural products or for the raising of livestock.[46] In this arrangement, the donor contributes a remainder interest in his or her home or farm to a hospital, retaining a life estate for the donor and spouse that permits them to live in the home for the remainder of their lives. Following the death of the life beneficiaries, title to the property passes to the hospital.

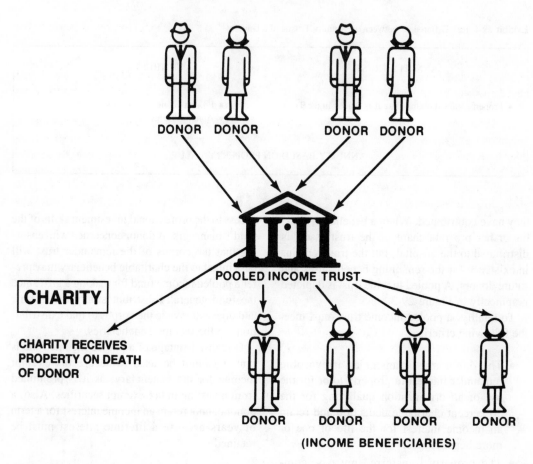

Figure 29-3 Pooled Income Trust. *Source:* © Arthur Andersen & Co.

Calculating the remainder interest value prescribed in the income tax regulations is quite complex.[47,48] Essentially, straight-line depreciation must be estimated on the depreciable portion of the property's total value. The resulting value is discounted to the date of the gift at the prescribed rate of 6 percent.

Charitable Lead Trust

In contrast to a charitable remainder trust, a charitable lead trust[49] involves the transfer of an immediate *income* interest to the hospital while the *remainder* interest remains with the donor or is transferred to a noncharitable donee of the donor's choice.

There are two uses of a lead trust in tax-planning programs. In the first, the donor receives an immediate income tax deduction for the actuarially determined value of the income that passes to the hospital. The donor is treated as the owner of the trust and must pay taxes on the annual income even though it is distributed to charity.[50] With proper planning, a donor realizes an immediate tax deduction in high-income years while reporting the income from the trust in later years, when the donor may be in a lower tax bracket. The donor may fund this type of lead trust with tax-exempt securities that would permit the same immediate tax deduction but not require taxable income to be reported in the future. An income interest gift is for the use of a hospital[51] and thus subject to the 30-percent deduction limitation.[52]

The second use of the lead trust is in a lifetime giving program or an estate planning program in which the donor purposely avoids a current income tax deduction by structuring the trust so that he or she is not its owner.[53] Although the donor foregoes the current income tax deduction, he or she is not taxed on the future trust income. In addition, the corpus still passes to noncharitable beneficiaries, typically a child or grandchild. The value of the noncharitable gift subject to tax, or the value of a decedent's property subject to estate tax, is reduced by the present value of the income that passes to the hospital, as shown in the following example (Figure 29-4).

A father has $500,000 of stock he wants to give to his daughter. The stock is paying a dividend of 5 percent. Because the father is already in a gift and estate tax bracket of 55 percent, he has used his unified transfer tax credit. If he makes a gift now, he must pay a gift tax.

If the father gives the stock to his daughter today, the gift tax would be approximately $275,000. If he gives her the stock ten years from now, assuming the stock doubles in value, the gift tax (or, if he dies, the estate tax) would

be $500,000. The longer he holds property that appreciates, the greater the taxes will be on the ultimate stock transfer.

But if the father puts the stock in a 10-year lead trust, with the income for the period going to the hospital, and if at the end of ten years the stock goes to his daughter, the current gift tax would be approximately $190,500. Even if the stock doubles or triples in value by the end of ten years, neither the father nor the daughter will incur additional gift or estate tax.

In effect, the use of the trust freezes the value of the stock for tax purposes even though the beneficiary does not receive the stock until sometime in the future. Coincidentally, the hospital receives $25,000 per year for ten years.

Charitable Gift Annuity

With a charitable gift annuity, a donor actually sells his or her property to a hospital in exchange for a lifetime annuity.[54] The donor receives estate tax benefits from this arrangement by removing the property from the taxable estate. Also, no amount of the annuity is includ-

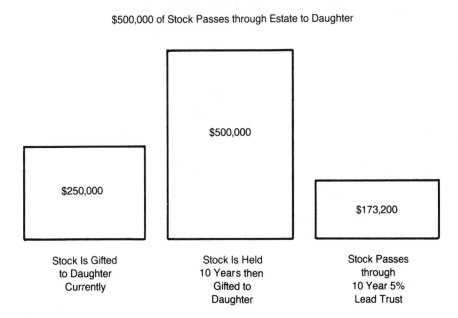

$500,000 of Stock Passes through Estate to Daughter

$500,000

$250,000

$173,200

| Stock Is Gifted to Daughter Currently | Stock Is Held 10 Years then Gifted to Daughter | Stock Passes through 10 Year 5% Lead Trust |

Figure 29-4 Stock Transfer Alternatives. *Source:* © Arthur Andersen & Co.

able in the estate, as the annuity was a lifetime interest only.

Using actuarial tables prepared by the Conference on Gift Annuities for this purpose,[55-57] the annuity retained by the donor is less than the value of the property transferred to the hospital. The difference in value represents a tax-deductible contribution by the donor in the year of the gift. The donor pays tax on the gain over an estimated lifetime while collecting the annuity.

SUMMARY

The principal means of making deferred gifts to hospitals is through charitable remainder trust arrangements. With careful planning by the donor and the hospital, and with tax and legal assistance, donors may receive substantial income and estate tax benefits and increase their cash flow by making a deferred gift to a hospital.

NOTES

1. *Giving U.S.A.* New York: American Association of Fundraising Counsel, 1986, p. 7.

2. *Bogardus v. Commissioner*, 302 U.S. 34 (1937).

3. *Threlfall v. U.S.*, 302 F.Supp. 1114 (D. Wis. 1969).

4. Treas. Reg. §1.170A-1(e) (1975).

5. Treas. Reg. §1.170A-1(g) (1975).

6. Rev. Rul. 58-240, 1958-1 C.B. 141.

7. Rev. Rul. 71-135, 1971-1 C.B. 95.

8. Internal Revenue Code (IRC) §170(f)(2)(B).

9. IRC §170(b)(1)(A).

10. IRC §170(b)(1)(B), (C) & (D).

11. IRC §170(b)(1)(C)(i).

12. IRC §170(b)(1)(C)(iii).

13. IRC §170(b)(2).

14. IRC §170(e)(1)(A).

15. Treas. Reg. §170A-1(c)(4) (1975).

16. IRC §170(d)(1)(A).

17. IRC §170(b)(1)(C)(ii).

18. IRC §170(b)(1)(D)(ii).

19. IRC §57(a)(6).

20. Treas. Reg. §20.2031-(2)(b) (1976).

21. 1984 Tax Reform Act, §155(a).

22. IRC §6050L.

23. IRC §6659(f).

24. Rev. Rul. 55-138, 1955-1 C.B. 223.

25. Rev. Rul. 68-69, 1968-1 C.B. 80.

26. Rev. Rul. 55-275, 1955-1 C.B. 295.

27. Rev. Rul. 55-531, 1955-2 C.B. 520.

28. *White v. Brodnick*, 104 F.Supp. 213 (D. Kansas 1952).

29. *Campbell v. Prothro*, 209 F.2d 331 (5th Cir. 1954).

30. Rev. Rul. 55-410, 1955-1 C.B. 297.

31. *Martin v. Machiz*, 251 F.Supp. 381 (D. Md. 1966).

32. *Magnolia Development Corporation*, 19 T.C.M. (CCH) 934 (1960).

33. IRC §§170(f)(2)(A), 2055(e)(2)(A), and 2522(c)(2)(A).

34. IRC §170(f)(3)(B)(i).

35. IRC §664(e).

36. IRC §664(d)(1).

37. Treas. Reg. §1.664-2(a) (1974).

38. IRC §508(e).

39. IRC §664(e).

40. IRC §664(d)(3).

41. Treas. Reg. §1.664-3(a)(1)(i)(b) (1972).

42. IRC §642(c)(5).

43. Treas. Reg. §1.642(c)-5(b) (1979).

44. IRC §170(f)(3)(b)(i).

45. Treas. Reg. §1.170A-7(b)(3) (1972).

46. Treas. Reg. §1.170A-7(b)(4) (1972).

47. Treas. Reg. §1.170A-12 (1975).

48. Treas. Reg. §25.2512-9 (1972).

49. IRC §170(f)(2)(B).

50. IRC §170(f)(2)(B).

51. Treas. Reg. §1.170A-8(a)(2) (1972).

52. IRC §170(b)(1)(B).

53. IRC §673(a).

54. Treas. Reg. §1.170A-1(d)(1) (1975).

55. Uniform Gift Annuity Rates adopted by Conference on Gift Annuities, May 5, 1977.

56. Treas. Reg. §1.170A-1(d)(2) (1975).

57. Treas. Reg. §1.101-2(e)(1)(iii)(b)(2) (1976).

Index

Page number in *italics* indicate figures and exhibits; those followed by "t" indicate tables.